THE PAPERS OF

WOODROW WILSON

VOLUME 27
1913

SPONSORED BY THE WOODROW WILSON
FOUNDATION
AND PRINCETON UNIVERSITY

THE PAPERS OF

WOODROW WILSON

ARTHUR S. LINK, *EDITOR*

DAVID W. HIRST AND JOHN E. LITTLE

ASSOCIATE EDITORS

EDITH JAMES, *ASSISTANT EDITOR*

SYLVIA ELVIN, *CONTRIBUTING EDITOR*

PHYLLIS MARCHAND, *EDITORIAL ASSISTANT*

Volume 27 · 1913

PRINCETON, NEW JERSEY

PRINCETON UNIVERSITY PRESS

1978

EDITING THE PRESIDENTIAL VOLUMES

With the beginning of this volume, Wilson moves on to the grand stage of presidential leadership for which all his earlier labors had been preparation. At this juncture, we believe that we owe our readers a new statement of our editorial purposes and objectives. Indeed, it is overdue, since the one set forth in the General Introduction in the first volume has long since ceased to be descriptive.

When we wrote that introduction, we were influenced by the traditional view that an individual's papers consisted of documents written or received by him or her. However, it became evident to us early in our editorial work that adhering strictly to the conventional definition would make it impossible to achieve our supreme objective—the presentation of as complete a record as possible of the development of Wilson's significant thought and activities in all their varied aspects.

For example, we said in the General Introduction that we would print only Wilson's most important speeches. It turned out a poor prediction, for we soon realized that the development of his thought could be seen in its steady accretion only by reading virtually all his speeches, or (when texts were unavailable) reports of them. An important development in his thought is signaled in a talk to the Philadelphian Society at Princeton and then more fully developed in an article. Which, then, is the more important—the speech or the article? We encountered the same difficulties in dealing with Wilson's political speeches from 1910 through 1912. In all of these, Wilson went from idea to idea and issue to issue while trying to rouse the people of New Jersey and of the United States to a heightened political consciousness and responsible exercise of the high duties of citizenship.

Yet most of the texts of those speeches were not papers in the traditional meaning of that word. A speech is a "paper" only when prepared in written form. Wilson had a profound aversion to delivering political speeches from a written text. Between 1910 and 1912 he gave only two speeches written beforehand—the one accepting the gubernatorial nomination in 1910, the other accepting the presidential nomination in 1912. All others he delivered from brief outlines. Whether those speeches were "papers" or not, it would have been unthinkable to omit them. They are the most important record of Wilson's political thought during the time when he was re-forming his political philosophy and laying the foundations in public opinion for his leadership in state and nation.

Moreover, as Wilson grew in stature in the educational and political worlds, his friends and associates began to record, in memoranda, diaries, and letters to third parties, his conversations with them. In many cases these are the most important records extant of Wilson's thinking at particular times about particular issues, and so we have included all of them that we have found to date, even though such documents are not, technically speaking, Wilson "papers." To mention a final example, we had to fall back upon news reports of Wilson's activities during the period 1911-1912 in order to compensate for the loss of most of Wilson's papers during this period.

In short, we have actually never felt ourselves bound by old definitional constraints and will not be so bound in selecting documents and records for the presidential period. On the contrary, we will seek to find and publish every important record of Wilson's thoughts and purposes without concern for the form in which the records have been preserved.

THE PAPERS AND RECORDS OF THE PRESIDENTIAL PERIOD

Before we explain our criteria and methods in selecting and editing materials for the presidential volumes, we present herewith a brief description of the major sources from which ·we have drawn and will draw these materials:

1. *The Papers of Woodrow Wilson in the Library of Congress*

This great collection has been and will continue to be our most important source. The Wilson Papers contain the letterpress and carbon copies of all outgoing correspondence typed by the White House staff. It also includes many original copies of Wilson letters donated by Wilson's friends and associates, the most important being the large group of handwritten and Wilson typed letters from Wilson to Mary Allen Hulbert (Peck).

The incoming materials in the Wilson Papers include most of the personal letters addressed to Wilson. In addition, there are the huge number and varied kinds of items that one would expect to find in a modern presidential collection—letters, telegrams, petitions, reports, memoranda, diplomatic dispatches, and so on. However, our research thus far has revealed that many important incoming letters are missing. Copies of some of these have been found in the writers' papers.

The Wilson Papers is also our major source for the texts of Wilson's speeches during the presidential period. These include Wilson shorthand drafts, Wilson typed drafts, transcripts typed by Charles L. Swem, printed reading copies, and official prints.

Finally, the Wilson Papers contain a huge volume of miscellaneous materials—for example, the diary kept by the head usher at the White House; the Executive Office appointment books; Wilson shorthand and Wilson typed drafts of messages and diplomatic notes, public statements, press releases, annual reports to Congress, and the like; and drafts of similar documents typed by Swem.

2. *The Woodrow Wilson Collection, Library of Princeton University*

Although more important for the pre-presidential period, this second largest collection of Wilson materials contains many documents from the presidential years: the letters between Wilson and Ellen Axson Wilson in 1913-1914; Wilson's own typed copy of his first inaugural; the originals of Wilson's letters to Cleveland H. Dodge; and numerous other items.

3. *The Papers of Edith Bolling Galt Wilson, Library of Congress*

This collection contains all of Wilson's love letters to Mrs. Galt; copies of diplomatic dispatches with Wilson's marginal comments, sent by Wilson to Mrs. Galt during their courtship; Mrs. Wilson's letters to her family during the Paris Peace Conference; and a large number of incoming personal and political letters.

4. *Materials in the National Archives*

The documents in the National Archives most important for this series are the thousands of pages of Wilson's diplomatic correspondence to be found only in the State Department files. Wilson maintained only a supervisory control over certain areas of foreign policy—relations with Central America, South America, and the Caribbean republics. However, in diplomatic relations in which he was intimately involved—relations with Mexico, Japan, China, Great Britain, Germany, France, Italy, Austria-Hungary, and Russia, and peacemaking, 1918-1920—Wilson personally wrote a large part of the diplomatic correspondence of the United States Government. He usually wrote a shorthand draft of a note or dispatch and then transcribed it on his own Hammond typewriter. Swem often made the final typed draft. The Wilson typed draft or Swem's copy was sent to the State Department where it was pasted on a "Telegram Sent" form, encoded, and then deposited in the department's files. Only rarely were copies of these dispatches kept in the White House files.

A second large group of Wilson materials in the National

Archives are the originals of Wilson letters addressed to depart-mental and agency heads and others. Even more important (be-cause we usually have letterpress or carbon copies of *Wilson's* letters) are the letters addressed to Wilson by his cabinet mem-bers and other officials, which Wilson returned to them with marginal comments and endorsements, or along with his own reply. After the outbreak of the World War, Wilson resorted more and more frequently to the practice of returning letters from his Secretaries of State to them, along with replies typed by himself.

Finally, there are in the departmental files of the National Archives thousands of letters addressed to Wilson which he re-ferred for information, recommendation, or action to cabinet heads and others.

5. *The Charles L. Swem Collection, Library of Princeton University*

This large and invaluable collection contains virtually all of Swem's shorthand notebooks. They consist of three series: (1) notebooks with shorthand versions of Wilson's speeches and cor-respondence from the beginning of the presidential campaign of 1912 through January 1913; (2) correspondence notebooks, 1913-1921; and (3) notebooks in which Swem recorded Wilson's speeches, press conferences, and public statements from 1913 to 1921. Swem also seems to have cleaned out Wilson's waste-basket every day, and his collection contains a large number of Wilson shorthand and Wilson typed documents, Wilson hand-written drafts, and miscellaneous items. Finally, Swem kept cop-ies of most of his transcripts of Wilson's speeches (some of them emended by Wilson for publication), press conferences, public statements, and so on. In many cases, these transcripts are the only ones in existence.

6. *Major Related Private Collections*

We have searched all private manuscript collections and dia-ries that might conceivably contain materials shedding light upon our subject. It would take more space than we care to use to list them all. Moreover, our search continues and is particularly fruitful in the recovery of single items or small groups still in private hands and public repositories. We hope that our readers will be content with a description of the following collections. They are singled out for special attention because of their su-preme importance: it would be impossible to publish a compre-hensive edition for the presidential period without them.

A. The William Jennings Bryan Collections.

The collection known as the Papers of William Jennings Bryan in the Library of Congress was originally a small collection with a few significant items from the Wilson era. It became very important for the Wilson Papers in 1966, when members of the Bryan family offered for sale about half the contents of Bryan's top secret file as Secretary of State and the Library of Congress purchased these documents and added them to the Bryan Papers. The addition consisted of some 1,400 items of the highest order of importance, including many Wilson handwritten and Wilson typed letters, memoranda, and drafts, and the originals of many Bryan letters and other documents.

An equally important Bryan collection is in the National Archives. It consists of the other half of Bryan's most secret file, which Bryan, on leaving the State Department, gave to his chief clerk, Ben G. Davis, as a memento of their friendship. Mrs. Davis donated these papers to the National Archives in 1947. They have been kept as a discrete collection.

B. The Papers of Colonel House, Yale University Library

Edward M. House, one of Wilson's chief advisers on foreign policy and often his roving ambassador, kept his papers with the intention of amassing a complete personal collection for the Wilson period. Magnificently arranged and catalogued, they contain, among other treasures, all of Wilson's 384 letters and telegrams to House. Many of these are Wilson handwritten or Wilson typed.

C. The Diary of Colonel House, Yale University Library

This, the single most important document of the Wilson era, runs to some 3,000 typed pages. Beginning on September 25, 1912, House began dictating (usually daily) his account of events of the day. He visited the White House frequently and was almost always present there during periods of crisis, and his records of conversations with Wilson are monumentally important because usually unique. However, other large sections of this diary—particularly relating to House's service as a roving ambassador and as an American peace commissioner in Paris—are of only slightly less importance.

It should be added that the House Diary varies greatly in reliability. Most persons keep a diary for a purpose. House went to great effort to keep this massive record with the main object of establishing his place in history. His egotism, always remarkably great, grew as the years passed. His diary should, therefore, be used with great caution, particularly when he was reporting on events in which he was personally involved or his own reputation was at stake.

D. The Papers of Robert Lansing, Library of Congress

Lansing was as methodical as House in saving his papers, and his collection in the Library of Congress includes, in addition to his letters, his appointment books, desk diaries, and a series of confidential memoranda, some of them recording discussions at cabinet meetings. Lansing kept possession of his top secret State Department files until his death in 1928. The department obtained this collection at a subsequent date and published it in two volumes in 1939-1940.

E. The Diary of Josephus Daniels, Library of Congress

Following the advice that he gave Wilson in a letter of March 1, 1913, Daniels started out bravely to keep a record of his activities and a full account of cabinet meetings. This diary is in two parts—a series of bound diaries in which Daniels made handwritten entries, and entries too long for the bound diary, which Daniels dictated to his secretary and were typed as separate documents.

Daniels kept full and revealing accounts of cabinet meetings through May 20, 1913. Then his energy, time, and resolution ran out, and he began to write only brief entries in the bound volumes detailing his personal and official activities. The next account of a cabinet meeting—a brief and cryptic one—is dated November 11, 1913. It is also the last entry until January 1, 1915. At this time, Daniels resumed writing in the bound diary and included brief but often revealing accounts of cabinet meetings. His record is crucially important for the period of Wilson's illness following his stroke in October 1919.

Since no other member of Wilson's cabinet is known to have kept a diary, Daniels' record, incomplete though it is, is an indispensable source. It is straightforward and, so far as we can determine, sturdily honest and reliable. It was edited by E. David Cronon and published by the University of Nebraska Press in 1963.

F. The Papers of Sir William Wiseman, Yale University Library

Wiseman was the direct liaison between Wilson and House and the British government during 1917-1918, and Wilson used Wiseman as his means of top secret communication with London. This collection contains not only all of these exchanges but the equally important correspondence on the British side.

7. *Diplomatic Materials in Foreign Public Archives*

Very important for the presidential period are the reports in foreign public archives of conversations between Wilson and diplomats, heads of state, special ambassadors, and so on. Wilson talked to diplomatic officers frequently. Eager to explain his attitudes and policies beyond any chance of misunderstanding, he would patiently and candidly explain them. There are hundreds of such reports in the archives of all the countries with which the United States had important diplomatic relations during the Wilson period. Often these reports are the fullest and best records that can be found of Wilson's plans and purposes in foreign policy. Moreover, they give us a revealing picture of Wilson's style as a diplomatist. In addition, these documents are full of news and comments about events occurring in the United States. They are prime evidence because their authors were highly trained reporters who often had access to the American elite. These foreign archives, particularly the British, also contain many Wilson handwritten and Wilson typed letters. Finally, the correspondence between diplomatic officers and their own governments and the memoranda of foreign office officials and their marginal comments on dispatches tell us much about how foreign leaders perceived Wilson's policies and the way American ambassadors communicated instructions from Wilson and the State Department.

8. *Newspapers and Periodicals*

These are an obviously important source for Wilson's interviews, public statements, and press releases. They are even more important as the source of Wilson's speeches. Experienced shorthand reporters recorded Wilson's extemporaneous speeches. Their usually complete texts enable us to determine (when the documents in the Wilson Papers and the Swem Collection do not reveal it) the degree to which Wilson and Swem edited the latter's transcripts of speeches for official publication. Newspaper texts also provide us with a check on Swem.

Newspapers are also the best source of information about Wilson's activities—his public appearances and addresses, meetings with congressional committees and leaders, daily activities, etc. Then, as now, little remained secret in Washington for very long.

PRINCIPLES OF SELECTION

How does one select documents for publication from among the millions that exist in the sources that we have just described?

The answer to this question—and the overriding principle of selection—depends altogether upon one's objectives in editing documentary series. Our first objective is to publish a comprehensive edition of the papers and records of the presidential period that emanated directly or indirectly from Wilson and shed significant light on his thoughts, purposes, and activities. To this end, we will publish:

1. All letters by Wilson that are essential to understanding his private life and personality. We will print all of his letters to Ellen Axson Wilson, Edith Bolling Galt Wilson, and Mary Allen Hulbert (Peck); most of his letters to old friends; and numerous samples of letters to others.

2. All of Wilson's political correspondence that seems to us to have enduring historical value, for example, letters to cabinet members and congressional leaders about important policies and legislation, most letters to ambassadors and Colonel House, and the like.

3. Enough of Wilson's correspondence to make clear his concern about patronage; they way he used appointments to promote legislation and reshape the Democratic party; and the constraints upon his appointment policies.

4. Those portions of transcripts of Wilson shorthand and Wilson typed documents which reveal significant changes between these first and the final drafts.

5. All of Wilson's diplomatic correspondence, omitting only what is obviously of ephemeral interest. Also all drafts of diplomatic notes, instructions to ambassadors, circular notes, etc., that Wilson decided not to send.

6. All of Wilson's speeches, omitting only casual remarks, for example, brief remarks to delegations visiting the White House.

7. All of Wilson's public statements and press releases.

8. Extracts from personal diaries recording significant conversations with Wilson, cabinet discussions, and the like, in spite of the obvious imperfection of this type of historical evidence.

9. Letters from Wilson's friends and associates to third parties recording significant conversations with Wilson.

10. Dispatches and reports by foreign diplomats that record conversations with Wilson, convey his thoughts or policies through a third person, or shed important light on Wilson as a diplomatist.

11. Those portions of the transcripts of Wilson's press conferences that reveal his relations with newspapermen, anything important about Wilson's thought and leadership, or provide the background for important news reports.

12. News reports of important events when they are the best records that we have of these events.

Our second objective is to publish all important letters, reports, diplomatic dispatches, and memoranda, not written by Wilson but which had a significant impact on his thought, policies, and programs. Along with this objective goes our principle of exclusion: all documents which Wilson never saw or knew about will be excluded on the ground that they could not have had any impact on him.

We know a good deal about White House routine and the way that Wilson handled his mail.

At least during the first fourteen months of Wilson's presidency, all mail (except a few personal letters) went to the Executive Office, where it was opened by the letter clerk and then screened by Tumulty. He laid the letters and other documents that he thought Wilson ought to see on the President's desk in the Oval Office. Swem told Ray Stannard Baker, in an interview in 1925, that "with the Mexican crisis" Wilson sought more and more to take control of his incoming mail. Finding that Tumulty's judgment of what was important often did not correspond with his own, Wilson directed that all letters addressed to him should be sent unopened to his study on the second floor of the White House.

There is no reason to doubt Swem's memory on this point. Indeed, beginning in late April 1914, Wilson began to write "personal file" in shorthand on certain letters; it is obvious that he was screening his mail by this time. However, it was not physically possible for Wilson to read all the mail that came into the White House on any single day, even if he had spent all his time at the task. He obviously selected letters from correspondents whom he knew personally or who were otherwise well known to him.

We can be almost completely certain that we know which documents Wilson handled and did not handle. The fact that a letter or report was in his personal file is conclusive evidence that he read it. In addition, Wilson's own replies give us a sure guide to a large portion of the letters that Wilson read; they often also indicate whether he had read them carefully or casually. Also, Swem typed virtually all of Wilson's letters; all the letters to which Swem typed answers bear the stamp "C.L.S." Thus it is easy to identify the incoming letters that Wilson answered in replies dictated to Swem.

Tumulty acknowledged most important letters that Wilson did not answer personally. In most cases, Wilson gave Tumulty written instructions for replies. Hence, obviously, Wilson read these letters.

As for the great bulk of White House mail, some of it was not answered at all, and the rest was acknowledged routinely by White House clerks, who stamped their own initials on these documents. They constitute the great bulk of incoming mail that will be excluded under our rule.

Many incoming diplomatic dispatches and reports were sent to Wilson or were handed to him by Bryan, Lansing, and other State Department officials. It is usually not difficult to determine which notes and dispatches Wilson read. His own diplomatic correspondence provides numerous clues. He often commented on diplomatic reports and dispatches in letters to the State Department. And there are times when one can see Wilson reacting in policy directly to a document.

Having segregated the documents that Wilson handled, we will make our choices among them for publication according to the rule of enduring historical and biographical significance. We will print only a small portion of or ignore several large types of correspondence. About one third of the incoming letters related to patronage. Wilson read most of them. We will print only enough, as we have said, to illuminate what we think are the important aspects of Wilson's patronage problems and policies. Another large part of the incoming mail—from cabinet members, the Civil Service Commission, the commissioners of the District of Columbia, and so on—concerned matters of day to day routine administration. We will print virtually none of these documents. The loss, which we regret, will be a view of the incredible burden of routine administration that Wilson (like other Presidents before Franklin D. Roosevelt) had to carry, in the absence of any special assistants except Tumulty. However, it is easy enough for any person interested in the mass of routine to satisfy himself by examining the microfilm edition of the Wilson Papers published by the Library of Congress and accessible in all major libraries. Finally, we will print only a small sample of congratulatory letters and telegrams following an address, legislative or diplomatic triumph, and so on—many of which Wilson read and acknowledged.

It remains only to be said that in following our rule of exclusion, we will not print thousands of interesting and important documents. For example, during the controversy over alleged segregation in the federal departments in 1913-1914, hundreds of black leaders and white civil libertarians wrote letters of protest to Wilson. Wilson replied to the ones that he saw, and the controversy is, we think, well documented in this series. However, Wilson did not see the great majority of these letters, and these we will not print because we are editing the *Wilson* papers, not a documentary history of the Wilson era. That task we leave to other scholars, and we hope that there will be many of them!

EDITORIAL METHODS

Our editorial methods have changed so little from the ones detailed in the General Introduction that it suffices to elaborate upon them, briefly, as follows:

1. We intend to follow, more strictly than we have in the past, the policy of printing documents *verbatim et literatim*, spelling and typographical errors and all; and to repair words and phrases in square brackets only when absolutely necessary for the sake of clarity.

2. We will excise passages of ephemeral interest from letters and other documents more frequently in the future than in the past. However, readers may be assured that we will not fail to print a document because it is long.

3. If incoming documents had a significant impact on Wilson, or if printing them is essential to understanding Wilson's own letters and diplomatic correspondence, we will usually publish them whether or not they have been printed before. Actually, many of the older printed versions are seriously flawed. For example, much of the diplomatic correspondence printed in the *Foreign Relations* series for 1913 to 1921 (excluding the special series—*The Lansing Papers*, the World War *Supplements*, and the Peace Conference series) is actually reproduced in paraphrase, with important omissions not indicated. To cite another example, Charles Seymour, in *The Intimate Papers of Colonel House*, made significant changes in the texts of House's letters to Wilson and considerably edited the House diary. The alterations in the letters sometimes completely changed the meaning of sentences. In any event, as we have said before, our purpose is to publish a complete and trustworthy edition of all documents that shed significant light on Wilson in order that they may be available in a single series.

4. Readers should be reminded that headings indicate the

authorship of documents. All documents with headings without attribution of authorship are Wilsonian. Thus the heading "A Circular Note to the Powers" or "To Walter Hines Page" means that Wilson wrote the circular and note even though they went out under Bryan's signature. Headings such as "A Draft of a Note" mean that this version was written by Wilson and was not sent.

In addition, evidence of authorship of documents not bearing Wilson's signature can be found in the description-location lines. Thus documents described as WWhw (Woodrow Wilson hand-written), WWT (Woodrow Wilson typed), and CLST (C. L. Swem typed) are always of Wilsonian authorship.

5. We will read all of Swem's transcripts of Wilson's speeches and press conferences against Swem's shorthand notes and continue silently to correct these transcripts. In addition, we will continue to compare Swem's transcripts against others when they exist.

6. Wilson often emended Swem's transcripts of his addresses for publication. We will print the texts as he edited them, on the assumption that anyone has the right to edit his writings and speeches before publication. However, we will indicate, either through notes or typographical devices any changes that could conceivably be regarded as significant. In addition the description-location line will indicate that the text printed has been edited by Wilson—for example, T MS (WP, DLC), with WWhw emendations.

7. From this volume on, documents cited in *future* volumes will be cross referenced only by date, not by volume.

ANNOTATION

The style and degree of annotation of any documentary series must depend upon a number of variable factors—the types of documents printed, the character of the individuals and events involved, the kinds of people who will most likely use the series, and the state of historical knowledge at the time the volumes are edited.

We are moving into a new and radically different period in Wilson's life, and this fact has important consequences for our annotation of this and following volumes. The biographical and historical literature on Wilson and his era is much more extensive for the presidential period than for the earlier years. The characters on our stage and the events in which they were involved are much better known. Hence we think that the need for annotation has decreased.

In the presidential volumes, we will try to make the documents intelligible by appropriate identifications and explanatory notes. Specifically we will:

1. Identify individuals who would not ordinarily be known to most readers, for example, congressmen and senators, governors, federal officials, etc., and of course more obscure persons, if we think that identifying them is necessary to understanding the document. However, we will not identify persons well known to most readers, for example, Theodore Roosevelt, George V, William Jennings Bryan, William II of Germany, etc.

The full names, when it is possible to find them, of all persons mentioned in the volumes will be printed in the indexes. In a few appropriate cases (for example, William Bayard Hale's report of June 18, 1913, in Volume 27) we will not supply full names in notes to a document but ask the reader to refer to the index for them.

2. We will not identify events and describe legislation about which there is a good historical literature but will, rather, refer the reader for background and orientation to the best books and articles on the persons and subjects involved. For example, when Wilson signs the Federal Reserve Act, we will not have a long note describing its various provisions but will refer the reader to the several excellent books that analyze that measure in detail. The same is true for all major legislation and events like the outbreak of the World War. However, we will provide annotation to explicate those documents revealing Wilson's participation in, for example, the drafting of the Federal Reserve bill and his role in securing its passage through Congress.

3. We will not write editorial notes of a biographical or historical character. We have neither the time nor the desire to write a history of the Wilson era in notes and editorial notes. It requires all our time and energies to search for missing documents, select the materials to be printed, analyze and criticize those materials, correct corrupt transcripts, and establish a reliable text. We will be satisfied if we can produce trustworthy texts of the significant documents essential to knowledge and understanding of Woodrow Wilson during his presidency. As for the rest, we are content to leave something for scholars of this and future generations to do.

THE EDITORS

Princeton, New Jersey
July 29, 1977

INTRODUCTION

WILSON, his vacation in Bermuda behind him, is in the midst of conferences with Democratic leaders and friends, laying the foundations for his legislative program and building the superstructure of his administration. After poignant farewells to the State of New Jersey and his neighbors in Princeton, he and his family, accompanied by several hundred Princeton undergraduates, board a special train at the foot of Blair Arch of Princeton University for the journey to Washington. From a stand on the east front of the Capitol on March 4, 1913, he reads his first inaugural. It affirms the fundamental soundness of American institutions and describes the things that should be done to restore public confidence in government and revive hope for a better life among the oppressed and downtrodden.

From this point on, the documents illustrate the life and activities of the new President in all their aspects. They show Wilson's effort to recruit only "the best men" for public service, and how this effort was often thwarted, particularly in ambassadorial appointments, by circumstances beyond his control. They reveal Wilson's determination of the essential provisions of the first two great domestic measures of his administration—the Underwood tariff and Federal Reserve bills—and his skill as a parliamentary leader in reconciling warring factions and uniting his followers in Congress. They reveal Wilson and Secretary of State Bryan as they repudiate the "realistic" foreign policy of their two predecessors and seek to formulate a foreign policy based upon moral principles and support for human rights and world peace. Then a controversy with Japan erupts over California's denial of the right of land ownership to persons "ineligible to citizenship," and Wilson and Bryan, as the documents reveal, move swiftly and deftly to solve the crisis. Finally, the materials give us an intimate view of Wilson at work, in the cabinet, and among his friends.

By the close of this volume, the Underwood tariff bill has triumphantly passed the House, Wilson has won agreement upon the Federal Reserve bill, and has brought the country safely through the crisis with Japan. The only dark cloud on the horizon is the Mexican problem—whether to recognize or oppose the government of the military usurper, Victoriano Huerta.

❖

We are grateful to Richard W. Leopold, August Heckscher, Pendleton Herring, and Richard D. Challener for participating in far-ranging discussions about the presidential volumes; and to Katharine E. Brand, Richard W. Leopold, August Heckscher, William H. Harbaugh, and John Milton Cooper, Jr., for reading and criticizing drafts of Volumes 27 and 28.

We express our warm thanks to the National Historical Publications and Records Commission for generous financial assistance in the publication of these and recent volumes. We also acknowledge with gratitude a grant by the commission to the Woodrow Wilson Foundation to enable us to have a researcher in Washington, Dr. Richard Wood, who, with consummate skill and doggedness, has found hundreds of Wilson letters and other documents long buried in departmental files.

We thank Professor Keiji Matsunobu of Kita-Kyushu University and Mr. Jun Furuya, a graduate student at Princeton University, for help in translating Japanese documents; and Professor Chihiro Hosoya of Hitotsubashi University for help in finding these documents in the Japanese Foreign Office; Manfred Bömeke, a graduate student at Princeton, and Dr. Reinhard Doerries of the University of Hamburg, for help in finding documents in the German Foreign Office; Professor John Milton Cooper, Jr., of the University of Wisconsin, and Professor Wilton B. Fowler, for help in locating materials in various British repositories; and Jane Serumgard Harrison for help in translating French documents. We welcome Judith May as our new editor at Princeton University Press.

M. Halsey Thomas, consulting editor since 1968, died in Princeton on July 7, 1977. He prepared the indexes for Volumes 6-12 and 14-23. In addition, he prepared the index section of Volume 13 and, in doing so, completely re-indexed Volumes 1-3 and revised those of Volumes 4 and 5. He was a master indexer, one of the greatest of his generation—meticulous, comprehensive, and brilliant in organization. Former Archivist of Princeton University, he was a storehouse of knowledge about the history of this institution. However, we remember him most as a gentle, quiet person, completely devoted to his work and to his colleagues. We bid him an affectionate farewell.

THE EDITORS

Princeton, New Jersey
July 14, 1977

CONTENTS

ILLUSTRATIONS

ABBREVIATIONS

ALS	autograph letter signed
CCL	carbon copy of letter
CCLS	carbon copy of letter signed
CLS	Charles Lee Swem
CLSsh	Charles Lee Swem shorthand
CLST	Charles Lee Swem typed
EAW	Ellen Axson Wilson
EBR	Executive Branch Records, National Archives
ELA	Ellen Louise Axson
EMH	Edward Mandell House
FO	British Foreign Office
hw	handwriting, handwritten
HwCL	handwritten copy of letter
JRT	Jack Romagna typed
MS	manuscript
PL	printed letter
RG	Record Group
SDR	State Department Records
T	typed
T MS	typed manuscript
TC	typed copy
TC MS	typed copy of manuscript
TCL	typed copy of letter
TL	typed letter
TLI	typed letter initialed
TLS	typed letter signed
WJB	William Jennings Bryan
WW	Woodrow Wilson
WWhw	Woodrow Wilson handwriting, handwritten
WWhw MS	Woodrow Wilson handwritten manuscript
WWsh	Woodrow Wilson shorthand
WWT MS	Woodrow Wilson typed manuscript
WWTLS	Woodrow Wilson typed letter signed

ABBREVIATIONS FOR COLLECTIONS AND REPOSITORIES

Following the National Union Catalog of the Library of Congress

A-Ar	Alabama Department of Archives and History
CoHi	Colorado State Historical Society
CtY	Yale University
CtY-D	Yale University, Divinity School
DLC	Library of Congress
DNA	National Archives
DeU	University of Delaware
FFM-Ar	French Foreign Ministry Archives
FR	*Papers Relating to the Foreign Relations of the United States*

GFO-Ar	German Foreign Office Archives
JFO-Ar	Japanese Foreign Office Archives
MH	Harvard University
MH-Ar	Harvard University Archives
MnHi	Minnesota Historical Society
NN	New York Public Library
NcMHi	Historical Foundation of the Presbyterian and Reformed Churches
NcU	University of North Carolina
NjP	Princeton University
PPAmP	American Philosophical Society
PPPrHi	Presbyterian Historical Society
PRO	Public Record Office
RSB Coll., DLC	Ray Stannard Baker Collection of Wilsoniana, Library of Congress
TxHR	Rice University
UA, NjP	Princeton University Archives
ViU	University of Virginia
WC, NjP	Woodrow Wilson Collection, Princeton University
WP, DLC	Woodrow Wilson Papers, Library of Congress

SYMBOLS

[Jan. 11, 1913]	publication date of a published writing; also date of document when date is not part of text
[*Feb. 3, 1913*]	composition date when publication date differs
[[March 1, 1913]]	delivery date of speech if publication date differs
⟨and visits to⟩	text deleted by Wilson

THE PAPERS OF

WOODROW WILSON

VOLUME 27
1913

THE PAPERS OF
WOODROW WILSON

To Mary Allen Hulbert

Dearest Friend,   Princeton. 1 Jan'y, 1912 [1913]

I will not wish you a Happy New Year: it might sound as if I were unmindful of your sorrow,[1]–of the change that must now seem to you to cast a shadow over all the years to come. I will only tell you what my thought of you is as I look forward and try to think *for* you,–now while you cannot think. It must seem to you as if the whole past had slipped away from you and was buried,– along with a great deal of yourself,–for with her was associated all your girlhood, all your free years, all the years of dreams and hope and wonder, and she was your anchor and your refuge in the years that followed and were so full of suffering and mortification and brave struggle. And now you seem to have cut *all* connections and to have left *yourself* behind! I can feel it as if it were my own experience, and it is terrible! The waters are very deep and very black. And so, with a clean slate and in a steel-grey world which does not seem the dawn of anything, but dull twilight, rather, and the *end* of the day, you stand facing,–what? Well, my dear, dear friend, remember that, while you have lost your comfort, your dearest one, and turned your back upon a whole life (as it must seem to you), all the things that haunted and hampered and humiliated and burdened you intolerably have gone with the rest, and you are *free*,–free to *serve* and let *go* in you all the things the release of which, as I have seen and know, give your [you] your real zest and happiness. It was touching that the first thing you were called on to do was to care for the poor dying woman on the steamer, but I could read between the lines of your account of it that it was sweet to you, too. And now, so soon as you rest and get hold of yourself, you can look about and *choose* what you will do. All the strongest and most beautiful things in you will come out. I predict that you will grow younger and more charming still as you find in your new free choice, the things that it will best please you to do, best satisfy the deep things in you that *are* you. You have never fully discovered yourself yet! Now you will *bloom*, as I have always foreseen that you would, and be most yourself by forgetting yourself, and discovering to the full those qualities which have made me

Your devoted friend   Woodrow Wilson

Love to Allen.

ALS (WP, DLC).
[1] Her mother, Anjenett Holcomb Allen, had died on December 2, 1912.

To William Bayard Hale

My dear Mr. Hale,   [Princeton, N. J.] 1 Jan'y, 1913.

Here's the first half of the galley proof of the book.[1] I have gone over it carefully and thank you for letting me have it in such convenient form.

In haste,   Faithfully Yours,   Woodrow Wilson

ALS (Berg Coll., NN).
[1] Of Wilson's book, *The New Freedom*.

To Carter Glass

My dear Mr. Glass: [Trenton, N. J.] January 1, 1913.

Thank you sincerely for your letter of December twenty-ninth.

My one time colleague, Mr. Royal Meeker of Princeton, has some views of the members of the Economic Association which he wishes to present to me, and I am going to try and see him very soon. After that I should greatly value another conference with you. I wonder what day of the week, if any, you are free to come to see me, now that Congress has resumed its sessions. If you will give me a tip on that matter I shall try to keep in touch with you.

It was a great pleasure to catch a glimpse of you in Staunton and I shall be interested to know your full ex[p]ressions of the event, particularly of the dinner.

In haste, with warm regards,

Faithfully yours,   Woodrow Wilson

TLS (C. Glass Papers, ViU).

From Royal Meeker

Princeton, New Jersey

My dear Governor Wilson: Jan. 1, 1913.

Please indicate a time when you will be at liberty to hear my report upon the opinions of eminent economists concerning bank-

ing and currency reform. Do you wish me to communicate with
Prof. H. P. Willis before reporting to you?

Sincerely yours,   Royal Meeker.

ALS (WP, DLC).

From Walter Hines Page

Garden City, New York
My dear Wilson: New Year's Day, 1913.

A suggestion: Commission the man in whose judgment you
have most confidence to master, condense, classify, and index all
the literature of our occupation of the Philippines; then to go
there and to study the people politically, socially, ethnologically;
let him have two or three or more most competent secretaries;
and let him bring you in the late summer not only his own opinion
but the opinions of all other men who have studied the subject.

Then by the opening of the regular session of Congress in
December you would have all the information best worth having
on the subject in the whole world.

Let such a man begin now to organize the work, to get at the
literature—silently—and let him sail March 5.

For reasons that I do not know this may be of no value; but it
is offered for whatever it may be worth.

Sincerely yours,   Walter H. Page

ALS (WP, DLC).

To William Howard Taft

My dear Mr. President,   Princeton, New Jersey 2 Jan'y, 1913

Allow me to extend to you, with all my heart, the best wishes
of the New Year. I hope it will bring to you satisfactions of the
most lasting sort. I trust that your trip to Panama brought you
refreshment and pleasure.

I am taking the liberty of writing to you, because Mrs. Wilson
does not wish to burden Mrs. Taft,[1] to ask your candid opinion
of the present housekeeper at the White House. I hope that you
will not deem it an undue liberty and that you will pardon so
intimate and domestic an inquiry! It is a piece of business from
which I know no escape!

With cordial regard,

Sincerely yours,   Woodrow Wilson

ALS (W. H. Taft Papers, DLC).
  [1] Helen Herron Taft.

To Walter Hines Page

My dear Page: [Trenton, N. J.] January 2, 1913.

Your suggestion about investigating the Philippine matter interests me mightily, but where would the money come from? Do you know of any funds that are available for such an expenditure?[1]

I am entirely uninformed on that point.

I was mighty sorry to cut off the engagement we had and was ashamed to fall sick at so interesting a moment. I wonder if you could find time to run down here on Monday the sixth, or Wednesday the eighth? I am sure I could find an hour on one or the other of those days, and I want very much to see you.

Faithfully yours,   Woodrow Wilson

TLS (W. H. Page Papers, MH).

[1] As subsequent documents will disclose, Wilson sent Henry Jones Ford on this mission. Wilson's old friend, Edward Leavitt Howe of the Princeton Bank, advanced some $7,000 to pay Ford's expenses.

To William Bayard Hale

My dear Mr. Hale,   Princeton, New Jersey 2 Jan'y, 1913

Here is the rest of the galleys. I have done my best with them and thank you for all your own careful work.

In haste, with all the best wishes of the season,

Cordially Yours,   Woodrow Wilson

ALS (Berg Coll., NN).

A Preface to *The New Freedom*

[c. Jan. 2, 1913]

I have not written a book since the campaign. I did not write this book at all. It is the result of the editorial literary skill of Mr. William Bayard Hale, who has put together here in their right sequences the more suggestive portions of my campaign speeches.

And yet it is not a book of campaign speeches. It is a discussion of a number of very vital subjects in the free form of extemporaneously spoken words. I have left the sentences in the form in which they were stenographically reported. I have not tried to alter the easy-going and often colloquial phraseology in which they were uttered from the platform, in the hope that they would seem the more fresh and spontaneous because of their very lack of pruning and recasting. They have been suffered to run their unpremeditated course even at the cost of such repetition and redundancy as the extemporaneous speaker apparently inevitably falls into.

The book is not a discussion of measures or of programs. It is an attempt to express the new spirit of our politics and to set forth, in large terms which may stick in the imagination, what it is that must be done if we are to restore our politics to their full spiritual vigor again, and our national life, whether in trade, in industry, or in what concerns us only as families and individuals, to its purity, its self-respect, and its pristine strength and freedom. The New Freedom is only the old revived and clothed in the unconquerable strength of modern America.

Woodrow Wilson.

Printed in Woodrow Wilson, *The New Freedom: A Call for the Emancipation of the Generous Energies of a People* (New York and Garden City, N. Y., 1913), pp. vii-viii.

To Henry St. George Tucker

My dear Mr. Tucker: [Trenton, N. J.] January 3, 1913.

I must admit that I am sorry that it should be thought by anybody that I was guilty of a breach of taste in the little (thoroughly good natured) squint I took at the earlier situation in Virginia before the nomination. I certainly was in the best humor about it as I had every reason to be. I did not intend anything venomous, but only speaking as I am in the habit of speaking at home, because I was among home folk.

It pleases me that you should think the speech made a profound impression and I was sorry that your engagements took you away so that I had only a glimpse of you.

In haste,

Cordially and sincerely yours,   Woodrow Wilson

TLS (Tucker Family Papers, NcU).

To Arthur W. Tedcastle

My dear Tedcastle: [Trenton, N. J.] January 3, 1913.

You may be sure that I appreciate very highly your letter of the fifteenth of December.[1] Unhappily I have to postpone my answers to letter[s] from friends who will understand, until I have taken care of strangers who will not.

There is one thing you can do for me which I would highly value, and it is quite in line with your own generous suggestion.

I want to get all the disinterested opinion I can collect about Mr. Louis D. Brandeis. He is a man of such originality and force and might be made so serviceable to the public that I want to know just what his neighbors whom he has not prejudiced by his action with regard to them personally think about him. Of course I know how some of the best men in Boston hate him, but I think I know the reason for that feeling, and I want to get outside of that circle.

It is fine to have somebody to whom I can turn whose reports I can rely upon as uncolored, and it is particularly delightful to feel your friendship.

Please give our warmest regards to Mrs. Tedcastle, of whom I hear the most glowing accounts from Savannah, and believe me,
                    Always faithfully,   Woodrow Wilson

TLS (WP, DLC).
  ¹ A. W. Tedcastle to WW, Dec. 15, 1912, ALS (WP, DLC).

To Abel McIver Fraser

My dear Dr. Fraser: [Trenton, N. J.] January 3, 1912 [1913].

We have settled again to our routine at home but it will be a long, long time before we loose the vivid impression of the pleasure we had in visiting you at Staunton. Your hospitality was of the truest, most generous and thoughtful sort, and we shall always be grateful to you for it and count ourselves among your friends and admirers. I wish there was some other way besides words in which I could express the real debt I feel under to you.

Mrs. Wilson is herself going to write to Mrs. Fraser,¹ but I wanted to give myself the pleasure of sending to Mrs. Fraser and you and the young people of your household² this warm expression of my deep appreciation.
                    Cordially and sincerely yours,   Woodrow Wilson

TLS (WP, DLC).
  ¹ Octavia Blanding Fraser.
  ² Nora Blanding Fraser, Margaret McIver Fraser, Douglas de Saussure Fraser, and Jean Blanding Fraser.

From William Jennings Bryan, with Enclosures

My Dear Gov,   Miami, Florida Jany 3 1913

I hope you will pardon me for writing with a pen. I do not like to dictate letters to you for fear the stenographer might draw conclusions from the contents. I enclose copy of letter recently rec'd from Aguinaldo—the leader of the Filipinos in their war for Independence. I met him several years ago when I visited the Philippines. He is a very interesting person and the most influential man in the islands. I also enclose my reply for correction or approval. It is my first "state paper" as it were. I thought it wise to restrain his eagerness a little first by showing him that we did not win by a *majority* but only by a plurality, and, second, by putting him to work advising others against impatience.

The Interior Dept seems to be the most coveted of the cabinet positions, to judge by the number of applicants. By the way, did you know that the forest reserves are under the Sec of Agriculture? I had forgotten this—that is the most troublesome question in the Mountain States.

Recommendations and protests still pour in upon me. The protests are not so numerous as the endorsements—some have questioned Teals progressiveness. One correspondent suggests Mr Sandles of Ohio[1] for Sec of Agriculture. He is a progressive and an excellent man but has not had as much experience as some others who have been brought to your attention.

Mr Lewis Post is recommended by another for the Interior Dept. Do you know Mr Post? He lives in Chicago & edits The Public. He is an advocate of the Single Tax—was converted by Henry George. He is a man of great intelligence, of high character and of sterling democracy. I do not know of any office he has held except that under Mayor Dunne[2] he was associated with Miss [Jane] Addams on the school board. He is competent for any position—he is a man who can be useful to you.

By the way, some one has called my attention to the fact that V. P. Gov Marshall has not been invited to confer. Might it not be worth while to cultivate closer relations between the Pres & V. P. than has been customary in the past?

Very truly yours   W. J. Bryan

P. S. The enclose[d] editorial from Wash. Star[3] emphasizes the importance of enlisting Aguinaldo as an aid.

ALS (WC, NjP).

[1] Alfred Putnam Sandles, long active in the Democratic party in Ohio, at this time secretary of the State Board of Agriculture.

[2] Edward Fitzsimons Dunne, Mayor of Chicago, 1905-1907; Governor of Illinois, 1913-17.

[3] "Philippine Independence," Washington *Evening Star*, Jan. 2, 1913. It warned that the Philippine plank of the Democratic platform of 1912, the "reported selection" of Bryan as Secretary of State, and Wilson's comment on the Philippines in his speech at the birthday banquet in Staunton on December 28, 1912, taken all together might encourage the "Aguinaldians" to new revolts and bloodshed to bring about immediate independence. The ultimate disposition of the Philippines, the *Star* asserted, lay in the hands of Congress, not in those of the President or his Secretary of State.

ENCLOSURE I

Emilio Aguinaldo to William Jennings Bryan

My dear Sir,   Manila, P. I. Nov. 15, 1912.

The triumph of your party is motive for rejoicing. Its bearing upon many questions and especially on the Philippine problem is of great importance. Never before have the Filipinos taken such a live interest in the outcome of the general election of the United States as at this one. The reason is easily understood when you take into account that the people of these islands have always looked upon the Democratic party as the standard bearer of justice, equality and liberty. May the right of the Filipinos to independence receive a friendly support in the Democratic party.

With the sincere wish that this success means an era of progress and prosperity, and that you will kindly accept my congratulations, I remain,

Yours very truly,   Emilio Aguinaldo.

ENCLOSURE II

William Jennings Bryan to Emilio Aguinaldo

My Dear Sir   Miami, Florida Jan. 2. 1913.

Your kind letter is at hand. The democratic vote while not a majority over all, gave us a handsome plurality and full control of the government.

I take it for granted, therefore, that the promises of the platform will be carried out, but it will take some time to pass the necessary measures and I trust you will use your great influence to encourage your people to be patient and to help us by showing self-restraint and confidence in our government.

The Republicans have been actuated by a desire to help your people, as shown by the interest they have taken in education, but they have differed from the Democrats as to the means that should be employed.

I, of course, prefer democratic methods.

With assurances of esteem &c. I am,

Very truly yours,   W. J. Bryan.

HwCL (WC, NjP).

From Carter Glass

Dear Governor Wilson: Washington. January 3, 1912 [1913].

I beg to acknowledge yours of January 1st asking when it will be convenient for me to come to see you on currency matters. We begin our hearings on Tuesday, January 7th, and will continue them on Tuesdays, Wednesdays and Thursdays of each succeeding week until that part of the work is ended. I will hold myself in readiness to come to Trenton, or to Princeton, at any time that may suit your convenience. Unless there is at least a probability for legislation at the extra session, there would be no necessity of pestering you now about this question, for I know you are overburdened with public affairs; but if there is a probability of action at the extra session I consider it all-important that we should have your definite views as early as possible. There is but one way to get legislation on this extremely difficult question and that is to have your thorough sanction of what the committee may propose.

With cordial regards,   Sincerely yours,   Carter Glass.

TLS (WP, DLC).

From Edward Mandell House

Dear Governor: New York City. January 3rd, 1913.

I received the enclosed letter from Mr. McCombs[1] this morning and I thought it would be of interest to you.

When I talked with him the other day he said that Hearst would want to be offered a place in the Cabinet, that he did not think he would take it but that he wanted it offered.

It will be a very pleasant pastime for you to offer the highest and most confidential places within your gift to your personal enemies and I sincerely hope that you will proceed at once to do so.

To be serious though I would not do anything about this matter until we can talk it over.

Among the pleasant things that McCombs told me was that you would soon not have a single newspaper of importance supporting you in New York City. He said he had learned through confidential sources that even the World was getting ready to turn. I trust the thought of it will not disturb you more than it does me.

I still have fever today and the doctor thinks it prudent for me

to remain in bed but he gives hope for very much better conditions tomorrow.

With affectionate regards, I am,

Your very faithful,   E. M. House

TLS (WP, DLC).
    ¹ W. F. McCombs to EMH, Jan. 2, 1913, ALS (WP, DLC), urging that Wilson
meet with William Randolph Hearst in order to avoid incurring his editorial
wrath.

William Howard Taft to Ellen Axson Wilson

My dear Mrs. Wilson: [The White House] January 3, 1913.

Mrs. Jaffray,¹ the housekeeper in the White House, has told me
that at your instance she visited you,² and that you would be
glad to hear from Mrs. Taft or me the impression we have of the
value of her services. Mrs. Jaffray is a Canadian, who has served
us well for four years. She understands the purchase of supplies,
is very attentive, and plans well ahead for entertainment. She
never makes herself conspicuous, and is never, so far as we have
seen, in the way. Mrs. Jaffray at first had the custody of government property in the White House, but a more satisfactory arrangement was made by appointing Arthur Brooks, a head colored
messenger, whom I had known in the War Department, to be
custodian, to have an office in the basement, and to record everything delivered to, and everything which went out of, the house.
In addition to this, Arthur Brooks, who is an excellent valet, has
assisted my Filipino boy³ in looking after my clothes. I shall take
my Filipino boy with me. Arthur Brooks is without exception the
most trustworthy colored man in the District of Columbia, and
has a very clear head for executive work. President Wilson, if he
retains him, will find him most useful in taking him upon trips
and in every possible way. Mrs. Jaffray and Arthur Brooks work
very well together. Brooks is especially useful in looking after the
wines and cigars to prevent their waste by waiters and others
at entertainments. He was Secretary Root's confidential messenger and man while he was in the War Department, and drew
all of his household checks.

Please present my compliments to President Wilson, and
believe me, my dear madam,

Sincerely yours,   Wm H Taft

Mrs. Taft has read this and approves.

TLS (Letterpress Books, W. H. Taft Papers, DLC).

¹ Elizabeth (Mrs. L. A.) Jaffray, a widow, formerly a household manager and social secretary in New York, who became housekeeper and general manager at the White House at the beginning of the Taft administration and remained in that position through the Coolidge administration. She wrote a brief book about her experiences, *Secrets of the White House* (New York, 1927).

² Mrs. Jaffray recalled that Mrs. Wilson asked her to come to Princeton in late November or early December 1912. At the conclusion of their interview, Mrs. Wilson asked her to stay on at the White House.

³ According to Mrs. Jaffray, his name was Monico.

To Mary Allen Hulbert

Dearest Friend,   Princeton, New Jersey 5 Jan'y, 1913

I find I must do as I did last winter, write on Sundays, when the world for a few hours lets me alone, quite regardless of the sailing times of the steamers. And I am going to assume that you know all the tiresome *public* news about us and that what you *want* is what is inside our hearts and our thinking boxes,—the things no one has the least claim to know except the friends who are most near and dear to us. I cannot tell you how often, how many times a day our thoughts turn to "Glencove" or with what affection and solicitude for the dear, dear friend who is there thinking her way to a new life, built on the present and on the things the people about her need from *her*, the things which only she can give, with her vivid nature and her extraordinary insight and sympathy,— for all sorts and conditions of people. I never knew a more perfect or more noble *sister to mankind* than that dear lady, now denied the infinite solace of receiving and laid under the noble necessity of *giving*, according to the infinite richness of her heart, of her whole nature. The other day I received a gift that was more welcome than the giver could possibly have divined. An old Confederate soldier in a Soldiers' Home down South somewhere sent me a dipper made out of *red cedar*. The bowl of it is made in the form of a beautifully formed, brass-bound little bucket,—my name on it on a brass plate,—and I drink out of it several times a day,— drink a draught of *Bermuda*, with a deep, sad pleasure,—a sort of renewal within me of all that Bermuda has meant for me. The water has a strange sweetness as it comes from the little bucket. And I fancy that you will yourself drink in a similar refreshment and renewal from the air that moves so freely and friendly about the little peninsula. (Watch for a chance for me to buy either Glencove or the point by the ferry) No small part of my pleasure and strength from day to day comes from thought of my dear friends. How I hope that thought of me supplies them sometimes with similar food for the heart. We are all well; and all unite in the most affectionate messages. Love to Allen.

Your devoted friend   Woodrow Wilson

This is just a message, not a letter. Do you like the kind?

ALS (WP, DLC).

From William Jennings Bryan

My Dear Gov,   Miami, Florida Jany 5, 1913

I am gratified that you are pleased with the suggestion regarding Gonzales. A friend of his wrote me a letter—a part of which I enclose.[1] Gonzales is a very modest fellow & would not press a matter in which he was personally interested but I know from him that it is the hight of his ambition to go to Cuba as Minister, and I am sure he would be of great service to us in dealing with the Cubans. His name is a prominent Spanish name and the service rendered by his father[2] in the earlier insurrections and by W. E. himself in the war for independence would make them welcome him as a friend. You are right, of course, in saying that there are cases where it would not do to send a man back to his home country—all rules have exceptions—but *where there are no objections* I think it is a good way of pleasing the foreign born element in the party. I am anxious that your administration shall strengthen our party—and we have been weak with the foreign element in recent years. I believe you have it in your power to so strengthen the party as to keep the party in power for a generation.

And, while on foreign affairs, let [me] say that I found our missionary cause embarassed by the immoralities of Americans and other representatives of the "Christian nations." I suggest for your consideration the propriety of selecting men of *pronounced Christian character* for China & Japan—these nations furnish the most encour[ag]ing missionary fields.

If you are considering Henry[3] in connection with Atty Generalship I beg to say that I believe he has sufficient ability and we are sure that his heart is right.   Yours truly   W. J. Bryan

ALS (WC, NjP).
  [1] This enclosure is missing.
  [2] Ambrosio José Gonzales (identified in WJB to WW, Dec. 25, 1912, n. 4, Vol. 25) had participated prominently in several abortive revolutionary expeditions from the United States to Cuba between 1848 and 1851. See Lewis Pinckney Jones, *Stormy Petrel: N. G. Gonzales and His State* (Columbia, S. C., 1973), pp. 6-8.
  [3] Robert L. Henry of Texas.

To Edward Mandell House

My dear friend: [Trenton, N. J.] January 6, 1913.

I am delighted to learn from Tumulty that you feel thar [that] you can come down and spend Wednesday night in Princeton. We have such a tiny house that there are no comfortable quarters which I would like you to occupy there, so I am going to ask you to be my guest at the Princeton Inn, which is near by and very comfortable, and spend all the time but bed time with us.

I hope you can plan to come down not later than the train (special Princeton t[r]ain) which leaves New York at 4:08.

Thank you for your note of the third.

In haste,   Faithfully yours,   Woodrow Wilson

Tumulty delights me with the intimation that Mrs. House may come with you. This will complete our satisfaction and enjoyment.   W.W.

TLS (E. M. House Papers, CtY).

To Albert Sidney Burleson

My dear Mr. Burleson: [Trenton, N. J.] January 6, 1913.

There is a natter [matter] I forgot to speak of this afternoon. I send this, therefore, as a memorandum.

I think it would be a mistake, nationally speaking, for the Committee on Appropriations, not to report favorably the bill providing money for the celebration of the Anniversary of the Emancipation Proclamation.

I know that you will pardon me for saying this to a close friend. I say this for the benefit of all my friends in the Comm.

In haste,   Faithfully yours,   Woodrow Wilson

TLS (A. S. Burleson Papers, DLC).

To Charles Scribner

My dear Mr. Scribner: [Trenton, N. J.] January 6, 1913

It was very thoughtful and courteous of you to consult me about a reissue of my little volume "An Old Master" and I thank you sincerely for it.[1]

I have delayed replying until I could look the little volume through. I find that at least one of the essays—the one entitled "The Char[ac]ter of Democracy in the United States" contains information which I have materially modified as I have come into contact with the actual conditions of politics. I feel, therefore, that the reissue of the volume now would be a little embarrassing to me. It could, of course, easily be explained that that essay, for example, was written in 1889 and that it did not represent my personal views entirely, but after all, that would be awkward and the essay would make more impression than the explanatory introduction. Since you are so generous as to leave to me the decision of the question as to whether the volume should be reprinted or not, I venture to express the hope that you will not reprint it. Some day it may come in with my collected works unaltered but then such volumes as a whole would explain themselves.

With warm regards

Sincerely yours   Woodrow Wilson

TCL (Charles Scribner's Sons Archives, NjP).
    [1] C. Scribner to WW, Dec. 24, 1912, TLS (WP, DLC).

From William Howard Taft

[The White House]

My dear Governor Wilson: January 6, 1913

The letter which, at the instance of Mrs. Jaffray, I wrote to Mrs. Wilson, has crossed your kind letter of January 2d, which I received this morning.

There is one thing with respect to Mrs. Jaffray which I did not note in my letter to Mrs. Wilson, and that is that she has been in the habit of having a room on the second floor with a bath attached, which at times it would be convenient, when you have many guests, yourself to use.

My family has been so small that I have not felt the necessity for it except once when I invited the whole Cabinet to stay a week with me. I give you a plan of the bed-rooms of the White House in order that you may get some idea of the room which can be occupied.

I was always anxious, and Congress would have been willing, to spend four or five thousand dollars to fit up a number of bed-rooms in the third story to accommodate male guests for a night or two; but Mrs. Taft always thought that the rooms on the second floor were enough for all that she wished to have in the house as house guests. It would be convenient, however, to have some extra rooms on the third floor, and if you agree with me on that subject and would like to have the matter attended to at once, I will have Colonel Cosby[1] make an estimate for that improvement so that it may be done conveniently during the summer of your first year.

There is another thing that I would like to bring to your attention, and that is that there is no specific appropriation for the military aide of the President. There is no question about having detailed for social occasions quite enough junior officers on duty in Washington from the Army and Navy properly to usher the entertainments that you have in the White House, but it has always seemed unfair to me that there should not be special provision for a military aide for the President who should receive some additional rank by reason of his selection, and some additional salary.

I have talked with Chairman Burleson of the committee of the Appropriations Committee and he has said that if I would invite the attention of the Committee to the necessity for and justice of this arrangement for my successor, he would see to it that it was provided for. I think that the aide of the President ought to be a colonel by rank, and ought to have a colonel's pay while he serves temporarily in the advanced rank, for I presume you will appoint a captain or a major to such a position.

If you will let me know your views about this matter, I think I can arrange it with the Appropriations Committee without publicity. It is impossible that a man should serve as aide to the President without having to spend more money than he would in his regular service; and I may add that it is impossible for the President to go anywhere without the presence and assistance of an aide. I can not tell you how much I miss Archie Butt,[2] who was ideal in this capacity, and how much I regret that I did not insist in the beginning of the administration that they should allow him a colonel's rank and pay for such an indispensable part of the Presidential household.

You will find, as I have had occasion to say publicly, that Congress is very generous to the President. You have all your transportation paid for, and all servants in the White House except such valet and maid as you and Mrs. Wilson choose to employ. Your flowers for entertainments and otherwise are furnished from the conservatory, and if they are not sufficient there is an appropriation from which they add to the supply. Music for all your entertainments, by the Marine Band or some other band, is always at hand. Provision is made by which when you leave in the summer time you may at government expense take such of the household as you need to your summer home, and the expense of their traveling and living is met under the appropriations. Your laundry is looked after in the White House, both when you are here and when you are away. Altogether, you can calculate that your expenses are only those of furnishing food to a large boarding house of servants and to your family, and your own personal expenses of clothing, etc. This of course makes the salary of $75,000, with $25,000 for traveling expenses, very much more than is generally supposed.

I have been able to save from my four years about $100,000. I give you these personal details because I am afraid I shall not have an opportunity, in view of your engagements, to meet you under conditions that will enable me to have a long talk with you, and I feel as if I should have liked the same kind of information when I came in.   Very sincerely yours,   Wm H Taft

P.S. I am sending the plan of the White House under separate cover.

TLS (Letterpress Books, W. H. Taft Papers, DLC).
    [1] Spencer Cosby, U.S.A., in charge of public buildings and grounds in Washington, with rank of colonel, 1909-13.
    [2] Major Archibald Willingham Butt, U.S.A., military aide to Presidents Roosevelt and Taft, 1908-12, who perished on the *Titanic*, April 15, 1912.

To William Howard Taft

My dear Mr. President: Trenton, N. J. January 8, 1913.

You are indeed kind and thoughtful and I thank you most warmly for your letter of January sixth. It gives me just the kind of information which I could get from no other source and which is most valuable to me. The floor plan of the White House is most useful to me.

I gladly avail myself of your generous suggestion that you have plans proceeded with for the finishing of several rooms on the third floor for extra guests.

I have taken the liberty of asking Colonel Cosby if he could find time to run up to Trenton for an hour and see me next week and inform me with regard to various matters of detail about which I do not wish to trouble you at all.

Your suggestion about provision for the temporary additional rank and pay of the Military Aide to the President is also most valuable to me and meets with my entire approval.

I cannot too warmly express the appreciation which Mrs. Wilson and I feel, of your thoughtfulness and friendly interest in our comfort and welfare. I hope I shall some time have the pleasure of thanking you in person just how we feel.

Let me thank you also for Mrs. Wilson's letter about Mrs. Jaffrey.[1] We find ourselves so inexperienced in all matters touching life at Washington that we are particularly grateful for information and suggestions.

Mrs. Wilson joins me in warmest regards to Mrs. Taft and yourself.

Cordially and sincerely yours,   Woodrow Wilson

TLS (W. H. Taft Papers, DLC).
¹ That is, W. H. Taft to EAW, Jan. 3, 1912.

From Alexander Walters

My Dear Sir: New York City January 8, 1913.

I wish you a happy and most prosperous New Year.

I was informed by Judge Hudspeth that he had called your attention to the work of the National Democratic League and that you had expressed yourself as being favorably impressed with our efforts.

He said also that you would give careful consideration to any suggestions that I had to make concerning matters relative to colored appointments.

It is my earnest desire to contribute all within my power to the success of your administration—this I hope to do by suggesting to you if requested the names of the very best prepared colored men, morally, intellectually and otherwise to fill such positions as you may deem it wise to give them.

I presume that Judge Hudspeth has spoken to you about the advisability of giving to colored democrats the positions now held by colored republicans.

It is the concensus of opinion that this should be done. This opinion is shared by Speaker Clark and a number of democratic Senators and Representatives.

There is so much uneasiness in our ranks about this matter that I would esteem it a great favor if you would indicate in some way what is to be your policy with regards to these appointments. I beg to assure you that I have the utmost confidence in your fairness, and believe you will do the best for all concerned.

My anxiety is so great for the perpetuation of the National Colored Democratic League and an enlargement of its influence that I have taken the liberty to intrude upon your valuable time to present to you the matters herein contained.

I am of the opinion that if any of the positions now held by colored men are taken from them and given to white men it will give the opposition the opportunity to discredit our movement and greatly injure our cause unless corresponding positions now held by white men are given to colored men.

I trust that I may not be transcending the bounds of propriety nor premature in my request in asking an expression from you on this subject.

Thanking you in advance for any consideration given the contents of this letter.

I beg to remain,

Yours most respectfully,   Alexander Walters

TLS (WP, DLC).

From the Diary of Colonel House

January 8, 1913.

We took the 4.08 train for Princeton and arrived there at 5.30 and was met by Mrs. Wilson. . . .

We drove to the Princeton Inn, dressed for dinner and reached the Wilson's at seven o'clock. I was struck by the extreme courtesy of the President-elect. He refused to either enter or go out before me. He was particularly solicitous as to my comfort and got up during the dinner to regulate the air.

Mrs. Wilson said: "Mr. House you are Woodrow's confidential adviser, let us have your opinion as to whether I should accept the silk which a Patterson [Paterson, N. J.] silk firm desires to present me for my Inauguration dress." She said she was satisfied that both Mrs. Roosevelt and Mrs. Taft have accepted silk from the same mill and for the same purpose. I advised its acceptance but spoke my mind pretty freely against the acceptance of presents of any value.

In order that the Governor and I might talk at dinner, I sat at his end of the table and Loulie sat next Mrs. Wilson. After dinner the ladies left us and the Governor and I sat in the living room for our conference.

He said Underwood pleased him greatly, that he seemed a whole-souled, frank gentleman. They had discussed the question of the time for the Special Session and Underwood wanted him to delay calling it until the Ways and Means Committee had formulated their tariff bill. He wished Governor Wilson to let some interim lapse between the death of the old Congress and the birth of the new, so that the members might go home and leave the committee free to work to the best advantage. He thought if the members were there, his time would be largely taken up in committee assignments and other matters.

The Governor thinks that the Special Session will be called around the 18th of March. Underwood said he would regret it if Mitchell Palmer were taken from the House, that he regarded him as his right arm. I am wondering whether Underwood really feels this or whether it was his purpose to defeat Palmer's ambition. While I do not question his sincerity, it is my purpose to find out from accurate sources.

We discussed the currency question and much to my surprise he said he had talked with Glass and Hoke Smith [about] some measure of this sort: The country to be divided into zones and each zone to issue currency and look out for its own affairs. The Governor said he knew this was not a complete measure but that it was like building three stories of a four story house, with the expectation that a fourth story would be demanded because of the needs of the situation.

I expressed myself very earnestly against any such measure. I told him he could not afford to lend his name to any measure that was unscientific, or that could be thought to be economically unsound by the other nations of the world. I said that banking had become a science, and that it could be worked out as closely as an insurance proposition, and in much the same way. That so much reserve had to be held; that currency should be bottomed on so much gold, and so much commercial papers and other assets.

It was my belief if he departed from what was known to be a sound currency, he would weaken his administration and that he would place himself in the eyes of the world very much as Mr. Bryan did when he advocated free silver.

The upshot of it was that he has agreed to put me in touch with Glass, Chairman of the Banking and Currency Committee and I am to help work out a measure which is to be submitted to him.

He spoke of his fear that Bryan would not approve such a bill as I have in mind. I said it was better to contend with Mr. Bryan's disapproval and fail in securing any bill at all than it was to get one which was not sound.

We then talked of men for the Cabinet and among them were, McAdoo, McCombs, Burleson, Mitchell Palmer, Walter H. Page, David F. Houston, A. S. Burleson, Josephus Daniels, Congressman Redfield, Teal of Oregon, Governor Burke of South Dakota, Governor Lind of Minnesota,[1] Fred Lynch and Joseph Davies. He eliminated Burleson and Palmer by saying that he did not want to take them from the House, and by the further remark that

[1] John Burke, Governor of North Dakota, 1907-13; John Lind, Governor of Minnesota, 1899-1901, congressman from Minnesota, 1903-05, at this time a lawyer in Minneapolis.

Tumulty had told him that Senator-elect Billy Hughes had said that Burleson did not have the confidence of the members of the House, that he was considered a schemeing and uncertain quantity. I believe Burleson would have been successful if this had not come to the Governor's ears. The Governor said he had never known Hughes to fail to correctly estimate anyone's popularity in Congress.

I thought if he did not appoint Burleson he should not appoint anyone from the House or Senate so that the blow would be softened. He said he agreed with this and that he would make a statement as to why he did not go to Congress for Cabinet material.

I was surprised to find that he had no prejudice whatever against Mitchell Palmer over what had happened at Baltimore.[2] McCombs had told him his version of it but he knew the true story and spoke in the highest terms and most affectionate way of Palmer.

He asked my opinion of Walter Page for Secretary of the Interior and of Houston for Secretary of Agriculture. I gave Houston unqualified praise but was somewhat guarded in regard to Page. We shifted them about several times, giving Page Interior, Houston, Agriculture, and then Houston Interior and Page Agriculture, where we finally left them temporarily.

He wondered if McAdoo would accept the Governor Generalship of the Philippine Islands. I thought he would not, and that it was a Cabinet place or nothing with him. We then talked of him for the Treasury. He asked if I thought he would make a good Postmaster General. I said he would make an excellent one, and for a moment it looked as we would pin his name to that post. We finally concluded that it would be scarcely fair since he desired the Treasury.

When we had McAdoo as Postmaster General, we placed Hous-

[2] On Sunday, June 30, 1912, when the Democratic convention at Baltimore seemed hopelessly deadlocked between Wilson and Champ Clark, political bosses Roger C. Sullivan, Thomas Taggart, Charles F. Murphy, and John J. Fitzgerald invited Wilson's floor managers, Albert S. Burleson and A. Mitchell Palmer, to a conference. The bosses suggested that if Burleson and Palmer could persuade Wilson to withdraw his name they in turn would throw their support to Palmer as a compromise candidate. Palmer rejected the proposal. See Arthur S. Link, *Wilson: The Road to the White House* (Princeton, N. J., 1947), p. 457. Stanley Coben, *A. Mitchell Palmer: Politician* (New York, 1963), pp. 60-62, has a slightly fuller account but misdates the conference on June 29; he suggests that Palmer "rapidly calculated" his chances of being elected to the presidency in 1912 before he turned down the offer. William F. McCombs, *Making Woodrow Wilson President* (New York 1912), pp. 163-64, argues that Palmer was sorely tempted by the proposal and that he, McCombs, that same evening warned Palmer that "if he did another thing I had fifty good husky Irishmen to throw him out of Baltimore." This was McCombs' version of the affair, referred to by House below.

ton in the Treasury. I told the Governor if we had two men like Houston and McAdoo in the Cabinet he could afford to have a fairly mediocre lot for the other places.

We spoke of Daniels, but somehow or other, Daniels did not fit in. The Governor wants to appoint him, but he does not size big enough for anything we could think of. He may, however, make him Postmaster General.

Chas. R. Crane of Chicago, was discussed and it is my purpose to suggest him for Postmaster General.

I told him he was now leaving Texas out of the Cabinet. His reply was, "I want you to go in the Cabinet." I answered by saying that I merely wished to be an ex-officio member, and that I had no desire to go into the Cabinet itself. He urged me not to give a definite answer for the present and said he very much wished me to be a member of his official family, that it seemed to coincide with the fitness of things.

He generously asked me what place I would like, evidently leaving me to choose. I regard this as a very high compliment for the reason that he has offered no one a place in the Cabinet up to now excepting Mr. Bryan, whom we agreed upon just after the election as a purely political necessity. With me it is different. He offers me anything within his gift before he has thought of tendering anything to anyone else. Of course, I shall not take any office although I would do much to oblige him and to be of service. My reasons are that I am not strong enough to tie myself down to a Cabinet department and, in addition, my general disinclination to hold office. I very much prefer being a free lance, and to advise with him regarding matters in general, and to have a roving commission to serve wherever and whenever possible.

I spoke of Gregory wanting to be Ambassador to Mexico and he asked if I thought Gregory would be good Cabinet material; that if I declined to come into the Cabinet, he wondered whether we could not fit Gregory in somewhere. I spoke highly of him and said that I thought he would be invaluable.

The Governor is getting a line on Brandeis. He is having someone in Massachusetts ask the rank and file of people there what they think of him. The report will probably be favorable to Brandeis, but even so, I think it would be a mistake to appoint him to any place other than Commerce or Labor, and even that is a doubtful expedient.

He asked if I thought it would be well to place Cleveland Dodge in the Cabinet. I thought Dodge was a republican and, if I were in his place, I would make him Ambassador to England.

I asked if he realized that he was taking too many men from

New York. There is McCombs, whom he has already offered the Ambassadorship to Austria, and there are McAdoo, Walter Page and Redfield.

We talked of Tumulty for Secretary to the President and he thought he would not appoint him. Tumulty has nearly all the necessary qualifications, but he has others that would not fit him for the Washington atmosphere in such a place as that contemplated. He also thinks that Tumulty is too provincial. He intends offering him a collectorship or something better which he hopes will be satisfactory. I am sorry for Tumulty for he has many qualifications for the job.

He spoke of Newton Baker as being a probable choice in the event he would accept. He called my attention to the fact that nearly all the men we had discussed were Southerners, even though some of them were now living in northern States. There is Walter Page, McAdoo, McCombs, Daniels, Houston, Newton Baker, Gregory and others.

I invited the Governor to come and stay with me some night. He promised to do so. I explained that we would have the apartment to ourselves and could talk undisturbed. I think he will come next week. Mrs. Wilson is coming to New York on Tuesday and on Wednesday she takes lunch with us and goes to a play. She is a strong woman but is beginning to show the effect of over work.

The Governor and I discussed the advisability of his seeing Hearst some time. He saw no purpose in it. He did not believe that it would do more than satisfy Hearst for a short while, and it would give him more power to do harm, so he is determined to let Hearst do his worst and pay no attention to his request for a conference.

McCombs has urged that he at least be permitted to refuse an appointment to the Cabinet, but the Governor has refused holding that he does not believe the National Chairman should go into the Cabinet, and he does not wish to stultify himself by offering him something that he could not accept.

To Carter Glass

My dear Mr. Glass: Trenton, N. J. January 9, 1913.

Thank you for your letter of January third. My present judgment is that it would be just as well to have a bill ready for introduction before the close at any rate of the extraordinary session so that it might be introduced if the situation seemed to warrant it.

I have had some very interesting conferences about the banking and currency question recently which make it very desirable that I should see you again for a further talk. I shall be leaving to-morrow for a hurried trip to Chicago but shall be back Monday to be present at the opening work of the State legislative session, but I shall take the liberty of getting into communication with you next week in order to suggest a time of conference.

In haste,   Faithfully yours,   Woodrow Wilson

TLS (C. Glass Papers, ViU).

To Willard Saulsbury

My dear Mr. Saulsbury: Trenton, N. J. January 9, 1913.

I wonder if you would be free at an early date to come up and see me for a little conference about the situation in Delaware?[1] I find myself more and more deeply interested in your fortunes there and would like to know if there is any way in which I can help without doing more harm than good. I am leaving to-morrow for Chicago but shall be back in Trenton by Monday morning and would be obliged if you would get into communication with me then so that we could make an engagement.

Cordially and sincerely yours,   Woodrow Wilson

TLS (W. Saulsbury Papers, DeU).

[1] In the election in November 1912, the Democrats won control of the lower house of the Delaware legislature, but the upper house remained Republican. However, in the joint balloting for United States senator, to commence on January 21, the Democrats would have a total of twenty-nine votes to twenty-three for the Republicans and hence would be able, if united, to choose a senator. Saulsbury was the leading Democratic contender, but there was considerable opposition to him in the state party, he lacked several of the fifteen votes needed to win in the party caucus, and some of his Democratic opponents in the legislature hoped to make the caucus vote non-binding, thus denying him the majority of twenty-seven votes needed for election by the joint session of the legislature. The opposition to Saulsbury was sufficiently well-known outside the state to cause the Baltimore *Sun*, in an editorial on January 10, 1913, to take the somewhat unusual step of directly urging Saulsbury's election. See the Wilmington, Del., *Every Evening*, Jan. 4, 6, and 11, 1913. For the outcome of the senatorial fight in Delaware, see W. Saulsbury to WW, Jan. 11, 1913, n. 3.

To Leonard Wood[1]

My dear General Wood: [Trenton, N. J.] January 9, 1913.

Thank you for your letter of January second[2] asking my preference with regard to the Guard of Honor.

I find that it has been customary for the Essex Troop, whose Headquarters are at Newark, New Jersey, to attend the Inauguration. They are a smart lot of fellows and make a capital appearance, and inasmuch as it seems to me appropriate that my Guard of Honor should come from the National Guard of New Jersey, I hope they will be designated. I am dropping a line to General Sadler, our Adjutant-General here, asking him to co-operate with you in this matter.

Sincerely yours,   Woodrow Wilson

TLS (L. Wood Papers, DLC).
  [1] Major General, at this time Chief of Staff, U.S. Army.
  [2] L. Wood to WW, Jan. 2, 1913, TLS (WP, DLC).

From the Minutes of the Board of Trustees of Princeton University

[Princeton, N. J., January 9, 1913]

On motion of the President of the University the congratulations of the Board to Governor Wilson on his election to the Presidency of the United States were offered and the following minute adopted:

"The Trustees of Princeton University offer to the Honorable Woodrow Wilson, one of the distinguished sons of the University, some time its President, and now President of the Board of Trustees, their congratulations on his election to the Presidency of the United States, and their wish for his health and happiness and for the largest usefulness and high distinction of the administration of the great office he is so soon to occupy."

"Minutes of the Trustees of Princeton University, April 1908 June 1913," bound minute book (UA, NjP).

From Edward Mandell House

Dear Governor: New York, Jan'y 9th, 1913.

Here is a slate to ponder over.

Sec'y State	W.J.B.	Nebraska
Secy Treas.	W. G. McA.	New York
Atty Gen'l	J. C. McReynolds	Tenn.
Secy of War } or } P. M. Genl	Chas. R. Crane	Ill

P. M. Gen'l or Secy War	T. W. Gregory	Texas
Secy Interior or Secy Agriculture	Walter H. Page	New York
Secy Agriculture or Secy Interior	D. F. Houston	Mo.
Secy of Navy	H. C. Wallace	Washington
Secy Com & Labor	Brandeis or Gardner	Mass Maine
In reserve	Daniels	N. C.
"	Thos. H. Ball	Texas
"	Redfield	New York
"	Burke	So. Dakota.

If I put in Crane I would leave out Brandeis, or vice versa. It would be too much La Follette. Mrs. House and I had a memorable evening with you. You can never know how deeply I appreciate you wanting me in your Cabinet. As an ex-officio member, however, I can do my share of the work and get a little of the reflected glory that I am very sure will come to your administration.   Your Affectionate,   E. M. House

This would give you a Cabinet well distributed geographically, and about the best available material.

ALS (WP, DLC).

Charles Lee Swem's Summary of a Letter from James Whitford Bashford[1]

[c. Jan. 10, 1913]

MEMO.

Long letter from J. W. Bashford, Bishop of Methodist Episcopal Church, Peking, China, in reference to the conditions in China. Says, "At the outbreak of the Revolution President Taft secured a signed agreement binding each of six foreign nations not to intervene with troops in China without the consent of the majority of the signatories. When President Taft proposed to recognize China some of the other powers asked that the agreement binding the six powers to concerted action be dissolved." The President refused.

The Bishop says that this agreement is already broken in letter and in spirit, that Russia and Japan are maintaining troops in Mongolia and Manchuria contrary to international law. He judges that the United States is unwilling to resort to arms to prevent this practical intervention upon the part of these two powers. He says, "There is, however, one other service which we can render China and which our entire traditions bind us to render, viz., the recognition of the Republic. Recognition has been delayed too long, and if granted, will help China both financially and politically.["]

Hopes that the first official act of your administration will be marked by the recognition of the Chinese Republic.

Second, discusses the practical importance of the appointment of a minister to China. Says Mr. [William James] Calhoun, the present minister, has rendered good service, but has not been in China long enough. Suggests Mr. Bryan as ambassador to China. If Mr. Bryan can not accept, Pres. Eliot might render conspicuous service. Another man is Prof. E. D. Burton of Chicago University.[2]

T MS (WP, DLC).

[1] This letter, which Wilson sent to the State Department, has not been found. James Whitford Bashford, President of Ohio Wesleyan University, 1889-1904, had since 1904 been bishop of the Methodist Episcopal Church in charge of missionary work in China. By this time a leading figure in the American community in Peking, Bashford was an enthusiastic advocate of the recently created Republic of China and as early as April 14, 1912, in a personal interview in Washington with President William Howard Taft, had urged that the United States recognize the Chinese republic. See Paul A. Varg, *Missionaries, Chinese, and Diplomats: The American Protestant Missionary Movement in China, 1890-1952* (Princeton, N. J., 1958), p. 137.

[2] The Rev. Dr. Ernest DeWitt Burton, head of the Department of New Testament Literature and Interpretation since 1892, prolific author and editor.

Ellen Axson Wilson to William Howard Taft

My dear Mr. Taft,   Princeton, New Jersey Jan. 10, 1913.

I cannot tell you how deeply both Mr. Wilson and I appreciate your friendly letters and the very great kindness and courtesy shown us by Mrs. Taft and yourself! It would also be difficult to express how helpful your letters and the chart have been to us in a practical way. I am naturally the most unambitious of women and life in the White House has no attractions for me! Quite the contrary in fact! But Mrs. Jaffrey and the wonderful ["]Brooks" will rob the immediate future of much of its terrors.

Thanking you again and again for your generous kindness, and with all the good wishes of the Season to Mrs. Taft and yourself, I am, my dear Sir,

Yours very sincerely,   Ellen A. Wilson.

ALS (W. H. Taft Papers, DLC).

An Address to the Commercial Club of Chicago[1]

[Jan. 11, 1913]

Mr. President,[2] ladies and gentlemen: I look back with the greatest pleasure upon the frequent occasions when I have dined with this club. Indeed, I dare say that I have experienced more pleasure on former occasions than I am experiencing now because it is more pleasant to tell men what they ought to do when none of the burden of it falls upon you, than to tell them what ought to be done when so much of the burden is likely to center upon yourself.

I remember the first visit that I paid to this club as a guest of one of your members, but not as a speaker. You were addressed by a certain Mr. Warner,[3] at one time a Senator of the State of New York, on the then proposed enterprise of cutting a canal through the Isthmus on the Nicaraguan route by private capital. And I remember that he had spread behind him a map that was most ingeniously contrived to show that all routes of trades ran through Chicago. It was not a map merely of the United States, it was a map of the world, and I reflected, even in those immature years, how subtle the human mind is, and how apt it is to the processes of flattery. But I also noticed that you listened with respect but not with credulity, because I never heard that his enterprise was at all set forward by any material assistance from Chicago. There were many gentlemen then as there are now in this company who were accustomed to the routes of trade in America and knew where they ran.

I have been reflecting as I sat here tonight that it would be futile for me to pretend that the chief routes of thought run through Chicago, but that I want to induce you, if I may, to travel, or perhaps, I should say, to forecast some of the routes of thought which must be traveled in this country if we are to settle the problems that are now immediately confronting us. But I am not here to tell you tonight what I am going to do. I

[1] Delivered in the Blackstone Hotel.
[2] Clyde Mitchell Carr, in the iron and steel business in Chicago.
[3] John De Witt Warner, congressman from New York, 1891-95, since that time a lawyer of New York City.

am not here to speak of the responsibilities which will fall upon me. I tell you frankly that if I permitted my thought to dwell on the responsibilities which will center upon myself, I should be daunted in facing the future.

I come here to ask for your counsel and assistance and to remind you of the responsibilities which lie upon you as representatives of the people of America. The business future of this country does not depend upon the Government of the United States. It depends upon the businessmen of the United States.

The government cannot breed a temper in men; the government cannot generate thought and purpose, and only the temper and the thought and the purpose of businessmen in America is going to determine what the future of business shall be.

There are many things to do which you can do without the assistance and also without the whip of law, and the thing which is done only under the whip of the law is done imperfectly, reluctantly, sometimes sullenly, and never successfully.

The hope of America is in the changing attitude of the businessmen of this country towards the things which they have to handle in the future. If thought and temper had not changed, the things could not have happened which have happened in recent months. For what you have witnessed within the last two months is not merely a political change, it is a change in the attitude and judgment of the American people. One of the reasons why there were not merely two parties contending for the supremacy at the recent election—one reason why the field of choice was varied and multiplied—was that the old lines are breaking up where they are oldest, and that men are no longer to be catalogued, no longer to be found by dead reckoning, no longer to be put in classes, as if their thinking had been concluded and they were no longer casting about for the things which they should have and the things which they should do. America has come upon a new period of independent thinking, and she is going to think her way out to a triumphant solution of her difficulties.

There are some perfectly clear lines that may be laid down. There are four sets of things which have to be done. In the first place, we have to husband and administer the common resources of this country for the common benefit.

Now, not all businessmen in this country have devoted their thought to that object. They have devoted their thought very successfully to exploiting the resources of America, but very few businessmen have devoted their thought to husbanding the resources of America. And very few, indeed, have had the attitude of those who administer a great trust in administering those natural resources. Until the businessmen of America make up their minds both to husband and to administer, as if for others as well as for their own profit, the natural resources of this country, some of the questions ahead of us will be immensely difficult of solution.

Why is it that the Government of the United States up to this moment has not hit upon a consistent policy of conservation? It has not. You must be aware that a mere policy of reservation is not a policy of conservation. It is in one sense a policy of conservation, for it conserves, but no nation can merely keep out of use its resources in order that they may not be squandered and dissipated. We must devise some process of general use. And why have we not done so? Why, if I am not very much mistaken, because the government at Washington was tremulously suspicious of everybody who approached it for rights in the water powers and forest reserves and mineral reserves of the western country which the federal government still controls. They looked with suspicion upon every applicant to use them. They cannot have looked with suspicion except because they believed that the men engaged in these great enterprises had not yet got the national point of view. If they had believed that the businessmen of that sort were purposing to husband these resources and regarded themselves, as in some sense they are, trustees for future generations who would need them as much as this generation needs them, there would have been no ground for suspicion. And they would have felt a free hand in the matter of framing a policy which they could have pursued. So that when the government at Washington undertakes in the future to develop a policy of this sort, the first thing it must know is the state of mind, the psychology, the purpose, the attitude of the men that it is dealing with. That attitude must be declared and open and transparent. Don't you see that is your responsibility, not mine? I shall sit there and try to preside over the matter, but I shall know what to do only as I can judge the men I am dealing with. The moment their purpose is declared to be for the general interest and shown by their procedure to be for the general interest, then the whole atmosphere of suspicion will be dissipated, and the government will come to a normal relation with the citizens of the United States.

Then there is another thing that has to be done. The raw materials obtainable in this country for every kind of manufacture and industry must be at the disposal of everybody in the United States upon the same terms. I don't mean that the government must determine upon what terms they must be available, but merely that they shall be available upon the same terms, whoever applies to use them or to purchase them, that there shall not be discrimination in respect of those who are to have access to these resources.

That, it is true, is merely a part and a specification under what I have already been talking about. If those raw materials are to be used in the spirit of those who would serve the whole country alike, without regard to section or individual, then our future is assured of an absence of the kind of discrimination which the whole temper of this country has sternly risen against. I want to take sternness out of the temper of this country. I want to see suspicion dissipated. I want to see a time brought about when the perfectly artificial condition now existing—when the rank and file of the citizens of the United States have a somewhat hostile attitude toward the businessmen of the country—shall be absolutely done away with and forgotten. Perfectly honest, upright, patriotic men, whom any one of us could pick out, are at a disadvantage now in America because business, business methods in general, are not trusted by the people, taken as a whole. That is unjust to you; it is unjust to everybody with whom business deals and everybody whom business touches.

They do not believe in the United States—I mean the rank and file of our people—that men of every kind are upon an equality in their access to the resources of the country, any more than they believe that everybody is upon equal terms in their access to the justice of the country. It is believed—I am not stating whether it is true or not, for a belief is a fact, and the facts that we are dealing with now are beliefs more than anything else—it is believed in this country that a poor man has less chance to get justice administered to him than a rich man. God forbid that that should be generally true. But so long as that is believed, the belief constitutes a threatening fact.

I have been told by some gentlemen with whom I have dealt in politics—and I have dealt with some gentlemen rather intimately in politics—that I am not treating them fairly because I understand their motives, and the general public does not understand their motives. And I consider myself privileged to say to them: "I can't deal with you until you make the general public understand your motives, because their belief that you are not acting upon high motives is the fundamental, underlying, governing belief of the way they vote, and you have got to clear yourselves before the general jury."

Now that goes hard. It goes hard with my heart. There are men whom I have a very warm feeling for whom I cannot encourage to take an active part in affairs because the general public does not believe in them. I am trying to set before you the psychology of the situation. That is the hardest nut we have to crack.

There are business problems which it would be easy to deal with if the people were in a temper to deal with them, but they are not, and we must get them in a temper to deal with them, and that job is yours, not mine. You are conducting the business of the country. I am not.

There is a third thing which you must do which has not yet been done. You must put the credit of this country at the disposal of everybody upon equal terms. Now, I am not entering into an indictment against the banking methods of this country. The banking system of this country don't need to be indicted. It is convicted. I am not aware of having a single indictment in my thought against any class of my fellow citizens; but there is reason to believe from things said under oath that there are inner circles and outer circles of credit in this country. There are regions of chilly exclusion, and there are regions of warm inclusion. You can't get into the game in some instances unless you are upon certain terms with the gentlemen who are running the game.

Now, I want to hasten to say that I believe that some of these gentlemen who are running the game intend to run it fairly, but there are gentlemen whom they know, and some whom they do not know. There are some whom they recognize as entitled to come in, and some whom they do not recognize as entitled to come in. And the future belongs to the men who are not yet recognized. This country is not going to grow rich in the future by the efforts of the men who have already got in. It is going to grow rich by the efforts of the men who haven't yet got in—a truism since it is going to get rich by the efforts of future generations after this generation is gone.

And generations don't come on by sharp cleavage. One generation doesn't end today and another begin tomorrow. They are interlaced. The next generation is now struggling for a foothold, and the next generation finds it extremely difficult to get a foothold.

The credit of this country must be opened upon equal terms, and with equal readiness upon the same terms, to everybody, and the bankers of this country, and the men who have the credit of this country in their control, must see to that first of all before they can expect to enjoy the confidence of the country and to have the problems peculiar to them settled without prejudice against them.

My dearest hope for my administration is that prejudices such as have been among this people may be dissolved and destroyed, the prejudices between sections, for example. The only advantage of having elected—I mean the only peculiar advantage of having elected—a man born in the South President of the United States is that men will realize that the South is a part of the Union, and that southern men—men born in the South—are not in the least inclined to draw sectional differences in guiding the policy of the nation.

I am free to admit that a great many able men have come from the South, but that is by the largess of nature. You know the Englishman who was talking to the Scotchman who appeared inclined to contend that everybody who had ever amounted to much in English history was either a Scotchman, or had a predominance of Scotch blood in him. The Englishman presently in irritation said: "You will be claiming Shakespeare next." "Weel, mon, he had intellect enough." And I am free to admit that I have met a great many men in the North who had intellect enough to be Southerners.

But quite apart from playfulness and jest, the happiest circumstances of my election is that I am the instrument, the innocent instrument, of bringing about an end of the old feeling that the Southerner was not of the same political breed and purpose as the rest of American citizens. And I would like to hope that there would be associated with the death of that prejudice the death of many another prejudice, particularly of these prejudices which are getting such formidable root amongst us as between class and class, as between those who control the resources of the country and those who use the resources of the country. These prejudices cut deeper than any sectional prejudices could cut. They are more fatal by way of obstacle to the happy solution of questions of difficult policy, and they, above all others, should be removed, and they can be removed only in one way—by having no substantial basis in fact.

If the credits of this country were open upon equal terms to everybody, the impression would never have got abroad that they aren't. The people of the United States don't have nightmares. They don't dream things that aren't so. They don't get them deeply rooted in their convictions with no cause and provocation. And then, in addition and on top of all this, we must see to it that the business of the United States is set absolutely free of every feature of monopoly. I notice you don't applaud that. I am disappointed because unless you feel that way the thing isn't going to happen except by duress, the worst way in which to bring anything about, because there will be monopoly in this country until there are no important businessmen in this country who don't intend to bring it about. I know that when they are talking about their business they say there isn't anybody in the United States who ever intended to set up a monopoly. But I know there were some gentlemen who did deliberately go about to set up monopoly. I know that they intended to do it because they did it, and because they did it in a way which inevitably led to monopoly. And we know it because they organized their business, or, rather, capitalized their business in such a way that they could not endure competition and had set up a monopoly.

You can't carry water against competition. I was accused the other day, and I am happy to plead guilty, of saying the same things after I was elected that I said before I was elected. Now, one of the things that I said most often during the campaign was this: I don't care how big a particular business gets, provided it grows big in contact with sharp competition, and I know that a business based upon genuine capital, that hasn't a drop of water in it, can be conducted with greater efficiency and economy than a business that is loaded with water. Just so soon as the gentlemen who carry water, some of them on both shoulders, are exposed to the competition of men of equal wits who don't carry water, the thing is settled, and I am willing to abide by the results. Then we can prevent monopoly and produce competition wherever men are strong enough to set it up. I am not interested in setting men up in business, but I am interested in leaving the doors open so that strong men at least can come in and set it up for themselves. And so soon as you produce that situation, then there won't be any necessity for government to come in and take a hand in administering the business of the United States. I, for my part, hope that the Government of the United States never shall take a hand in administering the business of a body of people who above all people in the world are prepared to take care of themselves—at least who used to be prepared to take care of themselves. They have been very much demoralized by the system of taxation which centers in the tariff.

I am alarmed at the number of businessmen able to beat the world who are afraid to go out and take the weather in a country the richest in the world, the richest in resources, and I am fain to believe the richest in brains, who say: "For God's sake, don't take the cover from over our heads; don't expose us to competition with the wits and the resources of other countries which we have all along claimed to be our inferiors in both." But there was a time—and it is going to come back—when this country was able to take care of itself. And it will be abundantly able to take care of itself when its energies are really realized and when no man is afraid of anybody else; when every man has the same right to conduct an independent business that every other man has; when every man knows that the business community is open for him to enter and be welcome. Then there is going to come a season of prosperity in this country which it has never known or dreamed of, but not until then. You can't have prosperity personally conducted. You can't have prosperity conducted by small circles of individuals. No body of men less than the whole manhood of the nation knows enough to be trustees for the rest. The only thing that makes society various and rich is that men who we never heard of can come in at any time and put us on our mettle to beat them.

I glory in democracy for that alone, that it is a competition which any man may enter, no matter what his antecedents, no matter what his training, no matter what his origins, no matter what his natural handicaps. The great pleasure of a college man is to see some awkward youngster, whose brain seems at first to run sluggish, come in among the smart set and put them to their mettle to beat him, not only at the use of his brain but in the use of his muscle, the skill of his hand, the adroitness of his address, his mastery in a company of cultivated men. It makes me proud when the men with a handicap win the race, and win it as if they had started at scratch.

So that what I have come to say to you tonight is this: Just so soon as you make up your minds that there shall be no monopoly in the United States, there won't be any monopoly in the United States. It is a purpose, and laws have to be devised in order to head off wrong purposes more than they have to be devised to head off wrong acts. Because, as I was just agreeing with one of my neighbors—and since there are gentlemen in the same profession which I am in myself at this table, I won't say which of my neighbors—one of the difficulties in politics is the shrewdness with which a certain sort of politician covers his tracks. You never know who his agent is; you never know whether you are dealing with him or somebody else. His approaches to you are so roundabout and so various, and he is so absolutely sleepless and adroit in the way he does things. And as long as you are suspicious you are safe.

Well, now, that ought not to be the case with law. Law ought not to be based upon suspicion. Law ought to be based upon the premise that only the exceptional man is going to try to circumvent the law—I do not mean the exceptional man in ability, but the exceptional man in character. If only the crooks tried to

circumvent the law in the United States, very much less law
would be necessary. But there are some men who have permitted
themselves to circumvent the law who are not crooks. The purpose is of the essence of the character of the nation.

Now, gentlemen, we are witnessing a new age. The nation has
awakened. We have asked for and obtained a change of venue.
We used to try every governmental case before a selected jury,
and the jury selected were always the same men. Now we are
trying it before the people of the United States, and the people
of the United States are going to reach a true verdict. There isn't
going to be any disagreement in the jury; it isn't going to be hung,
and it isn't going to stay out long. Just as soon as the facts are
laid before it, it is going to come in with its judgment, and its
judgment is going to be executed in the political action of the
United States. That is what I mean by a change of venue. The
jury is drawn from a wider panel, there are more names in the
hat, and that jury is now of the temper of the people who witnessed the setting up of the institutions under which we have
been so long free and so long happy.

I feel, and I believe, that everyone associated with me feels in
the atmosphere of this age the stimulation of that older day in
which men went about to set up a government which was not intended to serve their private interests, but which was intended to
serve mankind. Not merely to serve the people of America, for the
view of that older age was not confined to the three million people
then constituting a little fringe of civilization along the Atlantic
shore. The vision of those men was of the coming in of the nations
across the waters to this haven of freedom and of emancipation.
And they foresaw the day when men of every sort—and how their
vision has been fulfilled!—when men of every nation and every
sort should seek the shores of America in order to take a free
share in institutions intended not for the private benefit of anyone but for the elevation of the race as a whole.

Some of those gentlemen, whose names we remember with
such acclaim, who used to be in little neighborhood coteries down
in the Old Dominion of Virginia, met in order to devise changes
which were distinctly against the economic interest of Virginia,
and they contrived them upon the principle that it was their duty
to embark their fortunes and their honor in the enterprise of setting men everywhere free of every kind of trammel and restraint
and unfairness.

Ah, that day has come back! Don't you feel it? Do you look
at your business any longer within the four walls of your office?
Don't you feel the thrill that comes to you from the rest of Amer-

ica? Don't you know that men everywhere are looking to you with confidence and with hope in the assurance that you are not waiting for the whip of the law, but that you also are Americans, that you also are born with that unconquerable spirit of aspiration, which is the only distinction that ever belonged to the country that we love? America is not distinguished because she established a stable government—other countries have established stable governments—but because she established a government meant to be shot through with the hopes of humble men. The only glory of America is her spiritual glory, and when she takes down those ensigns of spiritual freedom she will have surrendered to the greed, the debased spirit that has wrecked so many governments, that has dissipated so many hopes, that has made it impossible to lift the race to the standards to which we all aspire. I believe that when I have the privilege of attacking some of the problems before me, I shall, if I can, conceive them in the spirit of America, speaking for you as well as for everybody else, for I believe a new age has begun.

I have no intimate knowledge of the processes of business. I never was engaged in business in my life. I must take counsel with the men who do understand business, but I dare not do that unless I know their purposes are the same as mine. I dare not. I am under bonds to the people of the United States. The man who does not hold their interests dearer than his own I cannot admit into my counsel. I would be faithless if I did. I have made promises which I regard as intimately involved with my essential honor. I can serve only one master, and no group of individuals can speak for my master. I am a trustee for the prosperity of the United States in counsel, and the counsel that isn't common counsel, the counsel that doesn't include you, is imperfect counsel, is counsel which will mislead. Won't you come in? Haven't you come in? Is it not your purpose to re-establish economic freedom in the United States? Aren't we all in the same boat? Can't I enlist you tonight in the common enterprise? There is no bright prospect otherwise.

I have preached this thing for twenty-five years. I preached it during a great many years when no particular heed was paid to what I said. The only value I attach to my present position is that men will listen to me; that they will listen to me whether they want to or not, that they have got to listen to me. And yet I am preaching the same thing that I preached as a boy; I purpose the same things that I purposed as a boy. I hope that the visions I had as a boy are about to be translated into fact, and that the great energies of the American people are about to be united in a thing which will set an example of emancipation from prejudice and constriction of every kind to the world. God grant it may be true!

I made this engagement before I was nominated. I haven't accepted any invitation to speak since I was nominated. I came here to redeem a promise which I would not have made if I had known I was going to be nominated. And I would not have come here then if it had not occurred to me that I might now say that I do not deem myself at liberty to go around and indulge in the pleasure of dining unless I may say to men after I have dined exactly what I think, and express what I think in terms of the general partnership of purpose and of honor which it seems to me we have now entered in. The bonds are now signed. We are of the same race, that splendid mixed race into which has been drawn all the riches of a hundred bloods. And now, as a united people, we are going to redeem the ancient pledges of America.[4]

T MS (WP, DLC), with corrections from the CLSsh notes (RSB Coll., DLC).
[4] There is a WWhw outline of this address, with the composition date of Jan. 4, 1913, in WP, DLC.

From Willard Saulsbury

Dear Governor,   Wilmington Jany 11, 1913

Thank you for your kind note of 9th. I should be delighted to come to see you whenever it will be convenient & think probably the newspaper announcement that I have been asked to visit you for a conference and afterward that I have done so, will have some effect of a favorable character on our members of legislature.

One of our newly elected State Senators[1] went to school with you & expresses his desire to be to vote for one who will support your policies. As yet I do not count this Senator, E. B. Carter, among my supporters & would like to have him, as the effort of the opposition now is to deadlock the legislature & thus prevent my election. I think I have about 2/3 of all the Democratic members & feel practically sure of the caucus nomination.

An early day for my visit[2] is I think desirable, as the caucus will be held one week hence

I will get Mr Tumulty on the phone at Trenton to-morrow, Monday, morning in accordance with what I understand the suggestion of your note.[3]

                    Yours very truly   Willard Saulsbury

ALS (WP, DLC).

¹ Edward Broadway Carter, Princeton 1883, state senator from Kent County, Del.

² Saulsbury lunched with Wilson in Trenton on January 14, 1913. See the Wilmington, Del. *Every Evening*, Jan. 15, 1913.

³ In the voting of the caucus of the Democratic members of the Delaware legislature on January 20, Saulsbury won easily, but four members from Kent County bolted and refused to support him, thus denying Saulsbury the majority needed for election in the legislative balloting which began on the following day. The deadlock continued until January 29, when the four insurgents, bowing to heavy pressure, finally cast their votes for Saulsbury. See the Wilmington, Del. *Every Evening*, Jan. 21, 22, and 29, 1913.

Remarks in Trenton to the New Jersey Electors[1]

[[Jan. 13, 1913]]

I feel a natural embarrassment on this particular occasion, because in view of what is likely to happen immediately after 3 o'clock, I am again placed in the position of a blushing candidate. I think that one can predict what the choice is going to be at 3 o'clock. Nevertheless, I feel that it would be unbecoming in me to make a speech in any other tone than that of a man who believes that he is speaking for the men with whom he is associated. Some men have been slow to observe, but the majority of us have seen, that the people of the United States have made a definite choice. I happen to be one of the instruments through whom that choice is expressed, but I am for the time, and that choice is for the long future. The people of the United States have turned their faces in a definite direction, and any party, any man, who does not go with them in that direction, they will reject—and they ought to reject.

Therefore, in looking forward to the responsibilities that I am about to assume, I feel first, last, and all the time that I am acting in a representative capacity. I am bidden to interpret as well as I can the purposes of the people of the United States and to act, so far as my choice determines the action, only through the instrumentality of persons who also represent that choice. I have no liberty in the matter. I have given bonds. My sacred honor is involved, and nothing more could be involved. Therefore, I shall not be acting as a partisan when I pick out progressives, and only progressives. I shall be acting as a representative of the people of this great country. And, therefore, it is a matter of supreme pleasure to me to find in every direction, as I turn about from one group of men to another, that men's minds and men's

¹ Delivered at a luncheon at the Sterling Hotel given by the Democratic State Committee in celebration of the meeting of the New Jersey presidential electors to cast their votes for Wilson and Marshall. State Chairman Edward E. Grosscup presided, and National Committeeman Robert Stephen Hudspeth introduced Wilson.

consciences, and men's purposes, are yielding to that great impulse that now moves the whole people of the United States.

I do not foresee any serious divisions of counsel in the Democratic party as a national body. On the contrary, I find every evidence of solidarity. I see every evidence that men who have not hitherto yielded their judgment to the movement of the age are now about to yield their judgment. I will not say their will. They do not seem to be acting under compulsion; they are beginning to yield their judgment to the common judgment of the nation. Because I find in discussing questions of business—contrary to the impression which prevails in some editorial rooms— that in speaking to men of business, I am speaking to men whose vision is swinging around to the path which the nation has marked out for itself.

This nation is full of honorable men who have been engaged in large business in a way in which they thought they were permitted to do so, both by their consciences and the laws. But they have had their eyes so close to their ledgers, they have had their energies so absolutely absorbed in the undertakings with which they were individually identified, that they have not, until the nation spoke loud, raised their eyes from their books and papers and seen how the things they were doing stood related to the fortunes of mankind.

Now, they are beginning to see those relationships, and as they see those relationships they are beginning to feel the refreshment of men who look away from a particular task and extend their eyes to the fortunes of men lying outside their usual ken and beyond their touch—the great bodies of men who would along with them hope and struggle and achieve. I believe that I am not mistaken in seeing this new purpose come into the hearts of men who have not permitted themselves hitherto to see what they now look upon. For the nation cannot move successfully by anything except concert of purpose and of judgment. You cannot whip a nation into line. You cannot drive your leaders before you. You have got to have a spirit that thrills the whole body, and I believe that that spirit is now beginning to thrill the whole body. Men are finding that they will be bigger men and bigger businessmen as they will spend some of their brains on something that has nothing to do with themselves, and that the more you extend the use of your energy, the more energy you have got to spend even upon your own affairs; that enrichment comes from the enlargement, and that with the enrichment comes the increase of power.

Men, in the last analysis, even in the narrower field of business, have a grip upon their fellowmen in proportion as they enjoy the confidence and admiration of their fellowmen. A man can accomplish a great deal more in business, as I need hardly tell you, by the belief that people have in him than by the fear that he inspires. And some men have made the profound mistake, so far as their individual success is concerned, of trying to succeed by fear and not by persuasion, not by confidence, but by creating the consciousness that they can spoil the careers of the men who do not work. They cannot get far that way. They may spoil a good many careers, but for every career they spoil this is the result:

Did you ever read that story of Poe's, that dreadful story of the man who was put in an iron room in a prison?[2] The room had seven windows, and after he had slept through the first night he became conscious that something had changed in the room, and there were only six windows. He believed that he must have counted wrong the day before, for the proportions of the room seemed the same. On the second morning there were only five windows, and the room was closing about him. Men who shut themselves up in selfishness ought to read that story and realize that their life is closing about them, and that the end is inexorable. The only way to increase the number of windows and let in the air and see the horizon is the way of fairness and equity and love of your fellowmen, and not the way of selfishness and of power.

This is not a new thing for America to see. She saw it at the first, but she forgot it for a little while. That is all. She diverted her energies. She thought that to be rich was to be great, and forgot that her only distinction is the way in which she uses her riches and her power; that she is great only as she differs from other nations, not as she resembles other nations. And she differed from other nations in setting up this standard of hope that was the standard of liberty, and so long as she can induce men to follow it as a standard of hope, so long will she lead the nations. We were just dreaming. We were astray in a dream. And now we have waked up and are recovering the road that we had gone aside from, and have set out again in the beginning of another century—for we choose a century as our dramatic unit in American history—rediscovering the standards of hope and liberty for mankind. And the Democratic party is privileged to lead in that quest. And New Jersey is privileged to stand at the front in the hosts of the Democratic party in that splendid enterprise. These are the things that make a man grateful who loves

[2] The Editors have been unable to discover this alleged Poe story.

his state and who believes in the men who are associated with him. These are the things that make fighting worthwhile.

I suppose some people have the idea that I love to fight just for the fun of it. I had a friend of mine tell me that I reminded him of a Highlander's dog who was looking very dejected one day, and his owner was asked what was the matter with him. He said: "He can no jus' get enuch o' fichtin'." He was not able to find any dog that would give him the satisfaction. Now, that is not in the least my temperament. I am really a very tame, amenable person; but I do love to feel in my blood the splendid satisfaction of fighting for something, something that is bigger than myself, and trying for the time at least to think I am as big as the thing I am fighting for. That is a solid satisfaction. And when I can for the time being represent the Democratic party and find that the nation as a whole is thawing out toward the Democratic party and more and more coming to believe that the Democratic party can do the thing which the country has been waiting for, then I enjoy the immense satisfaction of being part of a thing that is so much bigger than I am that I can dream, at any rate, that I am taking my own measure by the thing that I belong to.

Now, that is the kind of thought that I believe we are permitted to indulge in today, this common sense of being part of a new age and having our eyes forward and not backward, swearing allegiance to one another, that we are not going to allow ourselves or anything we are connected with to be caught in the old entanglements any more. That is what I have sworn to. And the enterprise is easy, because, as I told some gentlemen in another place the other night, we have asked for and obtained a change of venue. The jury is not now the selected jury that was always summoned and always consisted of the same persons; but it is a jury consisting of all the people of the United States; and that jury will stand by you to the last ditch. And with that jury back of you, you may smile at all the gentlemen who meet in corners and in private rooms and arrange to beat you. The thing cannot be arranged. The game cannot be set up. Because all the walls are taken down now, and you are out in the open now. If you want to set up your game, come here in the center of the ring and let us see you set it up. That is the only way in which you can set it up. And if it is the right kind of a setting up, you will not mind setting it up here in our presence, and in the presence, by representation, of the rest of the people of the United States.

And so, gentlemen, our satisfaction today is handsome because it is unselfish. There is nothing handsome about boasting. There is nothing handsome about crowing over anybody else.

That is a pretty mean business. But there is something very satisfactory in saying this: "Now we have left all those things behind; we have set forward in this journey that is ahead of us. We have found the old road, and we are going to follow it; and anybody is welcome to come along with us that wants to." And we are not going to remember whether he tried to find other roads or not, provided he comes along. But we are not going to take his word for it; we are going to look around and see if he is keeping step. Because he has got to get there when we get there, and he has got to get there by the same road we get there on or else he is not of our company. But he is welcome to come along if he will come along. And there is only one way to come along in this journey. There are inns and stages by the way, and there is good entertainment, I dare say, ahead, but the roll will have to be called occasionally, and we will have to see who is present or accounted for. It will not be military discipline, but we will all have to arrive at the same time.

I feel myself no bitterness about anything that has happened. There are some gentlemen who, I fear, think that I have entertained bitter feelings toward them, whom I would love to see and grasp hands with at the end of the journey.

Printed in the *Trenton Evening Times*, Jan. 14, 1913, with corrections from the nearly complete text in the *New York Times*, Jan. 14, 1913.

From Oscar Wilder Underwood

Washington, D. C.,
My dear Governor Wilson: January 13, 1913.

During our recent conference, I became so much absorbed with our legislative policy and program that for the time I overlooked mentioning another matter which I had planned to refer to. It is this:

I feel sure you concur with me in the importance of maintaining the most cordial relationship between the Executive and the majority members of the legislative department. With the view to maintaining at all times the necessary harmonious cooperation to insure this, I feel there must be in the Cabinet one or two persons who have the implicit confidence and esteem of the Democratic members of the House and Senate. I know of no man who so admirably meets this requirement as Honorable Albert S. Burleson. He has been in Congress fourteen years and for several years has proved a most valuable member of the Appropriations Committee of the House, where he has made a careful study of Government needs and requirements. Furthermore,

Mr. Burleson is, as you know, the Chairman of the Democratic Caucus and in that capacity has rendered valuable assistance in bringing about our present effective Democratic legislative organization. He possesses splendid administrative qualifications which, together with his comprehensive knowledge of Governmental affairs and ability to handle men, especially equip him for a Cabinet portfolio.

I trust you will pardon me for having written you so fully in this matter and that you will accept my high personal regard for Mr. Burleson and my interest in the success of your administration as a pardonable excuse for this letter.

With sincere good wishes, I am

Yours very respectfully,   O W Underwood

TLS (WP, DLC).

From John Franklin Jameson[1]

My dear Wilson: Washington, D. C. January 13, 1913.

I thought that I would wait, before writing you after the election, till the first million or so of letters of congratulation had been received and filed. Then I thought I would discreetly and kindly wait until you had had your vacation in Bermuda. Then there was Christmas, and the meeting of the American Historical Association, and the catching up of arrears on my return; and meantime I do not suppose that your mail has diminished, nor on the other hand your kindly feeling towards an old companion.

So I proceed to tell you, what it has been long on my mind and heart to say, that I rejoice very much at your election to this great office, the history of which we used to study together. It is for the country that I rejoice, more than for yourself. You will have labors and difficulties quite as much as pleasures, and very likely such as would outweigh all the pleasures but for the satisfaction there will be in great work conscientiously done; but for the United States it is a great thing to have in that chair a man of such character and such attainments, and I am very happy that it has come to be, though as a resident of the District of Columbia I could not even cast one vote to bring it about.

If, however, there is at any time during your administration any least thing in the world that I can do to help you in any small way, or any personal service to you or Mrs. Wilson by which I can show the affection bred of thirty years of friendship, you have only to command me.

With the heartiest good wishes for the New Year and for all

its successors and with kindest regards to Mrs. Wilson and the daughters, though the latter will hardly remember me, I am
Very sincerely yours,   J. F. Jameson.

TLS (WP, DLC).
¹ Director of the Department of Historical Research, Carnegie Institution of Washington.

An Annual Message to the Legislature of New Jersey

To the Legislature: Trenton, January 14th, 1913.

I trust that you will pardon me if the first note I strike in this my second annual message to your honorable bodies is a personal note. I can not forget that this, though only my second, is also my last annual message to you. I shall presently lay down the duties of Governor of New Jersey. I can not turn away from this great office or give up the privileges it has brought me without expressing my gratitude to the people of New Jersey that they gave me this opportunity to serve them, and my sense also of intimate comradeship and obligation towards the men in the Legislature of the State with whom I have been permitted to work in carrying out the reforms of the last two years.

They have been very full and eventful years, to which I' hope the people of the State will always look back with approval and pride. We have accomplished for New Jersey many things of high consequence which for many a long year had waited and cried out to be done. Our pride in their accomplishment has no touch of boastfulness in it, but only the deep gratification of having been privileged to do so much that was for the common benefit. The legislative session of 1911 will, I venture to say, long remain remarkable in the annals of the State for the number and importance of the reforms enacted, and those of us who were associated in the work of that notable session will, so long as we live, have the happiness of looking back upon it as upon one of the most satisfactory experiences of our public service. Certainly I shall never forget it; and I can not turn away from the great office in which I have enjoyed such satisfactions without avowing the pride I have taken in it and the deep obligation I feel to the fine public-spirited men who stood with me in the days of doubt and struggle. I am happy to have had a part in such things along with such men.

But not all that waited to be done was done by the Legislature of 1911. It was impossible that everything should be accomplished in a single session. The rapidly changing circumstances of the time, moreover, both in the political and in the industrial world, render it necessary that a constant process of adjustment should go on. It is my duty to call your attention to the further changes in our law which seem to be most immediately necessary.

The corporation laws of the State notoriously stand in need of alteration. They are manifestly inconsistent with the policy of the federal government and with the interests of the people in the all-important matter of monopoly, to which the attention of the whole nation is now so earnestly directed. The laws of New Jersey as they stand, so far from checking monopoly, actually encourage it. They explicitly permit every corporation formed in New Jersey, for example, to purchase, hold, assign, and dispose of as it pleases the securities of any and all other corporations of this or any other State and to exercise at pleasure the full rights of ownership in them, including the right to vote as stockholders. This is nothing less than an explicit license of holding companies. This is the very method of forming vast combinations and creating monopoly, against which the whole country has set its face; and I am sure that the people of New Jersey do not dissent from the common judgment that our law must prevent these things and prevent them very effectually.

It is our duty and our present opportunity to amend the statutes of the State in this matter not only, but also in such a way as to provide some responsible official supervision of the whole process of incorporation and provide, in addition, salutary checks upon unwarranted and fictitious increases of capital and the issuance of securities not based upon actual *bona fide* valuation. The honesty and soundness of business alike depend upon such safeguards. No legitimate business will be injured or harmfully restricted by them. These are matters which affect the honor and good faith of the State. We should act upon them at once and with clear purpose.[1]

The people of the State are at present, moreover, at the mercy of investment companies of every kind. Securities of any and every sort can be sold in New Jersey by irresponsible persons and the purchasers must depend upon their own investigations to ascertain whether they are bogus or based upon good business. They should have the protection of the law. Investment companies should be put under inspection and regulation by the State, and no one should be allowed to sell securities in New Jersey without public license issued from the department exercising the rights of inspection and regulation. New Jersey is very late indeed in affording her people this protection.[2]

[1] About the legislature's antitrust legislation, see the statement printed at Feb. 20, 1913.
[2] The legislature did not act on this suggestion in 1913.

There is another matter that cries out for reform and has long cried out for it. Why has no Legislature ever seriously and earnestly set itself to correct it? The drawing of grand juries, and even upon occasion the drawing of petit juries, is notoriously subject to political influence and control in this State, of whose processes of justice we are so proud and whose honor we are in most cases so quick to defend against question or slander. This can and should be remedied. You can not neglect it without seeming indifferent to justice and fair play in matters which are matters of life and death and reputation and honor and which cut to the very quick of human rights. The free, prompt, unbiased administration of criminal justice has been time out of mind at the very center of the fight for individual right and liberty. It is to be hoped that the commission now investigating the various methods of governing this all-important matter will presently submit a thorough and conclusive report.[3]

Another matter no less central, no less vital to the rights and opportunities of individuals and communities, is the method by which taxes are assessed and collected. New Jersey has suffered herself to drift into practices in this fundamental matter which might lead a critical outsider who knew nothing of the history and accidents of her legal development in this case to question both her fairness and her public sense. Her arrangements in respect of this, as of so many other interests and functions, are the result of mere patchwork and lack system and coherence altogether. It is not necessary to have both a board of assessors and a board of taxation; and it is ineffectual to have either if they are to have no administrative control over local assessors and collectors. The most extraordinary variety alike of rule and of practice obtains in the different counties and communities of the State, with this result among many others, that in many localities small property owners pay much heavier taxes in proportion to their holdings than large property owners pay and are practically without redress. Fortunately, this Legislature will have the benefit of a report from a commission specially appointed to make thorough investigation of these inequalities and this lack of system.[4] I hope that its recommendations will point out a wise and practicable way of reform.

There is an additional grant of power to the Board of Public Utility Commissioners which seems to me of capital importance and of pressing necessity. The many, almost innumerable, railway crossings at grade, which make travel on most of our country

---

[3] Many documents relating to the fight for jury reform follow in this volume.
[4] *Report of the Commission to Investigate Tax Assessments in the State of New Jersey, 1912* (Trenton, N. J., 1913).

roads so hazardous and the movement of traffic in so many of our town and city streets so dangerous and difficult, ought, of course, to be done away with as rapidly as possible, beginning with the most dangerous and proceeding without interruption from the more to the less dangerous until absolutely none is left. This cannot be done by the hard and fast precise terms of such a bill as passed the Houses during the last session and was prevented from becoming a law by my veto. No invariable rule can be laid down which will not lead to all sorts of impossible situations and the eventual interference of the courts. The proper solution of this very difficult matter is to empower the Board of Public Utility Commissioners to order the abolition of such grade crossings in such ways and at such a rate as will adjust their orders to each particular case and set of circumstances. The act conferring the power can and should make of that power a legal duty imposed upon the commission, the discretion of the commissioners to exist only in respect of their right to guide, direct, and adjust the processes of elimination in a thoroughly practical fashion. I can not too strongly urge this matter upon your attention.[5]

And while I am speaking of railways, permit me to urge another piece of legislation upon you which seems to me essential both to the safety of travel on the railways and to the fair protection of certain classes of railway employees. I refer to the so-called Full Crew bill, whose failure to pass the last Legislature was so much deplored by all who had noted its introduction and its significance. It is of the highest consequence that railway trains which pass through the State should be manned by adequate crews; and to me, for one, it is a matter of chagrin that they should now carry smaller crews through New Jersey than through Pennsylvania, with whom we are linked by so many important lines of railway. This is a matter which we can not afford to neglect. If it cannot be satisfactorily handled in an act, it might also very well be put in the hands of the Public Utility Commissioners by addition to their powers.[6]

The Legislature of 1911 went a long way towards recognizing the right of full self-government on the part of the municipalities of the State when it passed the excellent bill permitting the towns and cities of the State to adopt the commission form of

[5] For Wilson's veto of the grade crossing bill of 1912, see the veto message printed at April 11, 1912, Vol. 24. As mentioned in n. 1 to that document, the grade crossing bill enacted in 1913 (*Laws of New Jersey, 1913*, Chap. 57) embodied Wilson's recommendations.

[6] A full-crew bill was enacted by the legislature of 1913. It specified the number and job specialties of crewmen required for freight and passenger trains of various types and lengths. *Laws of New Jersey, 1913*, Chap. 190.

government at their pleasure. That was a great step in advance. It has been distinctly to the disadvantage of the cities and towns of New Jersey that the Legislature has undertaken to regulate their affairs and their powers so minutely from Trenton. Only the fullest and freest rights of self-government will stimulate them to serve their citizens as they should be served. The path of reform in that field is unquestionably the path of greater freedom. The question of municipal government is perhaps the most serious question concerning the organization of methods of government that now confronts us as a nation. I covet for New Jersey the honor of showing the way of liberty and self-respecting reorganization. We should set our municipalities free to organize their lives and exercise the functions of self-government with less dependence upon the Legislature of the State.

At the same time, there are matters in which uniform State regulation can be made of immense assistance to the municipalities. For example, it seems to me imperative that a uniform system and method of accounting and of public financial reports should be prescribed by statute for the financial authorities of our towns and cities. I hope that this Legislature will be able to formulate and pass such a measure.[7] The information and materials are at hand. In this matter, more perhaps that [than] in any other, students of municipal affairs have come to a substantial agreement, both as to methods and as to the practical advantages to be gained.

While the Legislature should give over its attempt to govern the cities from Trenton, there are other things to which it can turn its attention in which we are beginning to see a new and immensely beneficial function for the State. The farmer has not been served as he might be and should be. We have set up and subsidized agricultural schools, horticultural schools, schools of poultry breeding, and the rest, and they have done excellent work. Our support of them should be hearty and generous. But a more effective way still has been found by which the farmer can be served. Lectures and schools and experimental farms attached to schools like laboratories are excellent, but they do not and can not of themselves push their work home. Some States have gone much beyond this and we should follow them with zest.

The thing that tells is demonstration work. The knowledge of the schools should be carried out to the farms themselves. Dr. Seaman A. Knapp[8] found the way when he was sent into the

---

[7] No such legislation was passed in 1913.

[8] About Seaman Asahel Knapp (1833-1911) and his agricultural demonstration work, see Joseph Cannon Bailey, *Seaman A. Knapp: Schoolmaster of American Agriculture* (New York, 1945).

South to fight the boll weevil. Choosing a good farm and a good farmer here and there, he showed the farmer how to cultivate part of a field, gave him simple fundamental directions, brought him selected seed, and made frequent visits afterward to see that his directions were carried out. Of course, the neighbors promptly took notice and the next season did the same things,—with the same results, good crops, earlier crops, crops that the weevil was no match for. And fighting the weevil was only an incident. The work grew in every direction,—not work in the schools, but work suggested and directed by men sent out from the schools to take science to the farm, until the agricultural department could not supply the men called for from every direction. The countryman began once more to come into his own. When the farmer does fully take science into partnership and become his own master and fortune builder, the day will be gone once for all when the townsman can tax him and ignore him and absorb unto himself the powers of government at his pleasure.

It does not require a great deal of money to train men and send them out for this work; and when once it is begun it goes on of itself. Private persons, voluntary independent associations, county authorities, take it up. It is a thing that gives life as it goes. It awakens countrysides and rouses them to take charge of themselves. It is not help from the government, it is merely light from the government. The light does the rest. We should give ourselves the pleasure, the pride and satisfaction, of putting New Jersey forward to set an example in this truly great and intelligent work for relaying the foundations of wealth and prosperity in the United States.[9]

This is the way also to attack the problem of forest preservation and renewal,—demonstration work done throughout the State by way of example, until it is demonstrated not only how the forests can be preserved and renewed, but also how profitable they can be made without waste,—at once one of the most profitable and one of the most permanent sources of wealth, a permanent crop devoted to a thousand uses.

It is by such means that the people come to understand themselves and their own interests and assume their real sovereignty. Discussion of public questions becomes a very vital thing for them when the functions of government touch their daily lives and there is something of immediate consequence to them to discuss. Discussions must constantly clear the air and drive everything hidden from its covert. We ought, therefore, to afford the people every facility for discussion. Convenient and inexpensive meeting

[9] The legislature of 1913 passed an act "to provide for farm demonstration in agriculture" along the lines suggested by Wilson. See *Laws of New Jersey, 1913*, Chap. 364.

places ought to be supplied at the public expense. It ought not to be necessary to hire a hall whenever it is desired to have a public meeting. The owners of halls charge high prices when they can and are often partisans and will not let their halls at all to those whom they wish to defeat or embarrass. Every community has its schoolhouses. They should be available for every kind of proper neighborhood meeting out of school hours. If local school boards are illiberal or partisan or unreasonable, they ought to be commanded in their duty in this matter by statute. I recommend such legislation to you very heartily.

A great movement has sprung up in this country in recent years which centres around the schoolhouse as a place of neighborhood conference in all matters affecting the public or any local part of it. It is known as the social centre movement. It has the force and momentum of a great idea in it. Secret forces, corrupt forces, forces of evil of every kind are against it, are afraid of it. They fear neighborhood discussion. They do not wish to have local and neighborhood matters canvassed too much out loud. It is our duty as public servants to lend full and effectual aid to this movement. We can do it by making public-spirited men and women everywhere free of [in] the use of the schoolhouses. A very simple statute will accomplish the desired result.[10] The free forces of society will do the rest.

If such forces had been accustomed to act freely and thoroughly clear the air in New Jersey during the last twelve months, we could have settled some questions regarding the conservation of our natural resources which we have so far failed to settle. It would not have been possible, for example, for individual selfish influences at Lake Hopatcong and local influences in the city of Newark to block and defeat the prompt and reasonable settlement of the question of the abandonment of the Morris Canal. If a few men here and there had spoken out what they knew last session, the bill proposed for the settlement of that question would have passed, and they would have spoken out had there been the habit and place of local discussion. The use and conservation of our natural resources is a matter to which we must constantly devote ourselves, and watchful public opinion is always our best guide.

The pressure of intelligent opinion will soon be upon us in irresistible fashion concerning the business methods of the State also. I suggest that we do not wait for the pressure. The business of the State (I mean its administrative business) is conducted

10 The legislature did pass an act for the after-hours use of schoolhouses for the educational, social, and political purposes here suggested by Wilson. *Laws of New Jersey, 1913*, Chap. 309.

with a wastefulness, a duplication of effort, a confusion and conflict of function, which no business enterprise could survive for six months. There is an extraordinary multiplicity of boards, departments, commissions, and miscellaneous offices, overlapping, connected without being coördinated, independent of one another and yet naturally belonging to a single systematic whole, which ought to be drawn together, simplified, brought into their proper relations, pruned, and put upon a footing of efficiency which will also be a footing of economy and quick responsibility. A commission is now inquiring into this very matter by direction of the last Legislature. It has taken its duties seriously. It will no doubt show the way to many immediate reforms.[11] If its work is not finished, it should be continued and given funds sufficient to prosecute its work to a thorough completion.

We have lagged far behind other States in these matters. We are wasting the public moneys and are not getting the results good business methods would get. This has not been by deliberation. Our administrative methods have been developed piecemeal and at haphazard; but they are none the less worthy of condemnation and reform on that account, and we shall not have proved ourselves faithful and disinterested public servants until we correct them.

There are other things we have outgrown. The constitution of the State needs reconsideration in a score of parts, some of them of the first consequence. No doubt its provisions were considered wise and suitable at the time of its adoption, but that was quite two generations ago and the circumstances of our life have altered fundamentally within that time, politically, socially, economically. I urge upon you very earnestly indeed the need and demand for a constitutional convention. The powers of corrupt control have an enormous and abiding advantage under our constitutional arrangements as they stand. We shall not be free from them until we get a different system of representation and a different system of official responsibility. I hope that this question will be taken up by the Legislature at once and a constitutional convention arranged for without delay, in which the new forces of our day may speak and may have a chance to establish their ascendancy over the rule of machines and bosses.[12]

11 The self-styled "Economy and Efficiency Commission of the State of New Jersey" submitted a "preliminary report" to the legislature on February 18, 1913. It is printed in the *Journal of the Sixty-Ninth Senate of the State of New Jersey* . . . (Trenton, N. J., 1913), pp. 274-300. Further reports were presented in 1914, 1915, and 1916.

12 A bill providing for a constitutional convention passed the Assembly by a large majority on March 19, 1913. However, the rural majority of the Senate, faced with the loss of their privileged position (each county elected one senator),

Two great amendments to the Constitution of the United States await ratification by New Jersey, the amendment conferring upon the Congress of the United States in unmistakable terms the power to levy taxes on incomes, and the amendment providing for the election of Senators of the United States by the direct vote of the people. I can not too strongly urge upon the Legislature the ratification of both these amendments. We can not keep our place among the progressive States of the Union and reject them. Indeed, we shall be in a very small minority if we do reject them.[13]

There are many other subjects I should like to dwell upon,— the extension and systematization of the powers of the State Board of Health, the establishment by statute of an intelligent and thorough-going policy of road building, and the great interests involved in the prosecution of the plan for a ship canal across the State, part of a great inland waterway which is of vital importance to our shipping and commercial development, but these are things which speak for themselves. I have dwelt upon matters not yet enough considered which I deemed it my duty to press upon your consideration, and which I shall deem it my further duty to keep before your attention until they are acted on. They involve both party and public obligations.

May I not, in closing, express the satisfaction I feel in the knowledge that when I lay down the duties of Governor I shall leave them in the hands of Senator Fielder, a man of proved character, capacity, fidelity, and devotion to the public service, a man of a type to which the people of the State desire their public men to conform. I look back with the greatest admiration to that fine group of men in the Houses whose names all the State knows and honors, who set the pace in the days when the State was to be redeemed. It is men like these who have rendered the policies and reforms of the last two years possible. It is men like these who will carry them forward, and the people of the State will sustain them. They will sustain no others. Woe betide the individuals or the party groups that turn away from that path! The future is with those who serve, and who serve without secret or selfish purpose. A free people has come to know its own mind and its own friends.   Woodrow Wilson, *Governor*.

Printed in *Journal of the Sixty-Ninth Senate of the State of New Jersey* . . . (Trenton, N. J., 1913).

---

defeated the bill on March 26, 1913, by a vote of fourteen to four. See Arthur S. Link, *Wilson: The New Freedom* (Princeton, N. J., 1956), pp. 37-38.

[13] These amendments were approved, respectively, on February 5 and March 18, 1913. See Joint Resolutions Nos. 1 and 3, *Laws of New Jersey, 1913*.

From Joseph R. Wilson, Jr.

My dear Brother: Nashville, Tenn. Jan. 14, 1913.

I am informed through a letter from Woolley that Senator Gore, Col. House and perhaps others have arranged for him to be the Secretary of the Senate,[1] the position I at first understood was picked out for me.

In a letter from Mr. McAdoo he said the other day there were reasons, without giving them, why it seemed it would not be best for me to be a candidate for the Secretaryship. This was a surprise to me and I did not understand it until I received Woolley's letter stating that he was in the fight to a finish.

Mr. McAdoo said he had other plans for me which would have to develop but gave no intimation of what they are. I suppose they still have in mind that Historianship[2] which does not appeal to me and is not to your own liking, either.

The first formal ballots for U.S. Senator were taken today without result and indications now point to a dead lock. If the fight is long drawn out, there is a slight chance for me to come in on the home stretch, but I cannot feel that there is more than a bare chance.[3]

I am getting rather restless for it is hard to sit off at this distance and wait for friends in New York and Washington to decide what they want to do. What I have in the past accomplished has been the result of my own efforts and I cannot leave it for others to do and decide for me everything at a time when I feel that the future is possibly opening opportunities for at least some successful venture. I must confess I would like to go to the Senate if that were possible, for there I could aid you, my state and the country, I think, to some extent at least. I would certainly be in a more influential position than possibly elsewhere to back you up in your progressive policies and this would, I need not tell you, be a great pleasure to me personally for I believe you are right in the things you stand for.

I must confess that I am becoming somewhat depressed over the outlook just now for it is hard to sit idle and wait for "something" to turn up. If I knew what that something was most likely to be, then I could be making plans accordingly. Now my hands seem tied.

I did not intend writing a blue letter to you, but my original purpose was simply to further acquaint you with the situation in my individual case, feeling confident of your interest even in the midst of the busy period through which you are now passing.

I suppose we three will attend the inauguration. We certainly will if the future seems to hold out anything worth while which will make the trip possible. Alice has just had a bad spell of grip which kept her in bed for a week and left her much run down, and Kate is passing through a time of nose treatment. Fortunately my health has kept good. I am rushed to death all the time and you cannot realize what a mass of correspondence I have had with Tom, Dick and Harry since the election, many letters being from office-seekers who are after my endorsement and "influence" to accomplish other desired ends. Applicants for appointments from Second Assistant Post-Master General down to those for country post-offices are after me red hot all the time. You see what you have done for me?

All join me in warmest love. Please write when you can spare a moment. I am always so anxious to hear from you and now especially when I feel I need your advice.

Before closing pardon one suggestion just to bring the matter to your attention. You know you will have to select from the army a personal aide. Have you ever considered George McMaster in this connection? I thought he might be a congenial man to have in this rather intimate position.

Your aff. Brother,   Joseph.

TLS (WP, DLC).
    [1] Robert Wickliffe Woolley did not become a secretary of the Senate.
    [2] Of the Democratic National Committee.
    [3] The senatorial election fight in the Tennessee legislature was the latest episode in the long and bitter political conflict in that state centering around the issue of prohibition, about which see J. R. Wilson, Jr., to WW, Nov. 5, 1908, n. 2, Vol. 18. In the senatorial contest, the anti-prohibitionist "Regular" Democrats were arrayed against a prohibitionist fusion of "independent" Democrats and Republicans led by Republican Governor Ben Walter Hooper. The balance of power lay with a group of Democrats controlled by Edward Hull Crump, mayor and political boss of Memphis. Though Crump was strongly opposed to state-wide prohibition, he made an alliance with the fusionists to organize and control the legislature of 1913. This coalition had already forced the withdrawal from the senatorial contest of former Democratic Governor Malcolm Rice Patterson, an anti-prohibitionist, despite the fact that Patterson had run unopposed in the Democratic senatorial preference primary in November 1912. Though the senatorial balloting went on for over a week, the contest did not become deadlocked. On January 23, 1913, some of the fusionists united with the Regular Democrats to elect John Knight Shields, chief justice of the Supreme Court of Tennessee and an independent Democrat, to a full, six-year term in the Senate. On the following day, the fusionist-Crump coalition elected William Robert Webb, headmaster of the Webb School of Bell Buckle, to fill the unexpired term (to March 3, 1913) of the late Senator Robert Love Taylor. See Paul E. Isaac, *Prohibition and Politics: Turbulent Decades in Tennessee, 1885-1920* (Knoxville, Tenn., 1965), pp. 204-205, 210-213, and Everett Robert Boyce (ed.), *The Unwanted Boy: The Autobiography of Governor Ben W. Hooper* (Knoxville, Tenn., 1963), pp. 132-36. The Editors have found no evidence that Joseph R. Wilson, Jr. was seriously considered as a compromise candidate.

From the Diary of Colonel House

January 15, 1913.

Mrs. Wilson and Eleanor came in again after the matinee and remained with us until train time, seven o'clock. We gave them a little supper before they left, and took them to the station.

I talked to Mrs. Wilson about Tumulty for Secretary to the President, and found that she liked him very much and had a good deal of confidence in him. She brought up the question of his being a Roman Catholic. I thought the fact that he was already the Governor's private secretary would seem to make it the natural thing for him to continue in that capacity. She said she had received a great number of letter[s] concerning the matter, that the writers were afraid to send them to Governor Wilson because they thought that Tumulty would intercept them and that they would never reach him. I replied that I thought when the Governor made the appointment, opposition would cease. She wanted to know if I would appoint Tumulty if I were President, and whether I would advise "Woodrow" to do so. I evaded this and said that the Governor knew Tumulty better than I did, that I had known him for less than a month, and that I hardly liked to give a positive opinion. I said, as an original proposition, I would prefer Newton Baker, but that it was not an original proposition, and that I was very loath to swap horses in crossing a stream. I said that Governor Wilson had been very confidential with Tumulty, that he knew all the ins and outs of his public and private affairs, and on that account his appointment would be singularly fit.

We then discussed McCombs. She said he had the strangest effect upon the Governor, that when they went to Staunton and McCombs was with him for an hour or more, he told her that he felt as if he had been "sucked by a vampire and had been left weak and ill." She wanted to know whether I thought the Governor should continue to refuse him a Cabinet place. I did not think it was any longer a question for speculation because the Governor had definitely made up his mind upon the subject and there was no use in discussing it further. I also thought it would not do to put both McCombs and McAdoo in the Cabinet which she of course understood.

To William Jennings Bryan

My dear Mr. Bryan: [Trenton, N. J.] January 16, 1913.

Thank you warmly for your recent letters and for your generous telegram about my speech to the New Jersey electors.[1] Is it not singular how it disturbs some business men to have me say after the election exactly what I said before it?

I warmly concur in your judgment that I ought to send to China and Japan men of pronounced Christian character. These nations are very much on my mind and I think there are certain distinct services which we can render them, and that those services can best be rendered through such men. I also received a letter from Bishop Bashford which made a great impression on me.

I think that the questions you ask concerning the Commoner and concerning Chautauqua work[2] need give us no trouble, and that we can easily agree concerning the best way of meeting them when we have a little conference.

I think that the letter you wrote Aguinaldo was of just the right sort.

I shall certainly act on your suggestion about sending for the Vice-President. I am going a little slowly in my conferences just now because I am wholly absorbed in the session of the State Legislature, which has just opened.

Mr. Lewis Post has attracted my attention more than once and I am particularly interested in what you yourself say of him.

Mrs. Wilson and my daughters join me in warmest messages to Mrs. Bryan and yourself.

In haste,

Cordially and faithfully yours,   Woodrow Wilson

TLS (W. J. Bryan Papers, DLC).
    [1] This telegram is missing.
    [2] The letter in which Bryan discussed continuing as editor of *The Commoner* and as a lecturer on the Chautauqua circuit is missing.

To Winthrop More Daniels

My dear Daniels: [Trenton, N. J.] January 16, 1913.

This is just a hasty line to ask if you could find the time and would be kind enough to draw a bill with regard to the carrying of full crews on the railroads in conformity with the ideas that I know you have reached in the matter. That is to say, a law which would put the matter, in proper form, in the hands of the Public Utility Commission.

In haste,

Cordially and faithfully yours,   Woodrow Wilson

TLS (Wilson-Daniels Corr., CtY).

A News Report

[Jan. 17, 1913]

WILSON OPPOSES INAUGURAL BALL

President-Elect Believes Time-Honored Function
Has Outlived Its Usefulness

For the reason that it entails unnecessary expense upon the Government, President-elect Wilson has come out strongly in opposition to the Inaugural ball, the time-honored institution by which the Washington Committee finds a means of meeting the expenses of the big ceremonial. The President-elect has been informed, semi-officially, but none the less reliably, that [t]he balls have in recent years become mere feminine clothes shows, sometimes not much to show, either.

Time was that the ball was the most important item of the quadrennial induction of the President into office, but opinion worth counting is now declared to be that all its old-time glory and effectiveness socially have departed and that its commercial aspect is the one chief cause for retaining it. The President-elect is understood to realize fully just what he is doing in thus attacking an institution about which so much glamor has been cast, but his friends declare that he is doing it with wide-open eyes, displaying that quality of courage and fortitude that has been so conspicuous in his career.

The ball is always held in the Pension Building. To get the ballroom in shape it has always been necessary to discontinue work in the building for two weeks previous to the inauguration. The estimated cost of the ball to the Government in this way alone was about $95,000 for Mr. Taft's inaugural. This does sot [not] include the expense of the Inaugural Committee. Governor Wilson has been against any such wanton waste of money and feels that he will not be interfering with any one's pleasure if the affair is done away with.

The following letter to William Corcoran Eustis, chairman of the Inaugural Committee, expresses the Governor's feeling in the matter:

"My Dear Mr. Eustis: After taking counsel with a great many persons and ascertaining as well as I could general opinion in the matter, I have come to the conclusion that it is my duty to ask you to consider the feasibility of omitting the inaugural ball altogether.

"I do this with a great deal of hesitation, because I do not wish to interfere with settled practices or with reasonable expectations of those who usually go to enjoy the inauguration; but it has come to wear the aspect of a sort of a public duty, because of the large indirect expense upon the Government incidental to it, and because these balls have ceased to be necessary to the enjoyment of the visitors.

"I hope most sincerely that this request will in no way embarrass you and that I have not too long delayed in making the suggestion."

Printed in the *Trenton Evening Times*, Jan. 17, 1913.

To Charles Richard Crane

My dear friend: [Trenton, N. J.] January 17, 1913.

Thank you for your letter of January fifteenth.[1] I was hoping to get some direct echo from my address in Chicago, and I know that you have given me the real impression that it made. I think that it accomplished just what I had in mind, though one can never be sure that he does these things in exactly the right way.

I had a letter yesterday from Mr. Lawrence Godkin[2] about Horace Plunkett[3] and am trying to arrange to see him. I should be very sorry indeed to miss him.[4]

With warmest regards to all including of course Mr. Brandeis if he is still with you.

Cordially yours,   Woodrow Wilson

TCL (RSB Coll., DLC).

[1] It is missing.

[2] L. Godkin to WW, Jan. 11, 1913, ALS (WP, DLC), saying that Sir Horace Plunkett would be visiting Godkin, January 16-22, 1913, and asking if both men might come to see Wilson during that period. Godkin, a son of Edwin Lawrence Godkin, was a lawyer of New York.

[3] Sir Horace Plunkett (1854-1932), Anglo-Irish statesman; rancher in Wyoming, 1879-89; leader in Irish agricultural reform; M.P. from South County Dublin, 1892-1900; vice-president of the Department of Agriculture and Technical Instruction for Ireland, 1900-1907. At this time, chiefly occupied with publicizing the agricultural cooperative movement in the British Empire and elsewhere. A close friend of many prominent Americans, notably Theodore Roosevelt, and an advocate of Anglo-American understanding and cooperation.

[4] The visit took place on January 21, 1913. Plunkett recorded in his diary: "Went with Godkin to see Governor Woodrow Wilson at Trenton. He was being inundated with the stream of office seekers, but gave us a good interview. I told him of my interest in the Rural Problem of the U. S. and he listened attentively and apparently interested. He asked me to write in anything that occurred to me from time to time." Quoted in Margaret Digby, *Horace Plunkett: An Anglo-American Irishman* (Oxford, 1949), p. 137.

To Arthur W. Tedcastle

My dear Tedcastle: [Trenton, N. J.] January 17, 1913.

I send this letter to your home address to await your return. It happened that just after you left Princeton I got a letter from

Norman Hapgood, who until recently was Editor of Colliers, in which the charges against Brandeis to which you referred the other evening, were absolutely disproved, so far as anything connected with Colliers is concerned.[1] I knew that this would interest you.   Cordially and sincerely yours,   Woodrow Wilson

TLS (WP, DLC).
  [1] The letter from Hapgood is missing.

From William Corcoran Eustis

Washington, D. C. Jan 17 [1913]

Your letter in reference to the omission of the inaugural ball has not reached [us] but I hasten to assure you of our desire to comply with your wishes in every way.

William Corcoran Eustis.

T telegram (WP, DLC).

From the Diary of Colonel House

January 17, 1913.

I met the Governor upon the arrival of the 5.56 train. He had a number of reporters and three secret service men with him. We took the three secret service men with us in the automobile and drove to our apartment at 145 East 35th Street. We talked nearly an hour before dinner, going over the political situation pretty thoroughly. I explained to him that the tentative Cabinet we had outlined the last time we were together, were nearly all irregular, that Wallace was practically the only regular one of the number. That McAdoo, Page, Crane, Houston, Brandeis and some of the others had voted for Taft four years ago, and that some of them had not voted a democratic national ticket for sixteen years. I thought it was positively necessary to put in some rock-ribbed democrats; that it would not do to name more than McAdoo, Houston and Crane and perhaps Walter Page.

We then talked of Burleson and Palmer for the Cabinet. The Governor was insistent that his position was the correct one, that is he should not go to Congress at all but he should keep these men as his most active lieutenants or, as he termed it, his Congressional Cabinet. He said it was his purpose to be in the President's room at the Capitol several days a week, and that it was his purpose to confer freely with both Senators and Representatives. That of course such men as Palmer, Burleson, Gore, Culberson, Henry and others would be his active lieutenants. There is no gainsaying the correctness of this point of view, and I suppose Palmer and Burleson will have to be content with it, for his determination seems to be fixed.

I told him I wanted to do whatever was best to increase his influence with both houses of Congress, and that it seemed to me by putting Palmer and Burleson in, this might be accomplished. He thought, however, the plan he had in mind was much more effective.

We went over practically every Cabinet place. Unless there is some change in the slate, Bryan, McAdoo, Houston, Crane and perhaps Daniels will go in. We discussed the Attorney Generalship and we practically eliminated Brandeis from any Cabinet place. It was my opinion that it would be unwise to put him in. McReynolds he is to send for, ostensibly to discuss the appointment of a District Attorney for New York, but really to size him up for the Attorney General's office.

I called his attention to the importance of the British Mission, in which he fully acquiesced. We could find no man who suited either of us for that place. He spoke of President Eliot for the Chinese mission. He thought it would be a wonderful thing for a man like Eliot to go to China to help uplift them in their general struggle to help themselves. He expressed a profound sympathy for the Chinese and he wished to do all that was possible to aid them. I told him that Jesse Grant[1] desired the place, but the matter dropped there.

He asked what I thought of Rudolph Spreckles[2] for the German mission. I thought it was the best place he could send him. He showed me a letter from Spreckles in which he proposed that the Government should inaugurate a weekly paper to be sent to every voter in the United States.[3] I considered it an Utopian scheme and impracticable, and to this he agreed. I thought it would give an abnormal power to whatever administration was in, and that it would not accomplish the purpose which Spreckles had in mind.

The President-elect announced that he did not intend to give

[1] Jesse Root Grant, youngest son of President Grant, who at this time gave as his address the Democratic Club, New York. Grant had played a minor role in Wilson's presidential campaign.

[2] Rudolph Spreckles, president of the First National Bank of San Francisco and heir to much of the great fortune from sugar manufacturing and real estate amassed by his German-born father, Claus Spreckles. Rudolph Spreckles was active in civic reform in San Francisco and had largely financed the graft prosecutions of 1906-11 (about which see G. L. Record to WW, Oct. 17, 1910, n. 5, Vol. 21). During the campaign of 1912, Spreckles headed the Wilson National Progressive Republican League.

[3] Spreckels's letter is missing.

the ambassadorships to the merely rich who were clamoring for them. He spoke particularly of Judge Jas. W. Gerard and said that under no circumstances would he give that type of man recognition.

He spoke of McCombs and of how he tired and exhaus[t]ed him with his interviews. I feel sorry for this. There is no compatibility between them. He spoke of an old college friend who came in to see him the other day. He said he spent an hour or more harrowing him with the enormous responsibility which confronted him, and the almost certainty of failure. He could not understand how a friend could bring himself to talk in this way. He said if he gave way to his fears and apprehensions, he would lose his reason. I encouraged him and said that he would make make [sic] a great success; that it could not be otherwise; that his steadfastness of purpose; that the righteousness of his cause, would enevitably mean success. I was glad that the dominant note throughout his administration was to be the giving of equal opportunity to all classes, thereby leavening the entire social fabric; that it was better worth while to do something for your fellow man than it was to do something for yourself. I believed that this had never been done, as far as I knew, and he said "no, not since Jefferson." This pleased me greatly for I am more interested in that *motif* than in anything. I pointed out that it could not be accomplished by law, but if he would say it often enough, it would set people to thinking who had never thought along those lines before, and that it would make them feel ashamed of their selfishness and their lack of thought for their fellow man. I thought it would do untold good.

We went to the Cort Theater with two of the Secret Service men to see Laurette Taylor in Peg O My Heart.[4] The Secret Service men sat in the box with us. The audience almost immediately recognized the president-elect, and throughout the evening he was the center of attraction. He enjoyed the play immensely, for it was well acted and very diverting.

We came home at eleven o'clock and a Secret Service man was left on guard down stairs for the night. We had a few sandwiches and a little further conversation and by twelve o'clock were ready for bed.

[4] A comedy about an Irish girl in English high society written by John Hartley Manners. After a successful run in Los Angeles, the play opened at the Cort Theatre in New York on December 20, 1912. It ran until May 30, 1914, setting a new record of 604 performances. The play established the reputations of Manners and his wife Laurette Taylor, who played the title role, and earned a fortune for them through numerous touring companies. Miss Taylor also appeared in a highly successful London production of the play in 1914-15 and starred in a moving picture adaptation in 1922.

January 18, 1913.

This morning we arose and breakfasted at eight o'clock. The Governor eats a cereal and two raw eggs in which some lemon or orange juice was squeezed. He takes neither coffee nor tea.

We talked about Mexico and I expressed the opinion that Madero[1] was an idealist and was trying hard to uplife [uplift] the Mexican people and that he should have his sympathy and support. Diaz[2] had done nothing along these lines, that it was only along the lines of physical development that he was great, but Madero was trying the other end of it.

I said that my friend, T. W. Gregory of Texas, wished to be Ambassador to Mexico and that while it had heretofore been thought that a Texan was ineligible for that place, the time had come when I believed a Texan would be acceptable to the Mexican Government. He asked me to ascertain whether Gregory would be acceptable to Madero.

I told him that I wanted to go to Florida at the end of next week, and he said he would come over again next Friday and spend the night with me and go to the theater just as we did this week, and that then I could go and see Mr. Bryan at Miami. We talked a good deal about Bryan and how admirably he had acted up to now. I thought it would be well for me to discuss with Bryan currency reform and some of the men he had in mind for the Cabinet. He agreed to this and said I could talk to him freely, but that it was to give him, Bryan, information *and not to ask his advice*.

[1] Francisco Indalecio Madero (1873-1913), Mexican political reformer and revolutionary leader, President of Mexico, November 6, 1911, to February 19, 1913. Two excellent studies of Madero and the movement he led are Charles Curtis Cumberland, *Mexican Revolution: Genesis under Madero* (Austin, Texas, 1952), and Stanley R. Ross, *Francisco I. Madero: Apostle of Mexican Democracy* (New York, 1955).
[2] Porfirio Díaz (1830-1915), "President" in name, dictator in fact, of Mexico, 1876-80, 1884-1911. The standard biography in English is Carleton Beals, *Porfirio Diaz: Dictator of Mexico* (Philadelphia and London, 1932).

To Mary Allen Hulbert

19 Jan'y, 1913, Princeton

Please forgive me, my dearest friend, for my apparent neglect. I know how lonely you are,—how your spirit pines for the dear one who is gone, and looks about in vain for some thing—some interest,—in which to take refuge from the loneliness,—and I know how letters from those who understand and deeply sympathise relieve the sense of standing stark and alone in the midst of the desolation; and when these inexorable days lay their grip upon

me and leave me not a minute, not an ounce of energy, from the time I get up in the morning till I drop into bed at night, as they have been doing for the past two weeks, I feel deeply guilty, as if I were a useless and unworthy friend. I am stealing the few minutes for these hasty lines from my bed-time, after guests and callers have relented and gone to bed. I am sure, all the time, that you understand. My thoughts are every day over the water with you. Even as the tireless politicians talk to me hour after hour, with pitiless iteration and endless self-absorption, my thoughts elude them, and travel down the seas to the dear brave lady who is making so gallant a fight against dismay and wonder by what message of confidence and cheer they may comfort and reassure her. We talk of you constantly, and if "absent treatment," if affection and confidence and solicitude and sympathy and full comprehension given with the full heart, even if with unspoken words, can avail to sustain you and revive all the fine spirit, all the capacity to serve and enjoy that is in you, you would grow into your old vital, self-reliant, light-hearted self again apace. You will come to it! You were not gifted and equipped to bless and to enjoy those about you for nothing,—to have your spirit snuffed out at last. Do not lose heart for a moment. Remember those who believe in you and depend upon you and would feel the world infinitely poorer without you, and see if the thought of them does not make living seem worth while to you again. Live again and live to the full for those who, like myself, can sign themselves
Your devoted friend   Woodrow Wilson

ALS (WP, DLC).

To Charles William Eliot

My dear Doctor Eliot: [Trenton, N. J.] January 20, 1913.

Thank you sincerely for your thoughtfulness in sending me the extract from Mr. Edwin C. Green's letter embodied in your letter of January seventeenth.[1] I am very much concerned that our representatives in China and Japan should be of the best quality the country affords. I believe that there is probably nothing more nearly touches the future development of the world than what will happen in the East and it ought to happen, so far as our influence extends, under the best possible guidance.

I wonder if you are expecting to be in this part of the country at any near date? I should greatly value a conference with you about this very matter.[2]
Cordially and sincerely yours,   Woodrow Wilson

TLS (C. W. Eliot Papers, MH-Ar).
¹ C. W. Eliot to WW, Jan. 17, 1913, TLS (WP, DLC). Actually, the extract was from a letter written by Daniel Crosby Greene, missionary to Japan for the American Board of Commissioners for Foreign Missions (Congregational) from November 1869 until his death in September 1913, and a sympathetic student of the Japanese people and their culture. In the extract, which formed the bulk of Eliot's letter, Greene listed in detail the attributes which he considered necessary to a successful American ambassador to Japan.

² Wilson conferred with Eliot in New York on January 24. See the extract from the House Diary printed at that date.

To Winthrop More Daniels

My dear Daniels: [Trenton, N. J.] January 21, 1913.

Thank you warmly for your great kindness in drafting a full crew bill. I shall try to get the Attorney-General's office to go over it for any crudeness of form that may be in it, if you are right in supposing that there is any such crudeness.

In haste,   Faithfully yours,   Woodrow Wilson

TLS (Wilson-Daniels Corr., CtY).

To Oscar Wilder Underwood

My dear Mr. Underwood: [Trenton, N. J.] January 21, 1913.

May I ask your forgiveness in treating you like an old friend and seeking to impose upon you a diplomatic office in a matter, not much in itself, and yet that might have some political significance.

The ladies of the Southern Democratic League, of which I believe Mrs. Underwood is one of the Directors, are proposing to have a Ball on the evening of the sixth of March, to which they are asking Mrs. Wilson and my daughters to come. The occasion they are planning is delightfully conceived, and of course Mrs. Wilson and my daughters would enjoy it immensely, particularly since they are promised that they would meet a great number of their Southern friends. But some instinct makes me feel that it is not wise to plan it as the first social function the ladies will attend after the Inauguration. Perhaps you will catch my point without my making it. While I myself am deeply glad to be a Southern man and to have the South feel a sense of possession in me, we shall have to be careful not to make the impression that the South is seeking to keep the front of the stage and take possession of the administration. There are jealousies in other parts of the country that would be quick to be excited.

I am, therefore, taking the liberty (I fear it is a great liberty) of enclosing a letter from Mrs. Wilson to the Secretary of the

League, with a view to ask that you would be so generous, as well as so kind, as to act as our diplomatic spokesman in suggesting to the ladies concerned that the carrying out of their plans be postponed until a later time. I am at a loss just how to do this, except through someone who like yourself can find the right channels, because there is not a single thought of criticism in my mind of the ladies concerned, but only a desire to do the right thing in the most courteous way. If you, therefore, could have Mrs. Wilson's letter conveyed to the Secretary of the League with the right diplomatic intimations, and have the whole thing kept within the bosom of the family, I would be your debtor.

Cordially and sincerely yours,   Woodrow Wilson

TLS (O. W. Underwood Papers, A-Ar).

To William Jennings Bryan

My dear Mr. Bryan: [Trenton, N. J.] January 22, 1913.

Thank you for the pains you have taken to inquire about Farrar.[1] I had ascertained practically the same things and had virtually dismissed him from my mind. I find no search quite so difficult as that for an Attorney-General, because I want a man of experience and balance and yet a man thoroughly on the people's side.

I am delighted that you should feel as you do about my recent speeches.

In haste,   Faithfully yours,   Woodrow Wilson

TLS (W. J. Bryan Papers, DLC).
[1] WJB to WW, Jan. 17, 1913, ALS (WP, DLC).

From James Marshall Head[1]

Dear Sir: Boston, January 22, 1913

If, as suggested in some of your recent utterances, where new appointments are to be made, none but "Progressive Democrats are to be put on guard," (and in this sentiment I most heartily concur) you will, of course, require the advice and assistance of a man at the head of your legal department who is at heart in full sympathy with Progressive ideas as applied to all the departments of government—who has both the capacity and courage to put those ideas into affirmative, constructive operation, and who, if need be, is willing to make the personal, professional and political sacrifices necessary to accomplish those ends.

Such an adviser you can find in the person of Mr. Louis D. Brandeis, of this City, who, while he has always been independent in politics, has heretofore generally acted with the Republican party, and recently supported Senator La Follette for the Republican nomination for President. Failing in this, after the Chicago fiasco, he loyally and earnestly, publicly and privately, advocated your election.

Such a selection in my judgment, as a Democrat who has always voted and acted with the regular organization, will meet with general approval at this time, strengthen the Democratic organization, and your administration.

I have known Mr. Brandeis since we were in the Harvard Law School together, where he was certainly one of, if not the leading man in his class, and is now recognized as one of the leaders of the Boston Bar, where he has made many earnest friends and admirers, and, as might be expected, a number of bitter enemies, who have felt the force of his intellectual power and genius.

This letter is written without the knowledge of Mr. Brandeis and is a voluntary suggestion from one of your many admirers and friends, anxious to see your administration a success. I do not even know whether or not Mr. Brandeis desires such recognition at your hands, but having seen his name mentioned in this connection, take the liberty, as one of your fellow citizens, in adding my personal endorsement of his eminent qualifications for the position of Attorney General.

Very truly yours   J. M. Head

TLS (WP, DLC).
[1] Mayor of Nashville, Tennessee, 1899-1903; lawyer of Boston since 1904.

To Jenny Davidson Hibben

My dear Mrs. Hibben: Princeton, 23 Jan'y, 1913

Your note,[1] just received, has caused me genuine distress. I beg you to believe that neither to-day nor at any other time have I been guilty of any conscious or deliberate discourtesy to you; I hope that I am incapable of so gross and inexcusable a thing as that would be,—and so contrary both to my principles and to my feelings. I must have done something of which I was wholly unconscious, for I have no recollection of seeing you to-day, except when I took my seat at the rear end of the car on the 9.33 train this morning and noticed that you were sitting at the front of the car. When I entered the train at Trenton this afternoon I was looking for Nellie, who usually is on that train, and saw no one but her. I did not know till afterwards from her, that you had been sitting immediately behind us. If I had seen you or had been conscious of any discourtesy of any kind, I would beg you, with all my heart, to pardon me. As it is I can only express my heart-felt distress that I should have unconsciously and entirely without intention, caused you the least pain or embarrassment. I was as much startled as dismayed by what your note made me aware of.

Most sincerely Yours,   Woodrow Wilson

ALS (photostat in WC, NjP).
¹ It is missing.

To Edward Mandell House

My dear friend: [Trenton, N. J.] January 23, 1913.

I am to be in Philadelphia to-morrow morning at the Dentists but am planning to leave Philadelphia at 12 o'clock on the train which reaches New York at 2. There I am going to join Mrs. Wilson in some shopping, see my tailor, and call on ex-President Eliot, all of which I hope to accomplish before 6 o'clock. Please do not trouble yourself about me one way or the other in the meantime.

In haste,   Affectionately yours,   Woodrow Wilson

TLS (E. M. House Papers, CtY).

Ellen Axson Wilson to William Howard Taft

My dear Mr. Taft,   Princeton, New Jersey Jan. 23, 1913.

I beg that you will pardon my almost inexcusable delay in thanking you for your second letter,¹—a delay due entirely to my rather constant absence from home of late.

I have no words in which to express my sense of your kindness in writing me again,—and with your own hand too! I shall keep it "forever" as my little girls used to say.

And the letter is so full of useful suggestions that it would be invaluable to me just now whoever had written it.

With warmest thanks and good wishes to Mrs. Taft and yourself, I am,   Yours most sincerely,   Ellen A. Wilson.

ALS (W. H. Taft Papers, DLC).
¹ It is missing.

From the Diary of Colonel House

January 24, 1913.

Governor Wilson came at 5.45 and we talked over the Cabinet and foreign appointments for about an hour until it was time to dress for dinner. He had just come from seeing Dr. Eliot of

Harvard to whom he offered the Chinese post. He placed it before Dr. Eliot in such a complimentary way that he promised to take it under consideration, intimating that he would probably accept it provided Mrs. Eliot[1] gave her consent.

The President-elect expressed his purpose of elevating our foreign service by appointments as nearly akin to that of Dr. Eliot as he could find favorable material.

McCombs asked him why he suggested Austria to him. As a matter of fact, the reason was that McCombs had at one time told me that he would like to go there, and I in turn conveyed the information to the Governor. However, he told McCombs that it was one of the most interesting places he had to offer on account of the Balkan situation. The Governor is very earnest in his desire that the United States should express itself sympathetically towards the new Confederation of Balkan States. McCombs said he would prefer Italy. To this the Governor replied that he would be perfectly willing to send him there, it was a question for McCombs to decide. McCombs was still insistent that he be offered a Cabinet place in order that he might say he had declined it. The Governor was quite as insistent upon maintaining his original attitude that no Chairman of the National Committee should be elevated to a position in the Cabinet. So the matter stands.

We discussed the various candidates for Ambassadorial honors but came to no conclusion, for the matter is not pressing.

We then took up the Cabinet and after much discussion we made this slate: W. J. Bryan, Secretary of State, M. G. McAdoo, Secretary of the Treasury, Mitchell Palmer, Attorney General, A. S. Burleson, Secretary of War, D. F. Houston, Secretary of Agriculture, Newton Baker, Secretary of the Interior, Redfield, Commerce & Labor, Lewis of Maryland,[2] Postmaster General, and Wilson of Pennsylvania, Secretary of Labor, in the event Commerce and Labor are separated which is probable. Josephus Daniels as Secretary of the Navy has crowded Wallace out, but the Governor wants Daniels in and it could not be helped. This slate may be revamped, but it seems now as if it will go through largely as it is.

I urged McReynolds for Solicitor General and that may be offered him. We left out Cras. R. Crane, whom the Governor had put down tentatively for Secretary of the Treasury. I told him I did not believe Crane could fill the place satisfactorily and that he had better return to McAdoo. I suggested that he send Crane abroad, also Phelan or Teal of Oregon so as to satisfy the Pacific Coast if he did not put Wallace in.

[1] Grace Mellen Hopkinson Eliot.
[2] David John Lewis, congressman from Maryland since 1911.

We wanted to know what we could do with Burke and I suggested making him Chairman of the Canadian Boundaries Commission. The Governor had never heard of this Commission and I could not myself give him much information but I shall look it up.

We had dinner together quietly and enjoyably. I did not permit the telephone to be connected and no one was allowed to come to the apartment.

We talked of Brandeis and the Governor suggested him for Solicitor General. I told him again that it would not be wise to appoint him to anything of a legal nature, and in this view I think he finally concurs.

We discussed Tumulty for Secretary to the President and I think this appointment will finally be given him.

I asked him concerning his views in regard to the Panama Canal tolls controversy with Great Britain. I was glad to find that he took the same view that I have and that is that the clause should be repealed. We discussed Senator O'Gorman's attitude in this matter and we both thought it entirely untenable. Neither of us believe that O'Gorman is maintaining himself well as Senator and we expressed the opinion that he would be crus[h]ed between the reform element of our party and the machine end of it. I also asked if he had suggested to Gore the creation of two more Supreme Judges which Gore is advocating. He said he had not[,] that he did not approve it unless they divided into a triangular court, three justices being able to give a final opinion in any matter. This is in accordance with the English system and would greatly facilitate business.

He asked me to tell Mr. Bryan of his offer of the Chinese post to Dr. Eliot, and also those whom he had tentatively slated for the Cabinet. It was understood that I should remain away for sometime provided Mr. Bryan did not have an urgent message for me to bring back. In that event, I shall return immediately.

The Governor and I went to the Little Theater to see "Rutherford and Son."[3] It is a well acted but gloomy play.

We came home and had a little supper of sandwiches. While eating them he told me something of his troubles at Princeton. He said that Princeton was really for sale, and if he could find some man with ten millions of dollars to invest, he would like to have him take Princeton out of its present influence and make it what it should be. He did not show the slighest bitterness

---

[3] By Githa Sowerby. This was a "realistic" drama about an English north-country industrialist who permitted his singleminded devotion to the family business to destroy his home life. First produced in London in January 1912, the play opened in New York with a British cast on December 24, 1912.

towards anyone, not even to those who have so constantly as-
sailed him. He spoke of his relations with President and Mrs.
Hibben. He said that up to the time of his trouble they were close
friends and that it was a matter of real sorrow to him that Hibben
had gone over to his enemies.

I talked to him about George Harvey and he spoke of him
most kindly and asked that I convey to Harvey his assurance
of friendship. We talked a good deal about the Harvey-Wat-
terson incident but there was no new light thrown upon it.

January 25, 1913.

We breakfasted at eight o'clock. The Governor expressed a
desire to see the Morgan Collection at the Metropolitan Museum.[1]
We found upon inquiry that it did not open until ten o'clock but
I arranged with the officials to open it earlier. Mr. Kent[2] kindly
showed us through. We then went to the Battery where the
Governor took boat for Ellis Island. He expressed the keenest
regret at my departure for Florida, but we agreed if he wanted
me that I would return at a moment's notice.

The play last night was of Scotch middle class life. This
started the Governor talking of his Scotch ancestry and of his
visits to Scotland.

I telephoned Burleson at Washington and told him to send
Congressman Lewis over to see me tomorrow morning. I also
asked him, Burleson, to meet me at Baltimore with Mitchell Palmer at five o'clock Monday afternoon and ride with me as far as
Washington.

I have been bothered all day with people trying to make engagements but I have steadily declined to see any excepting those
whom it was absolutely necessary to see.

I suggested to the Governor that he appoint George Gordon Battle[3] as District Attorney for this district. The suggestion seemed
to meet his approval but he later said "he is another Southerner."
It looks as if that fatality was pursuing me.

In speaking of patronage, I asked him what his attitude would
be regarding consulting Senators and Representatives. The practice was to consult the Senators regarding district attorneys,
marshals and collectors, and the Congressmen as to postmasters.
He said it was his intention to consult with them before making
appointments, and that when a state was represented by republican senators, he would consult them to the extent of asking
them whether they knew of any reason why an appointment
should not be made. In the event they objected, it was his purpose
to inquire further into the fitness of the applicant.

¹ An exhibition of twenty-nine paintings from the collection of J. Pierpont Morgan was opened to the public at the Metropolitan Museum of Art on January 14. Only recently brought from Morgan's London home to New York, the exhibition included works by Raphael, Rubens, Van Dyck, Rembrandt, Hobbema, Velázquez, Gainsborough, Reynolds, Constable, and Turner. There was also a separate exhibition of drawings from Morgan's collection, including examples of Michelangelo, Raphael, and Dürer. See the *New York Times*, Jan. 14, 1913, and the *Bulletin of the Metropolitan Museum of Art*, VIII (Jan. 1913), 2-17.

² Henry Watson Kent, officially assistant secretary to the board of trustees of the Metropolitan Museum of Art; actually chief factotum and a principal organizer of the modern Metropolitan Museum.

³ Born Edgecomb County, N. C., in 1868, lawyer of New York since 1891; assistant district attorney of New York County, 1892-97. At this time a law partner of Senator James A. O'Gorman.

From Samuel Baker Woods¹

Dear Wilson:　　　　　　　Charlottesville, Va. Jan. 36 [26], 1913.

In answer to your favor this is on my mind. Some years ago a number of us went to work in Virginia for a new constitution to introduce much needed reforms.² Against the opposition of the machine we succeeded, and we could have had any of the offices in the state we wanted, but as most of us did not desire office and thinking the new constitution safeguarded everything we allowed the offices to go without contest to the machine men who had opposed the movement. The result was that in a few years almost every reform was negatived, the constitution having left to the legislature a wide discretion. We won a victory and lost its fruits.

Now the same game is being worked in national affairs. Already Martin, Hay,³ Flood etc., saying that you are going to leave to congressmen the nomination to Federal offices, have announced the men they will appoint and invariably they are men who live, move and have their being in the machine, men it can "trust," enemies of yours. As I wrote you before the nomination the machine is against you. I do not expect what follows to prejudice you, for I think you too good a Christian and too magnanimous a man to desire personal vengeance but it discloses the character of the opposition, and the principles which actuate it.

In the beginning of your canvass I went to Washington to see what could be done with "the powers that be," in Virginia. The brother and secretary of Senator Martin I found strongly opposed to you, and when I urged that his state pride should lead him to support you he answered that you had no more claim to be a Virginian than a snowbird to be a citizen of hell. Tom Martin said that you had done nothing to recommend yourself for the presidency unless it was to disorganize and ruin the party in

New Jersey, that you had been treacherous to Smith who was his personal friend and who was a more valuable man than you; and later at the Baltimore Convention he announced that the Democrats would elect Harmon or Underwood or anybody but Wilson. Hay and Flood both insisted that Ryan was a better Democrat than you. When you declined to consider a campaign subscription from Ryan, you settled your hash with the Virginia machine though you inspired confidence in millions of your countrymen. A year or so ago Ryan gave Flood a carriage and horses worth thousands of dollars and he has given Martin and Hay money whenever they wanted it. They have often gone to Mr. Ryan's place, Martin and the others, to confer about political actions. These men have been bitter against you, they are so still, and are not the crowd to accept defeat. While calling themselves Democrats they stand in every essential principal opposed to you, and by direct or indirect means they have uniformly attained their end. They have no use for any man who has an independent conscience and who will not be subservient and obedient to the bitter end. If they fill the Federal offices you may expect a growing criticism and opposition from Virginia, and a persistent undermining of progressive sentiment. The machine belongs to the trusts and the corporate interests and, while it gives out a certain amount of anti-trust talk for public consumption, it is always found, whenever a pinch comes, doing just what the trusts need and in the most subtle way killing reforms. It would not dare to appear in open opposition, nor to openly antagonize you, especially if it had no offices with which to pay its henchmen. The only way to be sure of these people is to chain them, shorn of power, to your chariot. I do not believe in the spoils system but I feel at this juncture that your administration, if it is to effect promised reforms, must be backed loyally by executive officers. I know too that without patronage the machine would speedily go to the junk pile. As I am free from any desire for any office I feel the more at liberty to urge you, for your own sake, to see to it that Simon-pure, original Progressives be put in the offices in your gift. With regards and best wishes for your success,   Your friend,   Sam'l. B. Woods

While dictating this to my daughter my wife came in & said that this would do you no good & do me harm. I feel, however, that it is my duty to tell you what I know & believe for what it may be worth.

TLS (WP, DLC).
   [1] President and treasurer of the Albemarle Orchard Co. of Charlottesville, Va. He and Wilson had been students together in the Law Department of the University of Virginia, 1879-80.

2 One "reform" sought and achieved in the Virginia Constitution of 1902 was the effective disfranchisement of blacks in an effort, "reformers" said, to purge the rolls of venal and purchasable voters. Recent scholars also agree that the Democratic "machine" politicians were the ultimate beneficiaries. For studies of the constitution, its origins, and its effects, see Allen W. Moger, *Virginia: Bourbonism to Byrd, 1870-1925* (Charlottesville, Va., 1968), pp. 181-230; Richard L. Morton, *The Negro in Virginia Politics, 1865-1902* (Charlottesville, Va., 1919), pp. 147-62; and Raymond H. Pulley, *Old Virginia Restored: An Interpretation of the Progressive Impulse, 1870-1930* (Charlottesville, Va., 1968), pp. 66-131, 152-70.

3 James Hay, congressman from Virginia, 1897-1916.

A News Report

[Jan. 27, 1913]

WILSON CAPTURES SOCIAL WORKERS

Holds a Secret Conference with Them
at Mrs. Alexander's Castle Point Home.

At a conference held yesterday at the home of Mrs. Caroline B. Alexander in Hoboken, Gov. Woodrow Wilson met the "social welfare" advocates, in whose behalf Col. Roosevelt and his Bull Moose Party were so solicitous in the last campaign, heard their demands, and made an impromptu speech of a most encouraging character.

Though the arrangements were all made a week or more ago, and though the conference was a formal one, with set subjects for discussion, and with a prearranged order of procedure, such secrecy was enforced on the participants that no hint of it leaked out. Newspaper men were not admitted, and only when the meeting was over did the conferrees consent to give out a statement of what had occurred. Even then newspaper men were not admitted to see any one, and the statement given out consisted of a summary of the arguments made by the social workers and a stenographic report of Gov. Wilson's reply. . . .

In the supreme effort to keep the meeting a secret the participants did not even dare to take a stenographer into their confidence, and so when it came to reporting the Governor's speech they were obliged to rely on one of the social workers present who had a knowledge of shorthand. Her version, which was given out on the steps of the Alexander mansion to the newspaper men, is the official one. Nevertheless one of the conferrees insisted when the official version was read to him that this stenographer had failed to get the Governor's meaning in his utterances about the National Board of Health. She had left out all he had to say about sanitation, which, this conferree asserted, was the point of his argument. . . .

Following is the report given out as official:

"At the home of Mrs. Caroline Alexander, at Castle Point, Hoboken, yesterday afternoon, Gov. Wilson heard the views of a number of experts on industrial questions of the day and made a brief speech in outlining his own point of view.

"A. J. McKelway described the complicated system by which the District of Columbia is governed. 'It is a triangle of profit and power manned by a triumvirate. Of this triumvirate one is President of a National bank, with connections in speculative real estate. The second is President of a trust company, with connections in speculative real estate. The third is also President of a trust company, with connections in speculative real estate. The situation is controlled in three ways: By control of taxation, which is lowest in the privileged district and highest in the home districts; by control of credit—investments within the speculative area are encouraged, those in other districts discouraged; by control of Congress, through the committees of the District, in seeing that improvements ordered by Congress work for the pockets of the triumvirate.'

"Owen R. Lovejoy said that Congressmen needed to be educated as to the purposes and scope of the National Child Labor bill[1] and the appropriation increased.

"Miss Lillian D. Wald thought the public underrated the value of the immigrant, largely because there are insufficient methods for protecting him during the first year or two. 'There should be inter-State arrangements for distributing immigration. Our laws for exclusion are sufficient. Much of the agitation against the amount of immigration is hysteria.'

Miss Josephine Goldmark, of the National Consumers' League, author of the recent monumental work, 'Fatigue and Efficiency,'[2] spoke in favor of a bill now pending before both branches of Congress, to limit the hours of women working in the District of Columbia.

"Mrs. Florence Kelley reviewed some of the court decisions which interfere with the protection of the consumer and mentioned legislation now before Congress to remedy some aspects of the situation.

"Homer Folks told of the number of preventable deaths, described the opportunity of the Federal Government to take the lead in scientific and professional sanitary work, and urged the passage of the Owen bill for the establishment of a Federal health

[1] The text was garbled by the reporter. The intended reference was to the Children's Bureau.

[2] Josephine Clara Goldmark, *Fatigue and Efficiency: A Study in Industry* (New York, 1912).

service[3]—a step to which all three parties are committed by their platforms.

"Prof. Seager[4] described the defects in the present Federal Employers' Liability act, and said a bill was about to be presented remedying these defects.

"Prof. Lindsay[5] spoke of the unsatisfactory make-up of the present industrial commission,[6] and hoped the Senate would not confirm the nominations, but keep the matter open for the incoming Administration.[7]

"Gov. Wilson said in reply:

" 'Several of those who have spoken have described this as a valued opportunity to them. I can speak of the opportunity as mine rather than theirs. It is seldom a man in my position hears from so many who know what they are talking about. I have the opportunity every day of hearing from those who do not.

" 'Every subject treated here to-day engages my deep interest and enthusiasm. My enthusiasm is in proportion generally to the practicability of a scheme. I have always been eager to forward general principles, but I do not feel the breath fill my lungs until I see the practical plan. I hope you will always come to me with plans, and you may count on me to consider those plans with interest and with friendliness.

" 'Dr. McKelway excited me, because he put under my nose a fresh trail, and the kind of a trail that I always follow with zest.

" 'Most of the things that you have spoken of are without politi-

3 Introduced on February 1, 1910, by Senator Robert Latham Owen of Oklahoma, it provided for the creation of a cabinet-level Department of Public Health. This new department would have charge of "all matters within the control of the federal government relating to the public health and to diseases of animal life" and would incorporate all existing federal agencies "affecting the medical, surgical, biological or sanitary service, or any questions relative thereto," except those in the Departments of War and Navy. The bill was the subject of lengthy public hearings but was not enacted then or later. However, numerous public health advocates continued to push for the passage of this or a similar measure. See Laurence F. Schmeckebier, *The Public Health Service: Its History, Activities and Organization* (Baltimore, 1923), pp. 35-37.

4 Henry Rogers Seager, Professor of Political Economy at Columbia University.

5 Samuel McCune Lindsay, Professor of Social Legislation at Columbia University.

6 That is, the United States Commission on Industrial Relations, established by Congress on August 23, 1912, with sweeping powers to investigate the whole area of the relationship between capital and labor in the United States. For the origins and creation of the commission, see Graham Adams, Jr., *Age of Industrial Violence, 1910-1915: The Activities and Findings of the United States Commission on Industrial Relations* (New York and London, 1966), pp. 25-41.

7 President Taft made public his nominations to the nine-member commission on December 17. However, the Democratic minority in the Senate prevented confirmation through a filibuster, thus leaving the incoming Wilson administration free to make new nominations. *Ibid.*, pp. 41-49.

cal embarrassment. One that does have political embarrassment is the Health Department project. Already in dealing with medical education in New Jersey we have had political difficulties, because of the various independent schools of medicine that have sprung up on all sides. There is a fear in many minds that we are about to set up what has been called a medical trust, and it is very desirable to remove that idea. I have never seen any serious proposal to put any particular school of medicine in charge of the National health.

" 'With regard to the Children's Bureau another similar difficulty exists. My own party in some of its elements represents a very strong State's rights feeling. It is very plain that you would have to go much further than most interpretations of the Constitution would allow if you were to give to the Government general control over child labor throughout the country. It is important to make it generally understood that the purpose of your bureau is to collect and co-ordinate information on the subject.

" 'I want above all things to enjoy the confidence of, and to have at my service the information and counsel of, those who are engaged in these fundamental things. Most of the vitality of public action comes from outside the Government. The Government does not originate. It responds to public opinion. You are all to regard yourselves as forces playing upon the Government, and I hope that during the next four years you will find a sensitive part of the Government at the top.' "

Printed in the *New York Times*, Jan. 27, 1913.

To Oscar Wilder Underwood

Personal and Confidential.

My dear Mr. Underwood: [Trenton, N. J.] January 27, 1913.

You have indeed played the part of a real friend, and I thank you for it most warmly. I had my own misgivings along just the lines you trace in your letter,[1] and I shall present the matter to Mrs. Wilson as you present it to me. I am sure she will agree with you, as I do, that you have suggested the best way.

It is rewarding to have such friends.

Cordially and sincerely yours   Woodrow Wilson

TLS (O. W. Underwood Papers, A-Ar).
[1] It is missing.

From Carter Glass

Personal.

Dear Governor Wilson: Washington. January 27, 1913.

I received a letter from you under date of January 9th stating that you considered it desirable that you should see me for a further talk on the currency question and that you would in a few days suggest a time for another conference. For fear that failure to promptly acknowledge your letter may have produced the impression that I did not think the matter of sufficient importance to pursue immediately, I am writing to say that I shall be glad to confer at any time that may best suit your convenience. In my view it is very important that we should know your conclusions on currency matters as soon as they are reached, as it would be futile to proceed upon lines that might be contrary to your convictions. Indeed I am inclined to think that it is going to be a little difficult to enact legislation even with the full power of the administration behind any bill we may agree upon.

I am right much encouraged, however, by the changed attitude of some of the influential bankers who have appeared before our subcommittee. After being courteously, but firmly, informed that the committee felt precluded from consideration of the Aldrich scheme or a central bank plan, these gentlemen, as I am privately told, concluded that they could not carry out Mr. Warburg's[1] purpose of "battering the committee into a repudiation of the Democratic platform," and they are now writing me, after conference among themselves, that they are willing to cooperate with the committee in trying to secure the best remedial legislation that it is possible to obtain. They are expressing a good deal of anxiety for immediate action, and men like Hepburn, of New York, Forgan and Reynolds, of Chicago, and Wade, of St. Louis,[2] have written that they will be glad, at the word from me, to assemble the currency commission of the American Bankers' Association for the purpose of getting behind any sound measure that our committee may construct.

There are, of course, two sides to the question. Too pronounced activity by the organized bankers might arouse suspicion and hostility among those who regard banks as essentially evil. We shall, therefore, have to proceed discreetly in everything we do. I am, as chairman of the committee, receiving numerous invitations from bankers and business bodies to make addresses. Several of these I have accepted; but I shall have to talk guardedly and discursively, as I did before the National Chamber of Commerce last Tuesday night. This is both awkward and unsatisfactory; and the situation in all respects would be much improved if we could get on a little more definite basis. You will readily understand that this cannot be done until I can know something more of your views.

    With cordial regards,

Sincerely yours,   Carter Glass.

TLS (WP, DLC).

  1 Paul Moritz Warburg, partner in the investment banking firm of Kuhn, Loeb & Co. of New York, one of the authors and a leading proponent of the Aldrich plan for a central bank, about which see n. 3 to the interview printed at Aug. 26, 1911, Vol. 23.

  2 Alonzo Barton Hepburn, chairman of the board of directors, Chase National Bank, New York; James Berwick Forgan, president of the First National Bank of Chicago; George McClelland Reynolds, president of the Continental & Commercial National Bank of Chicago; and Festus John Wade, president of the Mercantile Trust Co. of St. Louis.

From Charles William Eliot

CONFIDENTIAL.

Dear Governor Wilson: Cambridge, Mass., January 27, 1913.

    I have consulted my wife, my son,[1] and my surviving sister (now eighty-five)[2] on the proposal you made to me last Friday afternoon. They unanimously advise against it, and have presented arguments which convince me that I ought not to accept, at my age,[3] the important work to which you invite me. They saw clearly that the service would be highly honorable, and possibly highly useful; but they urged that I had plenty of such work to do at home, and that home was the best and most appropriate working-place for me. I find their arguments just, and so I accept their conclusion, and respectfully decline your invitation, though I thank you for the confidence in me which your giving it implies.

    I have not mentioned the subject except to the persons named above; and neither they nor I will make further mention of it.

    I am, with high regard,

Sincerely yours,   Charles W. Eliot

TLS (WP, DLC).

  1 The Rev. Dr. Samuel Atkins Eliot, president of the American Unitarian Association.

  2 Mary Lyman Eliot (Mrs. Charles Eliot) Guild.

  3 He was born March 20, 1834.

From Edward Mandell House, with Enclosure

Dear Governor: New York City. January 27th, 1913.

    I asked Lane to tell me something of Lewis of Maryland and I enclose you his reply.

I also asked Billy Hughes concerning him and he promised me that he would talk to you today or tomorrow and tell you what he knows. I shall see some people in Washington this afternoon and get further information and will send you a line from there.

As to Lane I wish you would invite him over in the next day or two. He is to be in New York at the Vanderbilt Hotel. He is one of the big men of our Party and after talking with him you might think it advisable to use him.

I hope you will also send for McReynolds within the next day or two. He can give you invaluable information concerning the District Attorney's office here and the Attorney General's office in Washington. I really think it is important for you to see him for more reasons than one for you can get some information that you cannot get elsewhere.

Please remember that I stand ready to return from Florida at an hour's notice and also remember that if you call for me, the pleasure will be all mine.   Your very faithful,   E. M. House

Macauley[1] has just brought Judge Freschi[2] to see me. If he is capable it would be a *fine* appointment for reasons which will doubtless occur to you. I am sending them down to McReynolds to have him look him over.

TLS (WP, DLC).
  [1] Charles Raymond Macauley, cartoonist for the New York *World*.
  [2] John J. Freschi, lawyer and city magistrate of New York, and prominent in Italian-American affairs in New York.

E N C L O S U R E

Franklin Knight Lane to Edward Mandell House

Dear Mr. House,   Washington [c. Jan. 26, 1913]

Lewis of Maryland, Congressman, is a useful man, of ideals and great earnestness,—which is a rare virtue these days,—but he has the fatal gift of being logical, that makes him most dangerous to follow. You know we Anglo Saxons make government "go" by being illogical while others like the French are constantly failing, —bumping their heads against the sky or the ground by going the limit with an idea.

I like Lewis but he sees nothing but straight lines—and so in talking to him I break the lines now and then, and throw in curves and things so as to allow for human nature, for things as they are—etc.

Good time to you.   Lane

ALS (WP, DLC).

From Joseph R. Wilson, Jr.

My dear Brother: Nashville, Tenn. Jan. 27, 1913.

I find it now as I have always found it in the past, natural to turn to you for advice. I do this now with some hesitation, however, because of the fact that you are soon to become President. I want you to know, however, that I write to you freely and candidly. as your brother and not to you as the next President of the United States. I do not desire to worry you at a time when your thoughts are so fully occupied, but I have reached a period when I feel the need of your advice.

You know the outcome of the Senatorial fight. I feel convinced I could have been elected had I been willing to compromise myself with promises and in other ways, but I stood fast, occupying an uncompromising position throughout it all and not giving countenance, even, to any of the many schemes which were worked with more or less success and about which I desire to fully inform you when the earliest opportunity offers, for I feel it my unpleasant duty to keep you informed as to actual conditions in this state. I had the chance to receive endorsements which I refused because not certain in my own mind they were entirely proper. I was offered the short term in the Senate with every indication of election, and this I refused because I was not willing to be made a "sop" for those who desired to secure any possible or imaginiary advantage my friendship might give with the coming administration. I have since learned that those in control of the situation, or one side of it, have been deeply regretful of the fact that they did not press me forward as a compromise candidate. I never announced my candidacy but took the position that I would be willing to accept as a compromise provided that I could enter the Senate entirely free from all promises and obligations, implied or real. This was not exactly the kind of a fellow some people wanted.

Now as to the Secretaryship of the Senate. You have probably noticed from the press dispatches that my boom has been started by Luke Lea. He seems enthusiastic and determined to put me over, declaring there will be no difficulty. I recently wrote you that for some reason Col. House, Senator Gore and others had thought it best for Woolley to enter this race. It now develops that the reason for this was some fear that my being Secretary of the Senate might cause possible embarassment in case the Senate should, in executive session, discuss some of your official appointments or some other action on your part while President. Lea and other friends here can see nothing in this. I have not myself officially announced my candidacy, but Lea and others have gone systematically to work and seem already to have made good progress. They have certainly secured a considerable amount of publicity. I feel I am fitted for the position and that I may be of assistance to you in Washington, for I feel you will need some friends who will tell you the unvarnished truth about things, not as a personal representative of yours to watch what is going on, of course, but as an observer of political events throughout the country.

Now here is the feature of the situation about which I feel a delicacy in speaking. The people of Nashville of all ranks and callings, are expressing an earnest desire to keep me here. For some reason, they have apparently decided that I will most likely get the local post office. I am informed that petitions asking that this appointment be made have already been started although the local office will not be vacant for a year yet. My desire is to keep this matter from being put up to you if possible. From a financial standpoint the local office would be far better for me than the secretaryship of the Senate, for it will, after June 1 next, pay $6,000 per annum and this in Nashville would mean much more to me than $6,500 in Washington where my social obligations as the brother of the President would be far more exacting than they could possibly be here with our modest way of living. My election as Secretary of the Senate would, of course, relieve you of all necessity for even considering me in connection with official preferment even in the minor office of post-master at Nashville.

Now Mr. McAdoo, in whose friendship and good sense I have entire confidence, and Col. House and others, say they are working in my behalf and I can rest assured that "something will develope." This is good so far as it goes, but I cannot be content to be idle myself for I am not in the position of a man who is merely seeking "a job." I merely desire to take advantage of circumstances and better my condition if possible at the same time ridding myself for a time, at least, of the newspaper grind which is very wearing and is telling on me, I fear, gradually.

I regret greatly that Woolley has entered this race for I do not want to antagonize him and to cause the slightest friction between those of us who were so pleasantly associated in the work of the recent campaign at the New York headquarters. He was informed, however, some time before he entered the race that I had been mentioned. He says, however, that he knew nothing of the plans for him until all had been arranged by House, Gore et als. I can say with truth, however, that Lea had set the machinery going in my hebalf [behalf] before he came home from

Washington to participate in the recent Senatorial struggle, and now my friends are doing all the work that is being done in my behalf. Lee Douglass is very active and useful among others.

I am sorry I have taken so much of your time, but I feel I must have your advice. I was pleased at the interest Malone has taken in me and with the liberal offer he has secured for me.[1] I wrote him candidly, however, I had had no experience in the business suggested and was not willing to enter any line of work unless I could give full value received. I expected to receive a wire from him today telling me whether to come on to New York, but have heard nothing so far.

I wrote Walker Vick about tickets to the inauguration. Kate, Alice and Kate's sister will be with me. He did not know how many of us would be with your personal party on the reviewing stand and could not tell what he could do in the way of securing tickets I want for some of my personal friends and some of Kate's relatives, together with the kind friends who will entertain us for a few days when we first reach Washington and before we can go to be with you for a very brief stay. Can you give me information on these points?

Please let me hear from you soon. Kate and Alice join me in great love to you all.

Your aff. brother,   Joseph R. Wilson.

TLS (WP, DLC).
  [1] The Editors have been unable to discover what employment Dudley Field Malone had found for Joseph R. Wilson, Jr.

To Carter Glass

My dear Mr. Glass: [Trenton, N. J.] January 28, 1913.

Thank you for your letter of yesterday. I find that I shall have a comparatively free day on Thursday next the thirtieth. If it is not too short a notice for you, I would be very much obliged to you if you could come up and see me at half past two o'clock in my office here on that day.

I am very much pleased and encouraged by your report of the changed attitude of the men who have been appearing before your sub-committee. I have a growing hope that we are going to work this difficult question out to a successful issue.

Cordially yours,   Woodrow Wilson

TCL (C. Glass Papers, ViU).

An After-Dinner Talk to the New Jersey Senators[1]

[Jan. 28, 1913]

Mr. President[2] and gentlemen: I must confess that it has been a little hard for me to keep my spirits up this evening because I realize with a good deal of anxiety the fact that I am not likely to meet you again, and certainly not to meet you socially in an official relationship; because some of the happiest months of my life have been spent as Governor of New Jersey.

No small part of that happiness has been due to the kind relationship I have borne to my colleagues in the legislature. I think I shall always recall as one of the turning points of my administration, an evening memorable, that when I led Senator Nichols in the Cake Walk.[3] I think that was one of the earliest cases, if it was not the very first case, when the gentlemen in the Senate two years ago realized that my long, solemn face was not a real index to my countenance, and that I was something different from the ascetic schoolmaster; that I was a human being, and that I greatly enjoyed, perhaps enjoyed more than anything else, the intimate comradeship where men get at each other's minds in informal debate. I have enjoyed this privilege.

I realize that the Senate of New Jersey is perhaps unique because it is so small as to make relationships of this sort possible. It would be impossible to have relationships, such as I have had with the senators on this subject, if this body were twice or two or three times its size. I am not now arguing the question of what may come but merely expressing my satisfaction with the [size] of this body.

I feel that one of the most shining moments of my life was about a week ago, when I was conferring with a number of my colleagues in the Assembly and the Senate, in my office. And after rising from a conference with a little group of them, one of the men grasped me by the hand and said, "Governor, I haven't had an opportunity to congratulate you," and I said, "About what?"

I had become so absorbed in the ordinary affairs of New Jersey that I had utterly forgotten that I had been elected President of the United States!

That, I think, is a genuine expression of the way I am feeling tonight.

It would be a real wrench to separate myself from this state

[1] At the annual dinner of the New Jersey Senate, in the Marlborough-Blenheim Hotel in Atlantic City.

[2] James F. Fielder.

[3] About this episode, see WW to Mary A. H. Peck, April 2, 1911, Vol. 22, p. 532.

and my association with your work. There are many reminiscences that come over me as I sit here tonight. I have been only two years Governor of New Jersey, and I think it seems a very much longer time than that and, judged by events and sensations, it is a very much longer period than that.

I feel that the real foundation of every man's usefulness is his intense affection for some particular part of the country. You can't entertain the sentiment of patriotism if you spread it thin over the whole continent. I entertain a sentiment for all parts of the United States, but there are two parts of the United States with regard to which that sentiment is very intense indeed. One is the state in which I was born, and the other is this state, because I have been bred to it in the principal part of my political experience.

And so I shall always think of myself as a Jersey man. That doesn't mean the same thing in all parts of New Jersey. There are Jersey men who are easily detachable from the state, and there are other Jersey men who are not detachable. For a large number of our fellow citizens, New Jersey is a mere dormitory. It is a place where they sleep but where they do not think. It is a place where they keep their families and occasionally resort to their families, but it is not a place where they do their business or expend their energies or entertain their ambitions. Now your energy and your ambition must be centered upon a particular place if you are to feel a vital and everlasting connection with it. . . .

I have reflected, as I have been sitting here tonight, that the only glory of a particular state of the Union, the only immortality that a state can enjoy, is its example, and that the only way it can exercise an example is by its legislative policy and by the actual careers of the men whom it produces.

When you think back through the history of New Jersey, the thing you really love to do is to recall those men who, forgetting their own interests, devoted themselves to the interests of the state and the nation. We are all perfectly aware that those are the only individuals who illustrate any degree of greatness on the part of New Jersey. It is not necessary that they should have been statesmen. If they devoted themselves to science, if they devoted themselves to philanthropy, if they devoted themselves to big concepts that had nothing to do with the advancement of their personal interests, they are the lights that have been blessed on high, to show where New Jersey was and what New Jersey bred and illustrated. . . .

One of the things that I have been gratified over recently in the

Assembly, with reference to legislation, is that we were by the mere introduction of a series of bills, which contained attempts to meet the corporation question, able to get the attention of the whole of the United States, for we are the first state to introduce a series of bills addressed to the settlement of this infinitely difficult question.

If we can successfully pass these measures and establish their feasibility, we shall have again set an example for the country of what a state can do.

Now every state in the United States is a sort of experimental station. What has given distinction to the great State of Wisconsin is that it has blazed the way, shown the method, established the feasibility of particular lines of legislation. One of the prides of the State of Oregon—everybody has heard of the Oregon idea— whether they have subscribed to that idea or not. That idea is that the people must have direct access to their own government, by one route or another, and every man feels just a little bit bigger that he belongs to the state that has supplied an idea to the nation.

To my mind, as a university man, it is delightful to know that the great State of Wisconsin, which has been one of the great, leading states of the Union, is the state of the Union which comes nearest to being governed by its university. I don't mean governed by its university in any formal sense as it is by its governor, but governed by its university's influence.

The University of Wisconsin stretches its tentacles out into every part of that state by one process or another of university extension. It carries knowledge and science abroad as an invaluable commodity. And because it's supported by the taxes of the state, it is fruitful of information to the humble and the educated alike throughout that great commonwealth. That has been an incomparable source of fertilization and stimulation. That is the reason that men have come out of that state who have to know something in order to answer. Mr. Robert La Follette, for example, may be very tedious in insisting upon speaking never less than two hours at a time; but he speaks for two hours at a time because he intends, when he starts out, to give you the full case. And when he is through with his case, you have got to know more than he does to answer it. That is the reason some people don't like him. They have not been able to answer him. They have never known enough to answer him when he got through. . . .

Now along that line, the challenge of the state nowadays is to know what you are doing and to do it without fear and with knowledge, because sound sense and absolute fearlessness seem to me to sum up the demands of public life just now.

In the first place, sound sense. Again let me refer to a recent experience. Those recent experiences are always the most vital. I took the liberty of asking one of the most experienced jurists of this state[4] to take counsel with me with regard to the bills, of which the corporation bills were part, and at every phrase our question was not "What will this disturb?" but "Does this disturb anything that should not be disturbed?" And it required experience. It required very much more experience than I personally had gotten. It required a sound balance of judgment and a recollection of complicated transactions, something like the sympathetic connection with the business of the state, in order to answer that question.

Whether we answer it successfully in all cases or not is another matter. But the purpose, it seems to me, in our minds, is to serve the facts, not to serve any radical tendencies in ourselves which would satisfy, as a boy would satisfy himself by tying a pack of firecrackers to a dog's tail. Nobody in his senses wishes to uproot anything sound in our modern life. Nobody wants to see anybody run for the fun of seeing him run. . . .

Now I do believe in sound, free, competitive business. And therefore it is with great ardor, to try and serve that idea, if New Jersey can serve it, that New Jersey has seen a new light. My love, therefore, for New Jersey is a very practical love, and I turn away from her with this deep regret, that I have got to give up working directly in the interest of her reputation and her influence.

It is a great thing when you have got a mother to let other people feel the benign and guiding influence that emanates from her. And when you believe in her and believe in the sources of your nourishment, it is a pretty fine thing to try and give other persons access to those sources.

I believe in the soundness, I believe in the wholesomeness, of the people of New Jersey. I believe that as their energies are released, so will the country profit and New Jersey grow great and illustrious, and grow more great and illustrious for having again and again contributed to the progress of the nation.

You know that New Jersey has always, historically speaking, enjoyed a peculiar reputation. She has always had two elements in her, very marked in their development. There were some of the most outrageous Tories and Loyalists of the Revolutionary period in New Jersey. But there were also some of the most rampageous and active patriots in New Jersey. She has never done anything by halves, and she has always had all the elements in a very pronounced state of development. And that adds to

---

[4] Edwin Robert Walker, Chancellor of New Jersey.

the greatness of nations and also adds to the progress of affairs. . . .

It is with all these things in my mind that I am about to turn away to a new sphere of influence. For the present, the happiest part of the week for me is the early part of the week when I am absorbed in the business of the state. The latter part of the week I shall turn away to such questions that have been asked by telegrams which come as near to giving me nervous prostration as they do the gentlemen who originated the inquiries.

I anticipate that there will be some greater difficulties in getting a complete and intimate understanding with the United States that I would not feel in getting a complete and intimate understanding with New Jersey; but the sum and substance of it is that I value evenings like this where I may sit with you in intercourse of this sort.

I want you to know, gentlemen, that if I permit myself to think of my impending task as a whole, I should be very much daunted and dismayed. I don't permit myself to think of it as a whole. It is a new beginning. It dismays the imagination. I try to think of one subject at a time. It is only by thinking of one subject at a time that I can have the least hope that I will comprehend any of these subjects and succeed in handling them. I am going by the rule of thumb, the rule of experience, the rule of development, and not by the rule of imagining at the outset that I know the whole thing or know where I am bound for.

I feel somewhat in the condition of the man described in a story I once heard. There were a couple of gentlemen who went fishing somewhere in one of the northern states, I think it was New Hampshire. And up there they were beguiled into partaking, perhaps too liberally, of a beverage which was known there as "squirrel" whiskey. The name was explained by the circumstance that if you drank it, you felt like climbing a tree.

One gentleman imbibed more freely than the rest and preceded his friends in going to the railway station, where they were to embark for their train, and got on a train going north instead of a train going south. They missed him, so they telegraphed the conductor—they said, "Send back that man who is inebriated and named Thompson, who is on the northbound train and should be on the southbound train." They soon got a telegram from the conductor saying, "Further instructions necessary. Six men on the train who know neither their name nor their destination."

Now I know my name, but not my destination.[5]

JRT transcript of CLSsh notes (C. L. Swem Coll., NjP).

[5] "After dinner, Gov. Wilson proposed a midnight stroll along the board walk. The Senate accepted the proposition en masse and led by the Governor the

twenty-one Senators marched along the walk before the brisk breeze until the Governor's 'right face,' when they wheeled and returned. They got back to the Marlborough-Blenheim at 12:20 A.M., after a walk of two miles." *New York Times*, Jan. 29, 1913.

From Arthur W. Tedcastle

My dear Wilson   Milton [Mass.] 1/28/13

It was very kind of you, busy as you are, to write me the information direct from Colliers. That is far better than things "believed but not proven." And it is always good to have a lie "nailed"

On the other hand there is much sure information, and the generally accepted fact that the community in which a man lives forms a pretty correct estimate of his character. I therefore see no reason to change my views already expressed. If you ever get up against the so called "Pure Shoe" law[1] I should like to explain a few things. There is much "bunkum" in that idea and it could be very easy to have "high cost of shoes" without a corresponding benefit to anyone unless possibly to the leather man.

I cannot tell you how much we enjoyed our quiet evening with you and your dear family[.] Give our love to them all. We had a very pleasant trip South and now I go into harness again. It will be more than a pleasure to me if I can be of service to you at any time. It is not necessary to acknowledge my notes or I will not feel at liberty to write

The "Seven Sisters"[2] were *fine* and our friend this evening is beginning to understand, nay! even applaude

Sincerely   Arthur W Tedcastle

ALS (WP, DLC).
    [1] A movement for the passage of so-called pure-shoe laws, on both the state and national levels, which would require shoe manufacturers to stipulate the composition of their products and, more specifically, whether or not they were made entirely of leather.
    [2] Wilson's New Jersey antitrust bills.

From John Miller Turpin Finney

My Dear Mr. Wilson: Baltimore January 28 13

I thank you for your kind letter of January twenty-third which should have been acknowledged earlier but for press of professional and other duties. It was good of you to take the trouble to write as you did about Mr. Fine. His name has been prominently before the Board in connection with the Presidency of Johns Hopkins from the beginning. The idea at present is to get a younger man, if possible. For many reasons, it seems best to do this if the proper man can be found. Just at present, owing to the condition of President Remsen's health, (he has recently had to undergo a serious surgical operation), it has become necessary for him to retire permanently from the Presidency, in which capacity he has been acting since his resignation took effect. It has been decided, therefore, to place the management of the University in the hands of a governing committee of the Faculty of which Dr. Welch is Chairman, which means that Dr. Welch, for the present, will be virtual President. This arrangement will be in effect until the new President has been selected. I had a talk with Mr. Keyser[1] yesterday with reference to your letter and Mr. Fine's fitness for the place. Personally, I know of no man whom I had rather see as President of the Johns Hopkins University and I have been, in every way, using what influence I possess in favor of Mr. Fine's selection. If, however, it is thought best to secure a younger man, I feel sure that Mr. Elliott[2] possesses qualifications that would render him a very acceptable candidate. I should be delighted with the selection of either one of them for President.

May I take this opportunity of asking whether it would be possible or agreeable for you to give Dr. Welch and myself an half hour of your time, which I know is already more than taken up, in order that we can place before you just what is the true position of the Medical Profession in the matter of legislation with regard to public health. No one can give you so concise and correct an idea of conditions as they actually exist as can Dr. Welch who is the most representative man in the Profession in this Country. I believe such a talk would be of great assistance to you in a proper decision of the matters which will, sooner or later, come before you in this connection. This suggestion upon my part is prompted solely by my interest in proper legislation as regards public health, and my earnest desire that your administration may be marked by the same progress in matters which affect so vitally the health of the Nation as, I am sure, it will be along all other lines. We should be glad to meet you any day and hour in Trenton or any evening in Princeton that you may designate.[3]

With kind regards,   Sincerely yours,   J. M. T. Finney.

TLS (WP, DLC).

[1] Robert Brent Keyser, president of the Board of Trustees of The Johns Hopkins University.

[2] Edward Graham Elliott.

[3] The proposed meeting did not take place. See W. H. Welch to WW, Jan. 24 and Jan. 29, 1913, ALS (WP, DLC).

To John Wesley Wescott

My dear Judge: [Trenton, N. J.] January 30, 1913.

Thank you for Mr. Youngman's letter and for your suggestion about Mr. Dodges' knowledge of Mr. Brandeis.[1] What puzzles me is that a man can have one reputation in the city in which he lives and an absolutely different reputation throughout the rest of the country.

In haste,   Faithfully yours,   Woodrow Wilson

TLS (J. W. Wescott Coll., NjP).
   [1] J. W. Wescott to WW, Jan. 28, 1913, TLS (WP, DLC): "I beg to say that Mr. Cleveland Dodge, of New York, is quite familiar with some matters explicating the real character of Mr. Brandeis, as I have heard. Your relations with Mr. Dodge will no doubt warrant the transmission by him to you of his knowledge. I am quite aware that Mr. Brandeis is a man of remarkable ability, but, if one-tenth of what is published about him is true, his association with you as a cabinet advisor would be calamitous. The attitude of Mr. Brandeis towards the public is one of exulted patriotism, but there cannot be so much smoke without some fire. Upright men cannot have so many adverse things circulated about them without some justification. There are many good and very capable men free from every form of suspicion."

To Charles William Eliot

My dear Doctor Eliot: [Trenton, N. J.] January 30, 1913.

I am genuinely distressed that you find it unwise to accept the mission I urged upon you. I think that you must have seen that I urged it with all my heart and my disappointment is proportionate. I would not do anything, however, to imperil your health and I yield to your judgment in the matter with as much respect as reluctance.

I feel sure that fields of the highest usefulness lie open to you in every direction and that if you do not serve the country in the way I suggested, you will certainly serve it in many other ways.

With the warmest regard,
          Cordially and sincerely yours,   Woodrow Wilson

TLS (C. W. Eliot Papers, MH-Ar).

From Norman Hapgood

My dear Governor: [New York] Jan. 30 [1913]

The Brandeis matter seems to me so important that I shall not apologize for jotting down my most recent thoughts on the subject, especially as Crane estimates fully as highly as I do the amount Brandeis could do.

The idea that he is difficult or exacting I imagine had two sources of origin:

1. It is being industriously spread for a purpose.

2. It is true that lawyers who have been on the opposite side of cases have criticised him for lack of professional courtesy. There is much nonsense in legal ethics and the point seems to me of minor importance.

One thing that brought home to me his nature was that nobody except Crane has been as devoted to me since I left Colliers. Brandeis has been much more affectionate, and has put himself out much more for me, since I have had no power to help him than he did before.

Men who have had sufficient experience to know how easy and pleasant he is to work with are: La Follette, Ollie James, Rep. Graham of Illinois,[1] [William] Kent, Gifford Pinchot, Amos Pinchot, Fisher,[2] Crane, [Francis J.] Heney, Steffens,[3] [James R.] Garfield, and I should say probably [Augustus O.] Stanley and [Irvine L.] Lenroot,—but unfortunately not many of these, I suppose, are among those with whom you happen to come in touch.

Mainly, I think, the men who are working up the feeling against Brandeis are the men who will oppose you any way, as soon as the first serious struggle is on.

Yours sincerely　Norman Hapgood

ALS (WP, DLC).

[1] James McMahon Graham, Democratic congressman from Illinois since 1909.

[2] Walter Lowrie Fisher, Secretary of the Interior, 1911-13.

[3] Lincoln Steffens, muckraking journalist.

A News Report

[Jan. 31, 1913]

WILSON DISCOURSES ON CABINET POSTS

Almost Tells Something That Sounds Like Bryan For Secretary of State

That he does not want college presidents in his Cabinet was one of the points reluctantly yielded to the sifters of Presidential news by Governor Wilson yesterday. As a matter of fact, the Governor talked a little more than usual, and came mighty near saying something definite about his plans. He said enough, indeed, to indicate that Col. William J. Bryan, the Nebraskan, is about the only settled fact as to the make-up of the Cabinet. That probability had been about agreed as settled by those who have been trying to dig something out of the plans of the President-elect, but there came near being a direct declaration on that score from one of the two living men who know. The Governor was asked: "Will you say whether any other name than that of Mr. Bryan has been presented to you in connection with the Secretaryship of State."

"Oh, yes," was the reply, "at least half a dozen."

"Will you name some of them?" The Governor looked up toward the ceiling, "Well, strange as it may seem," he answered slowly, "I cannot recall the name of a single one of them." He paused, then added: "That may be because the names I have in mind may be shifted about, you see."

"Has anyone personally offered himself as a candidate for a Cabinet position?" he was asked.

"No one has committed that indiscretion."

"Will you appoint men who have been prominent in politics in the past, or men who have led more retired lives, such as yourself?"

"Well, I have both sorts under consideration, so I cannot say." Then, after a slight pause, "I will not name a Cabinet of college presidents, if that is what you mean. What I am seeking to get is a team." The Governor emphasized the last word.

It was called to the Governor's attention that Colonel House, at whose home he has stopped every time he has gone to New York, had gone to Miami, Fla., where Mr. Bryan now is. To a direct question Governor Wilson asserted that Colonel House was not stopping with Mr. Bryan, that no message from himself to Bryan was being carried by House and that no particular significance is attached to the coincidence. . . .

During the discussion of the Cabinet the President-elect asserted again that he would fill his "list," as he calls it, and then ask the men he desired to appoint whether they would serve. He was told that former Presidents had adopted a plan of putting out names confident[ial]ly as "feelers" to ascertain how the appointments of such men would be regarded.

"And this is how that plan works," said the Governor. "I don't think very much of it, for very often it works great unfairness. When a man's name is thrown into the light in that way, every one who has anything against him immediately jumps on him. Much that is untrue is asserted, and the man may be injured for years in his business and otherwise as a result. In making my appointments I don't intend to let this occur. It is surprising how much people know that isn't true about men. I can investigate these matters first and then make the appointments after I have satisfied myself of the untruth of the reports. If the reports are made after the appointment, the falsity of the charges will be shown. You would be surprised to see the reports that come to me even when a man is mentioned as a possibility for some office."

Printed in the *Trenton Evening Times*, Jan. 31, 1913.

To Mary Allen Hulbert

Dearest Friend,   Princeton, New Jersey 2 Feb'y, 1913

Last Sunday was anything but a day of rest for me. Ellen, Jessie, Nellie, and I spent the week end (which I try to devote to catching my breath and getting the ache out of my mental bones, after the pounding of the week) with Mrs. Alexander at Hoboken. Mrs. A. is a lovely woman, lovely both in person and in character, and is devoted to good works. She was many years ago shamefully betrayed by her husband and last summer she lost her only child,[1] a son whom she adored—a handsome youngster whom I had made my personal aide. We *thought* she was offering us a week end of rest, and we went to her thinking her lonely and in need of our company! What happened? On Saturday she organized an expedition to Ellis Island, to inspect the Immigrant Station and see hundreds of immigrants put through the mill; that evening gave us a dinner; on Sunday took us to see the Stevens Institute of Technology, had people in to lunch who talked shop, had a conference of social workers in the afternoon to unfold before me some of my minor (!) tasks at Washington, and in the evening gathered a lively dinner party! *This* week, therefore, I've been living on my nerve: I began it frazzled at the edges! But yesterday and to-day, after a little real rest, stolen in the intervals of calls from many quarters for this, that, or the other scrap of my energy, I am normal again, and turn to you with, oh! so much zest and pleasure,—and yet with a gnawing anxiety. For it is a long time since a letter came to reassure us about you; we fear you have been ill; and there is no joy in thinking of you unless we can know that you are well and coming into your own again,—your own wonderful spirit and command, not only of yourself, but of all about you as well. There is one thing I cannot *imagine* of you: I cannot imagine you *succumbing*: I can only imagine you *dominating*[.] There is such brilliant and compelling *life* in you! No matter what may befall for a little while, give it but time and half a chance, and it will bloom out again as incomparable as ever. We are well, all of us,—dreading the plunge we must make next month into unfamiliar waters and harassed by a life now that we cannot reduce to any sort of order and from which we cannot extract anything for our private selves,—but well in spite of it all; and within us a deeply quickened love of and dependence on all the old friendships and intimacies that have made our lives sweet. God bless you and help you in every effectual way! All unite in messages of deep affection. My love to Allen.

Your devoted friend   Woodrow Wilson

ALS (WP, DLC).
¹ Archibald Stevens Alexander, Princeton 1902.

A News Report

[Feb. 3, 1913]

CABINET QUERIES UPSET WILSON'S CALM

TRENTON, N. J., Feb. 3.—"I am not here to amuse the newspapers," said President-elect Wilson crisply when a reporter of The New York Times reminded him that there was a good deal of interest throughout the country in the make-up of his Cabinet.

"I am here," he went on, "to select a Cabinet for the people of the United States. If the newspapers think they can make me conduct myself in any other way they are wrong."

The Times correspondent told Mr. Wilson that he could prevent the publication of erroneous reports, such as one or two he had just denied, by announcing the facts concerning his selections. He replied:

"I cannot make myself over to please the newspapers. You will have to take me as you find me. I cannot assume a personality."

"But, Governor," said The Times correspondent, "only an hour or so ago you denied a report printed in The New York American to the effect that Bryan was to be Secretary of State, Palmer of the Treasury and Henry Attorney General. If you would let the public know what men you intended to have in your Cabinet you would be under no necessity of denying unfounded rumors."

"I am doing," answered the Governor, "what I believe to be best for the country and for myself. If the newspapers expect me to do anything else, I'll be damned if I will."

The Governor's face flushed a little as he said this, and he brought his hand down hard on his desk. Then, relaxing a little, he smiled and said:

"Pardon me for blowing up. These stories about Cabinet appointments are all false. I have told you men here in Trenton that I have made no selections for the Cabinet, and to keep on questioning me about it is to doubt my veracity."

The Governor announced to-day the appointment of Joseph P. Tumulty as his private secretary after he goes to Washington. Tumulty has been his secretary since he became Governor. He is a rosy-cheeked Irishman with slightly gray hair and a fine fund of humor. He is only 33 years old, and he has six children. His education was gleaned in St. Bridget's Parochial School and the Jesuit College in Jersey City,[1] where his father, Philip Tumulty, was a prosperous contractor.

Printed in the *New York Times*, Feb. 4, 1913.
  [1] St. Peter's College.

From Alexander Mitchell Palmer

PERSONAL.

My dear Governor: Washington, D. C., February 3, 1913.

You have doubtless noticed the action of the Senate in passing the Joint Resolution providing for a submission of a constitutional amendment limiting the presidency to one term of six years.[1] The Speaker has not yet referred the Resolution, but I think it will go to the Committee on the Judiciary, of which Hon. Henry D. Clayton[2] is Chairman. The form of the amendment, and perhaps the fate of the proposition, can be controlled by an intimation from yourself as to your own views, if you desire to give it. Clayton's Committee will undoubtedly do what you desire, if you wish to give a hint.

With best regards, I am,
                    Yours truly,   A Mitchell Palmer

TLS (WP, DLC).
  [1] For the background of the movement for a single-term amendment, see Link, *The New Freedom*, pp. 22-23.
  [2] Henry De Lamar Clayton, Democratic congressman from Alabama.

To Alexander Mitchell Palmer, with Enclosure

My dear Palmer: [Trenton, N. J.] February 5, 1913.

I hope that you will use the enclosed letter as you think best among your colleagues in the House. Before I publish it I should like to know your opinion of it.

In haste,   Cordially yours,   Woodrow Wilson

To Alexander Mitchell Palmer

My dear Palmer: [Trenton, N. J.] February 5, 1913.

Thank you warmly for your letter of February third. It was characteristically considerate of you to ask my views with regard to the Joint Resolution which has just come over from the House to the Senate with regard to the Presidential term.

I have not hitherto said anything about this question because I had not observed that there was any evidence that the public was very much interested in it. I must have been mistaken in this, else the Senate would hardly have acted so promptly upon it.

It is a matter which concerns the character and conduct of the great office upon the duties of which I am about to enter. I feel, therefore, that in the present circumstances I should not be acting consistently with my ideals with regard to the rule of entire frankness and plain speaking that ought to exist between public servants and the public whom they serve if I did not speak out about it without reserve of any kind, and without thought of the personal embarrassment.

The question is simply this: Shall our Presidents be free, so far as the law is concerned, to seek a second term of four years, or shall they be limited by constitutional amendment to a single term of four years, or to a single term extended to six years?

I can approach the question from a perfectly impersonal point of view, because I shall most cheerfully abide by the judgment of my party and the public as to whether I shall be a candidate for the Presidency again in 1916. I absolutely pledge myself to resort to nothing but public opinion to decide that question. The President ought to be absolutely deprived of every other means of deciding it. He can be. I shall use to the utmost every proper influence within my reach to see that he is, before the term to which I have been elected is out. That side of the matter need disturb no one.

And yet, if he is deprived of every other means of deciding the question, what becomes of the argument for a constitutional limitation to a single term? The argument is not that it is clearly known now just how long each President should remain in office. Four years is too long a term for a President who is not the true spokesman of the people, who is imposed upon and does not lead. It is too short a term for a President who is doing, or attempting, a great work of reform, and who has not had time to finish it. To change the term to six years would be to increase the likelihood of its being too long, without any assurance that it would in happy cases be long enough. A fixed constitutional limitation to a single term of office is highly arbitrary and unsatisfactory from every point of view.

The argument for it rests upon temporary conditions which can easily be removed by law. Presidents, it is said, are effective for one half of their term only, because they devote their attention during the last two years of the term to building up the influences, and above all the organization, by which they hope and purpose to secure a second nomination and election. It is their illicit power, not their legitimate influence with the country, that the advocates of a constitutional change profess to be afraid of, and I heartily sympathize with them. It is intolerable that any President should be permitted to determine who should succeed him—himself or another—by patronage or coercion, or by any sort of control of the machinery by which delegates to the nominating convention are chosen. There ought never to be another Presidential nominating convention; and there need never be another. Several of the states have successfully solved that difficulty with regard to the choice of their Governors, and Federal law can solve it in the same way with regard to the choice of Presidents. The nominations should be made directly by the people at the polls. Conventions should determine nothing but party platforms and should be made up of the men who would be expected, if elected, to carry those platforms into effect. It is not necessary to attend to the people's business by constitutional amendment if you will only actually put the business into the people's own hands.

I think it may safely be assumed that that will be done within the next four years; for it can be done by statute; it need not wait for constitutional change. That being done, the question of the Presidential term can be discussed on its merits.

It must be clear to everybody who has studied our political development at all that the character of the Presidency is passing through a transitional stage. We know what the office is now and what use must be made of it; but we do not know what it is going to work out into; and until we do know, we shall not know what constitutional change, if any is needed, it would be best to make.

I must speak with absolute freedom and candor in this matter, or not speak at all; and it seems to me that the present position of the Presidency in our actual system, as we use it, is quite abnormal and must lead eventually to something very different. He is expected by the nation to be the leader of his party as well as the chief executive officer of the government, and the country will take no excuses from him. He must play the part and play it successfully, or lose the country's confidence. He must be prime minister, as much concerned with the guidance of legislation as with the just and orderly execution of law; and he is the spokesman of the nation in everything, even the most momentous and most delicate dealings of the government with foreign nations. Why in such circumstances should he be responsible to no one for four long years? All the people's legislative spokesmen in the House of Representatives and one-third of their representatives in the Senate are brought to book every two years; why not the President, if he is to be the leader of the party and the spokesman of policy? Sooner or later, it would seem, he must be made answerable to opinion in a somewhat more informal and intimate fashion,—answerable, it may be, to the Houses whom he seeks to lead, either personally or through a cabinet, as well as to the people for whom they speak. But that is a matter to be worked out,—as it inevitably will be, in some natural American way which we cannot yet even predict.

The present fact is that the President is held responsible for what happens in Washington in every large matter, and so long as he is commanded to lead he is surely entitled to a certain amount of power,—all the power he can get from the support and convictions and opinions of his fellow countrymen; that he ought to be suffered to use that power against his opponents until his work is done. It will be very difficult for him to abuse it. He holds it upon suffrance, at the pleasure of public opinion. Everyone else, his opponents included, have access to opinion, as he has. He must keep the confidence of the country by earning it, for he can keep it in no other way. Put the present customary limitation of two terms into the constitution, if you do not trust the people to take care of themselves, but make it two terms (not one, because four years is often too long) and give the President a chance to win the full service by proving himself fit for it.

If you wish to learn the result of constitutional ineligibility to re-election, ask any former Governor of New Jersey, for example, what the effect is, in actual experience. He will tell you how cynically and with what complacence the politicians banded against him waited for the inevitable end of his term, to take their chances with his successor. Constitutions place and can place no limitations upon *their* power. They may control what Governors they can as long as they please, as long as they can keep their outside power and influence together. They smile at the coming and going of Governors, as some men in Washington have smiled at the coming and going of Presidents, as upon things ephemeral, which passed and were soon enough got rid of if you but sat tight and waited. As things stand now the people might more likely be cheated than served by further limitations of the President's eligibility. His fighting power in their behalf would be immensely weakened. No one will fear a President except those whom he can make fear the elections.

We singularly belie our own principles by seeking to determine by fixed constitutional provision what the people shall determine for themselves and are perfectly competent to determine for themselves. We cast a doubt upon the whole theory of popular government. I believe that we should fatally embarrass ourselves if we made the constitutional change proposed. If we want our Presidents to fight our battles for us, we should give them the means, the legitimate means, the means their opponents will always have. Strip them of everything else but the right to appeal to the people, but leave them that; suffer them to be leaders; absolutely prevent them from being bosses. We would otherwise appear to be going in two opposite directions. We are seeking in every way to extend the power of the people, but in the matter of the Presidency we fear and distrust the people and seek to bind them hand and foot by rigid constitutional provision. My own mind is not agile enough to go both ways.

I am very well aware that my position on this question will be misconstrued, but that is a matter of perfect indifference to me. The truth is much more important than my reputation for modesty and lack of personal ambition. My reputation will take care of itself; but constitutional questions and questions of policy will not take care of themselves without frank and fearless discussion. I am not speaking for my own re-election; I am speaking to redeem my promise that I would say what I really think on every public question and take my chances in the court of public opinion.

Again thanking you for your great courtesy and consideration,

Cordially and faithfully yours,   Woodrow Wilson[1]

TLS (WP, DLC).
[1] There is a WWsh draft of this letter, with the composition date of Dec. 12, 1912, and a CLST draft with WWhw emendations, dated Feb. 4, 1913, in WP, DLC.

To Edward Mandell House

My dear friend: [Trenton, N. J.] February 5, 1913.
    I send you a very important letter which I have just written to A. Mitchell Palmer. Will you be kind enough to show it to

Mr. Bryan, whom I think ought to be one of the first to see it. You know my mind in this matter so thoroughly that you can lay the matter before him in just the right way, and I am sure that he will not feel that you have laid it before him with any doubt as to the spirit in which I acted or the motives which have prompted it.

I am promising myself a further note to you precently [presently]. I shall need a talk with you next week for final judgments. I will telegraph you.

Thank you with all my heart for the delightful notes you have been writing me full of your own spirit and your own faithful counsels.   Affectionately yours   Woodrow Wilson

TLS (E. M. House Papers, CtY).

From Norman Hapgood

My dear Governor: [New York] Feb. 5 [1913]

Victor J. Dowling, one of the most honorable of the Tammany leaders, told me last night that Mr. Bryan had written to one or two friends of Dowling's, asking about the propriety of both serving in your cabinet and running next time for the Presidency. I have no doubt that Mr. Bryan, in whose character I fully believe, has been entirely lucid with you, but I did not quite dare to take anything for granted.

                    Yours sincerely   Norman Hapgood

ALS (WP, DLC).

To Edward Mandell House

Dear Friend,   University Club [New York] 7 Feb'y, 1913

I feel the need of seeing you, for a final conference about the official family. If you do not deem the weather too severe then (for your health is the first consideration, with me) will you not spend Thursday, the 13th, with me at Princeton? I can put you up at the Inn, if, as I hope, you will spend the night. There is much to talk over.

The enclosed letter will,[1] I am sure, interest you, and add to the matter of our conference.

Meantime would you be kind enough to sound H[ouston]. of St. Louis on the Secretaryship of Agriculture for me? On that case I am clear and my choice made; but I think it best for you to open the matter with him, if you will be so kind. The Treasury has been offered and accepted, as we planned.

I am in town for an evening with Cleve. Dodge.

With warmest regard from us all to you both.

Affectionately   Woodrow Wilson

ALS (E. M. House Papers, CtY).
¹ It is missing.

From Alexander Mitchell Palmer

My dear Governor Wilson: [Washington] February 7, 1913.

I was obliged to leave Washington yesterday and will remain at Stroudsburg until Monday evening, returning to Washington Tuesday morning. Judge Clayton, Chairman of the Committee on the Judiciary, to which the single term resolution has been referred, has assured me that nothing will be done by his committee until he has learned your views, which I have told him you would commit to writing. Your letter came after I left, and it was forwarded to me here, but I will show it to Judge Clayton upon my return to Washington, Tuesday morning. It may not be necessary to show it to anybody else.

If the communication of your views to Judge Clayton shall prove sufficient to keep the resolution where it is now, during the remainder of the session, I would think it not only [un]necessary, but unwise for you to give public expression to those views, either by the publication of your letter to me or otherwise.¹

Your reasoning is unquestionably sound and I entirely agree with your conclusions. The whole force of the argument in support of a single presidential term has been broken by the election of 1912. It has been demonstrated that the people will cut a President off with a single term, where he has failed to make good, and the use of all the patronage at his command in such case, is insufficient to save him. It has been demonstrated also that the wise custom, which since the foundation of the government, has limited the presidency to two terms, will be preserved by the people, even under conditions where the unprecedented personal popularity of the candidate makes it seem peculiarly difficult to preserve such custom. In other words the people have shown that they can be trusted to take care of themselves upon this matter, and there is no necessity for a constitutional restriction of their right to exercise their own judgment as the conditions at the time may require.

Aside from the merits of the proposition, however, the political aspect of the thing gives me much concern. The Baltimore platform declared:

> "We favor a single presidential term, and to that end we urge the adoption of an amendment to the constitution, making the President of the United States ineligible for re-election, and we pledge the candidate of this convention to this principle."

Of course, I do not subscribe to the doctrine that a resolutions committee, in a national convention, drafting a platform between sunset and sunrise, which is adopted in the confusion of the dying hours of the convention, unconsidered, even unheard by the vast body of the delegates, can bind me, unless it be by a statement of a fundamental principle of the party, long recognized as such.

The peculiar circumstances which surrounded the preparation of this particular plank in the platform and its significant wording are sufficient, however, to give us pause. Mr. Bryan, if he did not write it, was responsible for it. My information is that he did actually write the last clause. At any rate he made much of it in the campaign, repeating and reiterating it throughout his campaign tours, that the party had committed itself to the single term amendment and pledged the candidate to it as well. Your silence on the subject during the campaign was unquestionably construed, by his friends at least, as acquiescence.

You are in a better position than I to judge what Mr. Bryan's attitude will be in the face of the publication of your views, as expressed in your letter to me. My guess is, that having made so much of it during the campaign, he will insist that your position is a repudiation of a pledge to which you were committed, both by the platform and by your silence, while he was proclaiming it as the party's promise.

Would it not be most unfortunate, just at this time, to have such a marked difference of opinion and purpose between yourself and Mr. Bryan? I do not mean at all to suggest that your judgment should give way to his, and if it becomes absolutely necessary for you to give public expression to your views, it should, of course, be done without regard for the opinion of any other men. But, if the expression of your views now should result in a condition which would make it impossible for you to start your administration with the full support and cooperation of Mr. Bryan and his supporters throughout the country, you would be heavily handicapped at the very time when support of that kind will be most needed. If you could get past the special session of Congress with a real Democratic tariff law on the statute books, and monetary and anti-trust legislation on the ways, I would have little fear of the result of a difference of opinion upon a matter of this sort between yourself and Mr. Bryan. The country would unquestionably sustain you, and the work of your administration would have received so favorable a start that the rest of the program would be comparatively easy of performance.

Perhaps I am taking too seriously the possibility of trouble growing out of Mr. Bryan's supposed attitude on this suggestion. I know, however, you want me to express my views with frankness, and I give them to you for what they may be worth.

With best regards,

Very cordially yours,   A. Mitchell Palmer.

TCL (WP, DLC).

[1] As it turned out, Wilson did not publish the letter until January 1916, when it was rumored that Bryan would oppose Wilson's re-nomination on account of the one-term plank in the platform of 1912. See Link, *The New Freedom*, p. 23.

To Mary Allen Hulbert

Dearest Friend,   Princeton, New Jersey 9 February, 1913

My pen hand is exceedingly weary, and you have already graciously given me leave to use my machine in writing to you. It is almost as familiar and intimate to my hand as my pen, anyway. It and I have gone through many thoughts together, and many emotions!

I need not tell you how your latst [last] letter[1] affected me, with its new burden of anxiety about the boy who is all in all to you! It struck into my heart. I have prayed for you and for him every day since as I pray for my own salvation. What would I not give to know what to say and what to do to help you and him! You have been a burden bearer all your life, my sweet friend, and how steadfast and noble you have been! I know what a dun colour it wears to your eyes as you look back upon it, but to me it looks very beautiful indeed. You have been *giving*, giving, giving all your life, and you have had so much to give! Your wonderful vitality, your wonderful charm, your beauty and vivacity—all gifts which seemed intended for other uses,—have made it possible for you to accomplish the impossible, meet situations no one else could have met, keep a household going which no other woman *could* have kept going without absolute surrender and the loss of every right of her own, and have a surplus over with which to brighten and stimulate other lives, as if incidentally and casually,—sheer largess of sympathy and insight and love. It quickens me to think of it; it makes me proud to be your friend; it makes me wonder what I have ever done, or can do, to compare with it by way of spending myself for others! And so, it would seem, it is to be to the end. The fruit of it all no one can foretell and no one can doubt. I do not doubt that you will see the fruit of your present devotion in something that will mean happiness and reassurance. The lad, I am sure, *feels* your love. There are depths in him which will presently be stirred. Is there anything *I* can do, do you think? Would I have any influence with him? Is there any word I could speak that would avail? I do so long to help you—and him! Will you soon get away from Bermuda and go where he can take up some sort of work,—does he think of that and *wish* to turn to some business? Bless Mrs. Parrish! She is a brick. Ellen saw the fine metal in her and liked her, too, as much as I do. Indeed she and (in a less degree, of course) Mrs Eels seemed to us stuff of which friends could be made. It is delightful that there is *some* one at hand who understands and can be depended on. Please give Mrs. Parrish my love.

Our trial draws nearer and nearer, and we dread it—especially Ellen. It will be much less trying in reality than it is in anticipation, I hope and believe and there will be a wholesome reaction which will bring the blood back to our hearts after the cold plunge, but for the time we shrink and are uncomfortable. How I wish you might be at hand to steady us—or that we were as resourceful as you! We are well, in spite of the increasing daily demands upon us,—and have plenty of time to think of you and think a thousand messages and prayers. Give my love to Allen and let him know that I believe he can win.

Your devoted friend   Woodrow Wilson

WWTLS and WWhw (WP, DLC).

  [1] It is missing, as are all of Mrs. Hulbert's letters for the period covered by this volume.

To Norman Hapgood

My dear Hapgood: [Trenton, N. J.] February 10, 1913.

You are a friend worth having. I say that for myself as well as because of your attitude towards Mr. Brandeis, and I thank you heartily for everything you have sent me. It has served to clear my thought in many directions. Pray never apologize for sending anything you choose to bring to my attention.

Faithfully yours,   Woodrow Wilson

TLS (WC, NjP).

From Owen Reed Lovejoy

My dear Governor Wilson: New York, February 10, 1913.

Sometime ago Dr. Felix Adler wrote to you on behalf of the National Child Labor Committee inviting you to become an honorary member. It was during the heat of your Presidential campaign and no doubt, this with many other letters was necessarily put aside.

I should explain that we have but two honorary members thus far, Colonel Roosevelt, who was President when the Committee organized, and President Taft.

We gratefully acknowledge the sympathetic interest you have taken in the work of this Committee from the beginning and assure you that it will be a source of strength to us to have your name thus identified with it.

As a concrete illustration of the service you could thus render may I say that last week a friend in North Carolina inquired whether you were connected with the Committee as he wanted to use that fact in an argument for a bill to protect women and children against night work in the North Carolina mills.

No added burdens will be placed upon you in accepting this invitation and I hope you are sufficiently familiar with our work through Dr. Adler, Dr. McKelway and others to have confidence that we should in no way misuse your endorsement.[1]

Trusting we may have your early response, I am
                          Sincerely yours,   Owen R. Lovejoy
                                          General Secretary.

TLS (WP, DLC).
[1] Wilson's reply not found; he accepted the honorary membership.

From Charles Richard Crane

Dear Governor Wilson: Chicago, Feb 10, 13.

A recent visit to La Follette at Washington brings up a matter that I feel I should write to you about. La Follette has made up his mind to devote himself to progressive legislation. He has great talents for this sort of work, he is in fine physical condition and believes that, with you at the White House and Gore to work with in the Senate, he has the best of opportunities to serve the country. He is, however, like all other progressives, most anxious to have Brandeis, to work with. He has worked with Brandeis for several years and greatly prizes Brandeis' wisdom, patience and sympathy. He also believes that Brandeis, more than any one else, in Washington and in authority can pull together the progressives

—whether La Follette, Democratic or Bull Mooser—and harmonize progressive legislation.

I, myself, want to put in a word about one of Brandeis' rare qualities not generally noted. Brandeis is the only important Jew who is *first* American and then Jew. All of the other important Jews are first Jews and then Americans and do not hesitate to sacrifice real American interests at any time for what they conceive to be Jewish ones. Brandeis has grown up and developed as an American and, now that he has become a man of importance, the other Jews are trying hard to control him but they will not succeed.

I can bear testimony to his real patriotism, sweet reasonableness and clear forsightedness. He is just but impersonal.

I shall not tell you now of the many warm hearted messages I have received for you from the finest people in the land, but only send all possible good wishes to you and the family.

Yours faithfully   Charles R. Crane

TLS (WP, DLC).

From Alexander Jeffrey McKelway

Dear Mr. Wilson: Little Rock, Ark. Feb. 11, 1913.

I have been away from Washington for ten days, visiting the legislatures of Texas and Arkansas in the interest of our uniform Child Labor Law. I noted in today's [Memphis] Commercial Appeal the following clipping which I send you, concerning the campaign Mrs. Robert W. Wickliffe[1] appears to be conducting for the position of Chief of the Children's Bureau. I do not know anything about Mrs. Wickliffe, but I do know Miss Julia Lathrop, who was appointed Chief by President Taft last summer, and who has just suceeded in organizing the Bureau with the full force allowed by law. I happen to know that she has been most conscientious and painstaking in seeing that the Bureau was organized with absolute disregard of politics, and she has succeeded in securing a force of most intelligent and well trained workers, both men and women. Miss Lathrop was appointed upon the recommendation of the National Child Labor Committee, which had been charged with the duty of persuading Congress to create the Bureau. She has also the backing of the Federation of Women's Clubs, certainly a large number of the members of the National Conference of Charities and Correction, and I might say of social workers generally throughout the country. I believe it would be a calamity from many points of view to allow her to be disturbed in her position, and I feel sure that a protest of this sort will be all that you will need in order to give due consideration to the question of removing her.

I have been intending to write to you also about making a new appointment for the Judge of the Juvenile Court of the District of Columbia, when you shall have time to attend to that matter. The present incumbent, Judge DeLacey,[2] was appointed by President Roosevelt for reasons which it seems to me were not concerned with the best interests of the unfortunate children of the District. Nearly every social worker in the City of Washington is on record against the re-appointment of Judge DeLacey, and although his term expired last summer, President Taft has thus far declined to send in his name for re-appointment, as I understand upon the advice of Attorney General Wickersham, the Department of Justice having investigated the matter. Judge DeLacey will serve until his successor is appointed, and this again is just to ask that the wishes of those who come daily in contact with the unfortunate children of the District of Columbia shall be considered in making an appointment to this important post.

You can have no idea how your words in reply to my little talk at Mrs. Alexander's in Hoboken two weeks ago, stirred up the banking and real estate interests of Washington. The reporters beseigned [beseiged] me when I returned to the city, but I declined to add anything to the account of the meeting that had been sent out in a semi-official way. The real friends of the District of Columbia, who are not concerned with exploiting it, have been tremendously encouraged by your determination to investigate these matters fully.

Cordially yours,   A. J. McKelway.

CCLS (A. J. McKelway Papers, DLC).
  1 Lydia Cooke Wickliffe. Her husband, Robert Charles Wickliffe, had been a congressman from Louisiana from 1909 until his accidental death in Washington on June 11, 1912. The article, which actually appeared in the Memphis *Commercial Appeal*, February 6, 1913, stated that Mrs. Wickliffe had launched a "campaign" for the position of chief of the Children's Bureau, arguing that the place should go to a loyal Democrat.
  2 William Henry De Lacy.

From the Diary of Colonel House

February 13, 1913.

I went to Princeton on the twelve o'clock train and the Governor met me at Princeton Junction on his way from Trenton. We had a long afternoon and evening together.

He read me his Inaugural Address which seems to me a masterpiece of its kind, it is off the beaten track and is full of spirituality. It is a document which should be of far-reaching good. It out-lines the purposes of his administration. He was exceedingly gratified by my complimentary estimate of it.

We talked of the Cabinet and of the foreign appointments. He said that Dr. Eliot had declined the Chinese mission and that he would now offer it to John W. Mott of the Y.M.C.A. which is doing so much to bring about reforms in China. He intends also to ask Prof Fine of Princeton to accept the Ambassadorship to Germany. His reason for this is that Fine is well suited for the post and he is not happy under conditions where he is. He has no money but Cleveland Dodge has generously offered to supplement his salary with $25 000. a year for four years.

Governor Wilson asked Dodge if he would take a post abroad but he declined. He said it would cost him $100,000. a year and he would rather give it to his old friend Fine and let him take the post.

We spoke of Richard Olney as Ambassador to the Court of St James, and the only objection is his age, which is seventy-eight.

We passed from those matters for the present and thought of Thos. Nelson Page for France or Italy. He would be an admirable man for Italy, and I told the Governor that I thought he fitted in there better than in France. He spoke of Frederic Penfield,[1] and decided to send him to Belgium, Holland or perhaps Spain. He decided definitely that he would not appoint Justice Gerard or any man who was conspicuous for his money.

McCombs wants him to appoint de Saulles[2] as Minister to Chile. He said the trouble with McCombs was that he was only in-terested in second or third rate men,—men whom he could not ap-point or did not desire to. That he only presents to him the "cheap-est" type of men. He regretted very much that he was to have another sitting with McCombs on Saturday evening. He thought he would probably stay until twelve o'clock, and they would get no further than they were now.

In speaking of the Cabinet he said he had investigated Bran-deis' record and he could not bring himself to believe that he had done anything to cause criticism,—certainly not of the virulent kind he was getting. I argued against putting him in the Cabinet for the reason that so large a part of the reputable people of New England think ill of him. It does not matter whether they are right or whether they are wrong, they believe he is dishonest and his value of service would be minimized. The President-elect spoke ardently in his favor and criticized Brandeis' critics. I thought the same group would be glad not to see Mr. Bryan in the Cabinet, but no one questioned Mr. Bryan's integrity.

We dropped the matter for awhile and took it up later and I reluctantly acquiesced in his appointment to the Bureau of Commerce.[3]

We went over names from one end of the country to the other, revamping former tentative decisions.

Tumulty came in for dinner. He pointed out that Redfield had not been a Wilson man before the campaign and had said some things in disparagement of the Governor. We discussed putting Daniels in the Postoffice Department, but the question of patronage came up and some one suggested that he was too ardent a Bryan man and that he would be more loyal to Bryan than to Wilson. The Governor expressed himself as not desiring patronage used either in his own behalf or in behalf of anyone else.

My advice was to make Burleson Postmaster General. He thought Burleson would build up a machine. I replied that if he did it would be a Wilson machine, and he could be restrained from even doing that. He was rather distrustful of Burleson being able to hold down the place. I reassured him by saying that if he would appoint Burleson I could get him to appoint Lewis or Redfield as assistant.

We finally discontinued our conference because the Governor was tired, and I could see that we were not reaching any conclusions. I braced him up by telling him that he now had the nucleus of a strong Cabinet and not to think or worry about it again until we met again, and we would then place each in the proper niche.

[1] Frederic Courtland Penfield of New York, wealthy gentleman of leisure, former journalist, vice-consul general at London and consul general at Cairo in the Cleveland administrations, and a large contributor to Wilson's preconvention and election campaigns. Wilson appointed him ambassador to Austria-Hungary on July 7, 1913.

[2] John Gerard Longer de Saulles, former Yale football captain, New York socialite, active in the real estate business. He was a friend of McCombs, who appointed him president of the Wilson College Men's League during the campaign of 1912. He had represented a railroad-building company in Chile in 1910-1912 and married a Chilean during his stay there. Wilson appointed him Minister to Uruguay on March 10, 1914, but he resigned on May 28, 1914, without having proceeded to his post.

[3] House meant the Department of Commerce.

To William Jennings Bryan

My dear Mr. Bryan,   University Club [New York] 14 Feb'y, 1913

Here, in the inner recesses of a big club, is the only place I can ever get, nowadays, a few minutes to myself, and a chance to write a few lines with my own hand.

I have already, in a dictated note, told you how sincerely I appreciated the memoranda sent me by you through Mr. House, and how much I was assisted by them to think out difficult choices. I want to say this again now, and in this more personal way express my pleasure and obligation.

I hope that your visit to Cuba proved enjoyable and profitable, both to Mrs. Bryan and to yourself.

I have been thinking much, of late, of foreign appointments. I want to find exceptional men, out of the common run, for all the chief posts. Men who will *see* and think. Mott, of whom I wrote, is one out of a thousand, and I have others to discuss with you.

I shall see Mr. House this evening. It is delightful to have him again at hand.

My warmest regards to Mrs. Bryan.

Faithfully Yours,   Woodrow Wilson

ALS (W. J. Bryan Papers, DLC).

From the Diary of Colonel House

Feburary 14, 1913.

I returned on the eight o'clock to New York. At five in the afternoon Governor Wilson came to spend the night with me.

We had two hours before dinner discussing the Cabinet. It was fairly definitely determined then to arrange it in this way:

Bryan for State, McAdoo for Treasury, Houston for Agriculture, Palmer for Attorney General, Burleson for Postmaster General, Brandeis for Commerce, Wilson for Labor, Newton Baker for Interior and Daniels for Navy.

I urged that he put in Franklin K. Lane for War or Interior. He asked if I knew Lane's views on conservation. I did not but I knew they were sound. I suggested that he let me find out. He asked how I would do it. I said I would send for him and in order to be certain that he met the extreme Eastern view, I would have Norman Hapgood drop in and let them meet as if by accident. He was pleased with this plan and told me to go ahead. We spoke of the foreign appointments again, and he reiterated his determination to lift up the standard.

We went to the Belasco to see "Years of Discretion."[1] We had a lower box, and after the second act the audience began to applaud. The Governor asked if I thought he should arise. I advised him to pay no attention to it, but the applause continued and he whispered that it was becoming embarrassing. I then suggested that he arise and bow, which he did and the applause ceased.

[1] A romantic comedy by Frederic and Fanny Locke Hatton, which had its New York premiere on December 25, 1912. The plot concerned a proper suburban Boston widow who went to New York to recapture her lost youth.

We discussed the difference between England and the United States as to such matters. In England the King and Royal Family can go to the opera or theater and not a head will be turned towards them by anyone excepting foreigners. The British sense of fair play is something our people have yet to learn. The King can go to Newmarket and mingle with the crowd and no Englishman will turn his head to stare at him. We left by a private entrance to avoid the crowd.

When we reached the apartment and were munching our sandwiches before retiring, we fell to talking about various matters. The Governor said he thought that lying was justified in some instances, particularly where it involved the honor of a woman. I agreed to this. He thought it was also justified where it related to matters of public policy. I mildly dissented from this view telling him that it opened up too wide a range; that I thought the best thing to do when inpertinent questions were put to you, was not to make any reply. He said perhaps I was right and that in the future he thought he would do that. This attitude of mind is interesting to me, for the reason that he has so many times grazed the truth in answering questions in regard to his appointments.

Another thing he talked of was war. He said he did not share the views of many of our present day statesmen that war was was [sic] so much to be deprecated. He considered it, as an economic porposition ruinous, but he thought there was no more glorious way to die than in battle. This coming from the son of a minister and an ex-college president surprised. It strengthened my opinion though as to his unusual courage both moral and physical.

We spoke of his brother's candidacy for Secretary of the Senate. I was again surprised to see that he could find no impropriety in his making the race. He said the question of his brother being present at the executive sessions was an excuse, that the President always knew what happened at executive sessions; that if his brother had been elected a Senator from Tennessee no question would have been raised as to his sitting in executive session, and the objection would be as great in the one case as the other. Now that his brother was in the race he saw no reason why he should not continue, and that if they failed to elect him, it would be no worse than a withdrawal which would be a confession that he was beaten.

The President-elect does not seem to see that it is a case of nepotism of a peculiarly offensive character. He, himself, has just been elected to the greatest office within the gift of the people. The Senate has not been democratic for a score of years; the

Secretary of the Senate is the only piece of patronage of any consequence belonging to it, and to have his brother given the position, would leave a very disagreeable impression.

He told me he had written a letter to Mitchell Palmer concerning the bill now pending before Congress in regard to restricting the length of time a President of the United States should serve. He had sent me a copy of it to Florida with a request that I read it to Mr. Bryan. I replied that I was very glad it had not come before I left, for I thought it would have made a disagreeable impression upon Mr. Bryan; that I believe Mr. Bryan was entirely sincere in his belief that a President should serve only one term, and to show that he was unselfish in the matter he was willing for the bill not to include the President-elect.

We then argued the question as to whether any restriction should be made. He took the ground that the objection was puerile; that it should be left to the people as to how long a man should serve them; that no nation on earth restricted its public servants to office. He further said that it seemed to him that the people could always regulate this themselves, and that even if a man "on horseback" should attempt to over-ride the desires of the people, it would meet with failure. He thought if Roosevelt should attempt it, the attempt would be a fiasco and look like overa [opera] bouffe. I took the opposite ground, I could see clearly how the failure to restrict the term of office which one man could hold might end disastrously. I thought in the first instance our Presidents had too much power, as Commander of the Army and Navy, and entrenched in power for four years, and subject to no removal excepting by impeachment; with an enormous patronage at his command, and with the power practically to make war with a foreign country, his term of office should be restricted.

I thought we should have a change in the form of our Government, in as much as the power of the President should be restricted, and that he should be held in a way subject to the control of the Lower House, much as the English and French Premiers are now held. He replied, even so, if a Cromwell or a "man on horseback" appeared he would pay no attention to the mandates of a parliament. I put this situation before him: Suppose a man of limitless ambition, unrestrained by patriotism should become President. Supose he desired to perpetuate his power and suppose such an opportunity as this presented itself:— Strikes should become prevalent throughout the country both among railroads and minds [mines], a condition might easily be brought about which would border upon revolution and chaos. As soon as the people began to feel the pinch of high prices and the lack of necessities because the output of the mines were restricted, and because transportation facilities were at a standstill, they would demand that the Government proceed to open up transportation and products by force. To do this a large and ever increasing army would be necessary, since it would have to be scattered from one end of the land to the other.

The sympathy of the rich and well-to-do would be with the strong arm that was directing affairs and, being backed by no inhibition of the Constitution as to the length of term, he could go on indefinitely and with dictatorial powers.

It was twelve o'clock before we went to bed, and we had a busy morning before us.

February 15, 1913.

Governor Wilson had sent for Mr. Maubrey[1] of Maryland to meet him at our apartment. He wishes to persuade him to enter the Senatorial race in Maryland. He also wished to see Jas. W. McReynolds and look him over. I invited McReynolds down ostensibly to discuss the appointment of a District Attorney here.

The Governor liked McReynolds, but he had to leave before McReynolds did. I went with him to the elevator and downstairs, and during that time we discussed him. He authorized me to offer him the Solicitor Generalship if I thought best, although he said he thought perhaps this should not be done until he had conferred with his Attorney General whomever he might be. He told me however to use my judgment.

I spoke to McReynolds about it, and he said the Governor was right in believing the Attorney General should be spoken to first. He was not inclined to accept it. He had had so much work of that character already and it had no attraction to a man of fifty, who had already had experience of that sort. I told him that Palmer was slated for Attorney General and he said he would look up his record. He did this during the day and came to see me later.

Before leaving the Governor authorized me to ask George Gordon Battle if he would accept the District Attorneyship here. I asked McReynolds to do this and Battle said he could not take it on account of commitments he had already made. McReynolds, according to our agreement, then asked him if his partner Snowden Marshall[2] could take it and he promised to ascertain.

[1] William Luke Marbury, lawyer of Baltimore.
[2] Hudson Snowden Marshall, law partner of Senator James A. O'Gorman and George Gordon Battle.

February 16, 1913.

Then came . . . afterwards McReynolds. McReynolds had looked up Palmer's record and thought it would be absurd to appoint him Attorney General; that he had had no experience whatever to qualify him for the position. Not only that, he represented the D. L. & W.[1] and the Lehigh Valley Railroads and that Attorney General Wickersham had, at his suggestion, gotten him, McReynolds, to draw up a bill against one road and that suit against the other would be brought within a week or two.

He said Palmer also represented a little railroad running out from Straunsburg [Stroudsburg], Pa. and that this road belonged to the Paint Trust. I asked McReynolds to put this in writing in concrete form so I could present it to Governor Wilson.

The Governor called me up at nine o'clock and asked me about Lane. I was delighted to tell him that matter was in fine shape. I then told him about McReynolds and Palmer. He seemed depressed and said "that may necessitate a rearrangement." I asked him not to worry, that the getting of Lane in the Cabinet was of much more importance than the losing of Palmer for Attorney General; that Lane could take that place if necessary, and fill it with distinction and that we could keep Baker for the Interior.

[1] The Delaware, Lackawanna, and Western Railroad Co.

To Mary Allen Hulbert

Dearest Friend,   Princeton, New Jersey 16 Feb'y, 1913

The days hurry on and bring us near the time when we must say good-bye to dear old Princeton, where we have enjoyed and suffered so much, and dear old New Jersey, of which I now seem a part, much faster than we any of us relish. Frankly, we dread the change,—not so much the new duties as the novel circumstances in which they must be performed. But the comfort is, that nothing essential *can* be changed. The *enjoyment* of old friendships may be sadly interfered with, but the friendships themselves cannot be touched or altered,—will always constitute the sweet, lasting *substance* of our life. I find that they are always in the background of my thought, no matter what is in the foreground. They are always there to fall back on and draw refreshment from, however fierce and trying the strain of the day. The airs of Bermuda soothe me in the midst of the bleakest winter day because you are there and my thoughts turn so often to you. They would always be altogether happy and refreshing thoughts (for that is your effect on those who need cheer and refreshment) did I not feel so poignantly the anxiety you carry at your heart and the deep loneliness amidst which you move, wistful and a bit dismayed,—*you*, who more than anyone else I ever knew, can dispel loneliness, were made to impart to all about you a sense of the fulness of life,—a sense of its being full of quickening thoughts, full of interesting persons, full of things, big and little, that it is a joy to look upon and think about. I never knew anyone more interested in *life* or better able to give interest to it. That you, who are such perfect *company*, should be *lonely* has a touch of pathos about it that is, to me, beyond words. I believe that your life will yet go out into the boy again and give him the strength and the spirit to conquer himself and his temptation. Please do not hesitate to write to me, whatever your mood or the burden of thought you are at the time carrying. God knows I am carrying all but a breaking weight now, but the load is increased, not lightened, if I cannot know what those I constantly think of, and *for*, are doing or thinking or suffering. Write to me, if only to release the misery that is in your heart. I shall always esteem it a privilege to be so confided in and allowed to help carry!

All send most affectionate messages. My love, and confidence of his success, to Allen.

Your devoted friend,   Woodrow Wilson

ALS (WP, DLC).

From the Diary of Colonel House

February 18, 1913.

Tumulty called me over the telephone to say that the Governor would leave Trenton on the 4.32 train and would reach New York at 5.56 to spend the evening and night with me.

Newton Baker, Mayor of Cleveland, also rang me up to say that he had arrived. When I was in Princeton, the Governor wrote him a note asking him to come to New York on Tuesday or Wednesday, as was most convenient, and to telephone me and that I would make an appointment for him to meet the Governor at my apartment. I asked Baker to dine with us at seven o'clock and I requested him not to let his presence in New York be known and above all things, not to let anyone know he was coming to my apartment or was having an appointment with the President-elect.

Edward S. Martin and Charles Ferguson,[1] one of the editors

---

[1] He listed himself in *Who's Who in America* as an "editorial writer Hearst newspapers, 1908-1913"; formerly a Protestant Episcopal minister and lawyer.

and a writer for Hearst, lunched with me. Martin and I were amused at Ferguson whom we both met for the first time. Ferguson smothered his ideas in such a splendid flow of eloquent verbiage that it was almost impossible to gather what he was trying to say. After two hours, I got a glimpse as to the *motif* running through his conversation. Martin never did because, as he said, he could not keep from lapsing into commonsense every now and then.

I met Governor Wilson and brought him to the apartment. We had about forty minutes before Baker came, and we discussed the Cabinet and other appointments. I told him that Snowden Marshall would accept the District Attorneyship.

I related my interview with Morganthau and asked him to give Morganthau something and suggested that he make him Minister to Turkey. He laughingly replied "there ain't going to be no Turkey."

Baker came and we had a very delightful dinner; politics were not discussed at all, stories were told, Mark Twain and various other persons and matters were talked of. After dinner I left the Governor and Baker for a few minutes. I could hear the Governor telling Baker about me and of his regard for me, but I did not care to listen and went into another room further away. In about a half hour I returned. The Governor said he had offered Baker the Secretaryship of the Interior and that he was considering the matter. Baker finally decided he could not take it. He said there was no one to carry on the work in Cleveland which he had begun, and he thought the government of our American cities was the greatest disgrace to our citizenship, that Cleveland was emerging from that state and would soon be an example to her sister cities throughout the land.

Both the Governor and I urged him to take a broader view of the situation and do the bigger work. He finally decided to take the matter under consideration for the night, and said if he changed his mind he would wire me tomorrow quoting a line from Shakespeare which I would understand. When he left I expressed my disappointment in him stating that he was too local. He is a high minded fellow, and a man of ability, but I am afraid he is not constructive enough to handle the Interior Department.

Baker did not leave until after ten, and for a half hour or more the Governor and I discussed various matters. I showed him the editorial by Edward S. Martin written for the next issue of Life. He asked me to read it to him. Above the editorial was a little cartoon showing an elephant and a donkey sitting in a car and underneath was written "After the Inauguration." The Governor laughed and asked me if I saw anything wrong about it. I looked at it carefully and discovered that the elephant was sitting on the right-hand side which, of course, would be wrong after the Inauguration. I braced the Governor up again and told him not to mind Baker's refusal and that we could arrange without him.

February 19, 1913.

We were up at half past six and had breakfast at half past seven. We discussed McCombs. I urged him to let McCombs say that he had been offered a position in the Cabinet if he desired to do so. He replied that it would not be true. I thought that McCombs' lookout, and he need not say anything himself. My reason for this was that it would gratify McCombs, and there would be no necessity of making any explanation to the country as to McCombs.

When the mail came in, I found a letter from McCombs asking to see me. I have made an appointment with him for five thirty.

I asked Governor Wilson to come and be my guest on Friday and go to the theater to which he readily consented. I told him that we could arrange to have Mitchell Palmer over Saturday morning in order that he might offer him the Secretaryship of War.

Morganthau told me yesterday that Secretary of War Stimson wanted to have a private interview with the President-elect. I offered to ascertain the truth of this. I telephoned Wallace at Washington and had him call up Stimson. Stimson said he had not made the request, but had merely said he thought it important that as soon as Governor Wilson had named his successor they should confer together. This is on account of the Mexican situation.[1] Secretary Stimson also expressed the belief that Governor Wilson should put a very strong man in that portfolio.

When Governor Wilson comes Friday he is to see Melville Stone of the Associated Press at the Universit[y] Club and then come directly to the apartment. We will then discuss Cabinet appointments and later go to see "The Sunshine Girl"[2] at the Knickerbocker Theater.

In our talk last night with Newton Baker the Governor ex-

[1] General Victoriano Huerta, commander of federal troops in Mexico, in cooperation with Felix Díaz, nephew of Porfirio Díaz, had just overthrown the constitutional government. Huerta proclaimed himself Provisional President on February 18. Madero and Vice-President Piño Suarez were murdered four days later.

[2] An English musical comedy with music by Paul Rubens and book and lyrics by Rubens and Cecil Raleigh, which had its New York premiere on February 3, 1913.

pressed a desire to have in the Cabinet a man of general constructive ability so that he, himself, would not have to carry the weight of every Department. He also expressed a desire for men who had idealism, and yet with all, practical. He pointed to Mr. Bryan as one who had idealism without being practical. . . .

I talked to Governor Wilson over the telephone later in the evening and told him of this conference with McCombs. He seemed pleased that there was some prospect of McCombs and McAdoo coming together. We call them Damon and Pythias in order to conceal their identity. He advised me in dealing with McCombs to use "the iron hand," that he thought it was necessary in his case. I believe he is right.

I reported that I had sent Wallace to the Secretary of War in regard to his request for a meeting, and that Stimson had said he had made no request, but had told someone who had told Morganthau that he thought it advisable to have a talk with the next Secretary as soon as he was chosen.

I also informed the Governor that I had not received a telegram from Newton Baker, therefore, that incident was closed.

A Statement on Signing Seven Bills Regulating New Jersey Corporations[1]

[Feb. 20, 1913]

The Legislature has passed the seven anti-trust bills recently introduced into the Senate, and they have received Executive approval. I congratulate the Legislature and the people on their passage. These laws mark a new era in our business life.

A good deal of criticism was leveled at the bills during the hearings while they were in the committee stage. A few amendments, thought to be just and reasonable, were made, but criticisms seeking to cut through the issue were answered and disregarded.

First it was urged that the provisions of the amendment of Section 51 of the corporation act would prohibit one corporation from acquiring the bonds, securities and other evidences of indebtedness of other corporations in the regular conduct of legitimate business. Those who made the objections quite overlooked the provision that the act should not operate to prevent any corporation from taking such securities from a non-competing corporation in the payment of debt.

It had even been said that the act would prevent a company

which may lawfully loan money from taking a bond and mortgage to secure a payment. This was palpably untrue. A loan creates a debt, and security for a debt, legitimately created, can always be taken by a loaning corporation from a borrowing corporation under the plain meeting of the act.

Besides, the bill does not invade the rights already acquired by corporations under Section 51 of the act. Every established business can go on without interruption as heretofore, but cannot hereafter expand by the acquisition of the stock and bonds of other corporations for the purpose of controlling them; and no corporation can in the future be organized to take over, hold or control other corporations.

Carefully considered clauses in the new legislation permit corporations to invest their surplus earnings, reserved as a working capital, as well as funds reserved for the benefit of their employes by way of insurance and otherwise, or for rebuilding or to offset depreciation.

It has been suggested that these acts would prevent a bank from acquiring and discounting the promissory notes of a corporation. They could have no such effect. The corporations whose notes are discounted by banks do not compete with those banks, and when a bank discounts a note it loans its money on the strength of the note and takes it to secure payment. Besides, banks are not organized under the general corporation act. Banking powers shall not be exercised by any corporation formed under it.

The amendment to Section 51 describes only corporations formed under the general corporation act. Furthermore, Section 49 of the corporation act still stands, though appreciably restricted by the amendments made by Senate 45. It still permits any corporation to purchase property, real and personal, necessary for its business, or the stock of any company owning or producing property necessary for its business; provided, only, that the property purchased shall be of like character and use to the property used by the purchasing company in the direct conduct of its own proper business. Heretofore, under Section 49, the stock and property of rival concerns could be acquired for the purpose of lessening competition and creating monopolies. That is now prohibited.

Senate 43, the act defining trusts and designed to promote free competition and commerce in all classes of business, makes it criminal to make an agreement which directly or indirectly precludes a free and unrestricted competition in the sale or transportation of any article or commodity, either by pooling, withholding from the market, or selling at a fixed price, or in any other manner by which the price might be affected.

It was urged upon the Legislature that the bill be amended by adding the word 'knowingly' so that it would read that 'any person or persons who wilfully and knowingly makes an agreement in restraint of trade' should be punished. I do not see how agreements can be made without the knowledge of those who make them, but I do understand how exceedingly difficult it is to prove knowledge to the satisfaction of a court; and it was perfectly evident that the proposal to superadd the word 'knowingly' was merely a plausible scheme devised by those who would escape the just penalty of illegal acts, by compelling the prosecution to prove that the inhibited act was done knowingly.

I understand that it is a general principle of law that there must be a guilty mind to constitute a guilty act. It seems to me that this affords ample protection to any honest man.

It has been said in some quarters that these laws will help big business and hurt the small dealers. That is, of course, not the intention, and it cannot be the effect. The purpose is to strike down monopoly and restraint of trade, big or little, and I confidently predict that these laws will prove a blessing to the whole people.

The salutary provision of the act defining trusts is that it makes it unlawful to make any agreement, directly or indirectly, which will preclude free and unrestricted competition in business.

Monopolies have too often accomplished by indirection what they could not do directly. The holding company is an example of this. When two or more companies, by existing law, could not make an agreement in restraint of trade, they hit upon the scheme of fusing and merging into a holding company, which regulated the business of the subsidiaries in such a way as to restrict trade and increase prices. Honest business and honest men have nothing to fear from these acts. Those who would engage in the heartless practices of ruining rivals and filching from the pockets of the people more than they ought reasonably to demand are the only ones who will have cause to regret their enactment.

I predict that under them the people of New Jersey will enter upon a new era of prosperity.[2]

Printed in the *Newark Evening News*, Feb. 20, 1913.

[1] They were chapters 13-19 of the *Laws of New Jersey, 1913*. For a description and analysis of these laws, see Link, *The New Freedom*, pp. 34-36.

[2] There is a typed draft of this statement, with extensive WWhw emendations, in WP, DLC.

From Oscar Wilder Underwood

My dear Gov. Wilson: [Washington] February 20, 1913.

Some time ago I promised I would advise you as to the progress that was being made by the Ways and Means Committee in preparing a tariff bill. We have made fairly good progress and have completed the first reading of the bill, but I think that the condition of business in the House of Representatives is such that from now until the end of the session it requires my attention. We are meeting at eleven o'clock in the morning and running most every night until ten or eleven o'clock so the Ways and Means Committee will be compelled to postpone the second reading of the bill until after the fourth of March. In the meantime, our experts and clerks are putting the bill in shape.

At the request of the committee, Mr. Burleson has called a caucus of the new House to meet on the fifth of March to organize a new Ways and Means Committee so that the work can proceed at once. As far as I am able to estimate, I think that it will take us about thirty days from the fifth of March to properly draft the bill.

On account of the increased membership in the new House, it will be necessary to take out the old desks and change the seating arrangements for the members. The Supervising Architect has made a contract to have this work completed by the fifteenth of March but he advised me the other day that he did not think the work can be done in that time and asked for at least a week longer in which to complete the work. Under these circumstances, I write to suggest that if it is in accord with your plans that the date of the extra session be fixed some where about the first of April.

There are a great many members of the House who desire to make their arrangements to go home between the sessions and are coming to me every day for information as to when the extra session will be called and are very anxious to know the exact date. I suggest that it will accommodate these gentlemen if you can make the announcement before the fourth of March.

I thank you very much for postponing the fixing of the time for the calling of the extra session until I had an opportunity to do the preliminary work on the tariff bill and ascertain with some definiteness when we could have it ready.

With kindest regards, I am
                    Sincerely yours,   [O W Underwood]

CCL (O. W. Underwood Papers, A-Ar).

To William Jennings Bryan

My dear Mr. Bryan: [Trenton, N. J.] February 21, 1913.

The case of our representation in China is giving me a great deal of thought and concern and I write to ask your comment upon the following suggestion.

In the first place, President Eliot of Harvard was unable to accept the appointment.

The thing most prominent in my mind is that the men now most active in establishing a new government and a new regime for China are many of them members of the Y.M.C.A., and many of them also men trained in American univers[i]ties. The Christian influence, direct or indirect, is very prominently at the front and I need not say, ought to be kept there. Mr. John R. Mott, whom I know very well and who has as many of the qualities of statesman as any man of my acquaintance, is very familiar with the situation in China, not only that, but he enjoys the confidence of men of the finest influence all over the Christian world. I am thinking of cabling to him (for he is now in China) to ask if he would be willing to remain there and represent the United States as our Minister.

I would be very much obliged to you for your comment upon this.

With warmest regard,

Faithfully yours,   Woodrow Wilson

TLS (W. J. Bryan Papers, DLC).

James Bryce to Sir Edward Grey[1]

Sir,   Washington, February 21, 1913.

I have the honour to inform you that the opportunity of seeing Dr. Woodrow Wilson for which I had been watching for some time presented itself last week when I was in New York. Through the kindness of a common friend I met the President Elect in the University Club of that City without our being observed, and had a conversation with him. As instructed by your telegram No. 206 of November 7, 1912, I conveyed to him The King's congratulations on his election, making it clear that the good wishes which I was directed to express had no party political character. Dr. Wilson was evidently much gratified by this mark of His Majesty's good will and asked me to express his very warm and deep appreciation of it and his sincere desire that the relations of Great Britain and the United States should be altogether cordial in the days of his own Administration. He mentioned incidentally that he had a personal tie with England in the fact that his mother was born a British Subject.

He observed that the friendship of the United Kingdom and the United States could not but be of the greatest service to the maintenance of the peace of the whole world and added that he deplored the attempts which he saw from time to time made, as in connection with the present Panama Tolls question, to sow discord between the two countries. These attempts however proceeded from small sections only. I expressed the hearty concurrence of His Majesty's Government in his opinion that our good relations were of high significance for the preservation of general peace, and mentioned to him many recent instances in which the two Governments had been able to act together as in reciprocally extending protection to one another's citizens and subjects, and in which they had in other ways cooperated for the aims which they had in common and which they found conducive to the general welfare.

I have the honour to be, With the highest respect, Sir,
Your most obedient, humble Servant, James Bryce

TLS (FO 371/1857, No. 9908, PRO).
1 British Undersecretary of State for Foreign Affairs, 1892-95, Foreign Secretary, 1905-16.

From the Diary of Colonel House

February 21, 1913.

Governor Wilson arrived at six o'clock. I immediately took up the McCombs matter. I urged him to let me invite McCombs to go to the theater with us. I thought he was in a docile humor and that it would be a mistake not to meet him half way. I expressed my strong belief that he did not realize just what a break with McCombs would mean. McCombs could not hurt him politically, but I was afraid the country would feel that he, the Governor, had proved ungrateful. Our people are a sentimental people, and sometimes go to extreme lengths when their feelings are stirred.

He answered that he never got anywhere with McCombs; that he was weak and vain; that he had no suggestions of value to make, and that he wanted to discuss with him appointments and offer for his consideration second or third rate men. He said it was becoming unbearable; that he had made a mistake while President of Princeton in trying to reconcile that kind of people, and that he did not intend to make such a mistake again. He consented, however, for mc to do as I liked. I called up McCombs and he was very pleased. I told him to be ready at 7.45, but as usual he was late and kept the President-elect waiting.

After the theater we left McCombs at his hotel, and while eating our sandwiches before going to bed we talked of many things.

I told him that Lane wanted to know what kind of man he was, and whether he would be given a free hand in his department. I answered that it would depend entirely upon him, Lane, that if he was capable of handling the department without any assistance, the President would soon find it out and would give him a perfectly free hand; that he really wanted his Cabinet to be able to carry on their departments without his help, but if he found them lacking, he would keep his hand upon them. The Governor replied that I had exactly stated his views to Lane.

We went over some of the letters which I had picked out from the many I am receiving. We discussed some of the minor offices. He desired Dudley Field Malone to be in Washington, and we decided to put him in the Department of Justice if nothing else suitable could be found.

I suggested Obadiah Gardner for Commissioner of Pensions which met his approval. I also suggested Governor Burke for Treasurer of the United States which also pleased him. I suggested Governor Osborne of Wyoming for one of the Philippine Commissioners. This place pays $15,000. a year and I was sure Mr. Bryan would be pleased if he gave it to him. Mr. Bryan wants Osborne for his First Assistant in the State Department. Governor Wilson and I both think him entirely unfit for that place. He has neither the culture nor the training for it.

I discussed currency matters with him and we went over the new memoranda which Paul Warburg had given me.

February 22, 1913.

Mitchell Palmer came at ten o'clock. The Governor offered him the War Portfolio. Palmer was visibly disappointed and will probably not accept it. In my opinion he will make a mistake not to do so. His view is rather narrow and selfish. He wants to be Attorney General in order to advance his own fortunes as he thinks it would be possible for him to obtain a lucrative practice after four years of service under the Government. I tried to convince him that this might occur if he were Secretary of War. I called his attention to his predecessors, mentioning Stanton and others in former years, and Taft[,] Dickinson, Root and Stimson more recently.

I took the Governor to the station and left Palmer in the apartment. On the way I suggested that he offer Walter Page the Interior and put Lane into War. He authorized me to interview Page and see whether he would take it.

Before we left the apartment, McCombs had called me up and said he had a notion to go abroad and wanted to know if that place was still open to him. I said it was. He then said he would like to go to France and wanted to know if I thought I could arrange it. I answered I thought I could and would try. I spoke to the Governor about this on the way to the station. He seemed to think the post far beyond his capabilities, but I urged him to give it to him. He finally said I might make the tender.

I shall call up McCombs later and have an interview with him. I feel sorry for the poor devil. He has brought his troubles upon himself, but nevertheless, they are many and real, and he has my profound sympathy. I am really very fond of him and I shall do what I can to save his feelings and his face.

The Governor said he would appoint Gregory to the Mexican mission. I called Burleson up and he was delighted with the news.

McCombs called at half past five. He asked if I would accept the Chairmanship of the National Committee if he resigned. I declined to do so. We then discussed a proper person to place in charge in the event he should resign and go as Ambassador to France. My choice was Hugh C. Wallace and his, Mitchell Palmer, although he does not seem to wholly trust him. . . .

McCombs said the idea of being "sent into darkest Austria" did not appeal to him, but he thought he would like to go to France. I told him to give me a definite answer on Monday, because I did not care to take the matter up with the Governor until he had made up his mind.

I called the Governor over the telephone and told him I had telegraphed Walter Page to be here on Monday. I also told him of my conversation with McCombs.

To Albert Sidney Burleson

My dear Mr. Burleson,   Princeton, New Jersey 23 Feb'y, 1913

I am writing to ask if you will accept the post of Post Master General in my cabinet. If I wrote a thousand lines I could not say more of my confidence in you or of my desire to have the best men at my side.

Please let this remain confidential between us for the present.
        Cordially and faithfully Yrs.,   Woodrow Wilson

ALS (A. S. Burleson Papers, DLC).

To William Jennings Bryan

My dear Mr. Bryan,   Princeton, New Jersey 23 Feb'y, 1913

How contemptible the efforts of the papers are, the last few days, to make trouble for us and between us,—and how delightful it is—to me, as I hope it is to you—to know, all the while, how perfect an understanding exists between us! It has been to me, since I saw you, a constant source of strength and confidence.

I had nothing in particular to write to you about to-day. I have written these few lines merely by impulse from the heart.

Mrs. Wilson joins me in warmest messages to Mrs. Bryan and yourself.   Your sincere friend,   Woodrow Wilson

ALS (W. J. Bryan Papers, DLC).

To Josephus Daniels

My dear Friend,   Princeton, New Jersey 23 Feb'y, 1913

I have been sweating blood over the cabinet choices, and have decided to beg of you that you will do me the very great service of accepting the Secretaryship of the Navy. I know of no one I trust more entirely or affectionately; and I am sure that you will trust and believe me when I assure you that you will, in my judgment, best serve the party and its new leader by accepting this post. I cannot spare you from my council table.

Faithfully & affectionately Yours,   Woodrow Wilson

May this be confidential between us for the present?

ALS (J. Daniels Papers, DLC).

To Mary Allen Hulbert

Dearest Friend,   Princeton, New Jersey 23 Feb'y, 1913

We are growing very anxious about you! It has been several weeks since we had sight of one of your welcome letters, and we fear,—we scarcely know what,—chiefly that you are ill and unable to write, or, maybe, too sick at heart. But surely *that* would not prevent! Surely that is what real friends are *for*, to pour out the heart to and be allowed to suffer the sorrows with you as well as the glad things! Write when you can. Our hearts wait for the sound of your voice.

We are not as light-hearted as we might be. Much as we have suffered in Princeton, deep as are the wounds our hearts have received here, it goes hard with us to leave it—and *next* Sunday is our last day here,—on Monday, the 3rd. of March, we start down to serve out our sentence at Washington. No doubt when the plunge is over we will fare well enough, but just now we hold back with genuine shivers. And *what* a comfort it is to think of all the old, established things, particularly of the friendships which can never alter or fail. They are so deliciously familiar, so dear to the taste and habit of our hearts. As the pressure of life increases, as the rush and hurly-burly grow more and more bewildering, old friends are not swallowed up and lost in the confusion: they stand out more distinct and lovely than ever; they are the solace of our souls. I think I should lose heart if it were not for them. God bless you! It is so sweet to think of you. I wish I could hand some of the sweetness of it on to you. When I woke up this morning, at dawn, a great wind was abroad and yet it was not cold. The airs that came in at the open window were mild and sweet and the curtains made the quiet rustling sound against the window sides that have so often been in my ears when I wakened in Bermuda. With my eyelids half closed, I could imagine myself in the dear islands of enchantment again, and my thoughts were cheered and refreshed with the delightful memories stirred by both sound and sense. I wonder if the magic has ceased to be magic for you?

A friend of ours, whom we have a very warm feeling for, Mrs. Winthrop M. Daniels,[1] is going down by the next boat, and hopes to stay either at Newstead or at Inverurie. If you are well enough could you look her up? She goes down with her boy[2] and for his sake, but needs the rest and change as much as he does. But do this *only* if it will not be a burden. We think of you constantly and long to know that your spirits are picking up. Love to Allen.

Your devoted friend,   Woodrow Wilson

ALS (WP, DLC).
[1] Joan Robertson Daniels.
[2] Robertson Balfour Daniels.

From the Diary of Colonel House

February 23, 1913.

Burleson called me from Washington and said he had had a long talk with Mitchell Palmer. That Palmer did not want to go into War because he was a Quaker, but that does not seem to be his real reason. Burleson said Palmer would take the Treasury. He thought McAdoo might possibly be persuaded to take War and give the Treasury to Palmer. I told him I would talk the matter over with Governor Wilson but I thought unless Palmer took the War Department, he might as well conclude to remain out of the Cabinet.

I asked Burleson to write Gregory and add his persuasions to mine that he accept the Solicitor Generalship instead of going as Ambassador to Mexico.

Tumulty came over at half past twelve to discuss Cabinet matters. Neither of us is satisfied with Brandeis, and neither of us thought that Walter Page should go into the Interior Department. There is the complication of my having wired Page to come here, and the uncertainty of what to do with him.

I called the Governor over the telephone and told him Page would be here Monday morning, but I was very doubtful about his putting him in the Interior. I thought no Southern man should be given that place because the Pension Bureau would be under him. He thought Page had been living in the North long enough to bar that objection. I disagreed with him. I promised to telephone later in the day.

I went to see Melville Stone at the Lotus Club and we talked of the next administration and of its policies. We fell to discussing the Monroe Doctrine. In speaking of his interview with Governor Wilson the other day he said that the Governor remarked that he thought it would be a good idea for this country to have a sympathetic understanding with England and Germany. This is the same idea I gave him some two weeks ago, and it showed that it fell upon fallow soil. . . .

I called the Governor on the Telephone again to see if we could settle upon a satisfactory man for War and Interior. . . .

After Tumulty came I called up the Governor and told him of my talk with Burleson and of his conversation with Palmer. The President-elect declined to give Palmer the Treasury, saying that the matter was closed. We then discussed over the telephone the propriety of asking Redfield to be First Assistant in Commerce and Labor, and he authorized me to find out whether he would accept that place.

We also discussed Walter Page for Interior and it was decided that I should consult with Burleson and have him ask Palmer for his opinion.

I called up Burleson and gave him the two commissions and asked him to report as soon as possible. He said he could not see Redfield before tomorrow, but he would see Palmer at once.

At about eight o'clock Burleson reported that Palmer said when he first mentioned the matter, "I am not one of the cards in the game, but one of the discards, and I do not know why my opinion should be asked for or be of any value." This does not indicate a very fine spirit. However, Burleson soothed him and Palmer told him he did not think that any Southerner should be appointed to the Interior. He also expressed to Burleson his desire to cooperate cordially with the administration even though he were not in the Cabinet.

I reported this conversation to the Governor and we decided to keep Lane in the Interior and pick out another man for War. I urged H. C. Wallace of Washington, and we finally let the matter go over until tomorrow.

To John R. Mott

My dear Mr. Mott: [Trenton, N. J.] February 24, 1913.

I have just sent you a cablegram with which go my best hopes for China and the Orient. I have set my heart on you to accept the Ambassadorship to China and this hope is shared by Mr. Bryan who will be the Secretary of State. I beg to assure you that any arrangements will be made which will enable you to fulfill your immediate present obligations.

I think that even you yourself will see how eminently fitted you are for this particular post. I will not argue to you of your character but you must understand your own influence and how intimately you can tie yourself in with all the best things that are going on in the new Republic. I beg with all my heart that you will accept this mission which seems to me so important for China and for the world.

Cordially and faithfully yours,   Woodrow Wilson

Photographic copy printed in *Addresses and Papers of John R. Mott*, Vol. vi (New York: Association Press, 1947), p. 534.

To Oscar Wilder Underwood

Personal.

My dear Mr. Underwood: [Trenton, N. J.] February 24, 1913.

Thank you sincerely for your letter of February twentieth. I would have answered it immediately had I not been absent from my office for a day or two.

Following your suggestion I shall announce that I will convene Congress in extraordinary session on Tuesday the first of April.[1]

I am very much interested indeed in what you tell me of the progress of your work and am warmly obliged to you for letting me know of it.

In haste,   Cordially yours,   Woodrow Wilson

TLS (O. W. Underwood Papers, A-Ar).
[1] He issued the call on March 17 for Congress to meet on April 7.

From Alexander Mitchell Palmer

Washington, D. C.

My dear Governor Wilson: February 24, 1913.

I have, as you requested, given further consideration to your offer to make me the Secretary of War.

I deeply appreciate the great honor which you have done me in tendering the appointment to this high office, but feel that I can not accept. The more I think of it, the more impossible it becomes. I am a Quaker. Many generations of my people have borne strong testimony against "war and the preparations for war." Of course, as a Representative in Congress, I vote for the great supply bills to maintain the military establishment and thus, in a sense, participate in the work of preparation for war but I do this in response to the sentiment and opinion of a vast majority of the people whom I represent. My mind, however, revolts at the prospect of filling an executive position where my time and thought and energy would be almost wholly devoted to the details of the improvement of our military establishment as an adequate preparation for possible war. As a Quaker War Secretary, I should consider myself a living illustration of a horrible incongruity.

I hope you understand. I am as patriotic as any man who ever lived. In case of foreign invasion of our soil, or in case our country should come to armed conflict with any other, I would go as far as any man in her defense; but I can not, without violating every tradition of my people and going against every instinct of my nature planted there by heredity, environment, and training, sit down in cold blood in an executive position and use such talents as I possess to the work of preparing for such a conflict.

I shall hope that my continued service in the House will afford me many opportunities to show that my declination of this high honor is not caused by any lack of desire to serve you and the cause you represent.

With assurances of my high personal regard and best wishes for the entire success of your administration, I am,

Yours very truly,   A. Mitchell Palmer.

TCL (WP, DLC).

From the Diary of Colonel House

February 24, 1913.

Wallace called and I told him that I had urged him for War, but I doubted whether he ought to take it since he is not a lawyer and, at this particular time, the duties of that office were un-usually onerous. I told him to think about it and to let me know by one o'clock the conclusions he reached. . . .

Wallace rang me up and said he thought it inadvisable for him to accept War. I conveyed this to the Governor through Tumulty. We are going to look up a New Jersey man, Vice Chancellor [Lindley M.] Garrison, and see whether he will fill the bill. . . .

Walter Page came after dinner and told of his trip to Trenton. He regretted that it was too late to keep Daniels out of the Cabinet. The President-elect had already written him. I knew this, because he told me he intended writing McReynolds Daniels and Burleson notes on Sunday. I was in hopes he had not mailed the one to Daniels. He said to Page, "you do not seem to think that Daniels is Cabinet timber." Page replied "He is hardly a splinter.". . .

Tumulty telephoned while Page was here, saying that the Governor had sent for Vice Chancellor Garrison and was very much pleased with him, and had offered him the post of Secretary of War.[1] Garrison had taken it under advisement until today.

[1] In an interview with Ray Stannard Baker many years later, Garrison said that he had been much surprised by Wilson's offer and had protested that he knew nothing of the army, was a lawyer by training, and was temperamentally unfit for a cabinet position. R. S. Baker, interview with L. M. Garrison, Nov. 30, 1928, RSB Coll., DLC. Felix Frankfurter, who served briefly under Garrison as law officer of the Bureau of Insular Affairs, later recalled that it was not by chance that Wilson had turned to an equity judge for Secretary of War. According to Frankfurter, Wilson said to Garrison, at their interview on February 24, that the administration of the Philippines was the most important responsibility of the War Department and that he therefore believed that the Secretary of War should be "a man with a very sensitive fiduciary equipment, and a man with a very strong sense of responsibility as a trustee." *Felix Frankfurter Reminisces: Recorded in Talks with Dr. Harlan B. Phillips* (New York, 1960), pp. 69-72.

Tumulty's account of Garrison's appointment in *Woodrow Wilson As I Know Him* (Garden City, N. Y., and Toronto, 1921), pp. 137-38, is obviously inaccurate and self-serving.

To the Legislature of New Jersey

To the Legislature: [Trenton, N. J., Feb. 25, 1913]

I wish to call your attention to the imperative necessity of effecting an immediate reform of the present system by which grand and petit juries are chosen in this State. Many honorable and notable men have occupied the office of sheriff in our several counties; many men of the highest character now fill that office, but again and again[,] by obtaining control of the office of sheriff[,] the interests which have corrupted this State, which have defied the laws, which have built up selfish private interests, which have sought to get the State in the clutch of personal political machines, have bent the law to their own uses, and I speak with absolute confidence when I say that I know the public opinion of this State now cries out for and demands reform of no hesitating or doubtful character, which shall take the selection of grand juries out of the hands of the sheriffs and place it elsewhere. A bill is pending before you which seeks to perfect this object in a way which has proved excellent in operation in other States, and which seems to afford us our only present escape from what is[,] in more than one of our counties, an intolerable situation.

Permit me to urge you[,] in the name of the people whom I know that in this matter I represent, to redeem the expectations which have been formed of us and to bring this matter to a conclusion so definite and speedy that no man's purpose can be called in question. Those who hesitate in this matter will lie under a very grave responsibility.

Respectfully,   Woodrow Wilson,   *Governor.*

Printed in *Journal of the N. J. Senate, 1913,* pp. 413-14.

To Alexander Mitchell Palmer

My dear friend: [Trenton, N. J.] February 25, 1913.

Of course I understand, sorry as I am and disappointed that I shall not have the pleasure as well as the benefit of being associated with you constantly in my immediate counsel. I understand perfectly and thank you with all my heart for your letter of yesterday. We shall have many talks over these things when I get to Washington.

Your recommendation of Honorable George W. Guthrie for the post I am sincerely sorry to say reaches me just too late to consider it. I have offered the position to a very highly valued friend here in New Jersey who I hope will accept it to-day. If he does not, you may be sure that my thoughts will willingly turn to the consideration of Mr. Guthrie, whom I greatly admire.

Cordially and faithfully yours,   Woodrow Wilson

TLS (WP, DLC).

From Josephus Daniels

Dear Governor: Raleigh, N. C., Feb. 25th., 1913.

From the day it was my pleasure to accompany you to Chapel Hill and hear your inspiring address to our University boys,[1] it has been my hope and belief that you would be called to the great work upon which you are to enter next Tuesday. The privilege of working with you in last year's campaign to win the people's approval of the principles you incarnate was cherished as an opportunity to render service for a cause dear to us both. It is my conviction that your administration, under the blessings of the Almighty, will mark a new era in our Republic. Sharing your faith in the people and sharing your ambition to make easier the path for those who toil and have been forgotten by those in power, I count it an honor to be asked to sit in the councils where the policies for carrying out our pledges will be formulated. More than that: I prize your confidence and esteem as evidenced by your invitation to become Secretary of the Navy. With grave doubt as to my ability to measure up to the high duties of that responsible post, I will accept it with the earnest desire that in this portfolio and in the councils my service may be as acceptable as my endeavor will be sincere and patriotic.

Your expressions of affection are most grateful to me and to my wife, and your letter of friendship will be handed down to my boys. It makes me happy to have come into close relationship with you—a relationship which has sweetened my life. I confidently look forward to a strengthening of the friendly ties in the yoke-fellowship in labors during the coming days.

With warmest regards to your wife and daughters, I am, with life-long sentiments of affectionate regards,

Faithfully your friend,   Josephus Daniels

ALS (WP, DLC).
  [1] When Wilson spoke on Robert E. Lee on January 19, 1909. See Josephus Daniels, *The Wilson Era: Years of Peace, 1910-1917* (Chapel Hill, N. C., 1944), pp. 3-9.

From Albert Sidney Burleson

My dear Gov. Wilson,   [Washington, D. C.] Feby 25th, 1913

Your letter tendering me the Post Office portfolio in your Cabinet has been received. I accept, realizing the full weight of responsibility assumed in doing so.

It shall be my purpose, within the limit of my ability, to discharge the duties of the high office with fidelity to you and absolute devotion to the public service.

I await the opportunity to express in person my appreciation of the confidence you have reposed in me.

Sincerely Your Friend   Albert S. Burleson

ALS (WP, DLC).

From James Clark McReynolds

My dear Governor,   New York, Febry. 25th, 1913.

Your cordial and peculiarly esteemed invitation to accept the Attorney Generalship in your cabinet reached me last evening.

I am deeply sensible of the high regard and confidence which your action implies and appreciate to the full the importance of the office to which you call me.

Association with you in counsel will surely bring to me a continuous sense of gratification, and I like to hope may enable me to be of some service to you as the chief officer of our country.

It gives me great pleasure to accept the place which you so graciously tender; and I beg to assure you of loyal cooperation and the exercise of my best efforts worthily to discharge its exacting duties.   Sincerely Yours,   J. C. McReynolds

ALS (WP, DLC).

From Lindley Miller Garrison

My dear Governor: Jersey City, N. J. February 25, 1913

I have determined to accept the offer you made me yesterday.

I have been over-working of late and had planned to go to Atlantic City today and stay until Sunday evening, and then return to Jersey City. I will be at Chalfonte Hotel, Atlantic City, until the time named and then 266 Barrow St. Jersey City. Kindly let me know just when my presence at Washington is desired.

It is not necessary for me to repeat what I said to you yesterday, that I am deeply appreciative of the confidence you have reposed in me.   Sincerely Yours   Lindley M. Garrison

ALS (WP, DLC).

To Albert Sidney Burleson

Personal and Private.

My dear friend: [Trenton, N. J.] February 26, 1913.

Your letter accepting the appointment has given me genuine pleasure and I was glad to have the little chat with you over the telephone yesterday.

A friend of mine, at my request, approached your colleague, Mr. Lewis of Maryland, as to whether he would be willing to accept the Assistant Postmaster-Generalship in order to apply his unusual knowledge of the transportation expenses connected with the postal service to the problems which we shall have to work out. It was his feeling at that time that he would not care to undertake a post in which he would not have a free hand. I wonder if you would be willing to talk with him and see whether you could change his attitude. Not by persuasion but perhaps by letting him know how willing we should be to give him as great freedom as possible in developing the parcels post service.

In haste,

Cordially and faithfully yours,   Woodrow Wilson

TLS (A. S. Burleson Papers, DLC).

From William Jennings Bryan

My Dear Gov,   Miami, Florida Feb 26 [1913]

Your generous letter just rec'd. It is a great pleasure to be associated with one who moves so steadily forward and is so little disturbed by criticism issuing from irresponsible sources. I have feared that you might be annoyed by the indiscretion and over-zeal of some of my friends, if not by the rantings of my enemies. I am used to these things and do not mind them. I would not accept a place in your official household if I did not feel as deeply interested in the success of your administration as you do your-self—as solicitous about your place in history as your good wife is. They do me injustice who represent me as disappointed that the Presidency did not come to me. I am glad to have the burden of leadership borne by another. I would prefer to hold no office at all but I am pursuaded that I can render more service near you. Mr House says you may want to announce my name first. I would prefer no special compliment in the announcement but I leave that entirely to your judgment

With cordial good will to you and your family—in which Mrs Bryan joins—I am   Very truly Yours   W. J. Bryan

ALS (WP, DLC).

From the Diary of Colonel House

February 26, 1913.

Burleson called me from Washington and said that Redfield had reconsidered his decision to accept the place of First Assistant Secretary of Commerce. I communicated this to Tumulty for Governor Wilson, and urged him not to lose Redfield's services but to appoint him to the first place instead of Brandeis. I called up McAdoo and told him what I had done. He sanctioned it. I told him the Governor knew I was right, but the enemies of Brandeis had made him angry and he had become stubborn over his appointment.

To William Cox Redfield

My dear Mr. Redfield,   Princeton, New Jersey 26 Feb'y, 1913

I write to ask if you will not accept the post of Secretary of Commerce and Labor (of Commerce, should Labor be set apart as a separate Department). It would be a real pleasure to me to be associated with you—and, what is better, a great advantage to the Department of Commerce to have you take charge of it.

Cordially and sincerely Yours,   Woodrow Wilson

P.S. May I ask that for the present you regard this as confidential?   W.W.

ALS (W. C. Redfield Papers, DLC).

Ellen Axson Wilson to Helen Herron Taft

My dear Mrs. Taft,   Princeton, New Jersey, February 26, 1913.

Your very kind note[1] is just at hand and I hasten to express my pleasure that we are to have the opportunity of meeting you on Monday. Six o'clock will suit us perfectly.

I am very glad that the President can be with us on Tuesday at luncheon, and very sorry that you cannot; but I understand perfectly the difficulties, due to your early departure. We appreciate greatly Mr. Taft's courtesy in remaining with us. It will add very much to the pleasure of the occasion.

With kindest regards in which Mr. Wilson joins me, I am

Yours very sincerely,   Ellen A Wilson.

ALS (W. H. Taft Papers, DLC).
[1] It is missing.

To William Jennings Bryan

My dear Mr. Bryan: [Trenton, N. J.] February 27, 1913.

The passage you send me[1] from the speech is very inspiring and I of course entirely subscribe to it. I do not see how better sentiments could be found for what you propose to say.

I think that Brandeis has been very grossly aspersed but of course I am looking into the matter very carefully and shall do nothing to bring the administration into question in any way.

In haste,   Faithfully yours,   Woodrow Wilson

TLS (W. J. Bryan Papers, DLC).
[1] WJB to WW, Feb. 24, 1913, ALS (WP, DLC).

From the Diary of Colonel House

February 27, 1913.

I talked with Governor Wilson at Princeton. He was to go to Philadelphia this morning and would be in New York at two, having a sitting for his portrait with Seymour Thomas[1] until five, then see McCombs at the University Club until six and would come to our apartment for dinner and the theater tonight. I told him McCombs wanted him to say that he had offered him a place in the Cabinet. The Governor replied "I cannot lie about it." I also told him of my plan to have McAdoo and McCombs join us at the theater. He thought the idea excellent, and hoped I could encompass it.

We received an invitation from the President-elect and Mrs. Wilson to lunch with them at the White House at two o'clock, Tuesday, March fourth.

[1] Stephen Seymour Thomas, Texas-born portrait artist, who resided in Paris but maintained a studio in New York.

From William Cox Redfield

Washington, D. C.

My dear Governor Wilson   February 28. 1913

Your kind favor dated 26th reached me this morning.

I do not find it easy to express my appreciation of the compliment you pay me. To fill such a post is an honor. It becomes doubly so when it takes place at your request.

In the most grateful spirit for your confidence I frankly accept the service and will perform it in a loyal spirit and to the utmost of my powers.

Very sincerely yours   William C. Redfield

ALS (WP, DLC).

From Franklin Knight Lane

My dear Mr. Wilson,   Washington Feb 28 [1913]

I hope that I may prove of help to you and of service to the Nation. Your confidence so graciously extended will stimulate me to do my best.

With sincere appreciation of the honor done me I beg to remain

Faithfully yours   Franklin K. Lane

ALS (WP, DLC).

From the Diary of Colonel House

February 28, 1913.

Governor Wilson came at six o'clock. The Brandeis matter is settled. Redfield will go in as Secretary of Commerce. This makes the list complete.

The Governor had just left McCombs and he said the interview was rather pleasant. He agreed to say that McCombs did not want to go into the Cabinet, and that he had offered him one of the posts abroad. I called McCombs over the telephone and asked him whether he was going to the theater with us. He did not think it advisable[.] I rather urged him to do it, but the Governor said in an undertone "do not urge him." McCombs finally said it [if] he could break an engagement he would ring me up in fifteen minutes which he did while we were at dinner. He drooled along for fifteen minutes, and I finally had to cut him off. He decided not to go and show himself with McAdoo. Both the Governor and I thought he made a mistake.

White [While] dinner was in progress we discussed many matters but principally poetry. He quoted several selections from Wordsworth, and again quoted James Whitcomb Reily's "Man in the Moon."

Before going into the dining room I handed him the article entitled "To Woodrow Wilson, Greeting" written by William Garrott Brown for the next edition of Harper's Weekly,[1] the proofs of which Martin had given me. The Governor stood under the light, I by his side, and read the three columns in a quiet, well modulated voice. He was deeply stirred and said "It is a noble utterance. It is a classic." He asked me to arrange for its publication in Washington as a companion piece to his Inaugural Address and I promised to attend to it.

We went to the theater to see "Within the Law."[2] The audience recognized the Governor and applauded enthusiastically. He liked the play very much. At the end of the third act, Mr. Villiers the author came to our box to meet the Governor. The audience applauded again, and the Governor presented to them Mr. Villiers. They continued cheering until he arose and said "my friends, the newspaper men, who are seated in the box opposite, understand that I am now making a virtue of silence" and then sat down.

We discussed the play and the low wages of women. When we reached home we had our sandwiches as usual, and sat until midnight talking of various matters. I told him Dudley Malone wanted to be Collector of the Port of New York. We then fell to talking of friends who uncovered their desires from time to time, and he said he had become almost skeptical of friendship because there were so few who were disinterested. That sooner or later the self interest motive would crop out.

We discussed the Maryland situation in connection with Senator Smith and Mauburg.[3] He was afraid he had made a mistake there, and I thought he had, but that it was more Mauburg's fault than his; that he should not have come out in the way he had. I thought his general course in that matter was subject to two opinions. I was sure it would be charged that he was trying to assume dictatorial powers. I said "if you go into states for the purpose of urging upon the people any particular man for the Senate, why not do the same thing in each congressional district? If that is done and your wishes prevail, then we would be in the same condition that Mexico was under Diaz." That Diaz never permitted the states to elect a governor or senator, or any public official with[out] his visé.

The Governor said he saw the point, but thought there was another side. I admitted that there was, but I wondered how many of the Cabinet would agree with him in the matter and how many would be against him.

[1] "To Woodrow Wilson: Greetings!," *Harper's Weekly*, LVII (March 8, 1913), 7.
[2] A melodrama with a social message by the American playwright and producer Bayard Veiller, which opened at the Eltinge Theatre on September 11, 1912. The involved plot centered on a shopgirl wrongly imprisoned on a charge of stealing, who, following her release, took her revenge on her former employer and also married his son.
[3] The Baltimore *Sun* reported as early as February 21 that Wilson opposed the re-election of Senator John Walter Smith and would openly support a progressive Democrat for the nomination. William L. Marbury, on February 25, announced his candidacy for the seat held by Smith and was quoted as saying: "In reaching this determination I am responding to the desire of the President-elect of the United States." Baltimore *Sun*, Feb. 26, 1913.

A Farewell to New Jersey[1]

[[March 1, 1913]]

I cannot pretend that I am not moved by deep emotions to-day. I had not expected to say anything. It would, indeed, have been my preference not to say anything because there are some feelings that are too deep for words and that seem to be cheapened by being put into words.

I already loved the State of New Jersey when I became its Governor, but that love has been deepened and intensified during these last two and a half years. I now feel a sense of identification with the people of this State and the interests of this State which have seemed to enlarge my own personality and which has been the greatest privilege of my life.

Therefore, in resigning, I want to utter these few words of poignant regret that I cannot serve this great State directly any longer. I wish for the moment that the traveling from New Jersey were less facile than it is, and yet I have the greatest feeling of confidence in the man to whom I am about to hand this seal. I have been associated with him with unusual intimacy of counsel. I have found in him qualities of honesty and courage which commend men more than any other qualities do in public life.

The rarest thing in public life is courage, and the man who has courage is marked for distinction; the man who has not is marked for extinction, and deserves submersion. The people of this country are going to be served by consciences and not by expediency. When you strike a man of courage you feel that you have struck the bedrock of our institutions. It is, therefore, with a feeling of confidence and affection for him personally that I hand him the seal of office.

Printed in the *New York Times*, March 2, 1913; with corrections from the text in the *Newark Evening News*, March 1, 1913.

[1] The occasion was the swearing in of James Fairman Fielder, President of the Senate of New Jersey, as Acting Governor of New Jersey. The oath of office was administered by William Stryker Gummere, chief justice of the New Jersey Supreme Court, in the Assembly chamber before the full Senate and Assembly and many state officials and guests. Following this ceremony, John Warren Davis of Salem County, floor leader of the Democrats in Senate Democrats, made a brief speech and then invited Wilson to speak.

Remarks to Neighbors in Princeton[1]

[[March 1, 1913]]

I feel very deeply complimented that you should have gathered here to-night to say a good-bye to me and to bid me godspeed. I have felt a very intimate identification with this town. I suppose that some of you think there is a sort of disconnection between the university and the town, and perhaps some of you suppose it is only since I became Governor of this State that I have been keenly aware of the impulses which have come out of the ranks of the citizens of this place to touch me and inspire me—but that is not true. I think you will bear me witness that I have had many friends in this town ever since I came here, and that one of the happiest experiences I have had day by day has been the grasp of the hand and the familiar salutation which I have met at every hand.

I experienced only one mortification in this town. I went into a shop one day after I became President of this University and purchased a small article, and said, "Won't you be kind enough to send that up?" I had purchased it of a man with whose face I had been familiar for years, and he said,

"What is your name, sir?"

That was my single mortification, and that is the keenest kind of mortification: because if there is one thing a man loves better than another, it is being known by his fellow citizens.

Now, my friends, I said the other day, and I said it most unaffectedly, that I was going keenly to enjoy these three days as a plain and an untitled citizen. I have admitted that many times. I said I was going to enjoy these days and I am enjoying them. Not because they are days when I am not particularly responsible for anything, but because they are days that remind me of the many years I have spent in this place going in and out as one of your own number; and I want you to believe me when I say that I shall never lose that consciousness.

I would be a very poor President if I did lose it. I have always believed that the real rootages of patriotism were local; that they resided in one's consciousness of an intimate touch with persons who were watching him with a knowledge of his character.

You cannot love a country abstractly; you have got to love it concretely. You have got to know people in order to love them. You have got to feel as they do in order to have sympathy with them. And any man would be a poor public servant who did not regard himself as a part of the public himself. No man can imagine how other people are thinking. He can know only by what is going on in his own head, and if that head is not connected by every thread of suggestion with the heads of people about him he cannot think as they think.

I am turning away from this place in body but not in spirit, and I am doing it with genuine sadness. The real trials of life are the connections you break, and when a man has lived in one place as long as I have lived in Princeton and had as many experiences as I have had here—first as an undergraduate and then as a resident—he knows what it means to change his residence and to go into strange environments and surroundings.

I have never been inside of the White House, and I shall feel very strange when I get inside of it. I shall think of this little house behind me and remember how much more familiar it is to me than that is, and how much more intimate a sense of possession there must be in the one case than in the other.

One cannot be neighbor to the whole United States. I shall miss my neighbors. I shall miss the daily contact with the men I know and by whom I am known, and one of the happiest things

144   MARCH 1, 1913

in my thoughts will be that your good wishes go with me. I shall always look at this beautiful cup with the greater pleasure because it reminds me of this occasion, and of all that you have meant to me.

You have said very kind things about me, but no kinder than I could say about you. With your confidence and the confidence of men like you, the task that lies before me will be gracious and agreeable. It will be a thing to be proud of, because I am trying to represent those who have so graciously trusted me.

Printed in the *New York Times*, March 2, 1913.
¹ Some fifteen hundred townspeople and college students marched from Nassau Street to Wilson's home on Cleveland Lane on the evening of March 1. They burned red flares and carried Japanese lanterns, and a band played "Hail to the Chief" and accompanied the singing of "My Country, 'Tis of Thee" and "Auld Lang Syne." David M. Flynn, president of the First National Bank, presented Wilson with a silver loving cup inscribed: "Presented to Woodrow Wilson, President of the United States, by the Citizens of Princeton." The students closed the affair with the singing of "Old Nassau." See the *New York Times*, March 2, 1913 and the *Princeton Alumni Weekly*, XIII (March 5, 1913), 421-24.

John R. Mott to Cleveland Hoadley Dodge

[Hankow, China, c. March 1, 1913]

Please convey to President Wilson that my careful study of whole situation, wide contact with different sections and intercourse with Chinese leaders and well-informed disinterested men of other nations living in China have convinced me that time has come when America should promptly recognize Chinese Republic. FIRST, China has won right to recognition by progress achieved in most difficult year and by grasp of situation.
SECOND, China presents evidences of stability. Country has become quiet. No serious troubles continue. Elections for house of representatives have already taken place without disturbances in twenty one of twenty two provinces. New provincial assemblies all elected which are electing senators this month. Good feeling between sections. Whole country united. Principal possible rivals to Yuan¹ are strongly supporting him. Country prosperous. Past year record year in crops and custom receipts. Best men in power.
THIRD, Recognition now would give America position of unique influence.
FOURTH, Recognition would accord with our best traditions and with our greatest helpfulness to all other republics.
FIFTH, American ideals prevail in China more than those of any other land. China speaking of us as the great sister republic and looking to us as to no other country.

SIXTH, Students returned from America wielding predominant influence and therefore render it peculiarly appropriate that a nation which afforded them their inspiration and training should strengthen their hands.

SEVENTH, If America is ultimately to recognize China why not now when recognition would mean far more than at any later time. If America has been restrained by international agreement has not that arrangement been nullified by action of Russia, and, in any event, should new administration be bound by it?

I find spreading among best men keenest disappointment and dismay as result of inexplicable delay, and confidence in Americas disinterestedness being greatly shaken.

Those at home cannot realize what eager expectations are centred upon Wilsons inaugural message. Prompt recognition by new administration would enormously enhance our prestige in the East.   Mott

TC telegram (J. R. Mott Coll., CtY-D).
    [1] Yuan Shih-k'ai, military and political leader, who succeeded Sun Yat-sen as Provisional President of the Chinese republic on March 12, 1912.

From the Diary of Colonel House

March 1, 1913.

We breakfasted at 8.45. Before going in I showed him some of the letters and memoranda I had placed in his pigeon-hole for attention such as personal letters, important requests, etc. etc.

William Bayard Hale called at half past nine. The Governor had sent him to Washington to get some information in regard to Central America and other affairs. We went over these matters at length.

We saw in the paper that Castro had announced that while he had not been invited to the Inauguration, he intended coming anyway.[1] The Governor asked me to have it conveyed to Castro that it would be embarrassing to him, Castro; that he would be snubbed, and that he had better keep away. I conveyed this (through Gordon Auchincloss) to O'Gorman, Battle & Marshall who acted as Castro's attorneys when he was trying to obtain entrance into this country. Gordon saw Snowdon Marshall who was the only member of the firm in, and he promised to notify Castro at once. He said, however, that they had not represented Castro excepting in the one case of admission, but they would wire him anyway.

    [1] Cipriano Castro, dictator and President of Venezuela from 1899 until deposed and forced into permanent exile in 1908. Castro, who had recently paid

a brief visit to the United States, was at the moment in Havana, amid the usual rumors that he was planning a filibustering expedition to Venezuela. He told reporters on February 28 that he intended to return to the United States to attend Wilson's inauguration, while freely admitting that he had not been invited by Wilson. Castro was in Washington on inauguration day, but only as a spectator. See the *New York Times*, March 1 and 5, 1913.

To Mary Allen Hulbert

Dearest Friend,   Princeton, New Jersey 2 March, 1913.

This is our last evening in this little house, and we find our hearts very heavy. We leave familiar scenes, which we may possibly never know again, and go out to new adventures, amongst strangers. New adjustments must be made all along the line,—a new life must be worked out,—a life full of strain and anxiety. Our joy lies in the ties that *cannot* be broken,—our dear, dear friends from whom we cannot be parted in thought or sympathy.

These lines, into which I do not know how to put our hearts as I would, go to you laden with greetings which are mingled with the feeling that Bermuda is just outside the window, while Washington is on the far side of the globe. You are our permanent possession—always our friend and neighbour.

Your last letter pleased me because of the way your humour lightened as you wrote. Please think always of our deep affection, make us your own, and take life from our thought of you.
          Your devoted friend,   Woodrow Wilson

Alas, it was too late to send Allen a ticket.

ALS (WP, DLC).

From George Mason La Monte

My dear Mr. Wilson: Bound Brook, N. J. Mch 2nd 1913.

I want you to get this letter between the acts as it were so that I can tell you as man to man just how much I have valued the association of the recent years. I felt, as you know, when we started out in 1910 that we had serious business ahead of us and I am glad to have had the privilege of having had a part in its successful accomplishment.

Association with you has made public service a very real duty and devotion to it has been a source of genuine satisfaction.

Those of us who remain here have real problems to continue to stimulate us to action—not so large as those ahead of you and only less serious than yours because their effect is not so far reaching. I hope time will permit us to have an occasional exchange of experiences and that it will be a source of satisfaction to you to know that you have "started something" in New Jersey that will not easily die. I also feel sure that the fact that "the folks at home" are sympathising with you in your larger endeavors will be a bulwark of strength in the days to come. Your success will be ours and we will always follow you with love and confidence.

Affectionately yours   George Mason La Monte

ALS (WP, DLC).

From Felexiana Shepherd Baker Woodrow

My dear Tommy: Columbia, S. C., March 3, 1913.

May our Heavenly Father's richest blessings rest upon you.

May He protect you from all harm, and may He guide and direct you in all things.

With best love to all,   Affectionately,   Aunt Felie.

ALS (WP, DLC).

Remarks at a Princeton Smoker in Washington[1]

[March 3, 1913]

Fellows, I hadn't expected to say anything tonight, because the only appropriate thing to say I can't say, because there are no words for it. There are some emotions that are very much deeper than a man's vocabulary can reach, and I have a feeling tonight that moves me very much indeed.

We have often spoken of our comradeship together as Princeton men, and I have spoken so often that I am ashamed almost to repeat it, of the part that Princeton has played in public life and of the part she ought to play in public life, and I have spoken so often of that sense of having a great invisible brotherhood that binds a man by uncommon standards of honor and of service. Now I stand here upon the eve of attempting a great task, a profoundly great one. I rejoice that there are so many men in the United States who know me and understand me and to whom I don't have to explain anything.

Members of the family don't have to be told what is going to happen, and therefore it isn't necessary to make a speech to the family. I have only to say that my feeling tonight is a family feeling, of being among men trained as I was trained, looking upon life as I do and ready to give me that sympathy that buoys a man up more than anything else in the world. I thank God that it is so, and thank you profoundly for this evidence of it.

T MS (C. L. Swem Coll., NjP), with corrections from the complete text in the *New York Times*, March 4, 1913.
    [1] A reception and smoker in Wilson's honor, held at the New Willard Hotel under the auspices of the Princeton Alumni Association of the District of Columbia. Some eight hundred alumni from all parts of the United States attended, and Wilson is reported to have shaken hands with all of them. For the most detailed report, see "The Inauguration Smoker," *Princeton Alumni Weekly*, XIII (March 12, 1913), 446-48.

From William Frank McCombs

My dear Governor: Washington March 3 1913

    I have thought carefully over the means of accomplishing the accepting of the great compliment you have paid me in offering to me the ambassadorship to France. Happily after conference with my family today I am glad to say I can arrange to accept the great honor you have offered me. I shall try to fulfil the function of the great office to the utmost of my ability.

                              Yours Sincerely   W F McCombs

ALS (WP, DLC).

An Inaugural Address

                                              [March 4, 1913]

    There has been a change of government. It began two years ago, when the House of Representatives became Democratic by a decisive majority. It has now been completed. The Senate about to assemble will also be Democratic. The offices of President and Vice President have been put into the hands of Democrats. What does the change mean? That is the question that is uppermost in our minds today. That is the question I am going to try to answer, in order, if I may, to interpret the occasion.

    It means much more than the mere success of a party. The success of a party means little except when the nation is using that party for a large and definite purpose. No one can mistake the purpose for which the nation now seeks to use the Democratic party. It seeks to use it to interpret a change in its own plans and point of view. Some old things with which we had grown familiar, and which had begun to creep into the very habit of our thought and of our lives, have altered their aspect as we have latterly looked critically upon them, with fresh, awakened eyes; have dropped their disguises and shown themselves alien and sinister. Some new things, as we look frankly upon them, willing to comprehend their real character, have come to assume the aspect of things long believed in and familiar, stuff of our own convictions. We have been refreshed by a new insight into our own life.

We see that in many things that life is very great. It is incomparably great in its material aspects, in its body of wealth, in the diversity and sweep of its energy, in the industries which have been conceived and built up by the genius of individual men and the limitless enterprise of groups of men. It is great, also, very great, in its moral force. Nowhere else in the world have noble men and women exhibited in more striking forms the beauty and the energy of sympathy and helpfulness and counsel in their efforts to rectify wrong, alleviate suffering, and set the weak in the way of strength and hope. We have built up, moreover, a great system of government, which has stood through a long age as in many respects a model for those who seek to set liberty upon foundations that will endure against fortuitous change, against storm and accident. Our life contains every great thing, and contains it in rich abundance.

But the evil has come with the good, and much fine gold has been corroded. With riches has come inexcusable waste. We have squandered a great part of what we might have used, and have not stopped to conserve the exceeding bounty of nature without which our genius for enterprise would have been worthless and impotent, scorning to be careful, shamefully prodigal as well as admirably efficient. We have been proud of our industrial achievements, but we have not hitherto stopped thoughtfully enough to count the human cost, the cost of lives snuffed out, of energies overtaxed and broken, the fearful physical and spiritual cost to the men and women and children upon whom the dead weight and burden of it all has fallen pitilessly the years through. The groans and agony of it all had not yet reached our ears, the solemn, moving undertone of our life, coming up out of the mines and factories and out of every home where the struggle had its intimate and familiar seat. With the great government went many deep secret things which we too long delayed to look into and scrutinize with candid, fearless eyes. The great government we loved has too often been made use of for private and selfish purposes, and those who used it had forgotten the people.

At last a vision has been vouchsafed us of our life as a whole. We see the bad with the good, the debased and decadent with the sound and vital. With this vision we approach new affairs. Our duty is to cleanse, to reconsider, to restore, to correct the evil without impairing the good, to purify and humanize every

process of our common life without weakening or sentimental-
izing it. There has been something crude and heartless and un-
feeling in our haste to succeed and be great. Our thought has
been "Let every man look out for himself; let every generation
look out for itself," while we reared giant machinery which made
it impossible that any but those who stood at the levers of control
should have a chance to look out for themselves. We had not
forgotten our morals. We remembered well enough that we had
set up a polity which was meant to serve the humblest as well
as the most powerful, with an eye single to the standards of justice and fair play, and remembered it with pride. But we were
very heedless and in a hurry to be great.

We have come now to the sober second thought. The scales of
heedlessness have fallen from our eyes. We have made up our
minds to square every process of our national life again with the
standards we so proudly set up at the beginning and have always
carried at our hearts. Our work is a work of restoration.

We have itemized with some degree of particularity the things
that ought to be altered, and here are some of the chief items: A
tariff which cuts us off from our proper part in the commerce of
the world, violates the just principles of taxation, and makes the
government a facile instrument in the hands of private interests;
a banking and currency system based upon the necessity of the
government to sell its bonds fifty years ago and perfectly adapted
to concentrating cash and restricting credits; an industrial system which, take it on all its sides, financial as well as administrative, holds capital in leading strings, restricts the liberties and
limits the opportunities of labor, and exploits without renewing
or conserving the natural resources of the country; a body of
agricultural activities never yet given the efficiency of great business undertakings or served as it should be through the instrumentality of science taken directly to the farm, or afforded the
facilities of credit best suited to its practical needs; watercourses
undeveloped, waste places unreclaimed, forests untended, fast
disappearing without plan or prospect of renewal, unregarded
waste heaps at every mine. We have studied as perhaps no other
nation has the most effective means of production, but we have
not studied cost or economy as we should either as organizers of
industry, as statesmen, or as individuals.

Nor have we studied and perfected the means by which government may be put at the service of humanity, in safeguarding the
health of the nation, the health of its men and its women and
its children, as well as their rights in the struggle for existence.
This is no sentimental duty. The firm basis of government is jus-

tice, not pity. These are matters of justice. There can be no equality of opportunity, the first essential of justice in the body politic, if men and women and children be not shielded in their lives, their very vitality, from the consequences of great industrial and social processes which they cannot alter, control, or singly cope with. Society must see to it that it does not itself crush or weaken or damage its own constituent parts. The first duty of law is to keep sound the society it serves. Sanitary laws, pure food laws, and laws determining conditions of labor which individuals are powerless to determine for themselves are intimate parts of the very business of justice and legal efficiency.

These are some of the things we ought to do, and not leave the others undone, the old-fashioned, never to be neglected, fundamental safeguarding of property and of individual right. This is the high enterprise of the new day: to lift everything that concerns our life as a nation to the light that shines from the hearthfire of every man's conscience and vision of the right. It is inconceivable that we should do this as partisans; it is inconceivable we should do it in ignorance of the facts as they are or in blind haste. We shall restore, not destroy. We shall deal with our economic system as it is and as it may be modified, not as it might be if we had a clean sheet of paper to write upon; and step by step we shall make it what it should be, in the spirit of those who question their own wisdom and seek counsel and knowledge, not shallow self-satisfaction or the excitement of excursions whither they cannot tell. Justice, and only justice, shall always be our motto.

And yet it will be no cool process of mere science. The nation has been deeply stirred, stirred by a solemn passion, stirred by the knowledge of wrong, of ideals lost, of government too often debauched and made an instrument of evil. The feelings with which we face this new age of right and opportunity sweep across our heartstrings like some air out of God's own presence, where justice and mercy are reconciled and the judge and the brother are one. We know our task to be no mere task of politics but a task which shall search us through and through, whether we be able to understand our time and the need of our people, whether we be indeed their spokesmen and interpreters, whether we have the pure heart to comprehend and the rectified will to choose our high course of action.

This is not a day of triumph; it is a day of dedication. Here muster, not the forces of party, but the forces of humanity. Men's hearts wait upon us, men's lives hang in the balance; men's hopes call upon us to say what we will do. Who shall live up to the great trust? Who dares fail to try? I summon all honest men, all patriotic, all forward-looking men, to my side. God helping me, I will not fail them, if they will but counsel and sustain me![1]

WWT MS (WC, NjP), with a few corrections from *Inaugural Address of President Woodrow Wilson and Vice President Thomas R. Marshall* (Washington, 1913).
[1] There is a WWsh draft of this address, with the composition date of Feb. 6, 1913, in WP, DLC.

From Victoriano Huerta

Mexico City, Mexico, March 4, 1913.

En nombre del pueblo y gobierno Mexicano y en el mio propio tengo la honra de ofrecer a vuestra excelencia las mas cordiales felicitaciones por su exaltacion a la primera magistratura de esa gran republica.   V. Huerta.

T telegram (SDR, RG 59, 811.00/2269/8, DNA).

From the Diary of Colonel House

March 4, 1913.

The President-elect telephoned and asked Loulie and me to meet his family party at the Shoreham Hotel at 9.45 in order to accompany them to the Capitol for the Inauguration Ceremonies. I took Loulie to the Shoreham and left her with the Wilsons, but I did not go to the Capitol myself. I went instead to the Metropolitan Club and loafed around with Wallace. Functions of this sort do not appeal to me and I never go.

We lunched at the White House at two o'clock. Ex-President Taft and his Cabinet, President Wilson and his Cabinet, and the heads of the Army and Navy were among the guests. It was a notable function.

We went from the dining room directly to the President's reviewing stand in front of the White House. I remained there for awhile chatting with the members of the Cabinet and other friends, and then went back to the Wallaces.

Mrs. Wilson invited us to the White House to see the fireworks. When we arrived we found the President was over in his office. I went there and was with him for a few minutes in order to tell him that I had investigated John H. Marble[1] for Interstate Commerce Commissioner in place of F. K. Lane, and had found him satisfactory. The President had never met Marble and had made no inquiries concerning him further than mine. He said he would send his name in tomorrow along with the names of his Cabinet.

He made the appointment in this way in order to avoid the great pressure which would be made upon him by candidates for this important office.

We talked about McCombs and McAdoo and the war that Mc-Combs was making upon him. I advised the President to send for McCombs and have him stop it.

After my interview with the President I said a few words to Mrs. Wilson and then went to the Shoreham to see McAdoo, Walter Page and several others. I told McAdoo what the President had said regarding McCombs and he seemed satisfied.

[1] John Hobart Marble, lawyer of Washington, at this time secretary of the Interstate Commerce Commission.

A Warning to Office-Seekers

[March 5, 1913]

The President regrets that he is obliged to announce that he deems it his duty to decline to see applicants for office in person, except when he himself invites the interview. It is his purpose and desire to devote his attention very earnestly and very constantly to the business of the Government and the large questions of policy affecting the whole nation; and he knows from his experience as Governor of New Jersey (where it fell to him to make innumerable appointments) that the greater part both of his time and of his energy will be spent in personal interviews with candidates unless he sets an invariable rule in the matter. It is his intention to deal with appointments through the heads of the several executive departments.

T MS (Letterpress Books, WP, DLC).

From the Federal Council of the Churches of Christ in America

[c. March 5, 1913]

To Hon. Woodrow Wilson, President of the United States:

The Federal Council of the Churches of Christ in America extends to you the good will and the prayerful sympathy of the Churches of Christ, and tenders you the serious and earnest cooperation of the forces represented by the churches, as you take up the task, as the chief magistrate of the nation, of guiding the moral forces of the people, and of the leadership of the nations of the world.

Your warm and sympathetic sense of our democracy; your

conviction expressed in so many ways, both by utterance and execution, that our social order must be fashioned after the Kingdom of God as taught by Jesus Christ; together with your public faithfulness and your personal faith, lead the churches of the nation to look with confidence to the performance of the serious and solemn duties of the coming years.

The beginning of your First Quadrennium as President is almost coincident with the beginning of the Second Quadrennium of the Federal Council. While you are planning for these four years, the Federal Council is also projecting for the same term of years, larger movements in the interest of the spirit and realization of Christian unity expressed by the Council. It is to be hoped that, without unwise embarrassment, with both sympathy and discrimination, with social vision and social emotion, the political forces of the nation, and its moral forces as embodied in the churches of Christ, may feel and serve together for the social and spiritual wellbeing of the people.

For the Council,   William I. Haven,
                        Chairman of Administrative Committee.
                        Rivington D. Lord,
                        Recording Secretary of the Administrative
                        Committee.
                        Charles S. Macfarland,
                        Secretary of the Council.

Printed in the Utica, N. Y., *Presbyterian Advance*, VII (March 13, 1913), 31.

From Abram Woodruff Halsey

My dear Wilson,   Washington March 5, 1913

Your loyalty to '79 was never better attested than when at the close of the great day of your life you gave us such a delightful half hour.[1] On behalf of the class, and of the committee and personally I wish to thank you for your gracious act. We all knew what a strenuous day you had, and not a word would have been said had you felt unable to meet with us. Nothing in all your career has endeared you to us more than this fine expression of devotion to all that the class holds dear. Let me assure you that we will do our best to aid you in the great tasks which lie before you   Always yours   A. W. Halsey

ALS (WP, DLC).
    [1] The Class of 1879 had a dinner in Wilson's honor at the Shoreham Hotel during the evening of March 4. It is described in David Lawrence, "The Inauguration of President Wilson," *Princeton Alumni Weekly*, XIII (March 5, 1913), 421. For a list of those who attended, see *ibid.*, p. 452.

Frederic Yates to Emily Chapman Martin Yates
and Mary Yates

My dear Blesseds,   The White House 5th Mar. '13

What a host of experiences to tell—it has all gone beautifully.
I arrived here on the 3rd about 5.30 and at 6.30 was "dressed all
in my best" and by 7 was seated next to Mrs. Woodrow Wilson
at a table of 32.[1] Mr. John A Wilson is a cousin of W.W. My
instructions were to come here on leaving the train[.] It was a
beautiful table, and a wonderful dinner. We had hardly begun
than the everlasting photographer arrived[.] Washington Bristles
with Photographers. I am going to get all I can in the way of
newspaper versions. Next to Mrs. Wilson was John A Wilson and
at the far end of the table was the President-Elect, Jessie, Nellie
& Margaret all looking lovely as queens, princesses rather.

Early next morning the President Elect was taken from the
Hotel Shoreham by 1000 Princeton graduates,[2] all wearing a
badge [of] orange. We followed later, coming on in motor cars
and taxies. All went to the Capitol and then later to the swearing
in of the President. I was in the President's party everywhere—at
the Senate first where we heard the swearing in of the Vice President Marshall and the swearing in of the newly elected Senators.
Then after all the Ambassadors and the Ministers had left the
Senate the galleries gradually emptied, and we were all congre-
gated around the grand stand where the incoming President was
to take the oath administered by the Chief Justice[.] I was three
rows off and could see the President's face all the while. The
address created a profound sensation. Back of him and seated
all around on the stand were the outgoing and incoming cabinet,
President Taft &c. Then back to the White House to a standing
up lunch at which there were 189 people. Then the Parade of
the Troops—a function that the President witnessed from the
grand stand at the south side of the White House—enormous
stands & thousands of thousands of people. 4¼ hours the dear
President stood there raising his hat as the colours passed they
slightly bending as they passed him. Mrs. Wilson standing by
looking like an angel[—]how beautiful she looked now and again
in her old enthusiasm waving a little lace handkerchief and
smiling her radiant smile. Then came dinner at 7.30—the first
dinner at the White House. We were all of the family except myself and as I entered the President said "Fred go and sit on Mrs.
Wilsons left." There I was for my second dinner sitting next to
that dear darling. We numbered on[ly] 14. As you may imagine
we talked often of you two dear darlings at home, the President

sitting across the table from Mrs. Wilson, flowers galore on the table.

After dinner a big display of fireworks the most wonderful I think that I ever saw. I got to bed at 10.30 & wrote letters till 12. Got up at 7 and wrote again, and at 8.30 I had breakfast alone with the dear President[.] He had two eggs—unbeaten—and swallowed them in orange juice—whole—like oysters—that and some porridge & coffee. He is looking very well and weighs more than he has ever done in his life—179 lbs. I played accompaniments for Margaret to sing and at lunch time we sat down again—33— when again I find myself again at Mrs. Wilsons left—and a gay time we had I can tell you, with the President in fine story form seated in front. He had to leave for a series of deputations before we had quite finished lunch. And at 4, he took Mrs. Wilson for a short auto drive round the Washington Monument and after about ¼ of an hour we brought her back. I alone was with them and the man—the body guard who sits by the chauffeur. Great crowds cheering. Then when we left Mrs. Wilson, the President took me off alone with him round the park. We were gone about an hour and you may imagine your dear husband's distinction! Getting back I hastily got away. Mrs. Wilson most lovingly asked me to stay longer and the President said, "Why surely Fred you are not going to leave us." I said Yes I am, my cup is filled to the brim, and I did the square, for I know the crowds of relatives they want my room for.

It was palatial, and Lordy, how well I slept awaking this morning not in the least bit realizing where I was, nor that our dear friend was actually the President of America. . . .

[Fred]

ALS (F. Yates Coll, NjP).
¹ Wilson, his immediate family, a number of relatives, and a few close friends, were dinner guests of John Adams Wilson at the Shoreham Hotel on the evening of March 3. For the guest list and a description of the affair, see the *New York Herald*, March 4, 1913.
² Actually, they were undergraduates, many of whom had accompanied the Wilson family from Princeton to Washington on a special train. For a good description of the extensive role played by Princeton students and alumni in Wilson's inauguration, see David Lawrence, "The Inauguration of President Wilson," *Princeton Alumni Weekly*, XIII (March 5, 1913), 418-21.

To Abram Woodruff Halsey

My dear Halsey: [The White House] March 6, 1913

Your letter from the Shoreham gave me deep gratification and touched me very much indeed. You may be sure that I only followed the dictates of my heart on Tuesday night and that my visit to the '79 dinner was the best part of the day for me.

Affectionately yours,   Woodrow Wilson

TLS (Letterpress Books, WP, DLC).

To Champ Clark

My dear Mr. Speaker: [The White House] March 6, 1913

May I not drop you this line of sincere congratulation on your renomination to the Speakership? It is what every Democrat desired, and I think the country and the House as well as yourself are to be warmly congratulated. It gives me great pleasure to look forward to my intimate association with you.

I wish I might have been at the Missouri dinner last night.

Cordially and sincerely yours,   Woodrow Wilson

TLS (Letterpress Books, WP, DLC).

From the Diary of Josephus Daniels

March Thur 6 1913

As soon as I received the letter from the President tendering the appointment as Secretary of the Navy, I immediately thought of Franklin D. Roosevelt, of New York, as Assistant Secretary. He had supported Wilson for the nomination, and taken an active part in the campaign, and I found him a singularly attractive and honorable and courageous young Democratic leader. I believed in him and was desirous of being associated with him in the Navy Department. And so this morning I went to the White House and told the President that I had decided upon Mr. Roosevelt. He said "capital" and heartily approved. This was gratifying to me.

That afternoon I consulted Senator O'Gorman, of New York, and asked him [his] opinion. He spoke in high terms of Mr R and said his appointment would be acceptable. He had not been gone long before a New York gentleman[1] came and warned me against naming R as Assistant Secretary, saying that every person named Roosevelt wishes to run everything and would try to be the Secretary. I listened and replied that any man who was afraid his assistant would supplant him thereby confessed that he did not think he was big enough for the job. I related the conversation to the President who expressed about the same opinion I had entertained.

Bound desk diary (J. Daniels Papers, DLC).
   [1] Senator Elihu Root. See J. Daniels to WW, March 11, 1913, TLS (WP, DLC).

To Victoriano Huerta[1]

Washington, March 7, 1913.

I thank you for your cordial congratulations.

Woodrow Wilson

T telegram signed (SDR, RG 59, 811.00/W69, DNA).
   [1] After much discussion, Wilson and Bryan decided to address this telegram "General V. Huerta, Mexico City, Mexico," in order to avoid any semblance of diplomatic recognition.

To Eugene Elliott Reed

My dear Mr. Reed: [The White House] March 7, 1913

I am deeply anxious about the situation in New Hampshire with regard to the election of the United States Senator, and I want to send through you a message to those of my friends in the Legislature who still have doubts as to the wisdom of voting for Mr. Hollis.[1]

I hope that they will not think that I am taking an undue liberty in this matter. I feel to the bottom of my heart my responsibility to the country and to the party, and I know what the difficulties of the party are likely to be if the margin of Democratic votes in the Senate of the United States is too narrow. Any accident might impair or destroy that majority, and even the illness of a man or two might change the complexion of affairs. For this reason I feel it to be the solemn obligation of every Democrat to cast aside personal feeling, and even individual judgment, and stand with the party in a united effort to make the most of its opportunity.

I, therefore, make this earnest appeal to the friends to whom this letter is addressed through you to support Mr. Hollis. I wish that I could make the appeal in person, but in no circumstances could I make it more solemnly or earnestly than I now do. My duty and their duty to the party and to the country is involved.[2]

Cordially and sincerely yours,   Woodrow Wilson

TLS (Letterpress Books, WP, DLC).
   [1] Henry French Hollis had been nominated by the Democratic legislative caucus on January 8, 1913. The legislature had begun balloting on January 14 and had voted on every legislative day thereafter without an election because of the refusal of several Democrats to vote for Hollis.
   [2] Hollis was finally elected on March 13 by a narrow majority, when most of the Democratic defectors swung to his side. He also received the votes of nine progressive Republicans.

From the American Philosophical Society

Sir: [Philadelphia, March 7, 1913]

The American Philosophical Society extends its cordial congratulations to you, as one of its fellow members, upon your
accession to the Presidency of the United States. You carry into
public life the ideals of the scholar and you will show in the
new world, as had been proved so often in the old, that scientific
training, in the best and broadest sense of the term, is a help to
the practical statesman. Your studies in history and in political
science will illuminate your task of giving to the Nation a wise
and strong government.

It was Montesquieu, the good genius of the makers of our
National Constitution, who said that for a safe voyage for the
Ship of State the spirit of the laws should serve as compass and
history should be the chart. This Society confidently believes
that you have at your command this compass and this chart;
that with your firm hand at the helm the Ship of State will safely
ride the seas, and that, like those of your distinguished predecessors in the Presidency, who were its members, you will help
to make the future history of the Nation worthy of its past.

Seven times since the founding of the Republic The American
Philolosphical Society has had cause for congratulation in the
selection of one of its members as President of the United States.
Washington, Adams, Jefferson, Madison, the second Adams,
Buchanan and Grant were honored names upon its Roll before
the popular vote inscribed them in the list of American Presidents. To you, the eighth in turn of its members to enter upon this
high office, this Society extends its warmest greeting.

Given under the Seal and in the name of The American
Philosophical Society held at Philadelphia for Promoting Useful Knowledge, this seventh day of March, 1913.

William W. Keen   President

Attest: I. Minis Hays, Secretary

Printed letter (WP, DLC).

From Frank Morrison

My dear Mr. President: Washington, D. C., March 7th, 1913.

In a few words in your inaugural address you indicated in the
most certain terms the reforms needed to turn the tide of discontent among our people to something akin to the feeling that

the human equation will soon be solved, and when solved, the answer will be equal protection and opportunity for each citizen.

When Congress enacts legislation in harmony with your inaugural address, it will kindle afresh in many, and for the first time in the hearts of millions of our citizens the hope that enactment of wise legislation will gradually eliminate from our present civilization the many inequalities and injustices which bear heavily upon many of our people.

You said to Mr. Gompers and myself that you thought we would be satisfied with your address. I am satisfied, and will do what I can to have Congress enact the legislation necessary to secure the splendid reforms which you have clearly outlined in your address.   Yours very truly,   Frank Morrison

TLS (WP, DLC).

From the Diary of Josephus Daniels

March Fri 7 1913

The first regular meeting of the cabinet was held. One of the topics for discussion was whether the order of President Taft putting fourth class postmasters under the civil service should be revoked or modified. A few days before President Taft was defeated, he issued an order that if it stands keeps Republicans in office who were appointed because of their service to that party. The opinion prevailed that the merit system was not advanced by such use of the civil service regulation. But the virtual decision was that Post Master General Burleson should draw up a paper to be presented to the cabinet embodying his views.

I presented the request of the naval board that the ships sent to Mexico should be returned so as to enable them to take part in the target practise off Hampton Roads about the 22nd. of March. It was the opinion of the President that, inasmuch as the ships were sent because of troubles, if withdrawn now, it would be construed as proof that the Government was satisfied because of present conditions. It is not satisfied and it was therefore determined that no order for their return be made.

Bound desk diary (J. Daniels Papers, DLC).

Viscount Sutemi Chinda to Baron Nobuaki Makino

1092　暗　華盛頓発　大正2年3月7日　后4・15
　　　　　本省着

牧野外務大臣

　　　　　　　　　　　　　　珍　田　大　使

第29号

（前略）次ニ大統領ハ常ニ日米ノ親交ヲ念トスル旨ヲ語レルニ付其ノ機会ニ乗シ本使ハ両国間ノ関係カ目下極メテ親善ナル状態ニ在ルヲ切言シ唯当国一部方面中今尚日本国ニ対スル誤見ヲ抱ク者アルハ本官ノ解スルニ苦シム所ニシテ従来日本側ニ在リテハ終始当国ニ好意ヲ有シ日本ノ桑港博覧会ニ参同ノ如キモ主トシテ国交ノ親善ヲ顧念スルノ意ニ外ナラサルニ拘ハラス太平洋沿岸ノ州議会ニ於テハ現ニ幾多排日ノ性質ヲ含ム法案ノ繋属スルアリ若シ此等法案ノ通過スル如キコトアレハ其ノ影響ノ重大ナルヘキヲ思ヒ深ク憂慮ナキ能ハス就テハ可成速カニ国務長官（「ダブリュー、ジー、ブライアン」）トモ面会シ篤ト本件ニ関スル意見ヲ交換シタキ考ナルモ大体ニ於テ新行政部モ従来ノ行政部ト同シク両国ノ親交ニ顧ミ適当ノ手段ヲ尽シテ排日法案ノ防止ニ努力セラレンコトヲ切望スル旨ヲ述ヘタルニ大統領ハ本使ノ所言ニ謝意ヲ表シ只当国々体上中央政府ハ各州ノ憲法上ノ権利ニ干渉スルコトヲ得サルモ米国政府ニ於テハ及フ限リノ勢力ヲ用テ本使ノ期待スル目的ノ為メニ斡旋スルコトヲ辞セスト答ヘタリ

Hw telegram (MT 3.8.2.274-2, pp. 103-106, JFO-Ar).

T R A N S L A T I O N

Confidential
No. 29.

Dispatched from Washington
to the Ministry of Foreign Affairs.
Received at 4:15 p.m. on March 7th,
in the 2nd year of Taisho [1913].

(Dispensing with the foregoing part) Then the President said that he had always concerned himself about friendly relations between Japan and the United States of America. I took this opportunity of presenting my argument as follows: Although I had no intention of denying that the two countries had enjoyed very good relations recently, I have difficulty understanding the reason why in some parts of this country there are some persons who have misunderstanding about Japan. Japan has always had good will toward the United States, and, in such cases as the San Francisco Exposition,[1] Japan took part in them in order to promote this friendly relationship. Nevertheless, many bills of an anti-Japanese character are being introduced in the state legislatures on the west coast.[2] I could not help worrying about the grave effects which these bills would produce if they were passed. Therefore I would like to meet the Secretary of State (W. G. Bryan) as soon as possible and have a full exchange of views regarding this matter. Finally, I urged the President as the new executive to have as much consideration for friendly relations between the two countries as his predecessors had had, and to devise an appropriate means of preventing the passage of these anti-Japanese bills. The President expressed his thanks for my statement and then answered that, although under the constitution of this country, the central government could not infringe upon the constitutional rights that each state enjoys, the American government will use all good offices in its power in behalf of the objective I had mentioned.

1 The Panama-Pacific International Exposition planned for 1915.
2 See WJB to WW, March 24, 1913

To Richard Olney

My dear Mr. Olney: The White House March 8, 1913

Thank you very much indeed for your kind letter!¹ I am delighted to learn that my Cabinet selections and my inaugural address have found such favor with you.

With an assurance of my deep appreciation of your congratulations and good wishes, pray believe me to be
        Cordially and sincerely yours,   Woodrow Wilson

I hope with all my heart that you will accept the offer of my
telegram²—for my heart is in it.   W.W.

TLS (R. Olney Papers, DLC).
  ¹ It is missing.
  ² See WW to R. Olney, March 10, 1913.

From the Diary of Colonel House

March 8, 1913.

The President asked me to be at the White House this morning at nine. The offices were nearly deserted at so early an hour.
The President was dressed in a very becoming sack suit of grey,
with a light grey silk tie. It was rather an informal looking cos-
tume, but very attractive. I sat with him for nearly an hour and
we had a delightful talk. We discussed the Cabinet mainly, and
he laughingly told me his estimate of each one and how they
acted at the first meeting. Burleson, he said, was the most constant talker and would have to be suppressed if he kept it up.
Houston, too, wanted to have his say. The President spoke finely
of Bryan and said their relations were exceedingly cordial, and
the only thing he was stubborn about was the appointment of
the Ambassador to Mexico. I then told him of Gregory's withdrawal and he seemed relieved. He wanted to know if there
was not something else we could do for Gregory. I was afraid not.
    I pointed out to the President how necessary it was for him
to have a man like John Bassett Moore in the State Department
with Mr. Bryan. He said Mr. Bryan was still insisting upon Governor Osborn as his Assistant. We both feel that it would be an
entirely unfit appointment, but I thought if John Bassett Moore
would take the place of Counsellor in that office it would go far
towards remedying the situation.
    I urged the President to be careful concerning the recom-
mendations Mr. Bryan made, because of his notoriously bad
judgment in regard to men.
    He asked if I knew a good man for Solicitor in the Agricul-
tural Department, someone who was able and honest and who
would enforce the pure food laws with intelligence and vigor. I
replied that Houston had asked me the same question the night
before, and that I had recommended Samuel Huston Thompson
Jr. of Denver. He remarked that Thompson was a republican. I

thought that did not matter, that he was fit for the place and that he supported him, the President, cordially.

We discussed whether it would be better for me to remain in Washington or to live elsewhere. That is in which way I could be more helpful. We agreed that I could be of more service to him if I remained away from Washington, than if I stayed there continually. We both realize that one soon becomes saturated with what might be termed the Washington viewpoint, and that everything is colored by that environment. So we concluded that I could be of more service if I should come to Washington whenever sent for, and keep in touch by telephone and letters.

The President suggested that we could have a cypher between us, so when we talked over the telephone or wrote we could discuss men without fear of revealing their identity. He took a pencil and started out with Bryan, whom he said "let us call him, Prime." McAdoo is already known as Pythias—McCombs being Damon. Garrison he suggested as "Mars," McReynolds "Coke," Burleson "Demosthenes," because he talked so much. Daniels he thought to call "Lion" on account of Daniel in the lions den, but I thought "Neptune" was better so we adopted that. "Alley" was the name he suggested for Lane, and Houston he called "Mansion." "Bluefields" seemed good for Redfield, and Wilson we called "Vulcan."[1]

I suggested very few of the nicknames, for the reason that I wanted to see how his mind was running in regard to his Cabinet, and I got some sort of bearing upon his estimate of them from these names.

[1] William Bauchop Wilson, Secretary of Labor. No documents relating to his appointment seem to be extant.

Charles Willis Thompson to Reuben Adiel Bull

My dear Rube: Washington, March 8, 13.

. . . I have put in the last three or four months at Princeton and Trenton, N. J. with a very amiable gentleman who is possessed with a quick temper. I have had several run-ins with him. Despite that little characteristic of his, I have taking an immense liking to him, and I believe that if he does not make a successful President of the United States it will be the fault of others rather than himself.

I have come to entertain a profound affection for Wilson, though I am still as red hot a Bull Moose as ever. He is so darned human, although you wouldn't think that when you first got acquainted with him. At first we fellows down there used to hate him, and I don't know how long it took to make us realize that he was right there with the goods. Why, you take his way of apologizing when he has done a man an injustice. He won't apologize. He flares up and says something nasty, and then spends the rest of the day brooding over it and kicking himself. He won't apologize, but the next time he sees that man he will go out of his way to say something nice to him just to make him feel good. That's the kind of man Woodrow is.

Then look at the way in which he takes care of the bunch that's been around with him. They charge him with ingratitude, but I never saw a man more punctilious about looking after the crowd. His chief telegraph operator in the White House is Jack Mendelson; his chief stenographer is Charlie Swem; his second stenographer is Warren Johnson,[1] and his secretary is Joe Tumulty, all of whom went through the campaign. But before he appointed them he made careful inquiries about whether he could get places for the persons whose jobs they were to take. Salome Tarr, the 18 year old girl who has been Swem's assistant, was bitterly disappointed when she found she couldn't come to the White House. What do you think the President did? At his first Cabinet meeting he devoted a large part of his time to instructing each one of the ten members of the cabinet to hunt through their departments with a fine tooth comb and find a job for Salome. Do you wonder that I am strong for him.

The last time we went to New York I printed a story to the effect that McCombs had gone to see him and criti[ci]zed some of his Cabinet slate. The story was dead true but they put a misleading head on it to the effect that he and McCombs quarrelled. The president read the head and not the story. The following morning when the bunch went over to Princeton Wilson looked for me, and not finding me, said "Where is the fictionist?" Then he followed that up with some pungent remark about liars who invent stories out of whole cloth and print them in newspapers. I got to Princeton several hours later and when I heard about it I decided it was all off between me and Wilson. It was hardly worth my while to go down to Washington with me [him]; that he would probably never speak to me again. That night the citizens of Princeton turned out 2,000 strong to give Wilson a loving cup with the usual accompaniments of red fire and brass band, and Wilson on a soap box making a speech. Without the slightest occasion for it, right during the middle of the ceremonies, Wilson suddenly turned from the Soap box to me, gave me the glad hand and a genial smile and said, "Mighty glad to see you here, Mr. Thompson, how are you." It was altogether uncalled for and just his way of showing that he was sorry he said a lot of mean things about me in the morning. I want to tell you Rube that this President we've got is one of the most human propositions I ever went up against. . . .

Ever yours   [Chas.].

CCL (C. W. Thompson Papers, NjP).

[1] Warren Forman Johnson, "correspondent" on the White House staff, who served mainly as Tumulty's secretary.

To Mary Allen Hulbert

Dearest Friend,   The White House 9 March, 1913

The first week here has come to a close; the first novelty and excitement has worn off; we are beginning to look about us and take our bearings like those who have accepted the situation and come to stay; and at last, with the comparative quiet of Sunday, has come the opportunity, for which I have waited with such impatience, to write to my dear, dear friend of whom I have thought so often the days through,—and for whose happiness I pray every night of my life with a depth of earnestness and anxiety which I am sure even she cannot realize. How *real* the dear friendship seems that has grown up between us, and how your pain and travail of spirit has seemed to deepen and intensify it! As events and distractions thicken about me, *that* seems to grow more distinct, more permanent, more real, like a verdant isle in the midst of shifting seas,—a place to rest up, and from which to look forth with reassurance, with freshened spirits, with a heart made stout and calm again! If only it could seem the same to *you* and give you rest and peace! It *will*, I am sure. You have not got your bearings yet, since the dear lady, upon whom you used, I think unconsciously, to lean, was taken away. How self-confident and unconquerably strong you used to seem as you fought the days through when I first met you! It was all so complex, and you were so surrounded with tasks and difficulties. And now it is all so simple, all reduced to a single situation, with Allen at the centre, and the problem for you is only watchfulness and endurance,—an understanding heart, sympathy, patience (oh, so *much* patience!) and no action (for you, who are so used to action and so fitted for it) until an occasion come which you cannot anticipate or prepare for! Courage, dear lady, courage of the new kind, in quietness and waiting! We are with you in thought and in prayer—comprehending always.

All goes well with us. What I have done, and the men I have

chosen are approved with most unusual cordiality and accord. God give me a clear head, good counsellors, and a pure heart; and bless all the dear people who, like yourself, hearten and support and dignify me with your confidence and affection. All join in love. Love to Allen.

Your devoted friend   Woodrow Wilson

ALS (WP, DLC).

To Richard Olney

The White House March 10, 1913

May I not have the very great pleasure of proposing your name to the Senate and to the Court of St. James as Ambassador to Great Britain? The party would be deeply gratified, the country honored, and I myself greatly strengthened.

Woodrow Wilson

T telegram (WP, DLC).

To Henry Burchard Fine

My dear Harry: [The White House] March 10, 1913

I am sending you a cable today[1] which refers to this letter.

I have consulted with Mr. Bryan, who cordially concurs with me in the desire that you should remain in Germany as Ambassador from the United States, and I drop you this line to tell you that in a recent talk with Cleve Dodge he said, in his characteristic generous way, that he very much desired, if you thought that the salary of the post would be insufficient for your proper support, to supplement it, if necessary, up to fifteen or twenty thousand dollars a year. You know how genuine this offer is, and it makes me happy to transmit it.

In haste   Affectionately yours,   Woodrow Wilson

TLS (Letterpress Books, WP, DLC).
[1] WW to H. B. Fine, March 10, 1913, T telegram (Letterpress Books, WP, DLC).

To Cleveland Hoadley Dodge

The White House March 10, 1913

Feel it imperatively necessary Mott should go to China.[1] Can you not bring proper pressure to bear on him from his most influential friends? I do not know where else to turn.

Woodrow Wilson.

T telegram (WP, DLC).
[1] Mott had just declined the Chinese post in a telegram which is missing.

From Cleveland Hoadley Dodge

Douglas, Ariz., March 10, 1913.

Telegram received. Will do my best. Have telegraphed Jenkins[1] to see Halsey and others confidentially and obtain their assistance and to cable Mott you will not accept his decision and consider imperative he accept and urging him in name of myself and others to reconsider and reply direct to Jenkins who can communicate promptly to you. Have further asked Jenkins to consult you if necessary and send you copy of message sent. I will be New York twentieth.   Cleveland H. Dodge.

T telegram (WP, DLC).
[1] Edward Corbin Jenkins, Mott's secretary.

From Richard Olney

PRIVATE AND CONFIDENTIAL.

My dear Mr. President,   Boston, 10 March, 1913

Your telegram is received and I am quite overcome by the great honor you suggest doing me and by the very complimentary terms in which you express your offer.

Yet, in fairness to my family and myself and in justice to the administration and you, I must take a brief time to consider whether I ought to undertake the responsibilities of so great an office as those involved in becoming the American Ambassador in London.

I will give you a definite answer by the end of the week. If you ought to have it earlier, I will answer at any time you may suggest.

With thanks for your kind consideration, I am
                    Very sincerely yours,   Richard Olney

TLS (WP, DLC).

To Richard Olney

My dear Mr. Olney: The White House March 11, 1913

It rejoices me that you are willing to consider the invitation I took the liberty of sending you by telegraph, and I am happy to say there is no such hurry about your decision as would make it necessary for you to let me know your conclusion before the end of the week.

May I not add as urgently as possible my strong hope that you will see your way to accept? The post is most difficult to fill and you are the only man Mr. Bryan and I have had in our thoughts who would ideally satisfy the requirements of the post. I feel that it is of the utmost consequence to the country and to the party that you should accept.

With apologies for this urgency, which is prompted by my full knowledge of the case, I am

Cordially and sincerely yours,   Woodrow Wilson

TLS (R. Olney Papers, DLC).

From Henry Burchard Fine

Muenchen, March 11, 1913.

Heartiest thanks, but cannot accept. Am writing.

Harry.

T telegram (WP, DLC).

To Henry Burchard Fine

The White House March 11, 1913

Do not decide until letter reaches you.

Woodrow Wilson

T telegram (WP, DLC).

From the Diary of Josephus Daniels

March Tues 11 1913

The cabinet devoted the day to consideration of a letter or statement presented by the President outlining the policy of the administration with reference to Central and South American states. During the campaign, there grew up a feeling in some of those countries that a Democratic victory would be hailed by those seeking to foment revolution as an encouragement. The President and Secretary of State thought it necessary to make a statement. All were agreed. The point of difference was as to whether the statement should be delivered to the official representatives of those countries or whether it should be given to the press. It was suggested that it would not be appreciated by those countries having stable governments, and if sent to those only where revolutions were imminent or where there were troubles, those countries would be offended by being singled out. The importance of making known this country's attitude known [sic] as encouraging stable government where it is based on the consent of the governed was stressed by the President, whose original idea was to send the declaration to official representatives. After a discussion of nearly two hours, it was unanimously agreed that the President should give it out to the press in a way to make it authoritative and impressive. It is a singularly clear and uniform declaration and is as follows: (Insert here)[1]

This statement will do much good and ought to stop those who foment troubles for personal aggrandizement in the hope of America winking at revolution or holding hands off.

Bound desk diary (J. Daniels Papers, DLC).
  [1] There is no insertion in this entry.

Count Johann Heinrich von Bernstorff[1] to Theobald von Bethmann Hollweg[2]

Washington, den 11. März 1913.

Gestern wurde das hiesige Diplomatische Corps in corpore am Vormittage von Staatssekretär Bryan und am Nachmittage von Präsident Wilson empfangen.

Nachdem Herr Bryan jedem von uns mit einigen freundlichen Worten die Hand gedrückt hatte, hielt er eine kleine Rede, in welcher er sagte, daß es ihn besonders gefreut habe, das Staatsdepartement zu übernehmen, weil er dadurch Gelegenheit zu haben hoffe, die Beziehungen der Vereinigten Staaten zu allen fremden Ländern noch freundlicher als bisher zu gestalten. Zu einer solchen Politik des Friedens seien die Vereinigten Staaten vielleicht mehr als irgend eine andere Macht befähigt, weil sie weder durch Bündnisse noch durch nachbarliche Interessen-Gegensätze in einer bestimmten Richtung festgelegt seien. Zum Schluß sprach Herr Bryan den Wunsch aus, daß wir uns in jeder auftauchenden Frage persönlich an ihn wenden möchten. Der französische Botschafter[3] antwortete als Doyen in wenigen allgemeinen Worten. Das erste Auftreten Herrn Bryans als Staatssekretär machte auf mich und sämtliche Kollegen, mit denen ich sprach, einen günstigen Eindruck. Er scheint zugänglicher sein zu wollen als sein Amtsvorgänger, welcher für das Ausland bekanntlich ein sehr geringes Interesse hatte.

Der Empfang bei dem Präsidenten spielte sich in der gleichen Weise ab mit der Ausnahme, daß Herr Wilson eine viel kürzere Rede hielt, die keine Antwort des Doyens erforderlich machte. Als der Präsident mich begrüßte, sprach ich ihm meinen allgemeinen Instruktionen gemäß in [im] Namen der Kaiserlichen Regierung die aufrichtigsten Gratulationen zu seinem Amtsantritte aus sowie die besten Wünsche für seine Administration, wofür er herzlichst dankte.

Morgen Nachmittag wird das ganze Diplomatische Corps mit Damen einer Einladung von Mrs. Wilson zum Tee Folge leisten, um bei dieser Gelegenheit mit den neuen Kabinettsmitgliedern und deren Damen zusammenzutreffen.

Bernstorff

TLS (Dept. I A, USA No. 11: The President, Vol. 21, GFO-Ar).
[1] German Ambassador to the United States, 1908-17.
[2] Imperial German Chancellor, 1909-17.
[3] Jean Jules Jusserand, French Ambassador to the United States, 1902-25.

T R A N S L A T I O N

Washington, March 11, 1913.

Yesterday the Diplomatic Corps in this country was welcomed in a body in the forenoon by Secretary of State Bryan and in the afternoon by President Wilson.

After Mr. Bryan, with a few friendly words, had shaken the hand of each of us he made a little speech in which he said that he was especially happy to take charge of the State Department because he hoped thereby to have the opportunity to make the relations of the United States with all foreign countries even friendlier than heretofore. The United States probably would qualify for such a policy of peace more than any other power because she is not committed to a fixed course either through alliances or things that conflict with neighborly relations. At the end, Mr. Bryan expressed the wish that we might turn to him personally in any question that arises. The French Ambassador, as the dean, answered in a few general words. Mr. Bryan's first appearance as Secretary of State made a favorable impression on me and all colleagues with whom I spoke. He appears to want to be more approachable than his predecessor who, as is well known, had little interest in foreign countries.

The reception by the President went in a similar manner with the exception that Mr. Wilson gave a much shorter speech, which made unnecessary an answer by the dean. When the President greeted me, in accordance with my general instructions, I offered him, in the name of the Imperial Government, most sincere congratulations on his assuming office, as well as best wishes for his administration, for which he heartily thanked me.

Tomorrow afternoon the whole Diplomatic Corps with wives will accept from Mrs. Wilson an invitation to tea in order to meet with the new Cabinet members and their wives on this occasion.   Bernstorff

A Statement on Relations with Latin America

March 12, 1913.

In view of questions which are naturally uppermost in the public mind just now, the President issued the following statement:

One of the chief objects of my administration will be to cultivate the friendship and deserve the confidence of our sister republics of Central and South America, and to promote in every proper and honorable way the interests which are common to the peoples of the two continents. I earnestly desire the most cordial understanding and cooperation between the peoples and leaders of America and, therefore, deem it my duty to make this brief statement.

Cooperation is possible only when supported at every turn by the orderly processes of just government based upon law, not upon arbitrary or irregular force. We hold, as I am sure all thoughtful leaders of republican government everywhere hold, that just government rests always upon the consent of the governed, and that there can be no freedom without order based upon law and upon the public conscience and approval. We shall look to make these principles the basis of mutual intercourse, respect, and helpfulness between our sister republics and ourselves. We shall lend our influence of every kind to the realization of these principles in fact and practice, knowing that disorder, personal intrigue and defiance of constitutional rights weaken and discredit government and injure none so much as the people who are unfortunate enough to have their common life and their common affairs so tainted and disturbed. We can have no sympathy with those who seek to seize the power of government to advance their own personal interests or ambition. We are the friends of peace, but we know that there can be no lasting or stable peace in such circumstances. As friends, therefore, we shall prefer those who act in the interest of peace and honor, who protect private rights and respect the restraints of constitutional provision. Mutual respect seems to us the indispensable foundation of friendship between states, as between individuals.

The United States has nothing to seek in Central and South America except the lasting interests of the peoples of the two continents, the security of governments intended for the people and for no special group or interest, and the development of personal and trade relationships between the two continents which shall redound to the profit and advantage of both and interfere with the rights and liberties of neither.

From these principles may be read so much of the future policy of this government as it is necessary now to forecast; and in the spirit of these principles I may, I hope, be permitted with as much confidence as earnestness to extend to the governments of all the republics of America the hand of genuine disinterested friendship and to pledge my own honor and the honor of my colleagues to every enterprise of peace and amity that a fortunate future may disclose.[1]

T MS (Letterpress Books, WP, DLC).
[1] There is a WWsh draft of this statement and a CLST draft with WWhw emendations in WP, DLC.

From Henry Burchard Fine[1]

My dear Tommy:　　　　　　　　　　Munich, March 12, 1913.

Your letter of Feb. 24th[2] reached me on Sunday Mar. 9th. Yesterday came your cablegram of March 10th to which I cabled a reply and then began a letter which was not finished when your second cablegram arrived asking me not to decide until letter reached me.

I can not express the pleasure I felt that you should think me the proper man for so important and distinguished a post as the German Ambassadorship and that you should desire me to fill it. In making me the offer you have paid me one of the greatest compliments it is in the power of the President to pay one of his fellow citizens and you do not need to be assured that I appreciate it and am gratified to you for it.

But while I shall consider your letter with an open mind when it arrives the reasons against my accepting the appointment now seem to me so weighty that I doubt whether I can arrive at any other conclusion than the one already cabled you.

In the first place, I am convinced that you can find a better man than I for the post. All that can be said for me is that I am a scholar of some reputation in a field rather remote from general human interests, that I possess a fair amount of judgment and tact, and that in university work I have shown good administrative ability. I have had no training in statecraft and have no real knowledge of jurisprudence, economics or international law. My German, on which I fear you may have reckoned, answers well enough for conversational purposes, but would not show to advantage in public speech.

Again, while I do not know the salary attaching to this ambassadorship, I have often heard that it is insufficient to meet the requirements of the representative of the American Government

in such a European capitol as Berlin, even when these requirements in mode of life, entertaining, and so on, are reduced to
terms as simple as it is reasonable to make them. If my understanding of these conditions be correct, I can not financially afford to be the Ambassador.

Nor can I afford to resign my Princeton professorship which
carries with it an assured income for life to accept such an appointment. But would it not be necessary for me to resign the
professorship if I did accept the appointment? The trustees of
Princeton might be willing to grant me leave of absence for a
brief period, but to ask them to hold my professorship open for a
period long enough to enable me to render any real service at
Berlin would be unreasonable.

And finally, and this is the chief consideration, so far as the
question of my own personal happiness is concerned, I am more
deeply interested in mathematics than in anything else. To be
compelled to terminate my career as a mathematician would be
to me a catastrophy. To interrupt it for a few years to enter upon
a life which seems to me too full of social obligations to be attractive and my fitness for which I regard as problematical is a step
which I could only be persuaded to take from a sense of duty. And
I can not imagine any public service which I am better qualified
to render, as ambassador to Germany, than other men whom you
could appoint.

I have stated the case as it now lies in my mind. When I have
read your letter it is possible that I may feel differently. At all
events I shall think the whole question out again in the light
of what you say before cabling you my final decision.

I can not conclude this letter, full as it is of myself, without
telling you how proud we all are of the magnificent way in which
you have begun your administration.

With love from us all to you all, as ever,
Sincerely yours,   Henry B. Fine.

TCL (WP, DLC).
[1] Wilson did not receive this letter until about March 25, 1913.
[2] It is missing.

From the Diary of Josephus Daniels

March Wed 12 1913

The cabinet held its longest session to-day. It was called at the
request of the Secretary of State to discuss the question of the
Chinese loan. The European powers had agreed to furnish the
new Republic of China money to pay its army and indebtedness
upon condition that the money should be disbursed by or under

the direction of the foreign governments. A group of American bankers, including what is known as the banker's trust, had stated to the Secretary of State that if requested by the administration they might take that portion of the loan allotted to this country. One of the stipulations made by those offering to make the loan was that if China wished to borrow more money it could be borrowed only from those making this loan. The Taft administration had approved the plan.[1] The matter was discussed two hours, and was opened by Mr. Bryan who luminously stated the objections to the plan. The Secretary of the Treasury thought we could not agree to request the banker's trust to subscribe to the loan. Secretary Lane, who had made a long study of Chinese affairs, thought it would be a mistake to approve this old time favoritism method after China had declared for new ways, and that this country should not be a party to helping China upon condition that it should be beholden to a group of financiers in the biggest nations. Secy Redfield feared if we failed to help in some proper way, the loan would be made by the other nations, and America would lose the chance for building up a large trade. My idea was that we ought to find some way for this Government to help China coupled with the recognition of the Republic of China. The President was clear in his conviction that we could not request the trust group of bankers to effect the loan, and that we ought to help China in some better way. It was decided that the President should draw up a statement to be presented at the next meeting of the cabinet.

Bound desk diary (J. Daniels Papers, DLC).
[1] About this matter, see Tien-yi Li, *Woodrow Wilson's China Policy, 1913-1917* (New York, 1952), pp. 24-48; Roy Watson Curry, *Woodrow Wilson and Far Eastern Policy, 1913-1921* (New York, 1957), pp. 18-27; and A. Whitney Griswold, *The Far Eastern Policy of the United States* (New York, 1938), pp. 133-75.

To John R. Mott

The White House March 13, 1913

Beg that you will await advises before confirming decision communicated through Dodge.   Woodrow Wilson

T telegram (WP, DLC).

To Henry Burchard Fine

The White House March 13, 1913

Dodge desires to supplement salary up to fifteen or twenty thousand. Hope that will make a difference in your conclusion.
          Woodrow Wilson

T telegram (Letterpress Books, WP, DLC).

From Richard Olney

PRIVATE & CONFIDENTIAL

Dear Mr. President,   Boston, 13 March, 1913

I have anxiously considered accepting the English mission. The temptation to service under your administration is very great and severely tests my self-restraint.

But there are obstacles of a personal and family nature, which I will not trouble you with but which are serious, and in view particularly of the necessary residence abroad, are not to be ignored. They force me to the conclusion that I am not warranted in making the experiment of assuming the duties and responsibilities of the office you so kindly and persuasively tender. In the nature of things it *would* be an experiment, with the chances largely against success. I am unwilling to subject to any chances an administration which promises, and I believe will accomplish, so much for the country's lasting welfare.

With the highest appreciation of the honor done me by your proposal, and with infinite regret that I cannot reach any other result than that above indicated, I am

                    Sincerely yours,   Richard Olney

TLS (WP, DLC).

From Joseph H. Stewart[1]

Mr. President: Washington, D. C. March 13, 1913.

We congratulate you for your splendid Inaugural Address. It is teeming with expressions of justice and equal rights for each and every citizen. It expresses the ideals of equal rights as conceived by the founders of our Government. Being representatives of that class of American citizens who are habitually controlled by the forms and practices of the slavery of the past, we rejoice in your grand expressions of equal rights for every citizen. We assure you, Mr. President, of our activity and help in aiding you to make those noble sentiments of justice delivered by you on March 4th, 1913, a practical realization among the citizens of our great and grand country. No citizens are more patriotic and no citizens are more true and loyal to the stars and stripes than those we represent and we will always be willing and ready with whatever power we possess to uphold the equal rights of the citizens so well announced by you.

We thank you, Mr. President, for this interview[2] and we hope that your administration will go down in history as one of the best in the United States of America.

Respectfully,   Joseph H. Stewart

TLS (WP, DLC).
¹ Secretary of the National Negro Democratic League, organized in 1886.
² Wilson received a committee of the National Negro Democratic League at the White House on March 14.

To Richard Olney

My dear Mr. Olney: The White House March 14, 1913

I am genuinely grieved that you find it necessary to decline the British mission. I had set my heart upon it, as had everyone else with whom I had consulted, and I turn with the greatest reluctance away from what would have been an ideal appointment.

I do not feel like debating with you a matter which, of course, lies clearer to your mind than it possibly can to mine, but I do want to express my very deep and sincere regret and my cordial personal regard.

Faithfully and sincerely yours,   Woodrow Wilson

TLS (R. Olney Papers, DLC).

To Oscar Wilder Underwood

My dear Mr. Underwood: The White House March 14, 1913

Would you be kind enough to have prepared for me, so that I may have it at the same time with the tariff bill, a conspectus of the importations under the present tariff?

If it does not involve too much labor, I should like to have a table showing the estimated proportion of the importations under each schedule to the domestic production and consumption of the several articles.

Perhaps you will see what I am driving at: I want something that will enable me to tell how far competitive conditions already exist.

Hoping that this will not carry your clerical force beyond what they have already in hand, I am

Cordially and faithfully yours,   Woodrow Wilson

TLS (O. W. Underwood Papers, A-Ar).

From William Eaton Chandler[1]

Washington, D. C.,
March 14, 1913.

My dear Mr. President Wilson:

The New Hampshire legislature having elected a Democratic Senator, Hon. Henry F. Hollis, will now be anxious to adjourn. It ought not to do so without passing, of the "Seven Sisters" bills, at least the first of the series, that which defines trusts and provides criminal penalties for the destruction of free competition. As a Republican I have considered that bill and am in favor of its adoption in New Hampshire. I notice that you say the election of Mr. Hollis was a good thing. It will also be a good thing if you use your reasonable influence with the Democratic Senator, Governor and Members of the Legislature in favor of the passage of the bill above mentioned.

There is no time to lose.

I make the suggestion in the spirit shown in the Journal-Transcript of Franklin, N. H., whose editor, Mr. Omar A. Towne, says:

"The difference between the two great parties today is not one of principle. Time was when this was different, and that was the time for men to fight strenuously for their principles. Today the great majority desire only what is best for the country, and their faith in a man of the character of President Wilson leads men to trust him as one who will endeavor to do what is right."

I concur in the desire above expressed.

Very truly yours,   Wm. E. Chandler

TLS (J. P. Tumulty Papers, DLC).
[1] Former Secretary of the Navy and Republican Senator from New Hampshire.

To Eugene Elliott Reed

My dear Mr. Reed: [The White House] March 14, 1913

I need not tell you how deeply gratified I have been by the action of the New Hampshire Legislature in electing Mr. Hollis Senator. But apparently it is not permitted progressives to be satisfied with anything, and I am writing to urge that you will use your utmost influence with the powers that be in the state government to push forward the pending legislation with regard to corporations, particularly that legislation modeled upon the statutes we have just so successfully put through in New Jersey. I feel that it is distinctly in the line of Democratic principle and practice that the states should undertake legislation of this kind, and I am very glad to see New Hampshire one of those that lead the way.[1]

If you could point out to me any proper way in which I may use my influence in this matter, I should be very glad indeed to take your lead.[2]

In haste

Cordially and sincerely yours,   Woodrow Wilson

TLS (Letterpress Books, WP, DLC).
 [1] Wilson mistakenly inferred from Chandler's letter that antitrust legislation was pending in the New Hampshire legislature. That body did not consider or adopt any such legislation in 1913.
 [2] If Reed replied, his letter is missing.

From Edward Corbin Jenkins

Mr. President: New York March 14, 1913.

Mr. C. H. Dodge has telegraphed me to aid in bringing additional influence to bear upon Mr. Mott to accept the position. I had already suggested to him that if any further pressure was needed, though your own and Mr. Dodge's words can hardly be supplemented, I would mention Mr. Cyrus McCormick, Mr. C. R. Crane, Dr. James L. Barton,[1] secretary of the American Board, and Professor J. W. Jenks[2] as those who would probably count for most.

I can follow Mr. Dodge's suggestions with reference to seeing Mr. McCormick and Dr. Barton, unless you prefer that I do not do so, and I myself can talk freely with Professor Jenks, if you think wise. Mr. Dodge suggests that you perhaps could influence Mr. Crane. Though deeply regretting to trouble you, I do not like to make moves that may be blunders.

Messages from these men can be sent to me here, coded, and thence forwarded or they can be sent in plain language, deferred service, as follows:

Committee, Shanghai

Mott. * * *

I should be glad of a brief word from you as to whether you desire to modify in any way these suggestions.

Respectfully,   Edward C. Jenkins.

ALS (WP, DLC).
 [1] James Levi Barton, foreign secretary of the American Board of Commissioners for Foreign Missions (Congregational) since 1894.
 [2] Jeremiah Whipple Jenks, Professor of Government and Public Administration at New York University. He served on numerous federal commissions on labor affairs, immigration, and economics; authority on currency reform in China; prolific author of works on economic, political, and social subjects.

From Samuel Gompers

Sir: Washington, D. C., March 14, 1913.

Since current discussion of the past few days has been largely upon a matter of vital importance to many millions of people whose welfare has been entrusted to your keeping, and since the newspaper press is undertaking to place you in a position before the public entirely at variance with the contentions of Labor, thereon, there rests upon me an imperative duty not only to those upon whom the dead weight and burden of industry have ever fallen, but to you, that there may be avoided your being placed in apparent opposition to Labor's contentions without having had them fully and completely presented for your consideration.

The matter to which I refer was embodied in an amendment, proposed by Congressman Hughes, of New Jersey, on June 2, 1910, to a section of the Sundry Civil Appropriation bill for the year 1911, and which amendment was later proposed by Representative Hamill of New Jersey to the bill (H.R. 28775) entitled: "An Act making appropriations for the sundry civil expenses of the Government for the fiscal year ending June 30, 1914, and for other purposes." The amendment in both instances reads as follows:

"Provided, however, That no part of this money shall be expended in the prosecution of any organization or individual for entering into any combination or agreement having in view the increase of wages, the shortening of hours, or bettering the condition of labor, or for any act done in furtherance thereof, NOT IN ITSELF UNLAWFUL."

The bill was adopted by both houses of Congress, but vetoed by President Taft.

I am addressing you to explain briefly why the workingmen demand as a matter of social justice and humanity that they be given relief from possible prosecution by the Department of Justice for acts not in themselves unlawful and to protect you from possible embarrassment that might result from only partial presentation of the legislation and that from the viewpoint of those opposed to Labor.

Owing to circumstances entirely beyond my control, I have been unable to request an interview with you for the presentation of the matter, even though you might have been in a position to accord it to me. By reason of the responsibility and the importance of the subject which I am discussing in this letter, I ask that you will overlook its length.

The history of those who toil has been one of pathos and bitter struggle, one of great suffering and indomitable courage. In the earlier centuries the toilers were compelled to work at the will or caprice of masters who owned their bodies and their labor power; living beings with human hearts and brains were legally and socially rated as things, property. As a result of the Barbarian Invasions that overturned the social, economic and political institutions of Europe and produced feudalism, it was expedient that changes be made in conditions of the workers— they were made serfs and villeins. Although their bodies were made free, the overlord retained an ownership in their labor power. From this status, this semi-thraldom, the workers struggled to secure more definite and more advantageous terms affecting the services they owed, until finally they reached the level of freedom of contract.

Yet liberty, equality in justice, equal opportunity, had then not been won, nor is it yet assured to those who have always been the oppressed, wherever or whenever oppression exists. They had no voice or influence in determining the laws of the land, or in selecting the administrative agents who made them effective. The laws of the land had been made by those whose interests, environment, experiences, in no way touched the world of the workers; political and judicial theories, precedents, were in accord with the convictions and viewpoint of the controlling classes; intellectual life and interests were isolated from the work-a-day world; ethical and moral standards were as yet untouched by enlightened and merciful humanitarianism. It was the task of the workers to present their pleas and conceptions of justice so that established practices and standards might be broadened to include the welfare of all the people. This was the task laid upon untutored, undisciplined workers. Opposed to them were the keenest, most subtle forces vested interests could retain. Each forward step was fiercely contested. The controlling interests would not abandon its special privileges even when once lost, but sought to regain them by circumvention, sophistry, and legal chicanery.

As you know, the law is a product of two elements—the imperative and the traditional. Most of our difficulties have arisen through the second element. Precedents and judicial interpretation determined by the individual bias of the judge or by the prevailing economic and political philosophy, have been obstacles to the adoption of newer ideals of justice and to the shifting of standards to suit changing conditions.

These are some of the difficulties which we workers of today inherit from the past ages. They explain why the workers of today have to combat legal and economic theories which accord to employers certain rights to labor power, and why greater consideration has been paid to safeguarding wealth than to safeguarding the freedom of the men who help to create that wealth. The workingmen of our country ask most seriously and solemnly whether it is just that property be hedged about by inviolable sanctity, while they are denied normal activities in furtherance of the interests of human beings.

When feudal regulation of labor conditions was broken down by the disturbances resulting from the Black Death, a system of State regulation was inaugurated. This was never very effective and completely failed under the changes set up by the Industrial Revolution. With the coming of the factory system individual relations became ineffective, obsolete and powerless to protect the interests and lives of the workers. Collective action by workmen in furtherance of their own interests as opposed to those of the employers was legislated against as "conspiracies." The old political and economic theories of justice considered that employes had no right to withhold labor power necessary to the operation of the employer's business—the influence of the former periods when workmen were the master's property. We, in our country, inherit many of the problems and theories from the old country, and some are of our own making. It took years to secure relief from the old conspiracy laws which curbed and restricted the workers in protecting and promoting their industrial rights and interests. When at last it seemed that efforts of the toilers were to be rewarded, then the Supreme Court of the United States, by an interpretation which amounted to judicial legislation, applied the Sherman Anti-Trust Law to trade unions in a way which virtually revived the conspiracy laws.

When the court applied the Sherman Anti-Trust law to labor organizations, it created an offense never intended by the makers of that law. As has been repeated again and again, but never refuted, as an investigation of the Congressional Record will prove, the men who drafted the Sherman Anti-Trust Act, Senators Sherman, Edmunds and George, did not intend that it should apply to organizations instituted not for profit. On March 25, 1890, when the bill was before the Senate, Senator Sherman insisted upon the following amendment:

"Provided, that this act shall not be construed to apply to any arrangements, agreements, or combinations between laborers, made with a view to lessening the number of hours of labor or the increasing of their wages; nor to any arrangements, agreements, or combinations among persons engaged in horticulture or agriculture, made with a view of enhancing the price of their own agricultural or horticultural products."

Senators George and Edmunds did not oppose the amendment, but regarded it as surplusage. The amendment was agreed to while the Senate was sitting in Committee of the whole. On March 26, when the bill came up again for consideration, Senator Stewart of Nevada said:

"The original bill has been very much improved and one of the great objections has been removed from it by the amendment offered by Senator Sherman which relieves the class of persons who would have been first under the prosecution under the original bill without amendment * * * The bill ought now to be satisfactory to every person who is opposed to the oppression of Labor and desires to see it properly rewarded."

In advocating the amendment Senator Hoar said in part:

"I hold we may constitutionally and wisely allow laborers to make associations * * * for the sake of maintaining and advancing their wages * * * their contracts are made with corporations who are but associations or combinations of capital on the other side. When we are promoting and even encouraging that we are encouraging what is not only lawful, wise and profitable, but absolutely essential to the existence of the commonwealth itself."

Afterwards the bill was referred to the Committee on the Judiciary, where the amendment was suppressed.

Because of the failure to include this amendment in the law, organized labor was always apprehensive that attempts would be made to pervert the act from its real purpose. Nor were we mistaken, and that is why we now seek legislative relief that organized labor may not be prohibited from doing things "not in themselves unlawful."

That which we seek is not class legislation. It is a common custom in speaking to couple together the words "labor and capital," as though they stood for things of similar natures. Capital stands for material, tangible things, things separate and distinct from personality; labor is a human attribute, indissolubly bound up with the human body. It is that by which man expresses the thought, the purpose, the self that is his own individuality; if he is a free man, he has the right to control this means of self-expression. This he values above all, for if he lose this right to decide the granting or withholding of his own labor, then freedom ceases and slavery begins.

Under the present industrial order, the individual working man is unable to maintain his right of self-assertion unaided, hence the workers instituted organizations, and have banded together to secure for themselves wider freedom of action. To classify these combinations, not for profit, and without capital stock, in the same category with corporations, trusts and monopolies, is forcing an indefensible classification and grouping together things not of the same nature.

The associations of working people, commonly known as labor unions, are dealing not with property, material things, but with labor power alone, with lives, happiness, rights and welfare of men, women and children. They are striving for the uplift and conservation of the nation itself.

The corporations, trusts and monopolies aim to create monopoly conditions, to manipulate capital and production to secure monopoly profits. It is most unjust to try to co-ordinate these two inherently different kinds of organizations and to apply to them similar regulations. Justice does not necessarily result from the application of identical provisions to all people. On the contrary, it works injustice if the conditions are dissim[i]lar and the people unequally situated. Theoretical justice only becomes real justice when the men as well as the deeds are taken into consideration.

It is impossible to legislate equitably for labor and capital under the same law. Certainly it is not class legislation to make different provisions for two things inherently different, aiming at different purposes and employing different methods. The provisions of no law will admit of universal indiscriminate application.

This is no "special privilege" or "exemption" that organized labor has been asking. Our demand for justice is that working men and their organizations shall not be prosecuted for entering into any combination or agreement having in view the increasing of wages, the shortening of hours, or the bettering of conditions of labor, or for any act done in furtherance thereof "NOT IN ITSELF UNLAWFUL."

Your attention is respectfully and particularly called to those last four words that have been so persistently and unfairly suppressed by the press and our opponents. We are not seeking to be permitted to do unlawful acts, but are demanding that the rights of which we have been deprived by judicial interpretation be restored to us. We are not asking to be "exempt" from the application of a law of a law [sic] which properly applies to labor organizations as well as to other voluntary associations organized not for profit, but we are asking that inherent differences that exist be recognized by the laws and the courts as well as by reason.

The mere fact that a law or a legal precedent exists, does not necessarily imply that it works justice. Oppression and wrong may become established, and under the cloak of authority and regularity take on a prestige and a sanctity usually ascribed to accepted rules of justice. These are the insidious forces that have fought labor under the guise of conspiracy laws, and now seek to accomplish their purpose by interpreting the Sherman Anti-Trust law as a modernized conspiracy act.

Those rights which we wish restored are rights necessary to conducting the normal activities of labor organizations. Labor organizations are formed to protect the workers and their rights against the cupidity of employers and combinations of employers dealing in the products created by labor power. The right to strike, to withhold labor power, is essential to the maintenance of the freedom of the workers. It would be impossible to retain present advantages, or to increase wages or better conditions of work without the right or the power to strike, not only as individuals but as organizations. Organized labor does not advocate strikes. On the contrary we deplore the necessity for them, but we know, and we know from actual experience, how powerless and helpless workmen would be to protect themselves without the right and the power to strike. To make acts in furtherance of these purposes either enjoinable or punishable both by fines and imprisonment takes from organized labor that which gives it virility and effectiveness.

The men and the organizations that have instituted suits against labor unions under this law, the methods that have been employed and the charges made, make it manifest beyond a doubt that the purpose of the prosecutions is not to prevent restraint of trade or competition, but to disrupt or make ineffective labor organizations.

Those who have been out in the ditches, the factories, in the grinding toil of modern industry, know what the labor movement has done for human progress and welfare. Those who work for the Steel Corporations, the Tobacco Trust, know what it is to deal with organized employers without collective self-protection. In the light of these facts, which you well know, would it not be well to consider seriously whether or not this fear of alleged "conspiracy" of labor associations should be allowed to prevent an effort to arrive at standards of justice that do not sacrifice human rights to the right to conduct business?

Peaceful, rightful attempts to secure advantages for labor have been deemed "combinations in restraint of trade." The workingmen's Amalgamated Council of New Orleans struck to

induce the employers to employ none but union labor—a purpose
certainly not in restraint of trade. No violence was charged,
and yet the court ruled "the defendants were in restraint of trade."
In the case of Loewe vs. Lawlor, it was offered and accepted
as evidence of "conspiracy" that out of 82 manufacturers of hats
in the United States, 70 were in agreement with the union of hat
makers to maintain the highest standards of wages and other
labor conditions. Is it any wonder that the men of labor have
been forced to the conclusion that judicial interpretation of conspiracy is synonymous with successful hostility to the humaniz-
ing conditions of unionism? It is absurd to argue that activities
of organized labor are intended to destroy or injure business;
such a result would defeat the very purpose they have in view.

Even should the activities of labor organizations be right-
fully classified as conspiracies, has not the time come when it
must be considered whether these "conspiracies" of organized
labor do not do more to further the advancement of humanity and
national welfare than the property interests which have been
heretofore carefully safeguarded? It is no man of straw that we
fear in the application of the Sherman Anti-Trust law to organized labor. While it is unthinkable that the organized labor movement could be crushed out of existence, yet the repression of
normal activities, rousing of resentment at injustice among the
workers, denial to them of legal methods of redress, would lead
to situations and conditions which thoughtful, patriotic citizens
could not consider without dread.

This struggle of the working people to secure individual rights
and liberty has not been confined to our own country. In England
the same problems have been confronted and solved. In 1824
Parliament enacted that no workman should be "subject or liable
to any indictment or prosecution for conspiracy, or to any other
criminal information or punishment whatever, *under the common or statute law*, for entering into any combination to obtain
an advance, or to fix the rates of wages, or to lessen or alter the
hours or duration of the time of working, or to decrease the
quantity of work, or to induce another to depart from his service
before the end of the time or term for which he is hired, or to quit
or return to his work before the same shall be finished, or, not
being hired, to refuse to enter into work or employment, or to
regulate the mode of carrying on any manufacture, trade, or
business, or the management thereof."

For a while the toilers were released from "legal shackles," but
the courts by judicial legislation and interpretation, there, as
here, sought again to bind on some of the chains. As soon as the
legislative relief was given against the judicial theory of "criminal

conspiracy" under the common law, the interests took refuge behind the doctrine of "civil conspiracy." Finally the workmen won their fight by securing the Trade Disputes Act of 1906, which forbids action for

1. Any act done by a combination of persons which would not be actionable if done without such combination (s. 1)
2. Any act which merely induces a breach of a contract of employment, or interferes with trade, business or employment, or the right of some other person to dispose of his capital or labor as he wills. (s. 3)
3. Any alleged responsibility by a Trade Union, as a body, for the tortious acts of its officials or members (s. 4)

Nor is it amiss when I take the liberty of respectfully calling your attention to the declarations of the Democratic party national conventions of 1908 and 1912 upon this, the subject matter under discussion.

My presentation of the cause of organized labor has not been from the legal viewpoint, for I am not a lawyer. But even could I present the legal phases, I doubt whether that would aid in determining justice for the workers. Often justice is obscured in the mazes of legal theories and technicalities. The law is not an unfailing source of justice, it can only approximate that ideal as it is rendered flexible enough to adjust to new conditions and needs. That is what we ask for in the legislation we seek.

As I have already stated, it is not my purpose to present here a legal argument in defense or in futherance of Labor's position with respect to the principle involved in legislation of this character, nor can I, in this letter, make a sociological or an economic presentation of the subject. My main purpose is that you may give this letter the consideration it deserves at the present time, that you may arrest your final judgment, defer the determination of your course until an opportunity is afforded when you may accord the privilege of a conference in which a more complete and comprehensive presentation of this matter may be made to you.

It is earnestly hoped that your final conclusion upon this entire matter, which is fraught with such far-reaching consequences to the rights and the welfare of the toilers of our country, will be reached only after the most complete consideration of it in all its bearings and all that is involved therein.

I have the honor to remain,

Very respectfully yours,   Saml. Gompers.
President
American Federation
of Labor.

TLS (WP, DLC).

To Rudolph Spreckels

My dear Mr. Spreckels: [The White House] March 15, 1913

Thank you warmly for your letter of March 12th, written en route from Chicago.[1] It has given me a great deal of pleasure, and I want to send a word of reply at once to assure you of my full realization of the danger of being guided by the wrong persons in making appointments in California, and also of my genuine interest in the Seaman's bill.[2]

I did not know about the bill in any detail until yesterday, when Senator La Follette called my attention to it.[3] I hope sincerely that it will be possible for Congress to take it up at an early date. It seems to me of capital consequence.

It was kind of you to send the reassuring lines about Mr. Brandeis, but since I saw you I have had a delightful talk with him[4] and, happily, did not need the assurances you give me. I shall keep in touch with Mr. Brandeis and shall look forward with genuine pleasure to doing so.

You may be sure that I shall value the opportunity of resorting to you for suggestions.

Cordially yours,   Woodrow Wilson

TLS (Letterpress Books, WP, DLC).
   [1] It is missing.
   [2] Subsequent documents in this series will disclose Wilson's interest in this measure. For its background and course through Congress, see Hyman Weintraub, *Andrew Furuseth, Emancipator of the Seamen* (Berkeley and Los Angeles, Cal., 1959), pp. 108-32; Belle Case La Follette and Fola La Follette, *Robert M. La Follette* (2 vols., New York, 1953), I, 521-36; and Link, *The New Freedom*, pp. 269-74.
   [3] Wilson conferred with La Follette at the White House on March 14 and assured him that the bill would have his sympathetic support. *Robert M. La Follette*, I, 524.
   [4] Wilson conferred with Brandeis at the White House during the evening of March 10.

From Henry Burchard Fine

Muenchen, March 15, 1913.

Cablegrams received. Will await letter and cable reply.

Harry

T telegram (WP, DLC).

From Henry Jones Ford

Sir: San Fernando, Pampanga, P. I. March 15, 1913

I beg to report that I arrived in Manila, Friday, 14th inst. by the Pacific Mail steamship Mongolia. Among the passengers

were many Philippine officials from whom I obtained information
of value. I left Manila today for Pampanga province, where I
shall spend several days. On Thursday, the 20th, I start for
the southern islands and shall spend some six weeks in a tour
of the archipelago. After returning to Manila I shall go to Baguio
—the summer capital. It is my plan to acquaint myself first with
conditions before discussing matters with administrative chiefs.
I have escaped all publicity and so far have been able to get information without appearing inquisitive. Indeed, there is so much
tension of feeling as regards the Philippine policy of the Democratic administration that one has only to be a good listener to be
in the way of copious supplies of fact and comment. As I shall
devote careful study to the situation before attempting to draw
conclusions it may be two months before I shall be ready to begin
my report. My cable address is Howford, Manila. I am
                    Very respectfully yours   Henry J. Ford

ALS (WP, DLC).

To Mary Allen Hulbert

Dearest Friend,   The White House 16 March, 1913.
    I wish with all my heart we *could* take the house at Nantucket,
but we had already gone more than half way in committing ourselves to engaging a house in New Hampshire;[1] and we have
felt all along that if we did take a house by the sea it must be in
old New Jersey, which would not easily forgive us if we went
elsewhere. It is dreary to think of your going abroad next summer
and putting the *whole* sea between you and us; and yet, when
I look at the question unselfishly, I know that nothing could
freshen you up or take your thoughts out of the dreary, lonely
round they have been in since the last sadness fell upon you.
I had a letter the other day from that honest, but very light-
weight person, Jaffray,[2] the other day. He said he had seen you
at the races (?) and that you were looking very well. That pleased
me mightily, and I wondered (with a gleam of hope) whether
your letters to me were not like a school-boy's Sunday letters
home, filled with all that a consciousness of friends shut away
by distance and of deep sympathy excites. They make my heart
ache! For I know what they mean coming from a person of such
extraordinary vitality and natural high spirits as you are,—a person intended by a generous Providence to cheer and sustain and
stimulate others—everybody that comes within her radius. You
may be sure that the sympathy they excite, and the comprehen-

sion, is quick and deep, and lasts through every day and hour of the week! But I want to see the life flooding back into your veins! I know it will, and that every one about you will be blest accordingly.

The days pass without variety. The work is hard and incessant. But it grows gradually familiar. The old kink in me is still there. Everything is persistently *impersonal*. I am administering a great office,—no doubt the greatest in the world,—but I do not seem to be identified with it: it is not me, and I am not it. I am only a commissioner, in charge of its apparatus, living in its offices, and taking upon myself its functions[.] This impersonality of my life is a very odd thing, and perhaps robs it of intensity, as it certainly does of pride and self-consciousness (and, maybe, of enjoyment) but it at least prevents me from becoming a fool, and thinking myself *It*! Everything has gone well, so far, and very generous opinions are expressed of the start the new administration has made.

We are all well. We think often, very, very often, of you, and all unite in messages of deep affection.

Your devoted friend,   Woodrow Wilson
Love to Allen.

ALS (WP, DLC).
[1] Harlakenden House, the American novelist Winston Churchill's home in Cornish, N. H.
[2] Reginald Jaffray of Paget West.

To Edward Corbin Jenkins

My dear Mr. Jenkins: [The White House] March 17, 1913
Thank you for your note of the 14th. I hope that you will carry out Mr. Dodge's suggestions, as they seem to me excellent.

May I not beg that you will send the following message in code to Mr. Mott:

"Feel that my duty to the public interest obliges me to urge reconsideration on your part. The interests of China and of the Christian world are so intimately involved."

Cordially and sincerely yours,   Woodrow Wilson

TLS (Letterpress Books, WP, DLC).

To John Warren Davis

[The White House, March 17, 1913]
I feel very strongly our party's unequivocal commitment to jury reform and that the terms of referendum in the present bill are a

virtual nullification of the reform.[1] Can we not give the people what they demand without qualification?[2]

Woodrow Wilson.

T telegram (Letterpress Books, WP, DLC).
[1] Wilson was herewith in the act of removing himself from the horns of a dilemma. In his eagerness to achieve some kind of jury reform legislation before he left for Washington, he had told a Democratic legislative caucus in February 1913 that he would yield to the majority and accept a bill providing for the selection of jurors by commissions appointed by the governor. This was in direct violation of the Democratic state platform pledge of a nonpolitical jury system. The bill was immediately attacked alike by Wilson's friends and foes. Anti-Wilson forces in the Assembly, seeking to delay consideration of the measure until Wilson was in the White House, managed to attach an amendment requiring that, before it could go into effect in any county, voters of that county had to approve it in a referendum. Wilson felt obliged to accept this, saying, according to the Jersey City *Jersey Journal*, February 26, 1913: "I believe in the referendum. If the people don't want this measure I don't want it." Then, on March 13, with Wilson safely out of the state, opponents moved to kill the bill entirely by calling for a new referendum amendment with provisions so cumbersome as to constitute, to use Wilson's words, "virtual nullification" of any jury reform. It was this tactic that prompted Wilson, now convinced that the earlier agreement concerning an "honest" referendum had been violated, to send this telegram to Davis and, *mutatis mutandis*, to Governor Fielder on the same date. For the full details of his prior and subsequent gyrations on jury reform and the ultimate resolution of the issue, see Link, *The New Freedom*, pp. 38-48.
[2] There is a WWhw draft of this telegram in WP, DLC.

To John Bassett Moore

My dear Mr. Moore: [The White House] March 17, 1913

The Secretary of State and I are both deeply gratified that you have seen your way to accept the position of Counselor to the State Department.[1] It will strengthen us greatly.

There will be no sort of trouble about meeting the conditions you lay down. They all seem to be entirely consistent with the public interest and the performance of your duties.

Cordially and sincerely yours,   Woodrow Wilson

TLS (J. B. Moore Papers, DLC).
[1] Moore, in J. B. Moore to WJB, March 13, 1913, TLS (WP, DLC), accepted, provided that he be permitted to continue meeting his classes at Columbia University until June 1, 1913, and that, as counselor, he not be subordinate to the assistant secretaries and be permitted to continue as a member of the International Commission of Jurists and of the Permanent Court at The Hague. He was commissioned on April 21, 1913, and took up his duties two days later.

To Samuel Gompers

My dear Mr. Gompers: [The White House] March 17, 1913

You may be sure your letter of March 14th will receive my most careful consideration. I am sincerely obliged to you for writing it, and you have no occasion to apologize for the length of the letter. I shall take it home with me and go over it very carefully indeed, for I am sure you know my disposition in matters of this kind.   Cordially and sincerely yours,   Woodrow Wilson

TLS (Letterpress Books, WP, DLC).

To Charles Henry Grasty

My dear Mr. Grasty: [The White House] March 17, 1913

If you were naming a postmaster for Baltimore, whom would you name? I should very much value your advice on the subject, in any form in which you choose to give it.[1]

Cordially yours,   Woodrow Wilson

TLS (Letterpress Books, WP, DLC).
[1] In his reply (C. H. Grasty to WW, March 19, 1913, TLS [WP, DLC]), Grasty recommended S. Sterett McKim, vice-president and cashier of the National Union Bank of Baltimore. However, a short time later Grasty wrote (C. H. Grasty to WW, March 28, 1913, TLS [WP, DLC]) that he had changed his mind and now supported Sherlock Swann, president of the Druid Oak Belting Co. of Baltimore, who was an active candidate for the post and whose claims had been "impressively presented to the Postoffice Department and to the public." Wilson appointed Swann on April 24, 1913.

From Oscar Wilder Underwood

My dear Mr. President: Washington, D. C., March 17, 1913.

I am in receipt of your letter of the fourteenth instant, in reference to the data you desire prepared for you when you take up the consideration of the tariff bill. I have had prepared for the use of my committee the information suggested in your letter relating to each paragraph. I expect to have it brough[t] up to date shortly and will have it ready to lay before you by the time that the tariff bill is in shape for your consideration before we introduce it in the caucus. I do not think that I can get the matters ready in less than a week but as soon as they are ready, I will phone Mr. Tumulty and ask you for an appointment and bring them down.   Sincerely yours,   O W Underwood

TLS (WP, DLC).

A Statement on the Pending Chinese Loan

[March 18, 1913]

We are informed that at the request of the last administration a certain group of American bankers undertook to participate in the loan now desired by the government of China (approximately $125,000,000). Our government wished American bankers to participate along with the bankers of other nations, because it desired that the good will of the United States towards China should be exhibited in this practical way, that American capital should have access to that great country, and that the United States should be in a position to share with the other powers any political responsibilities that might be associated with the development of the foreign relations of China in connection with her industrial and commercial enterprises. The present administration has been asked by this group of bankers whether it would also request them to participate in the loan. The representatives of the bankers through whom the administration was approached declared that they would continue to seek their share of the loan under the proposed agreements only if expressly requested to do so by the government. The administration has declined to make such request because it did not approve the conditions of the loan or the implications of responsibility on its own part which it was plainly told would be involved in the request.

The conditions of the loan seem to us to touch very nearly the administrative independence of China itself; and this administration does not feel that it ought, even by implication, to be a party to those conditions. The responsibility on its part which would be implied in requesting the bankers to undertake the loan might conceivably go the length in some unhappy contingency of forcible interference in the financial, and even the political, affairs of that great oriental State, just now awakening to a consciousness of its power and of its obligation to its people. The conditions include not only the pledging of particular taxes, some of them antiquated and burdensome, to secure the loan, but also the administration of those taxes by foreign agents. The responsibility on the part of our government implied in the encouragement of a loan thus secured and administered is plain enough and is obnoxious to the principles upon which the government of our people rests.

The government of the United States is not only willing, but earnestly desirous, of aiding the great Chinese people in every way that is consistent with their untrammeled development and its own immemorial principles. The awakening of the people of China to a consciousness of their possibilities under free government is the most significant, if not the most momentous, event of our generation. With this movement and aspiration the American people are in profound sympathy. They certainly wish to participate, and participate very generously, in opening to the Chinese and to the use of the world the almost untouched and perhaps unrivalled resources of China.

The government of the United States is earnestly desirous of promoting the most extended and intimate trade relationships between this country and the Chinese republic. The present administration will urge and support the legislative measures necessary to give American merchants, manufacturers, contractors, and engineers the banking and other financial facilities which they now lack, and without which they are at a serious disadvantage as compared with their industrial and commercial rivals. This is its duty. This is the main material interest of its citizens in the development of China. Our interests are those of the open door—a door of friendship and mutual advantage. This is the only door we care to enter.[1]

T MS (WP, DLC).
  [1] There is a WWsh draft of this statement, with the composition date of March 13, 1913, in WP, DLC.

From the Diary of Josephus Daniels

March Tues 18 1913

Nothing of great importance came up in cabinet meeting today. The President, speaking of the fact that a dozen new Federal judges were to be appointed, outlined his idea of the sort of men who should be appointed to the bench. It was illuminating. He said a very different sort of men were needed from those who had too often been appointed. He is in favor finding able lawyers who have no strings tied to them and who are not so in sympathy with large corporations or trusts as to bias them in favor of the Big interests rather than the superior rights of all the public. He expressed his difficulty in knowing exactly how to find the best man in every State, but urged all the cabinet to assist the Attorney General in finding lawyers of the highest type who would hold the scales of justice equally.

Bound desk diary (J. Daniels Papers, DLC).

To Charles William Eliot

[The White House] March 19, 1913

I venture to inquire whether you would be willing to consider the appointment as Ambassador to Great Britain. It would give me great gratification if I felt that you would.

Woodrow Wilson.

T telegram (Letterpress Books, WP, DLC).

To William Williams Keen

My dear Dr. Keen: The White House March 19, 1913

May I not express to you, and through you to the members of the American Philosophical Society, my deep and sincere appreciation of the cordial message brought me from the Society by you and your associates this afternoon? Nothing has gratified me more. I do not know of any association whose confidence I would rather enjoy. It has been a matter of peculiar pride to me to be associated with the American Philosophical Society, and that that distinguished body should feel honored by my elevation to the Presidency is a source of genuine satisfaction to me. I can only say in reply to their gracious address that I shall hope and strive at all times to deserve their respect and confidence.

Cordially and sincerely yours,   Woodrow Wilson

TLS (Archives, PPAmP).

From David Starr Jordan

Stanford University California

My dear President Wilson: March 19, 1913.

Let me congratulate you most sincerely on your treatment of the "Six-power Loan" to China. The "Dollar Diplomacy," which would involve our national authority and even the force of arms in connection with foreign loans was, it seemed to me, one of the most dangerous features of the late administration.

Sincerely yours,   David Starr Jordan

ALS (WP, DLC).

From Huntington Wilson[1]

My dear Mr. President: Washington March 19, 1913.

In view of all the circumstances, I feel that the resignation which I had the honor to submit to you on March fourth must be effective today. I have accordingly handed over the charge of the Department of State to Mr. Adee, the able and experienced Second Assistant Secretary of State. If I had felt that my continuing in office or not would affect in any way the interests of the country which I have had the honor to serve, I should not have today reached the decision which I beg leave now to communicate to you; but it seems now demonstrated that my remaining can serve no useful purpose.

It today becomes the duty of the Acting Secretary of State, in despatching instructions to the representatives of this Government abroad and as the channel of communication with the representatives of foreign governments at Washington, to be the spokesman of the President in regard to a new Far Eastern policy which is apparently deducible from your statement issued to the press last night. Inasmuch as I find myself entirely out of harmony with this radical change of policy as I understand it, I trust that you will sympathize with the view that it was not appropriate that I should longer retain the responsibilities of the office which I have now relinquished.

When I consented, at the request of Mr. Bryan and in deference to what I understood to be your wishes, to continue in the office of Assistant Secretary of State for these few weeks longer, I believe I was justified in assuming that there would be no radical departure from the practice of this and other countries whereby the knowledge and experience of the various officials of the foreign office is made use of in the study of great questions of foreign policy. I had no reason to suppose that the officials on duty in the Department of State would learn first from the newspapers of a declaration of policy which I think shows on its face the inadequacy of the consideration given to the facts and theories involved and the failure clearly to apprehend the motives leading to and the purposes of the policy superseded. I had no reason to suppose that the fate of negotiations which had so long had the studious attention of the foreign offices of the six great Powers would be abruptly determined with such quite unnecessary haste and in so unusual a manner. These methods, against which I respectfully protest, are the very extraordinary circumstances which I feel vitiate my understanding with Mr. Bryan and completely relieve me of any further obligation in the premises.

The repeated utterances of the last administration must have made it perfectly clear that the motive and purpose of the policy now abandoned were first and primarily the protection of China's integrity and sovereignty, the uplift of the Chinese people, morally, materially and governmentally, the development of China's resources, and the maintenance of our traditional policy of the "open door," or equality of opportunity for American enterprise. Precisely because of the ultimate possibility of a measure of foreign control of China's finances, which may be inferred from a study of other countries which have found themselves in a similar situation, it was deemed imperative that there should be American participation in the rehabilitation of China's finances, in order to make sure of the presence of the potent, friendly and disinterested influence of the United States. The only practicable method of such participation was by the use of reliable American bankers.

In the consideration of the Far Eastern policy, I have felt that so much should be premised and that the problem of the Government's using American bankers, while still scrupulously avoiding any material monopolistic feature, might now, as before, be found one of the most difficult preoccupations. I have always thought that, in the work of advancing the national interests and promoting the welfare of other nations, the financial force of the United States could be marshalled in some manner to present a safely united front abroad, where it would be like the apex of a triangle, but would have at home at its base broad equality of opportunity, both for citizens desiring to invest and for bankers desiring to engage in these difficult and relatively risky ventures. It seems, however, that the conclusions reached are expressed upon other grounds.

You will readily understand, Mr. President, that in view of all the considerations indicated in this letter and of the practical necessity that one charged, even temporarily, with the administration of the Department of State should be in entire and complete accord with your foreign policies, I feel it my duty at once to vacate a post in which one not in harmony with your foreign policy would be in danger, even with the best intentions, of failing accurately to reflect your views.

In retiring from the service I beg leave to take the liberty of referring to the phrase in your Inaugural address by which you summon "all honest men, all patriotic, all forward-looking men to your side" and of assuring you that when you apply to the Department of State for technical advice in formulating your policies you can nowhere find men more truly described by that phrase than the patriotic, intelligent, high-minded and non-partisan gentlemen whose association I am leaving with so much regret.

With every good wish for the success of your administration, I have the honor to be, Mr. President, with great respect,

                    Yours very faithfully,   Huntington Wilson

TLS (WP, DLC).
    [1] Assistant Secretary of State, appointed March 5, 1909, by President Taft. Wilson changed his name in 1922 to Francis Mairs Huntington-Wilson.

To William Jennings Bryan

[The White House] March 20, 1913

Huntington Wilson insists upon immediate resignation in a letter which makes it impossible that he should remain. Things will go on perfectly well without him so that this need not disturb your vacation.[1] Will not trouble you with details at present.

Woodrow Wilson.

T telegram (Letterpress Books, WP, DLC).
[1] Bryan had been filling several speaking engagements in the Middle West. He spoke in Des Moines on March 20, and Wilson's telegram was addressed to him there. He was about to go to his home in Lincoln "for a few days' rest." *New York Times*, March 21, 1913.

To Huntington Wilson

My dear Sir: [The White House] March 20, 1913

Allow me to acknowledge the receipt of your letter of yesterday, and to say that I accept your resignation, as you suggest, as of the present date.   Very truly yours,   Woodrow Wilson

TLS (Letterpress Books, WP, DLC).

From Charles William Eliot

Cambridge, Massachusetts, March 20, 1913.

I thank you sincerely, but still believe I had better work in familiar field during the rest of my life.

Charles W. Eliot.

T telegram (WP, DLC).

From the Diary of Colonel House

Washington, D. C. March 20, 1913.

I used Houston's carriage and went to the White House. The President was not well and had not come down. Tumulty and I talked of McCombs whom he said was generally thought crazy; that he drank a bottle of whiskey a day, and never knew his own mind one hour at a time. McCombs had written the President accepting the French Mission; the next day had withdrawn it, and that he had accepted and withdrawn it several times since.

Senator Hughes stated that McCombs was driving him mad, and he could not stand the strain of dealing with him. I told Tumulty that I had the job for six months and am glad it has been transferred to someone else. McCombs, among other things, told the President that he supposed he knew that in a fight between Bryan and himself, I would be on Bryan's side. This amused the President, but it is another instance of McCombs' insane jealousy.

When the President came down he asked me into his office. The night before, while he was in bed, he received the resignation of Huntington Wilson, Assistant Secretary of State. It was a four page typewritten document, but the President insisted upon reading it to me. It was very impertinent and gave as his reasons for resigning, the administration's attitude upon the Chinese loan.

The question then came up as to what action should be taken in regard to the letter. I advised its immediate publication. Tumulty seconded this, and the President acquiesced. He dictated a two line reply, curtly accepting the resignation to take effect at once. He also dictated a telegram to Mr. Bryan, who is now in the West, telling him that Wilson had resigned, but not to let it make any difference as to his vacation. I suggested that he also tell Mr. Bryan that he had accepted the resignation at once on account of the tenor of the letter. I thought if he did not do this, Bryan might express regret.

We discussed at length Wilson's successor. The President said Mr. Bryan was still insisting upon ex-Governor Osborne of Wyoming and the difficulty was that he had no one himself to suggest in lieu thereof.

The Secretary of War and the Governor of Porta Rica[1] arrived as I left.

The President has offered Chas. W. Eliot the Ambassadorship to the Court of St James. I asked if he would like me to go to Boston and urge him to accept, and he said he would appreciate it. . . .

I took McAdoo to dine at the Metropolitan Club and afterwards we walked to the White House. The President asked us to his library. We discussed the currency bill and the appointments McAdoo has to make. I mentioned what Glass had in mind and how pleased I was at the suggestion he had made as to the proper way to handle the currency bill. The President laughed and said that he had made the suggestion to Glass. I then congratulated him.

The President said Malone had obtained some business which would enable him to take a position in Washington which would pay him much less than he could otherwise have afforded. He suggested him as one of the Commissioners of the District of Columbia. I did not think well of it. He suggested him for one of the Assistant Secretaries of State. McAdoo thought that would fit him well. McAdoo's idea was clear to me. He thought if he could get rid of Malone in the State Department, it would not be necessary to give him a place in the Treasury.

We spoke of the ambassadorships and we both urged Walter Page for London. The President said Eliot had declined it. He wanted to know what I thought of Charles Francis Adams. I considered him too old and too irascible; that he had nothing now to conjure with except a name.

He said he had decided not to appoint Thos. Nelson Page to any post, on account of his reactionary tendancies and associations, and instead he was considering Willard of Virginia.[2] He suggested Frederic Penfield for a small post. McAdoo did not think he was big enough for anything. He thought if the President intended using that kind of material, Gerard would be better.

The President expressed regret that he could not find proper material for these places. I think he will eventually offer the London mission to Walter Page. We talked of McCombs and he expressed concern regarding his health and the whole miserable condition of affairs connected with him. While the country thought he was a veritable young Napoleon of politics, only a few of us knew the real facts. I thought more than a few knew them, and that his incompetency was becoming generally known. We all expressed sincere sympathy for him; McAdoo going so far as to tell the President that he would resign and let McCombs have his place in the Cabinet if the President so desired. I can imagine McAdoo's consternation if he should be taken at his word.

When we arose to go I congratulated the President that he could now indicate when an interview was ended, which would give him the advantage over office seekers and officials generally since he could dismiss them at will. He laughed and said the Supreme Court called the other day[3] and Colonel Rhoades[4] said they would remain until he dismissed them. When President Taft first received the Court they remained for two hours and a half waiting for him to indicate when they should depart.

The President showed us all over the White House. He particularly admired the dining room and the blue room, and said the electric elevator was a joy to all the family. He insisted upon my preceding him in leaving the room, and laughingly said he could not bring himself to think of himself as President of the United States. He administered the office, but as to the dignity of it, it had never impressed itself upon him.

McAdoo and I were saying very much the same thing as we walked up to the White House. Neither of us could realize that we were playing a part on so large a stage.

During the evening Mrs. Wilson came in to show us photographs of the Winston Churchill house in Cornish, New Hampshire. It is a beautiful place with 200 acres of ground.

I promised the President to be back in Washington Monday in order that we might go over some matters. McAdoo and I walked over to the Cosmus Club and soon after I left on the midnight train for New York.

¹ George Radcliffe Colton, Governor of Porto Rico (its official name in 1913) since 1909.
² Joseph Edward Willard, prominent member of the progressive faction of the Democratic party in Virginia.
³ Wilson received the Supreme Court on March 8.
⁴ Thomas Leidy Rhoads, Medical Corps, U.S.A., military aide at the White House, and surgeon in charge at the Walter Reed General Army Hospital.

To Duncan Upshaw Fletcher

My dear Senator,   [The White House] March 21, 1913

It has given me peculiar pleasure to commission you as one of the delegates of the United States designated to study rural credits abroad, and I hope sincerely that it will be possible for you to undertake the duty.

I venture to express, however, the very strong desire that the Commission shall not begin its trip until after the close of the special session of Congress. I do this because it would be, in my judgment, a serious mistake if you should be absent from the approaching session, where our full force and counsel are needed. This need not interfere with the plans of the delegates of the Southern Commercial Congress, and I am sure that our own delegates could join them at a later season without any material loss to the main objects of the mission.

Hoping sincerely that my views coincide with yours in this matter, I am

Cordially and sincerely yours,   Woodrow Wilson

P. S. The Commission is as follows:
Hon. Duncan U. Fletcher, U. S. Senate,
Hon. Thomas P. Gore, U. S. Senate,
Hon. Ralph W. Moss, House of Representatives,
Col. Harvie Jordan, Atlanta, Georgia,
Dr. John Lee Coulter, Census Bureau,
Dr. Kenyon L. Butterfield, Amherst, Mass,
Mr. Clarence J. Owens, Southern Commercial Congress.

TLS (Letterpress Books, WP, DLC).

From William Jennings Bryan

My Dear Mr President   Lincoln [Neb.] 3/21 [1913]

I have just secured authentic information on two subjects 1st that Pres Madero *resigned*, the consideration being a promise of life & free passage from the country. The second piece of information I give in blue code cipher below my signature. Do not suppose it will be necessary for you to act before I return but thought I had better communicate this information. With assurances of esteem I am, my Dear Mr President,

Very truly Yours   W. J. Bryan

Unfixing overbend *Madero* Jossa strung loses. Smooth foretasted Judaical hotels multum *Madero* triton Jossa. Smooth *Medoros* evidence inserving preengage Mexico.[1]

ALS (WP, DLC).
   [1] As written above the cipher, the decode reads: "While in prison Madero killed [by] two men. The family do not know how or when Madero was killed. The Maderos do not intend to return to Mexico."

From John R. Mott

Darien [Manchuria], March 21, 1913.

Will await advices before making final decision.

Mott.

T telegram (WP, DLC).

To John R. Mott

[The White House] March 21, 1913

It would help rather than interfere with your work as representative of this government if you retained your posts of guidance in your present work. It would be quite possible also to allow you in all ordinary circumstances such leaves of absence as are necessary. I am eager to unite what you represent with what this government means to try to represent. I have set my heart on the appointment because of all it will imply no less than because of my complete confidence in your character and ability.   Woodrow Wilson

T telegram (WP, DLC).

From James Bryce

My dear Mr. President,   Washington. March 21, 1913.

Knowing how heavy is the pressure upon your time, I have hitherto abstained from approaching you on public matters, but as my Government requested me to remain here beyond the date originally fixed for my departure in order that I might do what I could to settle with you and your Administration such questions as are pending between the United States and Great Britain, and as the time when I must leave is now fast approaching, I will venture to ask you for an early opportunity of mentioning to you —the Secretary of State being absent—the most important of those questions viz: that of the Panama Canal Tolls, in order that I may briefly convey to you the views of my Government regarding it. Whenever therefore you find that you can spare me a few minutes for this purpose, I shall be at your disposal. I do not wish to ask you for any further expression of your own views than you may feel yourself in a position to give me, but merely to convey to you the views of my Government.

Believe me to be   Sincerely yours   James Bryce

P.S. I hope to bring the Canadian Minister of Fisheries to-morrow morning to you for the purpose of letting him say a word about the Freshwater Fisheries Treaty, but should not propose to ask you to enter then upon the Panama Tolls question, reserving that for such a time as you might fix.

TLS (WP, DLC).

From Charles Richard Crane

Chicago, Ill., March 21, 1913.

Sincere congratulations on obtaining the services of Mr. Moore for the State Department. Your Chinese policy is wise American and popular, and recent changes in the Department will aid you greatly in quickly righting ourselves. At no time has the dismemberment of China proceeded so rapidly as since the formation of the six power group. Think of Professor Paul Reinsch of Wisconsin[1] for the post of Secretary for the South American states. Easter greetings to you all.   Charles R. Crane.

T telegram (WP, DLC).
    [1] Paul Samuel Reinsch, Professor of Political Science at the University of Wisconsin. He had been a delegate to the third Pan-American Conference in Rio de Janeiro in 1906, the fourth Pan-American Conference in Buenos Aires

in 1910, the first Pan-American Scientific Congress in Santiago in 1909, and was a member of the Pan-American Commission. He was also the author of several books on far eastern affairs. Wilson appointed him minister to China on August 5, 1913.

From Royal Meeker, with Enclosure

My dear Mr. President,   Princeton, New Jersey March 21, 1913

I have been much delayed in submitting the results of the questionnaire prepared by Prof. E. W. Kemmerer[1] and myself and sent to several economists of some note in matters of banking reform. I enclose the digest I have made, together with the letters received in reply.[2] Trusting that these may be of use to you I beg to remain,   Yours to serve,   Royal Meeker

P.S. I am preparing a new questionnaire to be based on more accurate knowledge of what the Committee on Currency and Banking propose to put before Congress.

ALS (WP, DLC).
  [1] Edwin Walter Kemmerer, Professor of Economics and Finance at Princeton University since 1912.
  [2] The letters are not printed.

E N C L O S U R E

QUESTIONNAIRE ON BANKING REFORM

A. QUESTIONS ASKED

I Do you believe that our banking system should be revised so as to grant to some agency or agencies, with or without further limitations, the more important functions assigned to the National Reserve Association, i. e. (1) to hold reserves of banks so as to mobilize funds where needed; (2) to extend credit to banks by rediscount; (3) to issue an asset currency; (4) to act as a depository of government funds; and (5) to regulate the foreign exchanges?

II Do you believe that the plan of organization and government of the National Reserve Association (including district and local associations) is in the main well adapted to an institution with such functions, and reasonably immune from the danger of selfish exploitation by special interests?

III If you are opposed to any fundamental feature of the National Monetary Commission's plan, state your objections and suggest such amendments as would remedy the defects you point out

(1) as to functions

(2) as to organization and control?

IV Would a plan for the division of the country into districts, and the creating in each district of an independent Reserve Association with functions similar to those assigned to the National Reserve Association meet with your approval?

V Should the capital necessary to make effective the plan outlined under either (I) or (IV) be provided by banks exclusively, by banks and the public, by the public exclusively, or in some other way?

B. GENERAL SUMMARY OF ALL REPLIES.

Question I.

Yes, unanimously.

Question II.

A substantial agreement that a larger measure of non-banking control, secured either by more government representatives or otherwise, is desirable.

Question III (a)

As regards fundamentals there is essential agreement in favor of the functions assigned; as regards important details, however, many believe that the plan can be greatly improved.

(*b*) A substantial agreement in favor of a larger element of non-banking control.

Question IV.

Substantial agreement that such a plan would be undesirable if such district associations are to be absolutely independent.

Question V.

General agreement that matter is not of great importance so long as there is effective government control.

C. SUMMARY OF INDIVIDUAL REPLIES.

Name	Q. I	Q. II
Agger, L.E. *Columbia U.*	Yes.	Yes.
Barnett, G.E. *J. Hopkins U.*	Yes. Asset currency should be severely limited	Yes. Directors & officers should be appointed by the President.
Barrett, D.C. *Haverford C.*	Yes	In main well adapted. Not reasonably immune from danger of selfish exploitation
Breckenridge, R.M. *Authority on Canadian banking.*	No reply	No reply
Clark, W.E. *College of City of N.Y.*	do.	do.
Dewey, D.R. *M.I.T.*	do.	do.
Droppers, G. *Williams C.*	Yes. Objects to "asset currency." Notes should be based on cash & liquid assets	An inferential No, mingled with some Yes.
Scott, W.A. *Univ. Wisconsin.*	Yes	Plan is cumbersome & can be much improved.
Sprague, O.M.W. *Harvard U.*	Yes, but credit extension and note issue should be more definitely limited.	Yes. Not approved by people. Plan should be changed so as to give more government influence.
Taylor, F.M.* *Univ. Mich.*	Yes	Yes
Whittaker, A.C. *Stanford U.*	Yes	Yes
Hollander, J.H. *J. Hopkins U.*	Yes	Yes. Concessions should be made to existing rights & prejudices

* No letter. Questions were answered on questionnaire form as given.

Q. III	Q. IV	Q. V
Central assoc to deal also with public.	Yes, with machinery for cooperation.	Mostly by public.
In substantial agreement.	No	Immatèrial
Favors plan outlined in Q. IV.	Step in right direction; not so effective, but centralization can be effected later if desirable. Directors chosen by nonbanking interests.	Banks and public.
No reply	No reply	No reply
do.	do.	do.
do.	do.	do.
Plan is cumbersome. Method of appointing Governor bad. Should not be owned by banks.	Not answered. An inferential No.	By public
Defective in important provisions. See letter.	Entirely feasible.	By banks. Public would not buy stock limited to 5% dividends.
Opposed to certain features. See letter.	No, if strictly independent. Management less efficient. Different discount rates an advantage.	Not important Any plan satisfactory to public should be adopted.
Not answered	No opinion	By banks
Legal definition of commercial paper needs more careful statement. Favors direct election of board by banks.	No. An inferior substitute.	By banks exclusively.
	Not answered. Inferentially opposed.	Not answered.

Johnson, J.F. *N.Y. Univ.*	Yes	In main well adapted, but not free from suspicion
Kemmerer, E.W. *Princeton U.*	Yes.	No
Kinley, D. *Univ. Ill.*	Asks to be excused.	. . .
Meeker, Royal *Princeton U.*	Yes.	Needlessly clumsy. Not free from suspicion.
Laughlin, J.L. *Univ. Chicago*	Replied saying that no satisfactory answers were possible.	
McCrea, R.C. *Univ. Pa.*	Yes	Plan of organization should be more democratic.
Fairchild, F. *Yale U.*	Yes, altho result may be achieved without creating any new institution.	No
Fisher, Irving *Yale U.*	Yes	Yes as to functions; no as to selfish exploitation
Fisher, Willard. *Formerly of Wesleyan Univ.*	Yes	In main well adapted, but not free from danger of selfish ex[p]loitation.
Glasson, W.H. *Trinity C., N.C.*	Yes	In main satisfactory. Favors stronger government control.
Goodhue, W.H. *Colgate U.*	Yes, without further limitations.	Yes, Kemmerer's views followed.
Holdsworth, J.T. *Univ. of Pittsburg.*	Yes.	Yes.

	Not able to answer. Probably No.	Not vital. By public exclusively.
All non-banking directors, of which there should be a good number, to be appointed by government. One bank one vote, regardless of size. Smaller directorate.	No, unless there is a reasonably strong central body. Otherwise it would mean control, under cover, by the N.Y. district.	By banks exclusively, provided there is effective government control.
. . .	. . .	. . .
A simpler method of choosing directors. A larger governmental control.	Yes, if a central agency be impossible.	By banks.
	Might succeed. Considerable concentration needed.	By banks & public.
Cannot answer.	No, certainly	Not vital. Stock ownership will not prevent selfish control.
	Probably	Inclined to think banks Control not given entirely with ownership
A larger measure of non-banking control desirable.	Not if the districts are to be entirely independent.	Banks & public Public control
Government to appoint in addition 3 economists. Governor to be removable by President. Directors to be chosen differently.	Yes, as a substitute for the N.R.A. if latter cannot be secured.	By banks.
Stock voting disapproved, directors in part to be chosen by Government.	No. Makeshift. Must have nation wide cooperation.	By banks.
Not opposed.	Yes, if N.R.A. cannot be secured. Would help discount market, & cooperation of banks. Might not prevent struggle between districts for reserves.	By banks exclusively.

T MS (WP, DLC).

From the Diary of Josephus Daniels

March Fri 21 1913

All the members of the cabinet were present at to-day's meeting except the Secretary of State. The fiasco of Huntington Wilson's resignation as Asst Secy. of State, because the President had repudiated the Taft program of requesting the banking trust to share with the bankers of other countries the control of the fiscal affairs of the new Republic of China, created only amusement. He took himself very seriously, but nobody else did. Before he left for Nebraska, Mr. Bryan requested Mr. Wilson to remain to look after details. I suggested to Mr. B that it was of doubtful wisdom for him to leave Wilson in charge of his department because he was not in accord with anything in our policy and might take some action that would not be approved. The general opinion is that Huntington Wilson is a great egotist and that his letter of resignation, under the circumstances, was a piece of pertinence and impertinence. The press generally said that for an under secretary, already notified that he was to stay only a few weeks, to seize the opportunity to try to rebuke a new President was unheard of and most out of place. In this city he is generally regarded as having made an exhibition of himself.

Bound desk diary (J. Daniels Papers, DLC).

Remarks to Reporters at the First Press Conference

March 22, 1913

I feel that this gathering has a degree of formality which I wish it might not have. If there were any other room[1] in which we could have met, it would have been more pleasing to me. I asked Mr. Tumulty to ask you gentlemen to come together this afternoon, because the other day when I saw you, just after the fatigue of the morning, I did not feel that I had anything more to say; and if it is agreeable to you, I would be obliged if you would regard what I say this afternoon as just between ourselves. Because I want an opportunity to open some part of my mind to you, so that you may know my point of view a little better than perhaps you have had an opportunity to know it so far.

I feel that a large part of the success of public affairs depends on the newspaper men—not so much on the editorial writers, because we can live down what they say, as upon the news writers, because the news is the atmosphere of public affairs. Unless you

[1] The East Room.

get the right setting to affairs—disperse the right impression—
things go wrong. Now, the United States is just now at a very
critical turning point in respect to public opinion, not in respect
to parties, for that is not the part that is most interesting. They
may go to pieces or they may hold together. So far as the United
States is concerned, it does not make much difference whether
they do or not, because a party hasn't any vitality whatever unless
it is an embodiment of something real in the way of public
opinion and public purpose. I am not interested in a party that is
not an embodied program based upon a set of principles; and
our present job is to get the people who believe in principles to
stand shoulder to shoulder to do things from one side of this
continent to the other.

Now, that being the case, I can illustrate one of the bad things
that the newspapers may do in order to speak of the good things
they may do. If you play up every morning differences of opinion
and predict difficulties, and say there are going to be so many
factions of this and so many groups of that, and things are going
to pull at such and such cross purposes, you are not so much
doing an injury to an individual or to any one of the groups of
individuals you are talking about as impeding the public business.
Our present business is to get together, not to get divided, and
to draw a line and say, "Now, you fellows who do not believe that
genuine public government will work, please stand on that side,"
(I choose the left because it is scriptural) "and you fellows who
do believe that it will work, get on that side. And all the fellows
who get on this side, then get together and just put these fellows
to rout in such fashion that they will not stop until Doomsday."

Now, in order to do that you have got to have a lot of fellows
who in the news try to interpret the times and to get the momentum in things without which they will not go. I do not mean in
the least to imply that any of you gentlemen are interested in
making trouble. That is not the point. I would be a mighty proud
man if I could get it into your imaginations that you can oblige
people, almost, to get together by the atmosphere with which
you surround them in the daily news. And the atmosphere has
got to come, not from Washington, but from the country. You
have got to write from the country in and not from Washington
out. The only way I can succeed is by not having my mind live in
Washington. My body has got to live there, but my mind has got
to live in the United States, or else I will fail. Now, you fellows
can help me and help everybody else by just swathing my mind
and other people's minds in the atmosphere of the thought of the
United States. The great advantage that you enjoy is that you

represent papers all over the country, and therefore you can import the opinion and the impulse of the country into Washington, and import them after a fashion that nobody else can employ. A congressman has to import opinion according to the repairing of his fences—or, at least, he thinks he has; I do not think so, but he thinks he has. Now, you have not got any fences to repair or to keep in order. Your interest is simply to see that the thinking of the people comes pressing in all the time on Washington. It would help me immensely, and it would help every man in public life immensely, should you do that.

So the thought I have in dealing with you fellows is this, that you, more than any other persons, can lubricate—quicken—the processes by which you are going to do what? Serve the people of the United States. If we do not serve them (the "we" now applies to politicians), if we do not serve them, then we will go out of business; and we ought to go out of business. We will go out of business with the applause of the world; because if we do not serve the people of the United States, there is going to be so radical a change of venue—and it will be an entirely new kind of trial for public men. So that I do not feel that I am engaged in a partisan enterprise or a party enterprise, or in anything except interpreting what you men ought to make it your business to bring to them—the country. I have got to understand the country, or I will not understand my job. Therefore, I have brought you here to say to you this very simple thing: "Please do not tell the country what Washington is thinking, for that does not make any difference. Tell Washington what the country is thinking; and then we will get things with a move on, we will get them so refreshed, so shot through with airs from every wholesome part of the country, that they cannot go stale, they cannot go rotten, and men will stand up and take notice, and know that they have got to vote according to the purposes of the country and the needs of the country, and the interpreted general interests of the country, and in no other way.

I sent for you, therefore, to ask that you go into partnership with me, that you lend me your assistance as nobody else can, and then, after you have brought this precious freight of opinion into Washington, let us try and make true gold here that will go out from Washington. Because nothing better will go out than comes in. It is the old law of compensation, the law of equivalence. In proportion that Washington is enriched, so will the fruition in Washington itself be rich. Now, all this is obvious enough to you gentlemen. I am not telling you anything that you did not know before, but I did want you to feel that I was depending upon you, and from what I can learn of you, I think I have reason to depend with confidence on you to do this thing, not for me, but for the United States, for the people of the United States, and so bring about a day which will be a little better than the days that have gone before us. I think we can cooperate with enthusiasm along that line, and if you agree with me, I shall be very happy.

Transcript (CLSsh notes, C. L. Swem Coll., NjP).

To James Bryce

My dear Mr. Bryce: [The White House] March 22, 1913

It will give me real pleasure to see you, if it is convenient to you, at the White House on Monday at 2:30 in the afternoon, to discuss the matters mentioned in your kind note of yesterday.

With cordial regard, I am

Sincerely yours,   Woodrow Wilson

TLS (Letterpress Books, WP, DLC).

To Samuel Gordon[1]

My dear Sam: [The White House] March 22, 1913

When I left Trenton I did not speak to you about coming down to Washington with me, because I was not sure what there was to offer you.

I now find that there is in this office a position very similar to the one you have occupied at Trenton and it would give me a great deal of satisfaction if you could come down and take it, for we have all come to like and trust you in a very unusual degree.

The post pays $1200 a year. I am not sure that it will be worth your while to take it, but I am so anxious that you should know how highly I have valued your services that I want to offer it to you in the earnest hope that you may think it worth your while.[2]

Mr. Tumulty and all join in cordial messages.

Sincerely yours,   Woodrow Wilson

TLS (Letterpress Books, WP, DLC).

[1] Doorkeeper, messenger, and general factotum in the New Jersey State House for some thirty-seven years.

[2] Gordon apparently never went to Washington.

To Joseph H. Stewart

My dear Mr. Stewart: [The White House] March 22, 1913

   Allow me to thank you most sincerely for the letter of March 13th which I yesterday found upon my table. It has given me a great deal of pleasure and satisfaction.

                              Sincerely yours,   Woodrow Wilson

TLS (Letterpress Books, WP, DLC).

From Thomas Davies Jones

                              Chicago, March 22, 1913.

   Can I safely cable Dean Fine about offer of Germany? Hesitate to act on newspaper dispatches.   Thomas D. Jones.

T telegram (Mineral Point, Wisc., Public Library).

To Thomas Davies Jones

                              The White House Mar. 22 [1913]

   Yes would be glad if you would.   Woodrow Wilson.

T telegram (Mineral Point, Wisc., Public Library).

From Thomas Davies Jones

My dear Mr. President: Chicago March 22, 1913.

   I have an inward conviction—whether born of desire or not, I do not know—that there is basis of fact for the rumor that appeared in yesterday's papers here and for the positive statement that was made in this morning's paper that the ambassadorship to Germany has been offered to Dean Fine. It would be awkward for me to cable him if the offer has not actually been made, even though it be under consideration, and I have therefore telegraphed you this morning asking whether I could safely cable him.

   Assuming that the offer has been or will be made, I want to tell you how deeply pleased I am. I am delighted in all my dimensions. The offer itself, whether he can accept it or not, will be a splendid and merited tribute to a man of rare intellectual distinction and of really lofty character.

   I very much hope also that Mr. Mott will accept the appointment to China. And apropos of China, let me say that your statement with regard to the policy of your administration toward

Central America and your subsequent statement with regard to China are in my judgment admirable in form and substance. A great many people have come to feel that something sordid has been creeping into our relations with foreign countries, and there is general rejoicing at the approach of better things.

Faithfully yours,   Thomas D. Jones.

TLS (WP, DLC).

From Jacob Harry Hollander[1]

My dear President Wilson,   Baltimore, Md. March 22, 1913.

I should like very much to have a brief interview with you in regard to affairs in San Domingo. As you are perhaps aware, some years ago circumstances made it necessary for me to investigate in great detail the economic and political condition of that country, and eventually to effect a drastic scaling down of its semi-fraudulent debt, and to establish its public economy upon a sound basis.

This wholesome situation has been gravely impaired by the blundering policies of the State Department in the past three years—with which I have had no connection whatever—whereby the United States has become seriously and unnecessarily involved and the prosperity and progress of San Domingo arrested.

Whatever new policy or whatever change in policy is now contemplated, I am sure that it is your desire that this course should be based upon a full knowledge of the situation. It is with no wish to obtrude suggestion, but only because no one else has had the opportunity—or the inclination—to endeavor to master the facts that make up the Dominican tangle, that I am impelled to address you.   Very respectfully,   Jacob H. Hollander.

TLS (WP, DLC).
[1] Professor of Political Economy at The Johns Hopkins University, Hollander had been sent to the Dominican Republic by President Roosevelt in 1905 to investigate that country's public debt. He was subsequently instrumental in its readjustment, was a confidential agent of the Department of State with respect to Dominican affairs during 1906 and 1907, and became financial adviser to the Dominican Republic in 1908.

From the Diary of Colonel House

March 22, 1913.

Mr. Frick[1] came at eleven. He wished to know whether I thought it was possible to settle the U. S. Steel Corporation suit[2] outside of the courts. He declared that he came of his own initiative and no one knew he was doing so. He wanted the matter kept confidential excepting the President and Attorney General. We discussed the matter at some length. I pointed out the difficulties, to which he concurred. He seemed fair. I promised to mention the matter and to see what could be done. I thought there would have to be considerable dissolution and readjustment, and he addmiited [admitted] this. He spoke of the fact that the President was not unfavorable to large corporations *per se*, and that was what the Steel Corporation was willing to make itself; they were willing to dissolve all holding companies and form it into a single unobjectionable corporation. I thought the difficulty here was that the corporation did not grow into a large and unobjectionable corporation from mere efficiency, but that it was formed contrary to the Sherman Act and that would have to be taken into consideration. He admitted it. I asked him of Mr. Farrell, the new President.[3] He considered him the ablest and best man they had ever had; that they were fortunate in getting rid of Schwab,[4] whom he did not consider a good man for the place. He also spoke of Judge Gary in uncomplimentary terms. He said Morgan had favored him and given him the influence he had with the company.

We spoke of Morgan, Carnegie and Rockefeller and their different characteristics. We agreed that Carnegie had given his money unwisely and that Rockefeller had used good judgment. He spoke of Rockefeller as being a good man, and one who was looking out for other people. He said that he often received letters from Mr. Rockefeller recommending men to work on the new house which he, Frick, was building on Fifth Avenue, and which showed his kindly interest in other people.

My impression of John D. had been the reverse, and nothing Mr. Frick said has changed that opinion. I think he has given more wisely than any man we have had in this country, but I doubt whether he has any lovable, personal characteristics.

Mr. Frick also spoke of J. P. Morgan and of what a poor trader he was. He said Carnegie out-traded him in the sale of the Carnegie Steel Company. He thought, however, Morgan was a perfectly honest man. He apologized for remaining so long which was not more than a half hour. I promise to let him know after I had talked with the President and Attorney General.

[1] Henry Clay Frick, chairman of the board of directors of the H. C. Frick Coke Co.; chairman of the board of managers of the Carnegie Steel Company; and a director, among many other concerns, of the United States Steel Corp.
[2] See n. 6 to the second address printed at Oct. 28, 1911, Vol. 23.
[3] James Augustine Farrell, president of U. S. Steel since January 1911.
[4] Charles Michael Schwab, president of U. S. Steel, 1901-1903; at this time president and chairman of the board of directors of the Bethlehem Steel Corp.

A Statement

[[March 23, 1913]]

I am very sorry indeed that Mr. McCombs cannot accept the appointment to France.[1] I was particularly anxious that he should. My admiration for his abilities, my knowledge of his singular capacity for grasping complex situations, my confidence in his tact and resourcefulness, as well as my affection for him and the intimate relations that of course exist between us, combine to make my disappointment very great indeed. But I, of course, appreciate the force of the reasons given. He would have accepted at an unreasonable sacrifice, and I could not further press the offer upon him.

It is a great pity that the country has to ask such sacrifices of those who are invited to serve it abroad—a service which every year becomes more exacting and more important. The sacrifice of time, of means, and of opportunity at home is very serious for any but men of large means and leisure, and the diplomatic service is unnecessarily hampered.[2]

Printed in the *New York Times*, March 24, 1913.
    [1] In his statement of declination, which he gave to the press on March 21, McCombs said that, although no position within the President's gift could be more attractive to him, he felt "impelled" to decline because it would entail "greater sacrifices" than he should make. "I do not feel," he added, "that I can afford to leave my life work, the practice of the law." *New York Times*, March 22, 1913.
    [2] There is a WWhw draft of this statement in WP, DLC.

To Mary Allen Hulbert

Dearest Friend,   The White House 23 March, 1913

Our third Sunday in Washington, but alas! only one letter from our dear, dear friend in Bermuda since we came,—and that means that we are deeply discontented! There are some things that we *must* have, and amongst them is constant news of you. Do you suppose that we need our friends less, and miss them less here than we did before? If so, pray, my dear Madam, dismiss the idea from your pretty head,—for it is false. On the contrary we miss and need them more—*much* more, if I may speak for the male member of the group with especial emphasis. Do you really want to know what the present President of the United States lacks and *must* have, if he is to serve his country as he should and give the best that is in him to his tasks? He needs *pleasure* and the unaffected human touch! He cannot live on duty. He cannot feed his heart on "great questions." He must have the constant tonic of personal friendships, old and sweet and tested, that have nothing to do with him as a politician, have no relation to his, or any, career, but touch him only as a man, ante-date his public responsibilities and will outlive them,—that *belong* to him, are part of his private and essential life! You said the other day that you felt very lonely and (foolish lady!) very useless, a looker on at a life that was not yours but that of another generation. Well, suppose that is true in Bermuda (as of course it is not!) here is a job for you in America which you can perform from Bermuda,— not as easily or as completely as you could in America, but so well that you may add to the success of a national administration. I am not jesting! I am in as dead earnest as I ever was in my life; and this is what I mean, that one Mary Allen Hulbert may be of infinite use and benefit to one Woodrow Wilson by merely drawing him aside from politics *at least once a week* into the realm of personal comradeship, into which politics can come only by way of an impertinent and irrelevant intrusion! She has the talisman by which all the magic of friendship and comradeship may be wrought, namely her own personality. I *know* what it can do for me for I have *felt* it shoot back every bolt in me and re- lease me from the pent house of my own cares and respon- sibilities. If you want to escape from Glencove, send your spirit over sea to Washington, to give me a holiday, and I shall rejoice as only he can who is privileged to subscribe himself

Your devoted friend   Woodrow Wilson

Love from all. Love to Allen. We are well.

ALS (WP, DLC).

From William Jennings Bryan

My Dear Mr President   [Lincoln, Neb.] Mch 23 [1913]

The papers have reported that Mr McCombs has declined the Paris Embassy & that Mr Augustus Thomas[1] is being considered. I know that but little reliance can be placed on newspaper reports but I venture to say that I regard Thomas as both competent and deserving[.] He is an accomplished fellow and a progressive of the first water.

I have yet to find the first man who dissents from your posi- tion on the Chinese loan and I believe you have won the lasting gratitude of China. With this nation setting such an example no other nation can force her into unfair terms. They will now be- come rivals for her friendship.

With assurances of esteem I am, my Dear Mr President,

Very truly yours   W. J. Bryan

P.S. I would like to present for your consideration for Gov of the Canal Zone Mr Metcalfe[2] my associate editor on The Commoner. Of all the men I know there is no one who comes more to my ideal as to the kind of a man needed there. I shall take great pleasure in telling you of his qualifications for the position. I understand that one of the commission acts as Gov[3]

ALS (WP, DLC).
  [1] In addition to being a prolific dramatist, Thomas was an ardent Democrat, who spoke at party dinners and meetings.
  [2] Richard Lee Metcalfe, editor of the *Omaha World-Herald*, 1896-1905, and associate editor of *The Commoner* since 1905.
  [3] He was appointed commissioner and head of the Department of Civil Administration of the Canal Zone.

To Thomas Davies Jones

My dear Friend: The White House March 24, 1913

Thank you for your letter of March twenty-second. As I wired you, I shall be only too glad to have you urge Dean Fine to accept the post I have offered him. I am deeply anxious to have him identified with my administration and his acceptance will give me real pleasure.

The same thing holds true with respect to Mr. Mott, and I hope you will use any influence you may have with him, for I have set my heart on having him represent us at Pekin.

With deep appreciation of the help you so generously offer, I am   Faithfully yours,   Woodrow Wilson

TLS (Mineral Point, Wisc., Public Library).

To Jacob Harry Hollander

My dear Dr. Hollander: [The White House] March 24, 1913

At present it would seem that interviews that are worth while are out of the question for me, but if you would be kind enough to dictate a pretty full memorandum for me about the mistakes you think have been made in the last three years with regard to San Domingo, I would be greatly obliged to you.[1]

Sincerely yours,   Woodrow Wilson

TLS (Letterpress Books, WP, DLC).
  [1] See WW to WJB, April 8, 1913, n. 1.

From William Jennings Bryan, with Enclosure

My Dear Mr President,   [Lincoln, Neb., c. March 24, 1913]

I have, in accordance with your suggestion, written Gov Lister[1] of Washington in regard to the proposed land law discriminating against the Japanese (I enclose a copy[2]). Gov Lister is a Democrat & will I doubt not go as [far] as local conditions will permit in carrying out your suggestions. I am also writing State Senator Caminetti[3] at Sacramento along the same line,[4] but as the Gov of California[5] is a Roosevelt Republican I think you had better ask Senator Works of Cal[6] to come to the White House & you can lay the matter before him verbally. As we have two Democratic Senators from Oregon would it not be well for you to see them and lay the matter before them. It is better than writing. The interest of the Pacific coast in the Exhibit at San Francisco ought to lead them to avoid any that disturb our amicable relations with Japan. This may require early action. With assurances of esteem etc I am my dear Mr President

Yours truly   W. J. Bryan

ALS (WP, DLC).

[1] Ernest Lister, elected governor in November 1912, the only winning Democrat on the state ticket.

[2] It is missing. Bryan was unaware of the fact that the discriminatory Washington bill limiting ownership of land to aliens "eligible to citizenship" had been superseded by one permitting all resident aliens to own urban land. This measure, submitted to the voters as a constitutional amendment, was overwhelmingly defeated on November 3, 1914.

[3] Anthony Caminetti, prominent California Democrat, member of Congress, 1891-95, of the California Assembly, 1883-85 and 1896-1900, and of the state Senate, 1885-87, and 1907-13.

[4] Anti-Japanese sentiment, based on fear of Japanese economic penetration of the state as well as racial prejudice, was of long standing among California farm and labor groups. The immediate problem facing the Wilson administration stemmed from the efforts of Democrats and some Progressives during the campaign of 1912 to attract the farm and labor vote by proposing legislation to curtail Japanese ownership of land. Although Wilson lost the state to Roosevelt, the Democrats made their best showing since 1892, capturing 44 per cent of the presidential vote, an increase that leading Democrats attributed to the party's stand on the Japanese question. Feeling was running strongly in favor of some kind of restrictive land measure when the legislature met in January 1913, and several bills were immediately introduced. They progressed slowly through the legislative process; and, at the time Bryan wrote this letter, there were two kinds of alien land bills pending. One prohibited all aliens from owning land; the other barred only aliens who were ineligible to citizenship, that is, Orientals. Subsequent documents will relate the administration's reaction to the developing crisis. For a detailed discussion of the entire issue, see Roger Daniels, *The Politics of Prejudice, The Anti-Japanese Movement in California and the Struggle for Japanese Exclusion.* (Berkeley and Los Angeles, Cal., 1962), and Link, *The New Freedom,* pp. 289-302.

[5] That is, Hiram Warren Johnson.

[6] John Downey Works, progressive Republican senator, who had supported Wilson in 1912.

ENCLOSURE

William Jennings Bryan to Ernest Lister

My Dear Gov,   Lincoln Neb Mch 23 [1913]

The Japanese Ambassador has called my attention to a bill before your legislature discriminating against the Japanese in the matter of owning land.

After talking with the President I write to urge you to use your influence with the legislature to prevent *discrimination—* that is urge that the bill be so drawn as to make ownership depend upon something other than race. The President hopes that the Pacific States will go as far as they can in helping him to promote amicable relations with the Asiatic nations. He thinks it better to make this personal and confidential appeal than to address you publicly through an official communication. Please regard this as personal and let me know confidentially what the situation is. With assurances of esteem I am

Very truly yours   W. J. Bryan

HwCL (WP, DLC).

James Bryce to Sir Edward Grey

Sir,   Washington, March 24, 1913.

I have the honour to inform you that I had an interview today with the President of the United States, in which I conveyed to him the views of His Majesty's Government with regard to the present position of the Panama Canal tolls question, and their desire that progress should be made towards its settlement, with as little delay as possible.[1] I pointed out that the time was no longer far distant when commercial vessels would begin to pass through the canal; that it was of importance that the pending controversy should be disposed of before that time; and that if the issue were to be settled by arbitration, a considerable time would necessarily be required for proceedings of that nature; and I observed also that in the interests of perfect goodfeeling between the two countries it was desirable that an early and friendly adjustment of their differences should be reached. I added that the importance of the matter was to be measured not by the material interests involved, but by the effect upon the sentiment of the peoples of the two countries, and indicated the surprise that had been felt in Great Britain at the adoption by Congress and the President of an interpretation of the Hay-

Pauncefote Treaty not only quite unexpected by us, but also quite different from that held by Mr. Choate and Mr. Henry White, who had been concerned in the negotiations of the treaty on the part of the United States. I adverted also to the omission of the late United States Administration to make to the protest of His Majesty's Government such a reply as might have been expected at the time or even to favour them with a statement of their view of the meaning of the treaty.

The President said that he had not yet had time to go into the matter but would take it up as soon as possible. He remarked that he did not think that Congress as a whole had intended to break the treaty. It had acted in the belief that as coastwise trade was already confined to vessels owned by citizens of the United States, legislation regarding it could not necessarily make a difference to British vessels, and its chief motive had been hostility to the United States transcontinental railways. (This is no doubt the fact.) I remarked that though what he said was true as to Congress generally, language had been employed by some Senators which had made an unfortunate impression im Great Britain, conveying the impression that the Senate meant to make itself judge in its own cause; and I remarked that although coastwise traffic was confined to United States vessels, the exemption of vessels carrying on that trade might seriously affect British as well as Canadian shipping passing through the canal by favouring the former in competition for the transport of goods. I also took occasion to contradict the fable assiduously propagated here that the Canadian railways had been the prompters of the protest of His Majesty's Government and were lobbying actively here against the coastwise exemption.

The President asked if the wish of His Majesty's Government was either that the exemption should be repealed or that the interpretation of the treaty should be referred to arbitration. I replied that such was their wish. He said that he would talk to Senators about it and see how the matter stood. I observed that it was believed that the bill for the repeal of the coastwise exemption, which is to be brought into the House, would pass easily, and that as to the Senate, the general opinion was that it would be guided by his wishes. I told him how the plank in the Baltimore Democratic platform relating to the subject had been introduced, and he said that it constantly happened that planks were so put in merely to please one or two persons without attracting any attention from the Convention at large or necessarily having their approval.

The President's tone throughout was entirely friendly and courteous.

I have the honour to be with the highest respect   Sir,
        your most obedient humble Servant,   James Bryce

TLS (FO 371/1702, No. 15574, PRO).
  1 For the background of this meeting, see J. Bryce to E. Grey, March 18, 1913, printed telegram (FO 371 / 1702, No. 12694, PRO), and E. Grey to J. Bryce, March 20, 1913, printed telegram (FO 371 / 1702, No. 12694, PRO).

From the Diary of Colonel House

Washington, D. C. March 24, 1913.

I went to the White House this morning at about half past nien [nine] o'clock. The door-keeper said the President was then trying to reach me over the telephone. When I went into his office he had the Commission of Captain [John H.] Rogers for U. S. Marshal of the Western District of Texas, on the desk before him. He did not know who Rogers was, and asked me if he was all right, and whether that was not Captain Bill's place. I explained that Bill lived in the Northern District and that I had already spoken to McReynolds about him. He then signed Rogers' commission.

We discussed Sague[1] for Collector of New York, and the relative merits of Marshall and Gibboney for U. S. District Attorney. We both thought Marshall the abler man of the two, but Gibboney was a Wilson man and was warmly advocated for the place by McAdoo. We came to no conclusion because it was decided I should see the Attorney General in the afternoon and thresh it out with him.

I then told him about Mr. Frick's call and his suggestion in regard to the United States Steel Corporation suit. Before the President replied, I said "you had better let me tell Frick that you referred me to the Attorney General and suggested that whatever proposal came to you should come through the Attorney General's Office." The President smiled and said "You may consider it has been said."

We discussed it at some length. The President thought that the Steel Corporation should have the same consideration as any other, neither more nor less, and that they should be allowed to make a proposition for an agreement as to a decree of court in the suit.

Our further talk was of McReynolds, Gregory, O'Gorman and others. He does not admire O'Gorman. Neither do I. He has not sufficient stamina. I predicted that he would go out of office at the end of his term; because the Tammany machine will not have him, and our friends will not support him, and between the two he will lose out.

The President asked me to speak to McReynolds about appointments and tell him of the complaint being made that anti-Wilson men were getting all the offices. He thought we should look into such matters more carefully. He has no personal feeling in regard to this, but is wise enough to know that it will hurt his administration to discard its friends when they are fit and appoint those who were unfriendly.

¹ John Kelsey Sague, cashier of the Poughkeepsie Savings Bank and Mayor of Poughkeepsie, 1907-12.

From Alvey Augustus Adee, with Enclosure

Mr. President: Washington March 25, 1913.

I have the honor to enclose herewith a memorandum of a conversation I had to-day with the Chinese Minister.¹ I informed the Minister that I would take great pleasure in transmitting to you the substance of the message from President Yuan Shih Kai but that I understood that it was your intention to defer any discussion of your recent statement with the foreign representatives in Washington until the return of the Secretary of State.

The Minister expressed his entire satisfaction with this arrangement, and I gathered from the conversation that on the return of the Secretary the Minister may request an opportunity of presenting the text of the message to you in person.

Very respectfully,   Alvey A. Adee

TLS (WP, DLC).
¹ Chang Yin Tang.

E N C L O S U R E

March 25, 1913.
Department of State.

MEMORANDUM

The Chinese Minister called at the Department to-day and informed the Acting Secretary of State, Mr. Adee, that he had received special instructions from President Yuan Shih Kai to make formal expression of the thanks of the people of China and of their appreciation of the just and magnanimous attitude of President Wilson indicated in the public statement recently issued by him which was accepted by the Chinese Government as an expression of sincere friendship toward the Republic and people of China whose aims and aspirations in the establishment of liberal institutions find such ready response in America.

The Minister further expressed the belief of the Chinese Government that the friendship now so happily existing between the two countries will be further strengthened as a result of this policy.

T MS (WP, DLC).

From Henry Burchard Fine

Muenchen 8 am [March] 25th [1913]

Letter not received but impossible to accept.

Harry.

T telegram (WP, DLC).

From Frank Ellsworth Doremus[1]

My dear Mr. President: Washington, D. C. March 25, 1913.

During our recent conversation, concerning the Panama Canal tolls controversy, I stated that the question whether the preference to our coastwise trade would contravene the Hay-Pauncefote Treaty was very carefully considered in the debates that preceded the passage of the Panama Canal Act. You suggested you would like to have me furnish you with excerpts from the Congressional Record, bearing upon this question, that you might peruse them at your leisure. Since then I have gone through the Congressional Record from the time the discussion of the bill began in the House, May 16, 1912, until its final passage in the Senate, August 9th, 1912, and am handing you copies of a few of the speeches reflecting both views of the Treaty.[2] There were many more, but I presume these will sufficiently show the character and scope of the debate.

Permit me to say that the discussion of the Treaty was directly precipitated in the Senate by the receipt of the British note of July 8, 1912, which was brought to the attention of the Senate by Secretary Knox July 12, 1912. A copy of Secretary Knox's communication (Congressional Record, page 8990) is herewith enclosed. From that time until the passage of the bill, August 9, 1912, the Record shows that the Hay-Pauncefote Treaty was the chief topic of debate, and the view of the Senate with reference thereto is shown by the vote on the bill—yeas, 47; nays, 15. The record of this vote is enclosed (Congressional Record, page 10590).

The Statement recently made in the Senate that the Panama Canal Act was passed without adequate consideration is unsupported by the Record. The question was carefully, earnestly and deliberately considered by men who realize the seriousness of violating a treaty obligation. In this connection your attention is respectfully invited to the enclosed copy of the speech of Mr. Mann,[3] minority leader, (Congressional Record, page 2201).

Enclosed you will also find a copy of the pamphlet issued by the State Department, containing copies of the diplomatic negotiations between the two governments. May I call your attention to the concluding paragraph of the first British note (page 12), from which it clearly appears that Great Britain does not seriously doubt our right, under the treaty, to exempt the coastwise trade from the payment of tolls, but questions our ability to frame regulations which would prevent the exemption from resulting in a preference to United States shipping generally, and consequently in an infraction of the Treaty. This statement was, of course, induced by the fact that under our navigation laws, foreign vessels can not engage in our coastwise trade, and would not, therefore, be adversely affected by any treatment we might accord vessels engaged therein.

With this admission at the outset of the negotiations, it is indeed unfortunate that thus far we have been unable to dispose of the controversy by the positive assurance, upon our part, that the exemption would be confined exclusively to the coastwise trade, and thus prove non-discriminatory as to British shipping.

It can scarcely be doubted this would have been the outcome, had not Secretary Knox been embarrassed and the British hand strengthened by the unseemly haste with which certain of our citizens, both in and out of Congress, denounced the Act as a violation of the Treaty, and urged its immediate repeal or its submission to The Hague Tribunal, in contravention of our arbitration treaty with Great Britain, which authorizes arbitration only after diplomacy has failed.

With assurance of my highest regard, I am,

Very respectfully yours,   Frank E Doremus

TLS (WP, DLC).
[1] Democratic congressman from Michigan since 1911.
[2] All enclosures mentioned in this letter are missing.
[3] James Robert Mann, Republican congressman from Illinois since 1897.

From the Diary of Colonel House

March 25, 1913.

I went to the White House at half past nine going directly to the President's room. Just as yesterday he had a Texas commission before him which the Attorney General had sent over for his signature. It was Judge J[ohn]. L[afayette]. Camp for the Western District of Texas.[1] The President remarked that "McReynolds is going too fast. I do not know who this man is." When I assured him that Camp was all right, he signed the commission.

I outlined my conversation with McReynolds regarding Gibboney, Marshall, the appointment of Wilson men and Mr. Frick's proposal.

The President asked me to dinner at seven o'clock, in order that we might go over some appointments. I suggested asking McAdoo to come in after dinner so we might discuss matters relating to his department. He asked me to invite him. . . .

I had an engagement with Carter Glass at five. We drove in order not to be interrupted. He wished me to aid in some Virginia appointments in his district or adjacent. I asked him to write out the list and promised to attend to it for him.

The purpose of our meeting was to discuss the currency measure and I urged him not to allow Owen and the Senate Committee change what we had agreed upon, or to destroy any of the essential features. He promised to be firm. I advised using honey so long as it was effective, but when it was not, I would bring the President and Secretary of the Treasury to his rescue.

I spoke to the President about this after dinner and advised that McAdoo and I whip the Glass measure into final shape, which he could endorse and take to Owen as his own. My opinion was that Owen would be more likely to accept it as a Presidential measure than as a measure coming from the House Committee on Banking and Currency.

When I went to the White House the President met me. Mrs. Wilson was a little late for dinner. It was again a family affair. The Wilsons are living simply. We had fish, veal cutlets, rice, peas and potatoes, a simple lettuce salad and ice cream. It is a household in which there are no pretenses and where everything is in good taste. I talked mostly to Mrs. Wilson and Jessie, very little to the President. Jessie wanted me to use my good offices in behalf of Dr. Henry Van Dyke for some foreign mission. After questioning her I think she understood that Van Dyke was hardly the man for her father to appoint. However, I told the President that Jessie and I had agreed upon Van Dyke for an appointment although we had not gone through the formality of asking him what he thought of it.

After dinner the President, Yumulty [Tumulty] and I went upstairs into the library. I asked him to recite for me again James Whitcomb Riley's "The Man in the Moon." We looked at pictures and discussed the historic things in the library. The desk, at which he sat, was made from wood taken from the Resolute which went in quest of Sir John Franklin and his unfortunate party. The President seemed interested to learn that my father owned jointly with the Confederate Government the celebrated gunboat "Harriet Lane" which was captured off Galveston during the Civil War.

We first took up foreign appointments. He thought that Walter Page was about the best man left for Ambassador to Great Britain. I was pleased to hear this, for I had been urging his appointment. I was not only the first to suggest Page for this place, but since Eliot and Olney declined it, I have advocated him earnestly. He asked if I thought Page would take it. I assured him that he would, and promised to find out definitely tomorrow.

We discussed a great number of other people for foreign appointments, among them Jos. E. Willard, St George Tucker and Thos. Nelson Page. He declared that he was almost of a mind to appoint these three. I thought Thos. Nelson Page should have Italy, and he agreed. He spoke of Rudolph Spreckles for Germany, since Fine has declined it, and of Chas. R. Crane for Russia. We practically agreed upon Phelan for Ambassador to Austria and Henry Morganthau for Turkey. Augustus Thomas was spoken of for France merely tentatively. I told him, too, about Lewis Hancock[2] of Texas, for a small post like Switzerland or Belgium. He wrote his name on the list. I considered him admirably fitted for such a post.

He said that Guthrie of Pennsylvania did not want to go to Mexico but wanted a European post. He remarked "I am inclined to give him nothing."

McAdoo wanted to know why he did not persuade Bryan that Gregory was the man to go to Mexico. The President replied, "I have tried to convince him six separate times, and Mr. Bryan can only give a theory for an argument. When anyone insists upon doing that, there is no use to argue." He said it was the only thing Bryan was obstinate about and he supposed he would have to let him have his way.

We agreed upon Dudley Field Malone as Third Assistant Secretary of State if he would take it. He has been one of our most difficult problems. We went over the collectors of customs, etc.

etc. It is wearying work and one which neither the President nor I enjoy. I urged him to give us a list of names and let us thresh the matter out with the departments and so place the people he wanted to have appointed, and not worry about it himself.

I promised to come over again next week and stay long enough to go over it more thoroughly. He expressed regret that I did not live in Washington. He seems to have changed his mind regarding the viewpoint I was to obtain by being away, and now wants to have me near him. I took the midnight for New York.

[1] As federal attorney.
[2] Lawyer, banker, gentleman scholar, long prominent in the cultural and civic life of Austin; mayor, 1895-97.

An Appeal

The White House March 26, 1913.

The terrible floods in Ohio and Indiana have assumed the proportions of a national calamity.[1] The loss of life and the infinite suffering involved prompt me to issue an earnest appeal to all who are able in however small a way to assist the labors of the American Red Cross to send contributions at once to the Red Cross at Washington or to the local treasurers of the Society.

We should make this a common cause. The needs of those upon whom this sudden and overwhelming disaster has come should quicken everyone capable of sympathy and compassion to give immediate aid to those who are laboring to rescue and relieve.   Woodrow Wilson

T MS (WP, DLC).
[1] A torrential rainstorm, representing the eastern edge of a severe storm that had earlier battered the Plains states, hit Indiana and Ohio on March 25, causing flooding, the worst being in central and southern Ohio. First reports of the disaster in the *New York Times*, March 26 and 27, 1913, for example, placed the loss of lives in the thousands and property damage in the hundreds of millions. After the storm had abated by the end of the week, the figures on the loss of life were scaled downward to several hundred, but property losses were incalculable. Governor James M. Cox of Ohio, for example, put the figure for losses in his state alone at $300,500,000. The swollen Ohio River also wrought considerable havoc in Kentucky, as did subsequent heavy rains in several eastern states.

To Thomas Staples Martin and John Joseph Fitzgerald[1]

[The White House] March 26, 1913

I am directing the War Department to extend the necessary aid to the sufferers from the floods. May I assume that I will have your approval in seeking the subsequent authorization of Congress and the necessary funds?   Woodrow Wilson

T telegram (WP, DLC).
1 Chairmen of the appropriations committees of the Senate and House.

To James McMahon Cox and Samuel Moffett Ralston

[The White House] March 26, 1913.
I deeply sympathize with the people of your State in the terrible disaster that has come upon them. Can the Federal Government assist in any way?   Woodrow Wilson

T telegram (Letterpress Books, WP, DLC).

From James McMahon Cox

Columbus, Ohio, March 26, 1913.
We have asked the Secretary of War this morning for tents, supplies, rations and physicians. In the name of humanity see that this is granted at the earliest possible moment. The situation in this State is very critical. We believe that two hundred and fifty thousand people were unsheltered last night and the indications are that before night the Muskingum Valley will suffer the fate of the Miami and Scioto Valleys.
James M. Cox, Governor

T telegram (WP, DLC).

To James McMahon Cox

[The White House] March 26, 1913
Your telegram received. Have directed the Secretary of War immediately to comply with your request, and to use every agency of his Department to meet the needs of the situation.
Woodrow Wilson

T telegram (Letterpress Books, WP, DLC).

To Royal Meeker

My dear Meeker: [The White House] March 26, 1913
Thank you very warmly for your kindness in sending me the answers to the Questionaire. They are most useful to me, and I warmly appreciate all the trouble you have taken in getting this material together.   Cordially yours,   Woodrow Wilson

TLS (Letterpress Books, WP, DLC).

To Charles Stedman Macfarland[1]

My dear Mr. Macfarland: [The White House] March 26, 1913

Allow me to acknowledge more formally than it was possible the other day when you called at my office the receipt of the several papers you then handed me.

I need not tell you how deeply I appreciate the address of confidence addressed directly to me on the part of the Federal Council of the Churches of Christ in America,[2] or how greatly it adds to my sense of being supported and guided to have such feelings and confidence expressed.

I appreciate also the weight and significance of the resolutions of the Council with regard to the early recognition of the republic of China.[3]

The memorial with regard to the assignment of the proper quota of chaplains to the various divisions of our land and naval forces impresses me very much indeed.[4]

For all of these interesting and important papers, allow me to thank you and your colleagues.

    Cordially and sincerely yours, Woodrow Wilson

TLS (Letterpress Books, WP, DLC).

[1] Congregational minister and executive secretary of the Federal Council of the Churches of Christ in America.

[2] The document is missing in WP, DLC. A copy is printed at March 5, 1913.

[3] This document is also missing. It read:

"RESOLVED[,] one[,] that this Federal Council hereby records its gratitude to God for the wonderful providence which has given to our fellow-Christians in China and the Chinese people a new government which has as its fundamental principles liberty, both civil and religious, equality, enlightenment and progress.

"RESOLVED, two, that we extend to the Christian churches of the new Republic our heartiest congratulations upon the extraordinary opportunity now afforded them to glorify God and serve their nation by helping to lay a foundation of truth and righteousness for the newly established Republic, and that we assure the Christians of China that they have the hearty Godspeed and the unceasing prayers of the Christians of the United States of America.

"RESOLVED, three, that this Federal Council respectfully requests the government of the United States to take early action for the recognition by it of the Republic of China, and that the President of the Council be entrusted with this duty associating with himself such other members as he may select." "Administrative Committee Records, 1913-1916" (Papers of the Federal Council of the Churches of Christ in America, PPPrHi).

[4] The memorial, deploring the assignment of only twenty-one chaplains for 53,375 men in the navy and sixty-seven for 95,000 men in the army, appealed "most earnestly" for an increase in the number so that each battleship, cruiser, schoolship, and navy yard and each occupied army post would have at least one chaplain. Shailer Mathews et al. to the President et al., March 25, 1913, TC MS (WP, DLC).

From the Diary of Colonel House

New York, March 26, 1913.

Mr. Frick rang up at six and asked me to dine with him alone. I agreed to do so if he could have dinner as early as half past seven since I had an engagement for half past eight. He promised to have dinner very promptly, which he did. . . .

We talked of the United States Steel Corporation suit. I explained in a few words the President's attitude, which was that the matter must come to him through the Attorney General who would be glad to receive any offer looking to a settlement of the suit by a decree of court. He asked if I would meet with himself and Judge Gary. I declined to do this, saying they would have to thresh it out between themselves; that my position was that of adviser to the President and I did not wish to be thought of in any other capacity.

He seemed to see that this was best, and asked if I would arrange for him and Gary to meet with the Attorney General. I promised to speak to the Attorney General about it when he lunches with me on Sunday.

I asked him to give me in detail the component parts of which the Steel Corporation was formed. This he did in the frankest way possible. He spoke of Mr. Morgan's health and said it was very bad, worse than people thought.[1] He spoke well of Jack Morgan.[2]

[1] J. Pierpont Morgan died on March 31, 1913.
[2] J. Pierpont Morgan, Jr.

To James McMahon Cox and Samuel Moffet Ralston

[The White House] March 27, 1913.

I have directed the Secretary of War to proceed at once to the flood districts with the necessary staff in order to extend every possible assistance to the sufferers more promptly than would be possible if they had to overcome the present imperfect means of communication with Washington.   Woodrow Wilson

T telegram (Letterpress Books, WP, DLC).

To Franklin Knight Lane

My dear Mr. Secretary: [The White House] March 27, 1913

Mr. Tumulty has handed me your note of March third, sending me the enclosed.[1] I entirely agree with the writer. I think we would be doing a great disservice to a fine cause if we were to displace Miss Lathrop, and I had quite made up my mind that it is out of the question that we should permit anybody to push her out.[2]

In haste   Cordially yours,   Woodrow Wilson

TLS (Letterpress Books, WP, DLC).
    [1] Lane's note and the enclosure are missing.
    [2] Wilson did not replace Julia Clifford Lathrop as chief of the Children's Bureau in the Department of Labor. She retained the post until her resignation in 1921.

To James Fairman Fielder

My dear Governor: [The White House] March 27, 1913

We are watching with the deepest interest down here the course of business here at Trenton. The feeling grows upon me every day that it is absolutely necessary for the prestige of the party not only, but for the vindication of the reforms we all stand for, that the Jury Reform bill should be put through in its integrity. Nothing that we have done in the past two years will be safe without it. The enforcement of the Corrupt Practices Act, the effective administration of the Geran law, will be impossible unless we put this bulwark between the people and those who try to break down those wholesome measures of control, enacted in the people's behalf.

I feel these things so deeply that I think it would be fatal to submit to any kind of defeat. I take the liberty of suggesting with great earnestness that if it should prove impossible to get the bill through at this session, you call an extra session for a very early date for the special purpose of putting that through, and also a plan for a constitutional convention. We can not escape the responsibility for these.

If you desire, I might make it possible in between the regular and the extra session to come back and make at least one address to the people.

With the deepest desire to help, I am

Faithfully yours,   Woodrow Wilson

TLS (Letterpress Books, WP, DLC).

From Samuel Moffett Ralston

Indianapolis, Indiana, March 27, 1913

Your first message delayed. Could not get reply through. Your second message stating you have ordered prompt assistance and relief to flood sufferers through the War Department is just received. The stricken people of Indiana appreciate your prompt and practicable assistance and they appreciate even more the generous spirit of sympathy that lies back of your action. In their name and for myself I thank you.

Samuel M. Ralston,   Governor.

T telegram (WP, DLC).

From the Diary of Colonel House

March 28, 1913.

Walter Page telephoned around nien [nine] o'clock that "I have decided to turn my face towards the East" which meant he would accept the post to Great Britain. I felicitated with him, and expressed my pleasure. He wished to know the next move. I told him I would notify the President, and that he would write him a formal note offering him the Ambassadorship.

I called up the President at Washington a little after nine to tell of Page's acceptance. He replied "that is fine, I am very glad." He promised to write Page at once.

I telephoned Page to let him know how pleased the President was. Page expressed great appreciation for what I had done.

To Walter Hines Page

My dear Page,   The White House 28 March, 1913

I am writing to ask whether you are willing that I should send your name in to the Senate, when it meets again, as Ambassador to Great Britain. I hope with all my heart that you are. It would give me the deepest satisfaction to have in London a man whose character and ability and tact and ability to comprehend a situation and the men who formed a part of it I could so absolutely rely on; and it would be of the greatest advantage to the country and to the party. Pray say Yes and make me content!

Cordially and faithfully Yours,   Woodrow Wilson

ALS (W. H. Page Papers, MH).

From James McMahon Cox

Columbus, Ohio, March 28, 1913.

We are more than grateful for the good things you are doing for our State.   James M. Cox.

T telegram (WP, DLC).

From James Fairman Fielder

My dear Mr. President: [Trenton, N. J.] March 28, 1913.

I am glad indeed to receive your letter of yesterday and to know that those of us who are in favor of real jury reform and proper constitutional convention bills can have your personal assistance. I am satisfied there are enough votes in the Assembly to pass the sort of a jury commission bill I have been urging, if the joint conference committee will report it, and I assure you that no other kind of bill will become a law with my approval. I have already considered the possibility of a special session and should the legislature adjourn without performing what I believe to be its duty on these two important subjects, it is my idea that an extra session should be called about May first, so that there shall be sufficient time between adjournment and reconvening, for public meetings at which the peoples' demand can emphatically be made known. In case such meetings are necessary, we would want your presence and I am glad to be assured that we can have it.

Not knowing whether you would desire me to make your letter public, I at once wired Mr. Tumulty, requesting him to do so and have myself declined to give copies to the press. I do not yet know whether Mr. Tumulty has made your letter public[1] and I shall not hand copies of this to the papers, leaving it to you to so use it if you desire.   Very sincerely,   James F Fielder

TLS (WP, DLC).
  [1] In fact, Tumulty had already given a copy of Wilson's letter to the correspondent of the *Newark Evening News*. It appeared in that newspaper on March 28.

From the Diary of Josephus Daniels

Friday, March 28, 1913

The President read his message to be presented to the Congress when it convenes on April 7th. It is brief, comprehensive, and illuminating. The opening sentence gave the reason why he had called the Congress in extraordinary session and the chief reason given was that the business interests of the country might know what changes would be made in the tariff so they might adjust themselves to it.

Secretary Bryan suggested that it might be well to add to the other reason given "and that the consumers ought to receive the benefit to be derived from the (reduced) tariff reduction at as early a date as practicable." The President said that he thought that that would be generally understood without being specifically stated and would be glad to incorporate Mr. Bryan's suggestion in the completed draft when it was finished. I suggested that the allusion to possible currency legislation to follow tariff legislation might not be the wisest. I had talked to some of the leaders of the House who felt that it was exceedingly important that after the House had passed the tariff bill or bills that the whole country's attention would be focused on the Senate so that the Senate would have no matter before them except the passage of tariff bills. These leaders of Congress felt that the suggestion in the message of currency legislation would divide the attention of the country and make it easier for the Senate to follow the past precedents and cut the heart out of tariff bills because the public attention would be centered upon currency legislation rather than tariff legislation. President Wilson stated that he had given consideration to this thought and discussed it with members of Congress but in his opinion the currency legislation ought to be enacted at this session of Congress if there could be an agreement and it would be a help to the tariff situation if the suggestion was made in the message that currency legislation badly needed would follow. "In the past," said the President, "when tariff reduction bills were enacted, the question was, if trade expansion follows, where is the money with which to do the increased business of the country? By holding out the expectation of salutary currency legislation, this question would not be asked and the promise of [that] it now would be probably taken up as the tariff bills are enacted would be helpful.["]

There was a general discussion on the tariff situation. Secretary McAdoo thought that the President ought to add the word "labor" to the word "industry" in his message, in view of the fact that in the last campaign the republicans made much of the suggestion that the democrats would not give the same care to labor that the republicans had done. Secretary Wilson expressed the opinion that the word "industry" included "labor" and it ought not to be added separately. Secretary Redfield gave statistics of the exports of manufactured goods showing an increase of 20% in the last year. Secretary McAdoo called attention to the fact that the President used the term "competitive tariff" several times and seemed to indicate that the democratic tariff would open the door to competition and asked whether this would be wise. The President said that his message was exactly along the line of his pledges before the election and any suggestion that he should not demand now what he promised then recalled a cartoon recently appearing in a Chicago paper after he made his speech in Chicago on his return from Bermuda. Underneath the cartoon were the words "This fellow actually talks after the election just as he talked before," as if that were a reprehensible thing. "I propose," said the President, "to urge the tariff along the lines of my pre-election promises."

Secretary Bryan read a letter which was to be sent to the representative of the bankers that had been requested to take part in the Chinese loan. It suggested to the bankers that they ought to give China further time to pay the obligations already incurred. There was some question as to whether this was wise in view of the Cabinet's refusal to request American bankers to lend China money on the terms proposed by the banking syndicate. President Wilson said, "I feel so keenly the desire to help China that I prefer to err in the line of helping that country than otherwise. If we had entered into the loan with other powers we would have got nothing but mere influence in China and lost the proud position which America secured when Secretary Hay stood for the open door in China after the Boxer Uprising.["] He declared he believed that our position would be stronger not to be in partnership with other countries but to stand ready to aid China and to be able to say to Russia "what are your designs on Manchuria," and to Japan, "What are your wishes on this part of China," and to England, Germany, or any other country, "What are your designs," and being free, this country could help China and restore the relationship which this country occupied toward that country and the world when Mr. Hay was Secretary of State.

The President said in connection with the refusal of the Cabinet to request the American bankers to lend China money under terms which would give the lending powers control of Chinese affairs that after his publication the Japanese Minister called at the State Department and asked to be informed of the mind of the United States and it developed then that the United States had asked Japan to take part of the proposed loan to China and Japan had acceded to this in the Taft administration. "It seems," said the President, "in speaking of this matter, that the United States had invited Japan to dinner and than [then] absented itself when dinner was served and Japan did not understand it." Of course he laughed. Mr. Bryan and I both feel this a mistake we made and we ought to have informed the other governments of our actions, but he did not believe any serious result would follow. . . .

The President said he had a talk with Mr. Rea[1] who had a power of attorney from Sun Yat Sen, whose imperial company had the right to build 10,000 miles of railroad in China and was here

[1] George Bronson Rea, technical secretary of the Chinese National Railway Corp.

to get money to finance this construction. It seems Mr. Rea, who has long been Sun Yat Sen's financial manager, wished to assure the President that the loan as proposed by certain syndicates would not go through and [if] the loans were not made to China on those hard terms the railroad company could get American capital to build the railroads in China, because they had good security. The President said he told Mr. Rea that his public statement was sufficient evidence of what this government stood for in the way of loans and he thought nothing more was needed and he said Mr. Rea seemed to assent to this. Secretary Redfield said he had just seen a letter from a great manufacturing concern in America saying they sent six modern engines to China and this is very good evidence that America leads in the Chinese situation.

Just as the Cabinet meeting closed, Attorney General McReynolds announced that the republican marshall in Texas had resigned thus opening the way of appointing Captain Bill McDonald marshall in Texas. Captain McDonald was the bodyguard of the President in the campaign and won his spurs as a ranger, as a scout and confederate soldier. The whole Cabinet rejoiced that the way was open and the President [was] advised to send it in as a recess appointment without waiting for Congress. Speaking of the fact that Captain Bill carried in his body many bullets and had been wounded in war and other conflicts, President Wilson said, "you may recall when my scalp was injured in an automobile accident last fall, Captain Bill was with me, and he suffered a severe wrench in his back, and when the automobile was righted and on the way to the doctor, Captain Bill said 'I certainly hate to be hurt—in an accident. I don't mind it when I have a fair chance and some fellow shooting at me, but being hurt running into a stump is a kind of injury[.' "]

T MS (J. Daniels Papers, DLC).

Three Letters to Albert Sidney Burleson

My dear Burleson: [The White House] March 30, 1913

At Corsicana, Texas, there lives a Miss Alice Johnson, who was the adopted daughter of the late Rev. Dr. J. Leighton Wilson. Doctor Wilson was in no way related to me except by his intimate and lifelong affectionate friendship with my father. He was one of the noblest men that ever lived, and this lady whom he adopted seems to me an exceptionally fine woman. She very much wants to be postmistress at Corsicana (the post falls vacant next February) and I hope sincerely that you will keep her in mind.[1]

I foresee that I will have to make a number of personal appointments.   Cordially yours,   Woodrow Wilson

TLS (Letterpress Books, WP, DLC).
[1] She did not receive the appointment because Congressman Rufus Hardy, also from Corsicana, supported another candidate, and eventually Wilson yielded. See WW to A. Johnson, March 5, 1914.

❖

My dear Burleson: The White House March 30, 1913

I think it will be best for me to drop you a note from time to time as items affecting the Department come to my attention. I write this morning to say that when the post office in Murfreesboro, Tennessee, falls vacant I am anxious that Mrs. Margaret Elliott[1] of that place shall be appointed postmistress. The reasons are many, and I shall be very happy to explain them to you when I see you. Judge Houston[2] is the Congressman from that district, but I hope he will have no objections to my making a personal choice in that case.[3]

                Cordially and sincerely yours,   Woodrow Wilson

[1] Margaret Graham Johnston (Mrs. William Yandell) Elliott, mother of Wilson's brother-in-law, Edward Graham Elliott.
[2] William Cannon Houston, congressman from Woodbury, Tenn., since 1905.
[3] Wilson sent her nomination to the Senate on May 22; she was confirmed on June 10, 1913.

❖

My dear Burleson: The White House March 30, 1913

I do not know whether or not I spoke to you about the post office in Gainesville, Georgia. There seems to be a pretty fight on down there, because Hardy,[1] who represents that district, is purposing to oust Mrs. Longstreet,[2] the present postmistress, who is the widow of General Longstreet. General Longstreet was a gallant soldier, and although he angered his people very much after the Civil War by aligning himself with the Republicans, I think we should be very slow indeed to disturb the tenure of Mrs. Longstreet.

                Cordially and faithfully yours,   Woodrow Wilson

TLS (A. S. Burleson Papers, DLC).
[1] He probably meant Thomas William Hardwick, congressman from the 10th Georgia district; however, Gainesville was in the 9th congressional district, represented by Thomas Montgomery Bell of Gainesville.
[2] Helen Dortch (Mrs. James) Longstreet, who retained her post.

To James Fairman Fielder

My dear Governor: [The White House] March 30, 1913

Thank you warmly for your letter of March twenty-eighth which is laid before me this morning.

It is very cheering to hear what you say of the prospects of the Jury Reform. I think the whole state will be aroused about the matter before we get through with it, and it is something that is worth rousing it about.

I am sincerely obliged to you for your permission to publish your reply, which I shall do with pleasure. I congratulate you on the decision of calling an extra session if it should be necessary.

May I suggest that you consult with Gaskill[1] about the form in which the bill shall finally be put through? I have just received a letter from him which has made a very great impression on me,[2] and I know you would be glad to hear what he has said to me.

              Cordially and faithfully yours   Woodrow Wilson

TLS (Letterpress Books, WP, DLC).
  [1] Nelson Burr Gaskill, Princeton 1896, assistant attorney general of New Jersey since 1906.
  [2] The letter is missing.

To Robert Brent Keyser

My dear Dr. Keyser: [The White House] March 30, 1913

I feel it a sort of duty on my part in view of your present search for a president for the Johns Hopkins to speak once more of Dr. Henry B. Fine, whom I have just been trying in vain to induce to accept the post of Ambassador to Germany. My disappointment in not being able to persuade him is very keen indeed, because I know of no man who could represent the country with greater dignity or efficiency or distinction. His own tastes dictate that he should come back to his post at Princeton and continue his teaching work, and it would seem as if I ought not to set my judgment against his in a matter of that kind, but I feel so strongly that it would be a great and unnecessary loss to the academic world to be deprived of the use of his administrative ability and of his capacity to govern men and attach them to himself that I am venturing once more to urge upon you the consideration of his name for the presidency of the Hopkins.

I am prompted perhaps as much by my affection for the Hopkins as by my admiration for Fine. I think if you were to ask men like Pritchett of the Carnegie Foundation, you would find that they think Fine one of the greatest of the men whom our recent college life has developed.

With the most cordial good wishes for the future of the University, I am　　　　Sincerely yours,　Woodrow Wilson

TLS (Letterpress Books, WP, DLC).

To John Coates Eastman[1]

My dear Mr. Eastman:　　　[The White House] March 30, 1913

Now and again at very rare intervals a moment of leisure comes to me, when I can turn to those who have been especially generous in their support of me and of the things I believe in and tell them how earnestly and sincerely I appreciate the work they have done. May I not take a moment today to send you a very cordial message of this sort? Men caught in the hurry of public business are apt to be supposed ungracious and ungrateful, simply because their whole days are engrossed in matters not personal to themselves. As a matter of fact, I venture to say they often turn with very genuine gratitude in their thoughts at least to those who have upheld them.

Cordially and sincerely yours,　Woodrow Wilson

TLS (Letterpress Books, WP, DLC).
1 Owner and publisher of the Chicago *Daily Journal*.

To Mary Allen Hulbert

Dearest Friend,　　　　The White House 30 March, 1913

What shall I say to speak adequately our sympathy, our admiration, our deep desire to help? Your letter—so full of the tragedy of your struggle for Allen—went to our hearts like the cry to which we would respond with everything that is in us. Our prayer is, that these words (how it *hurts* us that there is nothing but words!) may come to you freighted with what they are meant to carry, love and reassurance and comfort. You have done all that was possible,—have acted with courage, with wisdom, with a quick power to see what there was to do. We are so thankful the Wallaces[1] were there to help—in every way, and wish that we had been there to help also; tho. I must see [say] I cannot think of anything we could have done or suggested that you did not see and act upon. How fine you are, how fit for an emergency! You do not succumb to *anything*, however daunting or tragical even, but *act*, act with your heart and mind and will, and save the situation as far as it is possible to save it. Our hearts go out to you and our admiration no less. *You* always do the fine thing no matter how everything tumbles about you and threatens to go to wreck. So that there is something inspiring about this poor distracted letter of yours. It does not leave us wholly sad. It tugs at our hearts all the harder because we seem to act and feel with you at every step of the narrative and yet there is a sort of tonic in it for us, coming straight from you! God bless you and help you! He *cannot* mean to wholly break so noble and loving a spirit! You are to come here, straight, just so soon as you set foot on this continent again, and are to stay until you *feel* the healing effect of what we shall give you—are giving you—out of our hearts. You have nothing to regret or chide yourself for. You did *all* that could be done and did the right things well. I believe the boy is saved from the toils and the experience may be the making of him when once he has got into harness in Boston. I am sure that Mr. Wallace will do the best possible for him. Hurrah for a heroic mother who is the real thing! That is just at this moment my uppermost feeling. We are all well. The business, anxious as it often is, seems to agree with me. How fine it will be to see you here! Tell us everything and take in return all that you need of reassurance and affection.

Your devoted friend   Woodrow Wilson

ALS (WP, DLC).
  [1] William Wallace and Jouett Lee Wallace of Boston. He was an insurance broker.

From Paul Underwood Kellogg and Others

Dear Mr. President: [New York, March 31, 1913]

On the eve of the convening of the Sixty-Third Congress in special session, the undersigned desire to bring to your attention certain bills of importance which have received the favorable consideration of the last congress, but which owing to various reasons failed of affirmative action.

Nothing could set more vividly before the country the urgency of such measures than the words of your inaugural address in which you pointed out the need for perfecting the means by which government may be put at the service of humanity in safeguarding the health of the nation, the health of its men and its women and its children, as well as their rights in the struggle for existence. The country has been stirred by your declaration:

"This is no sentimental duty. The firm basis of government

is justice, not pity. These are matters of justice. There can be no equality of opportunity, the first essential of justice in the body politic, if men and women and children be not shielded in their lives, their very vitality, from the consequences of great industrial and social processes which they cannot alter, control, or singly cope with. Society must see to it that it does not itself crush or weaken or damage its own constituent parts."

The undersigned are aware that the time and energy of Congress will be largely expended upon the revision of the revenue and currency statutes. Without in any way meaning to minimize the importance of these subjects, we wish to lay emphasis upon what we believe to be the necessity for the passage of certain other measures directly affecting the health and happiness of hundreds of thousands of citizens. The legislative proposals which we present to you are not new; several of them have met with little open opposition; some have been passed by one house of Congress; others by both; all have been prepared by experts and are based upon tried principles already embodied either in the federal laws, in the laws of the various states, or in the laws of other nations. An example is the bill which aims to compensate workingmen employed in interstate commerce for accidents to life and limb. Another is the eight hour bill for women in the District of Columbia, which was lost through an accident in the closing hours of the last Congress.

The measures which had not passed when Congress adjourned and which are herewith advocated are as follows. It is the principles underlying these several bills rather than the specific provisions of any measure that we wish to be understood as urging upon the attention of the President and Congress:

Providing compensation for federal employes suffering injury or occupational diseases in the course of their employment.

Providing compensation for employes in interstate commerce suffering injury in the course of their employment.

Harmonizing conflicting court decisions in different states by giving the state itself the right of appeal to the Supreme Court of United States.

Establishing the eight hour day for women employed in certain occupations in the District of Columbia.

Co-ordinating the federal health activities and strengthening the public health service.

Providing in the immigration act for mental examination of immigrants by alienists; safe-guarding the welfare of immigrants at sea by detailing American medical officers and matrons to immigrant-carrying ships.

Providing a hospital ship for American deep-sea fishermen.

Providing for the betterment of the conditions of American seamen.

Establishing a commission to investigate jails and the correction of first offenders.

Abolishing the contract convict labor system by restricting interstate commerce in prison-made goods.

Legislation giving effect to the principles underlying such proposals as these would constitute, we believe, an important step in the accomplishment of the forward-looking purposes which you have placed before the American people.

Respectfully,

Frederic Almy	Arthur P. Kellogg
Louis D. Brandeis	Paul U. Kellogg
Howard S. Braucher	John A. Kingsbury
Allen T. Burns	Constance D. Leupp
Charles C. Burlingham	Samuel McCune Lindsay
Richard C. Cabot	Charles S. Macfarland
Richard S. Childs	W. N. McNair
Charles R. Crane	Henry Morgenthau
Edward T. Devine	Frances Perkins
Abram I. Elkus	Charles R. Richards
H. D. W. English	Thomas W. Salmon
Livingston Farrand	Henry R. Seager
Homer Folks	Thomas A. Storey
John M. Glenn	Graham Romeyn Taylor
Josephine Goldmark	James R. West
T. J. Keenan	W. F. Willoughby
Florence Kell[e]y	Stephen S. Wise[1]
Howard A. Kelly	

TL (WP, DLC).

[1] John Rogers Commons also endorsed this circular which reached him too late for his signature. See P. U. Kellogg to WW, April 3, 1913, TLS, enclosing J. R. Commons to P. U. Kellogg, April 1, 1913, TLS (WP, DLC).

To Frank Ellsworth Doremus

My dear Mr. Doremus: [The White House] April 1, 1913

I am sincerely obliged to you for the material you furnished me on the Panama treaty. It is very carefully selected and affords me an opportunity to go over the matter very thoroughly indeed.

Cordially yours,   Woodrow Wilson

TLS (Letterpress Books, WP, DLC).

From Walter Hines Page

My dear Mr. President: Garden City, New York April 1. 1913.

I have full and most grateful appreciation of the great honor you do me and of the trust you put in me; and I welcome the opportunity to do my best to be of some wider service to you personally and to the country—if the Senate and the British Government consent.

I have had serious misgivings; but now I must use them only as a spur to diligence and to my utmost effort. Your confidence in me greatly sustains me. If I declined so flattering a command I should have to acknowledge to myself that all the spirit of high adventure had gone out of me; and, since you so rouse me to this high opportunity, I am not willing to make such a confession.

Thus even things never dreamed of come true—in this glad year.

I was surprised yesterday morning to receive telegrams from every part of the United States and even from Europe indicating that information of your offer to me had been given out at Washington. I said nothing till it became evident that it was already published all over the world. Then I saw no frank way of denying it. Of course I said only that it is true and that I await the Senate's action and your instructions.

Most gratefully and loyally Yours,   Walter H. Page.

ALS (WP, DLC).

From James Aloysius O'Gorman

My dear Mr. President: [Washington] April 1, 1913.

I beg to offer for your consideration, in connection with the office of Collector of the Port of New York, the following names:
    John G. O'Keeffe,
    Michael J. Drummond,
    Thomas M. Mulry, and
    John Jerome Rooney.
All of these gentlemen are residents of The City of New York, have had large and varied business experience and are well qualified for the position.

Mr. O'Keeffe was in the firm of H. L. Horton & Co., of 66 Broadway, New York, well known bankers and brokers, from 1898 to 1907. He is at present a trustee of the Emigrant Industrial Savings Bank of this city, and a director of the Bellevue and Allied Hospitals. He is a man of large means, and has been active in civic and charitable movements in New York. Like all the other gentlemen named in this letter (with the exception of Mr. Rooney), he is not a candidate for the place, and does not know that his name is being mentioned in connection with it. Mr. O'Keeffe is a native and a life-long resident of New York, and was active on the Finance Committee in your campaign.

Mr. Drummond has been a merchant and manufacturer and has also been engaged in banking activities for more than thirty years. He is at present Commissioner of the Department of Charities in the City Governmrnt under appointment of Mayor Gaynor.

Mr. Mulry is a native of New York, and has been engaged in business and banking for many years. He has been President of the Emigrant Industrial Savings Bank for several years back.

Mr. Rooney, before his admission to the Bar, twelve or fifteen years since, was a custom broker for some years. He is a tariff expert, and is at present Presiding Judge of the Court of Claims of the State of New York. I believe he possesses administrative capacity, and, from his experience and general equipment, ought to fill the office very acceptably.

In connection with the office of United States District Attorney for the Southern District of New York, I beg to invite your attention to the following names:

William B. Ellison,
George J. Gillespie,
Bartow S. Weeks,
James W. Osborne, and
Thomas W. Churchill.

All of these gentlemen are lawyers of recognized ability.

Mr. Ellison was a member of the legislature about twenty years ago, and, under Mayor McClellan, was Corporation Counsel of the City of New York, a far more important post than that of District Attorney.

Mr. Weeks and Mr. Osborne had experience as assistant prosecutors years ago in the office of the District Attorney of the County of New York.

Mr. Gillespie was employed in the customs service at this port for about five years before his admission to the Bar, nineteen or twenty years ago. For several years past he has been a member of the Board of Education of this city.

Mr. Churchill was also connected with the Custom House, in the Legal Department, for some years before his admission to the Bar about fifteen years ago; and he is now President of the Board of Education of The City of New York.

Any one of these gentlemen possesses, in my judgment, all the qualifications needed for capable and efficient service in the office of District Attorney. All of them have been successful in their profession; none of them is a candidate, and none of them is aware that I am presenting his name for your consideration.

I expect to return to Washington on Thursday or Friday, and shall be glad to confer with you, if you desire any further information regarding these names.

With kind regards,   Sincerely yours,   J. A. O'Gorman

TLS (J. P. Tumulty Papers, DLC).

From Cleveland Hoadley Dodge, with Enclosure

My dear Mr. President: New York April 1, 1913.

I received your very kind letter this morning,[1] and thank you heartily for writing so cordially. It is needless to say that I regret exceedingly Harry Fine's decision regarding Germany, and on top of that comes, this morning, a long telegram from Mr. Mott, at Tokio, the gist of which I have already given to Mr. Tumulty this morning over the telephone. I enclose you a copy of his cablegram, which is a little garbled, but which expresses very definitely his decision.

I have been so sanguine, in view of the long message which we sent him ten days ago incorporating your message, that he would finally decide to accept, that his decision comes as a great blow to me, and I am almost broken-hearted about it. We will probably find that during the past few months when he has been holding a series of great conferences in different countries he has probably committed himself to certain things which he cannot give up. In any event, we can be thankful that the mere fact of your wishing to have Mott in China has made a great impression both here and abroad, and has announced to the world, more definitely than anything else could have done, the kind of policy which you intend to adopt in your dealings with China.

In this connection I have heard that a number of good missionaries want to urge you to appoint a journalist named W. T. Ellis,[2] as Minister to China, in case of Mott's refusal. I have, however, been warned against this man by two or three people in whom I have confidence. He has spent some time in China, and has written a good deal for the papers and magazines, but my informants say that he is a man of very light calibre, and they do not think that he would be fitted at all for the position of Minister.

Trusting that your patience has not been too deeply tried by

the long delay in hearing from Mott, believe me, with warm regards,

Very cordially and faithfully yours,

Cleveland H. Dodge

TLS (WP, DLC).
    [1] WW to C. H. Dodge, March 30, 1913, TLS (WC, NjP).
    [2] William Thomas Ellis, a writer of Swarthmore, Pa., who regularly contributed
to the religious press and to various Philadelphia dailies and was active in the
municipal reform movement. In the winter of 1906-1907, he toured the Chinese
areas of famine and raised over $1,000,000 for relief. In 1906-1907, and again
in 1910-1911, he investigated social, religious, and political conditions throughout the world for a syndicate of American newspapers.

E   N   C   L   O   S   U   R   E

John R. Mott to Cleveland Hoadley Dodge

Tokio [April 1, 1913.]

Tell president deeply regret that as result prolonged thorough
reconsideration must decline truly great opportunity   appreciation present this done with profound situation and full sympathy
with his policy[1]   could not fulfill serious obligations already assumed and do justice to new position.   Mott.

TC telegram (WP, DLC).
    [1] In the telegram as sent, this sentence read, "This done with profound ap-
preciation present situation and full sympathy with his policy." T telegram (J. R.
Mott Coll., CtY-D).

From the Diary of Josephus Daniels

Tuesday, April 1, 1913.

The meeting of the Cabinet today will be historic. Secretary
Bryan read a letter written by the syndicate of American Bankers
who had agreed to loan money to China, if the administration
should request it, stating that they were unable to give China
the six months she had requested on the loans already advanced.
This decision was reached after consultation with the bankers of
the other five great powers. They stated that they had written to
these powers and had asked them to cooperate in giving China
the time requested. This letter was in reply to one from Secretary Bryan expressing the hope that those who had advanced
money to China would give her six months to pay the loan. Secretary Bryan remarked that this letter was another proof of the
wisdom of President Wilson in refusing to sanction the loan to
China in that it showed that if we had gone into the agreement

with the other powers the United States would have been bound to stay with the powers in all of China's matters and this might have put this country in a position where it would be obliged to do things that it ought not to do.

This letter and comment, however, were only preliminary to the greater problems involved with reference to China. President Wilson made the statement that he had been thinking about the Chinese situation and had reached the conclusion that this country ought to recognize China as a Republic and suggested that this should be done next Tuesday when the constitutional representatives elected by the voters of China would meet to fully organize that Republic.

A discussion ensued as to the best method of doing this. Mr. Bryan was inclined to the opinion that the Secretary of State should state to the Ambassadors of the great powers that America would recognize China next Tuesday and would ask the powers to do likewise. Mr. Bryan's idea was that it would be well to inform the public that this had been done after he had talked with the Ambassadors and Ministers. There was dissent among several members of the Cabinet to the suggestion that it should [not] be made public until the Ambassadors and Ministers had been given an opportunity to communicate with their governments.

The Russian Ambassador[1] had suggested that Russia had intended to recognize Mexico in accordance with the action of this government; it might be well for us to follow Russia and recognize the Chinese Republic.

The President thought the conditions were not at all similar in this country and that we should not wait for the other countries to recognize the Republic before this country should do so.

Attorney General McReynolds thought it would be best to ask the powers it [if] they would cooperate with this Republic in recognizing China. The President was not agreeable to this. He thought it was best to announce confidentially to the Ambassadors that they could communicate with their government and say to them that it was his purpose to recognize the Republic of China and he hoped that their countries would take like action. He was not willing to make it a conference in which the powers should have equal voice or by which America would be bound by the action of others. He wished it to be understood that this country was going to recognize China on the great day in its history when the Parliament or Congress of the new Republic will meet, and ask other countries to do likewise and that he did not wish this country's action to be at all dependent upon them. It was finally determined that Mr. Bryan should see the Ambassadors of the powers who have been conferring together about the loan of the money to China and let them cable to their governments in the hope that they would take action in recognizing the Republic of China at the time America does and that after the great powers had agreed that the representatives of the smaller powers should be notified.

T MS (J. Daniels Papers, DLC).
  [1] George Bakhméteff.

A Draft of An Aide-Mémoire

[April 1, 1913]

The President wishes me to announce to you, and through you to your government, that it is his purpose to recognize the gov't of China on the 8th of April upon the meeting of its constituent assembly. He wishes me to say that he very earnestly desires and invites the cooperation of your gov't and its action to the same effect at the same time.[1]

WWhw MS (WP, DLC).
  [1] This was circulated to the representatives in Washington of countries having treaty relations with China and is printed in FR 1913, p. 108.

From the Diary of Colonel House

Washington, D. C. April 1, 1913.

I returned to the White House for luncheon. The President had not come from his office, so I went there and we walked back together. The luncheon was a simple affair. Bouillon, some veal and vegetables and fruit afterwards. I like the simplicity of their living. It is a relief after the long and formal meals one gets elsewhere.

I told the President about McCombs and we fell to laughing about him. Mrs. Wilson wanted to know if he intended leaving the post of Ambassador to France open for McCombs, and the President answered, "I am going to let him have just as much rope as he requires to hang himself." I told her that while it was hard on the French people, something was due the Governor and me. No one was present at luncheon excepting the family.

After lunch we went upstairs in the electric elevator. The President likes to run it. I told him it reminded me of the picture in Life which represented him as an elevator boy, and saying, "Miss Tariff, I am going to take you down."

We went into the library and immediately began a discussion of foreign appointments. We went over the entire list from top to bottom, and almost every post was decided upon.

The next thing under discussion was the tariff, particularly the sugar and wool schedules. I advised the President to take the position of keeping one cent per pound on sugar for a limited period. He suggested three years, and that was agreed upon. I gave him in detail the situation of the growers in the South and that of the beet-root growers in the West. He then wanted to know whether I thought the tariff bill should be introduced as a whole or in separate parts. Underwood was with him last night and wanted the bill to go in as a whole. The President thought, perhaps, that his object in this was to have it known as the "Underwood Bill"; whereas if it went in as separate measures, its identity would be lost.

The President said that Redfield had suggested putting the bill in, in five different groups, that is, putting the subjects that related, more or less, to one another. I favor this plan and so does the President. He is to see Underwood again and tell him of his decision.

The trouble is not in the House, but in the Senate. We discussed many provisions of the bill but not at great length. When we had finished with it, he wished to know whether or not I would act as Chairman of a Committee composed of McAdoo, McCombs, Gore, Burleson and Tumulty to make out lists of appointments in each State for him to make. I expressed myself as being willing to do anything I could to help him. After discussing it a few moments he finally said he thought it would be better if I would take the matter entirely in my own hands, and do it in any way I thought besy [best]. He thought perhaps that the others coming in would cause more or less confusion and jealousy; that if I did it alone I could do it more effectively, and could get what advice I needed in my own way. I think he is right, but I loathe the thought of it, and will probably get from under it. I wondered whether he realized that he was practically placing the entire patronage of the Government in my hands.

I handed him an editorial to read concerning Lloyd George and the Marconi stock affair in England.[1] The editorial said that the interests were always ready to raise a hue and cry against the advocates of the people if they transgressed in the slightest degree along the lines that, they, the interests, considered entirely honorable in their own representatives.

---

[1] About this controverted, if ephemeral, affair, see W. J. Baker, *A History of the Marconi Company* (London, 1970), pp. 143-48, and R. C. K. Ensor, *England, 1870-1914* (Oxford, 1936), pp. 456-59.

I cautioned the President against such pitfalls; I told him that where commerce and politics met, the waters were deep and troublous. I, myself, was afraid to buy or sell anything in any way connected with legislation, either present or prospective.

He told me then that he had nine shares of United States Steel, preferred stock, and wanted my advice. He thought if he sold it, it would look as if he were trying to "get from under" what might happen in the Steel Trust suit, and if he held it he might be criticized if the settlement of it was favorable to the Steel Company. I advised selling it. I also advised that he ask Mr. Bryan to suggest someone as additional counsel in the Steel Trust suit. I told him Mr. Bryan would suggest Jos. W. Folk, and if he did not, that he, the President, should suggest him. If this were done at once, and a settlement made in the courts either by decree or decision, it would prevent any of the Bryanites from criticizing him. He made a note of it in shorthand.

I then talked to him about saving a part of his salary and suggested that he save as much as $35,000. or $40,000. He replied "I thought I might save as much as $50,000. in the four years." I told him I was speaking of a single year, and not four years, that in the four years I hoped he would save as much as $150,000. He said he would speak to Mrs. Wilson, as she was the economical member of the family.

I talked to him at lunch about Mexico and along the lines Mr. [Edward Norphlet] Brown [president] of the National Railways had suggested,[2] and advised him not to remove Ambassador Wil-

[2] "Brown came and I got some interesting information. He is president of more than 8000 miles of railway, which is owned jointly by the Mexican Government and American, English, French and German capital. The Mexican Government owns a slight majority of the stock. He said it was the general opinion that sad as Madero's death was, that it was the only solution of the situation. He said Huerta claims that Madero tried to have him assasinated just before he, Huerta, arrested him. Huerta went to the palace for a conference with Maredo, and was urging Madero to resign so as to bring about peace. Madero declined and asked to be excused for a moment, stepping towards an open door. Huerta looked around and saw through some transoms three or four men with carbines leveled at him and about to fire. He threw himself down and the bullets went over his head. Huerta rushed out of the room, and immediately afterwards had Madero arrested. He claims that Madero's death was brought about by his attempted escape, but Brown thinks that it was the usual Mexican way of getting rid of an enemy.

"Brown wanted me to urge upon the President the retention of Ambassador [Henry Lane] Wilson until after the July election occurred because Wilson was Dean of the Diplomatic Corps, and it was through his efforts that the status quo was brought about between Huerta and Felix Diaz, and an agreement was made that Huerta should become Provisional President and should support Diaz for permanent President when the election occurred.

"In the meanwhile, a Cabinet was to be chosen to serve under Huerta and afterward to become the Diaz Cabinet. This agreement had been signed in triplicate and was brought about by Ambassador Wilson.

"Brown thinks it would be inexpedient to remove Wilson until after this agreement goes into effect. He thought two things would certainly happen in Mexico if this administration of Huerta's was not a success. One was intervention, and

son until after the election occurred.[3] He said he would not do so. I told him that Brown thought if the present government did not succeed, it meant either intervention or disintergration into smaller states.

The President left me and went into the East Room for about twenty minutes, during which time he said he had shaken hands with six hundred people. When he returned I was reading Kipling's poems and I handed him "L'Envoi" which begins "When Earth's last picture is painted" and asked him to read it. He did so with much feeling, and we fell to discussing religion for a moment and the imagination of men.

He had finished with his budget, and I took up mine, and by four o'clock we were ready to drive. We circled the City of Washington and stopped for a moment at the Cemetery just beyond the Old Soldiers Home. He wanted to show me the Adams statue by Saint Gaudens. We walked across the Cemetery and sat upon a granite bench in front of the marvelous figure depicting Grief. He called attention to the beautiful outlines and the look of resolution upon the face. I thought she seemed of the kind to send sons to the wars and bear with fortitude the news of their death.

I asked him why he thought the early Greeks were such marvelous sculptors and why the teeming millions of modern times could produce so few who were able to conceive and execute anything worth while. He thought there was one thing in favor of modern scul[p]ture, and that was, the work had more poetry and imagination in it than the ancients gave to theirs. He spoke of the Greeks depicting action and beauty of form rather than emotion. We sat for a long while before the statue, which affected me much as some mournful strain of music would.

We returned to the automobile and drove through the park. Among other things I asked him his estimate of his Cabinet and of their different characteristics. He said that Bryan was a constant surprise to him; that he was amenable to advice, did not talk unduly much and was altogether different from what he had anticipated.

Redfield possessed much the best analytical mind; that Lane had an analytical mind plus imagination, which Redfield lacked. McReynolds was quiet and said but little, but when he talked it was effective. He did not comment upon the others.

I called his attention to the pleasure people felt when a great

the other was a disintegration of the Republic into smaller units. It was the general belief that if this Government could not maintain itself, no other could." House Diary, March 27, 1913.

[3] That is, the election for the presidency of Mexico.

leader did things differently from what they had been done before. I thought a leader could do such things, and it would please,
but if the ordinary human diverged from the beaten track, he was
considered a crank and derided. I advised the President to do the
unusual thing when it was the sensible thing, regardless of
whether it conformed to custom.

I spoke of efficiency, and called attention to the enormous
amount of business we had done that afternoon in one hour and
twenty-five minutes, because we wasted no time in talk. He, in
turn, complimented me by saying that I was the most efficient
man he knew, or had ever known with the exception of one or
two, and in this way we tossed bouquets at one another and became thoroughly satisfied with ourselves and the world as it was.

I again congratulated him upon the high note he had struck in
his Inaugural Address, and I spoke of the good he could accomplish, and of the opportunity that was being given him to further
the cause of humanity.

He left me at the White House at six o'clock and I returned
to the Wallace home.

To Walter Hines Page

My dear Page,   The White House 2 April, 1913
Hurrah! I knew that I could count on you! Your letter of
yesterday has made me deeply content.

The Lord only knows how things get into the papers from here
the minute I *think* them. This was something I was glad to have
known. We did not give it out.

More anon!

                    Yours with great content,   Woodrow Wilson

ALS (W. H. Page Papers, MH).

From James Bryce

My dear Mr. President   Washington. April 2nd 1913
I do not know whether you have yet decided if you will dine
outside the White House, in Washington, during your term of office: and possibly you may wish to leave the question undeter-
mined for the present. If however you have considered the point
and have not resolved to exclude the possibility, may I say that it
would give my wife and myself the liveliest pleasure to receive
you and Mrs. Wilson under our roof tree here before we leave

Washington, either quite alone, or with a very small number of friends, which ever you might prefer. In the latter event, perhaps you would kindly let me know if there are persons in particular whom you would like to have asked to meet you, and if you would also say whether Friday April 11th or Monday April 14th would be a suitable day for you.

If you think it better not to dine out at all, we shall of course quite understand the grounds of your decision, and will hope some day or other, if life is continued to us, to have the pleasure of receiving you in an English home.

Believe me   Very sincerely yours   James Bryce

ALS (WP, DLC).

From Lindley Miller Garrison

My dear Mr. President: Washington. April 2, 1913.

I am so firmly convinced that the appointment of Mr. Davies to be Governor General of the Philippines would be such a serious mistake, that I cannot refrain from writing to you in continuation of our conference of to-day.

The suggestion that Mr. Davies should be sent as Governor General to the Philippines caused an instant reaction in my own mind against it, as you know. For fear that that judgment which time served to intensify might be wrong, I called on the only person that I felt it proper for me to approach—Mr. Tumulty—and told him my state of mind.

I am so firmly convinced that this appointment would necessarily entail such disadvantageous consequences that I wish as quickly as possible to get your mind at work again upon this subject, so that the matter as it appeals to me may receive due consideration before it is finally settled. Since my judgment is practically entirely irrespective of the intrinsic character and worth of Mr. Davies, it is unnecessary, and it would be an impropriety for me now, to express any views with respect thereto.

For my purpose—that is, from my point of view—this appointment would be just as great a mistake from the Administration's standpoint if Mr. Davies were possessed of all the qualities that his most ardent admirer or supporter credits him with. I need not say that I admire Mr. Davies; that I like him personally; and that I credit him with the possession of capacity, probity and high character. However, to the country, which in this case is the jury, Mr. Davies is a young lawyer who has not as yet had time or opportunity to make for himself a prominent place at the bar. He is merely known as an energetic, political worker, who did valiant service in the last campaign and was a member of the National Committee and Secretary thereof.

The position of Governor General of the Philippines is one calling for a man of the very highest capacity that is capable of being enlisted for that place. Therefore, whatever Mr. Davies's intrinsic worth may be, his activities and reputation will, in my view, inevitably lead the country to the conclusion that a political worker has been rewarded with probably the most important position outside of your Cabinet, and a position which, above all things, should be free from the suggestion of politics. Whoever takes that position must be a man of very strong character, very well seasoned, firm of judgment, clear-eyed of purpose, and one able to cleave his way by sheer ability to the core of the many difficult questions which it will be his business to dissect and to display to us so that we may exercise our judgment upon the facts as presented by him. Said again, in other words, it clearly calls for and needs a man whose public reputation is different from that of Mr. Davies; and on the contrary, Mr. Davies's public reputation disappoints the expectations of those who have any knowledge of the requirements.

I need not waste time or space to tell you, in view of what I said and what I now write, that I am very desirous that your judgment, finally exercised, will be against the appointment of Mr. Davies to this position; I am, however, equally desirous that Mr. Davies should be utilized in the Government service where his capacities will find full scope. This leads me to make the following suggestion for your consideration:

Professor Ford, if appointed Governor General of the Philippines, would body forth in a public manner, and in his own personality, the Administration's policy towards the Philippines. His character, his aloofness from politics, his seasoning, the maturity of his judgment, the searching quality of his mind, and the irresistible way in which he pursues things to their ultimate reaches, when made known to the public by your statement thereof and confirmed by investigation, would gratify the expectations of the public concerning the man who should occupy that position. I would suggest, therefore, that since he is already in the Philippines, you persuade him to accept this office for a limited time only, if that is his wish and desire. He need not take up his duties at once, but a time in the future could be set, and in the mean time his prospective appointment could be announced and a time set when he could take office. He could disclose the situation to the present Governor General,[1] acquire a knowledge of the situation from him, and see the works in operation, and then go in at the appointed date. If he only went in for a short time, it would tide us over the existing embarrassment; and our search, I have no doubt, would disclose a man to undertake this most important work.

In the meantime I would suggest that Mr. Davies be appointed Governor of Porto Rico. No disappointment of public expectations would result there as would in the case of the Philippines. The situation is entirely different and would be free of the embarrassments which inhere in the other place. He could in Porto Rico learn in a most practical school the business of colonial administration. He could there show in a most effective manner his capacity for this class of work; and if he made good therein, I should see no reason why later he might not be transferred to the Governorship of the Philippines. This seems to me,—perhaps because the germ was born in my own brain,—to be a happy solution of an embarrassment from which I feel it necessary for the Administration to escape if a way of escape is open. I need not, of course, ask you to give most earnest consideration to this or to any other solution that may occur to you, but I do ask that you do not reach a final conclusion until you and I have had a full conference.

Sincerely yours,   Lindley M. Garrison

TLS (WP, DLC).
1 William Cameron Forbes.

To James Bryce

My dear Mr. Bryce,   The White House 3 April, 1913

Your note of yesterday gratified me very much—and Mrs. Wilson read me also Mrs. Bryce's delightful little note accompanying it.[1] How I wish that a President of this *free* Republic were a free man and could go to his friends when he pleased without provoking those *not* his personal friends to expect the same and risking their feeling hurt if he did not go to them. I dare not risk the consequences, brave as I try to be in most things! It does not help me that you will understand. I am vexed and deeply disappointed that I cannot accept your invitation to dinner. I suppose—I hope —that, if I wear the harness quietly and meekly at first, it will grow easy to bear and will not get on my nerves!

Thank you with all my heart. Mrs. Wilson joins both in my warm thanks and in my deep regret.

Cordially and faithfully Yours,   Woodrow Wilson

ALS (J. Bryce Papers, Bodleian Library).
1 Elizabeth M. A. Bryce to EAW, April 2, 1913, ALS (WP, DLC).

From William Frank McCombs

My dear Mr. President: New York April 3, 1913.

Since I saw you on Saturday, I have been making continuous efforts to dispose of my affairs so that I might accept your very flattering offer. I have been in touch with Tumulty from day to day to find out whether my delay was embarrassing you in any way, and he told me it was not. Of course, I did not want to inconvenience you.

As I have told you before, my difficulty in accepting the post has lain in the adjustment of my financial affairs here and in the forming of a connection which would continue, in some degree, my practice. The clientele which any lawyer has is very largely personal to himself, and it is almost impossible to arrange that the affairs of such a clientele be handled by others. This is the difficulty under which I have labored.

After intimations to my clients, I find my absence would, in their view, be prejudicial to their interests and that they would each seek separate counsel. This would mean my return to New York without any clientele whatsoever and a new start. After the statement which you so kindly issued, it occurred to me that I might make an arrangement under which my affairs could be handled. I am convinced now that it is impossible, and that I must remain here to maintain myself. During the past two years, I have been compelled to neglect my business to a very large extent, and I feel that it is absolutely essential for me to recoup. In view of the very great honor of the French post, I was quite willing to sacrifice almost anything. I now know that the sacrifice would be complete.

I was sorry to see in the New York papers of yesterday, under Washington date line, that I had accepted the embassy. It has placed me in a most embarrassing position, and has caused general comment of vacillation. I cannot imagine how the fact that I was re-considering became public. The press clippings I get in the matter are most annoying to me, and must be to you. I suppose the only thing to say in the matter is that my position is the same as it was when my statement was given out in Washington.

Let me again thank you very deeply for the great honor you have conferred upon me. I sincerely wish it were within my power to accept. It is such a thing as rarely comes in a man's lifetime.

Believe me as ever,
          Always yours to command,   Wm. F. McCombs

TLS (J. P. Tumulty Papers, DLC).

From the Diary of Colonel House

April 3, 1913.

Mr. Frick telephoned again to know what was the next move. I told him I had talked to the Attorney General late this afternoon over the telephone, and he would take the matter up directly with Mr. Stetson,[1] and that I, myself, thought that the best method of procedure. I want to drop the matter from now. . . .

Norman Hapgood came at six. I asked him of his plans for the future, and he said they were indefinate. He thought he would like to get out of the country for awhile. I asked if he would care for a foreign appointment and he thought he might. I asked what appealed to him, and he said Italy, Japan or China.

We spoke of Rudolph Spreckles and Charles R. Crane for Russia. He concurred in my opinion that Spreckles would not do for a diplomatic post. He is too opinionated, too dictatorial and altogether too uncertain for such important work. Hapgood thought Crane would be delighted with a tender, but said that on account of his father's death it would be impossible for him to accept.

I called the President over the telephone at Washington at eight o'clock, to tell him that Hapgood concurred in my opinion as to Spreckles. This eliminated Spreckles. I asked if he wanted me to get Hapgood to make a tender to Crane. He authorized me to do so, but cautioned me not to let his declination be known. I then suggested Hapgood for the Chinese mission. This seemed to surprise him. He asked if Hapgood was an orthodox Christian. I promised to find out.

I complimented him upon his proposed message to Congress, a copy of which he had sent me, and told him it was certain to make a happy impression. It was short, it contained everything that was necessary, and was a model of its kind. I asked him to do nothing about the Belgian mission until he heard from me further concerning it.

I telephoned Hapgood and asked him to tender the Russian Ambassadorship to Crane over the long distance telephone, but to caution him as to secrecy. Crane is in Chicago. I asked Hapgood to come and see me at ten o'clock in the morning to discuss the matter further. . . .

Houston fell to talking about Jos. Davies for the Philippines. He thought it a serious mistake and he expected to tell the President so tomorrow. I advised his seeing Tumulty before he talked to the President; that Tumulty agreed with him and could perhaps make some suggestion.

[1] Francis Lynde Stetson, general counsel for U. S. Steel.

To Albert Sidney Burleson

My dear Burleson: The White House April 4, 1913

For a long time I have thought that the government ought to own the telegraph lines of the country and combine the telegraph with the post office. How have you been thinking in this matter?

This is a large order to put into a small letter, but just because it is big we ought to be thinking about it, and I should value your ideas on the subject very much.

Always   Faithfully yours,   Woodrow Wilson

TLS (A. S. Burleson Papers, DLC).

To the Eighth Grade School Children of New Jersey

My dear young Friends: The White House April 4, 1913

In sending you this greeting I naturally think of what you may make of yourselves, and of the great good you may do the country by making something of yourselves that is noble and worth while.

I have had a great deal to do with teaching young people, and it has sometimes discouraged and saddened me to feel that they thought that the school work was a bore and that the only real thing was the thing they were set free to do after school hours. I have had as much fun as anybody in my time and hope that you will have unlimited good times, but I wish I could make you realize now that play has nothing in it unless back of it lies good honest hard work, fitted to harden the fibre of every part of the mind and make it an instrument that we can work with, achieve with, conquer with, and do what we please with. The really happy men and women are the men and women who can do their job, and the men and women who can do their job best are those who have given themselves the best discipline and training. If you make the most of yourselves, you will be able to give a great gift of duty finely performed to the country which we all love and which we all ought to try to serve by making our own lives what we should like to have everybody believe the life of every American to be. My exhortation is, be sample Americans and make the sample very fine.   Faithfully yours   Woodrow Wilson

CCL (WP, DLC).

From John R. Mott

Nara [Japan], April 4, 1913.

Pending anti-foreign California legislation seriously regarded here by all classes including Americans. Would seriously embarrass American interests.   Mott.

T telegram (WP, DLC).

From the Diary of Josephus Daniels

Friday, April 4, 1913.

The two matters of importance discussed in the Cabinet Meeting today were, first—The tariff question. At the last session of the Cabinet the President had read the first draft of his message to Congress. Today the matter came up as to the sugar schedule and the President stated that, after a conference with the members of the Ways & Means Committee and the Finance Comittee, he had a talk with the representatives from Louisiana who are chiefly interested in the sugar schedule. He felt that it was a great industry and that it would be proper and wise to give them some time to adjust themselves to free sugar and, therefore, he had told them that if the Louisiana delegation would support the democratic tariff bill, he would favor a tariff of one cent a pound on sugar for three years after which sugar should be free. He insisted on three years because he wished the free sugar to go into effect during his term and he had no authority to make an arrangement that would not be completed while he was President. The matter of the sugar schedule and its effect upon the industry and the maze of schedule[s] which had protected the sugar schedule so long was gone into fully by members of the Cabinet. They all concurred in the President's view that if the Louisiana people would accept the terms offered, it would be the best conclusion of the sugar schedule. The President intimated that he might deliver his tariff message in person in Congress but left it an open question to be decided whether he would do so.

The second important question was with reference to the Chinese situation. Secretary of State Bryan had notified the Ambassadors and Ministers on the 8th of April or on the date when the Constitutional Convention should meet in China, it was the purpose of this Government to recognize the Chinese Republic and it was the purpose of their Governments to recognize it at the same time. The Secretary of State reported that there was a suggestion from the Russian Ambassador to the effect that his Government would take whatever action we took with reference to Mexico and intimated that as his Government must do this about a country within the spher[e] of influence of the United States that the American government ought to follow Russia's example in China. This suggestion that America should be governed by Russia in the Chinese matter did not receive favor with the President or any Member of the Cabinet because of conditions in China and Mexico were in no way similar. The Secretary of State reported that he had heard from none of the other powers and could not state what would be the attitude of the other countries—whether they would join us in recognizing China upon the day when both houses of parliament or congress should convene.

The question was discussed as to whether China now really had a Government. The President had had [sic] assumed the range [reins] of power without an election by popular vote and there was a suggestion that he was a dictator and not a president, but the discussion brought out the fact that China had elected without any difficulty or any serious division of members of both houses of congress, and that this showed perfect acquiescence in the republic by all those people in China who wished to have a voice.

T MS (J. Daniels Papers, DLC).

From the Diary of Colonel House

April 4, 1913.

Norman Hapgood called and I asked about his religious views. He did not seem to have any worth while. I told him I had talked to the President, and I was sure he would offer him China provided he was an orthordox Christian. I explained that Mr. Bryan felt very strongly upon this point, and that it was necessary for the President to recognize it. Bryan merely desires it in the case of China where the uplift is being brought about by the missionaries, the Y.M.C.A. and like forces.

Hapgood had talked with Crane; that he was please[d] but could not accept. I hoped that he had made it clear to Crane that he must not talk. He had impressed it upon him as fully as he could. That is Crane's trouble—loquacity. I promised later I would see that it leaked out from Washington that he had been offered and declined it.

I told Hapgood I would see the President next week and would talk with him in more detail about an appointment for him, but for the present we would let the matter rest. He hoped the President would not think he was asking for anything. I said the President did not know that he, Hapgood, knew anything about it; that I was supposed to find out in a diplomatic way, his religious views, and that my diplomacy was usually of the direct kind. He expressed appreciation of my candor and directness.

To Cleveland Hoadley Dodge

My dear Cleve: [The White House] April 5, 1913

Mott's decision was a great blow to me. I don't know when I have been so disappointed. This is a difficult road I am traveling in trying to get the finest men in the country to serve us at foreign posts. I can not tell you, my dear fellow, how much I have appreciated your own activity and generous interest in the matter or how much I appreciate your letter.

You need give yourself no concern about my being impressed with the claims of W. T. Ellis. I shall seek for a different sort of man. But, in the meantime, I would value more than I can tell you any suggestions from you as to men who ought to be considered.

Harry Fine has declined to stay in Germany altogether. I am a bit disheartened in this field.

It is fine to feel that we are working together again in great business.

In haste, with warmest regards from us all,
Affectionately yours,   Woodrow Wilson

TLS (Letterpress Books, WP, DLC).

Remarks at a Press Conference

April 7, 1913

Did anything come out of the conference with members of the Senate this morning to which you might speak?[1]

No. We were discussing just the matter of handling the bill. We were not discussing the schedules or the contents of the bill at all.

Mr. President, did you get any idea as to what the chances are for the bill in the Senate, or did that come up?

That came up informally and I got the impression that the chances were very excellent. . . . I think that only eight of the ten members, ten Democratic members of the committee, were present when they discussed it, and those eight were in favor of it.[2] That's the way I remember it.

Mr. President, we are all very much interested in your going up to the Capitol tomorrow.

Yes.

We thought perhaps you could tell us something about it. We think we understand why—what the precedents are and all that. Perhaps you could throw some light on it. There might be some line I don't know about it.

> The reasons are very, very simply put. I think that that is the only dignified way for the President to address the houses on the opening of a session, instead of sending the thing up by messenger and letting the clerk read it perfunctorily in the familiar clerk's tone of voice. I thought that the dignified and natural thing was to return to precedent which, it is true, has been dormant a long time but which is a very respectable precedent.

Mr. President, in this morning's papers there was an intimation that there might be expected answers from Congress to the address.

> Oh, no, I think they were saying that because they were not looking for any answer except the legislative answer, that is all. I expect to do it just as simply as possible.

Do you expect a request from Congress to come here? There was an intimation also that they might send you a request that you come to address them.

> I simply asked Senator Kern and Mr. Underwood if it would be agreeable for me to come, and they both said that it would be entirely agreeable, and I don't expect any request. They felt sure they must speak to their colleagues in the Senate and that it would be entirely agreeable, that's all.

Mr. President, are you willing that we should quote you directly? That explanation of yours is exceedingly interesting. We further understand that we are not to quote you directly, but in that particular I think everybody would be glad.

> Certainly.

Would you follow that system, Mr. President, with regard to Annual Messages hereafter?

> An arrangement I would love to work with. To tell you the truth, I thought that that was the natural way to begin.

JRT transcript (WC, NjP) of CLSsh (C. L. Swem Coll., NjP).

[1] A meeting with Democratic members of the Senate Finance Committee about tariff legislation.

[2] The newspapers reported otherwise—that the senators warned Wilson that his entire program of tariff reform might be wrecked unless he agreed to separate the wool and sugar schedules from the Underwood bill. Link, *The New Freedom*, pp. 183-84.

From James Duval Phelan

Del Monte, Calif., April 7, 1913.

I have wired Secretary Bryan and Lane fully on Japanese situation. I beg to inform you that the problem is fundamental and most serious. It is this: a non-assimilable people, clever and industrious agriculturists working for themselves as owners and lessees takes farms from hands of white men in destructive competition. The tide must be checked, otherwise California will become a Japanese plantation and republican institutions, perish. The alien land bill is a reasonable law not repugnant to treaty, the legislature intends to pass it if not the people will be initiable.[1]

Jas. D. Phelan.

T telegram (WP, DLC).
  [1] That is, they would adopt the legislation by the initiative if the legislature did not.

From Jacob Harry Hollander

My dear President Wilson,   Baltimore, Md. April 7, 1913.

In accordance with your suggestion of March 24, I am enclosing a memorandum upon the present aspects of the Dominican problem.[1] I hope it may seem to you—as it is designed to be—a criticism of policies not of persons. The concern of those who believe in San Domingo and its people is less as to what has been done in the past, than as to what will [be] essayed in the future. I have had no access to recent departmental records and there may be some omissions in what I have written; but the essential facts are, I believe, as set forth.

Finally, may I express the earnest hope that the problem of Latin-America will continue—as I know it has already begun—to receive the sympathetic attention of your administration. The difficulties involved are so complex, the demands of our domestic concerns are so urgent, that there is the greatest danger, that at this particular juncture, when wise statesmanship is needed here as never before, recourse will be had to gunboat-and-marine opportunism.   Very truly yours,   Jacob H. Hollander

TLS (WP, DLC).
  [1] See WW to WJB, April 8, 1913, n. 1.

William Kent to William Jennings Bryan

Dear Sir: Washington, D. C. April 7, 1913.

The proposed legislation in the State of California directed against the ownership of land by aliens who are ineligible for citizenship appears to me a matter of greatest importance if we are to maintain a real democracy. The country has recognized the need of curtailing the right of Orientals to enter citizenship, in the interest of the white race.

Land-ownership means permanent rooting in our soil. It is of more importance than citizenship. The question of possession of land involves permanently the social life of any community. If the land is taken up by those who cannot mingle their blood with ours or who do not naturally affiliate with us in our institutions, we at once have a permanently alien element introduced which is hostile to such intermingling as is necessary to democracy.

The California situation is not academic but practical. There have been established certain Oriental communities in which white men are not welcome, and which white men regard as disagreeable communities in which to live. The permanence of such a condition must rest with land tenure.

I see no reason why Japan or any other Oriental nation should object to our control, in a matter so much our own peculiar business as is tenure of land. It is not for a moment because we feel our superiority or the inferiority of the Japanese that we object to their monopolizing, as they have done, certain sections of our State. We do not ask, and especially do not demand, that Japan modify her land laws to let us in. We merely recognize in frankness what they must recognize, although they do not wish to let the fact be known, that there are such things as racial lines that cannot be crossed except with peril and irritation. The negro problem under which this country labors is a sufficient proof of this fact. We cannot afford to have any more such problems with us. The bitterness involved in racial friction prevents the growth of domestic ideas and hampers our advancement.

It is distinctly in the interest of peace and good understanding and to avoid the irritation that is bound to occur that I strongly advocate the alien land laws of California. Any action taken ought to be taken in the most diplomatic, careful manner, free from offensive language or argument. If the Japanese pretend that they cannot understand the race argument, and bluster about unfriendly action, they are certainly taking offense where none is intended.

No loosely drawn treaty can stand for a moment against the patriotic desire of our people to protect the future of democracy and the integrity of the race, both of which are menaced by the prospective citizenship or permanent land occupation of those whom we cannot assimilate.

Yours truly,   William Kent

TLS (WP, DLC).

From the Diary of Josephus Daniels

Tuesday, 4/8/12[13].

At Cabinet Meeting today the President came in dressed up for the first time in his Prince Albert, looking spick and span— dressed up properly to break the precedent by reading his message to Congress. Some of us suggested that he had not deemed the members of his Cabinet important enough for him to dress up for them, but seemed to think he thought more of Congress than he did members of the Cabinet. He said he thought he ought to be allowed to dress up occasionally, and that this was the first time he had done so. The President stated that it was expected that the Chinese Government would be formed today and that the Secretary of the American Legation[1]—We have no minister or Ambassador there now—had been instructed as soon as the Government was organized to recognize it. . . . Secretary Bryan said he had a fatherly talk with the Chinese Minister and told him to impress upon the President and his people [not] to have [an] unseemingly spectacle on the occasion of the session of Congress or to do anything that would militate against causing the other nations in following America and recognizing Chinese Independence. So far only the United States, Brazil and Mexico have decided to recognize the Independence of China. Inasmuch as Mexico is in revolution and its President holds tenure by force of arms and not by election, it is doubtful if he has any right to extend any recognition to another country. The big powers are waiting and inclined to join us in recognition of the Independence of China. The President and the whole Cabinet devoutly hope that everything will go well in China today and the people will so demean themselves as to justify their recognition by the whole world and give the Chinese Republic an opportunity to take its place among the Republics of the earth.[2]

The Administration is sincerely desirous of promoting the peace of the world and to that end they are prepared to lead or inaugurate movements that will result in hastening the day when war shall be ended. The President stated that he had been talking with Mr. Bryan about the proposition which seemed to him to be a strong step in that direction and he gave a memorandum of the plan which the Secretary of State had suggested and gave a copy to each member of the Cabinet to be considered so that it might be discussed at some later meeting of the Cabinet. . . .

The President said the suggestion of Mr. Bryan reminded him of a rule once made by a great teacher of a military school[3] which was attended by his brother. The boys had a habit of fighting a good deal and he called them all in and said "boys, any boy in this school may fight another boy if he feels he has a grievance, but before doing so he must come to me and state his grievance and the fight must take place under my supervision or somebody representing me and carried on by the Queensbury Rules." The result was that there was no fighting in that school from that time forward. It was suggested that perhaps the other countries would not be able to agree to this. Upon that, the President said "let them say so, it will put them to their trumps to give a reason for not talking over the matter." The suggestion was made by Postmaster General Burleson that the United States ought to offer a conference of all the Powers looking to the purpose of securing uniform action that would be an end to the building of costly battleships and preparations for war. In other words, a conference to bring about disarmament. He thought this country should take the lead and now was the happy time. I agreed heartily to this, but suggested that the first step should be along the line of Mr. Bryan's memorandum. If we could get the nations to agree never to fight until they have talked over the matters in dispute, the day would not be far distant when we would be able to secure disarmament,

Upon the adjournment of the Cabinet, the President left the White House to deliver his message to Congress, thus breaking a precedent. Since John Adams' day, no President had read his message to Congress. Secretary Garrison asked the President whether he desired the Cabinet to accompany him. His answer was that some of the Senators declared in their speeches the day before that the President was reviving an old custom in the nature of an "address from the throne" and was restoring federalism in America.[4] The President laughingly said "the whole idea of a message from the President was an evolution of the address from the throne, but the only thing federalistic about it was delivering the message in person." But he thought it would be better for him to do it in as simple a way as possible without being attended by the Cabinet Ministers, leaving it for each Cabinet Minister either to pursue his duties at his office or go without going in a body.

Secretary Bryan stated that he would not go and that his wife had decided not to go. In view of the friction and the more [or] less feeling of Speaker Clark against the Secretary and inasmuch as the Speaker would be the officer to welcome the President to the Capitol, he thought it better on all lines for him not to be present. The President, in a very tactful way, voiced the hope that the feeling the Speaker seemed to have against the Secretary of State would pass away and that friendly relations would be resumed. Mr. Bryan's spirit about the matter all along has been most excellent and he has gone on his way ever since the Baltimore Convention without any criticism or even feeling any criticism against the Speaker who seems to be harboring resentment towards Mr. Bryan and holding him responsible for his defeat for the nomination at Baltimore. This is the only cloud that is as big as a man's hand on the political horizon in the Democratic Administration, but it will pass away.

Secretary Redfield stated he had some engagements which make it impracticable for him to be at the Capitol. All the other Members of the Cabinet stated arrangements had been made to go, so when the President entered, in a dignified way, to read his message, Members of the Cabinet were in the House Chamber scattered, some in the galleries, others on the floor, as citizens. It was an historical occasion with all the setting suited for the memorable message which the President was about to read. He was in fine form, and there was one spontaneous applause in his few opening sentences, and he read the message with a clearness and distinctness to all parts of the chamber. When he finished, he quietly withdrew amid applause. The precedent of a century had been shattered. Nobody was hurt and Congress heard the message that sounds the key-note of the government's fiscal policy—a key-note not burdened with a detail, but clear, ringing and direct. It was not only heard by members of Congress, but the diplomatic gallery was crowded and an audience representative of men political and governmental with such dignity as had never assembled in the House of Representatives.

T MS (J. Daniels Papers, DLC).

    1 Edward Thomas Williams.

    2 The United States extended recognition on May 2, 1913.

    3 Robert Bingham, headmaster of the Bingham School, at that time located in Mebaneville, N. C. See WW to ELA, June 29, 1884, n. 4. Vol. 3.

    4 Among them, John Sharp Williams, who said: "I for one very much regret the President's course. . . . I am sorry to see revived the old Federalistic custom of speeches from the throne. . . . The practice instituted by Jefferson was more American than the old pomposities and cavalcadings between the White House and the Capitol. . . . I regret all this cheap and tawdry imitation of English royalty." *New York Times*, April 8, 1913.

An Address on Tariff Reform to a Joint Session of Congress

[April 8, 1913]

Mr. Speaker, Mr. President, Gentlemen of the Congress:

I am very glad indeed to have this opportunity to address the two Houses directly and to verify for myself the impression that

the President of the United States is a person, not a mere department of the Government hailing Congress from some isolated
island of jealous power, sending messages, not speaking naturally and with his own voice—that he is a human being trying to cooperate with other human beings in a common service. After this
pleasant experience I shall feel quite normal in all our dealings
with one another.

I have called the Congress together in extraordinary session
because a duty was laid upon the party now in power at the recent
elections which it ought to perform promptly, in order that the
burden carried by the people under existing law may be lightened
as soon as possible and in order, also, that the business interests
of the country may not be kept too long in suspense as to what the
fiscal changes are to be to which they will be required to adjust
themselves. It is clear to the whole country that the tariff duties
must be altered. They must be changed to meet the radical alteration in the conditions of our economic life which the country
has witnessed within the last generation. While the whole face
and method of our industrial and commercial life were being
changed beyond recognition the tariff schedules have remained
what they were before the change began, or have moved in the
direction they were given when no large circumstance of our
industrial development was what it is to-day. Our task is to square
them with the actual facts. The sooner that is done the sooner we
shall escape from suffering from the facts and the sooner our men
of business will be free to thrive by the law of nature (the nature
of free business) instead of by the law of legislation and artificial
arrangement.

We have seen tariff legislation wander very far afield in our
day—very far indeed from the field in which our prosperity might
have had a normal growth and stimulation. No one who looks the
facts squarely in the face or knows anything that lies beneath
the surface of action can fail to perceive the principles upon
which recent tariff legislation has been based. We long ago passed
beyond the modest notion of "protecting" the industries of the
country and moved boldly forward to the idea that they were
entitled to the direct patronage of the Government. For a long
time—a time so long that the men now active in public policy
hardly remember the conditions that preceded it—we have sought
in our tariff schedules to give each group of manufacturers or
producers what they themselves thought that they needed in order
to maintain a practically exclusive market as against the rest of
the world. Consciously or unconsciously, we have built up a set
of privileges and exemptions from competition behind which it

was easy by any, even the crudest, forms of combination to organize monopoly; until at last nothing is normal, nothing is obliged to stand the tests of efficiency and economy, in our world of big business, but everything thrives by concerted arrangement. Only new principles of action will save us from a final hard crystallization of monopoly and a complete loss of the influences that quicken enterprise and keep independent energy alive.

It is plain what those principles must be. We must abolish everything that bears even the semblance of privilege or of any kind of artificial advantage, and put our business men and producers under the stimulation of a constant necessity to be efficient, economical, and enterprising, masters of competitive supremacy, better workers and merchants than any in the world. Aside from the duties laid upon articles which we do not, and probably can not, produce, therefore, and the duties laid upon luxuries and merely for the sake of the revenues they yield, the object of the tariff duties henceforth laid must be effective competition, the whetting of American wits by contest with the wits of the rest of the world.

It would be unwise to move toward this end headlong, with reckless haste, or with strokes that cut at the very roots of what has grown up amongst us by long process and at our own invitation. It does not alter a thing to upset it and break it and deprive it of a chance to change. It destroys it. We must make changes in our fiscal laws, in our fiscal system, whose object is development, a more free and wholesome development, not revolution or upset or confusion. We must build up trade, especially foreign trade. We need the outlet and the enlarged field of energy more than we ever did before. We must build up industry as well, and must adopt freedom in the place of artificial stimulation only so far as it will build, not pull down. In dealing with the tariff the method by which this may be done will be a matter of judgment, exercised item by item. To some not accustomed to the excitements and responsibilities of greater freedom our methods may in some respects and at some points seem heroic, but remedies may be heroic and yet be remedies. It is our business to make sure that they are genuine remedies. Our object is clear. If our motive is above just challenge and only an occasional error of judgment is chargeable against us, we shall be fortunate.

We are called upon to render the country a great service in more matters than one. Our responsibility should be met and our methods should be thorough, as thorough as moderate and well considered, based upon the facts as they are, and not worked out as if we were beginners. We are to deal with the facts of our own day, with the facts of no other, and to make laws which square with those facts. It is best, indeed it is necessary, to begin with the tariff. I will urge nothing upon you now at the opening of your session which can obscure that first object or divert our energies from that clearly defined duty. At a later time I may take the liberty of calling your attention to reforms which should press close upon the heels of the tariff changes, if not accompany them, of which the chief is the reform of our banking and currency laws; but just now I refrain. For the present, I put these matters on one side and think only of this one thing—of the changes in our fiscal system which may best serve to open once more the free channels of prosperity to a great people whom we would serve to the utmost and throughout both rank and file.

I thank you for your courtesy.[1]

Printed in *Address of the President of the United States. . . April 8, 1913* (Washington, 1913).
[1] There is a WWsh outline of this address, with the composition date of March 26, 1913; a WWsh draft of the address, with the composition date of March 26, 1913; a typed draft, with WWhw emendations, dated April 7, 1913; a WWsh draft of the first paragraph; and typed and printed reading copies in WP, DLC.

To Jacob Harry Hollander

My dear Dr. Hollander: [The White House] April 8, 1913.

Thank you sincerely for the memorandum on Dominican affairs which you were good enough to send me, and which I am glad to have. I was much interested in reading it.

Sincerely yours,   Woodrow Wilson

TLS (Letterpress Books, WP, DLC).

To William Jennings Bryan

My dear Mr. Secretary: [The White House] April 8, 1913.

I enclose a very interesting memorandum prepared by Dr. Hollander of Johns Hopkins in regard to the Dominican problem.[1]

Sincerely yours,   Woodrow Wilson

TLS (Letterpress Books, WP, DLC).
[1] The memorandum (SDR, RG 59, 839.51/1000, DNA) was a review of the Roosevelt-Taft policy toward the Dominican Republic. It stressed the beneficial effects of the United States customs receivership, 1905-1907, and of the American-Dominican Convention of 1907, which, Hollander said, had helped to restore financial and political stability to the country. He severely criticized Taft's recognition of revolutionaries who had won power in 1911 and 1912, because such recognition countenanced political violence and encouraged the idea that "if a patriot be dissatisfied with the constitutional government, he may take to the brush and eventually secure honor and emolument for his 'revolution.' " Hollander concluded by warning that the United States now faced a critical situation in Dominican politics and finance.

To Mary Allen Hulbert

Dearest Friend,   The White House 8 April, 1913

I was cheated out of a chance to write on Sunday, because business invaded,—the business of recognizing China, which is in the throes *to-day* of trying to get re-born, as a republic,—and the business of sugar on the tariff schedules, the inveterate trouble of every Democratic administration. The extra-ordinary session of Congress began yesterday. To-day I break another precedent by reading my message to Congress in person. The town is agog about it. It seems I have been smashing precedents almost daily ever since I got here—chiefly, no doubt, because I did not know how it had been the custom to do the several things it fell to me to do and was not particularly careful to inquire, and proceeded to do it in the most simple and natural way—which is always and everywhere contrary to precedent. The President has not addressed Congress in person since John Adams's day,—and yet what more natural and dignified? And a president is likely to read his own message rather better than a clerk would. Here is what I am going to say, by way of preface: ["]I am very glad indeed to have this opportunity to address the two Houses directly and to verify for myself the impression that the President of the United States is a person, not a mere department of the Government hailing Congress from some isolated island of jealous power, sending messages, not speaking naturally and with his own voice, —that he is a human being trying to coöperate with other human beings in a common service." It at least seems to amuse the town to have these unusual things done, and the newspaper men are very grateful!

Here I am, filling the sheet with talk about myself when I would a great deal rather talk about you. This is partly because my heart was a bit lightened about you by your last letter, which spoke of rest, real rest and quiet and of a partial recovery of spirits,—*so* delightful to read of and to *feel* in the very tones of the letter—as if your voice had grown steady and natural again and had something of its old, very beautiful elasticity in it once more. We had been very anxious. It is like you that duty performed, no matter in what distracting circumstances nor amidst what distress,—a piece of work well done for those you love,—sh. have calmed you and let refreshment in. Let dear Bermuda heal you now, and then come to the friends who so deeply admire you and cherish your friendship. In driving haste

Your devoted friend   Woodrow Wilson

ALS (WP, DLC).

From Lindley Miller Garrison

My dear Mr. President: Washington. April 8, 1913.

Mr. Davies of Wisconsin has just left me. He came in to explain to me in person that his situation at home was such that he did not feel justified in leaving it to come to Washington and accept the office of Assistant Secretary of War.

Incidentally he said to me that during my absence in the West it had been suggested to him that he might be sent as Governor General to the Philippines, but that he has since been told that this could not be.

With respect to the office of Assistant Secretary of War, I gathered from my latest talk with you on this subject that if Mr. Davies declined, Mr. Breckinridge[1] was to be appointed; and, as you know, he is entirely satisfactory to me.

With respect to the Governor Generalship of the Philippines, I am endeavoring to gather for your consideration the names of the very best men that can be procured for that service. I think that primarily, however, we should consider the question whether this office should be filled at once, that is, at this time, or whether you will decide that I had best go there before acting on these Philippine matters. You will recall that at our latest talk respecting this you said that you desired to seriously consider the matter before reaching a conclusion. Should you determine that I had best go, then I would seriously counsel postponing appointments until my return. I do not believe that any interests of the Islands or of this Government are suffering or will suffer by reason of delay in this respect. Of course, if you should conclude that you do not at the present time desire to have me absent from Washington for so long a period, then I think we should have a general talk upon the Philippine appointments and determine our policy and pick our men.

When you are free enough from your other engrossing duties, may I ask that you give the above matters consideration and advise me of your conclusion?

                    Sincerely yours,   Lindley M. Garrison

TLS (WP, DLC).
  [1] Henry S. Breckinridge, who was soon appointed.

From Cleveland Hoadley Dodge

Dear Mr. President: New York April 8, 1913.

I was just on the point of writing to you when your very kind letter of April fifth came to hand this morning.

I sympathize with you most profoundly in your efforts to secure the best men for important positions, and, regarding China, have been wondering whether you have thought of Prof. Jenks. I have seen quite a little of him lately and am very much impressed by his great knowledge of China and his high character and ability. He was intensely interested in our effort to secure Mr. Mott, and is strongly impressed with the feeling that it is necessary to infuse a little righteousness into the minds of the Chinese leaders. Moreover, the question there, for some little time, will be largely a financial and economic one, and his knowledge of the situation would help him very much.

I am going on to Washington next week Thursday, the 17th, to attend a meeting of the Executive Committee of the Carnegie Institution Thursday afternoon and a meeting of the Trustees of the Peace Foundation Friday morning. I shall be alone and hope sincerely that it will be possible for me to see you and the family, if only for a few minutes. I have no axe to grind but simply want to grip your hand and tell you how deeply interested I am in all that you are are doing.

Trusting that you can arrange for some time when I can see you, believe me, with warm regards,

Very cordially and faithfully yours,   C. H. Dodge

TLS (WP, DLC).

From John Downey Works

My dear Mr. President: Washington, April 8, 1913.

I went over the California situation very carefully last night with Mr. Lane. He is very strongly of the opinion that none of us should interfere with what is going on in the Legislature. He tells me that he is in close touch with Mr. Caminetti who can be thoroughly trusted in the matter and who is of the opinion that nothing will be done of which any foreign nation will have just reason to complain.

I am inclined to believe after this interview with Mr. Lane that he is right and that it would be better, at least for the present, to let things take their course. I think he was looking at it from a little different point of view than my own. He was considering it, I found, from the point of view of the Democratic party and the effect any interference by a Democratic President might have upon the future of that party. I had in mind more particularly the question of conflict that might arise, or complications between our government and other nations. Of course

Mr. Lane was broad-minded enough to take that feature into account also.

Unless you see some urgent reason for interference or suggestion on my part I shall feel inclined to follow Mr. Lane's suggestion and say nothing. Of course anything that I might do after the papers have published the fact of my being called to the White House to consider this question,[1] would be attributed to you and it undoubtedly would be maintained that you were taking the position in opposition to the best interests of California in opposing this measure intended to protect our people from the encroachments of citizens of another nation.

I shall be very glad to hear from you further on the subject if you should desire anything further at my hands.

Sincerely yours,   John D. Works

TLS (WP, DLC).
[1] Works saw Wilson at 6 P.M. on April 7. William Kent came at 6:15, Senator George E. Chamberlain and Secretary Lane at 6:25. Presumably they discussed the California situation together.
Kent later recalled that Wilson "suggested the extremely irritated state of affairs with Japan, admitted and endorsed the state's right to handle its own land questions, but deferentially submitted the fact that it might be framed in less offensive form." Would not Kent suggest to Governor Hiram Johnson "that a bill might be drawn excluding from land ownership those who had not made application for American citizenship, thereby leaving the way open for bonafide prospective citizens to participate in the privilege of owning California land, but excluding those who had no such intent, necessarily including the Japanese whose first papers would not be accepted." William Kent, "Some Reminiscences of Hiram Johnson," T MS dated Aug. 1, 1922 (W. Kent Papers, CtY).

William Jennings Bryan to Joseph Patrick Tumulty, with Enclosure

My dear Tumulty   [Washington, c. April 8, 1913]

Please show this to the President. Tell him that I have made the changes suggested. If this suits him I will ask Senator Bacon[1] to call a meeting of his Com & if I find the plan acceptable I can present it to the Amb[s] & Ministers before Mr Bryce sails.

Yours   Bryan

ALS (WP, DLC).
[1] Augustus Octavius Bacon of Georgia, chairman of the Foreign Relations Committee.

E N C L O S U R E

MEMORANDUM BY MR. BRYAN.[1]

The parties hereto agree that all questions of whatever character and nature whatever, in dispute between them, shall, when diplomatic efforts fail, be submitted for investigation and report to an international commission composed (the composition to be agreed upon); and the contracting parties agree not to declare war or begin hostilities until such investigation is made and report submitted.

The investigation shall be conducted as a matter of course, without the formality of a request from either party; the report shall be submitted within (time to be agreed upon) from the date of the submission of the dispute, and neither party shall utilize the period of investigation to change its military or naval program, but the parties hereto reserve the right to act independently on the subject matter in dispute after the report is submitted.

T MS (WP, DLC).
    1 This was the first formulation of Bryan's "cooling off" treaty, about which see Merle Eugene Curti, "Bryan and World Peace," *Smith College Studies in History*, XVI (April-July, 1931), 143-64; Paolo E. Coletta, *William Jennings Bryan* (3 vols., Lincoln, Neb., 1964-69), II, 239-49, and Link, *The New Freedom*, pp. 280-283.

To John Downey Works

My dear Senator: [The White House] April 9, 1913
    I am sincerely obliged to you for your note of yesterday and I entirely concur with the judgment it expresses. I find things are taking a more favorable form in the Legislature in California than I had supposed. The phraseology of the bill now pending appears to be almost exactly that which I suggested to you and Mr. Kent.
            Cordially and sincerely yours,   Woodrow Wilson

TLS (Letterpress Books, WP, DLC).

To James Duval Phelan

Confidential.

My dear Mr. Phelan: [The White House] April 9, 1913
    Thank you for your telegram. I think I understand the gravity of the situation in California and I have never been inclined to criticise. I have only hoped that the doing of the thing might be so modulated and managed as to offend the susceptibilities of a friendly nation as little as possible.
    In haste
            Cordially and sincerely yours,   Woodrow Wilson

TLS (Letterpress Books, WP, DLC).

A News Report

[*April 9, 1913*]

PRESIDENT VISITS CAPITOL AGAIN
TO MEET SENATORS

Meets the Democratic Members of the Senate Finance
Committee and Talks Over the Tariff Bill with Them
for an Hour and a Half with the Object of Insuring Harmony
and Keeping Party Promises.

WASHINGTON, April 9.—In a dignified and characteristically
Wilsonian way, the President to-day jolted custom and woke
up sleeping precedent by visiting the Capitol for a conference
with the lawmakers on pending legislation. For an hour and a
half he had a friendly consultation with the Democratic members of the Senate Finance Committee in the President's Room,
which is located in the Senate wing. In so doing he revived a
procedure that has lain dormant since the days of Grant, and at
the same time he carried out his announced intention of frequently occupying the room and holding pleasant conferences
with the Senators. That it was a profitable conference was
proved when it was all over and the President confidently said:
"We don't see any difficulty in standing together on any sort of
party programme."

The Tariff bill was the sole topic of discussion. The President
sought to reach an amicable arrangement by which necessary
amendments could be added to the measure with the least possible friction, both in the House and after it reaches the Senate.

In order to provide the maximum degree of harmony and
prevent possible wrangling during debate on the Tariff bill, the
President urged that every Senator be requested to advise him
personally just what amendments he desires to have incorporated in the measure. He would give them careful consideration
and either explain that they did not meet his approval or he
would request their insertion in the bill. He desires that no
amendments be proposed in the Senate by Democrats except
those offered by the Finance Committee.

At the request of the President, the ten members of the
Finance Committee present at the meeting promised to say
nothing regarding the conference, but refer all anxious inquirers
to the President.

When approached for information on the questions pending
during the ninety minutes passed in the President's room, and
before any interrogations could be propounded, Mr. Wilson
said:

"I suppose you fellows think this is another national crisis." Being assured to the contrary, the President continued:

"This conference was to discuss the tariff. I am glad I had it and I hope the Senators will let me come and consult them frequently. The net result of this meeting is that we don't see any sort of difficulty about standing firmly on our party programme."

"Will there be one bill or several? Will the sugar schedule be considered separately?" the President was asked.

"That is for the other house to decide," replied the President.

"Will the House be guided by the wishes of the Senate?" was the final inquiry.

"I haven't asked them," answered the President, as he moved away.

The sole purpose of the President's visit was to secure the greatest degree of harmony in the matter of amendments and to lessen those proposed by the Senate to the smallest possible number. The President frankly said that some amendments were absolutely essential. If these were not made in the House he desired the Finance Committee to take the subject up and remedy the apparent defects in the bill as printed.

The President pointed out that as framed the Tariff bill placed wool on the free list, but omitted mohair. He hoped this would be added in the removal of duties. He also urged that shoe machinery, now controlled by a trust, be added to the free list. The same, he said, was true of phosphoric acid, which is largely used in making fertilizers.

In addition, the President said a great many small items were permitted to retain duties. He thought these should all be added to the free list. He explained that in each instance but a trifling amount of revenue was derived and the expense of collection was greater than the sum realized by the Government. If any of these slipped through in the House he desired the Finance Committee to place them on the free list.

Beyond this point, and apart from the mass of suggestions which he expected to receive from Senators, the President hoped the Finance Committee would not go. He sought team work between the Senate and House in enacting the new tariff measure.

The Senators present replied that it was utterly impossible to give any pledge of the character indicated. They said the constitutional right of amending all House bills rested with the Senate and could neither be waived nor abrogated.

No resentment was manifested by the President at this plain

statement of the situation. He received the announcement seriously and said all these matters could be adjusted at conferences which would follow in the future.

And so it transpired that the President left his room smiling, self-possessed and seemingly happy, after shaking hands with his conferrees. He lifted his soft hat to the small crowd that awaited his reappearance, "jollied" the newspaper men and started on the return trip to the White House.

The President took the initiative in proposing a conference with the Democratic members of the Finance Committee. He selected an auspicious time. His statement yesterday that he came to the Capitol as a human being to confer with other human beings had generally disarmed all resentment and criticism. It placed the President in a light other than that of Executive usurpation and surrounded him with a feeling of friendly interest.

Some members of the committee explained that the meeting to-day was merely a continuance of the gathering at the White House last Monday and the President thought it easier for one man to visit the Capitol than to require ten Senators to see him at his offices.

An early adjournment of the Senate was taken in order that the Democratic members of the Finance Committee might have a "powwow" among themselves and prepare some plan of united action before the President came. A telephone message from the White House had previously announced that the President would be in his room, adjoining the Senate chamber, at 3 o'clock. . . .

Printed in the New York *World*, April 10, 1913.

From William Kent, with Enclosures

My dear Mr. Wilson: Washington, D. C. April 9, 1913.

Enclosed please find copy of my telegram to Governor Johnson, which was specifically intended to keep you and your administration free from any implication of interfering with California legislation. Appended please find the reply of Governor Johnson. In addition to sending to him this telegram, I requested Mr. William Denman, of San Francisco,[1] one of the most judicious men I know, to do what he could to keep down such action as might be offensive, sending to him copy of the telegram to Governor Johnson. If I can act further in this matter I shall be glad to do so, but the Governor evidently wishes first hand information.

I believe it would be sufficient if you wired to him the statement which I am sure you will be willing to make, that while recognizing the right of California to handle such of its internal affairs as are presented by this issue, it is your hope that the measure may be so general in character as to be free from offense to any people or nation.

Yours truly,   William Kent

TLS, (WP, DLC).
¹ Lawyer and municipal reform leader of San Francisco.

E N C L O S U R E   I

[Washington] April 7, 1913.

Legislation against alien land tenure in order to be void of unnecessary offense should exclude all aliens but should exempt from excluded classification those who have been permitted to file satisfactory first papers for naturalization.

Can state although not for publication that there is no denial here of the right or propriety of action by our state in this vital matter, but a heartfelt desire that action may be diplomatic and courteous.   William Kent

E N C L O S U R E   I I

Sacramento, Cal., April 8, 1913.

Thank you for your two telegrams of last night. I take it the one relating to alien land bill is authoritive but of course by its terms it cannot be communicated to those most interested. The two previous administrations have officially communicated their views to the Chief Executive of this State upon the subject of alien land bills and legislation affecting Japanese I see no reason why the present administration if it has views upon these subjects and desires our legislation to be in accordance with those views should not also officially express itself. I have assumed that the Federal Government thoroughly understands the measures that have been proposed at the present session of the legislature and indeed I have been informed that these measures have been the subject of discussion at Washington and I assume of course that the present national administration has no complaint regarding any of this legislation or that complaint would have been made in the usual manner and through the ordinary channel. I shall be pleased to transmit to you or to those you may suggest any information that may be desired.

Hiram W. Johnson, Governor.

T telegrams (WP, DLC).

To Hiram Warren Johnson

[Washington] April 10, 1913.

The President desires and intends to respect to the utmost the unquestionable prerogatives of the government of California in the matter of land tenure, but feels at liberty to request that you will be kind enough to have the full text of the pending Alien Land Tenure bill telegraphed to this department immediately upon its passage by the Legislature of the State and that you will allow this department as long a time as possible under the constitutional provisions of the State for the consideration of the measure in view of the treaty obligations of the government so that if necessary the questions and the possible embarrassments involved may be laid before you before the measure becomes law by your signature.   W. J. Bryan.[1]

TC telegram (WP, DLC).
   [1] There is a WWsh draft of this telegram in the C. L. Swem Coll., NjP.

To Oscar Wilder Underwood

My dear Mr. Underwood,   The White House 10 Apr., 1913

I hope that the understanding arrived at in the conference I held yesterday with the Democratic members of the Finance Committee lightened your work. I was very glad indeed to urge your judgment upon them and was happy to have [William] Hughes carry you the message which relieved you from a task from which I know your own best thought held back.

Cordially Yours,   Woodrow Wilson

ALS (O. W. Underwood Papers, A-Ar).

To Lindley Miller Garrison

My dear Mr. Secretary: [The White House] April 10, 1913

I quite agree with you that there is no particular haste in appointing a Governor General of the Philippines, and I shall wish to take up the matter with you very carefully. My own impression is that the more we look into the matter the more you will discover the reasonableness of the choice I have made, but we must cover the whole field before we finally decide. You are quite right in thinking that the time of the choice ought to depend upon whether you go to the Philippines or not. Just now it does not look to me possible to spare you from Washington for so long a time so early in the administration, when we are getting things into shape.

In haste   Cordially yours,   Woodrow Wilson

TLS (Letterpress Books, WP, DLC).

To William Kent

My dear Mr. Kent: [The White House] April 10, 1913

I am sincerely obliged to you for what you have been doing in the matter of the Alien Land Tenure bill in California, and also for keeping me so fully informed as to the news you get from the State. Things seem to be going quite satisfactorily.

Cordially yours,   Woodrow Wilson

TLS (Letterpress Books, WP, DLC).

To Cleveland Hoadley Dodge

My dear Cleve: The White House April 10, 1913

You must come straight here and stay with us when you come to Washington on the seventeenth. It not only will be delightful to us, but it is the only way I can hope to have a real glimpse of you. I wish that Mrs. Dodge were coming, too.

I shall discuss with you then your suggestion about Jenks, for I am going slowly in this matter of choosing someone else for China.

In haste   Affectionately yours,   Woodrow Wilson

TLS (WC, NjP).

From William Gibbs McAdoo

Dear Mr. President: Washington April 10, 1913.

The commission of Robert Smalls (colored),[1] Collector of Customs at Beaufort, South Carolina, expired July 31st, 1910. He was renominated by President Taft, but failed of confirmation by the Senate. The Senators and Representatives from South Carolina are very anxious to have a successor appointed. Senators Tillman and Smith and Representative Byrnes,[2] from the Beaufort District, recommend the appointment of Franklin Pierce Colcock, of Beaufort, South Carolina, age fifty-nine, occupation clerk. I am sure from what these gentlemen tell me that Mr. Colcock is well qualified for the position. I respectfully recommend that he be appointed.[3]

I may say that this is not an important port, the aggregate receipts for the fiscal year ended June 30, 1912, being $434.11.

Sincerely yours,   W G McAdoo

TLS (WP, DLC).

[1] Born a slave in Beaufort, S. C., Smalls became well known for his naval exploits on the Union side during the Civil War. He became prominent in South Carolina politics during the Reconstruction era and served as a Republican congressman from South Carolina, 1875-79, 1882-83, and 1884-87. He had served as collector of the port of Beaufort since 1889. See Okon Edet Uya, *From Slavery to Public Service: Robert Smalls, 1838-1915* (New York, 1971).

[2] James Francis Byrnes, representative from South Carolina since 1911.

[3] Colcock was appointed.

From Cleveland Hoadley Dodge

My dear Mr President   New York. April 10th 1913

As a loyal subject, I obey your command with the greatest alacrity and pleasure and will come next Wednesday on the noon train which reaches Washington about six o'clock, & if Mrs Wilson really wants me, I will spend that night and Thursday night with you, and have the Supreme satisfaction of seeing you all, in the place which I have longed to see you in, ever since that fateful day, in the Summer of 1910 when you decided to accept the profer of the Gubernatorial nomination.

I have recently been re-reading "Congressional Government," with the keenest interest, in view of what you are doing at Washington, in direct line with your thoughts of thirty years ago.

With many thanks for your awfully kind invitation

Your's aff'ly   Cleveland H. Dodge

ALS (WP, DLC).

Remarks at a Press Conference

April 11, 1913

Mr. President, have you taken up this question of continuing the Commerce Court with any definite idea?

I haven't. I am uninstructed, really, on the merits of the case.

Of course, I have been foregathering from citizens who have very distinct ideas on the subject—

Yes, I have had some intimations that there were such ideas, but I don't feel that I know enough about the merits of the thing to have a right to an opinion. I hope I haven't done anything else unprecedented lately, have I? (Laughter)

Have you any plans to break any precedents?

No, I haven't at any time had any plans. I was just saying to a friend today, I have a queer impression of what must have been done usually in the District of Columbia, because every time I do something perfectly natural, it turns out to be unprecedented.

Speaking of plans, Mr. President, have you decided yet when you are going to New Jersey?

No, I am waiting on the New Jersey people to make their appointments and I will go up and help.

What is this eight o'clock business,[1] Mr. President?

My only information about that was from the morning papers.

What does that mean?

At the cabinet meeting today not a word was said about any plan of the kind. I think it was a misunderstanding. At any rate, I have not heard a word about it.

Mr. President, what is the status of the Chinese situation?

Why simply this: For reasons which, speaking for myself, I don't understand, the constituent assembly met on Tuesday and then adjourned for ten days, I think. Why they adjourned, I am not informed, but they adjourned without a full constitution—I mean without electing officers, as I understand—and therefore, I suppose, to get acquainted and form their plans; because, of course, China isn't a homogeneous unit.

Or waiting for a few more assassinations!

Oh, there has been only one, hasn't there?

That is all.

That is enough, but I didn't know but that you had heard later news.

No, sir.

Mr. President, has there been any decision reached as to what you are going to do about fourth-class postmasters?

No, sir, that is still under discussion.

Mr. President, have you had any opportunity to give Alaska attention lately?

---

[1] News reports to the effect that government workers would be required to begin at eight o'clock.

Not any particular attention. Of course, I gave it a good deal of attention before I was inaugurated so as to inform myself just what was possible. The first thing I have to do is find a governor, and the governor has to be chosen from the residents of Alaska under the law; so I am trying to inform myself about the candidates.

Is that a new law?

I don't know.

The present governor[2] was the White House reporter for the New York *Sun*.

The candidates are before me, then! (Laughter) To tell you the truth, I didn't look the law up myself. I was taking it from Secretary Lane, who stated it to me, so that it must be a new law.

The new legislature may just have expressed that wish.

They did express that wish, but it was certainly the Secretary of the Interior's impression that that was the law.

The Democratic national platform declared for that.

Yes, I know it did.

Mr. President, did Colonel Ewing[3] cause you to change any views you may have had with regard to sugar. I understand the Colonel was here this morning.

No, he didn't try. He came in and the first thing he said was, "I haven't come to talk about sugar."

Mr. President, our understanding of the changes in the customhouse in Philadelphia[4] was that it was the beginning of changes in customhouses, or the important ones throughout the country, with an idea of having men there who were perhaps more in sympathy with the objects of the new tariff law—the forthcoming tariff law. Could you tell us anything about that?

No, that is too large a conclusion to draw. It really was an action with regard to that particular office.

I so understood.

I mean it wasn't part of the general policy.

Mr. President, I would like to ask something regarding this California alien land law. I have been looking into it a little. I find that the present treaty stipulates that the citizens of each country, while in the other country, shall have a right to own houses and factories and shops, and to lease land. It doesn't say anything about owning land. I also find that in Japan the old laws

2 Walter Eli Clark.
3 Robert Ewing, of New Orleans, newspaper publisher and Democratic national committeeman from Louisiana.
4 A reference to the announcement of the appointment of the new collector of the Port of Philadelphia, William H. Berry.

against foreign ownership of land were abrogated, and laws permitting foreigners to own lands were passed; but the necessary edict to put them in force has not been issued, so that citizens of the United States cannot now own lands in Japan; and it seems to me that if that was the case that the Japanese objections against the United States are possibly not well grounded.[5]

You see, the trouble about all those treaties is a trouble peculiar to ourselves because of our system. Nobody can for a moment challenge the constitutional right of California to pass such land laws as she pleases. Now, insofar as the federal government has gone beyond its powers—its domestic authority—in making a treaty, just so far is it liable to damages, but it is helpless in the premises. You see, that is the complication always in those treaties. The facts as you have stated them are the facts as I understand them.

[5] This was essentially correct. The correspondence between the American and Japanese governments during the negotiation of the Commercial Treaty of 1911 reveals that the Imperial authorities desired to avoid any treaty arrangements that would permit Americans to own land (as distinct from residences, places of business, etc.). As Ambassador Thomas J. O'Brien reported to the State Department, the Japanese Minister for Foreign Affairs, Count Jutarō Komura, had "stated in the Diet, and another member of the Foreign Office has informed the Embassy, that the Japanese Government desires to avoid treaty agreements regarding the ownership of land by foreigners and to regulate the matter entirely by domestic legislation." T. J. O'Brien to the Secretary of State, March 25, 1910, T telegram (SDR, RG 59, 711.942/50 1/2, DNA). However, under American pressure, and in anticipation of the completion of the treaty, the Imperial government on March 24, 1910, obtained passage of a law permitting limited land ownership of aliens on a reciprocal basis. However, the law had not been promulgated by early 1913 because the Japanese government said that it was still investigating the treatment of Japanese subjects with respect to land ownership in various countries.

The weakness of the Japanese legal case in the developing California controversy was exposed in detail in the Secretary of State to the Japanese Ambassador, July 16, 1913, about which see J. B. Moore to WW, June 29, 1913, n. 1.

Wilson's reply to the reporter's question was somewhat oblique. Once a serious crisis with Japan developed, he refused in public (the diplomatic correspondence with Japan was not published until 1920) to explain that the Japanese, in 1910 and 1911, had dragged their feet on reciprocity on land ownership and in fact in 1913 were not granting to American citizens rights that California denied to Japanese subjects. On January 27, 1914, Wilson, in an exclusive interview, told a New York Times reporter that the State Department files contained documents relating to the negotiation of the Japanese-American treaty which, if made public, "would at once establish the American contention in the California dispute." "The explanation offered as to why the State Department does not now produce that correspondence to shut off Japanese protests against the California law," this report continued, "is that, while such a course would be a final answer to the present Japanese Government, it would fan the fury of the jingo element in Japan and probably cause the overthrow of the Government after a bitter parliamentary onslaught. That would simply result in putting the jingoes at the head of the Japanese policy, and with them the United States would find it more difficult than ever to deal." New York Times, Jan. 28, 1914. About the source of this report, see n. 1 to the news report printed at Jan. 27, 1914.

That this was Wilson's motivation and strategy in 1913, following documents in this and the next volume will attest.

Do the Japanese really make representations regarding this matter? Are they still denying the same rights?

I want to say that the Japanese Ambassador has acted in a most proper and delightful way about it. He didn't so much make representations to Mr. Bryan and me as a government as treating us as friends of Japan who would wish to see the best relations prevail, and asked us to look into this legislation out there and see if anything could be done to take the sting out of it, or to make it acceptable to Japanese susceptibilities. And we have been trying to act in that spirit. That is really the whole situation.

Is the treaty construed as the right to own land?

No, it isn't construed as the right to own land. As a matter of fact, it guarantees that they shall be treated on the same basis with the most favored nations. It is that famous favored nation clause that is in so many of the treaties.

Mr. President, are they not supposed to take note of the fact that the Constitution of the United States would not permit such a treaty to be made—are they on notice?

Of course they know, because the Japanese Ambassador said that he understood our domestic constitutional arrangements, but we couldn't as a treatymaking power take it for granted that they had what one might call judicial notice of that.

That whole matter came up in the case in New Orleans.[6]

Yes, it did, and the federal government simply had to reimburse—

Mr. President, have you expressed yourself on the pending sundry bill that caused the trouble in the legislature?

No, I haven't.

Any development in the tariff situation today, Mr. President?

None that I have heard of.

Does it seem necessary to make some change in that provision which gives a reduction of 5 per cent for goods brought in American bottoms?

[6] The superintendent of the New Orleans police department, David C. Hennessy, was murdered on October 15, 1890, allegedly by members of the local Mafia who were seeking vengeance for Hennessy's investigation into their activities. When a jury failed to convict the Italian Americans accused of the assassination, an angry mob stormed the prison on March 14, 1891, and killed eleven of them. The Italian government protested to Secretary of State James G. Blaine and insisted that the federal government prosecute the lynchers and that monetary compensation be paid the families of the victims. Blaine replied that local authorities were entirely autonomous in this case but acceded to the demand for compensation; eventually an indemnity was paid to the families. About this episode, see Alexander De Conde, *Half Bitter, Half Sweet: An Excursion into Italian-American History* (New York, 1971), pp. 121-25, 412.

I haven't heard any suggestion that that change is necessary. As violating existing treaties with other countries?

No, I haven't heard that objection.

Republicans up there seem to be rejoicing over the inclusion of the antidumping clause of the bill,[7] which they say they could never get into the bill on account of Democratic opposition!

Well, since we are running the government, we know what is safe. (Laughter)

Mr. President, with the new tariff in the form in which it is proposed—with the reciprocity provision—[8] will there be any disposition to do away with the most favored nation clause?

I don't see why we should.

Is reciprocity recognized as a justifiable exception to the most favored nation treaty?

Yes, I think so; because the most favored nation clause doesn't exclude us from making special arrangements between particular nations.

There has been some difference between American construction and European construction. Are you liable to exclude this agreement between some states—Portugal, Italy, etc.?

Of course, that is so far in the future I hadn't taken that up in my mind. "Sufficient unto the day is the evil thereof."

When do you expect to come to New England, Mr. President?

As soon as I can get back from Panama.

What about the recognition of Mexico?

Well, I don't know. We don't decide that—that is decided between brawls! (Laughter)

Is it dependent upon the constitution?

I oughtn't to jest upon such a serious subject. Of course, what we are waiting for—what all the governments are waiting for—is the regular process by which they are expecting soon to constitute a constitutional government.

T MS (C. L. Swem Coll., NjP).

7 Section 4E of the Underwood tariff bill provided that, when any country should pay, directly or indirectly, any bounty upon the export of any item dutiable under the Underwood bill, then an additional duty equal to the net amount of the bounty would be levied on the item. This provision was almost identical to one in the Payne-Aldrich Tariff Act of 1909. See Report to Accompany H.R. 3321: A Bill to Reduce Tariff Duties, to Provide Revenue for the Government and for Other Purposes, 63d Congress, 1st sess., House of Representatives, Report No. 5, p. 436.

8 Section 4A of the Underwood bill authorized the President "to negotiate trade agreements with foreign nations wherein mutual concessions are made looking toward freer trade relations and further reciprocal expansion of trade and commerce." Such agreements would have to be ratified by Congress. Ibid., p. 431.

To Henry Burchard Fine

My dear Harry: [The White House] April 11, 1913

It was a deep, deep disappointment to me that you could not accept. In my opinion you are just the man for the place. You apparently do not know it but everyone who has spoken about the offer and who knew you has agreed with me enthusiastically. But I do not wish you to think for a moment that there is anything but regret that the country could not have had the benefit of your services. I deeply respect, as I thoroughly understand, the reasons why you declined, and in the turmoil of public affairs I can not help sighing to think that I can not turn, as you are turning, to study again and to the work that seems somehow to be part of the unbroken thinking of the world.

I can not tell you how deep a delight it was to me to have the opportunity to show just what I thought of you. There are not many pleasures connected with appointments to office, so far as the appointing officer is concerned, and, therefore, these rare occasions when I can turn to the men I really trust and believe in are very dear to me.

I want you to know that everybody regrets your having found it necessary to decline and speaks of the whole thing in just the terms that would make you happiest.

It was indeed fine in Cleve to make the offer he did. He made it with his usual heartiness and sincerity.

All join me in warmest and most affectionate regards, and we hope that you will all come back greatly refreshed by your vacation and give us the pleasure of seeing you as soon as possible after you return.

                    Affectionately yours,   Woodrow Wilson

TLS (Letterpress Books, WP, DLC).

From the Diary of Josephus Daniels

                              Friday, April 11, 1913.

The Postmaster General brought up a matter that is always the hardest matter to deal with—to wit: policies that are affected by race conditions. In the railway mail service there are a great many negroes who are employed and it often happens that there are four railway mail clerks in one car and when this happens, the white men might often have to do all the work. It is very unpleasant for them to work in a car with negroes where it is almost impossible to have different drinking vessels and different towels, or places to wash and he was anxious to segregate white and negro employees in all Departments of the Government, and he had talked with Bishop Walters and other prominent negroes and most of them thought it would be a great thing to do. Mr. Burleson thought the segregation would be a great thing as he had the highest regard for the negro and wished to help him in every way possible, but that he believed segregation was best for the negro and best for the Service. The matter then came up generally about negro appointments and how to use them. The President said he made no promises in particular to negroes, except to do them justice, and he did not wish to see them have less positions than they now have, but he wished the matter adjusted in a way to make the least friction. A negro is now Registrar of the Treasury, and Mr. Burleson, the Attorney General, thought it was wrong to have white clerks, men or women, under him, or any other negro. Secretary of the Treasury McAdoo doubted whether the Senate would confirm a negro even if the President appointed one for this place, and believed it would be very doubtful. As to the segregation of negro clerks in the Treasury Department under the Registrar, Mr. McAdoo feared it would not work. The difference in salaries, etc., would operate against it. The up-shot of it all was that no action was taken, but Mr. Burleson said he would work out the matter in the Railway Mail Service in an easy way that would not go into effect at once and negroes would be employed on railway mail cars in sections where the appointment of negroes would not be objectionable.[1]

The Secretary of Labor brought up the matter and the need of something being done in West Virginia. There is a strike out there between the mine workers and the mine owners[2] which is very aggravated, he said, by the fact that the owners of the mines employ Baldwin Guards, who go to every train and if a new man came to town, they kept him under surveillance, and asking him what his business was, etc., with a view to injuring the strikers. He said this condition had been aggravated so much and said if a striker was arrested and tried, he was tried by a military court and that the state court prohibited him from getting a habeas corpus proceeding, or having his trial by a civil tribunal, and that he was trying, through arbitration, to settle the matter and hoped to be able to secure it but has not yet been able to do so.

The President said he thought that it was unthinkable a man should be tried this way, but the beginning of all this was having a town controlled by a mine owner and the keeping out of people not desired by him. It was the root of the trouble. Secretary of

Labor Wilson also thought the trouble was aggravated because the mine owners compelled the men to buy at the mine owner's stores and compelled [them] to pay exorbitant prices. The President was very vigorously against the policy of excluding people from a town that did not give all people freedom to come a[nd] go. Secretary of War Garrison thought that the men who were tried by military courts without a jury could appeal to the Federal courts and that something might be done along that line. But, inasmuch as the state courts had held otherwise, there was not much chance.

At this juncture, the President arose and said he must be excused to dine with Mr. Bryce of England, not Ambassador Bryce, but his old friend who was shortly going back to England.

T MS (J. Daniels Papers, DLC).
    [1] Many documents relating to this matter will appear in this and following volumes. On the general subject, see Link, *The New Freedom*, pp. 246-52; Charles Flint Kellogg, *NAACP: A History of the National Association for the Advancement of Colored People, Vol. 1, 1909-1920* (Baltimore, 1967), pp. 161-77; Nancy J. Weiss, "The Negro and the New Freedom: Fighting Wilsonian Segregation," *Political Science Quarterly*, LXXXIV (March 1969), 61-79; Kathleen Long Wolgemuth, "Woodrow Wilson's Appointment Policy and the Negro," *Journal of Southern History*, XXIV (Nov. 1958), 457-71; and Morton Sosna, "The South in the Saddle: Racial Politics During the Wilson Years," *Wisconsin Magazine of History*, LIV (Autumn 1970), 30-49.
    [2] For the background and events of the violence-ridden strike in the West Virginia bituminous coal fields from April 20, 1912, to April 28, 1913, see John Rogers Commons *et al.*, *History of Labour in the United States* (4 vols., New York, 1918-35), IV, 326-35.

From the Diary of Colonel House

Washington, D. C. April 11, 1913.

McAdoo and I dined at the White House. At dinner the conversation ran along social lines, all of us trying to tell something to amuse. After dinner the President, McAdoo and I went to the library and discussed New York appointments. We decided upon Polk[1] for Collector. This was done largely upon my recommendation.

We then talked currency reform, and went over the Glass Bill in detail. It was agreed that McAdoo, Glass, Owens and I should meet Monday evening and go over it again and try and whip it in shape. We left the White House at ten and I returned to the Wallace's and found Walter Page.

    [1] Frank Lyon Polk, lawyer of New York and anti-Tammany Democrat.

Baron Nobuaki Makino to Viscount Sutemi Chinda

No. 56   [Tokyo, April 11, 1913]

The Imperial Government have learned with deep regret and concern of the two measures regarding alien land ownership now pending in the State legislature of California. Both measures appear to be directed against Japanese subjects and if enacted into law would undoubtedly give ground for serious complaint. The Japanese Government are well aware that the question is not at this time ripe for formal international discussion but ardently desiring that nothing shall be left undone tending to strengthen the good relations between the two countries, the Japanese Government have decided to approach the American Government on the subject at the present juncture in the hope that steps will be taken to prevent the adoption of the proposed legislation. Accordingly with this object in view you will see the President and Secretary of State regarding the matter. You will assure them that it has always been and still is the earnest desire of the Japanese Government to maintain relations of the most friendly and cordial nature with the United States. You will point out that it was in furtherance of that desire that the Japanese Government in a spirit of friendly accommodation and good neighborhood so readily and fully yielded five years ago to the wishes of the American Government respecting Japanese emigration to the mainland of the United States and that it is in pursuance of the same desire that the Japanese Government still continue scrupulously and satisfactorily to carry out the understanding then arrived at. You will add that with a view to promote the relations of friendly intercourse with the United States, the Japanese Government hastened at once last year to accept the invitation to take part in the forthcoming Grand Exposition[1] and are actively making all necessary preparation for the important event.

You will explain that the amount of land owned by Japanese subjects in California is very inconsiderable and that such amount must in any circumstances always remain a very negligible quantity but that that fact would not lessen the hardship of those who might be called upon to suffer from unjust and inequitable legislation on the subject. Reserving for the present the question of how far and in what particulars the contemplated enactments are in violation of the existing Japanese-American Treaty and hoping that it will not be found necessary to discuss that phase of the subject, you will impress upon the President and Secretary of State that the measures are clearly contrary to the spirit of good relations and good intercourse which Japan has done so much to foster and encourage and you will strongly urge them to take such steps as may be necessary to prevent the proposed bills from becoming law. You will say that the Japanese Government cannot but regard this question as most serious and important. The public opinion of the nation is deeply aroused and the enactment of either of the projected measures would be most unfortunate and prejudicial to the sentiments of good will and friendship which have always united the two countries, and would moreover be very injurious to their important commercial relations.

There are other anti-Japanese bills before the California Legislature which are equally objectionable. The Japanese Government are well aware that both the President and Secretary of State have exerted their endeavors to avert unfriendly legislation and it is sincerely hoped that they will continue to use their efforts in the same direction.   Makino.

T telegram (MT 3.8.2.274-2, pp. 277-80, JFO-Ar), sent in English.
  ¹ The San Francisco Exposition of 1915.

Remarks to the Gridiron Club of Washington

[April 12, 1913]

Mr. President and Gentlemen: This is my first night out since I came to Washington, and I want to say that I have profoundly enjoyed it. I have lived among good fellows all my life and I have found another bunch.

You have paid me a very deep compliment tonight, perhaps without being aware of it. You have interpreted, for I have gleaned that you have understood, my conception of the part that I have to play. The Presidency of the United States, gentlemen, is a very great office. We hope and believe that it is an immortal office, which may be lifted higher and higher for the guidance of a people and the guidance of free men throughout the world. But, pray, do not confound the man who occupies it with the office itself. The fundamental feeling that I have is that I am not identified with that office. I am the person for the time being allotted to administer it; and the only way in which I can administer it is by constantly feeling the grip of other men fastened upon my hand, not only to guide me, but to accompany me in the great task that is assigned me.

That is perhaps the reason why I have done some very unconventional things in this very conventional town! As I was saying to a large group of friends the other day,[1] I get a very singular impression of what has been the rule in the District of Columbia, because whenever I do a perfectly natural thing, I am told I have done something unprecedented. I am trying to get at the job by all the natural short cuts that I can think of, for the job is to understand and to be understood. It is not to stand off and imagine myself identified with the dignity and the immortality of a great office, but to think myself identified with the men with whom I am trying to cooperate, so that we may think common thoughts, for if we do not, we cannot have common purposes. Surely that is the reason why some of the men present have honored me with a peculiar confidence. They have paid me the compliment of not believing that I was fool enough to think that I knew the whole thing. They have paid me the compliment of recognizing that I was going about trying to learn from others, not trying to instruct those who have been longer in the game than I have. And there is one thing, and only one, that we have in common. That is our connection with the great impulses of the people to which we belong.

I have experienced in the last month a certain sense of isolation. One reason that I went up to the Capitol the other day is that it is lonely down at my end of the Avenue. I wanted to see some of the fellows, and see what they looked like; and I had a curious impression on Tuesday last that I was the only person present who was not embarrassed. The gentlemen in front of me all sat and looked at me as if I were a specimen at a horse show, as if wondering what this singular person was going to do, wondering if he had a bomb under his coat—saying that he had come there, the President of the United States, to deliver his message in person—not knowing that there is no living being whose pride would not be hurt by having his message read by a reading clerk, particularly when most of the members during that reading were quite excusably in the cloakroom, or that it was very interesting to the President of the United States, or at least to the person who is administering that office, to see what was going on among the bunch at the other end of the Avenue. Because what goes on there determines what is going to happen. Unless something is done on the hill, nothing will be done anywhere. And unless I understand their minds, I cannot be of any service to them, and if I cannot be of any service to them, I cannot be of any service to the country itself. This business of the division of powers, carried to the point of punctilio to which it has been car-

[1] At the press conference on April 11.

ried, amounts to a permanent misunderstanding, to a permanent incapacity to get together.

A singular thing about you newspapermen is that you are taking it for granted every day that it is incredible that there is not a fight on somewhere. You announced the interesting fact that, when I met the Democratic members of the Finance Committee of the Senate, it was for the purpose of having them tell me where to get off. One of the papers said that. Now, I do not remember being told where to get off. I distinctly remember that the result of the conference was a general understanding as to how we were all to stay on. Every morning I pick up the paper and see that there are all sorts of friction, if not already in existence, just about to be created. I must be exquisitely lubricated! I do not feel any friction. And I have not found any man who did. The fact of the matter is that the friction has been such a common excitement in Washington that it is incredible that it should not exist. Now, I want you gentlemen of the press to believe in the incredible. There ain't no friction. And there ain't gonna be no friction. The parts of this machine are so nicely assembled that they will not even need any Standard oil to lubricate them. There may be a fight, but it will be an orthodox, proper fight, the kind of fight that is set down in the billing, the kind of fight that always occurs between men who honestly differ with each other. It will not be a knockdown and drag-out fight, but it will be a fight to the finish; and at the finish everybody will stand up and smile serenely, and say, "Well, it was a bully fight and we got the job done." This is get-together business; that is all I can say now. Because this is not a speech, this is just a preliminary skirmish. I am going to make a speech presently, but it will be in New Jersey. My warpaint is at the White House, but I am going to carry it in my bag and not put it on until I get in the proper jurisdiction, where there is a fight going on. Then I will put it on, and I shall feel very much at home again.

There is not much fun standing up and making a speech when there is no business being transacted; but when there is business on the boards, then there is a lot of fun in making a speech. To make particular remarks about particular individuals, named by name, Christian name and all, as for example "Jim this and Jim that," gives spice and directness to discourse which is not set down in the books of rhetoric, but which is exceedingly serviceable for accomplishing the end in view, which is the concentration of public opinion upon certain gentlemen who have not very handsome wares to exhibit. The function of public speakers now is largely the function of swinging the searchlight. And the great fun in swinging the searchlight is to see the fellows who dodge and to see the fellows who stand up and face the light.

For the image is not an idle one, gentlemen; we are facing the light. I want to express in this public way the profound apprecia-tion I feel for what Senator Root said this evening.[2] Speeches like that make me feel that we are facing the light. You know it is easy to be discouraged about things. John Morley once said that anything will look black if you hold it up against the light that blazes in Utopia, but you do not have to hold it up that way. You have to let the light shine upon its face, and then the gleam will be returned by the shining surface you expose to it. And when I see men doing what they are doing now—forgetting party prejudices, turning to one another with honest disagreements and honest differences of opinion, and trying to work out a com-mon purpose by understanding each other—then I know that we are facing the light, and all we have to do is to move forward together in order to fulfill the hopes of a great people that wait upon us.

T MS (WP, DLC).
  [2] A news report of this affair in the *New York Herald*, April 13, 1913, indicates that Elihu Root was present at the dinner but says nothing about his speaking. The Editors have found no reports of the speeches at the dinner.

To John Bassett Moore

My dear Dr. Moore: The White House April 12, 1913

After a conference with the Secretary of State, I am glad to find that there is no sort of difficulty about making the arrange-ment you suggested in your conversation with me and in your letter to him when you were down here.[1]

I take it for granted that you did not contemplate in your sug-gestion the immediate publication of the arrangement or that it would be necessary to publish it as a standing order provided we always acted on it. I feel that it might cause some mortification to Governor Osborne, who will come in at the same time as Assistant Secretary of State, if at the very time of his confirma-tion by the Senate and induction into office this arrangement should be published, as if it were part of the understanding un-der which he assumes office. Of course it is part of it, as a matter of fact, but it would be neither kind nor wise to treat the matter in just this way.

I am more glad every day as I think of the prospect of your being associated with the Department.

   Cordially and faithfully yours, Woodrow Wilson

TLS (J. B. Moore Papers, DLC).
 [1] J. B. Moore to WJB, April 10, 1913, CCL (WP, DLC). Moore outlined the history of the position of Counselor of the Department of State, with particular reference to its lack of status within the department. He urged that the President issue an order making the Counselor the second-ranking officer in the department, thus making him eligible to serve as Acting Secretary of State in the absence of the secretary.

From Hamilton Wright Mabie

            Tokio, April 12, 1913.
 Deep feeling aroused here respecting legislation in California. Respectfully urge utmost influence to secure investigation Japanese population and holdings in California before legislation. Highest International feelings involved.[1] Mabie.

T telegram (WP, DLC).
 [1] About Japanese indignation at and protests against the pending California legislation, see Link, *The New Freedom*, pp. 292-93.

To Elihu Root

My dear Senator Root, The White House 13 April, 1913
 You were very generous last night and I want to thank you most warmly. What you said gave me fresh heart and confidence. I am moving amongst unaccustomed scenes and duties and am deeply grateful for such reassurance and encouragement.

   Cordially and sincerely Yours, Woodrow Wilson

ALS (E. Root Papers, DLC).

To Mary Allen Hulbert

Dearest Friend, The White House 13 April, 1913
 I have been lying in bed all day, not only because it was Sunday and I was tired and *could* rest, but because for the last forty-eight hours there has been a threat in my left shoulder of my old enemy, *neuritis*, as nasty a beast as ever attacked poor human flesh,—and a mean coward, besides, for the sneak comes only when a fellow is worn out and there is no fight in him. Maybe, this time, it is only a touch of cold. At any rate, this evening it is better and I am cheerful enough. This slight ailment of mine does not interest me as much as your own health. We

have had no letter from you this week, and that naturally makes us a little apprehensive lest you should have had a reaction after all your tragic struggle. *Please* let us know.

The week has been a very interesting one with us. The meeting with the two Houses in joint session went off famously, most naturally and pleasantly, and even the carpers were silenced. It was very simple. A long precedent was broken, but nobody heard the smash and no one was hurt or shocked. The next day I went to "the Presidents' Room" alongside the Senate chamber (which had not been made such use of since Lincoln's day) and conferred, on the tariff, with the Democratic members of the Finance Committee, without the least discomfort at doing an unusual thing. On Thursday I went to the opening game of the foot-ball season[1] and tossed out the ball to start the game. Last night I dined with the Gridiron Club (where public men are periodically grilled) and received my first public discipline as President, responsible to all who look on. It was very amusing and very instructive, in a way, and I was treated with singular sympathy and consideration, as if they really liked and admired me, and were a wee bit in awe of me! Fancy! Can you imagine it? I was a good deal moved, and very much stimulated. And so, step by step, am I being more and more thoroughly inducted into office. Meanwhile how constantly do our thoughts turn to the dear brave lady who has again proved her mettle against hideous odds—and her power of love, love that acts and succours and redeems! May God bless and keep her! Love from all

Your devoted friend   Woodrow Wilson

ALS (WP, DLC).

[1] Wilson meant the baseball season. The Washington Nationals defeated the New York Yankees by a score of 2 to 1 in the opening game on April 10.

From Edward Samuel Corwin

My dear Mr. President,   Princeton, N. J. Apr 13, 1913

I am sorry that you haven't taken the opportunity offered by the California Land Bill to knock in the head the silly idea that the Police Powers of the States comprise an independent limitation on the Treaty Power of the United States, or for that matter, any other power of the United States. That notion, besides making a solecism of Article II par. 2 of the Constitution, exposes our national good faith to a material danger.

Your Princeton admirers regard your course with the greatest enthusiasm, among whom is

Yours Sincerely   Edward S. Corwin

ALS (WP, DLC).

From William Frank McCombs

My dear Mr President: New York Sunday [April 13, 1913].

I wrote a letter on Friday night to Tumulty to be turned over to you. It was among a mass of other correspondence & one of my secretaries in charge of the correspondence became ill & neglected to send out my mail.

I saw in the papers a few days ago that Senator Bacon had introduced a Bill adding $10,000 to the regular salary of the ambassadors for house rent & etc. I inquired of Tumulty yesterday if the chances favored the passage of the bill. He replied in the affirmative. The passage of the Bill solves my difficulties and it will give us much pleasure to accept the great honor you have tendered me if that Bill becomes a law. In fact if the committees of the Senate & the House incline to look upon it with favor I am willing to take my chance upon its passage for I know a declaration from you in favor of that measure will insure its passage. At the same time it can be made the reason—as [it] is the fact—why I accept & in my mind it should be so stated.

I should prefer that no mention be made of my intention until the name is sent to the Senate so as to avoid comment which is distasteful to me & no doubt is to you.

I hope I have not embarrassed you in any way. The post is one of rare distinction & I shall make every effort to fulfil every requirement made or possible in connection with it.

I understand that you do not intend to send in your diplomatic appointments until the latter part of next week—of this Tumulty informed me. If consistent with your ideas that would suit me better. When the nomination is sent in perhaps it would be well to make some statement as to the Bacon bill as the reason why I have found it possible to accept. Meanwhile may I offer the suggestion that nothing should be said of the matter. I thank you profoundly for the great honor you have done me and for your great patience in allowing me time to work out my affairs in connection with this magnificent tender.

Permit me also to say that much of publicly stated friction between myself and a member of your cabinet[1] has been fomented by men about me & himself who thought they were befriending each of us respectively and I have remained absolutely silent. Further, whatever feeling there might have been, I am quite willing to forget, and I sent a message to you and to him that in your interest as well as that of party harmony no one would be more willing than I to establish a complete entente.

I hope in some way the Bacon bill may be reported & adopted

in the Senate prior to any public announcement. I hope more than that, I may be of value to your administration and always perform any function that you deem of value with honor as well as with satisfaction.

Believe me, With affectionate regards

Wm. F. McCombs

ALS (WP, DLC).
[1] McAdoo.

Remarks at a Press Conference

April 14, 1913

Mr. President, if we may be permitted to ask one or two questions that we trust are proper, the first being the tariff bill has now been before the country for just one week—have you reason to believe that in general it meets with the approval of the public?

> I think it does, that is to say, of the general public. Of course, there are people whose interests will be affected by it who disapprove of it, and I dare say they are somewhat numerous. But the impression I get is that it is regarded as a fair bill. I have heard a good many men say, for example, they didn't expect us to work out a good bill, that it was a very much better bill than was to be expected—and that not from very friendly sources—so that I am encouraged to believe that its reception has been very much better than might have been anticipated.

Do you see any reason, Mr. President, why there should be any business depression following the passage of this bill?

> None whatever.

Do you think that all healthy business should be able to continue without interruption?

> Oh, I am sure it should. I don't see where healthy business is cut to the bone anywhere in the bill.

Mr. President, have you had a good deal in the way of a direct response to yourself? I mean from people—Tom, Dick, and Harry, generally—writing to you?

> No, not much, unless in letters I haven't seen. There has been very little.

Nothing that especially impresses you in the way of a response?

> No. I have received several letters wanting to be heard, untimely, on the subject.

Mr. President, do you feel that the income tax[1] is also as popular as the tariff bill?

[1] Documents in Vol. 28 disclose the history of the income tax provision of the

I have seen very little comment on that, but I am sorry to say I don't have time to read many of the papers. I have to get my impressions more or less indirectly.

What is your main reason for deciding on free sugar, Mr. President?

My main reason is that it is fair to the consumer.

Do you think he will get it?

Yes, I do.

That he will get the benefit of it?

Oh, I am sure he will. You see, as I have said all along, that is one of the articles in which I am confident he will get the benefit at once. That will not be true as a rule. I was careful to say what I, of course, believed in the campaign—that I don't expect the tariff to effect an immediate reduction of the cost of living. But what I do expect, and confidently expect, is this—that it will bring about a competitive situation which will make it impossible by arrangements of price to keep up the present artificial levels of cost. So that, by a process more or less rapid, it will break down those combinations which now keep prices at so high a level and will redound to the general benefit before long, and that to a very great extent. But, you see, what we are fighting just now is an artificial situation in which prices are kept up by arrangements with which you are all more or less familiar. Now, those arrangements will become practically impossible when a truly competitive situation is created, and then the people will begin to get the benefit. But I think they will get it very promptly in sugar, because the competitive elements are there ready to contest with one another.

Mr. President, when you say there is criticism from interests that are affected, do you mean interests that are legitimately affected?

Yes.

Are there any legitimate interests involved in that?

Oh, yes, many of these are interests which I should call perfectly legitimate interests, but they feel that the cut in their cases is more than they can at present stand. That is all. I don't mean that they are illegitimate interests that are affected.

And you, yourself, don't look for any ruinous cut?

Oh, no, I don't see any cut that is ruinous at all. Because,

Underwood bill. In addition, see Davis Rich Dewey, *Financial History of the United States*, 12th edn. (New York, London, Toronto, 1939), pp. 448-91; Link, *The New Freedom*, p. 182, pp. 192-93; and Sidney Ratner, *Taxation and Democracy in America* (New York, 1967), pp. 321-38.

you see, these gentlemen on the Ways and Means Committee have been studying this tariff now for over two years,
and they have heard every person in interest, every party in
interest, again and again; and their votes are the results of
these hearings and their judgments based upon them.

Nine of ten of the Ohio Democrats feel that free wool will be
ruinous to the woolen industry.

Well, now, that is one of the subjects upon which I have
been trying to inform myself, and I have read as much as I
could lay my hands on, and I don't feel that that fear is
justified by the facts. For one thing, just the other day I
learned that the price of wool was the same on both sides
of the water; and one senator, who has been very much opposed to free wool—a Republican senator—said, "We hope
that it would not be put on the free list just now, because
our predictions wouldn't be verified." Because they certainly
would not, with the price of wool the same on both sides
of the water.

That has always been fixed in London.

I know, but these competitive conditions would of course
be affected by the whole thing.

Mr. President, it has been stated that you favor the re-enactment
of the sundry civil bill, with the labor exemption clause[2]—it is
printed in some of the papers.

That was a matter upon which I have not expressed any
opinion. Of course the bill will be renewed and put through.

You have expressed no opinion with reference to the exemption
bill?

I talked over it with Senator Martin and Mr. Fitzgerald the
other day, and they asked my opinion about that. And I told
them what my opinion of the clause was, but I didn't tell
them for publication.

More or less has been published—it is a very important matter.

Yes, of course it is. Where I stand will be found out eventually.

Mr. President, this bill authorizes you to start arrangements for
reciprocity with various countries. Will you take steps to that
end as soon as the bill is passed?

I should certainly hope so.

That would not mean that the United States would have to give
still lower rates to obtain anything from any other country?

Yes, very likely, or make arrangements of countervailing
duties, etc.

[2] That is, the Hughes-Hamill amendment to the sundry civil bill.

Mr. President, has it been decided whether the Commerce Court appropriation will be restored, or whether the jurisdiction of the court will be provided for?

> So far as I am informed on that subject, no; but I haven't discussed it with anybody, except that I got a letter from one member of Congress, asking my opinion on it, and I told him that my mind was "to let."

Mr. President, in connection with the tariff, does your confidence extend to the sugar factories, both beet and cane sugar—do you think they can all operate under free sugar?

> Yes, certainly I do. They may shut down for effect for a little while, but they will open for business later on.

Mr. President, we are all very much interested in the situation created in California by the interesting fact that the states, wholly within their own constitutional rights, can create an international situation. I hoped that you might be willing to say something about your own position toward that. It has been rather vaguely hinted at. Could you give us anything to clarify our own minds?

> I have felt this way about it: As President, I was not entitled, I had no right to intervene in the business against the undoubted constitutional powers of the State of California; but that, as an individual, and also as President, in view of my relations to foreign countries in that office, I was at liberty to seek counsel out there and to ask what was going on and to give intimations of what I thought would be just in the case. And I have been trying to do that in as tactful and proper a way as I could discover. I am not without hope that their legislation may be somewhat affected by the advice I make.

The impression that I had was that the best you could do was to get them to do what they did in a gentle rather than a rough way, that you wouldn't hope to affect the real essence of the thing very much.

> Well, I am afraid it won't be possible to affect it materially. The bill now provides that no alien shall own land for more than one year without taking out his first citizenship papers.

Making his first declaration.

And that, as I understand it now, gives offense to other nations that say that they have treaty rights with the United States, under which Americans shall hold land without citizenship in their country, and that this would compel foreigners to take out their citizenship papers here if they wanted to own lands.

> In one state only. Of course they all realize that it affects only a particularly small part of our territory. And, as I think

I was saying to you the other day, the awkwardness about all such treaty relations is that the federal government cannot promise more than it can deliver. If it does, then I don't see any remedy for it except payment of damages, as in the Louisiana case many years ago.

Do you get the impression, Mr. President, that Japan pretty well understands the peculiarities of the situation?

Oh, I am sure she does.

So that the government itself couldn't take any offense on the basis of a misunderstanding?

I think that the only fear is that there will be a very strong national feeling in Japan against this action. But I haven't heard any intimation that the government itself feels that this government is at fault.

Will we make an endeavor in treating with that government not to include something we can't enforce?

I haven't really got to that. My desire would be not to promise anything we could not deliver.

Mr. President, does Japan complain of the discrimination between Japan and China, particularly because their citizens could not become naturalized, and therefore are excluded from this?

When I saw the Japanese Ambassador some weeks ago the legislation was in another form. It was then directed explicitly against those who could not become citizens. And since then I haven't seen him, and just how he feels about the new form of it I cannot say.

Has there been any progress on that Russian treaty?[3]

No, not since this administration began. You see, we haven't any ambassador there yet. We shall have to wait until we have appointed a representative.

Mr. President, there seems to be some interest in the question as to how far the recommendations of senators and representatives will control in the appointment of men to office—with respect to postmasters particularly.

Yes, I understand it is particularly with those! I have nothing to say on that subject.

Do you contemplate a visit to the Capitol this week?

I don't know of anything that will take me there.

T MS (C. L. Swem Coll., NjP).
[3] That is, a new Russian-American commercial treaty.

A Welcome to the Daughters of the American Revolution

[April 14, 1913]

Madam President and Ladies of the Daughters of the American Revolution:

Mine is a very pleasant function this afternoon. I do not know that it is necessary to bid any American audience welcome to Washington, since Washington is their own; but I am in form, at any rate, your host today. I am one of the few persons in the District of Columbia who cannot in any circumstances be arrested, and, therefore, perhaps I occupy a somewhat unique position of privilege. May I not welcome you to the same privilege and assure you of immunity from arrest?

It is really delightful to see this company gathered together, and to realize what it stands for. I remember I used to be told by my teacher in psychology[1] (this is one of the few things he told me that I remember) that the function of memory was the function of identity, because if I did not remember who I was yesterday I would not know who I am today. Now, I regard organizations like this as part of the nation's lobe of memory. They remind us of the things that have gone by and of the standards to which we must conform if we would be true, loyal Americans. I would not undertake, at any rate in a single improvised address, to set up the canons of Americanism, though I think I can tell whether a man is an American or not when I talk to him. Americanism is now of so many varieties among the ladies that I am not so sure of my standards on that side of the house; and, therefore, I tread very gingerly when I try to set up standards there. But this I know —that so far as our recollections are concerned, so far as those things are concerned which we hold sacred in the past, so far as those things go that we intend to live up to and be worthy of, there is only one canon of Americanism. And the real, constant difficulty of American politics is to bring it back so that it will square with the standard set up at the first, when the Revolution was fought out and an independent nation was established in America.

We established an independent nation in order that men might enjoy a new kind of happiness and a new kind of dignity, that kind which a man has when he respects every other man's and woman's individuality as he respects his own, when he is not willing to draw distinctions between classes, when he is not willing to shut the door of privilege in the face of anyone. The dignity of your organization is measured by the dignity of the traditions which you are organized to maintain.

The American Revolution is worth remembering because it is one of the few struggles in the history of the world which was entirely devoted to the establishment of human liberty. We cut links with the past in that struggle which we hope will never be forged again. We cut the links that bound us to every system of privilege that had existed; and anybody who stands for privilege of any exclusive sort forfeits the title of Americanism. It is a stern doctrine, it is a doctrine at which some people wince, particularly those who think that the distinction will be drawn in their favor, but it is the only standard of gentility in America—that all men and women are equally genteel who are devoted to the interests of mankind. This is our only patent of nobility. This is the particular standard of nobility which I understand associations like this to be organized to maintain.

It is, therefore, as if I welcomed you to the place where you belong—that an organization that stands for the principles upon which the nation was based should be welcomed to the capital of the United States.

T MS (WP, DLC).
    ¹ Wilson took psychology during the first semester of his junior year at Princeton, 1877-78, and received a grade of 99.8. The lectures were given by President James McCosh. However, Wilson probably referred to the eminent psychologist, Granville Stanley Hall, whose course in pedagogy he took during the academic year 1884-85 while a student at The Johns Hopkins University. About this, see n. 1 to the newsletter printed at March 8, 1884, vol. 3, and WW to EAW, Oct. 6, 1884, n. 1, *ibid.*

To Joseph R. Wilson, Jr.

My dearest Brother: [The White House] April 14, 1913

I was so glad to get your letter of April tenth.¹ I have been wondering what you were thinking about and doing. Have you turned away from the proposal that we were discussing just before you left? I can't help hoping that you have not. It seemed to me thoroughly worth considering, and I think that the men concerned were willing to meet your wishes very handsomely. Please let me know what you have done and determined. McAdoo was speaking to me about it only the other day.

It is delightful to hear that you are all well and that Kate is getting her strength back after the distressing ordeal she went through. We are all quite well, though I have had a touch of neuritis in my left shoulder, perhaps due to cold as well as to fatigue.

It has been very gratifying the way in which the country has commented upon my action in addressing Congress in person, and everything seems to be going very well here indeed.

We wish for you again and again. It was delightful to have you even for a little while.

All join in the warmest love.

Affectionately yours,   Woodrow Wilson

TLS (Letterpress Books, WP, DLC).
    ¹ J. R. Wilson, Jr., to WW, April 10, 1913, TLS (WP, DLC).

From John Bassett Moore

My dear Mr. President: New York April 14, 1913.

I have had the honor to receive your letter of the 12th inst. referring to my conversation with you on Thursday last, the 10th of April, and to the letter addressed on the same day to the Secretary of State and communicated by copy to yourself, relating to the form of a permanent order to authorize the Counselor of the Department of State to act as Secretary in the latter's absence.

The question whether the order should be immediately published had not occurred to me, such publication being, so far as I am aware, the only way of making it effective; for, as was pointed out in my letter of the 10th instant, the authority to act is to be considered not so much an end in itself, as the means, and the only means, of fixing the position of the Counselor in his intercourse with the diplomatic corps, as well as with others who may have business with the Department. In other words, the office and its powers must publicly correspond.

You are justified, however, in assuming that I would not willingly do anything that you would consider "neither kind nor wise"; and I am, I trust, equally incapable of doing anything that might cause mortification or a sense of humiliation to anyone. On the other hand, I can conceive of no greater mortification to an official than to have the powers of his office habitually exercised by a person holding an inferior position.

It was for this reason that, before my name should be sent to the Senate, I presented both to yourself and to the Secretary of State the form of an order by which all possibility of misunderstanding was to be removed, by giving to the office of Counselor the position which I understand we were all agreed that it should have. In the absence of such an order, the occasional but habitual authorization of the Counselor to act as Secretary of State, in the absence of the Secretary, must necessarily bear the appearance of a reflection upon the competency of the Assistant Secretary. Still greater, it seems to me, would be the mortification to the Assistant Secretary, if, because of the non-publication of the order, his occasional but habitual supersession should be the cause of public surmise and comment.

In these circumstances, I feel that I must, in justice to you, to the Secretary of State, to Governor Osborne, and to myself, as well in the interest of a harmonious public service, withdraw myself, as I now do, from a situation which, having already given rise to forebodings of personal disappointment, manifestly can be relieved only by such action on my part. It is needless to say that to me it would be unendurable to figure either as having excluded Governor Osborne from the public service, or as having inflicted upon him a personal mortification in it.

Permit me in conclusion to say that if I can be of any service to the Department, out of office, I shall be glad to place myself at its disposal.

Believe me to be, my dear Mr. President,

Your sincere friend and most obedient servant,

John B. Moore.

TLS (WP, DLC).

From David Starr Jordan

Dear Sir: Stanford University, California, April 14, 1913.

Will you kindly permit me a word as to the anti-alien land bills now before the legislature of California? The motif of the proposed legislation seems to be the desire of the individuals to make political capital by nagging the Japanese. This comes up in some form with every Legislature.

The "gentleman's agreement of 1907" has been rigidly enforced in Japan. No Japanese laborers have come here for six years and none to British Columbia, Mexico or Hawaii. The number of Japanese does not increase. They are for the most part, with some unfortunate exceptions, quiet, industrious, clean and law-abiding people. Their ownership of land involves no visible "menace" to any one, and they are quite as "assimilable" as most of the people from Southern Europe. In view of the coming exposition, and in view of the exigencies of fair play there is every reason, I think, for letting well enough alone.

There is a strong feeling, which I share, against unchecked immigration of unskilled laborers from Japan or China. We do not want to see on the coast a stratification of labor, with a bottom layer of workmen underpaid because Asiatic—Asiatic because underpaid. But there is no question of this sort at present.

I take it that any and all statutes of the state directed against

Japanese or Chinese by name, or through the cheap subterfuge of "aliens not eligible to become citizens" are unconstitutional. No state has any right to deal with a foreign nation except through the federal government. No state can deal directly with the people of a foreign government as such nor with any group of them as members of another nationality.

A state must, I take it, treat all aliens alike, for aliens in the United States are, in a sense "wards of the nation," and derive their rights of travel or residence primarily from international treaties.

It may be that these proposed California statutes will assume the form of prohibition of land-ownership by all aliens.

This raises a large question of policy, and there is something to be said on either side. But in view of the large and undefined amount of British capital invested in lands, power plants and railways in California, it is not a matter to be decided off-hand, and as a side-issue to a petty anti-Japanese crusade.

I think that the State Department is wise in not dictating to the California Legislature. Mr. Roosevelt lost some points of advantage some years ago by over-emphasis. No one can say that a treaty has been violated or that rights under the federal constitution have been infringed until the courts have so decided.

Very truly yours,   David Starr Jordan.

TLS (WP, DLC).

James Bryce to Sir Edward Grey

Sir,   Washington April 14, 1913.

The condition of the State Department has been such that since the new Administration came into office it has been extremely difficult to find anyone with whom business can be done. The retiring officials say that they have no authority, and the new officials have not yet appeared upon the scene, their appointments not having been confirmed by the Senate until yesterday. In these circumstances the only person to whom one could go has been the Secretary of State himself; and he has been so much distracted and harried by office seekers and by general politics that he has been able to give comparatively little of his mind to his proper work; I may add that he has absolutely no knowledge of that kind of work and evidently feels the difficulties which his want of experience places in his way.

I took the opportunity, however, to speak to him more than once with regard to the Panana Canal Tolls question and to impress upon him the importance of his giving a definite expression of his views at the earliest possible moment. He promised to take it up and consider it but I suspect he has been waiting for the arrival of the new Councillor of the State Department, Mr. Bassett Moore, who has not yet appeared upon the scene; and believing this I have felt it would be unfair to press him too hardly on the subject. He has intimated vaguely that he has some large proposition to make but apparently he has not yet formulated it. I have also since the date of my former despatch referred again to the subject with the President when I was lunching with him last Friday and what he said, although said quite briefly and unofficially, was sufficient to indicate to me his own attitude and wishes. I gathered that he was endeavouring to take preliminary steps with a view to the passage of the bill for repealing coastwise exemption.

The general impression here is that opinion is progressing favourably on that subject and that the sentiment of the Senate is more in favour of repeal than it was two months ago. A leading Democratic Senator told me this a few days ago, and others have spoken in the same sense[.] How soon, however, any definite action can be taken may remain doubtful for some time.

I have the honour to be, With the highest respect, Sir,
Your most obedient, humble servant, James Bryce

TLS (FO 371/1702, No. 18718, PRO).

From William Jennings Bryan

My Dear Mr President   Washington April 15 [1913]

You were kind enough to say that you would call me over to the White House before sending your answer to Mr Moore's letter, but as I have talked with Mr Osborne I venture to address you a line in the hope that it may give you greater freedom of expression in replying to Mr Moore. Mr Osborne withdraws any objections he may have expressed to the publication of the order. He desires to relieve you of any possible embarassment and asks me to assure you that he appreciates most cordially your effort to save him from the unpleasant comments that publica[tion] may excite.

I need hardy add that Mr Osborne did not seek the office with which you have honored him. I mentioned it to him and presented the matter to you because of my earnest desire to have him associated with me. He was not only my choice but accepted at a pecuniary sacrifice because of his deep interest in your administration (He was, as you remember, an original Wilson man) added to his long-standing friendship for me. My affection for him is increased by his willingness to aid both you & me by consenting to that which Mr Moore regards as due to him. Mr Osborne joins me in urging you not to allow Mr Moore to withdraw his name. We shall be a happy family here in the department and I am [sure] he and Mr Osborne will be the best of friends when they become acquainted with each other. I have hesitated to write this letter but I feel sure that you will receive it in the spirit in which I write. Regretting if I have unintentionly added to your many cares I am, my dear Mr President, with assurances of regard etc.   Yours truly yours   W. J. Bryan

ALS (WP, DLC).

From the Diary of Josephus Daniels

Tuesday, April 15, 1913.

The matter that took up the most time in the Cabinet today, and it was of most serious importance at present, was with reference to what attitude the Admin[i]stration should take with reference to Canal tolls on the Panama Canal. England claims under the treaty that the law enacted by the last Congress permitted coast-wise American vessels to enter the Panama Canal without paying the same tolls exacted of ships carrying freight of other nations is a violation of the treaty. The President said he had it from pretty good inside information that when the American representatives offered in the treaty before the construction of the Panama Canal to give the same rights to people of all countries through the Canal, Pauncefote was surprised at the gift America was giving him. England did not ask for it and did not expect it, but [it] was offered by America and they eagerly accepted it. Having obtained it, England now, of course, feels that the law is a violation of the treaty.

Mr. Bryan stated that if the matter was to be taken up and discussed and a conclusion reached as to whether tolls should be laid or not and the whole question gone into on its merits, he would like to have time for consideration because he needed light on the subject. . . . The President said it was not his purpose to open it up in its general aspect, but only what was best to do at this time. The arbitration treaty with England expires in June and it was the general opinion that England would be slow to renew that treaty until there was some adjustment of the toll matter. I suggested that the Secretary of State should sound Mr. Bryce; explain to him the dif[f]iculties and the desire of the Administration to postpone the settlement of the tolls question until the next session of Congress[;] and to try to secure an extension of the treaty for one year so that it might be then taken up again after the Congress had a chance to pass upon the toll question.

The general sentiment, however, was that England would not consent to renew the treaty for one year with the Panama toll matter unsettled. The President was inclined to think that under the treaty we had no right to charge tolls on English or other vessels more than our own coast-wise trade, and that it was a better economic idea also to take that position. Mr. Burleston thought the bill passed Congress by a very narrow margin and Mr. Redfield said he voted for it under a misapprehension and there was a long debate whether it was best to try to secure the repeal of the law passed by last Congress on Panama Canal tolls as a matter of sound economic policy and try to secure that by this session of Congress, or to accept the construction that the treaty gave England the same right for its ships through Panama Canal that we had for ours.

It is a knotty question, and the knottiest that has come before the Cabinet or government in recent years. Why our government should have offered the provision under which England claims equal rights with us is a marvel, and it has involved us in an international complication that is going to be difficult to settle satisfactorily. It is believed that the Senate is strongly in favor of maintaining the present law and Senator O'Gorman has the strong conviction that as America paid money to build the Canal, the treaty does not give England any right except against discrimination, but as America put up money to build the Canal, it does not give England any better tolls than to France, or Germany, or any other country, and that is all the treaty means. England is willing to arbitrate. Mr. Burleson did not believe in arbitration. Mr. Bryan said he would arbitrate anything. Secretary Lane took the ground that it would not be wise to grant England's construction of the treaty but that the proper policy would be to repeal the bill as a matter of national policy. The Secretary of Agriculture thought that the bill passed by the last Congress savored of subsidies of American ships in which view the Secretary of the Treasury concurred and agreed with the President heartily that we ought not to exempt coast-wise trade from freedom of tolls; if we do exempt them, then, of course, foreign vessels will ship all the goods they wish to sell in this country or in the east to New York, put them on coast-wise vessels and escape the Panama Canal tolls. No decision was reached.

T MS (J. Daniels Papers, DLC).

To Oscar Wilder Underwood

My dear Mr. Underwood: The White House April 16, 1913

When you were with me this morning I forgot to mention a matter of, it seems to me, considerable importance about the income tax. If the lower limit of incomes is to be $4,000 would it not be wise and fair to exempt all persons receiving less than $3,000 a year income from the necessity of making income returns at all, in order to burden as small a number of persons with the obligations involved in the administration of what will at best be an unpopular law.

There is another feature of the law about which I am going to take the liberty of asking Mr. Hull,[1] who I understand was chiefly instrumental in drawing that portion, to consult with my colleague, Secretary Redfield.

In haste   Cordially yours,   Woodrow Wilson

TLS (O. Underwood Papers, A-Ar).
[1] Cordell Hull, Democratic congressman from Tennessee, chief author of the income tax provisions of the Underwood tariff bill. For a personal account, see Cordell Hull, *The Memoirs of Cordell Hull* (2 vols., New York, 1948), I, 70-71, 73-74.

To John Bassett Moore

My dear Mr. Moore: The White House April 16, 1913

I beg you to believe that I did not realize that I was suggesting in my last letter anything inconsistent with what you had yourself proposed. Your letter convinces me that I was mistaken. I have conferred with Mr. Bryan, and we wish to join in assuring you that we wish to meet your wishes in the matter in the fullest and frankest way. You need not fear, therefore, that there is any difficulty or complication in the matter. Your letter convinces me that what I was trying to do was in fact not kind or considerate of Mr. Osborne, and I thank you for your full statement of your own judgment in the matter.

Your name has already been sent in to the Senate and I have every reason to believe will be promptly confirmed, since everyone cordially approves of the choice.

Let me add that Mr. Osborne knew nothing of my effort to manage the matter in the way that would be most agreeable to him, and that I am sure that he heartily joins in this final settlement.

I have in my hand now a most cordial letter from Mr. Bryan expressed in terms which I am sure would gratify you very deeply. We could not in any circumstances think of foregoing the arrangements by which we feel we have given the Department of State added efficiency and distinction.

Cordially and sincerely yours,   Woodrow Wilson

TLS (J. B. Moore Papers, DLC).

Viscount Sutemi Chinda to Baron Nobuaki Makino

1835, 1840, 1844   暗   華府発 本省着   大正2年4月16日

牧野外務大臣

珍　田　大　使

第75号ノ1

４月15日予定ノ通大統領ニ謁見貴電第56号ノ全文ヲ読上ケ往電第71号国務長官ニ対シ陳述セル所ヲ繰返シタル後種々談話ヲ交換シタルカ其要領ヲ綜合スレハ概略左ノ如シ

本使ハ先ツ此際未タ法案各条ニ亘リテ条約上ノ議論ヲ試ミントスルモノニアラス只両国ノ親交ニ顧ミ正義公道ニ訴ヘ排日案ノ絶対的防止方ヲ懇請スル義ナル旨ヲ申述ヘ

(1) 帝国政府ニ於テハ夙ニ加州ニ於ケル排日感情ノ緩和ヲ図リ国内（不明語）上勘カラサル困難ヲ忍ヒテ移民禁止ヲ断行継続シタル結果在留日本人数著シク減少セル事実

(2) 在加州日本人カ従来ノ出稼的状態ヲ脱シテ永住的生業ニ傾注シタル結果実際在留地方ノ開発ト繁栄ニ貢献スル所勘カラサルコト

(3) 在留日本人ノ賃金ハ殆ト白人ニ匹敵シ最早低廉労働者トシテ排斥セラルル理由ナキコト

(4) 日本人ノ経営ニ係ル農業ノ発展ハ主トシテ白人ノ不得意ナル種類ニ属シ白人ノ生業ニ対シ直接競争ノ地位ニアラサル事実

等ヲ説明シ最早加州ニ於ケル今日ノ日本人ハ排斥セラルル
何等正当ナル理由ヲ発見スルコトヲ得サル次第ナリ況ンヤ
関係者カ日本人駆逐策タルコトヲ公然標榜スルニ於テハ全
然之ヲ人種的偏見ト見ルノ外ナシ以上ノ事実ヲ考量スルト
キハ今回本邦民論甚タシク沸騰シテ容易ナラサル形勢ヲ呈
スルニ至リタルハ已ムヲ得サルモノアルヲ見ルヘシ尤右排
日感情ノ発現ハ之ヲ米国側ヨリ見ルトキハ中央当局者カ直
接其衝ニアラサルハ勿論ナルモ苟モ事外国ニ関渉スル以上
ハ中央政府ハ結局其責ヲ免カルルコト能ハサルヘク又日本
側ニ於テハ加州当局者ト直接折衝スヘキ何等手段ヲ有セサ
ルニ顧ミルモ此際我ニ於テハ是非共中央当局者ノ尽力ヲ請
ヒ之ニ信頼スルノ外ナキ次第ヲ述ヘ今日迄ノ大統領及国務
長官ノ苦心ハ之ヲ諒トスルモ尚一層有効ナル尽力アランコ
トヲ要望シタリ

第75号ノ2

大統領ハ我諸般ノ事情ニ対シテハ一々之ヲ諒トシ自分一個
人トシテハ本案ノ正義ニ適セサルヲ認ムルモ一般外国人ノ
土地所有ヲ禁止スルト否トノ問題ハ各国ニ於テ自由ニ決定
スルノ権利アルト等シク米国ノ一州モ完全ニ其決定権ヲ有
スル次第ニシテ偶々日本人カ帰化権ナキ為不利ノ地位ニ立
ツノ結果トナルモノナレハ到底中央政府トシテ右立法ヲ制
止スルノ権能ヲ有セスト述ヘラレタルニ付本使ハ今回ノ法
案ハ日本人ニ帰化権ナキヲ前提トシタルモノナレハ区別的
待遇ハ偶然ノ結果ニハアラスシテ本案惟一ノ趣旨ナルコト
明白ナリ其目的タルヤ日本人生業ノ立脚地ヲ覆シ之ヲ州外

ニ放逐セントスルモノニシテ人種的迫害トモ称シ得ヘク其
正義公道ノ外ナルコト一点ノ疑ヲ容レスト述ヘタルニ大統
領ハ更ニ語ヲ継キテ行政部ハ決シテ冷淡ニ本問題ヲ看過ス
ルモノニアラス州権ニ干渉セサル範囲内ニ於テ能フヘキ限
リノ尽力ハ十分ニ之ヲ施シツ、アリ現ニ日々加州ニ於ケル
政友ト消息ヲ通シ居リ苟モ機会アル毎ニ之ヲ逸セサル積ナ
リトテ上院案中効力ヲ既往ニ遡ラシメ又ハ契約上ノ権利義
務ヲ変改スルノ嫌アル条文ハ合衆国憲法ニ違反ストノ理由
ヲ以テ之ヲ修正セシメ又外国人ノ条約上ノ権利ハ該法ニ依
リ毀損セラレサル旨ノ規定ヲ設ケシメタル等ノ事実ヲ例示
セラレタリ本使ハ仮令形式ニ於テ如何ナル改竄アリトモ土
地所有禁止ノ大綱ニ於テ改メラレサル限リハ依然トシテ不
都合ノ存スル次第ヲ説キ此際行政部ニ於テ活動ノ範囲ヲ其
政友ニ限ラス州知事一派ニモ之ヲ及ホスコトヲ切望スル旨
ヲ述ヘタルニ対シ大統領ハ国務長官前日ノ談話ト同様ノ趣
旨ヲ以テ答ヘタル上今日ノ場合此方面ニ向ヒテ何等運動ヲ
試ムルコトハ「ジョンソン」氏ノ感情的ニ成リ行ク性格ニ
顧ミ成功ノ見込ナキノミナラス却テ事態ヲ困難ナラシムル
ノ虞アリト説明シ尚大統領カ此頃加州選出国会議員等ノ意
見ヲ徴シタルニ何レモ該案成立ノ必要ヲ認ムルコトニ一致
シタルコトヲ説キ事態今日ノ如クナル上ハ其能フ限リノ尽
力モ遂ニ該案ヲ全然防止スルコト能ハス現在ノ形式ニ於テ
両院ヲ通過スルニ至ランコトヲ虞ルト述ヘラレタルニ付本
使ハ形勢愈切迫シ最早知事ノ感情ヲ顧慮スルノ必要ヲ見サ
ル場合ニ至ラハ同官ニ対シテモ機宜ノ交渉ヲ開カルヘキハ
勿論ノ義ト信スト念ヲ押シタルニ苟モ機会ノアラン限リハ
何時ニテモ之ト交渉スルヲ辞セサルヘキ旨説明セラレタリ

第75号ノ3

終リニ臨ミ大統領モ我方ノ事情及立場ハ十分ニ同情ヲ以テ
之ヲ考量シ従来同様今后ニ於テモ能フベキ限リ尽力ナスベ
キ決心ナルガ故此態度ハ能ク日本国政府ニ貫徹スル様本使
ヨリ伝達センコトヲ求メラレタリ右帰途国務長官ヲ訪問シ
謁見ノ顛末ヲ告ゲ重ネテ同官ノ意見ヲ叩キタルニ大統領ト
殆ンド同様ノ趣旨ヲ申述ヘタリ尚ホ同官ヨリハ本使ニ対シ
４月14日付公文ヲ以テ本件ノ上院案写ヲ送附シ来レル処右
ハ同官ニ於テ往電第60号末段所載打合セヲ誤解シ此際直ニ
該上院案ニ対スル本使ノ意見ヲ求ムルモノナルヤノ疑モア
リタルニ依リ本使ハ追テ法案ノ両院ヲ通過ノ上更ニ同官ヨ
リ其写ヲ送リ以テ知事ノ署名前確定案ニ付篤ト講究スル機
会ヲ与フベキコト、了解シ差支ナキヤト問ヒタルニ同官ハ
素ヨリ其趣意ニテ右上院未確定案トシテ単ニ予メ本使心得
迄ニ通報シタルニ過ギズト答ヘタリ右大統領及国務長官ノ
談話ニ関スル本使ノ所見ハ別ニ電報スベシ

Hw telegram (MT 3.8.2.274-2, pp. 397-408, JFO-Ar).

T R A N S L A T I O N

Washington, received
Confidential No. 75.   April 16 17 [1913]

On April 15, I met the President as planned. After I read the
full text of your telegram No. 56 and repeated the argument of
my telegram No. 71, which I had previously presented to the
Secretary of State,[1] we had a conversation of which the gist follows:

First, I said that I did not now intend to discuss each article of
the bill in light of the treaty but just wanted to ask the President
to devise a certain means of preventing passage of the anti-Japa-

nese bill on behalf of the friendly relationship between the two countries and in the cause of justice.

(1) The Imperial government has already imposed and continues a restriction on emigration at the cost of much difficulty in internal politics in order to assuage anti-Japanese feeling in the State of California. As a result, the number of Japanese residents has decreased extremely.

(2) Because Japanese residents in the State of California have worked their way out of unstable and temporary occupations and have been inclined to pursue permanent ways of making a living, they have come to contribute not a little to the development and prosperity of the communities in which they live.

(3) Considering that the wages of Japanese residents have become almost equal to those of the whites, there are no longer reasons for the exclusion of Japanese as cheap wage laborers.

(4) Because the Japanese are mainly engaged in the field of agricultural cultivation in which the whites are not so capable, therefore the former are hardly in competition with the latter in their employment.

Consequently, I said, no sound reason can be discerned for the present exclusion of the Japanese in the State of California. Moreover, since I heard the persons concerned in this matter bluntly declare that these bills had been devised as the means for the expulsion of the Japanese, I could not deny that they were products of racial prejudice. Taking all these considerations into account, I thought that Japanese public opinion had good reason to boil up seriously. Although, on the American side, the authorities of the central government were free from direct obligation, they could not totally avoid responsibility for this matter insofar as it affected foreign relations. And I said that, on the Japanese side, because of the lack of any means of negotiating directly with the authorities of the State of California, therefore nothing could be done other than to urge strongly the authorities of the central government to do their best and to trust it. Although I expressed my thanks for the efforts made by the President and by the Secretary of State up to now, I strongly requested this more effective effort.

The President said that he understood each circumstance on our side and that in his personal opinion the bill was not just. But he denied that the central government could prevent its enactment because, first, just as each nation has the right to decide for itself whether alien ownership of land should be prohibited or not, so did each state of the United States of America have a perfect right to do so, and, second, because it was an accident that the Japanese who had not been naturalized were placed at a disadvantage.

I refuted his argument as follows. Because the bill in question was drawn up on the premise that the Japanese had not been naturalized, the discrimination was not a result of an accident but a deliberate intention of the bill. The aim of the bill was to deprive the Japanese of the means of livelihood and to expel them from the state. So it could be called racial discrimination, and it was no doubt unjust.

The President replied that the chief executive was never a cool onlooker but was doing everything that he could within constitutional limits so long as he did not infringe upon state rights. He illustrated this by stating that he is keeping up a daily correspondence with his political followers in the State of California and would not lose any opportunities in this correspondence; and the fact that some articles of the bill pending in the Senate, which had retroactive effects or which effected changes in contractual rights and duties had been amended because of their unconstitutionality; and a provision saying that alien rights guaranteed by treaties should not be violated by this law had been added.

But I argued that, even if some alterations were made in the form of the bill, the problem still existed because the fundamental principle of the prohibition of the ownership of land had not been changed. And I asked the President to extend his activities as executive beyond his political friends to the Governor's party.

In answer to this request, the President repeated the same words as the Secretary of State had used in our meeting of the previous day. Considering the excitable character of Governor Johnson, he went on, to try to exert any influence on him not only had no chance of success but also might make matters worse. Moreover, he said that when he had met some congressmen from the State of California to hear their views on this matter, they all had agreed in the opinion that enactment was necessary. Now, he said, things had come to this pass already; he was afraid that in spite of all efforts enactment of the bill could not be prevented and it would pass both houses. Thus I emphasized that the situation had become so urgent that there was no longer any need to have regard for the Governor's feelings, and I urged upon him the

Leaving Princeton

A happy President with his successor

The inaugural parade

The inaugural address

After the inauguration

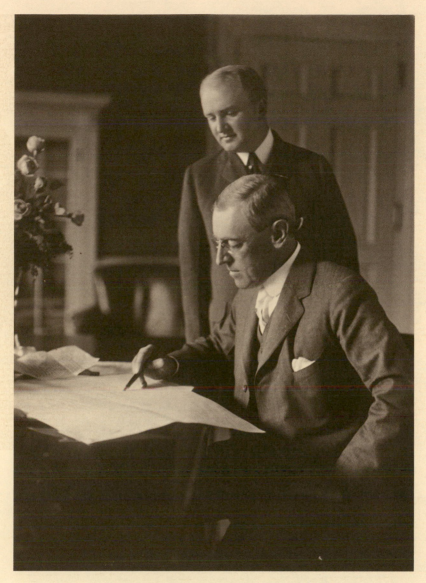

Wilson and Joseph P. Tumulty

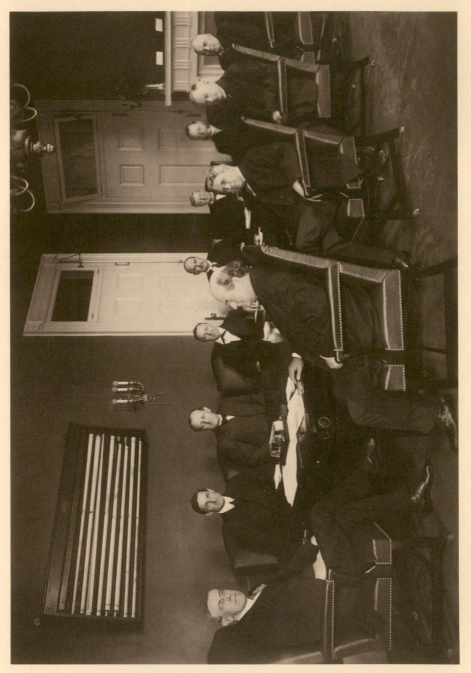

Wilson and his cabinet. Clockwise: the President, W. G. McAdoo, J. C. McReynolds, J. Daniels, D. F. Houston, W. B. Wilson, W. C. Redfield, F. K. Lane, A. S. Burleson, L. M. Garrison, W. J. Bryan

necessity of opening negotiations with him at the first opportunity. The President replied that he was ready to seize every opportunity to negotiate with him.

In the end the President said that he would consider our situation and position with complete sympathy and exert all possible efforts as before; and he asked me to inform the Japanese government fully about his intentions.

On my way back I visited the Secretary of State and gave to him an account of the meeting. Though I elicited again the Secretary's opinion, it was almost the same as the President's. And as to the copy of the senatorial bill on this matter sent officially from the Secretary, in order to dispel my suspicion that the Secretary had misunderstood our previous, which I communicated to you in the last part of my telegram No. 60 and might have intended eliciting my opinion about the senatorial bill, I asked him whether I could understand that he had meant to give me an opportunity to make a full investigation of the bill that had passed the Senate before it would be signed by the Governor. The Secretary answered that of course he had meant so and that he had sent it to me as a pending senatorial bill with no other intention than to call my attention to it.

My opinion about the statements of the President and Secretary of State, I will wire later.

[1] S. Chinda to N. Makino, received April 14, 1913 (MT 3.8.2. 274-2, pp. 348-58, JFO-Ar), reporting on a conversation with Bryan on April 12.

To James Clark McReynolds

                                        [The White House]
My dear Mr. Attorney General: April 17, 1913

One of the difficulties in handling the wool question is that, if I am correctly informed, the American Woolen Company is practically the only purchaser of wool, or at any rate purchases so large a proportion of it as virtually to control in some degree the price. If my information concerning this is correct, our best flank movement against high prices in that field would be to look into the legality of the operations of the American Woolen Company. Is this or is it not a promising lead?[1]

    Cordially and sincerely yours,   Woodrow Wilson

TLS (Letterpress Books, WP, DLC).
[1] His reply is missing.

From Oscar Wilder Underwood

My dear Mr. President: Washington, D. C., April 17, 1913.

I received your letter of the sixteenth instant yesterday, suggesting that we exempt all persons receiving less than $3,000 a year income from the necessity of making income returns at all. The committee bill as reported to the House, exempts all those having less than $3,500 a year income. I will take pleasure in calling your suggestion to the attention of the committee.

I have also spoken to Mr. Hull about the conference with Mr. Redfield and he says that he will call on Mr. Redfield.

The vote on the wool amendment in the caucus last night, was an agreeable surprise to me.[1] I had no doubt that we would win but we carried the point by a larger majority than I expected.
        Sincerely and cordially yours,   O W Underwood

TLS (WP, DLC).
[1] The Democratic House caucus approved Wilson's recommendation for free raw wool by a vote of 190 to 42, rejecting an amendment offered by Representative Martin Dies of Texas and actively promoted by the Ohio representatives, which set the duty at 15 per cent *ad valorem*. Underwood told the caucus that if the Dies amendment was adopted, every Republican newspaper would assert that the Democratic party was split and in disagreement with the President. "Out of the four thousand and more items in the bill," said Underwood, "the President only made two suggestions, those affecting the sugar and wool schedules. It seems to me that we should accept those suggestions from the President of the United States." New York *World* and *New York Times*, April 17, 1913.

From Samuel Rea[1]

My dear President Wilson: Philadelphia, April 17th, 1913.

I sincerely hope that the despatches from Washington, stating that you will not refuse to sign the Sundry Civil Appropriation Bill, with a rider attached exempting workmen and farmers from the Anti-Trust Act, are untrue.

To secure legislation of this kind through the irregular and vicious mode of attaching a rider to an appropriation bill, is wrong, and to exempt any class of people from the Anti-Trust Act is also wrong. It is well-known and has been stated by Senator Edmunds,[2] who was one of the chief framers of the Act, that it was not intended to apply to railroads, yet when it was considered by the Courts they decided that the Anti-Trust Law was universal in its application, and the Joint Traffic Association of Railroads was thereupon dissolved.

Every well-thinking person sympathizes with the effort to better the condition of labor, but there any [are] many other interests in this country as well as the laborers, organized and unorganized, and the farmers, and when the railroads are coerced by legislation such as the labor unions are securing in many of the States, notably the Extra Crew Laws in Pennsylvania, New York and New Jersey, thus providing places for men in idleness at the expense of the private Companies to whom have been confided the construction and operation of the railroads, it is time to scrutinize all such acts carefully and not allow our sympathies generally to outweigh our judgment. The editorial I enclose from the New York "Evening Post," (April 15th, 1913)[3] covers the situation quite fully, and I believe is endorsed by all good citizens, many of whom, like myself, are members of the Democratic Party and against "special privileges."

Respectfully yours,   Samuel Rea

TLS (WP, DLC).

[1] President of the Pennsylvania Railroad, an acquaintance of Wilson's from Bryn Mawr days.

[2] George Franklin Edmunds, Republican senator from Vermont, 1866-91. Edmunds explained the objectives of the drafters of the law in "The Interstate Trust and Commerce Act of 1890," *North American Review*, CXCIV (Dec. 1911), 801-17.

[3] A clipping of an editorial, "Special Privileges for Labor," saying that the Sherman Act ought not to be changed by rider legislation, and that in any event it would be "an enormous mistake" to give immunity from the law to any class or group.

Remarks at a Press Conference

April 18, 1913

Mr. President, have you taken a stand on the question whether there should be further hearings by the Senate concerning this tariff bill?

Oh, no; that is none of my business.

I thought some of the senators had asked—

I attend to my own business. . . .

Mr. President, are there any further developments in the California situation?

I got a memorandum this morning, but I haven't had time to look at it, sir. I don't know the details. It apparently was about the contents of the bill that was pending. And apparently there are two bills that are meeting half way, one coming up from the Assembly and another going down from the Senate.

Mr. President, have you looked into that matter of the analogy between the pending bills and statutes of states and the United States as applied to the District of Columbia?

Well, it would have involved, in order to do it accurately, a great deal of work that there hasn't been time yet to do. But

I had a digest before me yesterday of the laws of the several states[1]—not up to date quite, about four years old—that showed similar laws in several of the states; for example, one in New York, and one in Texas. And there is one in the District of Columbia. Of course, that latter would hardly be analogous, because the extent of the district is so small that there might be special reasons for not wishing the particular district of the national government to be owned by anybody but American citizens.

Doesn't that apply to all the territories over which we have jurisdiction—that is, federal jurisdiction?

The federal territories?

I am not sure about it at all.

I do not know.

Well, Mr. President, are you thinking of sending any member of the cabinet or any other representative to California in order to—

No, sir, though we are in constant touch with them as to what they are doing.

Have there been any communications from any European nation except Italy concerning that land law?

I saw in the morning's paper that there had been a communication from Italy, but it is the first I have heard of it. Mr. Bryan has not spoken to me about it.

He spoke to us about it!

It hadn't come to me in any form, except by the morning's newspapers. I do not know what the joke is. Do you mean that he spoke with some emphasis about it?

No, but it is the first time he has given us anything.

Mr. President, will these state laws that you looked at, do they prevent aliens from leasing lands?

This, as I said, was a mere synopsis, and I cannot give you the details of it at all.

Mr. President, what is the situation in Japan? It is stated that the imperial edict has never been issued whereby Americans and other aliens were allowed to own land.

That is true.

Mr. President, there is some interest about federal judges. Do you intend to appoint them very soon?

We are appointing them one by one, slowly.

I had in mind especially the situation in New England, where there is a vacancy caused by the election of Judge Colt.[2]

[1] Wilson probably referred to John Bassett Moore, *A Digest of International Law* (8 vols., Washington, D. C., 1906) IV, 32-50.

[2] LeBaron Bradford Colt of Bristol, R. I., presiding judge of the United States Circuit Court of Appeals for the first circuit, had just been elected to the Senate.

The Attorney General and I have conferred once or twice, briefly, about that, but we have not come to any conclusion.

Mr. President, is there any feeling because the British government has recognized the provisional government of Mexico?

Oh, no.

It is being stated in the papers that there was.

Oh, well, that is quite untrue. There is no feeling at all.

You had practically recognized this existing government, hadn't you, by transaction of diplomatic business with it?

Oh, no, no more than one would recognize a *de facto* government. But, of course, we haven't broken off diplomatic relations with Mexico, and are dealing with the *de facto* government just as any other government would deal with it.

That is practically recognition, isn't it?

I do not understand that it is by international precedent.

I thought when you carry on diplomatic relations, it was a recognition of the *de facto* government.

Well, we haven't carried on diplomatic relations except to this extent—that we have corresponded with Mr. Henry Lane Wilson about conditions there, and he has given us information, and we have made suggestions to him.

He is transacting business with the government, is he not—with the Mexican government?

Not of any sort that I have been directly connected with.

I see.

I cannot say what he has been doing; all that I know is that we haven't conveyed any messages yet to the existing government.

Mr. President, have you taken up the controversy over the Panama Canal tolls?

No.

Has there been any decision with regard to the Commerce Court, Mr. President?

By whom?

By the gentlemen upon whom the responsibility would fall of continuing or discontinuing that court.

You mean Congress. I cannot continue it or discontinue it. I do not know. You will have to ask that at the other end of the avenue.

Mr. President, I met a senator this morning, a brand new senator·with a fine set of whiskers,[3] and he seemed to think he knew

[3] James Hamilton Lewis of Illinois.

whom you were going to appoint as Comptroller of the Currency. Can you say anything about that at all?

> I should be very much interested to know, because I do not know myself.

Mr. President, have you fixed the date of your trip to New Jersey, or the length of the trip yet?

> No, I dare say Tumulty has; I haven't.

Mr. President, what is your attitude toward Senator Ashurst's plan for a direct primary for federal judgeships in Arizona?

> Why, you fellows must think I am an "attitudinarian." I haven't any attitude toward it at all.

Mr. President, it is reported today in some of the papers that this administration finds a number of men in the diplomatic service whose presence is not desirable because of some business connections they are supposed to have.

> I dare say that is a generalization from one or two cases. We haven't been finding anything startling.

Mr. President, has there been anything in the tariff legislation that you could comment on?

> Oh, it is going along all right, so far as I am informed. I see nothing to complain of.

Any district appointments?

> I am kept so busy with things, even just my business, that I haven't had time.

T MS (C. L. Swem Coll., NjP).

To Hiram Warren Johnson[1]

[Washington] April 18, '13

The President directs me to say that while he fully recognizes the right of the people of California to legislate according to their judgment on the subject of land tenure he feels it his duty to urge a recognition of the international character of such legislation. Being anxious to preserve and strengthen the long standing friendly relation existing between this country and the nations of the Orient he very respectfully but most earnestly advises against the use of the words "ineligible to citizenship." He asks that you bring this view to the attention of the legislators. He believes the Senate bill as telegraphed to the Department of State is greatly to be preferred. That bill limited ownership to citizens and to those who had declared their intention to become citizens.   W. J. Bryan.

TC telegram (WP, DLC).
  [1] There is a copy of this telegram in the CLSsh notebooks (C. L. Swem Coll., NjP).

To Oscar Wilder Underwood

My dear Mr. Underwood: [The White House] April 18, 1913.

Thank you very much for your note of the 17th. I congratulate you heartily on the vote on the wool amendment.

Cordially yours,   Woodrow Wilson

TLS (Letterpress Books, WP, DLC).

From John Bassett Moore

My dear Mr. President: New York April 18, 1913.

Your letter of the 16th inst. came into my hands last evening, and I deeply appreciate its kind expressions.

My withdrawal was intended to be in fact, as it was in terms, definitive; and I beg you so to treat it. By any other course, I cannot help feeling, after what has occurred, that a situation would be created which would soon prove to be untenable, with unfortunate consequences to all concerned, and particularly to the public service.

With a view to avoid comment and complications, I am willing, as a friend of your administration, (to say nothing of my great and long cherished regard for yourself) to take the place of Counselor just as it is, without any change whatever in its present status, with the mutual understanding (which, in order to prevent future misconception, I can in appropriate terms and on proper occasions make public) that I am within a few weeks to vacate it. Meanwhile a fit person can be chosen to fill the position, and I may be able to aid you in that direction.

Believe me to be, my dear Mr. President, ever with the highest regard,

Most respectfully and sincerely yours,   John B. Moore

TLS (WP, DLC).

From Elsworth Raymond Bathrick[1]

Sir: Washington, D. C. April 18, 1913.

I sought through your Secretary to secure an interview with you today and finally doubted the propriety of my calling upon you for the purpose set forth herein, but was assured by your Secretary that this letter would be delivered to you.

I call your attention to Paragraph 301, Page 74, in our Tariff Bill in which a 35 percentum ad valorem is placed upon cloth. This is the cloth which is used to make a suit of clothes. In Paragraph 304, Page 75, ready made clothing carries 35 percemtum ad valorem. These tariffs are still, in my opinion, prohibitive. Paragraph 304, carries ready made clothing from a $10 suit up to a Parisan gown if they contain wool chiefly. This places the high priced tailored suit on the same plane as the workman's $10 suit or the shop girl's shawl.

There should be no tariff upon these cheaper classes of ready made suits or if there is a tariff at all it should not be higher than fifteen percent.

There is no importation of any importance of men's and boy's ready made suits. These at least should be segregated from Paragraph 304 which might necessitate a change of Paragraph 301. However, even at 35 percent on cloth, 15 percent on men's and boy's suits would be sufficient compensatory duty.

I wanted to ask you if you would not urge a committee amendment changing the items of the cheaper ready made clothing.

On the floor of the Caucus yesterday I was accused of bad faith in making these amendments on ready made clothing. I assure you that had not this inconsistency of tariff rating on those articles which the poor people of this country must buy been apparent I would not have opposed free wool.

There is no condition in my District upon which to base such misconstruction of my motives and I am only asking this of you on behalf of the users of cheaper ready made clothing in this country.   Sincerely yours,   E R Bathrick

Kindly consider this confidential.

TLS (WP, DLC).
¹ Democratic congressman from Akron, Ohio.

From the Diary of Josephus Daniels

Friday, April 18, 1913.

As soon as the Cabinet met, Secretary Bryan said he wished to read what he regarded as the most remarkable official document that had been issued in a generation. He read from the Washington Post the following clipping:

"CHINA ASKS FOR PRAYERS—Government makes a Formal Appeal to All Christian Churches.

"Peking, China, April 17—An official appeal was made today by the Chinese government to all the Christian churches in China to set aside April 27 as a day for prayer that China may be guided to a wise solution of the critical problems besetting her. This act of the government is regarded here as striking evidence of the extraordinary changes which have taken place in the nation since the revolution.

"The appeal was distributed broadcast by telegraph today to the governors and high officials within whose jurisdiction Christian communities are to be found. It was also sent to the leaders of the various missions. Prayer was requested for the national assembly, for the new government, for the president of the republic, who is yet to be elected; for the constitution of the republic, for the recognition of the republic by the powers for the maintenance of peace, and for election of strong and virtuous men to office.

"The representatives of the provincial authorities are instructed to attend the services.["]

As soon as he finished reading it, he remarked upon the significant fact that official China was asking Christian churches of that country to pray for the success of the republic. Only a generation ago Christian missionaries could hardly find access to China and that in this generation they have been put to death. The revolution which changes all that and invokes the blessings of the Christians' God for the new republic shows what a tremendous revolution has been wrought in the feeling of the Celestial Empire.

The President said that he did not know when he had been so stirred and cheered as when he read that message in the paper this morning and he had in mind to request it though, of course, said he, "I had no right to issue the proclamation that all churches in America on that date will join the churches in China in the prayer for the success of a republic that feels the need of the prayers of Christians."

Secretary Redfield thought that the Chinese minds were so different from the minds of Europe and America that it might be well to consider whether the declaration was from the heart or whether it was not rather a play to secure the support of Christian nations and did not represent the real faith of the people. He also raised the question as to whether, in view of the fact that a majority of the people of China are not Christians, it might not hurt the republic if it became understood that the new Government was relying upon the Christian forces of the world for support. That the non-Christians in China, who outnumber the Christians by many thousands, would probably take advantage of this deep interest of the Christians of America and say beware of the republic. These foreign "devils," as they call Americans, are trying to get control of our country, and instead of helping, it might hurt.

This did not appeal to the President, who thought that while there might be something in that, we ought to accept the official appeal of wishing the prayers of the Christians as honest and earnest and join with the Christian people in China in praying for the peaceful organization of the republic and its success in administering the government for the people of China.

Secretary Garrison raised the question as to what we were going to do with reference to recognizing the republic of China. Mr. Bryan explained that he had sent a letter to our Secretary of Legation of China authorizing him to recognize China as soon as the Congress assembled and organized the government. It was expected then that a President would be elected on Tuesday of last week when the Assembly was scheduled to meet. That expectation had not been realized. . . .

The President said there had come into his mind a suggestion which might seem irreverent but which was not at all irreverent, i.e., that people would say if we pray that China may become a peaceful and progressive republic, why does not this country help answer its own prayers by immediately recognizing China? Secretary Garrison thought the country would say that you better recognize China first and pray afterwards. My suggestion was that faith without works is dead, that we ought to pray and also recognize China just as soon as we had enought facts to justify it. Secretary Bryan was requested to wire China and get all the facts. He has been hearing very little from China and we have no information of what is going on and the opinion was expressed by the President and others, particularly Mr. Bryan, in favor of recognizing China and that by Tuesday we would get enough information to recognize China by April 27th, on which date the churches would all offer prayers for the republic of that country.

The Mexican situation next came up for consideration. Some weeks ago when Secretary Bryan informed the the [sic] Ambassadors and Ministers from other countries that it was the purpose of the United States to recognize the republic of China as soon as the Assembly met and elected a President. He instructed his Secretary to notify all the Ambassadors and Ministers to come to see him and he made known his request. The American [Mexican] Ambassador[1] was included in that request and Secretary Bryan read a letter from our Minister at Mexico stating that it was contended by the Huerta Government that this was equivalent to recognition of that government although no act of recognition has never [sic] been given. The President suggested that Mr. Bryan say to the Mexican people that his summoning the Mex-

[1] Arturo de la Cueva, Mexican Chargé d'Affaires in Washington.

ican Minister was a courtesy and not recognition. What to do with Mexico is the great problem and was discussed at length.

Secretary Garrison had information which made him believe that conditions were worse than they had been and that it was doubtful whether the Mexicans could ever organize a government and that in this country it might be well to consider whether it would be well to recognize a brute like Huerta so as to have some form of government which could be recognized and dealt with. It was a general point of doubt that if we communicated with Huerta, he could not communicate with the northern states which are in revolution against him. The general opinion in the Cabinet was that the chief cause of this whole situation in Mexico was a contest between English and American Oil Companies to see which would control; that these people were ready to foment trouble and it was largely due to the English Company[2] that England was willing to recognize Mexico before we did. What to do as to property that had been destroyed in Mexico was earnestly discussed. American property is being destroyed. The President of the Harriman railroad had been to see the Cabinet officers and it was said that 300 men in their employ were retained at a place where their shops were located in Mexico (Guaymas, I think) and that property and life were in jeopardy. Mr. Bryan offered to give them a convoy or make it certain that they could be taken our [out] of the country and their lives be saved, but the President of the railroad did not wish that but wanted them to stay and protect the property. But, if they chose to stay and protect the property, Mr. Bryan could not see that this government could do anything. It was certain that this government could not send an army to make safe conduct and who wished to stay in order to protect their property.

The news from Mexico and our Minister and Consul General[3] is not as definite as is desirable and the question was whether a special man should be sent, a confidential man, to study the situation and get at the exact facts as they exist, but nothing went beyond discussion. This is Mexico's last chance at the President. Huerta and Diaz now have the opportunity to see if they can maintain a constitutional government. An election has been ordered to be held in a month or two and unless they can elect a constitutional government, there is no hope for it and when they throw their hands up, both parties will call upon America to interfere. If it should intervene without being called upon, it

2 The Aguila (Mexican Eagle) Oil Co., Ltd., controlled by S. Pearson and Son, Ltd., headed by Weetman Dickinson Pearson, 1st Baron Cowdray of Midhurst.
3 Arnold Shanklin, Consul General in Mexico City.

would have to go in and conquer Mexico which is unthinkable and it is greatly to be hoped that a constitutional government can be organized in Mexico so that America will not have to intervene.

Secretary Garrison thought that many Americans and Mexicans want intervention. Secretary Lane said he did not think there were 500 Mexicans who wished intervention. Postmaster General Burleson said the people in Northern Mexico, who are in opposition to Huerta, would like intervention provided they though[t] the Huerta government was going to succeed because they did not wish to be under his rule believing him to be a brute. But he was strongly against any intervention and thought the policy being pursued now was the only correct one and that this government should never intervene until Mexico saw there was no hope. . . .

The third big matter before the Cabinet, and this was a day for the discussion of real problems of world wide interest, was the statement of the conversation between Secretary Bryan and Ambassador Bryce. They had talked over an hour over the matter of tolls on the Panama Canal. Ambassador Bryce, whose term soon expires, urged upon the Secretary of State that the President should announce that unless Congress repealed the bill under which coast-wise vessels had an advantage through the Panama Canal over English vessels he would submit the controversy between England and America to arbitration. Mr. Bryce was very earnest about this matter and Mr. Bryan detailed the conversation and argument between them and he told the English Ambassador that after 20 years of struggle the democrats were now in power and were in the midst of a fight to secure a reduction in the tariff law and that in his opinion the President would not be justified in taking up any important matter that would divide his party in the midst of this great tariff struggle. He pointed out to Mr. Bryce that there was no hurry about this Canal matter as it would not be open to vessels for about a year, possibly longer, and this matter might well be postponed until the President had the opportunity to put the tariff fight behind him and that England ought not to urge that this matter be taken up and some statement made until the tariff matter was settled.

Mr. Bryan detailed his argument to Mr. Bryce along this line which was so convincing to the Cabinet as to lead me me [sic] to ask what answer Mr. Bryan could make to his argument on arbitration and Mr. Bryan answered that Mr. Bryce did not seem to be satisfied and did not understand why any man in America could oppose arbitration to which Mr. Bryan replied that it might be hard to understand but the fact existed and nevertheless it had to be dealt with. Although he could not speak for the President, he certainly would advise him that the only course would be not to permit this matter to be taken up now and make it an Administration policy until after the tariff measure had become a law. Mr. Bryce said in that event it might be that England would refuse to continue the arbitration treaty between that country and the United States which would expire in June. Mr. Bryan expressed surprise at this and quoted Mr. Bryce as saying that English leaders understood thoroughly the American favorable attitude toward arbitration and then asked Mr. Bryce if they understand it, why do you wish to press us to take it up now when the tariff matter is pressing?[4] Mr. Bryce replied that while he and the leaders understood it, the people did not understand, and he was urging their government for action. The President said, "I have talked all this matter over with Mr. Bryce, not as Ambassador of Great Britain but as my old friend, and I am determined that I shall not make any statement about the matter or permit it to interfere with the policy of the Administration until the tariff bill is out of the way.["]

T MS (J. Daniels Papers, DLC).
[4] For a similar report of this conversation, see J. Bryce to E. Grey, April 17, 1913, TLS (FO 371 / 1702, No. 19626, PRO).

From the Diary of Colonel House

April 18, 1913.

We [House and McAdoo] went over to the President's at four and remained with him for an hour. We took up the New York Collectorship first and discussed Senator O'Gorman's attitude. Both McAdoo and I urged the President to make the issue with the Senator even if he should oppose the nomination upon the floor of the Senate. I was sure it would come sooner or later and it might as well be fought out with him now, since it is clear that he and the President cannot make Tammany appointments and the sooner O'Gorman realizes it the better. He promised to "stand pat" and to send Polk's name to the Senate come what may. This is the way I like to hear him talk.

We discussed the other appointments that McAdoo and I had gone over last night and he consented to all of them with the exception of Hays of West Virginia[1] and Berry for Collector of Philadelphia. He wanted some data in regard to these two appointments which McAdoo is to get and then they will go in.

I went over my budget with him very quickly. I told him Fred

Lynch had telephoned me that Samuel Untermyer would like to become Ambassador to Germany. The President smiled and said it was interesting and he was glad to know that Mr. Untermyer would be pleased if he should be sent. I also said that Roger Sullivan would be pleased if it could be intimated to him that the President would see him the next time he visited Washington. The President replied the intimation could be given Mr. Sullivan if it were not done in writing under his signature.

The President seemed depressed and I tried to brace him up by telling him that everything was in splendid condition excepting himself; that was the only thing troubling me. He laughed and said he would try to reform if I would indicate the way. He promised to give himself more time for recreation. He spoke again of his desire to have me near him in Washington and said he was sorry whenever I told him goodbye.

[1] Samuel Augustus Hays, lawyer and businessman of Glenville, W. Va. He was appointed collector of internal revenue for West Virginia.

To James Clark McReynolds

[The White House]
My dear Mr. Attorney General: April 19, 1913

Mr. G. S. McFarland, who is the editor of Mr. Hearst's paper in Boston, came to see me the other day. He is a very earnest and genuine man, whom I greatly like, and who is doing his best to hold the papers with which he is associated back from mistaken policies.

He made a very interesting suggestion to me which I am inclined to consider very seriously, namely, the appointment of George Fred Williams as District Attorney for the Boston District. I would very much like to know your own judgment.

He also spoke very warmly of George W. Anderson,[1] once a partner of Williams, and once[2] also a candidate for the office of Attorney General on the Democratic ticket in Massachusetts.
                          Faithfully yours,   Woodrow Wilson

TLS (Letterpress Books, WP, DLC).
[1] George Weston Anderson, lawyer of Boston. He became district attorney for Massachusetts, Nov. 1, 1914.
[2] In 1911 and 1912.

To Oscar Wilder Underwood

My dear Mr. Underwood: The White House April 19, 1913

Ready made clothing under the proposed bill carries a duty of thirty-five per cent. ad valorem; and Paragraph 304 includes everything, apparently, from a ten dollar suit up to a Parisian gown if wool is the chief material. I suppose that this would include shawls and workmen's cheap suits.

I beg your pardon for calling your attention to this so late in the game, but I write chiefly to inquire if this were a deliberate arrangement, the consequences of which with regard to the price of the cheaper sort of clothing were analyzed.

I know that you will pardon my calling these matters to your attention as they come up.

Cordially and sincerely yours,   Woodrow Wilson

TLS (O. W. Underwood Papers, A-Ar).

To William Bayard Hale

My dear Mr. Hale: The White House April 19, 1913

I think that the situation of affairs in Central and South America is very much more difficult to get the threads of than the situation in California, and with the full acquiescence of Mr. Bryan I am writing to ask if you would be willing to undertake a tour of the Central and South American states, ostensibly on your own hook, in order that unofficially and through the eyes of an independent observer we might find out just what is going on down there.[1]

Will you not be kind enough to regard this inquiry as strictly confidential?

Cordially and sincerely yours,   Woodrow Wilson

TLS (received from W. H. Hale).
[1] As will soon become evident, Wilson sent Hale to Mexico instead of to Central and South America.

To Charles Albert Woods

My dear Friend: [The White House] April 19, 1913

I am expecting to give myself the pleasure of nominating you as circuit Judge for the Fourth Circuit. I can not tell you how sincere a pleasure it is to be able to do this. I have not consulted both of the South Carolina Senators, but I hope and believe that I shall get their willing assent.

In the meantime, I want to put to you very frankly what has been in the minds of the Attorney General and myself with regard to all judicial appointments. We think that it is wise and necessary for the efficiency of the judicial service of the country that we should ask those who are appointed if they would not be

willing to pledge themselves to retire upon reaching the age of
seventy. I put this to you in all frankness, because I know that you
will understand the spirit in which I do it and I am sure that
you will meet me with equal frankness in the matter.

I sincerely hope that Mrs. Woods[1] is growing stronger. We
think of you very often, and I only wish that the appointment
I have in contemplation would bring you where I could see more
of you.

With warmest regard to you both, I am

Faithfully yours,   Woodrow Wilson

TLS (Letterpress Books, WP, DLC).
[1] Salley Jones Wannamaker Woods. She died on September 5, 1913.

To Edward Samuel Corwin

My dear Corwin: [The White House] April 19, 1913

I do not feel by any means as confident as you do as to the
power of the Federal Government in the matter of overriding the
constitutional powers of the states through the instrumentality
of treaties, but I do not wonder you feel as you do about the
matter. The present case is a most perplexing and difficult one.

It is very delightful that the men at Princeton should be thinking about me as they do. It gives me a sense of confidence and
support which is of the greatest value to me.

Cordially and sincerely yours,   Woodrow Wilson

TLS (Letterpress Books, WP, DLC).

To James Aloysius O'Gorman[1]

PERSONAL AND CONFIDENTIAL.

My dear Senator: [The White House] April 20, 1913

I wish most cordially and unaffectedly that I could accept
your suggestion about the Collectorship of the Port of New York.
I distrust my own judgment when I find it differing from yours,
and my whole feeling about you, ever since I first knew you,
has inclined me to agree with you and act with you.

But in this case, I am deeply sorry to say, it is not possible. I
regard the Collectorship as in many ways as central and as intimately connected with my personal success as a place in the
Cabinet. Moreover, I would as soon think of asking the Secretary
of the Treasury to take a man whom he did not feel he could act
with as his first assistant in his Department as ask him to take
a man whom he does not feel he can act with as Collector of

the Port of New York. The post is, in fact, of much more importance to him in the administration of the Treasury than is the first Assistant Secretaryship.

He has known Mr. Polk for a long time and intimately. He trusts him, believes in his capacity, feels that he is especially adapted to the duties of the office, and desires there—indeed, deems it indispensable that he should have—someone with whom his relations may be personal and confidential from the first. I have had Mr. Polk very thoroughly looked up since I saw you and now feel sure that Mr. McAdoo is not mistaken in his estimate of him. He is just the man I was looking for. I deem it my duty, therefore, to send his name to the Senate for the appointment. I have reached the conclusion very deliberately and, I trust, with a full sense of my constitutional responsibility.

I beg you to believe that I do this in entire deference to yourself, and I hope most sincerely that you will generously support the vote of confirmation. If I did not see my duty very clearly in this case, it would give me real pleasure to act as you have suggested. I shall hope to have a talk with you again, for a fuller statement of my feeling and obligation in the matter, before I send the nomination to the Senate.

With great respect,
Cordially and sincerely yours,   Woodrow Wilson

TCL (WP, DLC).
    [1] There is a WWsh draft of this letter in WP, DLC. There is a note on the following typed copy that the original was in Wilson's hand.

Remarks at a Press Conference

April 21, 1913

Mr. President, did you notice that Senator Chamberlain said that he was going to introduce into the Senate a resolution to abrogate the Hay-Pauncefote Treaty?

No, I noticed that a newspaper published a dispatch from Washington saying that he had. That is all I know.

That hadn't been called to your attention before?

No, sir. It is so roundabout that I think it is not worth discussing. No, it had not been called to my attention at all.

Mr. President, I have seen some comment in connection with the appointment of the Director of the Census, upon the possibility of treating various so-called scientific bureaus as material for political appointments. I wondered whether you would say anything—draw any sort of line for us—as to the extent to which you think that is proper to do, or intend to do?

Oh, I think it is very proper and necessary to treat scientific bureaus on perfectly nonpolitical lines. The Census Bureau seems to me to stand on a footing of its own, because so much judgment is involved in it with regard to the various business developments and connections of the country; so that it is perfectly proper in my mind that a man should preside over it who has something besides the scientific statistical training that is so necessary in the general conduct of the bureau.

Mr. Willis Moore,[1] I think, took the stand that he was not bound by the custom of handing in his resignation, because that was a scientific bureau—he seemed to think so. And it did raise a very interesting question as to just where the line is drawn.

Well, the line there has nothing to do with that.

We have seen the line as far as that is concerned!

Mr. President, is there anything you can discuss with us with regard to the Japanese situation today—in regard to California?

I haven't any new information about it. I judged from what appeared in yesterday's newspapers that they are getting rather thoughtful about it out there—as to the possible improprieties of it—but I haven't heard anything more than the rest of you know about it.

The morning papers said that your memorandum to the governor[2] was very well received in Japan—that it had a very soothing effect.

I saw that, too. I hope it was.

Mr. President, have you received any advices as to whether the Senate bill[3] would be unobjectionable to Japan?

No, I haven't discussed any particular bill with them. It has just been the problem I have discussed with the Japanese Ambassador here.

But you thought that the Senate bill would be less objectionable than the House bill?[4]

Well, my whole thought is that there ought not to be discriminations in the bill.

Mr. President, are you at liberty to speak of the collectorship at Philadelphia—Mr. Berry's appointment?

No, I really have nothing to say about that, because there,

[1] Willis Luther Moore, chief of the United States Weather Bureau, 1895-1913.
[2] That is, WW to H. W. Johnson, April 18, 1913.
[3] The Thompson-Birdsall bill, which limited ownership of land to citizens and aliens who had declared their intention of becoming citizens.
[4] Adopted on April 15, it prevented persons "ineligible to citizenship" from owning land.

again, I have got it only through what is being said, and haven't handled it officially at all.

The same applies to the collectorship at New York?

Yes.

The appointment of the New York collector is not going to the Senate today, I judge?

We really are not ready with any appointments today.

Nor Philadelphia?

No. . . .

Mr. President, is there anything you can say on the progress of tariff legislation?

Why, it is making very satisfactory progress, if that is what you mean.

I thought possibly there was some development in it.

No, none whatever.

What time do you think the session will adjourn, Mr. President? Have you received any intimations?

You have been here much longer than I have, and you can make a better guess than I can.

Everybody is venturing a guess!

Mr. President, are you hearing any reports concerning the business and commercial status of the country in view of the present pending tariff legislation?

No, I can't say that I have heard anything that could be called reports—I mean, definite—from responsible sources. But I have got the impression from letters that I have got from editors, for example, ordinarily on the other side of the fence, that this is regarded as a most reasonable bill, a well thought out bill, and a bill from which nothing is feared that will be embarrassing to the country.

During its pendency there apparently is in certain financial centers somewhat of a contraction of credits and deposits, also reports of the reduction of prices, and I am wondering whether you have any observations to make on that.

Well, from the observations I have seen in the financial papers, they do not attribute those circumstances to the tariff at all.

To what do they?

To general market conditions and trade conditions.

Mr. President, have you been hearing from outside—I mean from business interests—regarding a tariff commission, whether they would care to have that?

No, I haven't heard anything along that line.

Some of the congressmen have; I didn't know whether you had.

> You see, as a matter of fact, the duties of the tariff commission were handed over by legislation to the Department of Commerce. But, of course, they are sleeping, because they made no appropriation.

Mr. President, you regard the reciprocity provision of the tariff bill as workable?

> Why, yes, I do not see why not.

Well, simply on this theory—where a tariff is made high to be traded down, reciprocity is safe; where it is calculated with respect to the American consumer, how are you going to trade it down?

> Well, that raises the question, which do you want?—the advantages to the American consumer, or do you want the tactical advantages in negotiating treaties of reciprocity? Of course, we are legislating first of all for our own people—for their relief and advantage—and it is a very secondary consideration whether we have the cards to play in a reciprocity negotiation. I say that is a secondary question.

It is except with regard, perhaps, to sugar.

> I don't understand.

I mean that sugar is the key to reciprocity with the tropical countries.

> How do you make that out? We don't get any sugar except from Cuba and Porto Rico and Hawaii.

Well, all these countries are—I know the conditions, of course, have changed since Porto Rico and Hawaii came in; it is emphatically true—

> I mean you can't find in statistics of sugar imports any countries with which we have important dealings. In that matter, practically all of the so-called raw sugar comes in—except from our own possessions—comes in from Cuba, and we have a reciprocal relationship with her under a treaty now. So that I don't see that that is a card of any consequence.

Mr. President, have there been any developments in China which would seem to make it necessary to postpone the day of recognition?

> Oh, no. They are, of course, delaying their final work—their constituent assembly—for various reasons which I don't fully understand. There is no delay on our part at all.

Nothing has happened that would affect the policy of this government?

> Nothing at all.

Mr. President, have you seen any reason to encourage or change your present attitude with reference to the introduction of currency legislation?

No.

Would you be willing to say whether you really expect that to be negotiated at this session?

Oh, that still depends on circumstances.

It stands about where it was before?

Just exactly.

I have talked with some congressmen today on that subject, and they say you can introduce it, but if you are engaged any length of time on the tariff, you can never get it through, because they do not want to stay too long, and you would simply be putting up your hand to let the other fellows know how to play at the other end of the table.

I never play with my hands under the table.

Well, it doesn't always do to show your hand.

I am perfectly willing to play with the cards face up.

Mr. President, have you any observations to make with regard to the suggestion that the fleet will make a trip around the world?

No, they are not flying kites at present.

T MS (C. L. Swem Coll., NjP).

To John Bassett Moore

Dear Mr. Moore: The White House April 21, 1913

I really can not let you insist upon the conclusion stated in your kind letter of April eighteenth, because it is based upon entire misapprehension. I know the men I am dealing with here so thoroughly that I can assure you that it is not possible "that a situation would be created which would soon prove to be untenable, with unfortunate consequences to all concerned and particularly to the public service."

What has happened was a mere misunderstanding from the first, and as much due to stupidity on my part as to anything else. Both Mr. Bryan and Governor Osborne would be genuinely distressed if you did not come to stay, and it would be a serious blow to the administration. Your announced acceptance of the post had drawn forth expressions from all sides which show how serious the impression would be if you now withdrew. A very brief time here will show you the genuineness and largeness of the men you are dealing with. I am as sure of that as that I am dictating this letter.

I am not begging you to reconsider a decision; I am only begging you to understand the real facts of an unnecessary blunder on my part, and I am sure that you have sufficient confidence in me to accept my assurances as to the real facts, as well as the disinterested devotion to the public service which would lead you to drop this little contretemps into oblivion.

With warmest regard, I am

Cordially yours,   Woodrow Wilson

ALS (J. B. Moore Papers, DLC).

To David Starr Jordan

My dear Dr. Jordan: [The White House] April 21, 1913

I thank you for your very full letter of April 14th, which I have noted with care. This matter is having our earnest and prayerful consideration, and I am hopeful that it will be concluded satisfactorily to all concerned.

Cordially and sincerely yours,   Woodrow Wilson

TLS (Letterpress Books, WP, DLC).

To Henry George, Jr.[1]

My dear Mr. George: [The White House] April 21, 1913

I am deeply sensible of the generosity of your kind letter of April 9th,[2] and tender to you my warmest thanks for your friendly words. I am delighted to know that you will so soon be restored to health. It will be a real pleasure to have you back in Washington and to work with you in the advancement of our common cause.

With regard,

Cordially and sincerely yours,   Woodrow Wilson

TLS (Letterpress Books, WP, DLC).
  [1] Democratic congressman from New York.
  [2] It is missing.

To Mary Allen Hulbert

Dearest Friend,   The White House 21 April, 1913.

I did not write yesterday because I thought that you had sailed for New York on Saturday, as you expected to do when you last wrote; but your letter, received to-day, postpones your coming till the boat that sails on the 29th. Remember that you are to write to us the moment you land (or telegraph) and that you are to arrange to come to us just as soon thereafter as possible! Ever since I knew that Allen was here and accessible every spare bed-room in the house has been occupied by guests or relatives and it has been simply impossible to have him come down, unless I were to put him up at a hotel—which would not count, for it would give me no chance at him. But we shall manage it later. I am eager to get hold of him for a little while. The worst of it is, that there is scarcely ever a day, except Sunday, when I can be sure beforehand that a single quarter of an hour will be mine to dispose of as I will. But I must try, and *squeeze* out a little for him! We shall see how things stand when you yourself get down. Ah! how jolly, how delightful that will be! And how my spirits have gone up, with yours, at the news that the engagement is broken.

You are a most efficient person! I wish I had you in my Cabinet! Is there *no* way, I wonder, in which I can attach you to the service? It is delightful to think that you will soon be at hand, at least, and *obtainable*. My mental (spiritual) barometer goes up with a great leap when I think of it. Bermuda is a long way off, after all. It is much better—at any rate selfishly much better—to have one's friends—at least one's *dear* friends, who are indispensable, on the same mainland! We must manage it better hereafter. All join me in messages of deep affection and in great happiness that we are to see you *soon*!

Your devoted friend,   Woodrow Wilson

ALS (WP, DLC).

To Hiram Warren Johnson and Others[1]

Hon. Hiram W. Johnson, Governor;
The President of the Senate,[2] and
The Speaker of the House,[3]
Sacramento, California.   The White House April 22, 1913

I speak upon the assumption, which I am sure is well founded, that the people of California do not desire their representatives— and that their representatives do not wish or intend—in any circumstances to embarrass the Government of the United States in its dealings with a nation with whom it has most earnestly and cordially sought to maintain relations of genuine friendship and good will, and that least of all do they desire to do anything that might impair treaty obligations or cast a doubt upon the honor and good faith of the Nation and its government.

I, therefore, appeal with the utmost confidence to the people, the Governor, and the Legislature of California to act in the matter now under consideration in a manner that can not from any point of view be fairly challenged or called in question. If they deem it necessary to exclude all aliens who have not declared their intention to become citizens from the privileges of land ownership, they can do so along lines already followed in the laws of many of the other states and of many foreign countries, including Japan herself. Invidious discrimination will inevitably draw in question the treaty obligations of the Government of the United States. I register my very earnest and respectful protest against discrimination in this case, not only because I deem it my duty to do so as the Chief Executive of the Nation, but also, and the more readily, because I believe that the people and the legislative authorities of California will generously respond the moment the matter is frankly presented to them as a question of national policy and of national honor. If they have ignored this point of view, it is, I am sure, because they did not realize what and how much was involved.[4]   Woodrow Wilson.

T telegram (Letterpress Books, WP, DLC).
  [1] This telegram was sent one day after Progressive leaders in the California Senate agreed to jettison the Thompson-Birdsall bill and to support a bill denying the right of land ownership to persons "ineligible to citizenship" and to corporations, the majority stockholders of which were aliens "ineligible to citizenship."
  [2] Albert E. Boynton, an attorney of San Francisco.
  [3] Clement Calhoun Young, a real estate dealer of Berkeley.
  [4] There is a CLST draft of this telegram, with WWhw emendations, in WP, DLC.

A Proposed Statement on Patronage[1]

Washington, D. C., April 22, 1913.

The policy of the Administration to be observed in making Federal appointments within the State was announced yesterday in a conference at the White House.

The rule receiving [permitting] recommendations and endorsements by Senators for Federal appointments to offices to be filled within the State, and permitting recommendations from Members of Congress for postmasters within their respectives Districts will be observed. These endorsements will be duly considered by the President, but he will not be entirely guided by them, and feels at liberty to make independent investigations of his own in deciding upon the fitness and efficiency of all applicants.

If he is not satisfied with recommendations he will decline to make the appointment and call upon the Senators or the delegation for the submission of other persons and names.

On inquiry as to what qualifications for office were desired, the President stated that only progressives would be considered or appointed. It was asked what is a progressive? In answering the President said it was rather difficult to define the term with exactness, but in effect a progressive was a Democrat who understood the principles of the common law as separable when necessary, from the construction and application made by the fathers from time to time, under the totally different circumstances which confronted them, and who recognizes that these same principles can and ought to be adapted and applied to meet present day problems and conditions.

It was suggested that the rule in Alabama has been to consult not Senators alone but the entire delegation in Congress as to Federal appointments within the State. The President said that it would be entirely satisfactory to him if the delegation desired to act together as a whole or through the Senators, that his course would be the same in either event.

It was also understood that Members of the Cabinet would be consulted and requested to make investigations upon all applications, and would be expected to receive proper consideration before final action in all cases.

The President is in no haste to make appointments, and time will be taken for thorough investigation before appointment.

It is understood that the present Federal officers in Alabama will be allowed to serve out their unexpired terms unless upon charges they may be sooner removed.

It is understood that in case of a postmaster where the applicants recommended by the Member is not appointed, then the Member who made the recommendation of the rejected applicant will be called on to recommend another applicant for postmaster.

T MS (WP, DLC).
  ¹ Written presumably by Henry D. Clayton for publication in Alabama newspapers, after a meeting between Wilson and the Alabama delegation at the White House on April 21. The statement was not published, and there was no correspondence about it.

To Joseph Edward Davies

[The White House] April 22, 1913.

May I hope that you will consider favorably the Commissionership of Corporations.¹   Woodrow Wilson.

T telegram (Letterpress Books, WP, DLC).
  ¹ He accepted.

To Samuel Rea

My dear Mr. Rea: [The White House] April 22, 1913

I, of course, realize the importance of the principle involved in the rider attached to the Sundry Civil Bill and agree that the wisdom of attaching riders is more than open to question, but you will notice upon an examination of the Bill that the rider applies to only a single special additional appropriation of $300,000 intended for the employment of additional counsel to do work already undertaken by the Department of Justice. It does not limit in any respect the expenditure of the general funds of the Department or restrict its discretion as to the character or object of the suits which it is to bring.

In these circumstances, I have not felt justified in embarrassing Congress, as it would be embarrassed if I asked them to open the bill and expose it to all the changes which would be sure to ensue were it not presented again in its original form.

Cordially and sincerely yours,   Woodrow Wilson

TLS (Letterpress Books, WP, DLC).

To Joseph R. Wilson, Jr.

My dear, dear Brother: [The White House] April 22, 1913

I never in my life had anything quite so hard to do as this that I must do about the Nashville Post Office.[1] Knowing as I do that a better man could not possibly be found for the place, and sure though I am that it would meet with the general approval of the citizens of Nashville, I yet feel that it would be a very serious mistake both for you and for me if I were to appoint you to the Postmastership there. I can not tell you how I have worried about this or how much I have had to struggle against affection and temptation, but I am clear in the conviction and I am sure that in the long run, if not now, you will agree with me that I am deciding rightly.

I can't write any more just now, because I feel too deeply.

With deepest love, I remain

Your affectionate brother,   Woodrow Wilson

TLS (Letterpress Books, WP, DLC).
[1] Wilson was replying to J. R. Wilson, Jr., to WW, April 19, 1913, TLS (WP, DLC), saying that his friends in Nashville were about to begin a campaign for his appointment as postmaster of that city.

From Hiram Warren Johnson

Sacramento, California, April 22, 1913.

Immediately upon receipt of your telegram of this date it was transmitted to both Houses of our Legislature. I think I may assure you that it is the desire of the majority of members of the legislature to do nothing in the matter of alien land bills that shall be embarrassing to our own government or offensive to any other. It is the design of these legislators specifically to provide in any act that nothing therein shall be construed as affecting or impairing any rights secured by treaty. Although from the legal standpoint this is deemed unnecessary if any act be passed it will be general in character relating to those who are ineligible to citizenship and the language employed will be that which has its precedent and sanction in statu[t]es which now exist upon the subject. I speak, I think, for the majority of the Senate of California, certainly I do for the vetoing power of the state when I convey to you our purpose to cooperate fully and heartily with the National Government and to do only that which is admittedly within our province without intended offense or invidious discrimination.   Hiram W. Johnson.

T telegram (WP, DLC).

From Oscar Wilder Underwood

My dear Mr. President: Washington, D. C., April 22, 1913.

I received your letter of the 19th instant this morning, in reference to Par. 304 of the new Tariff Bill. You are correct in stating that the taxes on clothing in the new bill are 35 per cent, but this is a reduction from 99 per cent on women's and children's dress goods and from 79 per cent on readymade clothing in the present law. I think it is impossible to arrange this schedule so that we could clearly differentiate between the articles covered by this paragraph on a valuation basis. Of course, the ad valorem duty adjusts itself to the value of the article and we have placed the tax on ready-made clothing at the same rate that is levied on the cloth from which it is made. I think it would be dangerous to make a reduction below the value of the cloth and I believe that the bill has reduced the tax on the cloth as low as it is safe to go at this time. It gave me pleasure to receive your suggestion.

With kindest regards, I am,

Cordially yours,   O W Underwood

TLS (WP, DLC).

From Charles Albert Woods

Personal.

My Dear Mr. President: Columbia, S. C., April 22, 1913.

The appointment to high judicial office from a President to whom devoted friendship and admiration attaches me is one of life's richest prizes. Knowing that you consider only the public welfare, I value the esteem and confidence implied even more than the office itself.

Quite aside from any personal consideration, I am in thorough accord with you and the Attorney General as to the propriety of retirement at the age of seventy and after ten years of continuous service as provided by the Judiciary Act of 1911; and I have no hesitation in committing myself to that course. While some men are quite capable after that age, the work of the judicial office is now so hard that it is safer not to expect it of a man who has reached the age of retirement.

Permit me to express to you, Mr. President, my sincere and enthusiastic admiration of the course of the administration. I should like to express myself on the subject in a private talk on the deck of the "Ethiopia."[1] At all events, I indulge the hope of a few minutes call at some early day.

You need no assurance that your expressions of personal regard gave Mrs. Woods and me great satisfaction. Her health is improved, and she takes the deepest interest in your success.

I beg that you will express to Mrs. Wilson my congratulations and good wishes.   Sincerely yours,   C. A. Woods

TLS (WP, DLC).
[1] On which they were fellow passengers en route to Glasgow in 1896.

From the Diary of Josephus Daniels

Tuesday, April 22, 1913.

As soon as the Cabinet met this morning, the President said he would like to ask the views of the members of the Cabinet as to whether it would not be wise for him to request the Secretary of State to go to California and confer with the Governor and Members of the Legislature with reference to the pending bill relating to alien ownership of land. Since the last meeting of Cabinet, there has been a distinct change in California. It looked a week ago that the legislature in response to the suggestion of the President and the Secretary of State that the legislature [sic] would pass an act that would apply to all aliens and not only to the

Japanese. But yesterday the Governor of the State, a Roosevelt Republican, gave out a statement in favor of the bill as originally introduced which excludes ownership of land by the Japanese and Chinese, but no other aliens. This is very offensive to the Japanese who are very sensitive and and [sic] feel that it is a reflection upon their race.

The President thought Mr. Bryan, who is very popular in California, particularly with the labor people and others who mostly give their expression to the hostility against the Japanese, could tell them the legislation desired by the passage of the bill forbidding alien ownership without making the bill apply only to the Japs, and that he could do this by his presence better than by writing.

Secretary Garrison raised the question that it might make a precedent that would come up to give trouble in the future as well as now. It was a very serious question for the Secretary of State to go into any state to confer about pending legislation and that there would be resentment against it. It would be contrary to the old democratic doctrine of "States Rights," and that it might inflame the people and do more harm than good.

The President did not think that this would raise such a precedent because it was not supposed [proposed] to take any action or do anything limiting the states in their rights, but only to point out to legislators and the Executive that the state ought not to do anything that might be contrary to the treaties which the federal government had made with any foreign power. He said that it had never been determined by the courts whether a state was bound by any treaty stipulations and this was a matter still to be decided.

Secretary Lane, of California, believed that the people of California wished the most drastic law against the Japanese that could be enacted and that they were not in a mood to have anything but drastic laws but as Mr. Bryan is very popular in California, and if anybody could persuade them that the Kaminetti Bill which forbade all alien ownership should become a law, Mr. Bryan is the man that could do it. According to Mr. Lane, the most unpopular people in California, led by Harrison Gray Otis,[1] who is despised by the labor organizations[,] had advocated a conservative course and Governor Johnson, a politician, had seized upon the advocacy of a conservative measure by the unpopular force to advocate a more stringent measure and doing this to strengthen himself politically and to strengthen the progressive party.

Secretary Wilson thought that if Mr. Bryan went out to Cali-

[1] General Manager and editor of the *Los Angeles Times*, reactionary, anti-labor Republican.

fornia, not to carry any word from the Administration, demanding something to be done, but in the spirit of cooperating with
the people to secure what they desire in a way that would be the
least objectionable, it would be very well, but if he went in any
other way it would be with bad effect.

Mr. Bryan discussed at some length the matter, prefacing by
saying it was not a job he would solicit and that he had but one
spirit in coming into the Cabinet and that was to help and [be]
ready to do anything that the members of the Cabinet and the
President thought he ought to undertake. His idea was that nobody should go from the Administration to California unless
invited to do so by the California people. He suggested that inasmuch as the California people had put in their constitution the
referendum, it might be well to advocate the submitting to the
people the choice between the two acts—the one forbidding all
alien ownership and the one forbidding ownership by the Japanese and then whatever action they took the Administration
could say to the Japanese that the Administration is up against a
fact and it could not fly in the face of a registered will of the people of a whole state.

Secretary Lane raised this question: What would you advise
the democrats in California to do? Would you advise them to
vote for the conservative bill forbidding all alien ownership or for
the bill advocating the forbidding only Japanese ownership?

The President brought out the fact that four years ago when the
Californians were passing acts forbidding the Japanese from coming to public schools and Mr. Roosevelt were asking them to hold
it up, the democrats made political capital out of this; and if this
Administration urge the more modern [moderate] measure, the
progressive party would make capital out of it and put the democrats in the hole because that was theirs when Roosevelt was trying to control the matter. Mr. Bryan's suggestion of a referendum
to the people of California would not meet with favorable consideration as the general opinion being that the people of California would vote for the most stringent legislation against the
Japanese and instead of helping the diplomatic situation with
Japan, would complicate it. Moreover, it would be embarrassing
to the democrats and if they stood by the Administration, they
would have to change their position of four years ago and it would
be embarrassing for them to join against the measure. The President stated that he had that morning sent a telegram, which he
had given to the Press, to the members of the Assembly of California to do nothing to abridge treaty rights. But the general
opinion was that the Governor of Cal[i]fornia was playing politics

and nothing was to be expected from him that would help the Administration but on the contrary he would take the opposite view. While Mr. Bryan was stating his views, the President wrote a message which he stated he thought of sending to the legislators in California suggesting that Mr. Bryan will come out to confer with them if they desired it. Secretary McAdoo agreed with me that it would probably be best to wait until the President heard from his telegram he had given out this morning before any further message should pass and that was the course pursued.

T MS (J. Daniels Papers, DLC).

To Hiram Warren Johnson

[The White House] April 23, 1913

Thank you for your patriotic telegram. We find it so difficult from this distance to understand fully the situation with regard to the sentiments and circumstances lying back of the pending proposition concerning the ownership of land in the State that I venture to inquire whether it would be agreeable to you and the Legislature to have the Secretary of State visit Sacramento for the purpose of counseling with you and the members of the Legislature and cooperating with you and them in the framing of a law which would meet the views of the people of the State and yet leave untouched the international obligations of the United States.   Woodrow Wilson.

T telegram (Letterpress Books, WP, DLC).

To James Henry Taylor[1]

My dear Mr. Taylor: The White House April 23, 1913

I write to say that Mrs. Wilson and my daughters and I are hoping to become regular attendants at your church, and to ask what arrangements it is customary for regular members of the congregation to make. Are pews assigned to members of the congregation? or are all the pews free to be used by the congregation as they come in? If pews are assigned, I would be very much obliged if you would have such an assignment made to us as may be convenient, and I should like to assume the full obligation of pew rent, etc.

Cordially and sincerely yours,   Woodrow Wilson

TLS (NcMHi).
[1] Pastor of the Central Presbyterian Church of Washington, affiliated with the Presbyterian Church in the U.S. (southern).

From Hiram Warren Johnson

Sacramento, Calif., April 23, 1913.

I shall at all times be pleased to consult with the Secretary of State and it will be entirely agreeable to me to have the Secretary visit Sacramento as suggested in your telegram.

Hiram W. Johnson.

T telegram (WP, DLC).

From Elihu Root

Dear Mr. President   Washington. April 23 1913

I am much gratified by your note & by knowing that my little speech was a cause of satisfaction to you.

I think what I said the great mass of our people feel

Perhaps the habit of thinking much about the benefit & credit of our country as a whole in Foreign Affairs makes that feeling more naturally find expression from me.

With good wishes & kind regards I am

Faithfully Yours   Elihu Root

ALS (WP, DLC).

Remarks at a Press Conference

April 24, 1913

Mr. President, as regards the Secretary of State's expression of policy in the Senate yesterday,[1] could you elucidate or amplify that—his proposition of world peace?

Well, he gave you the terms of it, didn't he?

Well, I don't know that he did.

Of course, it lies in our mind at present only in the most general form. Negotiation would have to bring it down to details and particulars. But the general proposal is this— that the contracting parties should never go to war before there had been an investigation of the facts involved and a report; with no further engagements on either side, that is to say, not binding the parties to abide by any decision, if a decision was involved, as to the merits of the controversy, but merely agreeing to wait until impartial persons had looked into the circumstances and made a report.

It is a question you have given, I presume, considerable study?

Yes; it seems to me an admirable suggestion.

Has there been any suggestion as to which country should be

consulted first, or whether it should be done through a commission of all nations?

> I understand that Mr. Bryan—perhaps you gentlemen will know—sent for the representatives of all of the countries and laid it before them in a body so as to avoid discrimination.

Mr. President, there was struck out in the draft which was handed to the diplomatic representatives one sentence which was included when presented to the Senate Foreign Relations Committee, and it bore upon the matter of suspending warlike preparations during the period of investigation.

> It was stricken out, as I understand it, not because the Senate committee took exception to it at all, but because they thought that that was one of the details which had better be arranged by negotiation with each particular nation. You see, this was what lay in their minds: Suppose that we were in danger of a collision with some other country. While that other country and we might agree not to increase our armaments as towards each other, the very fact that there was danger of war might lead some third party to increase her armaments so as to get ready to pounce on the one or the other of us when we got into trouble. That was the difficulty they suggested, so they said they feared it would be difficult to bring about such an arrangement unless there could be a somewhat general international agreement to that effect, so that a third party would not take advantage of the difficulties that someone had gotten into that didn't affect them directly.

That apprehension is wholly ours? it didn't come from any foreign nation?

> It is purely theoretical.

T MS (C. L. Swem Coll., NjP).

¹ When Bryan discussed his peace plan with the Senate Foreign Relations Committee.

To Louis Dembitz Brandeis

My dear Mr. Brandeis: [The White House] April 24, 1913

Would you be generous enough to act as Chairman of the Commission on Industrial Relations which it is my duty and privilege to appoint? I am sure you know the object and scope of the inquiry set for the Commission. There is no one in the United States who could preside over and direct such an inquiry so well as you could, and I wonder if it is possible for you to strengthen the whole thing by assuming direction of it. It would gratify me very deeply if you could.

Cordially and sincerely yours,   Woodrow Wilson

TLS (Letterpress Books, WP, DLC).

From Lindley Miller Garrison

My dear Mr. President: Washington April 24, 1913.

CONCERNING THE PHILIPPINES.

It is so difficult for us to get together for a real talk that I think it better for me from time to time, as I think of important matters, to write you for mutual benefit.

I have been giving all the time that I could possibly spare from other duties to considering the Philippine situation, which, in the minds of all those who know anything about it, is esteemed to be of great importance to this country and of supreme importance to the Filipino people.

I have not had time yet to allow my ideas to settle, but such of those as are prominent enough to recur whenever I consider the matter, I wish to state to you.

It must be remembered that there are at least forty islands large enough to merit separate consideration; perhaps thirty different languages spoken; and something like thirty different strains of blood among the people. An approximation to homogeneity of purpose will be necessary before a cohesive federal government, independent of all other governments, could have hope of success. Whether any such situation exists, I do not know. Absolutely contrary opinions are given by those who seem to have had practically similar experience as a basis for judgment.

What I individually would do, had I complete jurisdiction in the premises, would be along these lines:

I would search for and obtain the most wide-awake, vigorous, well equipped man of insight, judgment and broad vision, that I could find, and I would make him Governor General. In commissioning him I would have you take occasion to outline the attitude of the Administration towards the Philippines. This is esteemed to be extremely important by all who know, irrespective of what solution of the problem each reaches. Its importance consists in its quieting effect upon the situation there. It is represented that those people are in a state of disquietude and unrest because they do not know our attitude. My own outline at present would start with a brief, comprehensive, compact statement of the problem; then a reference to the fact that this Administration, if it is to act wisely—particularly in view of the fact that it is asked to act permanently and irretrievably—must have time to gather from disinterested and sympathetic sources information; and then make and enact a wise conclusion. Therefore, there should not be, in our judgment, any irretrievable legislative determination, pending the inquiry, consideration and deliberation just spoken of as necessary.

I should state that the unquestioned doctrine, based upon the American tradition, previous statements of the Executive, and the frequent declarations by our party, was freedom, governmentally, of the Filipino people. For the purpose of demonstrating, in the only way capable of being demonstrated, that the Filipino people were capable of self-government, I should advise that, either by Executive action, if that is possible without further legislative enactment, or by legislative enactment, the Philippine legislature in both branches should be given a majority of Filipinos, retaining a veto power either in the Governor General or the Secretary of War or the President—an executive veto and not a legislative veto as is contained in one of the present Acts which permits Congress to annul laws of the Philippine legislature. This would only require a change in the selection of the Executive Council. The Executive Council, as you know, is now composed of appointive officers selected by the President, and is practically the Senate with the Cabinet contained therein. I should not substantially alter the present form of government, but I should appoint Filipinos to enough of the positions in the Executive Council to give them a majority there. Of course, they already wholly compose the second chamber. With a majority in both branches they would set about governing legislatively, and through Cabinet ministers largely administratively, their country. Careful observation would then be able within a relatively short time to determine their capacity. I would not at present suggest so radical a change as the election of the Executive Council. Such an election would in any event take a long time and be cumbersome. The Christian population of the Islands is supposed to be about 7,000,000, and at the last election for members of the second chamber there were only 240,000 votes cast. I really doubt whether there is enough cohesion at present to enable them to select from the whole body of the electorate properly qualified men for the Executive Council. I think their selection by us should still be retained. We would endeavor, of course, in selecting Filipinos to serve on this Council, to get the very best men and those who are most satisfactory to the people there.

I am not wedded to this scheme, but I have not been able to devise any other that so nearly fits the situation and so nearly shapes the matter up for our judgment in a way to make our judgment of real value. I consider that such a proposition has every particle of merit that is in the Jones bill,[1] without the very positive perils that every one who is unprejudiced sees in that bill. I realize that if no definite period is fixed when we will surely grant independence, we are always open to the suspicion and charge that we are not acting in good faith; but if we *are* acting in good faith and wisely, I am not in favor of doing otherwise merely to avoid unfounded charges and suspicions; and I am not willing personally to hazard a guess as to the date when a so-far insoluble puzzle will be solved.

I have not discussed this situation at all with the Filipino representatives as yet, not wishing in any way to commit the Administration to anything, as I desire first to have a full understanding with you. I have discussed this matter with leading Americans, among others, Senator Hitchcock, the Chairman of the Senate Committee having charge of Philippine Affairs; Mr. Jones, and others; and no one has raised an objection thereto which seemed to me to have any real weight.

I am very averse to asking a man who is so overburdened as you are at the present time, to give me sufficient time to make our interview worth while. I realize that a hasty conversation upon this Philippine matter would be a waste of our time. When you find yourself in a position that you can readily give me as much time as we both know is necessary, will you advise me?

As at present informed, I think we should not do more right off than name the Governor General. If he could proceed there immediately, he could work in with the Vice Governor and the other members of the Commission until somewhat acquainted with the situation. We could utilize the time in sifting out the great mass of material necessary to be sifted before we can get satisfactory men for the other positions. I would not attempt to fill the entire Commission now. It might be well, of course, to send out some other one or two than the Governor General. All this will be made the subject matter of our talk and consideration.

Sincerely yours,   Lindley M. Garrison

TLS (WP, DLC).
¹ About which, see WW to O. W. Underwood, July 19, 1912, n. 1, Vol. 24.

From James Henry Taylor

My dear Mr President: [Washington] April 24th, 1913.

Your very kind letter has been received and we are very much gratified that you and your family are to be regular attendants at the Central Church. We want to assure you of a most cordial welcome to our church and of our sincere appreciation that you will worship with us.

I would like to express my personal gratitude to you and your family both for your past courtesies and for this renewed expression of confidence. I shall endeavor to be loyal to this responsibility in every way.

Though we have no pew rents, our people generally occupy the same seats regularly. We shall therefore be very glad to assign seats to yourself and family so that you may feel perfectly at home in our church.

With grateful appreciation and sincere regard,

Yours faithfully   James H. Taylor.

ALS (WP, DLC).

James Bryce to Sir Edward Grey

Sir,   Washington, 24th April 1913.

I have the honour to inform you that I to-day called upon the President of the United States to present my letters of recall. In the course of our conversation I asked him whether there was anything which he wished me to communicate to you and he replied that he did not think the time had yet come when he could usefully take action in the matter of the Panama Canal Tolls question. He explained in the same sense as, though more shortly than, the Secretary of State had done some days ago to me, the difficulties in which his Administration was placed by the Tariff Bill and the efforts he had to make to secure the passage of that measure and he observed that there would be so much desire to embarrass the Administration and to use the introduction of any new topic as a means of injuring the prospects of the Tariff Bill that he thought it was the course of prudence to wait until that question had been disposed of. His mind was evidently so made up upon that particular point that it was no use pressing him upon it, and it is not to be denied that the political circumstances which move him have some weight, for it would be all that the Administration can do to get the tariff bill through although at present its prospects are favourable.

When I asked him whether he thought that the Panama question could be taken up this session when the bill was fairly in port, he replied that he was afraid Congress would be too exhausted and the weather too hot to attempt that and that he did not think he could usefully act on the matter before the regular meeting of Congress in December. He observed that more progress would be made by endeavouring to get Congress and especially members of the Senate to see the thing in the way in which he saw it and to make the action that they took appear to be their own action rather than dictated by him, than there would be by his openly coming forward, and pressing them on the subject. I told him that I personally had never doubted what his own attitude and wishes would be and that I assumed it would be his endeavour to secure either the repeal of the coastwise exemption or else arbitration. He said that it was his desire and purpose to settle the matter in a way that would be satisfactory to us by arbitration or by the repeal of the coastwise exemption or in some other way such as a variation of the agreement and arrangement now binding on the two countries. On my remarking that if he liked to say something indicating his intentions in such a form that I could convey them to you he might do so, he did not take the opportunity of delivering himself categorically but on the other hand he gave a tacit consent to all the sentiments which I attributed to him as being those which I understood him to hold. I do not doubt his sincerity in the matter and those who know him share my opinion, so I do not think anything would be gained by a categorical summons to express himself in a categorical way, even confidentially.

In the course of our conversation the question of the renewal of the General Arbitration Treaty came up and he expressed the entire willingness of his Government that it should be renewed. I told him His Majesty's Government thought also that it should be renewed and we agreed that if this were to be done it had better be done soon. He expected no difficulty from its acceptance by the Senate and observed that several other countries were going to renew their treaties also. . . .

I may say that before writing this and the last preceding despatch I had conversations with two of those friends of ours[1] whose judgment I most value and that the line which I have ventured to indicate as apparently the best for His Majesty's Government to follow is the result not only of my own reflection but of what I have gathered from them.

I have the honour to be, With the highest respect, Sir,

Your most obedient, humble Servant, James Bryce

TLS (FO 371/1702, No. 20528, PRO).
[1] Undoubtedly Senators Root and Lodge.

To Charles Albert Woods

My dear Friend: [The White House] April 25, 1913
Thank you warmly for your letter of the twenty-second. It was quite like you in every respect. I thank you for it with all my heart. I sent in the nomination to the Senate yesterday, and hope and believe that it will be promptly confirmed.
With the warmest regard, in haste
Faithfully yours,   Woodrow Wilson

TLS (Letterpress Books, WP, DLC).

Remarks at a Press Conference

April 28, 1913
Mr. President, there has been considerable discussion, probably you have seen here in the last week, about the Panama Canal tolls. Is there anything that you can say on that, that you feel that you can say?
> There is nothing new on that at all. There is no pending action.
There is no pending action?
> No, I haven't taken it up within the last two or three weeks at all.
There is a general impression, Mr. President, that your view agrees with Senator Root's. Are you willing to say whether—what your own idea is?
> I must say that I think it is a very debatable subject. I thought at one time it had only one side, but I have come to believe it has two sides.
You are still considering the matter, Mr. President?
> Not actively, because it isn't pending.
Do you mind telling us, Mr. President, which side you thought it was?
> Well, perhaps I had better not tell you where I began or you might guess where I am going to land.
Mr. President, are we warranted then in assuming that your mind isn't made up?
> I want to say to you men very frankly that I try until the moment of action to keep my mind absolutely open on a subject and not make it up, because I don't think that is the way for public men to do when action isn't necessary. When action is necessary, I will have an opinion.
Is it a fair question, Mr. President—I mean it to be—do you regard limitation of armaments in the proposed peace treaties of Mr. Bryan as essential?

You mean the limitation of armaments as an essential feature?

An essential feature, yes, sir.

I think it is an essential feature. It may be embarrassing and difficult to get it embodied unless a very considerable number of nations combine in those agreements, because of the difficulty I was explaining last week of a third party going forward with exceptional preparations while the others were standing still, and so taking advantage of a situation unfairly. But I think everybody would admit that it was a very natural part of such an agreement that Mr. Bryan had in mind.

My notion of it is that it would be very difficult to get done.

I don't know. You never can tell until you try. I think that the whole temper of the opinion of the world now is so in favor of doing the reasonable thing for the promotion of peace that we needn't despair of accomplishing a great deal. Mr. Bryan's suggestion to the representatives of the other nations was very kindly received, and the one or two of them who made comment upon it—they made very favorable comment.

That was with reference to that idea—

With reference to that proposal on an agreement to have everything looked into before hostilities resulted.

Have you heard anything, Mr. President, from Secretary Bryan this morning or from the California end of it? There has been nothing new on the Japanese question?

Nothing at all, no. Nothing since we last spoke, or I mean since the interviews with the Japanese Ambassador that you all know about.

Last week?

Yes.

Is there anything new in the matter of the 5 per cent clause in the tariff bill that affects the treaties?

No, there is nothing new.

You anticipate going to the Capitol this week, Mr. President?

I don't know. I never know until a few hours beforehand whether it is convenient or not.

Mr. President, referring again to the California-Japanese situation, it appears from the dispatches that the California legislature is determined to utilize the phrase "eligible to citizenship" in some form in the bill. Would the use of that phrase, "eligible to citizenship," be still considered by the administration here and perhaps by the Japanese government, as a discrimination?

Well, I feel this way about it. I don't think we need discuss it on the basis of the speculations that come from Sacramento, because I don't think any of us knows the real state of mind out there, and I am waiting until Mr. Bryan gets here, and then I will feel that I really know what is going on.

JRT transcript (WC, NjP) of CLSsh (C. L. Swem Coll., NjP).

A Telegram and a Letter from William Jennings Bryan

Sacramento, Calif., April 28, 1913.

Spent two hours answering questions. Two questions which I was requested to submit to you were as follows: First, When the President advised against the words "ineligible to citizenship" did he know that Arizona passed a law in 1913 including those words, and that Washington passed a law in 1909 including those words, and if he did not know of those statutes then does he still advise against those words now that he does know of those statutes. Second, Did Japan protest when the law of Arizona and Washington were enacted and if not why does she protest against the passage of a similar statute in California. I answered the first that whether you knew of the Washington and Arizona statutes or not I felt sure that they would not change your views as to the advisability of avoiding the words "ineligible to citizenship." I could not answer second question. I would like an answer to both questions to submit tomorrow morning. I understand that Washington is considering a proposition to change her law and I am wiring the Governor of Washington for information. Think majority still incline to use words "ineligible to citizenship." I have been asked what you would do if legislature passed bill containing words, "ineligible to citizenship." I answered that I was not prepared to answer the question without further information from you.   Bryan.

T telegram (WP, DLC).

✧

My dear Mr. President: Sacramento, Cal., April 28, 1913.

I saw Mr. Phelan today and asked him whether he would consider an offer of the Austrian Embassy. He was pleased that you should feel such confidence in him and, while not deciding positively, felt that he would regard acceptance as a duty as well as a pleasure if he could accept with the understanding that he would not be expected to stay four years. He said that he did not care to make diplomacy his career, but that he could stay as long as a year and probably two years, but would not want to promise more than that. I told him that I felt sure that you would consent to his retirement at the end of two years and that I thought you would not insist upon his remaining longer than a year if at the end of a year he felt it necessary to resign. I told him to let you know at once in case he, upon reflection, decided that he could not accept. If you do not hear from him by next Monday, I think it would be safe for you to wire him offering him the place. As he is not married, I asked him whether his sister would go with him. She lives with him. I told him I thought he would find her necessary in the entertaining that is required. . . .

With assurances of respect, I am, my dear Mr. President,

Yours truly,   W. J. Bryan

TLS (WP, DLC).

To William Jennings Bryan

[The White House] April 29, 1913

It seems to me clear that the responsibilities of the administration in dealing with the case before it does not extend to state laws passed at other times and with reference to which it has not been called upon to take action. Replying to the inquiry what I would do if the Legislature passed a bill containing the words ineligible to citizenship or their equivalent I can only say that I can not assume that the representations heretofore made to the Governor and Legislature of California and which your presence in Sacramento must necessarily have greatly emphasized will be disregarded and so render it necessary to consider that question.   Woodrow Wilson.

T telegram (Letterpress Books, WP, DLC).

From William Jennings Bryan

Sacramento, Calif., April 29, 1913.

One of the members suggested yesterday that California might permit land ownership by the citizens of those nations which permit Americans to own land within their jurisdiction. I answered that the objection to it was that it allowed our land laws to be determined by the land laws of other nations adding that while the present laws of Japan prohibited foreign ownership the law was evaded by long term leases some as long as nine hundred and ninety nine years and that Japan had passed a law not yet in effect extending ownership on certain terms to foreigners. It occurs to me however on reflection that as a last resort it might be wise for you to advise the passage of such a bill instead of a bill containing the words "ineligible to citizenship." It might carry them through the present crisis and give time for diplomatic effort without seeming to. In other words it might meet the exigencies of the case and give us time to negotiate with the Japanese for the prevention of further ownership. The offer that has been suggested is as follows: quote. No alien shall be permitted to own or lease lands in California provided however that this prohibition shall not apply to the citizens of any nation which grants free and unrestricted right of land ownership to the citizens of this country. End quote. Such a law could not be objected to by the Japanese because in the law they now have under consideration they use the same condition for the protection of their citizens. As I said before this law could only be temporary in its effect because Japan would probably remove her restrictions in order to give her citizens acces[s] to the land unless we could by diplomatic negotiations prevent it. But as a temporary settlement of the question it commends itself to my judgement and I would like to have your opinion on the proposition as soon as possible.

Bryan.

T telegram (WP, DLC).

To William Jennings Bryan

[The White House] April 29, 1913.

Hope you will feel free to spend Wednesday in San Francisco, as you suggest. I feel that it is inadvisable to sanction particular statutes or forms of legislation. Our wise course seems to me to be to make it emphatically evident that we are acting just now not as the Federal government, sanctioning this or that but as the sincere friends of California, wishing to be of such service as possible to them in a critical matter whose importance and whose critical character we are better able to advise them of than others would be. The difficulty about sanctioning a particular form of words or of enactment is that it might estop or embarrass us in subsequent judicial action or international negotiation. Our advice should be along general lines and as if we spoke as sincere and by no means unsympathetic friends of California, and yet as [not] unmindful of our serious obligations to a friendly Nation. Whatever their final action, we must reserve our independence to pursue the course deemed best in the circumstances. In your present intimate association with the gentlemen there, you can easily make this clear.

With warm appreciation of what you are doing.

Woodrow Wilson.

T telegram (Letterpress Books, WP, DLC).

From William Jennings Bryan

Sacramento, Calif., April 29, 1913.

At Executive session held tonight I presented your answers and made clear your position. No vote has been taken but lines are being drawn. There will be a determined effort to pass a bill containing words "ineligible to citizenship" or words meaning the same thing. The effort will be opposed however, with possibility of defeating it. Your position has gained friends and they are prepared to fight. I am not sure that I can do anything further, but it might be well to return Thursday morning and look over the situation. After reading my speeches and my answers to questions you can inform me at San Francisco, tomorrow, whether I have left anything undone. Those who favor radical action spoke tonight as if they did not care to hear anything more, and were prepared to use "ineligible to citizenship," in spite of your advice.

Bryan.

T telegram (WP, DLC).

To William Jennings Bryan

CONFIDENTIAL.   [The White House] April 29, 1913

Answering your second telegram of today cordially approve your suggestions made in executive session; only beg that it be made clear that we are acting in a merely advisory character and not undertaking to settle beforehand questions of law or policy that may subsequently arise.   Woodrow Wilson.

T telegram (Letterpress Books, WP, DLC).

To George Wilkins Guthrie

[The White House] April 29, 1913

Hope that I may have your consent to nominate you minister[1] to Japan.[2] With your consent shall approach Japanese government on the subject immediately.   Woodrow Wilson.

T telegram (Letterpress Books, WP, DLC).
[1] Swem misread his notes. Wilson said "ambassador."
[2] Guthrie accepted the ambassadorship.

From Louis Dembitz Brandeis

My dear Mr. President: Boston, Mass. April 29, 1913.

With your permission, I will defer for about a week answering your most kind letter of the 24th tendering me the Chairmanship of the Commission on Industrial Relations; as the Interstate Commerce Commission hearings on our New England transportation monopoly are absorbing my whole attention for the present.

Meanwhile I shall be glad to have Mr. Tumulty send me a copy of the Act creating the Commission.

Very cordially yours,   Louis D Brandeis

TLS (WP, DLC).

From William Jennings Bryan

San Francisco, Calif., April 30, 1913.

Do not rely on newspaper reports. They are inaccurate. Indications this morning are favorable. Believe it possible to secure the passage of harmless law if action cannot be delayed. Number of strong men in Legislature will urge respect for your wishes. If a law must be passed am unofficially and without committing you expressing preference for law limiting ownership to aliens from countries permitting American ownership. This would temporarily stop land purchases and we could urge Japanese Government not to change law. If Japanese Government changed its law knowing California's feeling, it would become responsible for further agitation. I believe we could persuade Japanese to make restriction permanent by retaining their present law. Am strongly advising against new bill published this morning[1] because it contains discriminating language relating to citizenship. Am careful to emphasize fact that you (that you)—are not? —indorsing any measure but simply advising as friend. Governor Johnson much impressed by your attitude. He manifests growing inclination? respect your advice. He may (favor?) limiting ownership to aliens from countries permitting American ownership. Answer San Francisco.   Bryan.

T telegram (WP, DLC).

[1] Drawn by Ulysses Sigel Webb, Attorney General of California, it provided that all aliens "eligible to citizenship" might own land in California on the same terms as American citizens and that other aliens might hold land "in the manner and to the extent and for the purposes prescribed by any treaty now existing between the Government of the United States and the nation or country of which such alien is a citizen or subject." The California Senate unanimously approved the Webb bill on April 29. The full text of the statute, enacted on May 19, 1913, is printed in FR 1913, pp. 627-28.

To Hiram Warren Johnson

[The White House] April 30, 1913.

I take the liberty of calling your attention to the Webb bill which would involve an appeal to the courts on question of treaty rights and bring on what might be long and delicate litigation.

Woodrow Wilson.

T telegram (Letterpress Books, WP, DLC).

From Samuel Gompers

Sir: Washington, D. C., April 30, 1913.

Since the important matter concerning which, under date of March 14, I wrote you, is still a vital issue which must be determined in the near future, and I am still unavoidably prevented from seeking the privilege of a personal conference with you, yet as I am solicitous for the welfare of those whose interests I represent, the urgent necessity of the situation impels me to present in writing for your consideration further reasons why the enactment of legislation removing the working people as such from prosecution under and from the operation of the Sherman Antitrust law would be in the interest of justice and freedom, and a great service to humanity. . . .[1]

The fact, then, that organizations not for profit but for securing humanitarian benefits for the workers, would be exempt from the application of the provisions of the Sherman Antitrust law would not constitute a reason for declaring the measure unconstitutional—such a decision would depend upon whether there is a real and inherent difference between the voluntary associations of working people, (organized not for profit,) and monopolies or combinations whose sole purpose is profit; or upon whether the application of the law to the two kinds of organizations would produce similar results.

Such differences do exist. Organizations of labor have their origin in human need; they seek human welfare and betterment; they have to do with human labor power. Capitalistic monopolies have their origin in desire for great profits; they seek economic control and the elimination of competitive rivals; they deal in material things, the products of labor, wealth. Between wealth and labor there is a vital and fundamental difference, an under-

---

[1] In one paragraph of the omitted portion, Gompers quoted from one of Wilson's campaign speeches in 1912 to the effect that, since working people constituted the backbone of the nation, no legislation in their interest could be called class legislation.

standing of which is essential to those upon whom falls the responsibility of dealing with matters influencing the freedom of men. Wealth consists in material things, which are external, useful and appropriable. Wealth is that which a man has, not what he is. To classify skill, knowledge, labor power as wealth is an error that has crept into the thinking of some economists and political scientists. It is an error conducive to grave injury to the working people. . . .

Legislation recognizing the inherent difference between these two kinds of organizations could not be condemned as unconstitutional on the charge of unjustifiable discrimination. . . .

A free man has the right to bestow or withhold his labor power and his patronage whenever or wherever he may wish. To gainsay this right is to deny freedom. Since no individual is given any legal or inherent proprietary right in a man's labor power or patronage, he cannot be aggrieved or afforded grounds for action when they are withheld from him. Labor power and patronage are what make the individual workman effective and forceful— they constitute his principal protection and means of self-expression. They must be guarded as the foundation of individual freedom, the precious birthright of a man free to be himself and to possess his own soul.

Not only must the theoretical right to bestow or withhold labor power and patronage be maintained, but this must be given reality and effectiveness by permitting men to pursue lawful courses of action in exercising this right. If the end is lawful and worthy, then the means for attaining that end must also be recognized as legal and necessary. Justice must be reasonable and practical. There has been an attempt—it matters not whether consciously or unconsciously—to build up a legal fiction which tends to nullify these rights by discrediting and misrepresenting the means by which they are exercised. . . .

Hostile lawyers, lawyers paid to present the cases of their clients, judges under domination of the employer's and the legalist's viewpoint, have misrepresented and perverted acts and purposes of the workingmen to make them appear criminal and destructive, whereas the guiding purpose animating the labor movement is not destruction but construction, completion and perfection of general welfare. It is charged that workingmen conspire to destroy business when they withhold labor power or patronage, pending the securement of specific rights. As a matter of fact, destroying business would frustrate the end sought. This legal fiction, called destroying business, arises out of confusing the physical property with the immaterial something called good will which is dependent on reputation and patronage. This latter emanates from individuals outside business, it has a direct relation to business, but it is not business. For detracting from this, either individually or collectively, workingmen cannot any more be charged with destroying business than can competitors who build up their business at the expense of others engaged in the same line. Workingmen have the right to pursue policies for their welfare which may entail financial losses upon employers. To be sure, the employer has a right to his property and a right to do business, but that is a general right, not a specific one. He is not guaranteed the right to be protected against all hazards in a particular business. That, I take it, is the principle involved in the reduction of tariff, even though that may mean some decrease in the employers' profits. . . .

Since the Sherman Antitrust law has been so interpreted as to increase these limitations, Labor has found the right to unite for mutual protection but a mere legalistic expression of an ideal state. The law as now interpreted has the effect of stultifying labor organizations and prohibiting the exercise of necessary powers. What we seek is not special privilege, immunity from prosecution for crimes, but the right to do those things necessary to organizations accomplishing a real work for human workers. . . .

Our opponents simulate great alarm as to the disastrous effects of the boycott. But is that such a new and anarchistic device? Quite the contrary. It is a weapon that has been successfully used for good purposes by men of all times. Our revolutionary fathers used it most effectively to defeat what they considered the unjust demands of the English Government. Will you pardon another personal reference, for the placards as reproduced in the second volume of your "History of the American People," illustrate my point so nicely? The one on page 159 is an "unfair list"; on page 162 is a "conspiracy" agreement; on page 173, an unmistakable boycotting poster, though conceived in patriotism and ended reverently with "for ever and ever, AMEN.". . .

The boycott in itself cannot, it appears, be condemned as pernicious, illegal, or a class weapon. But Mr. Taft maintains that if the strike and the boycott should be used wickedly, deliberately and cruelly, there would be no recourse under the Sherman Antitrust law, should the provision Labor demands be made into law. Mr. Taft is quite right. That status is exactly right and proper. However, Mr. Taft fails to add that should the workingmen be guilty of violence or crime they can be and are punished under existing statutes. . . .

I must ask for your patience and forbearance in addressing such a lengthy letter to you.[2] I do not wish to appear as gratuitously offering you an argument upon this subject, upon which in all likelihood, you are as fully, if not more fully, informed than I. But I can only plead my deep concern for this legislation, a matter that lies very close to my heart and vitally affects the interests of those whom I officially represent and to whose welfare I have long devoted my thought and efforts. We represent great human interests, human lives and hearts that are seeking a better, higher life.

I have been encouraged to write this letter by two facts. First, the attempts of the press to pre-judge your position, to endeavor to anticipate and place you in a false position, and the attacks made upon you by every newspaper antagonistic to your election to the Presidency of the United States as well as those hostile to the rights and interests of the working people of the country, which will criticize, attack and misrepresent any one who may defend the rights of the toilers. In the second place, that you had an interview with Representative Fitzgerald and Senators Martin and Hughes—the latter the author of the original exemption amendment offered to the Sundry Civil Appropriations bill of 1910—and that Representative Fitzgerald, as chairman of the Committee on Appropriations, has introduced the bill containing the same amendments with which it was passed by both houses of Congress and was presented to President Taft, give me the impression, or lead me to draw the inference that the bill when passed by Congress will have, as I earnestly trust it will have, your approval.

A sense of duty and the obligation devolving upon me, impel me to offer you, in this way, whatever of information or experience I have bearing upon this matter. I feel it my duty to you, the chosen President of our people, to be helpful in every way that lies within my power, and I feel it my duty to the working people and all the citizens of the United States to present the cause of justice and human welfare as fully and as clearly as lies within my power, that our argument may be available for your use in determining your course upon this issue fraught with such tremendous possibilities for weal or woe directly to millions of people, and generally to all the people of our common country.

Sincerely and respectfully yours,

Saml. Gompers
President
American Federation of Labor.

TLS (WP, DLC).
[2] It is twenty-three pages long.

From Henry Jones Ford

Baguio, Philippine Islands

My dear President Wilson: April 30, 1913

I arrived at Manila on April 13th from the tour of the Southern Islands which I began on March 20th. I visited all the important points, my tour extending as far as Mati on the Pacific coast of Mindanao and as far South as Jolo, where I found a very strange situation. The American colony was virtually in a state of siege and we could not go outside of the walls without an armed guard. I arrived here at Baguio on April 16th and then for the first time I began to get information from official sources.

The notions with which I came from the States have long since been thrown overboard and I have acquired new ones that are now in such orderly shape, that I have been able to plan my report and I have it already partly prepared.

I expect to leave here on May 6th, for a trip of about a week along the western coast to the extreme North of Luzon. Speaker Osmeña[1] will be one of the party. After that excursion I shall go to Manila, of which city I have as yet seen little. There I expect to get some idea of views and opinions in the business world.

After a good deal of suspense and after passing through periods of perplexity, I now feel that I understand the Philippine situation quite as well as I should be able to do by remaining any longer in the Islands, so I am planning to start for home on May 28th by the Prinz Ludwig of the North German Lloyd, taking the Suez route. I shall bring my report with me, as I shall probably get it to you in person as fast as I could by mail. I expect to arrive in New York some time between the 10th and 15th of July.

A pretty thorough examination of the government departments has convinced me that in exactness of accounting and in integrity of official behavior, Philippine administration will compare favorably with anything we can show in the United States. Whatever else may be said about Governor General Forbes, he is a first rate business man, firm in his maintenance of high standards. This explains some of the bitterness of the attacks made upon him. One vendetta that is now operating against him in the United States is believed to arise from a transaction here in Baguio. An official who bought a lot, resold it in a few weeks to a Filipino at an advance of 650 pesos. Governor Forbes heard of the transaction and although the gain was small, ($325 in our money) he sent for the official and told him that for a person in his position to speculate in Baguio town lots was an impropriety that could not be tolerated and that he must turn over the profit to the town treasury. The official concerned did not comply until several months elapsed, when he finally succumbed to Governor Forbes' insistence, although not admitting that he had done anything wrong or that Governor Forbes had any right to interfere.

The situation in the Philippines impresses me as being very grave, and I believe that it requires radical treatment, but I think it would be a great mistake to imagine that the defects are due to administrative misconduct or that they could be remedied by putting in a better class of men. The defects are such as arise naturally out of the policy adopted, and the remedy lies far more in a change of policy than in a change of men. I have not been able to discover anything in administrative conditions that calls for present action nor indeed any reason why you should not postpone any administrative change until you have decided what policy you shall adopt as regards the relations between the United States and these Islands.

I have been so absorbed in the study of conditions here that I have lapsed into opaque ignorance as regards home politics, but I presume that you are immersed in tariff problems. My cordial sympathy and fervent good wishes are with you in your attack on the Augean Stables.

Howard[2] joins me in desiring that you present our compliments to Mrs. Wilson and your daughters.

Most faithfully yours,   Henry J. Ford

TLS (WP, DLC).
  [1] Sergio Osmeña, speaker of the Philippine Assembly, 1907-16; President of the Philippine Commonwealth, 1944-46.
  [2] His son, John Howard Ford.

Rudolph Forster to Joseph Patrick Tumulty

The White House [May] 1 [1913]

Following telegram received in cipher addressed to the President from Secretary Bryan Sacramento, quote: I have just conferred with the Governor and Attorney General Webb, author of the Senate amendment. They are considering your telegram and seem anxious to avoid as much as possible any language against which you advise. I have suggested that the phrase eligible to citizenship would be as offensive as the phrase ineligible to citizenship and that instead of using any discriminating words they might say that all aliens whose right to hold real estate had not been made a matter of treaty agreement could hold as citizens and that all aliens whose right to hold real estate had been made a matter of treaty agreement could according to the treaty. That would avoid the words eligible or ineligible but would not remove the necessity for judicial construction. I would be glad to have your opinion of situation wired you yesterday as to limiting the rights of aliens to hold land and the rights granted Americans in the lands from which the aliens come. This proposition also under consideration by the legislators end quote.   Forster

T telegram (WP, DLC).

To William Jennings Bryan

[Newark, N. J., May 1, 1913]

Think your suggestion that language be aliens whose right to hold real estate has been made a matter of treaty and so forth is excellent if immediate legislation is still insisted on as I earnestly hope it will not be. Please feel at liberty to use your own judgment as to how long it is necessary or best for you to stay. You can judge best and I shall heartily concur. Your presence and influence have had most excellent effect.

Woodrow Wilson.

T telegram (Letterpress Books, WP, DLC).

From William Jennings Bryan

Sacramento, Calif., May 1, 1913.

Have just seen Governor Johnson. He says that after bill reaches him for his signature, he will allow you a reasonable time to consider its language and to submit same to Japanese Ambassador. He will be pleased to have your views upon it.

Bryan.

T telegram (WP, DLC).

From the Diary of Colonel House

May 1, 1913.

I went to the Pennsylvania Station at 10.45 and had about one minute to get to the lower level when the President's special train came in. He was alone with the exception of Tumulty, Secret Service men and newspaper reporters. Two automobiles were waiting besides ours, but he got into ours with one Secret Service man in front with our chauffeur, and about ten others on motor cycles in front and as many more behind. There was a great tooting of horns, stoppage of traffic and a staring public as we motored swiftly through the streets.

When we came upstairs we had some sandwiches and while we ate them we talked for more than an hour about the collectorship and Senator O'Gorman's attitude. The President is afraid it [if] he antagonizes him at this particular time he may imperil his legislative program in the Senate. He said the situation was not good at best; that he had talked this morning to O'Gorman and some Western Senators, I think from the States of Colorado, Kansas, Montana, Oregon and Nevada.

We talked continuously about the O'Gorman matter until 12.15. He was much disturbed. I did not force any particular view upon him, although he could see that I was clearly of the opinion that he should make a stand against O'Gorman's contention that a Senator has practically the appointing power rather than the Executive. O'Gorman holds that it is necessary for the President to advise with the Senators before an appointment is made, and he believes that a Senator should suggest names. He believes that a President cannot go outside the list as suggested. It virtually makes the President abrogate his right of appointing.

An Address on Jury Reform at Newark, New Jersey[1]

[May 1, 1913]

Mr. Chairman and fellow citizens: It is with very deep and genuine pleasure that I find myself in New Jersey again. I know of no greater satisfaction than speaking for the people of this great state. For I have not come to speak *to* you. I know what you believe in; I know what you want. I have come to speak for you, and to these men with whom we are dealing. I want to tell them what it is their business to do. For we are their masters; they are not ours.

It made all my pulses beat quick again to think I was going to come back and speak for these people in this great County of Essex, that wants to govern itself and does not. The most amazing thing to me about Essex, through all my life in New Jersey, has been the number of aggressive, intelligent, independent men in this great county, and the failure of these men to grapple with the situation and master their own county and city governments. You are not governed by yourselves in Essex. But there come

1 Delivered at the New Auditorium. Louis Hood, prosecutor of pleas of Essex County, presided and introduced Wilson. Assemblyman John Alphonsus Matthews of Newark also spoke.

times when the great voice of the people of this county speaks out in such volume that even those who ordinarily dare to aspire to mastery cower under the voice of the real master. That is what has to be done now.

I have exercised a great deal of self-denial about New Jersey. When I had to make up my mind where I was going to spend next summer, after I got back from the Panama Canal, my great temptation was to come back and pitch my tent near where I used to pitch it on the shore. And I was withheld by this considera-tion, my fellow citizens: There is going to be a contest for the governorship of this state—for the nomination for the governor-ship—next summer, and I did not want anybody to suppose that I was coming back to try to boss the job. I have no candidate for the Democratic nomination for the governorship of this state; but I am opposed to whoever is desired for governor by certain gentlemen whom I shall have the pleasure of naming tonight. I do not want to see any more governors of New Jer-sey privately owned. I do not want to see any more governors of New Jersey privately manipulated by hands that were not dis-closed to the people themselves. I am going to New Hampshire next summer. New Hampshire is in telegraphic communication with New Jersey, and anybody who wants to know what I think can find it out by asking the question. But I am going just as far away from New Jersey as it is convenient to go, so that no-body may think I had come here as if to nominate a choice for a people that I have labored for as I have never labored for anything else, to set free to make their own choices.

That was the whole object of the electoral reform for which we fought so hard, and, thank God, fought so successfully, while I was Governor of New Jersey—to set the people free to make their own selections, not personally conducted; selections not suggested by people who undertook to make the government of the state their own private business, but exercised in the open, under discussion, under scrutiny, under canvass of all the worthy names that are to be considered in so great a connection.

I want to say a few words about the Democratic party. I want everybody to realize that I, at any rate, have not been "taken in" by the results of the last national election. The country did not go Democratic in November. It was impossible for it to go Republican, because it couldn't tell which kind of Republican to go. The only united and hopeful instrument through which it could accomplish its purposes was the Democratic party. And what it did was to say this: "There are certain things that we want to see done, not certain persons whom we wish to see

elevated. There are certain things that we want to have demonstrated; as, for example, that the Government of the United
States can no longer be controlled by special interests. Now, we
are going to have a trial at using the Democratic party as our
instrument to discover these things. If the trial is not successful,
we will never make it again. We want an instrument in our
hands by which to make ourselves masters of our own affairs,
and it looks likely in the existing circumstances that this is the
suitable and ready instrument. Therefore, we will try it—not
adopt it—try it."

You know what happened to the Democratic party in this
state. It got so confident of power about sixteen years ago—nearly
twenty years ago now—that it supposed that the people of New
Jersey had gone to sleep and had entrusted it with their fortunes,
and were asking no questions any more. Therefore, that power
was grossly and abominably abused, and the people turned away
from that party for twenty years almost, because it had betrayed
its trust. Then they turned to it again in 1910 to make trial
whether this long dwelling in the wilderness had purged this
party or not; to see whether the evil spirits had been baked out
of it under the sun of the desert; to see whether this was a
rejuvenated, a renewed, a chastened party. And the first thing
they wanted to know was whether the old gang still ran it or
not. Well, I will not go into the history of the two years that followed. Suffice it to say that the old gang did not run it; that they
kept under cover even in the lobbies at Trenton, knowing that
there were fingers that would point them out to the whole country
if they wished to come there and display themselves.

These gentlemen do not like the open. They don't like to have
the limelight shine upon them. They tremble in the spotlight.
Then I was told that just so soon as I went to Washington the
old gang would come back; and I didn't believe it—until I saw it.
Once more that bulky form of the gentleman[2] who used to personally lead the legislature of New Jersey into disgrace reap-
peared upon the very floor of the legislature, and again it was
known that his intrigues were successful in blocking the things
that he did not wish done. Am I mistaken? Have you not heard
it, that the same old gang that had for two years been scotched
had not been killed? It was the System, with a capital snake-
like S-s-s-s, that great s-s-sneaking, whis-s-spering s-s-system that
established itself again in Trenton. And why has it established
itself? Because something was afoot that it could not afford to
allow to be done.

[2] James R. Nugent.

As I came in Mr. Matthews was referring to the circumstance that at the hearing against the jury bill the room was lined with sheriffs of the various counties or with their representatives. Nothing has distressed me more than that. New Jersey is at present full of honest sheriffs. But they are not all honest, and we are not gunning for the honest ones. But the ways of the dishonest are just as astute as they are devious. They can let their grand juries indict at the strategic and dramatic moment, and they can also withhold their grand juries from indicting when everything is quiet and there is no storm on the horizon. And you know perfectly well that the mastery in politics of some gentlemen who assume to dominate New Jersey would be impossible if the things that they did were subjected to the ordinary scrutiny of discretionately-drawn grand juries. We passed a very stringent electoral reform, intended to put the government of the state in your hands, but if the grand jury's hand is withheld at chosen moments, what good is it that you go to the polls and vote? Who counts the votes? Who controls the management of the polls? How, then, will the crimes committed against the ballot be brought before your judges? I managed to give you two judges[3] who were not afraid of the system. At last, in the fullness of time, I managed to give you a prosecutor[4] who was not afraid of the system. And that prosecutor saw without spectacles things which I myself from a distance had pointed out to the authorities of this city as much as a year before. It did not require spectacles to see them! Everybody knew that they were there; but the hand of the law was withheld.

Do you want a system under which it is possible to withhold the hand of the law? Do you want a system under which it is possible to choose when the hand of the law shall be withheld and when it shall not? Ah, gentlemen, I tell you the process of corruption in the justice of this country does not lie so often where it is supposed that it lies—with the men who preside over the trial of cases—as it lies with the system which determines who shall feel the pinch of the law and who shall not. And the poor man, the uninfluential man, the man who does not stand in with the gang, will feel the pinch of the law and the other man will not. It is a disgrace to the judicial system of the state and of the Union, and I come here to protest against it, as a representative American citizen, that such things should be allowed to exist. And look at the apparent reasonableness of the whole thing—how honest men allowed themselves to be played upon. "Yes," they

3 William P. Martin and Harry V. Osborne.
4 Louis Hood.

say, "the Democratic platform of the state promised jury reform, but it did not say what kind of jury reform; and we can so divide the forces up into kinds that no kind can have a majority."

I foresaw that before I left the governorship, and I requested that I might be present at a conference of the members of the present legislature. We came to that conference. We debated and fought out on that floor in the most candid possible manner the form of jury commissions which a majority of us could agree upon, and I, for my part, yielded my personal judgment with regard to the form. I believed then, as l believe now, that the safest thing is to make this a judicial process from top to bottom and that it is perfectly safe, and that it would be wise, to have jury commissions chosen by the justices of the Supreme Court of New Jersey. There were others quite as thoughtful as myself—certainly quite as honest as myself—who thought that it would be better to lodge the power of choosing the commissions in the hands of the judges of the circuit courts. And then there were others, and they turned out to be in the majority at that conference—or they seemed at the end of it to be in the majority—who thought that the governor ought to be given the right to name a jury commission in each of the counties. I, myself, though I had been governor of the state, did not think that that was the wisest form, but when the majority of my colleagues in that conference declared their preference for it, I yielded my preference, and other gentlemen present seemed to yield their preferences. And it was settled, so far as the expression of the opinion of that conference was concerned, what the Democratic platform meant. It meant jury commissions in the several counties appointed by the governor.

Ah, but there is a little string attached to a conference! If the governor is not present, it is a caucus and the members are bound. If the governor *is* present, it is not a caucus, but a conference, and the members are not bound. A very neat and significant distinction! In a public conference, where they are bound to show their hands, they do not bind their consciences. In private, where it is possible to make arrangements, they do bind themselves—not to the public, but to each other. And therefore, it seems, when this conference was over, and every man there had a chance to express his full convictions and his reasons for them, that everything was just as fluid as it was before. And some perfectly honest men allowed themselves to be made the instruments for defeating this measure, because they were persuaded that it was not in the form which they had favored. So it is that a very subtle Machiavellian hand has been thrust into this affair, and men have been persuaded that they were following their own convictions when they were making it impossible for the party to fulfill its pledges to the people.

Ladies and gentlemen, does anybody doubt that the people of New Jersey want this critical business put into other hands? I find in the state nowhere any doubt upon that subject, and if there were an election between now and next Tuesday, there would be no doubt what would be done next Tuesday, and there would be no doubt that, if the election were to be next Tuesday, some of the gentlemen who would try to defeat it would not be there to try. I have a little list. I can point out to you some gentlemen; but it is not worth pointing out to you many of the gentlemen in the Essex delegation, because they are all in a lump. They are not distinguishable from one another. They are in the condition of fluid candy that has been too close neighbors. They are one lump, plumped into the box by the impulse of one will, and that will not their own. Therefore, I would not take the pains to discriminate among that select eleven. It is not worth a thoughtful man's while. But there are gentlemen elsewhere, who can be pointed out by name, in other counties, and if I should visit their counties, I would take pleasure in pointing them out.

It does not do to be groping in this business. You want to know whom you are talking about, as well as what you are talking about. These gentlemen ought to be described according to their orbits. They don't belong to any solar system. They are erratic comets, and the attraction of gravitation which governs their courses is to my mind incalculable. But it is worthwhile to point them out so that you may keep your eyes upon the evening sky and see to it that your community, at any rate, is not devastated by their fall. For their fall is easy to predict by one who is not an astronomer.

There are two things that the people of New Jersey determined to have and have not got. They determined to have jury reform, and they determined to have a look at their own constitution. But the gentlemen who made the present constitution of New Jersey looked a long way ahead. They said, "We may need this constitution some day, and we will make it of such a fashion that nobody can monkey with it, not even the people themselves." They limited the number of times we could suggest an amendment of the constitution within a given period of years. They said, "This thing is too exciting; don't try it too often. This is your own constitution, but your own constitution will not stand the pace. You had better live on your by-laws for a time; and five years at a time is not a bit too long to live on your by-laws and keep quiet. And when you begin to touch this delicate constitution, you have got to touch it twice, not once. You have got to pass it through two legislatures in order that it may still have the chance of surviving the examination which its own makers, theoretically, have subjected it to."

Now, a constitution which is made in one age is not suited to the circumstances of another age. And the circumstances of the year 1913 are as unlike the circumstances of the year 1844 as the twentieth century is unlike the seventeenth century. Our whole economic, social, and political system has been altered within the period during which this constitution has served the people of New Jersey. And in my opinion it is just about time that the people of New Jersey asked themselves if they don't want to rejuvenate things and bring their fundamental regulations up to the circumstances of today. There is only one barrier, I am told, to that, and that is that Essex County, for example, has so many more people in it than Cape May County, for example, that it wants more representatives in the Senate of this state than Cape May, that it wants as large a representation in the Senate in proportion to Cape May as the population of the county is in proportion to the population of Cape May. And certain astute gentlemen, who are afraid that certain other sacred parts of that constitution will be changed, are relying upon that in order to prevent any constitutional change whatever. I say let's call their bluff and propose to the legislators at Trenton that we allow the counties of this state equal representation in the constitutional convention. Because I would rather sacrifice one point than sacrifice the chances of the people of New Jersey to modernize their constitution.

The gentlemen who work politics in this state live in the very populous counties, and they are working this very natural, and I must say, it may be, very just, argument for the purpose of preventing the things that they do care about by making more important the things that they do not really care about. They would like, it is true, to have in proportion as many senators to manipulate as there are assemblymen. If you leave the political machinery of the county in their hands, they will have just that many more pawns to play on the board. And they are interested in this question, if they are interested honestly at all, merely from the point of view of their numerical advantage in making the arrangements and interchanges of favors which they choose to make in the legislature of the state. Well, what are you going to do about it? Are you going to hold meetings? Are you going to listen to these men and tell them what is the matter? Is that enough? This meeting is not going to change the result next Tuesday in the least,[5] unless you see to it that your neighbors are just as much in earnest about this thing as you are; unless, perchance, the things that I am fortunate enough to have the opportunity to say tonight may kindle a little fire underneath these gentlemen. You have got to kindle fire under them. There used to be a time when there were only two things that would move them—fodder held just before them and a fire built underneath them. Fodder has gone out of fashion.

Nobody suspects—at any rate, I do not suspect—direct corruption of any kind in this matter. It is the astute misleading of the will that is being done in Trenton. Men are being lined up upon their private convictions, when every man who loves his public duty ought to pull his private convictions with other men's and get the main thing out of the result, like a sensible and honorable man. But all these intricate suggestions of differences of individual opinion are made to hold up the whole process and chill the whole atmosphere, and make men look at each other as those who are in love with their individual prescriptions against earthquakes. And there is going to be an earthquake unless something happens to settle the earth before that time. I am not speaking in jest. I am speaking in earnest. The people of this country and of this state are going to have what they know they ought to get by one process or another. I pray God that it may not be the wrong process! I have the greatest confidence in the self-control, the public spirit, the legal conscience, of the people of America, and I do not myself believe that dangerous things will happen. But I warn these gentlemen not too long to show the people of this country that justice cannot be got by the ordinary processes of the law. I warn them to stand out of the sovereign's way.

I have traveled from one end of this country to the other, ladies and gentlemen, and I have looked into the faces of many audiences. I have never seen any symptom of riot. I have never seen any symptom that men were going to kick over the traces of the laws they themselves had sanctioned and made, but I have seen a great majesty seated upon their countenances, an infinite patience, but also an indomitable will. They are sitting now and watching their public men. And this is the test; this is the trial; this is the ultimate seat of judgment. And if these men will not serve them, they will be swept like the chaff be-

5 The Democratic caucus was to convene on Tuesday, May 6, just before the opening of the special session of the legislature, to work out an agreement on a jury reform measure.

fore the wind, and other men more honest, more brave, more wholesome, with the freshness of a new day upon them and with eyes that see the countrysides and the spaces where men are cool and thoughtful and determined, shall come to the front and lead them to a day of victory, when America will be crowned with a new wreath of self-revelation and of self-discovery. And these pitiful creatures who have put their ugly bulk in the way will have disappeared like the dust under the wheels of the chariot of God.

It is this hope, it is this confidence, that keeps a President of the United States alive. It is this confidence that makes it good to come back to Jersey and fight for the old cause.

T MS (WP, DLC).

William Jennings Bryan to Joseph Patrick Tumulty

Sacramento, Calif., May 2, 1913.

I believe a two year limit on law would be an advantage. It would give time enough for diplomatic effort with possibility of so improving situation as to prevent reenactment of law. Please secure President's opinion immediately. I desire to present suggestion this afternoon and then start home.   Bryan.

T telegram (WP, DLC).

Rudolph Forster to Joseph Patrick Tumulty

The White House May 2, 1913.

Following message just recd.

"Peking May 2 His Excellency Wilson, President of the United States of America, Washington[.] In the name of the Republic of China I thank you most heartilly for the message of recognition which you have sent to me through your honored representative in this capital. The sentiments of amity and good will which it bespeaks and the expressions of greeting and welcome which it conveys at once testify to the American spirit of mutual helpfullness and adds another brilliant page to the history of seventy years of uninterrupted friendly interiourze [intercourse] between China and the United States. Though unfamiliar with the republican form of governement, the Chinese people are yet fully convinced of the soundness of the principale which underlies it and which is so luminously represented by your glorious commonwealth. The sole aim of the government which they have established therefore is and will be to preserve this form of governement and to perfect its workings to the end that they may enjoy its unalloyed blessings prosperity and happiness within through the union of law and liberty and peace and friendship without; through the faithful execution of all established obligations.

"Yuan Shih Kai, President of the Republic of China."
Have sent copy to Acting Secretary of State.   Forster

T telegram (WP, DLC).

From William Jennings Bryan

Sacramento, Calif., May 2, 1913.

The Curtin resolution, the text of which I wired you delaying legislation in order to give you time to use diplomacy, has just been voted down in the Senate by a vote of 25 to 10. It was almost a party vote. There are ten Democrats in the Senate and thirty Republicans; eight Democrats and two Republicans voted for the resolution, and 23 Republicans and two Democrats voted against it. The Democratic platform in this state last fall declared strongly for a law prohibiting ownership by those ineligible to citizenship, and two Democratic senators felt bound to favor immediate legislation. The Senate is now discussing amendments to Webb bill, but the vote on the resolution probably indicates the division on the Webb bill. It is possible that the equivalent of Webb bill may agree to limit its operation to two years. But as the situation now stands it seems unlikely that any amendments can be made without the approval of the Progressive leader. The Senate may reach final action on the bill tonight.

Bryan.

T telegram (WP, DLC).

To William Jennings Bryan

[New York, May 2, 1913]

The Resolution proposed seems to me right and helpful except that I think the fine force and largeness of it marred by the implication that the governor might pending negotiations be obliged to put pressure to bear on the two governments by means of a special session of the legislature. Can you not delicately get that eliminated. The governor would be free to act as suggested in any case. Congratulate you on your admirable course. Am on political errand in New Jersey to-day. Will communicate with you again this afternoon.

WWhw telegram (E. M. House Papers, CtY).

From the Diary of Colonel House

May 2, 1913.

We had breakfast at 8.30. A number of despatches had come during the night from Mr. Bryan, who is in sacrimento, trying to get the Government officials there to disentangle the Japanese embroglio. We fell to talking of Mexico and the President wanted to know whether I thought intervention and war would be as bad as his Cabinet thought. I told him I did not. I believe that 50,000 men could do the work, but there would be considerable guerrilla warfare afterwards. He inclines to my opinion.

We then discussed whether it would be wise to recognize the Huerta Government. He said England had done so, which was significant. I told him that England had done so before Huerta had broken his promise in regard to Felix Diaz. I suggested that he try that situation out with Huerta before he recognized him. That is, that he ascertain whether Huerta intended to perform his obligations to Diaz and would call an election supporting Diaz for the Presidency as he had promised to do in writing. I thought if Huerta was recognized he would be able to borrow a large sum of money with which to maintain the fight against Diaz, and it was a question whether this was a good thing.

I again urged upon him the selection of a strong man for Ambassador to Mexico. He replied that he did not know where to find one. I suggested ex-Governor Adams of Colorado, but he did not consider him big enough.

I called his attention again to the necessity of keeping on good terms with England. He said there again O'Gorman was opposing him, and would oppose him in the Senate. I answered, "the more reason for a fight now."

I asked if he had given Ambassador Page special instructions along that line. He had not, but took it for granted that he would be diplomatic and conciliatory. I told him I had gone over the matter myself with Page, and had given him the reasons for having the good will of the British Government constantly on our side. We both deplored the short sightedness and ignoran[c]e of our public men. They talk and bluster and then are unwilling to maintain an army or navy in any way adequate to meet their pretensions.

The President started to go to New Jersey without answering Mr. Bryan's telegrams. I urged him to outline something, and then wire him more fully when he returned this afternoon. He suggested that I write it but I preferred to have him do so, and gave him a pad upon which he imparted our joint views. I afterward transcribed the telegram and sent it to Mr. Bryan. Its tenor and effect was that with some eliminations the resolution which the California Legislature was said to be prepared to adopt, would be satisfactory. I suggested to the President that he congratulate Mr. Bryan upon the good work he had done. He added such a clause.

McCombs rang up while the President was here and I talked to him for a moment, and then the President said a few words. McCombs is to accept the post of Ambassador to France unless he changes his mind in transit. He sails on Saturday on the Olympic, but his name will not go to the Senate until the other foreign appointments have been threshed out. McCombs wanted to arrange a meeting with McAdoo. I asked the President if he would like to have them here with us for dinner. He did not want them. He said it wearied him. I also told him that McCombs wished him to send a message to the steamer bidding him farewell, and wanted it couched in complimentary terms. The President laughed and said he would do it if I would remind him of it.

We left the apartment at 9.45 to start him on his Jersey tour. The streets were lined with people, the police and Secret Service men in plain clothes. It is arranged for the President to return between three and four o'clock, and remain until eight, when he is to go to Jersey City to speak. . . .

When I returned to the apartment I aroused the President for dinner. His stenographer also came to ask whether he should send the California despatch straight or in cypher. The President thought it might as well go straight, but after reading it I thought it best to send it in cypher which Schwem [Swem] did.

We talked of a multitude of matters at dinner. Among other things we discussed the City mayoralty situation,[1] and he again expressed his willingness for his friends to support an independent democrat against Tammany. He thought it inadvisable for McAdoo to take any part because he was in the Cabinet. I told him that something should be done for Morganthau or Elkus or perhaps both. He said he would offer Morganthau the Turkish

---

[1] About the formation of a fusion anti-Tammany ticket headed by John Purroy Mitchel, president of the Board of Aldermen, 1909-13, and Collector of the Port of New York, June-December 1913, see Edwin Ross Lewinson, *John Purroy Mitchel, The Boy Mayor of New York* (New York, 1965), pp. 78-103.

mission. I had heard that Morganthau did not want it and would not be complimented by the offer. He replied that nevertheless he would offer it.

We spoke of the Phillipines and Mexico, but he could not decide upon a proper person for Governor General of the one or an Ambassador for the other.

I urged him to make Walker Vick, Receiver General of Customs in the Dominican Republic, and he promised to do so. I also urged de Saulles for a small mission in South America. I thought he would be content with Uraguay or Paraguay although he wanted Chile. I told him that McCombs complained that he had not as yet made a single appointment for him, and he was insistent upon de Saulles. He said the reason was that McCombs presented such bad material, which I think is only partially the reason. As a matter of fact, he is prejudiced against McCombs, and I cannot blame him.

I suggested that McAdoo and McCombs dine with us, but he resolutely declined the pleasure.

When I came back from the Vanderbilt and told him of the reconciliation he exclaimed, "what children!"

I tried to hearten the President concerning the enormous responsibilities that are upon his slender shoulders, for he is anything but a strong man.

We did not go over the foreign appointments to any extent as we did not have time. We only touched on the Collector of the Port, but when we did I urged him to read the riot act to O'Gorman and to tell him he must get together with McAdoo and bring to him a suitable person satisfactory to them both. That if he did not, he, himself, would make the appointment without regard to his wishes.

We went over an infinite number of small matters which had to be taken up and disposed of. I told him, finally, that perhaps I was seeing him for the last time until Autumn unless we got together later during the summer when we were both in New England.

Tumulty came just as we were finishing dinner, and the conversation then fell upon Jersey matters concerning which I felt but little interest, further than as they related to the national welfare and to the President's prestige.

I told Tumulty that it was agreed between McCombs, McAdoo and myself that some mention should be made of their meeting but without calling attention to the fact that there had been any difference between them. I asked him to give it to the papers.

When we went down stairs several hundred people had

gathered to witness the President's departure. He left amid the cheers of the crowd and the tooting of the motor cycle horns of the Secret Service men.

He pressed my hand and said "I hope this is not goodbye, and that a north wind will blow you into Washington soon." This referred to my well known inability to stand excessive heat.

To William Frank McCombs

[New York, May 2, 1913]

A happy vacation and every kind of cheer and refreshment My best wishes go with you in all things.

Woodrow Wilson

WWhw telegram (E. M. House Papers, CtY).

An Address on Jury Reform at Jersey City, New Jersey[1]

[May 2, 1913]

Mr. Chairman and fellow citizens: Judge Hudspeth, as an old friend of mine, knows just exactly how to make me feel at home. He has given me just the introduction that I should have wished to have; and your very generous reception of me tonight, my dear fellow citizens, makes me feel very much more comfortable than I did this forenoon, for example, in another part of the city, where the tender sensibilities of one of the assemblymen from this county led me to conclude that he considered it an affront to his personal dignity that I should, without his invitation, have come into the county over which his influence so beneficently presides.[2] You do not make me feel that I come with so cold a welcome and to face so direct a rebuke.

I wish that you might do two opposite things tonight. I wish that you might forget that I am President of the United States, and that at the same time you might remember that I am President of the United States. I want you to forget it because I come here as a Jerseyman, fulfilling old promises that I made to Jerseymen. And I want you to remember it because it is the business of the President of the United States to see to it, wherever he

[1] Delivered at Dickinson High School. Robert S. Hudspeth called the meeting to order and introduced Governor Fielder and Mayor H. Otto Wittpenn, both of whom spoke for jury reform.

[2] In a conference of Democratic legislators at the Carteret Club of Jersey City earlier in the day, Assemblyman Walter Langdon McDermott had asked Wilson what plan of jury reform he preferred, and Wilson had refused to dictate a specific solution.

can, that the people get what they have a right to expect. I am not the servant of the Democratic party. I am the servant of the people, acting through the Democratic party, which has now undertaken some of the most solemn obligations that a party ever undertook. For it has stepped forward at a moment of universal disappointment and said, "We pledge you our honor as men and as patriots that you shall not be disappointed again." This is the situation in which the Democratic party finds itself, and in the midst of this situation there are particular promises which the Democratic party—for example, in New Jersey—has given to the people. One of the things which has made thoughtful men in this country most uneasy is that criminal justice was touched at its sources by perverting political influences, and that when a man stood in with the sheriff's office, he was safe against prosecution, and that when he did not stand in with the sheriff's office, he was in the position in which we all ought to be—responsible for everything that he did against the law of the land. This has not always applied. I would be ashamed of myself if I brought indictments against honest sheriffs, and in every county there have been sheriffs honest and dishonest. But what I want you to remember is that the political efforts of those men who wish to work their own private wills are always centered upon the capture of the sheriff's office; and that when they have captured the sheriff's office, then they feel at liberty not to be too scrupulous about the methods which they employ to work their own private purposes; and that here, there, and elsewhere, this threat of suspicion, if not of corruption, has touched the administration of criminal justice in this state, in which we should like to believe that all men's liberties are safe and that every man stands upon an equal footing before the judges who sit upon the bench.

The Democratic party undertook in its platform to see that that suspicion was removed. And if it doesn't do it, it ought not again to be trusted by the people of New Jersey. But gentlemen have their pet schemes. Gentlemen have their personal pride in their own proposals of reform. And unscrupulous persons play upon that pride, encourage and nurse the vanity that lies behind it, and say, "Go on and push your plan, for it will not be universally accepted; it will come into contest with other men's favorite projects; and we in the long run will prevent anything from being done." For it is proverbial, they remind you, that the Democratic party cannot get together. And so it is brought about that once more Hudson County is being played by the managers of Essex County. How long are you going to play second fiddle? How long are you going to elect men, who, whether they intend to do it or not, manage your affairs in such fashion that they are, as a matter of fact, subordinated to the purposes entertained by the managers—let us say, the governors of the party in the County of Essex?

I was present at a conference today at which one of the gentlemen in the Assembly from the County of Essex asked me if I had said that the greater part of the delegation from that county exercised no choice of its own, but took orders. He did not ask me in those words, but the words do not make any difference. That is what I said. And I said it not because I suspected it. I have lived in this state a good many years. I was an observer, and a very close observer, of the course of politics before I ventured upon that uneasy sea. And when I ventured upon that uneasy sea, I was not the landlubber that I looked. And I knew the gentlemen who controlled the politics of Essex County. Knew them! Why, the whole United States knew them. They were not hidden from anybody. Their names are synonyms of the corrupt management of politics from one end of America to the other. And because of the way in which your representatives have allowed themselves to be tied up by private politics of their own, they have, no matter how honest they are, no matter how well-intentioned they are, put themselves in the usual position of playing second fiddle to the managers of Essex. Look into the thing for yourself. The Democratic party had a platform, but these gentlemen had a little private platform of their own, in which they undertook to say how the Democratic party in this state should do the things which the Democratic party all over the state had promised to do. And because you elected them as Democrats, they told me today that you also voted for their private platforms. Did you? Don't you want the Democratic party to be an efficient body for giving the people what they demand? And don't you want these men to embark their fortunes with the great party which is now trying to serve the whole United States? Very well, then, tell them so. And tell them so out loud, so there cannot be any mistake about it. Because I have not come here to speak what is not in my heart—the least bitterness or the least criticism against these men personally. I think they have done mistaken things in some respects; but, then, like every man who has reached my years, at any rate, of discretion, I look back upon occasions when I also made mistakes; and the best friends I ever had were those who most emphatically told me that I had made a mistake. And the best friendship you can show for men who are not pursuing a practicable course of action to get what the people desire is to tell them that they are not pursuing the right course, whatever their right purposes may be.

And so I have come here tonight to plead with you to help us to see that the special session of the legislature, which convenes next week, does not end in disappointment and failure, but in the accomplishment of the great purposes for which it is called together. That is what we held a conference about this afternoon and this morning, and I think I can tell you that things are going to shape themselves and the party is going to get together. I have constantly to remind myself, so brief is the interval since I moved away from New Jersey, that I am not a part of the government of New Jersey, and that, therefore, it is not my business to make specific suggestions—in public. I have a little plan of my own, but I am not going to imitate the example of the numerous other gentlemen who have little plans of their own. I am perfectly willing to take any workable plan that accomplishes the substantial object we have in view. Any sensible, patriotic man ought to be equally willing to do that thing.

What is it that the Democratic party is expected to do? Is there a Democratic criminal justice in the United States? Is there a Republican criminal justice in the United States? Is there a Bull Moose criminal justice in the United States? Is justice measured by the standards of party difference? Why, what is the object we are talking about? It is the very heart and core of human liberty. It is the central object for which society was established. Society was established to see to it that every man had the same chance that every other man had, and that he was treated as every other man would be treated. And so we are not dealing with a party question here at all. We have gone back to the rudiments of human society. And the supreme test which the Democratic party has now to respond to is this: Is it ready to give the citizens of New Jersey final guarantees of disinterested justice? Did you ever hear a bigger question than that stated? Is there any suspicion abroad that equal justice is not administered in the United States? If there is such a suspicion, who ought of all others to remove it? The men who are responsible for the administration of justice, not only, but the men who make the laws which underlie the administration of justice. I do not know any more solemn thing that happens when these gentlemen get together in those chambers down in Trenton. There is the temple in which is worshipped the god of justice or the god of intrigue. And there is a high priest of intrigue, who is to be seen lurking about the corridors of that temple. He did not lurk in very obvious bulk a few months ago, but he lurks to the view of every casual observer now. Are you going to burn incense to his god, or are you going to burn incense to the God of mankind, the God of love and of justice and of purity and of righteousness?

You see, I want you to recognize that this is no trifling thing that has made me feel it was my duty to come up, perhaps to the neglect of my duties at Washington, in order to speak to my neighbors here in New Jersey and tell them what was up, what was involved, what it was that made it necessary for them to speak out about before next Tuesday. I wish I could go around from county to county of this state expounding this great theme. If there was ever anything to make a man's red corpuscles jump through his veins, it is this thing, in behalf of which men have not hesitated to shed their blood and to forfeit everything that they held sacred, in order that their fellows might be free, whether they themselves were liberated or not. Somebody told me that things were so tangled up here that jury reform was going to lose anyhow, and said, "Why go up and fight for a losing cause?" Well, I know my fellow citizens in New Jersey, and I deny that it is a losing cause. But suppose it was! I would rather have my body one of the first to fall by the wall than one of the last. Anybody can come on with the battalions that marshal millions strong before the war is over, but only men of sturdy courage can go with the little handful that starts the battle. And whether we win or lose, the battalions are coming on, and the eventual outcome of the day of battle is not in doubt. There is a God in the heavens, and all is well. And I am not going to be impatient.

There is something else I wanted to talk about. It is all very well to know what you want to do in a government, but it is another thing to know how you are going to do it. And the only thing that I am interested in in government is how you are going to do it, because no sane men will sit down long and soberly debate what ought to be done. Everybody admits that—at any rate in public. But what we want to debate now is how to get the thing done. You know it was my pleasure, at a time when it was not very popular to do so, to go into various parts of this state and speak for the commission form of government in cities, and I did so because I said I was tired of hide-and-seek government. I was tired of not knowing what men to put my finger on when things went wrong. I was tired of boards without number that were independent in function and sphere, some of which were appointed, some of which were elected, some of which had this function, and some of which had that; and over whom there was no common authority at all, except at the polls, when you have such a long ticket to vote that you did not know which man you were punishing and which man you were rewarding. And I did not see how to run a machine that you could not start without moving a hundred cranks at once, because I was not a centipede and had only two hands. I wished a real mechanical genius, such as characterizes this country, would show us how to make a machine that one cranked, started, and controlled. And therefore, I was in favor of a simplified government, where we could find the men who were responsible.

Now, I am in favor of the same kind of principle in the government of the state. And we have a constitution which, though more simple in its arrangements than the constitutions of some of our sister states, nevertheless does obscure, by scattering, responsibility in a way which makes it very difficult, indeed, for the people of this commonwealth to govern their own affairs. And therefore, I came up to suggest to you that after you get jury reform—which you are going to get—you insist upon having a constitutional convention, if only for the satisfaction of having a look at the inside of your own affairs. A great many learned and accomplished gentlemen are now rising in their places to protest against the modern rebellion against constitutions. I have not observed any rebellion against constitutions. I believe, as profoundly as any man can believe, in the ordered course of government under definite constitutional regulations. But I do not regard it as a rebellion against constitutions to desire constitutions that we can work with. I do not regard it as a reaction against constitutional government that we should desire to simplify responsibility and put the people more immediately in connection with their own affairs and the control of those affairs.

And my objection to the present constitution of New Jersey is this: It says you cannot even suggest an amendment of it more than once in five years, and that when you have suggested an amendment, you must take at least two years to put it through. For you must put it through one legislature, and then you must submit it to the people and elect another legislature and then put it through that legislature, and then at last the instrument which you yourselves made is at your disposal.

I am considered radical sometimes now because I venture to remind my fellow citizens of the principles upon which this republic was founded. And if it is radical to quote Washington, along with Jefferson; if it is radical to quote Hamilton, along with the leaders of the old Democratic party, then I am a radical. Because they all with one accord agreed that the essence of constitutional government was that the people had a right to change their own government when they chose. And some constitution makers, among the rest those that made the New Jersey constitution under which we now live, were of the opinion that the people ought to be discouraged from changing their own government, by having it made so difficult for them that they would get tied up into a hard knot if they tried it. I say, let's cut the knot, not with any sword of irregular procedure, but by means of a constitutional convention authorized by us to look this instrument over and suggest to us changes which may modify it in the interest of simplicity and directness of popular control.

Now, you know what stands in the way. Why, *you* do! Hudson County is one of the most populous counties in the state, and Hudson is inclined to say, "Oh, no, I will go into this scheme if you will promise that Hudson shall be proportionally represented in the Senate as well as in the House of Assembly, but it isn't fair that we shouldn't have any more members in the Senate than one of the less populous counties in the state has, or the least populous county in the state." Are you going to stick on that? Are you going to insist that your representatives stand for that to the point of making it impossible for you to get at anything else in the constitution? Aren't you going to be big and generous and say, "We will yield that point in order to get the other things we are interested in, and we are not going to let one matter of pride and self-interest on our part stand in the way of constitutional revision." Won't you take the big view of it like that? Don't let the populous counties of the state make the impression upon the rest of the state that they won't go into this great enterprise unless they get something out of it for themselves. That isn't the big point of view; that isn't the big attitude in politics. For there is coming a time, ladies and gentlemen—if it hasn't come now—when only the big attitude will be the winning attitude in politics in America. America is big. Her hospitable largess has furnished a home for everybody in the world that desired to change his station and have a new trial at the life of liberty. We have opened our doors wide to all mankind and said, "Come and share, and share alike, with us, in fortunes which are not built upon the interests of race, which are not built upon the standards of creeds, which are not built upon any antecedents, except that human blood is in your veins. Come and make a common cause with us, for mankind." That is the invitation of America! Her heart is as big as her hospitality, and her hospitality is the measure of her standards of justice.

And so at last a time has come when men in America look with contempt upon the little game of politics, look with absolute condescension upon the men who go about to establish their own fortunes, to press the interests of their own little circle, to see to it that the things that they are interested in have the pick in the things that are done and the things that are preferred. And they are more and more sitting like a great audience, saying, "We will laugh for a little time at this comedy. We will pretend to shed tears at your mock tragedies. But, after all, we want to see the real thing on the boards at present—the great pick of mankind."

And so I am reminded of some of the extraordinary misrepresentations that have been made with regard to the projects of jury reform. I am told that some of my friends among the laboring men have been told that this was a plan to see that they didn't get an equal share with the rest in the determination of what should be done in the courts of criminal justice. I ask them to answer me this question: In the game of politics, do they generally get the advantage? Do they generally determine in impartial fashion through their own representatives who shall have true bills brought against them and go before petit juries, and who shall not? Is the present arrangement altogether to their liking? I haven't heard it praised from their ranks. And what we are trying to do is to bring them, with all other men, into the partnership. I have never proposed, and I never shall propose, that a special class of society shall have a special preference in what ought to be a general partnership. I have again and again insisted that nobody ought to be excluded from the partnership, and I have again and again pointed out that the men who carry the heat and burden of the day—on our farms and in our shops and in the dull depths of our mines and in the forests and on the sea—constituted the greater part of our population and were, therefore, among the senior partners in the firm. But the game of politics has never gone in their direction that I have heard. And I have heard laboring men everywhere in this country say that their associations were now standing outside politics and asking this question: Who is going to perform justly, and who is not? What you ought to do, then, my dear fellow citizens, those of you who specifically describe yourselves as workingmen, though some of the rest of us work and don't have any limited hours either (if there was more than one President, I would form a union) but if those of you who choose to describe yourselves in some particular sense workingmen want to break up [into] this game in which you have joined in getting your share, then I advise you to go in for jury reform. But that, by the way, only illustrates what I was setting out to expound to you, namely, that this great government of ours was maintained as a general partnership. There is a very great peculiarity, though, about every partnership—there is always a talkative member and a silent member, and the talkative member is generally very much in evidence, and the silent member generally takes the consequences and pays the bills.

Some of my fellow citizens and some of my colleagues in Washington City now think that they are hearing the voice of the people of the United States, when they are only hearing the part that has become vocal by moving down to Washington and insisting upon its special interests. As I sit in my office in Washington, there are windows on only one side of the room, and those windows look out upon parks and upon the Potomac River and the shore of Virginia on the other side. And I cannot see Washington from those windows, and I sometimes thank God I can't. Because Washington behind me is seething with special representatives of little things who are almost storming at the doors of this office itself; whereas, out here are the cool large spaces of the United States. And I would rather hear the whispers coming in at those windows than the strident arguments coming in at those doors. And that is the enterprise upon which every man should keep his thought concentrated—walking as if in a vision, seeing things invisible, hearing voices inaudible, in love, not with his own ambitions or with his own interests, but with that thought of the pulsing heart of America, a heart which does not die with the generations, but pulses again as the children grow up, pulses as the new years come in, pulses with a greater and greater might as the population grows from million to millions, pulses in the folds of the flag—seems to be symbolized in everything that we look upon, except our own little selves and our own private ambitions. And those who dream of this nation will be able to serve it as those who forget themselves. There are men of this sort, there are a great many of this sort. Seek them out; sustain them; believe in them; swear by them. Don't go back on them if they make incidental mistakes. Just band yourselves together in a great body of Americans and say, "Hudson County is linked by every vital thong of living tissue with the State of New Jersey, and the State of New Jersey with the other states of the union, and the states of the Union with the great body of struggling mankind; and as we lift in New Jersey, so will men lift everywhere. As we stand by each other in New Jersey, so will men stand by each other throughout the Union. And those that we trust shall be lifted to places of authority in proportion as they love us and trust us."

T MS (WP, DLC).

Remarks to the New British Ambassador[1]

Mr. Ambassador: [May 3, 1913]

I am happy to receive at your hands the letter of his Britannic Majesty accrediting you as his Ambassador Extraordinary and Plenipotentiary to the Government of the United States, and to extend to you personally, as well as in your official capacity, a *most* cordial welcome. It is especially gratifying to me that His Majesty should have made choice for this mission of a gentleman whose former residence in ⟨and visits to⟩ this country *and whose repeated visits to it* have made him so thoroughly familiar with our Government and institutions and so well acquainted with our people.

I share in the wish of His Majesty that *warm* cordiality, *a ready sympathy and a quick understanding alike of policy and purpose* should characterize the intercourse between the two countries and I assure you that in your efforts to maintain and strengthen the friendly relations which have so long and so happily ⟨subsisted⟩ *existed* between the United States and Great Britain you will have my earnest co-operation to the end not only that amity and good will may prevail between them, but also that the cause of peace and justice throughout the world may be advanced.

⟨Fully appreciating the kind⟩ *I sincerely appreciate the kind* expression of ⟨sincere⟩ *personal* respect which you convey to me in behalf of Your Sovereign, ⟨I ask you to⟩ *and beg that you will* be so good as to ⟨confirm the reciprocal sentiment which I entertain for him⟩ *convey to him, for my countrymen and for myself, assurances of our highest regard.*

T MS (SDR, RG 59, 701. 4111/99a, DNA).
[1] See Cecil Arthur Spring Rice, British Ambassador to the United States, 1913-18. In the following text (prepared by the State Department), Wilson's additions are printed in italics, his deletions in angle brackets.

To William Jennings Bryan

[The White House] May 3, 1913.

Heartily share your opinion about a two-year limit.

Wilson.

T telegram (Letterpress Books, WP, DLC).

From William Jennings Bryan

Sacramento, Calif., May 3, 1913.

Senate passed the Webb bill at 12:45 tonight, the vote being 35 to 2, one Democrat and one Republican voting against it. Amended by permitting unlimited leaseholds of three years. The nearly unanimous vote shows Governor back of bill. The Democrats having tried to delay action and amend the bill voted for it when they found they could not change it. The House is quite sure to follow the Senate. I have decided to leave tomorrow afternoon unless something occurs tomorrow to change my plans. To remain here, after the Senate has taken the action it has, would in my judgment do no good and might irritate. Will arrange with both senators to keep me informed along the way, and I will wire you any suggestions which may seem necessary to fit the situation as it develops. I will go by the Southern Pacific, reaching Los Angeles Sunday morning; Tucson Sunday evening; El Paso Monday at noon; Chicago Wednesday morning, and Washington Thursday morning. I think I can be of more service to you in Washington during the time when the bill is in the hands of the Governor than I could out here.   Bryan.

T telegram (WP, DLC).

From William Bayard Hale[1]

Hotel Astor New York

Dear Mr. President: May the Third [1913]

I have wound up my affairs, closed my house, and secured passage to Europe (on Thursday) for Mrs. Hale and my son; and I wait here at the Hotel Astor for your instructions.

I am, dear Mr. President,

Sincerely yours   Wm. Bayard Hale

ALS (WP, DLC).

[1] Hale was about to leave on a secret fact finding mission to Mexico.

From Edward Mandell House

Dear Mr. President: New York City. May 4th, 1913.

I am afraid I did not express my convictions very forcefully the other day when we talked of the Collectorship.

Your concern over the situation caused me to want to bring about a solution that was, for the moment, less troublesome to you, and therefore I advised referring the matter back to the two gentlemen[1] at difference.

I was afraid that would be a mistake. If I were you I would name Polk. I believe that to do less would be construed as an unwillingness to confront the issue which the Senator from New York has raised.

Your mastery of Congress depends largely upon your maintaining that unflinching courage which our people rightly appreciate and which has made you the dominating figure upon this Continent.

You are clearly within your rights and I would not temporize with a situation that must be met either now or later, and reasons will occur to you why you should not postpone the seemingly inevitable.   Your very faithful,   E. M. House

TLS (WP, DLC).
[1] O'Gorman and McAdoo.

Remarks at a Press Conference

May 5, 1913

The Japanese situation?

> No, nothing at all. I haven't heard anything that is not in the papers. I haven't heard all that is in the papers.

The morning papers say that Mr. Bryan declared out on the coast that Governor Johnson would probably hear from you, or rather that he would withhold his signature until he heard from you. Have you intimated that you would send him some form of communication?

> I think you misunderstood. We asked Governor Johnson not to sign the bill until he had given us time to see the act in its final shape.

They said they expected some form of communication from you.

> I wouldn't give them any intimation that—

Has the bill been reported to you by telegraph?

> Not yet. Unless it has come in. It is coming in now.

Do you expect to wait until you see Mr. Bryan before advising Governor Johnson?

> I don't know how long Governor Johnson can wait before signing it, under his constitution.

Ten days, until the thirteenth of May.

> Then he would naturally wait until Mr. Bryan came back.

Mr. President, is there anything that you could say about the currency message, about the currency legislation?

> I have no currency legislation. No telling what—

The morning papers had a good deal about it, about your having a message coming on this week.

That is a most interesting invention.

That is in the morning papers now.

> Well, that is news to me, that is all I have to say. I learn a
> great deal about myself in the newspapers that I haven't
> [known] heretofore.

Mr. President, could you give us any idea as to when the—what
might be the—views of the administration about the currency
legislation which can be stated or authoritatively given?

> I tried to make that plain in answer to a previous question—
> I mean, some days ago. I am trying to see just how far
> the views of the members all together can be worked to-
> gether, or rather how far they can be brought to work in
> harmony with regard to this matter, so that we may know
> what momentum we may have for it. It is on that rather slow
> and vague process—I mean that incalculable process of the
> conference—that the whole thing is resting.

May I ask this: Would you say up to this time that there is a considerable degree of agreement on essentials?

> I think there is. I think there is a growing agreement—a very
> considerable agreement now. I mean, very general agree-
> ment.

I imagine you won't want to answer this question. Is that agreement substantially in accord with your own views?

> Yes.

Would you feel at liberty, can you give us any idea—

> I know that is not fair. Don't you see, gentlemen, I so
> honestly believe in common counsel to settle these things
> that I don't like to say whether or not these are my views.
> I want to see as many fellows come into it as possible.

I was not going quite as far as that. I am wondering if you would
feel it opportune to give us any notion of the general line of
your own thought rather than that of others.

> I would rather wait until there is a correlated, formulated
> message, what the details are and the scheme that con-
> stitute them, and whether it is workable or not workable
> according to the details.

I wasn't really honest in my question!

Mr. President, shall we look to the chairmen of the respective
currency committees for the formulated bills which will represent your views?

> Naturally. Yes, sir.

Mr. President, is it your idea to have currency legislation before
Congress adjourns?

Well, it is my hope that that may be, and I would know whether that—

These conferences are for the purpose of deciding that?

Yes.

That would give the House something to do while the Senate was wrestling with the tariff bill.

That would be very interesting.

JRT transcript (WC, NjP) of CLSsh (C. L. Swem Coll., NjP).

To James Aloysius O'Gorman[1]

My dear Senator,   [The White House, May 5, 1913]

I have been thinking a great deal about our recent conference, and the thinking has not reassured me, for I was disturbed by what you said. I am going to write you a few frank lines now in the hope that by so doing our thinking may never be at cross purposes again. I value your confidence and friendship too much to be willing to dissemble for a moment my real opinions or to withhold anything that is in my mind concerning matters which we must handle in common. I would rather speak than write, —partly because I always so much enjoy a conference with you, —but every time we meet (pending the determination of the chief appointment in New York) the newspapers put a false construction, of contest or compromise, upon our conference, and I am resolved they shall not embarrass us!

As I told you when we had our last talk, I cannot accept the interpretation you then put upon the constitutional relationship between the President and individual Senators in the matter of appointments in the several States. I am deeply conscious, moreover, of what the country has usually expected and demanded of the President in that matter and of its growing desire and insistance that he should hold himself free to exercise his independent choice in everything that concerned the fulfilment of his obligations as chief executive not only, but also as leader of his party, particularly when that party is in control of the government. It will hold him responsible in every particular.

But theoretical differences of opinion are not going to embarrass us. I know your *spirit* in this as in other matters; and I have no fear that we shall ever clash in practice because of any independence of choice I may feel it necessary to exercise. What .I want to make clear to you in this modest epistle is the principles upon which I shall try to act,—always with as much thoughtful consideration of the rights of others and of the full courtesy due them as I know how to show,—and the method I shall hope to pursue with your advice, and that of your colleagues, constantly in my mind.

In the first place, as to the advice of my Cabinet colleagues about appointments. You spoke the other day of the Secretary of the Treasury as a "subordinate." I do not look upon any member of the Cabinet as a subordinate. The offices they occupy are of the first dignity and consequence. Moreover, an "Administration" must be a unit in spirit and in action or it will fail and come to naught. If I were inclined to ignore the members of my Cabinet in these matters, or in any others that affected the administration and efficiency of their several departments, there could be no Administration at all. Men of pride and of reputation would not serve in the Cabinet. I have had long experience in cooperative administrative action where the partners were men of spirit and of parts, and I know that I must support my colleagues as loyally as they support me and must defer to them in every matter in which I do not disagree with them in principle or upon grounds of large public policy. It would be folly for me not to attach the greatest possible weight to the judgment and preference in respect of their subordinates, especially their chief subordinates, even if I were inclined to do so—except when I think them radically mistaken in their men. I must be guided by them so far as possible, if I am to have an efficient and successful administration.

But they are men of sense and discretion and good feeling and are as ready to defer to my wish and judgment as I could wish them to be. They respect the advice of Senators, besides, as sincerely and as habitually as I do, or as any one can who does not surrender entirely his right of individual choice and judgment, and they are as willing, as anxious, as I am that the recommendations of Senators should, as a rule, be accepted,—as a rule with as few exceptions as possible.

The solution, therefore, is, not clash or contest, but frank and frequent conference, in order that the choices to be made may be made jointly and by common counsel. All the forces involved are independent and self-respecting forces: they must be combined in the only way in which such forces can be.

And so we come to our own concrete instance. As you must have seen when you left me the other day, I was anxious, after our talk, to find it possible to agree with you and give the appointment to Mr. Lawson Purdy.[2] But I have made detailed inquiries in several directions since then and find that he would be regarded, whatever his personal character and quality, as representing a recognition by the Administration of the Tammany organization, now more than ever discredited in the eyes of the country. The difficulty is, not that the Secretary of the Treasury will claim any personal rights in this matter,—for I have talked with him again and find him most willing to accede to any choice which may seem wisest in all the circumstances,—but that *this* choice would violate a policy to which I feel I have no choice but to adhere. I shall hope, therefore, to have further conference both with you and with the Secretary about this selection.

We must use especial care in the future, that, in respect of all and every New York appointment of importance, cooperation between the three friends concerned, yourself, the Cabinet officer, and myself, will precede public mention of any person thought of in connection with it by any of us,—the actual cooperation of our minds in this delicate business,—and of course precede any conclusive judgment or individual commital by any one of us. No doubt, by the careful discipline of our office forces, we may have our consultations without mischievous talk from outside. We will work it out as friends should, and those who cordially and as a matter of course understand one another.

Cordially and faithfully yours,   Woodrow Wilson

TCL (WP, DLC).
¹ There is a WWsh draft of the following letter in WP, DLC. A note on the typed copy says that the original was in Wilson's hand.
² Lawson Purdy, president of the Department of Taxes and Assessments of the City of New York, 1906-17.

To John Purroy Mitchel

My dear Mr. Mitchell,   The White House 5 May, 1913

My friend Mr. Kerney, the bearer of this note, comes to you on a strictly confidential mission and one of the deepest interest and consequence to me. Please hear him as you would hear one who speaks my own mind.¹

Cordially Yours,   Woodrow Wilson

Printed in *Charles Hamilton Auction Number 41* (New York, 1970), p. 90.
¹ The "confidential mission" was to persuade Mitchel to accept the collectorship of the Port of New York. See James Kerney, *The Political Education of Woodrow Wilson* (New York and London, 1926), pp. 319-21.

From James Kerney

My dear Mr. President: Trenton, New Jersey May 6, 1913

I have just come from an hour's conference in New York and am to get a "yes" or "no" answer over the telephone before midnight. I will transmit it at once, so that before this reaches you, it is likely that you will have the message. If the answer is in the affirmative, he feels that he should have two weeks to finish up some big dock projects that he has had under way for two years or more, and which have required both state and city legislation. The announcement could be made immediately or as soon as you felt it desirable, but I take it that no harm would be done should he not take the oath of office for two weeks, and so informed him. He was particularly concerned about the obligation that he had to some of the forces that have been advocating him for the fall, but I cautioned him that any consultation with them was out of the question, and that the matter must be treated in a most confidential way. I took the liberty of suggesting to him that he could be saved any embarrassment of appearing in the light of a candidate, by having some little statement issued by yourself or the Treasury Department, should the appointment be made.

His every action bears the stamp of high-mindedness, and it was a real pleasure to have had the task. While he was fully appreciative of the confidence and high honor, it was very refreshing to watch him endeavor to work out the various phases of duty that he felt confronted him. He's a find.

Sincerely yours,   James Kerney

TLS (WP, DLC).

Joseph Patrick Tumulty to James Kerney

[The White House] May 5, 1913.

The President will not accept plan proposed by telephone this morning.   Joseph P. Tumulty.

T telegram (Letterpress Books, WP, DLC).

To John Purroy Mitchel

[The White House] May 6, 1913.

I am with great pleasure sending to the Senate this afternoon your name as Collector of the Port of New York.[1] I earnestly trust that you will serve the public interest by accepting this appointment. Woodrow Wilson.

T telegram (Letterpress Books, WP, DLC).
¹ Actually, he sent the nomination to the Senate in the late afternoon of May 7.

To Samuel Gompers

My dear Mr. Gompers: [The White House] May 6, 1913

Thank you for your letter of April thirtieth, with its full discussion of a very perplexing subject. The letter will be of real value to me in thinking things out.

Sincerely yours, Woodrow Wilson

TLS (Letterpress Books, WP, DLC).

From John Bassett Moore

My dear Mr. President: Washington May 6, 1913.

The Japanese Ambassador advises us informally that his protest is ready but doubts whether he shall present it at once or defer its presentation until the arrival of the Secretary of State in Washington. In view of the fact that the Secretary is hastening back from California in order that he may confer with you on the situation there, the Ambassador seems to feel that it might be appropriate to defer the filing of his protest until the Secretary shall have returned. The Secretary will, as I understand, arrive in Washington on Wednesday night or Thursday morning. I think that the Ambassador would be disposed to wait and would feel no difficulty in waiting if it were certain that Governor Johnson's promise to allow a "reasonable time" would embrace an opportunity for the Secretary to confer with the Ambassador and also with yourself. On this point the Secretary's telegram to you of May 4th from Yuma, Arizona, is not explicit. He says: "I think Governor will delay signing until I reach Washington. He has promised a reasonable time and he knows I desire to confer with you when I reach Washington."

Would you deem it proper to telegraph to Governor Johnson and ask him whether he will delay action upon the bill till you shall have had an opportunity to confer with the Secretary on his return to Washington? If so, the Ambassador might without formally presenting his protest communicate it to us personally and unofficially so that we may know what he will say when he comes to the point of actually making a protest.

If you should not feel disposed to communicate with Governor Johnson, the Ambassador would, I suppose, feel obliged to file his protest immediately, since he could not justify himself to his own government if any delay on his part should result in Governor Johnson's signing the bill without having been made acquainted with the objections of Japan.

Very respectfully and truly yours,   John B. Moore.

TLS (WP, DLC).

To Hiram Warren Johnson[1]

The White House, May 6, 1913.

Will you not be kind enough to advise me just how long a time you will be able to allow for the consideration by us and the presentation to you of the objections of the Japanese government before you will yourself be obliged to act on the alien land tenure bill. I wish to confer with Secretary Bryan in person before final action.   Woodrow Wilson.

T telegram (Letterpress Books, WP, DLC).
[1] There is a WWhw draft of the following telegram in WP, DLC.

From Edward Mandell House

Dear Mr. President: New York City. May 6th, 1913.

I am enclosing you three letters concerning the Mexico situation. One from Mr. Krunschnitt, President of the Board of the Southern Pacific,[1] one from Mr. James Speyer[2] and one from Mr. Ludlow,[3] whose opinion I value as he has lived in Mexico for the past ten or fifteen years.

The situation has about reached a point where it seems advisable for you to take a hand.

Your very faithful,   E. M. House

TLS (WP, DLC).
[1] Julius Kruttschnitt to E. M. House, May 6, 1913, TLS (WP, DLC). Kruttschnitt at this time was chairman of the executive committee of the Southern Pacific Co. His letter consisted primarily of a memorandum prepared by Delbert James Haff, which was soon incorporated, *mutatis mutandis*, in the latter half of the memorandum printed as an Enclosure with D. J. Haff to WW, May 12, 1913. Kruttschnitt's only addition was the comment that not only did he "concur most heartily" with Haff's plan, but that it had also been examined and "approved . . . enthusiastically" by Phelps, Dodge & Co., the Greene Cananea Copper Co., and Edward L. Doheny of the Mexican Petroleum Co.
[2] James Joseph Speyer [to E. M. House?], May 5, 1913, T MS (WP, DLC). Speyer was a German-American international banker and philanthropist of New York. He argued that, however much one might feel inclined to condemn the manner in which Huerta came to power, the General was the only man who could control the situation in Mexico. The Huerta government was badly in need

of money, but, Speyer declared, no responsible bankers either in the United States or Europe would lend to it until it was recognized by the United States. Speyer warned that the United States would be forced to intervene if the present chaotic situation in Mexico continued to worsen. Hence, he urged that the United States recognize the Huerta government.

3 Edwin Ludlow to E. M. House, April 29, 1913, TLS (WP, DLC). Ludlow, a mining engineer with many years of experience in Mexico and the southwestern United States, had been employed in Mexico as recently as 1911. Ludlow's view of the situation was very different from Speyer's. Not only did he express distaste for Huerta, but he also doubted Huerta's ability to control Mexico. He also offered a more realistic assessment of the strength of the Constitutionalist faction in northern Mexico (about which, see n. 1 to the Enclosure printed with D. J. Haff to WW, May 12, 1913) and of the Zapata movement in the State of Morelos. He warned that the only thing which could unite all of these factions was intervention by the United States, and that such intervention would lead to great destruction of American property and probably the loss of many American lives as well. He pointed out that, thus far, there had been little disruption of American enterprises in Mexico. His only policy suggestion was that the United States Government continue to maintain a large military force near the Mexican border, ready to intervene immediately should American enterprises be directly attacked by guerrilla bands. Beyond that, he said, there was nothing to be done except to wait until Mexico had achieved stability on her own.

From Hiram Warren Johnson

Sacramento, California, May 6, 1913.

If adjournment of Legislature shall occur within next week I will have thirty days before it is necessary to sign act, otherwise I have ten days. Our constitution provides Section sixteen, Article four, "If any bill shall not be returned within ten days after it shall have been presented to him, (the Governor) the same shall become a law unless the Legislature by adjournment prevents such return, in which case it shall not become a law unless the Governor within thirty days after such adjournment shall sign it" End quote. Mr. Bryan asked me to hold bill reasonable time before signature and of course I readily agree.

Hiram W. Johnson.

T telegram (WP, DLC).

Sir Cecil Arthur Spring Rice to Sir Edward Grey

Sir, Washington May 6, 1913.

I have the honour to state that I was today received by the President in audience and delivered my Letters of Credence.

Mr. Moore, who is acting as Secretary of State in the absence of Mr. Bryan, came to His Majesty's Embassy in order to accompany me to the White House in the President's automobile. Colonel Cosby of the President's Military staff came with Mr. Moore. The staff of His Majesty's Embassy attended. I was received at once and delivered the King's letter to the President.

reading to him the speech, copy of which is enclosed herewith. In reply the President read the speech copy of which is also enclosed. The text of my speech followed as closely as possible that of the speeches delivered by my predecessors. Mr. Bryce was good enough to advise me as to its wording, and I also followed some suggestions made by Mr. Moore, with whom I have a long and intimate acquaintance. As you, sir, will observe it is an eminently colourless document.

The President's speech was I understand considerably altered from the draft submitted to him by the State Department.

I requested the President's leave to present the staff of his Majesty's Embassy and after a few minutes conversation I withdrew.

The President was very cordial in his manner and expressed the hope that our personal relations might be of the pleasantest character. Nothing was mentioned which bore any relation to current politics.

I have the honour to be, With the highest respect,
Sir, Your most obedient,
humble servant,   Cecil Spring Rice

TLS (FO 371/1859, No. 22591, PRO).

To Alexander Mitchell Palmer

My dear Mr. Palmer: The White House May 7, 1913

I had a talk the other day with a Pittsburgh editor, Mr. Moore,[1] who seemed very much concerned about the way in which the Democratic members of the State Legislature in Pennsylvania were voting their opposition to the corrupt practices act, etc. I thought it would be wise to call your attention to the matter, because it is so important that we should at every point guard our lines and see to it that they are not broken into by the forces we have to fight at every turn.

Cordially and faithfully yours,   Woodrow Wilson

TLS (WP, DLC).
[1] Alexander Pollock Moore, editor of the *Pittsburgh Leader*.

From William Gibbs McAdoo

Dear Mr. President: Washington May 7, 1913.

In conformity with your suggestion, I take pleasure in recommending for appointment to fill the vacancy caused by the resignation of Hon. William Loeb, Jr., Hon. John Purroy Mitchell, of New York, as Collector of Customs for the District of New York. Sincerely yours, W G McAdoo

TLS (WP, DLC).

James Kerney to Joseph Patrick Tumulty

Trenton, New Jersey, May 7, 1913.

The statement that I agreed would be made was substantially as follows: That Mr. Mitchell has accepted appointment at the President's request and that he has at no time been a candidate for the office. Mr. Mitchell feels himself to be under obligations to conclude certain important matters now before Committee's of the Board of Estimate and Apportionment of the City of New York, of which he is Chairman, notably the organization of terminal facilities on the West Side of Manhattan Island and the organization of railroad and marine terminal facilities in South Brooklyn and is reluctant to surrender his present office while these remain unfinished. The President, recognizing the importance of these public works, has consented that Mr. Mitchell's assumption of office as collector be postponed until June first to permit him to complete his part in these matters. The President while reluctant to withdraw Mr. Mitchell from the city's service to which he has been elected, does not consider Mr. Mitchell's acceptance of the collectorship to be incompatible with his continued endeavor to promote efficient government in the city of New York. James Kerney.

T telegram (WP, DLC).

From the Diary of Colonel House

May 7, 1913.

McAdoo telephoned from Washington again to say that the President had decided to appoint Mitchel Collector of the Port, and to ask me to congratulate Mitchel for him. He also asked me to notify Frank Polk that he would not be appointed. He said O'Gorman had found out that Mitchel would be appointed and he went immediately to the President and suggested Mitchel's name himself. The President smiled and promised to appoint him at once. As a matter of fact, O'Gorman has but little fight in him, and if the President had appointed Polk, he would have yielded. I think the President must realize this now, for of all the men suggested, Mitchel is least acceptable to Tammany.

Remarks at a Press Conference

May 8, 1913

Can you tell us anything about currency legislation, Mr. President?

> That's a large order. I would have to hire a hall. Just which part of it do you want, a simple—

The bill in Congress—your views as to whether something should be taken up?

> I have always been expecting that we could take it up in the session.

Are you more hopeful now?

> I think the prospects are very good. . . .

The prospect is good for taking it up this session. Do you think the prospect is good for final action at the session?

> Of course, final action would depend upon how rapidly progress was made on the tariff bill in the Senate, to get that out of the way for the Senate to act on the currency bill. I don't suppose anybody in the House would have such "cruelty to animals" as to sit all summer.

You are used to that, Mr. President.

> I can stand it.

They have done it for several summers now.

> I know. That is what made them sick of it.

Do you hope for final action at this session, Mr. President?

> Yes, I do.

Wouldn't you hope for final action if the Senate should pass the tariff bill by the first of August?

> I don't know. I haven't gone into that. It depends upon whether we can all keep our momentum. We have got to have elasticity left in order to give elasticity to the currency bill.

Did Mr. Glass leave with you the measure he worked up?

> He left a preliminary draft with me. It is just a provision.

You haven't had time to look over it?

> Yes, sir, I have looked over it.

Is there anything you would care to say about it?

> No.

JRT transcript (WC, NjP) of CLSsh (C. L. Swem Coll., NjP).

To Carter Glass

My dear Mr. Glass: The White House May 8, 1913

Thank you sincerely for the copy of the bill.[1] I shall go to work on it at once, and shall consult with you again as soon as I have got through it.

In haste   Faithfully yours,   Woodrow Wilson

TLS (C. Glass Papers, ViU).

[1] A copy (T MS, WP, DLC) of the Federal Reserve bill later much modified. Wilson went through this draft and made a few handwritten marginal comments.

From John Purroy Mitchel

New York, May 8, 1913.

It is with a full sense of the responsibility laid upon me as well as the honor conferred by your nomination that I accept the appoi[n]tment at your hands of Collector of the Port of New York. It will be my constant endeavor in administring this office to reflect credit upon your administration and to justify the confidence which you have placed in me, and which I assure you I deeply appreciate.   John Purroy Mitchell.

T telegram (WP, DLC).

To John Purroy Mitchel

My dear Mr. Mitchel: The White House May 8, 1913

Thank you very warmly for your cordial telegram of today. I appreciate most highly the sense of devotion to public duty which has lead you to allow me to nominate you as Collector of the Port of New York, and I am delighted to have enlisted you in my administration.

Cordially and sincerely yours,   Woodrow Wilson

TLS (J. P. Mitchel Papers, DLC).

From James Kerney

My dear Mr. President: Trenton, New Jersey May 8, 1913

The Mitchel appointment is one of the very best things that has happened for us yet. When such staunch standpatters as the New York Tribune crowd fall over themselves in praise, it is easy to see what's going to happen in New York state. The foxy Senator may get away with some of the glory, but I am confident he will never get away with any of the man. It's going to clear things up in the state as I don't believe any other single move could possibly have done.

I had two long conferences with Mitchel and the views he entertains on public affairs are bound to make him a very shining force for the rest of the country, should conditions so shape themselves that he becomes the Mayor. To have him gradually assume command politically in New York is going to be not only of inestimable value to the common cause, but is going to add a most useful aide and ally to your own leadership in the rest of the country. He is a marvel for a youngster and so much aggressive independence at the head of our greatest city would be sure to have far-reaching results.

We had been taking such extra precautions to guard against any disclosures that I almost had heart failure when Mitchel called me on the 'phone at six o'clock yesterday afternoon and advised me that his nomination had been made. I had just reached home from New York, where, among other things, I had assured him that he would get twenty-four hours notice before anything was finally done. He and I were both naturally disturbed lest there had been a leak somewhere, but we finally agreed that it was one of those unusual coincidences that do sometimes happen. Dudley Malone was in to see Mitchell after I had left in the afternoon, and informed him that only the night before (Tuesday) he had been urging O'Gorman to take Mitchel as a compromise and that he felt that that was what O'Gorman would ultimately do. Dudley did not know that the name had already been forwarded to the Senate. It is our view that O'Gorman, to save his own face, decided to put the name up to you yesterday without having the slightest inkling that you were already so seriously considering Mitchel.

Let us hope for as favorable an outcome at tomorrow's special session here. All your friends are working hard.

Very sincerely yours,   James Kerney

TLS (J. P. Tumulty Papers, DLC).

To John Joseph Fitzgerald

My dear Mr. Fitzgerald: [The White House] May 9, 1913

I have been thinking a good deal lately of the possible business reactions which may occur as a result of the passage of the tariff, and would like to put this thought into your mind: Would it not be well for us to go forward as rapidly as our resources will permit with the erection of public buildings and the completion of other public works, in order that we may release as much money as possible for the sake of business and afford employment to a larger number of persons than would otherwise be employed? I would be very much obliged if you would think this over seriously.

Cordially and sincerely yours, Woodrow Wilson[1]

TLS (Letterpress Books, WP, DLC).
[1] WW to T. S. Martin, May 9, 1913, TLS (Letterpress Books, WP, DLC), is the same letter, *mutatis mutandis*.

From Robert Underwood Johnson

Dear Mr. President: New York May 9. 1913.

I am today completing the fortieth year of my service on the editorial staff of *The Century*. In all my dealing with public questions I have had no more agreeable work than to record appreciation of what you have done in the last year in instilling right principles into the public mind. I have done nothing appreciable for you, but you have done much for me in helping me stand firm for the ideals of this great institution:

"For he that feeds men serveth few;
He serves all who dares be true."

May I say to you, in all respect, therefore, that I am in a panic over the exemption provision of the Sundry Civil Bill—the persistent report that you are going to sign it. At this distance it seems to violate two important principles: (1) the opposition to the vicious method of forcing the hand of the Executive by "rider" legislation, as in the disgraceful Panama Canal Tolls Exemption— a thinly disguised subsidy avowed as such by the last Administration. On the apparently authoritative announcement that you were opposed to this method, I wrote in approval of your position in the May *Century* "Common Sense in the White House" (p. 149). If you yield your ground now, will you not have to meet the same situation again and again?

(2) I cannot see anything but class legislation in the exemption proviso. It reminds me of the Indiana farmer who was "in favor of the law but ag'in' its enforcement." It is even apologized for as an "offset" to the manufacturers' advantage in the tariff legislation of *cis-bellum* times, so to speak! Shall we never get back to considering legislation on its merits? That has not been the way the game has been played, but we look to you to give us the square deal, and to lift politics out of prejudice, and dicker-

ing, and log-rolling, and selfishness, and geographical provincial-
ism—all influences which hold us back in a kind of moral fog.

I have a very special reason for wishing to know what can be
said in defense of what seems to me a hobbling of the law officers
in their execution of the Sherman Anti-Trust Act. Mr. Root's
argument seems to me unanswerable, but if it does not convince
you I hope your reply to it will convince me.

Believe me, my dear Mr. President, respectfully and faithfully
yours,   R. U. Johnson.

ALS (WP, DLC).

To Robert Underwood Johnson

My dear Mr. Johnson: [The White House] May 10, 1913.

Your letters have afforded me a great deal of pleasure, and
I wish to assure you that I shall not take action on the Sundry
Civil Bill without giving the provision to which you refer my
most earnest consideration. Thank you very much for having
written.

Cordially and faithfully yours,   Woodrow Wilson

TLS (Letterpress Books, WP, DLC).

To Hiram Warren Johnson

Washington, D. C., May 11, 1913.

The President directs me to express his appreciation of your
courtesy in delaying action on the land bill now before you until
its provisions could be communicated to the Japanese Government and considered by it.

His Excellency, Baron Chinda, has, on behalf of his government, presented an earnest protest against the measure. As you
have before you but two alternatives, viz., to approve or to veto,
it will avail nothing to recall to your attention the amendments
suggested to the legislature; and as the President has already laid
before you his views upon the subject it is unnecessary to reiter-
ate them. He passes over questions affecting treaty rights for
two reasons, first, because the bill passed by the legislature is
avowedly intended to conform to treaty obligations and, second,
because any conflict complained of would be a matter for the
courts, but the President feels justified in expressing again his
desire that action on the subject be deferred for this session, and
he expresses the desire the more freely because the legislature

can be reconvened at any time if the welfare of the state requires it. He is fully alive to the importance of removing any root of discord which may create antagonism between American citizens and the subjects of Oriental nations residing here, but he is impelled by a sense of duty to express the hope that you will see fit to allow time for diplomatic effort. The Nations affected by the proposed law are friendly nations—nations that have shown themselves willing to co-operate in the establishment of harmonious relations between their people and ours.

If a postponement commends itself to your judgment the President will be pleased to cooperate in a systematic effort to discover and correct any evils that may exist in connection with land ownership by aliens. W. J. Bryan.

TC telegram (WP, DLC).

From the Diary of Colonel House

Washington, May 11, 1913.

Just before dinner I received a telephone message from the White House saying the President would like to see me after dinner at my convenience. . . . The President met me upstairs in his library, and we had our last interview before my sailing for Europe.

I talked to him particularly about the currency bill and advised what should be done. I told him that Mr. Bryan was waking up to the fact that the proposed bill was not to his liking and that it did not provide for direct Government issue.[1] We discussed at some length how this situation should be met. Mr. Bryan wants Carter Glass to go over the bill with him, but I asked Glass not to do so until after the President had talked with Bryan. It was my opinion the President was the only one who could influence Mr. Bryan or whose conclusions he would accept. I advised talking with him alone, rather than bringing the matter up in the Cabinet meeting because if it was brought up there Bryan would argue with his fellow members and would become set while if he, the President, would talk to him alone and in an earnest and direct way, I felt certain he could bring him around.

The President was greatly interested in this new phase of the situation. He admitted that if Mr. Bryan insisted upon his point of view that it might kill currency legislation at this session, and that when it was taken up at the regular session, Bryan might leave the Cabinet if the President was insistent upon putting the bill··through. I also told him that Mr. Bryan wanted to know what had become of his suggestion of employing Governor Folk in the Steel Trust suit, and that I had answered that McReynolds had thought that instead of employing other counsel it would be better to form a committee of which the President, Mr. Bryan and himself were the members. When I told Mr. Bryan this he turned to Mrs. Bryan and laughingly said: "Well Mamma they have got us there."

I also told the President that I had said to Mr. Bryan that I did not believe the suit would ever come to a point of serious discussion with the proposed committee, for the reason that I believed McReynolds would insist upon such terms as the Steel people would refuse, believing they would fare better if they took a decree from the Supreme Court.

I spoke to the President about conserving his strength, and suggested various means by which it could be done. I thought it was essential. He said it looked as if the people were trying to kill him, and he spoke of the lonliness of his position in a way that was saddening. He expressed again and again his regret at my departure. I said I felt like a deserter and that I would not go excepting that it had come to the point where I could no longer serve him, for I was broken down and it was absolutely necessary for me to get away for a few weeks.

He thanked me warmly for all I had done, and said he would feel unhappy until I returned. I expressed my gratitude for his kindness and said it had been the greatest pleasure of my life to be associated with him. I spoke of his probable renomination and re-election. He replied "do not let us talk about that now. My dear friend if I can finish up my legislative program I do not desire re-election." I urged him to keep up his courage for if he ever faltered in the slightest, he would lose his leadership and influence. He realized this and declared he would maintain his courage to the end.

I related that Captain Bill McDonald once told me that he attributed his still being alive to the fact that he had never hesitated the fraction of a second, but had always gone straight towards the point of danger, and the courage of the other fellow had always failed. I urged this attitude upon the President as strongly as I knew how, and told him it was the *most essential thing of all*. I am sure he realizes it, and I am also sure he will carry himself like a brave and gallant gentleman.

1 That is, of currency.

Remarks at a Press Conference

[May 12, 1913]

Mr. President, there is a very interesting dispatch in the papers this morning in which Mr. Bryan, in a telegram, refers to the action of the Japanese Ambassador as a very earnest protest. Can we know whether that is the description of the Japanese Ambassador's action by the Secretary of State, or whether it is the Japanese Ambassador's own description?

It is the Secretary of State's description.

The reason I ask is that the language of diplomacy is rather an exact science, and if the Japanese Ambassador himself described his action as a very earnest protest, it seems to me that a much greater degree of seriousness might attach.

No, that is the Secretary's own description.

It would not be possible, would it, Mr. President, to get a copy of the protest—or excerpts?

You see, we could not do that without the authority of the Tokyo government, and I do not understand that they desire it. The protest is not serious in the sense in which it was intimated just now.

Mr. President, then you would feel that Mr. Bryan's phrase, "very earnest," was colloquial rather than—

It was just to represent the character of it.

In the ordinary sense?

In the ordinary sense.

It seems to me in a situation like that, that the fullest publicity that was consistent with all the interests concerned is very much to be desired—that we ought not to be left to guess or hear rumors about that.

I think so, too. I quite agree with you there. Of course, as you know, I am a novice in international intercourse of this kind, and I do not know the exact science that has been referred to. The whole thing—if I may say this just among ourselves—is being managed in a very friendly way, but in a very frank way, setting forth the opinions, and so forth. And, of course, there are certain kinds of frankness which, if published, might give the thing a serious aspect which it is not meant to wear. And, therefore, it is in the best interests of all concerned to permit the greatest frankness, and that precludes publicity in some instances. But that is the present situation.

Is not the situation, Mr. President, such that we can eliminate the word "serious"?

Oh, yes. The word "serious" was not used—it was the word

"earnest." No, nobody is using the word "serious" as I know
of.
Mr. President, what remedy can Japan ask that is possible or—
        I would rather you ask John Bassett Moore that.
What remedy does she ask?
        She has not asked any remedy.
Mr. President, the morning papers—one or two of them in New
York—seem to indicate that Governor Johnson is practically cer-
tain to approve the bill today; that is, before noon, which is, I
believe, the hour of the limit.
        I thought it was tomorrow.[1]
But, anyway, in the event of his approving the measure, would
it be proper to state what would be the probable next step?
        No, I do not think If's are appropriate in a business of this
        kind. I don't think we ought to conjecture what we will do.
Mr. President, can we discuss certain things that are not conjec-
tural then, but which seem to be facts. As, for instance, the
real question at issue—as it has reached the stage where it is the
question at issue—is that of the denial by the Americans of the
right of naturalization to the Japanese?
        No, that has not been raised at all.
But isn't that the underlying, the fundamental, thing?
        In one sense that underlies the definition of the law as it is
        framed in California undoubtedly, but the law is scrupulous
        in observing the treaty obligations of the United States. It
        is founded on the treaty obligations.
If Japanese were eligible to citizenship, there would be no protest
against the California law.
        I don't know about that!
It would lose its strength. It would remove the discrimination
against them. So that the real question between Japan and the
United States is with the federal government, rather than with
the California government.
        No, I cannot say that, because there has been no intimation
        that that question has been raised. As you know, that is not
        explicit in the law. It is a matter of definition and inter-
        pretation.
That is a matter, as I understand it, of federal statute, is it not?
        The eligibility to citizenship? Yes. The naturalization.
Is it plain, Mr. President, that that bill is really not a violation
of the treaty?
        It can't be, because it is based on the treaty. It explicitly
        grants to present residents, but who are not eligible to cit-
        izenship, the rights that are granted to them by treaty.

Upon what, then, is the Japanese protest founded?

Why, I think just upon the feeling that there is an effort to discriminate against their people, on the ground of their alleged ineligibility to citizenship.

Has there been an intimation from Japan that they prefer not to go to court with the question of their eligibility to citizenship?

No, there hasn't been any intimation of any sort; just a very respectful calling our attention to this discrimination.

Mr. President, is any mention made of a treaty in Japan's formal protest?

I don't think that I ought in the circumstances to discuss the protest, but there would naturally be a reference to our treaty relations. I feel uncomfortable in seeming to try to conceal what is in the protest. There is nothing in it that need be concealed; only I just feel that if they want to confer with us in a way which will leave them free to say what they please, without offending any sensibilities, I should not discuss it. Therefore, I am acting as one gentleman would act with another.

Someone spoke to the Japanese Ambassador, also with the Secretary of State, regarding making public this protest. The Japanese Ambassador said that he expected the White House to do it, and the Secretary of State said that that matter probably would be considered.

Well, that has not reached me at all.

Mr. President, would it be possible—would you regard it as proper—to get the permission of the Japanese embassy to make it public?

Do you mean for me to seek it?

I do not mean in any formal way—to ascertain whether it would be in any way offensive to them?

I would rather you ask that of Mr. Bryan, rather than of me; because the whole thing is in his hands.

Mr. President, in view of the fact that you say the treaty, in the opinion of the Department of State, is not violated, doesn't the situation resolve itself where the government is called upon to defend the action of the California legislature? Isn't that what it amounts to?

I think you can answer that question as well as I can. That is a matter of opinion—a matter of judgment.

T MS (C. L. Swem Coll., NjP).
  [1] He signed the bill on May 19, 1913.

To James Kerney

My dear Kerney: The White House May 12, 1913
It was a most astonishing outcome. I know that Tumulty has already given you the details of it. It quite took my breath away. I am warmly obliged to you for the part you so generously played, and I have no doubt that it had not a little to do with getting Mr. Mitchel's consent. I am very happy about the outcome.
In haste
Cordially and faithfully yours,   Woodrow Wilson
TLS (WC, NjP).

To Nathan Philemon Bryan

My dear Senator: [The White House] May 12, 1913
Being shut out by the daily demands on me from reading the newspapers, I apparently have to find out what is going on from the weekly papers, which I look over at the week's end. I have just seen, therefore, in Collier's Weekly your correspondence with the Citrus Growers Association of Florida.[1] I want to express my warm and sincere admiration and to say that I congratulate the party and the country upon having a man to serve them who sees so clearly and does his duty so fearlessly.
Cordially and sincerely yours,   Woodrow Wilson

TLS (Letterpress Books, WP, DLC).
   [1] Extracts from Bryan's correspondence with the Florida Citrus Exchange appeared in Mark Sullivan's regular column, "Comment on Congress," *Collier's*, LI (May 17, 1913), 9. The Citrus Exchange had sent a telegram to Bryan demanding that he support a tariff of one cent a pound on oranges and grapefruit rather than the thirty-five-cents-per-box rate set by the Underwood bill. It further noted that "Louisiana has notified us that their Senators will help us on citrus tariff if you will help their Senators on sugar. *Will you consult with both Louisiana and Mississippi Senators in this matter, and see if such an alliance can be safely arranged?*"
   In his lengthy reply, Bryan declared: "Florida is Democratic and has endorsed . . . the position taken by the Democratic party upon the tariff question. *A very simple method of ascertaining whether a person believes in a principle is whether he will shrink from having it applied to himself.*" Rejecting any alliance with other senators, he declared that this kind of logrolling was exactly what had led to most of the protective tariff abuses of the past. Moreover, he asked, if it was his duty to make this particular alliance, would it not be equally his duty to make similar alliances with all other senators with special interests to protect? In closing, Bryan stated his position unequivocally: "*I had this question to meet when I was a candidate for the Senate and I can only say to you now what I said to the growers themselves then—that I will not vote for a protective tariff on anything, wherever grown, manufactured, or produced.*"

From Delbert James Haff,[1] with Enclosure

Personal

Sir: At Washington May 12, 1913.

As suggested in conversation this afternoon, I submit herewith a memorandum of certain facts regarding the present political condition of Mexico together with some observations and suggestions which Your Excellency may or may not deem of value, but which at least are submitted in good faith and with the deep desire that they may be of some service in the way of throwing some light upon the vexing Mexican situation.

I will take pleasure in communicating further, after my arrival in Mexico City, any information regarding the condition of things there which I deem to be of sufficient importance.

With the expression of my highest consideration, I remain,
Your obedient servant,   Delbert J. Haff

TLS (WP, DLC).
1 Lawyer of Kansas City, who specialized in representing American mining and railway companies before Mexican courts.

ENCLOSURE

MEMORANDUM

Suggestions bearing on the problem of the present
relations of the United States and Mexico,
growing out of the disturbed political
conditions of the lat[t]er country.

First. Armed intervention of the United States in the affairs of Mexico should be regarded by the people of the United States as a national calamity, as it certainly would prove to be, and is, therefore, to be avoided with the greatest care and by all honorable means. I make this statement as the result of an intimate acquaintance and knowledge of the Mexican people for more than twenty years, supplemented also by a knowledge of the Latin American prejudices and points of view. Intervention would cost the United States untold millions, and its disastrous consequences could not be measured. I have fought the intervention sentiment vigorously whenever it was manifest.

Second. The intimate commercial relations, however, between the two countries, the enormous investments of Americans in Mexico, the increasing commerce between the two countries, the jealousies of certain other foreign peoples interested in the country, and the responsibilities which the United States have assumed in Latin America growing out of the Monroe Doctrine, and which responsibilities are intensified in Mexico owing to its proximity to this country, as well as the world-old natural laws of national expansion, together make intervention in Mexico almost a certain destiny of this country which can be avoided only by a firm and clear policy on our part in carrying on political intercourse of the two governments.

The Mexican people give us no credit whatever for any philanthropic or disinterested motives in our attitude towards them. They believe us ready to avail ourselves of any excuse to deprive them of their independence and annex their territory; and so long as this belief continues on their part, the danger of intervention as well as the necessity will continue to be remote, since they will, to avoid this danger, discharge their responsibilities towards American citizens and American investments in that country and in protection of American commerce. Dispel that fear from their minds, and the natural antipathy between the Latin and the Anglo Saxon, increased by the feeling of jealousy which the inferior nation feels for the superior, and the lack of restraint among their people, due to the growing lawlessness, is likely to bring about some outrage against Americans domiciled in that country that will arouse the whole United States and force intervention and war, as did the incident of the blowing up of the "Maine." I regard it, therefore, as of prime importance, and in order to avoid the danger of intervention, to at all times hold the Mexican Government up to the strictest responsibility for the protection of the lives, the liberty and the property of Americans residing in that country. This should be demanded and insisted upon by our Government at all times. Any relaxation on our part of this rule, or any evidence of abandoning or waiving our strict rights, is invariably accepted by the Mexican people and the Mexican Government as an evidence of fear, cowardice or weakness on our part, and tends to encourage wrongs.

Third. The problem of the pacification of Mexico is not simply a political problem. That is a question not generally understood in this country; but it is a racial and a social problem which has been fostered by a caste system in force in that country since the Spanish Conquest. Ninety per cent of the population of the country are Indians who have been kept in a condition almost of peonage or species of slavery by a limited number of great land owners. They are unlettered, and have the natural hatred of the Indian for the white man, which has been increased by their treatment. The Madero revolution of 1910 was a revolution of the proletariat and in his interest. The present mental state of the common people of Mexico is one of confusion, false ideas and delusions. They have a wrong notion of the meaning of liberty, which they interpret rather as license. This is increased by their socialistic and communistic ideas. The Indian is originally, and by tradition, a communist, as is well known. He practiced it in its most perfect form in Mexico, and not until about the year 1900 was the communist system of land-holding among the Indians extinguished by the Government. Their attitude toward the Government is traditionally one of hatred, which, by force of circumstances, is extended to all foreign companies and enterprises because they were always protected and sustained by the Government, especially under General Diaz. Their notion, therefore, of democracy is a sort of socialism and communism, and the revolution has worked their complete insubordination to government and law. Add to this the fact that superior force is the only argument they have ever known or respected, and as they have, by the recent revolution, been taught that they could overthrow and dominate the Government, the cause of the continued revolutionary spirit and the difficulty of overcoming it and establishing order are very obvious.

Fourth. Their contact with the people of the United States has made the inhabitants of the border Mexican states more unruly and lawless.

The Present Peril in Our Relations

Fifth. It is to be regretted, I think, that the question of the recognition of the Huerta Government was raised by us, for the reason that non-recognition of the *de facto* government in Mexico has had a powerful effect in encouraging revolt against that government; indeed it is understood, in the north of Mexico, as a form of expressing sympathy with, and encouragement for, revolution against the de facto government. The resolution of Huerta not to recognize our Ambassador is also most unfortunate, and is apt to be interpreted by the people as inviting hostility and reprisal against Americans, and if this unfortunate misunderstanding between the two governments is long continued there is great danger of some explosion that will bring about the very intervention that we desire to avoid. I regard it as an ever-present peril until the question of recognition is settled.

Moreover, the continuance of revolution and war in Mexico for another year will utterly ruin the country, and destroy a large part of the one thousand million dollars of American investments there. The resources of the Government, as well as of the revolutionists, are being exhausted and the finances of the country are falling into disorder and confusion which will destroy the credit of the nation so that it will require a quarter of a century for the country to recover.

Sixth. Moreover, if the present de facto government of Mexico shall succeed in pacifying the country without the moral aid and sympathy of our Government, we shall lose the friendship and prestige which has required twenty years to build up, our commerce will be greatly injured and American influence undermined, a loss which I believe will extend to and be felt by us in all the Latin American States, for the Mexicans, as well as all Latin Americans, are highly emotional and sentimental and proud, and they will nurse a grievance and resent a real or fancied wrong for an indefinite period. It seems to me also that non-recognition would have the effect of barring the claims of American citizens for loss inflicted by both sides during the present revolution. It would seem that we could hardly hold the Mexican Nation responsible for the acts or omissions of a government that we ourselves repudiate as illegal, if that government, which the revolutionists denominate as illegal, falls.

Seventh. The present political situation in Mexico is briefly defined as follows: The governors of the States of Coahuila and Sonora, dominating the political machinery of these two states, and aided by a large following in Chihuahua, are in control of almost the entire area of the northern boundary states of Mexico, and are in rebellion against the administration of President Huerta, calling themselves constitutionalists.[1] They do not pretend, and have not pretended, to secede from Mexico, but they have denounced Huerta as a usurper and his administration as illegal, and are largely supported in that position by the attitude of the United States Government in refusing to recognize Huerta as the president *de jure* of Mexico. They pretend to exercise the federal authority and enforce the federal laws within the territory

[1] Venustiano Carranza, Governor of the State of Coahuila since 1911, declared on February 19, 1913, that his state would not recognize the Huerta regime. The State of Sonora, under the leadership of Acting Governor Ignacio Pesqueira, took similar action on March 5. The revolutionary movement in Chihuahua had several leaders, most notably Francisco Villa. The rebels soon organized military forces and, as Haff states, by mid-May controlled much of the territory of the northern border states. On March 26, Carranza and some of his associates from Coahuila formulated and proclaimed the Plan of Guadalupe, which again disavowed Huerta's government, pledged the signers to fight on to restore constitutional government, designated Carranza as "First Chief" of the Constitutionalist army, and stipulated that the First Chief would act as *ad interim* president for the purpose of holding elections once military victory had been achieved. Delegates from Sonora, Chihuahua, and Coahuila met with Carranza in Monclova on April 19 to draft and sign a statement of cooperation based upon the Plan of Guadalupe. See Cumberland, *Mexican Revolution*, pp. 15-72, *passim*.

of the State of Coahuila and Sonora in trust for the nation until
a constitutional president, as they call him, pledged to the support of the law, can be elected. The constitutionalists, however,
are practically without resources—that is, without funds—and
have exhausted, for the most part, their sources to obtain funds,
and I feel quite sure are in a position where a friendly intervening powerful influence like the Government of the United States
could bring about a suspension of hostilities and an agreement
between the constitutionalists and the federalists represented by
the Huerta administration. The constitutionalists steadfastly refuse to recognize Huerta or to treat with him.

Eighth. I heartily approve of the resolution of the President to
avoid the practice of so-called "Dollar diplomacy," which practice
I understand to mean converting the State Department into a
bureau for the aid of promoters of foreign undertakings. I do not
understand this declaration to mean, however, that the United
States Government has no duty and takes no interest in the protection of legitimate investments already made by Americans in
foreign countries at the invitation and on the promise of protection of the governments of those countries. Such investments are
the basis and principal stimulant of our foreign commerce and
are entitled to the same protection and are of the same interest
to our citizens at home as the foreign commerce itself. Kill the
former and you greatly injure the latter. There is great danger
of misinterpretation and misapplication of a popular phrase. And
if the practice of "Dollar diplomacy" should be understood to
mean the reasonable protection of American investments of all
kinds in foreign countries, it would be disastrous to Americans
both at home and abroad, and very injurious to our foreign commerce, which is one form of foreign investment.

Suggestions Based on the Foregoing Facts.

I will conclude these observations by repeating here a suggestion which I made a few days ago in writing, confidentially,
to a friend of the President, and which may have been transmitted to the President, but whether he is already familiar with it
or not I will take the liberty of repeating it; namely, that, in
my opinion, the United States Government has a great opportunity at the present time, by acting quickly, of presenting a plan
to Huerta, agreeing to recognize him on condition that he will
call an election at an early date, October 26 being too remote, and
that he guarantee a fair election in all those states of which he
has control, the constitutionalists to do the same and to participate in the election. The constitutionalists, on the other hand, to

agree that in consideration of this election being called and being fairly held, hostilities shall be suspended, and that they will loyally support the president who shall be chosen as the result of such election.

I do not think it necessary to insist that Huerta shall resign and some other interim president be appointed in his stead, because he is not pretending to hold the power in Mexico, except for the purpose of bringing about peace and a constitutional election, and to guarantee that a president legally elected may be installed. He is the de facto president at the present time, and is a man of energy and executive ability, is in command of the army, and is, better than any other person, able to carry out such an agreement; and I think, from my knowledge of the situation on both sides and the temper of both sides, that both the federalists and the constitutionalists might welcome the friendly intervention of the Department of State of our Government to bring about an understanding between the two factions and peace in the country, as the most graceful and practicable way of getting out of the difficult situation in which both sides now find themselves. It may be possible even that Huerta, if recognized by the United States, would consent if necessary to step aside and allow some other person acceptable to the constitutionalists to serve as interim president during the elections, if peace could in this manner be established. If this is not done, war will continue until the country is absolutely exhausted, banditism will grow and increase until there will be no security for human life and private property whatever in the Republic, and the millions of foreign property invested in the country will be depreciated, and in many cases absolutely destroyed. The losses now amount to millions of dollars per day and the situation cannot be much longer sustained.

In addition to that fact, foreign nations are becoming restive and are seeking to undermine the influence of the United States in Mexico. The British Government has already recognized Huerta in a most marked manner by autograph letter from the King, due to the efforts of Lord Cowdray (Sir Weetman Pearson) who has the largest interests outside of American interests in the Mexican Republic. He is using his efforts to obtain a large loan in England, and I am informed that he has succeeded on condition that the English Government would recognize Huerta, which has been done. If Mexico is helped out of her trouble by British and German influence, American prestige in that country and the commerce of the United States will suffer great damage.

I was in Cananea ten days ago, and saw the lawless condition of things. The people are in the same frame of mind that they were in the City of Paris in 1793, and are as ready to commit depredations against life and property. The want of opportunity for employment which is increasing daily is putting the people in a starving condition, and great looting may be expected in the near future, unless conditions can be speedily changed. Our Government has the opportunity to do a great service to humanity and gain lasting glory by it; in fact, a service far greater than that which was performed by President Roosevelt in bringing about an understanding between the Russian and the Japanese Governments in their late war.

Our Ambassador in Mexico is, in my opinion, the man to attempt this work. It might be found necessary to send a special envoy to treat with the constitutionalists, while entrusting our Ambassador in Mexico to treat with the Huerta Government. But in any event, it should be a possible task for the Department of State, because both sides will hesitate to repudiate the suggestion of the United States Government and its powerful influence presented in the form of a wish, and backed, as it necessarily is, with the moral right to demand that it shall be accepted and complied with, when it is considered that the interests of the United States in Mexico represent practically every industry of that country, excepting that of agriculture, and that the commerce of Mexico with the United States represents more than seventy-five per cent of her total foreign trade, all of which, so important to both countries, is now imperiled.

T MS (WP, DLC).

From the Diary of Josephus Daniels

Tuesday, May 13, 1913.

The discussion over the California situation occupied much of the time of the Cabinet and was generally participated in. The President read Baron Chinda's protest against the legislation in California.[1] The words of the protest were very strong—stronger than the circumstances seemed to warrant. The language, while diplomatic, was such as to cause Secretary Redfield to feel that it might imply that in the event this government was unable to meet the demands and wishes of Japan, the worst results might follow. All the members of the Cabinet seemed to think the language was stronger than ought to have been employed and should give

[1] The Japanese Ambassador to the Secretary of State, May 9, 1913, *FR 1913*, pp. 629-31.

them pause, but did not think it implied anything except a very earnest desire to secure the same rights for the Japanese in California that are given to other aliens. This protest, of course, will be made public when the President and the Secretary of State, Mr. Bryan, reply to it and it will take the subsequent results of history to determine whether the language really had in it the implication of possible force that the Japanese might employ. Secretary Redfield thought that what ought to be read into it was all which it implied by considering it in the light of diplomatic utterances. . . .

I brought up the question before the Cabinet as to whether the three ships, the SARATOGA, the MONTEREY, and the MONADNOCK,[2] which are in the Chinese rivers, ought to be ordered to the Philippines in accord with the suggestion of the Aid for Operations of the Fleet, Admiral Fiske.[3] I had read a statement on the possibility of war with Japan from the Aid for Operations to the Cabinet, which is appended hereto.[4]

Washington. May 13, 1913.

From: The Aid for Operations.
To: The Secretary of the Navy.

Subject: Possibility of War with Japan.

1. While I do not believe that our present tension with Japan will result in war, while I realize the reasonableness of the belief of many people that Japan does not desire war, and while I earnestly hope that war will not result, yet I beg leave to present the following statement of facts:

(I) The Islands of Japan are not at all fertile; the climate is very trying; the people have a hard time to subsist on the Islands.

(II) The Philippine Islands, which lie to the southwest of Japan, are extremely fertile, are very sparsely inhabited, and would be an extremely desirable possession for Japan as an outlet for their surplus population.

(III) From their geographical position with reference to Japan and to the east coast of Asia, the Philippines would be an extremely desirable possession for Japan as a strategic position from which to command the coast of China.

(IV) The Hawaiian Islands also are very fertile, and would be an extremely desirable possession for Japan. Japanese people

2 Actually, the ships were *Saratoga, Albany,* and *Cincinnati.*
3 Bradley Allen Fiske, Rear Admiral, U.S.N., at this time Aide for Operations, the chief military adviser of the Secretary of the Navy.
4 The original document is pasted in the diary.

are already on the Islands in great numbers; and it has frequently been stated that Japan declared, just previous to the Spanish War that she did not desire the United States to take possession of the Hawaiian Islands.

2. It is not impossible that Japan, in spite of her poverty, may decide that it is worth her while to go to war with the United States in order to secure possession of the Philippine Islands and the Hawaiian Islands.

3. Should she decide to go to war, she could at once occupy the Philippine Islands and the Hawaiian Islands, and hoist the flag of Japan on those Islands.

4. After doing this, after placing in the Hawaiian Islands, say, 60,000 men, and in the Philippine Islands 150,000 men, she could withdraw her fleet to Japan, and, to use a slang expression, "standpat"; that is, she would withdraw her fleet to a place in the Inland Sea, and not do any fighting whatever.

5. All the United States could do would be to send her Fleet to Japan; we could cut off most of the trade of Japan with the rest of the world by means of our Fleet, but not all of it. We could cut off her trade to the westward, and south'ard, and eastward, but probably we could not cut it off to the northwestward. Probably Japan would be able by means of mines and destroyers, even without the use of her battleship fleet, to keep the Sea of Japan sufficiently open for her vessels to communicate with Korea, and from there to make land communication with the rest of the world.

6. This would undoubtedly place Japan in a very distressing position; but her people are very frugal, and if they have to do so, can live in a very simple and inexpensive way. They have tremendous national feeling, a great deal of endurance, and determination, and probably could stand this condition for, say, two years, or even more.

7. During these two years our entire fleet, practically speaking, would have to be maintained off the southern coast of Japan. To do this would be enormously expensive; and even if no actual battleship battle were fought, it is probable that many of our ships would be lost through the agency of submarines, mines, and torpedoes.

8. What the issue would be would depend upon the relative state of mind of the people of the United States and the people of Japan.

9. It is possible that Japan may believe that there is so large a number of people in the United States who would be glad to get rid of the Philippine Islands, that they would easily come to terms

with Japan after an inglorious and expensive war that lasted, say, two years.

10. In other words, it is conceivable that Japan may conclude —*may have already concluded*—that, if she should go to war with the United States, she could, by enduring a period of privation and distress lasting about two years, acquire possession of both the Philippine Islands and the Hawaiian Islands. Her war against China supplies a precedent for such a procedure.

Bradley A. Fiske,
Rear Admiral, U.S.N.

There was considerable discussion of the matter. I recommended that no movement be made at this time. The "yellow press" in America are so aggravating and the Japanese are in such an inflammatory mood, I thought that any movement might give them an opportunity to inflame the people of Japan, who do not fully understand our attitude in regard to the movement of ships in the Yellow Sea, as evidence of our unfriendliness and our expectation of war. I have observed that if a man puts a gun on his shoulder and walks down the street, particularly down a street in which he knows there is a man with whom he has some misunderstanding, it is pretty likely to cause the other man to get a gun himself and that death or something else serious results, whereas if the man had not started out with the gun on his shoulder the difficulty would have ended peaceably.

T MS (J. Daniels Papers, DLC).

A Draft of a Note to the Japanese Government[1]

[May 14, 1913]

To His Excellency, Baron Chinda, Ambassador of Japan:

I have the honor to acknowledge the receipt of your note of May ninth, laying before my Government the representations of the Imperial Government of Japan with regard to the law just adopted by the State of California concerning the holding of agricultural lands by aliens.

The Government of the United States regrets most sincerely that the Imperial Government of Japan should regard this legislation as based upon an unfair discrimination against the Japanese settlers in California. Being apprised while that legislation was still under consideration by the Legislature of California that that might be the feeling of the Imperial Government, the President and I very earnestly attempted to induce the legislative authorities of California to reconsider, to forego, or radically to modify their plans in the matter. Under the Constitutional arrangements of the United States we could do no more than that, and we most sincerely regret that the authorities of California did not feel at liberty to act upon our representations. It would have been most agreeable to the Government of the United States to have succeeded, as the friendly interpreters of the feeling of Japan, in inducing the Legislature of California to change in many essential respects the terms of the legislation under discussion. Our failure to do so was a distinct disappointment to us.

At the same time, we feel that the Imperial Government has been misled in its interpretation of the spirit and object of the legislation in question. It is not political. It is not part of any general national policy which would indicate unfriendliness or any purpose inconsistent with the best and most cordial understanding between the two nations. It is wholly economic. It is based upon the particular economic conditions existing in California as interpreted by her own people, who wish to avoid certain conditions of competition in their agricultural industries. Their conclusions may be debatable, but their objects clearly fall within the well established limits of economic self-government recognized the world over.

The Government of the United States is very jealous to maintain its treaty obligations to the utmost point of scruple, and would itself have felt justified in protesting very vigorously against the law just enacted in California if that law had not seemed to it to safeguard to the fullest extent its treaty obligations to Japan. But the very terms of the act seem to the Government of the United States to remove all doubt and difficulty on that score. The act virtually embodies the terms of the treaty itself as its own terms in respect of the land owning rights of those aliens whose right to hold lands it seeks in some respects to curtail. No right or protection of right that could be claimed under the treaty is withheld or interfered with by the new law. Article XIV of the treaty, to which your Excellency refers, touches nothing, I would respectfully remind you, but the rights of commerce and navigation. These the legislation in question in no wise affects. The authors of the law seem to have been punctiliously careful to guard against any invasion of contractual rights. I need not assure your Excellency that this Government will cooperate with the Imperial Government in every possible way to maintain with the utmost cordiality the understandings which bind the two nations together in honor and in interest.

Your Excellency raises, very naturally and properly, the question how the case would stand should explicit treaties between the two countries expire or cease to be in force while, nevertheless, relations of entire amity and good will still continued to exist between them. I can only reply that in such circumstances the Government of the United States, so far as the present Administration can speak for it, would always deem it its pleasure, as well as a manifest mandate of its cordial friendship for Japan and the Japanese people, to safeguard the rights of trade and intercourse between the two peoples now secured by treaty. Its obligations of friendship would not be lessened or performed in niggardly fashion in any circumstances. It values too highly the regard of Japan and her cooperation in the great peaceful tasks of the modern world to jeopard them in any way; and I feel that I can assure your Excellency that there is no reason to feel that its policy in such matters would be embarrassed or interfered with by the legislation of any state of the Union. The economic policy of a single state with regard to a single kind of property cannot turn aside these strong and abiding currents of generous and profitable intercourse and good feeling.

In conclusion let me thank your Excellency for the candor with which you have dealt with this Government in this matter and express the hope that this episode in the intercourse of the two great countries which we represent will only quicken our understanding of one another and our confidence in the desire of each to do justice to the other.

T MS with WWhw emendations (WP, DLC).

[1] Wilson dictated the note printed below to Swem on May 14 from an undated WWsh draft (WP, DLC).

Remarks at a Press Conference

May 15, 1913

Could you tell us what headway has been made with currency in the past week, Mr. President?

> Well, none has been made, because the bill is still in process of being put together.

Hasn't a conference been arranged for some time next week, or rather this week?

> Not by me.

I understood that you were going to see Mr. Underwood and Representative Glass.

> No. I may see them, but I mean there is no conference arranged.

Do you expect the bill to be ready by the first of June?

> I hope so, but I really cannot tell yet.

Mr. President, your idea is to have the House take action on the currency bill now, isn't it?

My hope is, yes. My strong hope is that it will.

That is a strong possibility, isn't it?

I should say that it was, though I am not authorized to say that from any conferences with the leaders of the House.

Mr. President, is any particular bill being drawn with your knowledge, I mean a bill that would embody your ideas, and also the ideas of Mr. Underwood and Mr. Glass?

There are several tentative bills being drawn, and they are all of them with more or less consultation with me; and I suppose they all run along substantially the same lines.

You haven't brought in the chairmen of the two banking committees for that purpose?

Oh, no, sir.

Are these several bills you refer to one in the House and one in the Senate?

No; at least, those that I know of are bills that are being drawn one by a member of the House and one by outside parties, who are simply drafting it so that I can see what their idea is in detail, because, after all, the detail of the thing is the essential part.

Is the central idea the same, Mr. President, in the two?

I do not know what they will be, because I haven't seen them.

Can you give us any idea of what your ideas are of what legislation ought to be followed?

I could, but I don't think I will just now; because I think it is only fair to match my ideas with other men's before forming them finally.

Mr. President, is it fair to assume that they are all working along the same main line?

Yes, so far as I know they are. There is no contest that has yet disclosed itself on essential points.

Mr. President, did I understand you to say that someone outside the House is drawing up a bill?

Well, to be plain, a friend of mine, a professor of political economy.[1]

Would you tell us who that is, Mr. President? I thought that perhaps it might be Mr. Untermyer—someone associated with that committee?

No.

Mr. President, speaking with reference to Mr. Untermyer sug-

[1] Royal Meeker.

gested a question, and that is whether the bill will go so far as to the matters of clearinghouses and stock exchanges?

 Well, that has nothing to do with currency reform.

I know it wouldn't; it might with banking reform.

 This will be a strict currency reform bill. If that was taken up it would be for other statutes.

Mr. President, not to dwell on the point, will you tell us who the gentleman is?

 No, because I do not want him swamped by receiving all the correspondence I have received. This office can handle it, but his can't.

Mr. President, this bill will provide for the revision of national banking laws, will it not?

 Necessarily, you can't revise the currency without doing it.

Mr. President, we are all interested in the Japanese situation. There has been another turn given to it now. I think we would all like to know what the next step is.

 Well, the next step is to reply, of course, to the representations made by the Japanese government.

Has the Japanese Ambassador been furnished with a copy of the message of Governor Johnson?[2]

 Oh, yes.

Can you say anything about what the tenor of that reply will be?

 No, I can't say.

It will be delivered, I suppose, immediately, Mr. President.

 I don't even know that. It will depend upon circumstances. Of course, we want to observe all the deliberation that goes with courtesy.

Mr. President, is it your purpose to communicate any further with Governor Johnson?

 Not my present purpose.

Mr. President, how soon would the answer be sent?

 I couldn't tell you that; it will depend on circumstances.

It will probably be after the bill is signed—you will wait until the bill is signed?

 Again, I will just have to say I don't know.

Will the matter be one for cabinet deliberation tomorrow?

 Oh, well, we generally compare notes and opinions on all important subjects, but I don't know whether I shall formally bring it up or not.

Mr. President, when Mr. John Purroy Mitchel was here yesterday, it was said that he discussed with you the matter of economy

---

[2] H. W. Johnson to W. J. Bryan, May 14, 1913, *New York Times*, May 15, 1913. Johnson vehemently defended the bill and declared that he would sign it.

and efficiency; would you say along what lines, whether that was economy and efficiency of the federal government or of municipalities or making Washington a model city?

> Well, you know Mr. Mitchel and several other gentlemen came down some weeks ago on a double errand; one had to do with making Washington a model city, and the other had to do with a systematic study of economy and coordination in the departments of the government which would enable us to have a scientific budget; and it was only the latter question that he brought up yesterday.

Mr. President, have you expressed yourself with reference to public hearings on the tariff by the Senate Finance Committee?

> No.

Would you care to say whether you favor public hearings or not?

> Well, I feel that is the Senate's business. You know what Artemus Ward said. He said, "When I see a snake's hole, I walk around it, because I say to myself, 'That is a snake's hole.'"

Mr. President, a great deal of interest has been aroused by, first, Mr. Underwood's announcement in the House that the government would investigate any reductions of wages which seem to have been reduced for the purpose of politics, and then Mr. Redfield's very forceful speech last night; and I wanted to ask, sir, if you had any substantial or well-founded information that there was any purpose on the part of the manufacturers to reduce wages.

> No, nothing, except just the vague rumors that are always in the air at this stage of a tariff bill.

Mr. President, coming back to that matter of Mr. Mitchel, what I really had in mind was whether you were going to carry out some ideas that had been attributed to you to make Washington a model city, a model for the municipalities of the country.

> Well, I feel that all depends upon whether I show real good sense in the commissioners I choose. That is a starting point; and until I find my men I really do not feel that I have laid the basis for any plan. If I can find men that are right material for such purposes, I certainly would use all the influence I have to bring that about.

Have you considered changing the form of goverment for the district; giving a self-government to the district?

> You mean, proposed it to Congress?

Yes.

> No, sir, I haven't.

Do you plan, Mr. President, to have your own economy and

efficiency commission for the government, such as President Taft had?

> Do you mean appoint a new set of men? Well, you know there is no money for it at present, and no money in any of the pending bills.

Perhaps you could get it by asking for it.

> Perhaps so, but so many other people are asking for money, and I am modest!

Is there anything in prospect with regard to your Civil Service commissioners—changing the personnel of that commission?

> I haven't taken that up yet.

Their resignations are in your hands, Mr. President?

> Yes.

As a matter of formality?

> I think that always is the case, because their relations with the President are necessarily so direct.

Has there been any decision, Mr. President, as to whether the consul generals who were promoted from the consular ranks are to be regarded as under the civil service, or whether they are to be regarded as diplomatic officers?

> That has not been discussed.

Would you be willing to say what, Mr. President, your own thoughts are?

> My own sympathy and purpose is entirely in accord with what has been done to put the consular service under the civil service umbrella.

Would you include the consuls general in that?

> I suppose so; that is one of the subjects I haven't studied, and I am not entitled to a formal conclusion yet.

Mr. President, are you likely to make any move soon with regard to the Philippines in carrying out the plan in the Democratic platform giving independence to the Philippines?

> I don't know whether I can say soon or not. That depends altogether upon the way public business shapes itself.

I meant in the appointment of the Philippine commissioners.

> I hope to get to that as soon as possible. I haven't lost sight of it; I have simply not found the men I am looking for.

You haven't found a Comptroller of the Currency yet?

> No. There is one question which, if I am properly informed, I would ask me, if I were you! Am I correctly informed that any number of newspapers have been carrying the rumor that I was looking for some satisfactory compromise on the woolen schedule? Is that true? Somebody told me that this morning. I haven't seen it.

Wool and sugar both are mentioned, I think.

Was it said that I was considering compromising?
I have seen that.
That has been stated in a small number of papers; it isn't a general statement.

> Well, when you get a chance, just say that I am not the kind that considers compromises when I once take my position. Just note that down, so that there will be nothing more of that sort transmitted in the press.

Does that apply to both sugar and wool, Mr. President?

> Well, sir, I have taken my stand with the House leaders for the present bill. Enough said!

Would you say what you would do with a bill that came to you that materially changed those features?

> No, I won't say what I would do. I will simply say that I am not looking for or accepting compromises.

T MS (C. L. Swem Coll., NjP).

Draft of Instructions to Henry Lane Wilson[1]

[The White House, May 15, 1913]

CONFIDENTIAL INSTRUCTIONS.

Please represent to Huerta that our understanding was that he was to seek an early constitutional settlement of affairs in Mexico by means of a free popular election, and that our delay and hesitation about recognition has been due to the apparent doubt and uncertainty as to what his plans and purposes really were. Our sincere wish is to serve Mexico. We stand ready to assist in any way we can in a speedy and promising settlement which will bring peace and the restoration of order. The further continuation of the present state of affairs will be fatal to Mexico and is likely to disturb most dangerously all her international relations. We are ready to recognize him now on condition that all hostilities cease, that he call an election at an early date, the twenty-sixth of October now mentioned being, in our judgment, too remote, and that he absolutely pledge himself as a condition of our action in his behalf that a free and fair election be secured by all proper machinery and safeguards. Upon this understanding this Government will undertake the friendly office of securing from the officials of the states which are now refusing to acknowledge the authority of Huerta's government an agreement to cease hostilities, maintain the status quo until the election shall have been held, and abide by the result of the election if it be held freely and without arbitrary interference of any kind as we have suggested. It should be intimated to Huerta that the Government of the United States is not likely to assent to any method of settlement secured by the Government of Mexico making interest with European Governments to lend their countenance and assistance in consideration of special advantages accorded their citizens or subjects.

T telegram (WP, DLC).
   [1] President Wilson dictated the following draft dispatch to Swem on May 15 from a WWsh draft in WP, DLC.

From Edward Mandell House

Dear Mr. President: New York City. May 15th, 1913.

I saw Primus[1] today and had quite a talk with him.

He brought up the currency question and I am very much afraid that he is a long way afield from your views. He would like to talk to you but he wants the initiative to come from you.

I think it would be wise to discuss the question with him as soon as possible for there is no use letting it go further without some sort of understanding.

Curiously enough, Untermyer told me that he, himself, believed in the Government exercising the functions of issuing currency but he did not elaborate as fully as Primus. He said, however, that he and Primus intended to discuss the question today.

Primus also told me that he and Senator Owen were in accord. I can hardly credit this because Owen and Glass are not very far apart.

I should be very unhappy if anything should prevent your carrying through your currency legislation at this extra session but I am now less hopeful of it than at any time heretofore.

If you think it safe and would care to do so you might call me over the telephone tomorrow night so that I could give you more detail.

Referring to something more pleasant I am pleased to tell you that Brandeis and Hapgood are busy today drawing up some sort of plan to take over Harper's Weekly.

This is very confidential because there are one or two small snags which may prevent the consummation of the deal.

                    Your very faithful,   E. M. House

TLS (WP, DLC).
   [1] Bryan.

From John Bassett Moore, with Enclosure

My dear Mr. President: Washington. May 15, 1913.

I beg leave to enclose herewith copy of a memorandum on the Mexican situation which I communicated yesterday to the Secretary of State. Very respectfully & truly yrs J B Moore.

ALS (WP, DLC).

ENCLOSURE

The Mexican Situation.

For the Secretary: May 14, 1913.

1. The conditions resulting from our non-recognition of the existing government at the City of Mexico are producing serious inconvenience. There are matters pending between the two countries of which a solution should be reached, but of which none is now possible unless we deal with the government at the City of Mexico as the responsible government of the country, there being no other governmental organization professing to represent it.

We have a convention pending which affects the granting of water rights along the Colorado River. An agreement had practically been reached, but this is now held up and for the time being nothing can be done.

The Government of the United States refused to accept the award rendered two years ago in the Chamizal case,[1] and the Mexican Government agreed in a friendly spirit to enter upon a revision of it. Such a revision, acceptable to both Governments and to the parties in interest, had been substantially agreed upon. By the convention under which the arbitration was held the award becomes definitive within two years. The two years will be up on the 15th of June. The arrangement heretofore formulated can not now be concluded, because we do not recognize any responsible government in Mexico with which to sign it.

The case is the same with regard to claims, general and special. Negotiations are suspended, and no relief is obtainable.

2. The government at present existing at the City of Mexico is legally organized in conformity with the provisions of the Mexican constitution. This has not, however, in the practice of the United States been considered a prerequisite to the recognition of a new government. The Government of the United States having originally set itself up by revolution has always acted upon the

---

[1] About this arbitration and award, see Sheldon B. Liss, *A Century of Disagreement: The Chamizal Conflict, 1864-1964* (Washington, 1965), pp. 24-36.

de facto principle. We regard governments as existing or as not existing. We do not require them to be chosen by popular vote. We look simply to the fact of the existence of the government and to its ability and inclination to discharge the national obligations.

3. The government at present existing at the City of Mexico is the only government professing to be able and willing to discharge the international obligations of the country. It has no competitors. There are certain States along the northern frontier that refuse to recognize its authority, but none of them claims to be the national government of Mexico. It is said that Carranza, of whom among the opponents of the government we hear the most, has in all perhaps 8000 troops. However this may be, he is merely maintaining an opposition to the central authority, and does not profess to be maintaining a government which could in any sense be called the government of Mexico.

4. The opposition to the recognition of the central authority at the City of Mexico seems to be based chiefly upon the circumstances attending the killing of Madero two days after he had resigned the Presidency. Taking these to be as narrated in the press, we necessarily deplore them; but our deprecation of the political methods which may prevail in certain countries can not relieve us of the necessity of dealing with the governments of these countries. It might be possible, if reports, official and unofficial, are to be credited, to cite recent instances of much denounced despotisms with which we have been and possibly still are on very pleasant terms. In this we are not at fault. We cannot become the censors of the morals or conduct of other nations and make our approval or disapproval of their methods the test of our recognition of their governments without intervening in their affairs. The Government of the United States once boasted that the Pope, the Emperor of Russia and President Jackson were the only rulers that ever recognized Don Miguel as King of Portugal. This action on the part of President Jackson was ascribed to "our sacred regard for the independence of nations." We recognized, as did other powers, King Peter, of Servia, who actually gained his throne by means of assassination.

5. It is suggested that we cannot recognize the government at the City of Mexico, because we should treat that government and the leaders in the northern States in opposition to it, both alike. The answer to this suggestion is two-fold: First, that we are not at liberty to treat them alike in point of law; and secondly, that we do not treat them alike in point of fact. We can not treat them alike in point of law for the simple reason that the political

chiefs in the northern States do not represent a united governmental organization whose belligerency can properly be recognized. In the second place, we have at no time treated and are not now treating both sides alike. We have all along permitted and are now permitting the shipment of arms and munitions of war to the government at the City of Mexico, while we forbid such shipment to its adversaries.

6. An extraordinary stress seems lately to have been placed upon the act and effects of recognition. Perhaps this impression may partly be ascribed to the importance which was attached to the act of recognition by the Powers who were seeking to make a loan to China, recognition having been withheld for the purpose of inducing the existing government of China to take a particular course. This case is, however, to be considered as special and exceptional. The government of the United States once recognized five governments in Mexico within a few months, and did not injure its own interests or commit itself to any responsibilities by so doing. Recognition is purely and simply the avowal of an apparent state of fact, and the advantage gained by it is that the country is held responsible for the acts of the authority so acknowledged.

7. It is evident that the government at the City of Mexico will soon have been recognized by the principal European Powers. It has already been recognized by Great Britain and Spain, and we are advised that the recognition of France has been received and that that of Austria-Hungary is on the way. We are also advised that, as the result of this action, the government is enabled to obtain large sums of money in Europe. For some years past Mexican loans have been brought out in the United States, but a new loan is not attainable here under present conditions.

As I write this memorandum, official advices arrive of the recognition of the central government by Japan, Salvador, and Guatemala.

8. A suggestion has been made that the government at the City of Mexico and the insurgents, or "Constitutionalists," would both welcome a proposal from the outside for a cessation of arms with a view to the holding of an early and free election of a new President. Before such a step should be taken, it would be important to ascertain the precise grounds of the supposition that the proposal would be welcome. It would be most important for two reasons. In the first place, we know not only that in most cases of civil strife such proposals from the outside are unwelcome, but also that they are usually repulsed with more or less

heat by both sides, in order to conciliate popular feelings. In the second place, if such a proposal were made by the United States and declined by the Mexicans, it might be thought that we had tried the last peaceful expedient and that nothing but intervention remained.

9. It is also possible as the result of inaction to drift into intervention. During the past two months the United States has been represented at the City of Mexico by an Ambassador whose conduct apparently is not approved and whose recommendations have been disregarded. This is a situation which does not and cannot relieve itself. Ambassador Wilson has strongly advised the recognition of the central government, but such recognition has not been accorded. These facts are evidently well known to that government and to the public, and have contributed to the resentment which found expression in the recent conversation of President Huerta with the Ambassador.[2] There would appear to be an incongruity in keeping an Ambassador at a post, not for the purpose of transacting important business, but merely for the purpose of receiving and transmitting complaints against the attitude of his own government, with which attitude he does not himself agree.

Nor is the fact to be lost sight of that this state of things has, in Mexico, the double effect of producing anti-American feeling among the adherents of the central government and encouraging the enemies of that government.

10. In any event, it would not seem to be expedient or becoming, in view of the long delay that has taken place and of the recent conversation of President Huerta with Ambassador Wilson, for the United States now to recognize the former by answering his autograph letter.[3] The best course, if the reestablishment of normal relations should be determined upon, would seem to be to nominate to the Senate a new Ambassador to Mexico, who could present his letters in due course. Ambassador Wilson has repeatedly stated that he has no desire to remain in Mexico; and, assuming that the United States desires to avoid intervention, there is every reason for bringing to an end the present situation.

T MS (WP, DLC).
   [2] See H. L. Wilson to W. J. Bryan, May 8, 1913, *FR 1913*, pp. 799-800.
   [3] The letter cannot be found, but its gist was embodied in V. Huerta to W. H. Taft, telegram, Feb. 18, 1913, *ibid.*, p. 721.

From John Bassett Moore

My dear Mr. President: Washington May 15, 1913.

The Japanese Ambassador, Baron Chinda, called this morning. Being unacquainted with the purport of the conferences which he has held at the Department lately, I said little to him but hasten to report his representations.

1. He expressed regret that the points of his protest had not been communicated to Governor Johnson, seeming to think that they might have produced some effect on the latter's mind. He seemed to think that the substance of his protest might be communicated to the Governor confidentially, but I told him that it would be very difficult to avoid dealing with argumentative matters otherwise than publicly. I have not seen his protest and therefore do not know just what it contains.

2. He also intimated a desire to have a conference with you to-day. He seems to be very apprehensive lest he may appear to have left anything undone that possibly might prevent the signing of the bill.

I promised to communicate with you and advise him.

I may say that he seemed to be personally more disturbed than he has appeared to be at any previous time. This may be due to his sense of the responsibilities resting upon him in the present situation.

Believe me to be,
           Very respectfully and truly yours,   J. B. Moore.

TLS (WP, DLC).

From the Diary of Josephus Daniels

Thursday, May 15, 1913.

Yesterday the Joint Board of the Army and Navy[1] held a meeting and unanimously reported the conclusion that the three ships in the Yang-tze River, which were sent there about the time the Chinese began to change their form of government, should at once be sent to Manila. The War Department earnestly urged this on the ground that these ships could protect Corregidor Fort and that if these ships were there they could prevent the entrance of the Japanese Fleet which might come and it would be very difficult for the Japanese to take Manila if these ships were in Manila Bay or near by able to cover the approach to the Fort.

Admiral Fiske, Aid for Operations, who earnestly pressed this action of withdrawing these ships from China, gave me a

memorandum giving his reason and his argument on the possibility of war with Japan. This memorandum is appended
hereto.[2]

T MS (J. Daniels Papers, DLC).
  [1] Created in 1903 and composed of officers selected from the General Staff
of the Army and the General Board of the Navy, the Joint Board had the task
"of conferring upon, discussing and reaching common conclusions regarding
all matters calling for the cooperation of the two services." See Richard D.
Challener, *Admirals, Generals, and American Foreign Policy, 1898-1914* (Princeton, N. J., 1973), pp. 47-50.
  [2] B. A. Fiske to J. Daniels, May 14, 1913, TLS (Daniels Diary), strongly reiterating the opinions expressed in Fiske's memorandum of May 13, 1913.

Oswald Garrison Villard to Robert Hayne Leavell[1]

Private & Confidential

Dear Prof. Leavell: [New York] May 15, 1913.

    You will be delighted to hear that I had a most satisfactory
interview with the President yesterday in regard to the National
Race Commission.[2] He is wholly sympathetic and was glad to
grant the only request I made of him,—that he consider the matter with care until my return on July first. By that time he will be
able to judge better his relations with the Senate and Congress,
and what it will mean to him to antagonize the reactionary Southern politicians. As to the necessity of some such inquiry he was
quite clear; it was not necessary to convince him on that point.
You will be good enough to keep this entirely confidential. I am
to see the President again as soon as I return from Europe. I enclose herewith the finished programme.

                    Sincerely yours,   [Oswald Garrison Villard]

CCL (O. G. Villard Papers, MH).
  [1] Associate Professor of History and Economics at the Agricultural and Mechanical College of Texas (now Texas A & M University).
  [2] A project being pushed by Villard for a presidential commission, privately
funded, to investigate and report on race relations in the United States.

From the Diary of Josephus Daniels

                                   Friday, May 16, 1913.

    When the Cabinet met, the President presented a draft of his
reply about Baron Chinda's protest over the California-Japanese
legislation. It and the matters surrounding it were discussed for
nearly two hours and all the collateral matters were gone into,
particularly as to touching whether the Federal Government had
any powers it could assert to meet the feelings of the Japanese
Ambassador. Many suggestions as to changing the verbiage were

made and noted by the President, all looking toward trying to guard against any expression that might be taken up by jingoists in this country or Japan to make friction between the two nations.

On the day prior to the meeting of the Cabinet, the Joint Board of the Army and Navy held a meeting and had urgently recommended that the three largest ships in the Chinese rivers be sent at once to the Philippine Islands. Secretary Garrison approved the finding of the Joint Board. Secretary Garrison asked me to come over to his office to discuss this action of the Joint Board. He was very strongly in favor of its being carried out and having the ships moved at once and thought we ought to unite in a recommendation to that effect to the President, and I told him I could not do so chiefly for the reason that there was a very excited condition in Tokyo among those who are against the Government and hostile to the United States and the movement of any American ships now in the Yellow Sea would be taken up by the jingoists to inflame the popular mind there though these ships were not dreadnoughts and only one of them powerful. All Japan would be made to believe that we had mobilized our Navy in the Yellow Sea and it might so inflame the people of the Islands as to make possible a feeling that might provoke war. I told him that my feeling was that if the ships were moved out of Chinese waters to Manila there were not enough of them of powerful type as to be able to meet the Japanese fleet, that they could do very little good even if they got to Manila and that their movement would be heralded all over the world as indicative of the fact that we expected war with Japan and were getting ready to meet them in the Philippines. Even if we were expecting it, I went on to say, we could not prevent the Japanese Navy from taking the Philippines if they decided to concentrate their forces on those possessions. I told him that if I had known as much as I do now when I first became Secretary of the Navy, I would have taken steps to send our Fleet in the Pacific Ocean. Since I have been here, I learned that we came near having war with Japan in the Roosevelt Administration and was only averted by the most careful measures which caused Japan to think in a sense that America was afraid of it and that the action then opened the way for the Japanese jingoists to stir the people up now to the hatred of America. The last Administration should have had the Fleet in the Pacific and, of course, if we had foreseen the California legislation, they would have been despatched off the coast of California, Hawaii, or the Philippines, but until the Panama Canal is opened, the journey to the Pacific is such a long one that we could not now send the Fleet to the Pacific in time to save the Philippines if the Japanese Navy has any desire to strike a blow there.

Secretary Garrison took the ground that we had a perfect right to move our ships when and where we pleased and moving them from the Chinese waters to the Philippines was nobody's business and could not create any trouble and they could help protect the Philippines and back up the Army at Fort Corregidor in case of trouble and it would be a great mistake for us, who knew so little about military warfare, not to take the advice of the Joint Board. He put his argument along that line very ably and strongly but it seemed to me the weight of the argument was the other way and [I] could not sign the recommendations, but we agreed to go see the President and we did.

The Secretary of War urged upon the President that it was wisest and necessary to send the ships to the Philippines and to make every preparation for the protection of the Islands possible, and I advanced to the President the views I had put forth to Secretary Garrison, adding that I did not regard the Chinese situation in such shape as to make it wise to take the ships out of the rivers in China except in an emergency. After discussing the matter at some length, the President said that it was a matter of such importance that it would have to come up in Cabinet the next day but until then he would not consent to have any ship moved in the Pacific Ocean.

In the Cabinet Meeting Friday, this matter came up and was threshed out after lengthy discussion. Secretary Garrison presented his view with ability of the action of the Joint Board. I presented, briefly, the reasons why I could not agree with the Joint Board and while I believed at this time any such action which might inflame the passions of the people of Japan and lead to a war which we would all regret. Secretary Redfield was strongly supporting Secretary Garrison as did Secretary McAdoo. The Secretary of State and the Secretary of Labor took strong grounds against moving any ships in the Pacific and helped me hold up my end of the argument. Secretary Lane also indicated that it might be unwise to move the ships at this time. Attorney General McReynolds was inclined to agree with the Secretary of War. The Secretary of Agriculture took my side. I do not recall that the Postmaster General had any statement to make but I gathered that he was with me. On Mr. Bryan's earnest advocacy of peace, he could not approve any movement now that might make war. Most of the time of the discussion was taken up with the arguments of those who wished to withdraw the ships. When all was said and done the President said, "The Joint Board, of course, has presented the military aspect of the situation as it sees it and it may be right, but we are considering this matter with another light, on the diplomatic side, and must determine the policy. I do not think any movement should be made at this time in the Pacific Ocean and I will, therefore, take the responsibility of holding the ships where they are at present." He spoke at more length and made me very happy to find that he was in accord and agreement with the views I had made in supporting me in his clear and logical power.

In the afternoon the President and his wife held a garden party in the White House grounds, and I was made very happy by his taking me aside and saying, "I think we did right today. At one time I think we had a majority of the Cabinet against us, but when I looked down the table and saw you upholding what you thought was the right course, it cheered my heart. We must not have war except in an honorable way and I fear the Joint Board made a mistake."[1]

T MS (J. Daniels Papers, DLC).

[1] In fact, the Japanese government had no intention of going to war over the California alien land law. The British Ambassador in Tokyo, Sir Conyngham Greene, reported to the Foreign Office that Baron Makino on May 22 had "disclaimed anything in the nature of a forcible solution of the difficulty as out of the question under present conditions." Greene added that he himself thought that there was little danger of war. Sir C. Greene to Sir E. Grey, May 23, 1913, PL (FO 317/1667, No. 23167, PRO).

Nearly a year later, the British naval and military attachés in Tokyo prepared detailed memoranda on the military capabilities of Japan and the United States and the likelihood of war between them. The two attachés strongly agreed that Japan was in no condition, economically or militarily, to go to war with the United States, and that there was no disposition among any Japanese governing circles to do so. See Sir C. Greene to Sir E. Grey, April 20, 1914, PL, with enclosures (FO 371/2011, No. 22336, PRO).

To Edward Mandell House

My dear Friend: Washington May 17, 1913

Thank you for your full letter of yesterday about Primus. I have found since that he has been in conference with Untermeyer. I am going to try to see him at the earliest possible moment.

Don't worry yourself after you have once stepped on board. We shall work at the great tasks that confront us, and think often with deep affection of you.

In haste   Affectionately yours,   Woodrow Wilson

TLS (E. M. House Papers, CtY).

From the Diary of Josephus Daniels

Saturday, May 17, 1913.

After the Cabinet Meeting yesterday, I called in Admiral Fiske and told him that the President determined no ship should be moved in the Pacific for the present and that he was entirely in accord with the view I had expressed in this respect. The Admiral was greatly disappointed because he felt keenly that the wise course was to take the ships out of the rivers in China and send them to the Philippines. Nearly all the naval officers, including the Admiral, ever since the California matter came up, believed that no power would prevent the Japanese from taking the Philippines. Therefore I was surprised when the Joint Board unanimously demanded that these ships be moved and the movement of these ships might avert that disaster.

This morning Admiral Fiske came to me with a resolution which he said had been passed by the Joint Board which bore date of May 16th and he was very emphatic and earnest that whatever happened, the Joint Board wished it presented to the President so that the President might have before him their view upon what he thought was a very serious situation. He said that the Joint Board thought the President and the Secretary had made a great mistake in not having these ships brought out from the Chinese waters and now they presented a formal recommendation that at once all the torpedo boat destroyers and torpedo boats and a number of our other small craft on the California Coast be sent at once to Hawaii.

I told him that I thought the President's determination not to move anything in the Pacific Ocean had settled this matter for the present and thought it not worth while to re-open it, but the Joint Board seemed insistent, and he pressed it upon me to take it to the President so that he could have their point of view. Naturally in a matter of this importance I felt some little hesitation by standing on my own view when it was opposed to that held by the distinguished Army and Navy officers on the Joint Board, and action gave me pause and did not convince me at all, but later in the day the Admiral came to me with a map of the Philippine Islands and urged also that the two gunboats at Manila be taken away and sent to the Corregidor Fort so that they could mine the channel or entrance to Manila Bay and be ready for any emergency.

Shortly after these statements were brought to me the map and later the recommendations of the Joint Board. The correspondent of a big newspaper came in to see me and asked if I had approved the action of the Joint Board of taking all ships on the Pacific Coast and sending them to Hawaii or Manila. The question came to me like a clap of thunder from a blue sky. Evidently there had been a leak. Evidently the newspaperman knew what he was talking about and I was at a loss how to parry his inquiry and put it off by saying no action whatever had been taken to move any ship in the Pacific and none was contemplated. He pressed at the matter a little but went off.

I then sent for Admiral Fiske and told him about the interview and told him there was a leak in the matter somewhere. Of course, I knew that no employee of the Navy Department would consciously give out such important and confidential matter, but that it was a very serious matter. Of course, the Admiral was as much distressed as I was that anything had leaked but thought the newspaperman was talking about something else.

Late in the afternoon I went to the White House to see the President with the map and recommendation of the Joint Board urging the immediate removal of the Fleet on the Pacific Coast and told him about the leak. He was greatly put out, not only about the leak, but chiefly because after he had announced his policy on the Pacific Coast the Joint Board had a meeting and taken action relative to moving ships on the Pacific. He felt that this was a breach of military discipline and spoke his mind freely: He said in substance: "After we talked this matter over in Cabinet Friday and you and Secretary of War informed these Navy and Army gentlement that there was to be no movement now, they had no right to hold a meeting at all and discuss these matters. When a policy has been settled by the Administration and when it is communicated to the Joint Board, they have no right to be trying to force a different course and I wish you would say to them that if this should occur again, there will be no General or Joint Boards. They will be abolished."

We talked the matter over considerably and it was a glorious thing to see the President's determination that the policy of the Administration should be carried out and no officer in the Army or Navy should be permitted to make war plans along certain lines after they had been notified when such policy was contrary to the spirit of the Administration.

That night I called Admiral Fiske to state to him the President's spirit and purpose and to notify him that I wished no more meetings held until I returned to the city and could have a talk with him, but he had gone to the theatre, and I talked it over with my wife and as I was preparing to leave on the train, I communicated with my Naval Aide, Captain Palmer, and asked him to communicate this information to Admiral Fiske.[1]

T MS (J. Daniels Papers, DLC).
  [1] According to J. Daniels to WW, April 10, 1915, Wilson, "a few days thereafter," told Daniels "to say that meetings might be held but you wished no action decided upon in the Pacific pending the Japanese land discussion." The Joint Board met again in October 1913. Challener, *Admirals, Generals, and American Foreign Policy*, pp. 368-79.

From William Jennings Bryan

My Dear Mr President   Washington May 18 1913

I have had an hour & a half talk with Baron Chinda. He is very much disturbed as to the effect of our action on his government. He is very anxious to do any thing he can but hoped for something to offer as a consolation. He wanted to know if the gov't would test the California law in the courts or whether Japanese citizens would have to do it. I could give him no assurance that the national govt could help them in this matter. It has occurred to me, however, that we might consider whether we could pay any damages suffered by Japanese if the law causes the loss in value that they fear. This is a remote contigency but we might meet it with a promise to save them from loss, as we have paid for lives lost by mob violence.

He asked about naturalization (I see that, according to the dispatches from Japan, that subject was discussed at a public meeting in Tokio.) I told him that I could give no assurance of that.

He asked about arbitration & I told him I had no authority to consider it, but it occurred to me today that this might be an opportune time to offer to submit the matter to an international commission for *investigation* if his country would agree to the peace plan submitted to all the nations. It would give us a chance to test the plan & as Gt Britain France & Italy have accepted the principle, Japan could hardly refuse. It would give time for investigation during which passion could subside. What do you think of these two propositions?

I have asked him to get an answer from his govt if possible on the peace plan so that I can announce Japan with the other three. He asked me if our answer when delivered would be *final*. I told him that nothing was final between friends & that we would be glad to consider any proposition they submitted[.] They prefer that their protest & our answer be *not* published at present and I have promised that we would comply with their wishes and regard these papers as confidential. I submit that the assurance in regard to damages might be inserted in the reply or communicated orally. You have Blanchards[1] dispatch from Tokio.[2] I am sending the following reply.

"Blanchard

We are gratified that California law is being discussed calmly and that no feeling is being shown toward Americans[.] In conversation with Japanese government emphasize the extraordinary efforts made by the Washington government to prevent passage of law. Explain freedom of action allowed states under our constitution. Advise restraint and calmness. Suggest that nothing is final between friends and express confidence that a satisfactory solution can be found for all questions if the parties approach the subject with patience and in the right spirit"

As I have no one to send this by I will leave it myself as I take Mrs Bryan to the train. With assurances of respect etc I am My Dear Mr President   Yours truly   W. J. Bryan

ALS (WP, DLC).
  [1] Arthur Bailly-Blanchard, Secretary of the United States Embassy at Tokyo.
  [2] A. Bailly-Blanchard to the Secretary of State, May 17, 1913, T telegram (WP, DLC).

Remarks at a Press Conference

May 19, 1913.

Mr. President, is there anything new in the Japanese situation?
     Absolutely nothing new; nothing at all.
Mr. President, I would like to ask about that, whether you have any reliable information as to the state of public sentiment in Japan. That seems to be the troublesome thing.
     No, I haven't. Of course, we have the dispatches, and we have reports of public meetings—very insufficient reports. We don't know whom those public meetings represent. Altogether, we feel that it is a matter of conjecture still—what the real opinion over there is.
It seems to me that that is the real trouble spot over there.
     Yes, I think it is, and yet, so far as I can gather from recent dispatches, the later meetings are rather more reassuring, rather more moderate in tone. We got a message from the Chargé d'Affaires over there, who said that the meetings seemed very reasonable.
Mr. President, what is your impression about the sentiment in California in the case of a referendum attached to the bill?
     Really, there again, I don't know. Apparently, the sentiment in the northern and southern parts of the state is different. I mean in the north there is a distinct and very much

stronger support for this legislation than in the southern. There again you see I am conjecturing from what I hear, and don't know.

Mr. President, can you determine when our reply will go to Japan?

No; that is in the hands of the Secretary of State, who is in communication with Baron Chinda.

Is he going to communicate further with Governor Johnson?

No, not so far as I know.

Are we right, Mr. President, in the impression that that reply to Japan will not go in any event until the Governor has acted on the bill?

I have assumed that it would not until the Governor has signed the bill, and I have not learned yet that he has.

Mr. President, is there anything in that report from Sacramento that the administration has asked the Governor of California to take the full thirty days to act on that?

No. Has the legislature adjourned?

I think so.

Yes, sir, it has.

I had not learned that it adjourned.

A dispatch this morning spoke of it as a thirty-day affair.

And that out of thirty, nine had passed.

Mr. President, is it fair to inquire that the American reply is completed?

Well, it is provisionally completed.

You couldn't give us any notion of its general tenor?

No; simply for the reasons that I very frankly explained to you men before. We want to have the freest kind of interchange of views between the governments, and anything that is published, of course, becomes a formal thing, even the language of which would assume a new significance because it was published.

Is it considered, Mr. President, that the Ambassador has been pressing for a reply?

No; he has simply been anxious about the situation. That explains his frequent visits to the State Department. Baron Chinda is acting in an admirable spirit in the matter.

Mr. President, we have had nothing yet that was authoritative as to the matter of the Japanese Ambassador's protest; that is to say, as to the point of his protest. Is it possible to give us—

Well, I was saying to several of the men who asked me about that the other day, there is nothing in it that has not been again and again discussed. There is no new matter. It is all

the familiar matter that we went over from the time Mr.
Bryan went out to California until now.
I confess an inability to see what he can protest about in this
situation.

Perhaps it would not be polite for me to agree with you.
The thing that puzzles me, Mr. President, all the time, is the sug-
gestion that Japan, in taking any attitude in favor of giving the
Japanese rights of naturalization here, would be the idea that they
wanted to depopulate their own empire by making them all
American citizens. That has puzzled me right along.

Of course, this is a thing I could not in any circumstances
discuss out loud, but I am perfectly willing to tell you men
the way it lies in my mind. I do not think that the real
trouble arises out of any particular legislation. It arises out
of the implication in it that we do not want to have intimate
association in our life with the Japanese, which is but an
implication—a suggestion—of feeling on our part that they
are not on the same plane with us. That, of course, is something that diplomacy itself cannot handle. It is a fundamental, subtle, delicate, and yet radical thing. It touches a
man's pride; he cannot tell you just where you touched it, but
you have touched the sorest spot in him. That is at the bottom of it all, and you see in even the meager reports we get
from the meetings in Japan that that is where their feelings
go back to. Of course, it is a difficult thing to handle. I think
that America feels a genuine respect and friendship for
Japan, and I am sorry to have any question raised which
would seem to embarrass them.
Mr. President, the naval officers say, privately, and have said it
for years, that ever since the Russian-Japanese war, the Japanese
naval officers against whom they run have shown a sort of resentment against American naval officers, and not against the officers
of any other nation. It seems to resolve itself into the Japanese
not liking us or our not liking the Japanese. It all rests on that
basis; there has been some feeling there for years, because army
officers say the same thing.

I do not think you can say of Americans and the Japanese
in America that they do not like each other, because I think
there has been a great deal of admiration for the Japanese
and for Japan.
That is, for the individual Japanese.

No; I think for their extraordinary achievements and their
sagacity. They do some things, for example, so much better
than we do them, that they have commanded our respect.

Any nation that can go through a war, for example, and lose only 2 per cent from disease has a scientific superiority over any other modern nation which has to be admitted, and it impresses the imagination. And their practical capacity is extraordinary, and their adaptability and genius for taking up things that were unfamiliar to them in their earlier civilization, and then doing them at once almost as well as anybody else can do them.

They are peculiarly imitative.

Yes, but they are more than that, because they can adapt what they take to their own uses so perfectly. There is this that lies back of it: for some reason that I cannot fathom (of course I am saying this to you gentlemen just *entre nous* —these are things I ought not to discuss out loud) I get this information that they feel that we are in some way responsible for their not reaping a larger benefit from their war with Russia, because Mr. Roosevelt brought about the Portsmouth conference, and the Portsmouth conference issued them something less than they had been led to expect and hope for. And this act of generosity and peacemaking on our part is what they regard as the origin of their not having gotten an indemnity, for example, out of Russia.

I think Russia feels the same way, Mr. President.

It is just another illustration of when your neighbors quarrel, let it alone.

If they had given them an indemnity, they might be using it now for another purpose.

It is like a friend of mine who saw a man brutally beating his wife and intervened; and then the wife joined the husband and beat him. He then determined to let alone domestic quarrels. It is the irony of fate under the circumstances that that sort of feeling should arise out of a wholly disinterested act.

Mr. President, aren't the Japanese themselves to blame for that? They started the Portsmouth conference; they asked Mr. Roosevelt—

So I am told; I have no official knowledge of that, but I am told so.

Mr. President, is there any indication of sympathy with the Japanese government on the part of any other government? Has there been inquiry from Great Britain or China?

Oh, no, no. Of course, that would be an extraordinary thing for another government to do. There has been nothing done of that sort.

Mr. President, do you feel that the results of the tariff vote in the Senate last Friday[1] indicated anything you did not know before? Do you feel any encouragement about the bill?

Oh, no, I haven't felt anything about that. . . .

Are you going to stay on the ground this summer if necessary?

I am.

Will you feel glad when you get away for vacation?

I don't know. I intend to fight it out on this line if it takes all summer. . . .

How about currency, Mr. President?

Perhaps as the weather gets hotter, it will be unnecessary!

When do you expect to send your message?

I don't know. I haven't thought of that yet.

Is there no likelihood it will cause more difficulty?

You say the House—

You answered that before.

Which will then go into specific methods as to currency reform and not the guarantee of bank deposits?

Well, yes, the idea of bank deposits is another matter entirely apart from the currency.

Will you go into any specific matters in the message? Will it be a painless message?

Oh, I won't fire my arrows in the air, I will shoot at some mark.

Mr. President, it is reported in some quarters that an alternative measure to the Glass measure is being prepared outside of Congress with the administration's knowledge.

No, that is not true. The last part is not true.

But you previously acknowledged that was said.

No, no, I said I had been consulting a friend of mine, not with a view to an alternative measure at all, just as a side light.

T MS (C. L. Swem Coll., NjP).

[1] On May 16, 1913, the Democratic majority in the Senate rejected a resolution by Boies Penrose of Pennsylvania to hold public hearings on the Underwood bill. For comment on the significance of this event, see "The Tariff in the Senate," New York *Nation*, xcvi (May 22, 1913), 514.

To Baron Sutemi Chinda[1]

[c. May 19, 1913]

To His Excellency, Baron Chinda, Ambassador of Japan:

I have the honor to acknowledge the receipt of your note of May ninth, laying before my Government the representations of the Imperial Government of Japan with regard to the law just adopted by the State of California concerning the holding of agricultural lands by aliens.

The Government of the United States regrets most sincerely that the Imperial Government of Japan should regard this legislation as an indication of unfriendliness towards their people. Being apprised while that measure was still under consideration by the Legislature of California that that might be the feeling of the Imperial Government, the President and I very earnestly attempted to induce the legislative authorities of California to reconsider or to modify their plans in the matter, urging that the State should not act as a separate unit in this case but, rather, in coöperation with the federal government. Under the Constitutional arrangements of the United States we could do no more than that.

At the same time, we feel that the Imperial Government has been misled in its interpretation of the spirit and object of the legislation in question. It is not political. It is not part of any general national policy which would indicate unfriendliness or any purpose inconsistent with the best and most cordial understanding between the two nations. It is wholly economic. It is based upon the particular economic conditions existing in California as interpreted by her own people, who wish to avoid certain conditions of competition in their agricultural activities.

I have not failed to observe that your note calls attention to certain provisions of the California law which you conceive to be inconsistent with and to violate existing treaty stipulations between the two countries, and thus to threaten to impair vested rights of property. The law, however, in terms purports to respect and preserve all rights under existing treaties. Such is its declared intent. But in case it should be alleged that the law had in its operation failed to accomplish that intent, your Government is no doubt advised that by the Constitution of the United States the stipulations of treaties made in pursuance thereof are the supreme law of the land, and that they are expressly declared to be binding upon state and federal courts alike to the end that they may be judicially enforced in all cases. For this purpose the courts, federal and state, are open to all persons who may feel themselves to have been deprived of treaty rights and guarantees; and in this respect the alien enjoys under our laws a privilege which to one of our own citizens may not be in all cases available, namely, the privilege of suing in the federal courts. In precisely the same way, our citizens resort and are obliged to resort to the courts for the enforcement of their constitutional and legal rights. Article XIV of the treaty, to which your Excellency refers, appears to relate solely to rights of commerce and navigation. These the California statute does not appear to be designed in any way to affect. The authors of the law seem to have been careful to guard against any invasion of contractual rights.

Your Excellency raises, very naturally and properly, the question how the case would stand should explicit treaties between the two countries expire or cease to be in force while, nevertheless, relations of entire amity and good will still continued to exist between them. I can only reply that in such circumstances the Government of the United States would always deem it its pleasure, as well as a manifest dictate of its cordial friendship for Japan and the Japanese people, to safeguard the rights of trade and intercourse between the two peoples now secured by treaty. I need not assure your Excellency that this Government will cooperate with the Imperial Government in every possible way to maintain with the utmost cordiality the understandings which bind the two nations together in honor and in interest. Its obligations of friendship would not be lessened or performed in niggardly fashion in any circumstances. It values too highly the regard of Japan and her cooperation in the great peaceful tasks of the modern world to jeopard them in any way; and I feel that I can assure your Excellency that there is no reason to feel that its policy in such matters would be embarrassed or interferred with by the legislation of any state of the Union. The economic policy of a single state with regard to a single kind of property cannot turn aside these strong and abiding currents of generous and profitable intercourse and good feeling.

In conclusion let me thank your Excellency for the candor with which you have dealt with this Government in this matter and express the hope that this episode in the intercourse of the two great countries which we represent will only quicken our understanding of one another and our confidence in the desire of each to do justice to the other.

T MS with WWhw emendations (WP, DLC).

¹ Internal evidence indicates that John Bassett Moore wrote the revised fourth paragraph; however, J. B. Moore to WW, June 29, 1913, reveals that Wilson changed Moore's text without the latter's knowledge. The dispatch that went to Tokyo (Secretary of State to the Japanese Ambassador, May 19, 1913, *FR 1913*, pp. 631-32) conforms to the following text.

From Louis Dembitz Brandeis

My dear Mr. President: Boston, Mass. May 19, 1913.

Referring to our recent conference concerning the Industrial Commission:

First: Further deliberation confirms my conviction that I ought not to accept the appointment you so kindly offered.

Second: I have, as you suggested, considered carefully the selection of a Chairman, and am of opinion that, all things considered, President Van Hise of the University of Wisconsin, would be the best appointment. If you select him I suppose you would wish to select as the other two representatives of the general public, a sociologist and a social worker; and that one of these two would be a woman.

Third: As stated to you, it seems to me very important that one of the representatives of organized labor should be an I.W.W. man. I have talked over with John Graham Brooks, Lincoln Steffens and Walter Lippman, (men whom I deem the most competent to advise,) the question, who should be selected to represent the I.W.W.; I thought we had found the right man; but learn today that the man we selected has resigned from the I.W.W. I hope to report very soon further on this.

If you desire to talk with me, I shall, of course, be glad to go to Washington for the purpose.

                 Very truly yours,   Louis D Brandeis
TLS (WP, DLC).

From Matthias Cowell Ely

Dear Sir: Hoboken, N. J. May 19, 1913

One Frank Hague who for a year or two has been the leader of the Smith Old Gang in Jersey City has secured a nomination under the Walsh Act for membership in the Commission Government board. You have reason to know who he is and what his election would mean.

It would mean a foothold in this county for the Democratic reactionaries of Essex and the weakening of the wall which we have kept up against them since the Smith-Martine fight.

I sincerely hope that you will see your way clear, not to take any part for or against any other candidate, but to sound a rallying cry to the Progressive Democrats of Jersey City to defeat Hague and those whom he represents. Such a course on your part would be extremely helpful to us.

                 Yours very respectfully   Matt C Ely
TLS (WP, DLC).

From the Diary of Colonel House

May 19, 1913.

Then came Untermyer and we discussed the currency for an hour. He wished to see whether there was any chance to convince me that a currency bill could be constructed permitting the Government to issue currency instead of having it done by the banks. He is fairly sound in his financial views, and what he proposes is merely a guarantee by the Government of the currency to be issued upon bank assets. It is the same principle as the Aldrich and Glass bills, plus the guarantee of the Government. I think a plan could be worked out along these lines. I may call the President up tonight and ask him to get in touch with Untermyer. Untermyer has much influence with the House Committee on Currency, other than Glass, and it is exceedingly desirable that all the elements get together and agree on such a bill as the President can approve.

I called the President up at Washington around half past eight o'clock and gave him the substance of my interview with Untermyer. I suggested that he send for Untermyer and talk with him. He asked if McAdoo could not do it. I thought not, because the question of vanity entered so largely into these matters and the Jews were already more or less disgruntled because they had not been officially recognized. The President told me of his interview with Mr. Bryan, whom he referred to as "Primus." It was far from satisfactory and Bryan was absolutely set in his ideas as to the Government issuing the currency.

I promised to write him more fully regarding Untermyer's views, and to speak with McAdoo and arrange for him to get in touch with Untermyer. The President said not to worry about anything but to get on the boat and leave trouble behind. I expressed a willingness to return at a moment's notice, but hoped no occasion would arise demanding it.

To Joseph Taylor Robinson[1]

My dear Senator: [The White House] May 20, 1913

May I not give myself the pleasure of saying that I am proud to belong to a party consisting of such men as yourself, who can meet as you have met the suggestions of those who would have you prefer the interests of a locality to the interests of the nation and the party?[2]

With much respect, I am

Sincerely yours, Woodrow Wilson

TLS (Letterpress Books, WP, DLC).
    ¹ Democratic Senator from Arkansas.
    ² Robinson had opposed a request of his own constituents for an increased
tariff rate on rice. See Nevin E. Neal, "A Biography of Joseph T. Robinson"
(Ph.D. dissertation, University of Oklahoma, 1958), p. 127.

To Edward Mandell House

                                 The White House May 20 1913

My affectionate thoughts go with you and my prayers for your strength, refreshment and happiness.   Woodrow Wilson.

T telegram (E. M. House Papers, CtY).

From Edward Mandell House

Dear Mr. President: New York City. May 20th, 1913.

Supplementing our telephone conversation of last night I want to add that I believe that a sound currency bill can be worked out along the lines suggested by Mr. Untermyer and one which Primus and Senator Owen will probably accept.

His plan is not different from the one we have in mind excepting that it is his purpose to have the Government issue all currency and to be responsible for its payment.

After talking to you I explained it, over the telephone, much more fully to Phythias and he also thought that something might be worked out that would be satisfactory.

Untermyer tells me that some of the bankers here would approve such a measure.

The difficulty is that Untermyer wantes too large a share in the making of the measure but I think this can be overcome by bringing about a general agreement between Primus, Pythias, Owen and Glass, after first getting Untermyer committed to it.

I understand the objections to having him in conference, at the same time, an hour with you would do wonders towards bringing about the desired result.

Everyone goes with him and at the lunch that he gave Mr. Bryan the other day there met at his home people of all creeds and conditions. There was a strange mingling of the interests and the reformers and I do not believe that a conference with him would do any harm.

Pythias or Owen could get him to Washington and when he was there you could arrange to see him for an hour in the evening and it is quite possible that no one would know.

                                 Your very faithful,   E. M. House

TLS (WP, DLC).

From Norman Hapgood

My dear Mr. President: New York May twentieth, 1913.

I believe Colonel House has told you that I am about to go back to journalism, as editor of Harper's Weekly. I am anxious to have the paper become as active and popular as possible in the really progressive movements of the day. Of course, the best possible way of putting such a stamp on the paper, would be to publish something by you, but I am afraid the chance of your having anything on hand that you would be willing to have us use, is very slight. Possibly, however, if your rush lets up at all, you may be able to make a suggestion from time to time about desirable points for us to emphasize. I need hardly say that any assistance from you will be of the greatest value, and will be deeply appreciated.

I am sure that the enlightened public opinion of this country is most enthusiastically pleased with what you have been doing.

With very best wishes,

Yours very sincerely,   Norman Hapgood

TLS (WP, DLC).

From the Diary of Josephus Daniels

Tuesday, May 20, 1913.

At the Cabinet Meeting this morning the Secretary of State announced that immediately upon the signing of the California Alien Land Act he had delivered to Baron Chinda, the Japanese Ambassador the note in reply to the protest of Baron Chinda against the California legislation. This note was submitted to the Cabinet at its last meeting and gone over by them carefully after which the President rewrote it after conference with the Secretary of State. It ought to be satisfactory to the reasonable people of Japan and clearly shows that the spirit of the Administration is one of the utmost friendliness and that the good offices of the Administration have been employed to induce every American state to legislate in a way as to make as little friction as possible with any foreign country. Of course, the answer cannot give to Japan all that it desires, and under our Constitution the Federal Government has no power over land laws and each state may make laws to suit itself being bound thereto only by stipulations in treaties and in the Constitution. Japan cannot treat with California and, therefore, it must make its protest to the United States.

Mr. Bryan was asked how the Japanese Ambassador seemed to accept the answer to the protest of his government. He replied that he read it in the office of the Secretary of State, and from his manner one would not suppose that it caused him any great agitation. At a former meeting of the Cabinet when Mr. Bryan was absent and John Bassett Moore was present, Mr. Moore stated that the Japanese Ambassador seemed much agitated and so much so that when he left the room he seemed almost to stagger under some influence that oppressed him and, of course, the inference was that the outcome of this diplomatic controversy might be such as to greatly depress the Ambassador. No such feeling was shown by him or no such attitude at this meeting and Mr. Bryan felt from his attitude and bearing that there was cause for congratulation and encouragement though, of course, the Baron gave no such statement.[1]

In addition to the formal answer to the protest, Mr. Bryan stated, after consultation with the President, that he had told the Japanese Ambassador that the Federal Government, of course, would recognize that if the California Alien Land law brought any loss to any Japanese citizen, the President would recommend to Congress that money be appropriated to compensate for such loss. There are several precedents for this and Mr. Bryan said that he had told the Ambassador that the Administration would use all its influence to prevent any financial loss by the Japanese. Another addition was made to the formal note verbally to the Ambassador that was that this Government would use its good offices to insure and advance its hearings in the courts of any case that any citizen of Japan might bring who felt himself aggrieved. Mr. Bryan said he had suggested to the Ambassador that these verbal statements be not sent to the Government at once but wait until that Government had received and considered the formal answer to Japan's protest. He thought it wisest to let them consider that and determine their policy before adding anything. These might be added later. Of course, he did not say so but, of course, Mr. Bryan meant that if the Japanese Government is embarrassed by jingoists, he thinks more ought to be offered by this country. The Ambassador could then add these two expressions and offers of speedy trials and indemnity as reasonable assurance why Japan ought to understand the friendliness of this country and its sense of justice. . . .

Secretary Garrison, reverting to the Mexican situation, said he believed that recognition of the Huerta Government was the only alternative to intervention and that he would like to read to the Cabinet an editorial by Paul Hudson,[2] editor of the Mexican

Herald, which gave strong reasons for the recognition of the Huerta Government by this country. He said he entirely agreed with the editorial. The President said, "That reminds me of a statement made by Carlyle, who said that 'every man regarded an editorial in a newspaper as very wise and able if it voiced the opinion which he himself held,'" the intimation being that Secretary Garrison was applauding the editorial of the Herald because it was expressing the views he entertained. Secretary Lane said "You ought to know who owns Paul Hudson before you give much weight to what he writes." "I would not care who said it," replied Secretary Garrison, "if it came out of a phonograph; if it is sensible, I will take it just as quick." Then he proceeded to read the editorial, and in two or three places the President interjected remarks showing that some statements in the editorial were not true, and when he finished someone remarked that this was the first newspaper editorial that had been read at a Cabinet Meeting—(and I don't think it will be the last).

I asked Mr. Lane what he meant by saying, "Do you know who owns Editor Hudson," and he replied that it was well-known that Hudson and his paper had been long subsidized by people and parties and interests wishing special privileges in Mexico, and what he said should be taken with many grains of allowance. Mr. Lane thought that recognition of the Huerta Government would cause the northern states of Mexico, which are hostile to Huerta, would be so incensed with America that they would destroy the property of Americans in that country. Mr. Garrison thought that they could not destroy it any more than they were now.

T MS (J. Daniels Papers, DLC).
1 The French Ambassador, Jean Jules Jusserand, observed at this time:
"Le Vicomte Chinda, Ambassadeur du Japon aux Etats-Unis, consciencieux, modéré, bien équilibré, qui souhaite sincèrement un réglement amical de ces difficultés, ne dissimule guère ses anxiétés, visibles d'ailleurs sur ses traits. Il dinait à l'Ambassade, il y a quelque temps, et semblait si triste et en si mauvais état de santé, que je ne pus m'empêcher de lui demander s'il était souffrant. Il répondit: je ne suis pas malade, mais j'ai tant de préoccupations. Plus récemment, j'ai eu avec lui un bref entretien sur la situation; il m'a confirmé ce que les circonstances rendent évident quant aux motifs de plainte de ses compatriotes: 'C'est moins la loi californienne qui en est cause q'une multitude de faits s'ajoutant les uns aux autres.[']
"On peut croire, en effet, que toutes ces petites blessures se cicatrisaient tant bien que mal; l'inopportune décision californienne, avec surtout les considérants blessants dont elle fut l'occasion à la tribune et dans la presse, ont transformé ces petites blessures à moitié guéries en une grande, présentement à vif. Si fort qu'ils tiemment à leurs intérêts, les Japonais tiennent encore bien plus à leur honneur; vainqueurs de la Chine et de la Russie, alliés de l'Angleterre avec qui ils ont traité sur le pied d'égalité, patriotes à un degré que nul ne surpasse, ils sont, et celà se comprend, d'un orgueil ombrageux. C'est jouer gros jeu que de blesser un tel sentiment; quand il s'agit d'intérêt, on sait exactement où on en est et le calcul des réparations est facile à faire; quand il s'agit de sentiments, les données sont moins précises. D'aucuns s'en rendent compte; un

des hauts fonctionnaires du Département d'Etat me disait l'autre jour la loi
californienne respecte exactement le traité, et c'est même dommage; nous aurions
sans cela un moyen de donner satisfaction aux Japonais." J. J. Jusserand to S.
Pichon, May 20, 1913, TLS (N. S. États-Unis, Vol. 13, pp. 171-172, FFM-Ar).
    2 Born and reared in Kansas, Hudson had been associated with the Mexico
City *Mexican Herald* (published in both English and Spanish editions) since
1896 and was by this time the controlling owner of the paper.

To William Jennings Bryan

My dear Mr. Bryan: The White House May 21, 1913

My mind so confines itself to the chief things we are conferring about when we see one another that I find I must resort to
the expedient of dropping you an occasional line to call your attention to incidental matters.

Would it be possible to arrange soon for examinations for the
diplomatic service? You know, such examinations have been
held for some years now in order to recruit the secretaryships
and the lesser positions of the service, and Mr. Walter Page, just
before he left for England, called my attention to the fact that
there were several promising candidates for examination who
were seeking an opportunity. He himself seemed greatly interested in the matter.

    Cordially and faithfully yours,   Woodrow Wilson

TLS (W. J. Bryan Papers, DNA).

To Henry Means Pindell[1]

My dear Mr. Pindell: [The White House] May 21, 1913

I am writing to ask a very pointed question. Would you be
willing to accept the Collectorship of Internal Revenue for the
Fifth Illinois District? You see, I am aiming high, and will not
be content if I can not get the best, but I did not want to suggest
this to McAdoo before I felt that I had your permission to do so.

    With warmest regards, I am
    Cordially and sincerely yours,   Woodrow Wilson

TLS (Letterpress Books, WP, DLC).
    1 Editor and publisher of the *Peoria*, Ill., *Journal*; active in Illinois Demo-
cratic politics and an early Wilson supporter in 1912.

From Edward Mandell House

                                [New York] May 21st 1913.

I do not think you can ever know, my great and good friend,
how much I appreciate your kindness to me. All that I have tried

to do seems so little when measured by the returns you have made. I go only because of my desire to conserve my strength in order that I may serve you the better. I shall believe that you will be successful in all your undertakings, for surely no one is so well equipped as you to do what you have planned. My faith in you is as great as my love for you—more than that I cannot say.

E. M. House

ALS (WP, DLC).

Remarks at a Press Conference

May 22, 1913

Mr. President, in your last confidential statement to the newspapermen, you referred to a statement from the Chargé d'Affaires with reference to the feelings of Japan. Has there been any answer?

> I dare say we have continued to get them. I don't know that we have since that interview. All we get from him is reassurance as to the attitude of the government, on the question of the more thoughtful people, more people, people that will ultimately, I dare say, control the situation. I just remember, I had a talk with Mr. John R. Mott this forenoon who has just returned from Japan. He gave me very reassuring accounts of their entire comprehension of the situation.

Is that the government, Mr. President, or the—

> He made it a point to see so many sorts of ministers and university men, members of the official class. He didn't see any member of the government. I don't know whether he saw anybody in an official position or not.

Dispatches from Tokyo in the past three or four days invariably started off with the assurance that the conservative class, and newspapers generally, would prevent any high feeling, but the dispatches also nearly always insisted there is very strong feeling about the fundamental resentment against discrimination.

> Yes, that is just what I was saying the other day. That is fundamentally the difficulty, although you can't blame the feeling of the Japanese.

Is there not at present some discretion with regard to immigration?

> I sometimes wonder.

Well, there is what is generally known as a gentleman's agreement under which they restrict emigration.

> Still, that is a mere friendly understanding.

I know it is, yes, sir. Is that the reason it could be abandoned by them without consultation with us?

Oh, I dare say.

But you are not anxious to have their people come to the United States?

I wonder, I wonder.

I wonder whether the public sentiment there, if it was strong against discrimination, might not manifest itself against the arrangement, which is entirely in Japanese control?

Of course that is possible, but I have never heard anybody intimate that is true.

Of course, they have a similar arrangement in Canada. It seems to be based on their understanding that their people could live in close—

With ours, without any risks of disorders.

JRT transcript (WC, NjP) of CLSsh (C. L. Swem Coll., NjP).

To Herbert Putnam[1]

My dear Mr. Putnam: The White House May 22, 1913

Thank you sincerely for your courtesy in personally attending to my modest wish for detective stories. I am sure those that you sent me will keep me going for some time, since I have only odd moments in which to read.

You are quite right in saying that I do not wish, at any rate for the present, Conan Doyle, La Blanc, or Gaboriau.

In haste   Cordially yours,   Woodrow Wilson

TLS (H. Putnam Papers, DLC).
  [1] Librarian of Congress.

To Norman Hapgood

My dear Mr. Hapgood: [The White House] May 22, 1913

I am delighted to know that you are to take charge of Harper's Weekly, and I know how vital it will become out of your touch. You may be sure that I shall not be slow to send you any suggestions, such as you so kindly ask for, that may occur to me. I shall have you very much in mind.

Do you know Mr. Charles Ferguson (who lives at the National Arts Club, and who is struggling to endure his connection with the Hearst papers)? He is one of the most brilliant writers I know, and one of the most thoughtful and idealistic men. It occurred to me that he might, if you liked him, be very serviceable to you on the Weekly.

Is poor William Garrett Brown still going to be able to write? He is a wonderful fellow.

In haste, congratulating the cause on your return to the desk,
        Cordially and faithfully yours,   Woodrow Wilson

TLS (Letterpress Books, WP, DLC).

To Louis Dembitz Brandeis

My dear Mr. Brandeis: [The White House] May 22, 1913

Thank you sincerely for your letter of the nineteenth. The suggestion of President Van Hise is certainly a very interesting one. I have recently been thinking of Frank P. Walsh of Kansas City. What would you think of him as Chairman?

I shall await your suggestion about an I.W.W. man with the greatest interest.

In haste
        Cordially and sincerely yours,   Woodrow Wilson

TLS (Letterpress Books, WP, DLC).

Charles Willis Thompson to Reuben Adiel Bull

My dear Rube: New York, May 22, 1913.

. . . While I was in Washington I got the first line I have had on the President's attitude toward the Huerta Government in Mexico. He hasn't given a hint whether he will recognize it or not. But a friend of mine, Jim Doyle, who represents the Huerta folks, went to see the President to urge recognition, and the President replied, "I will not recognize a government of butchers." . . .   Sincerely,   [Chas.]

CCL (C. W. Thompson Papers, NjP).

To Julean Herbert Arnold[1]

My dear Mr. Arnold: [The White House] May 23, 1913

I have been very deeply gratified and very much moved by the receipt of the silk embroidered scroll presented to me by citizens of the Chinese Republic resident at Chefoo, China. My thoughts constantly turn to the great nation now struggling to its feet as a conscious, self-governing people, and it makes me very proud indeed that they should look to the United States as to their friend and exemplar in the great tasks which lie ahead of them.

I beg that you will take some means of conveying to the citizens who so graciously and generously send me this token of their respect my appreciation not only of their kindness and generosity but also my best wishes for their own happiness and prosperity and my earnest hope that not once in the recognition and first greeting of the Republic, but many times in the years to come, this country may have the opportunity to show its cordial friendship for China and all those who work for her lasting benefit.

The scroll will always be for me a momento of one of the most gratifying incidents of my incumbency of the Presidency of the United States.

With much respect, I am

Sincerely yours,   Woodrow Wilson

TLS (Letterpress Books, WP, DLC).
  ¹ American Consul at Chefoo, China.

To Robert Marion La Follette

My dear Senator: The White House May 23, 1913

I learned only last evening, and learned with the deepest distress, of the death of your brother, William La Follette. I learned to have a very warm feeling of friendship for him and I mourn his death most sincerely. May I not express my very great sympathy with you in this great loss?

Cordially and sincerely yours,   Woodrow Wilson

TLS (La Follette Family Papers, DLC).

From Henry Means Pindell

My dear Mr. President: Peoria, Ill., May 23rd, 1913.

I beg to acknowledge the receipt of your kind letter of the 21st inst. I confess it brought some embarrassment and the embarrassment arises out of my name being published throughout the country, in connection with the Comptrollership of The Currency and other great offices and, further, there has been a sentiment among a great many of those who fought the fight at Baltimore, that my name would be connected with some big office. I was not responsible for the connection of my name with any office, nor have I sought office or consented that my friends should address you in my behalf.

I have done some things in my life, which were no ordinary affairs. I have fought some issues in this community and in the state, which has brought me pleasure and some fame and they have been mighty vital issues to the people.

I perhaps have falsely allowed my friends to feel that my connection with your candidacy and nomination and election was far more important than it had any right to be and I am making no personal claim whatever.

Mrs. Pindell[1] and I have both felt that the only thing that I could do, in justice to my own interests here, was to decline any important office that might be tendered me, if I was fortunate enough to receive such an offer. I have enough self-confidence to feel that I could fill any office in your gift, not requiring technical knowledge.

My dear Mr. President, I am saying more than I ought to say. I prize my friendship with you above everything else. It was a joy to me to be fighting for you and that is what I told you the night you left Peoria, before the primaries.[2] I enjoyed the battle and have felt it a great honor to know you as I feel I do. I have only the most unselfish interest in the success and fame of your administration. I have studiously avoided bringing any burden whatever to you, even to the extent of answering my letters which I have frequently wanted to write you, concerning the interests of your administration, so I beg you not to give further consideration to my name in connection with any appointment.

With highest regards, I beg to remain,

Sincerely yours,   Henry M Pindell

TLS (WP, DLC).

¹ Eliza Adelia Smith Pindell.

² The Illinois presidential primary of April 9, 1912.

From Charles Richard Crane

Dear Mr. President: Chicago May 23, 1913.

We have completed our arrangements for taking over Harper's Weekly, and Norman Hapgood will begin editing it the middle of June. We have a fine list of shareholders, all your friends.

We are all happy at the way things are going, and only wish that you can take a little care of yourself.

Always faithfully,   Charles R. Crane

TLS (WP, DLC).

From Emilio Aguinaldo

Sir: Manila, Philippine Islands. May 23, 1913.

I have had real pleasure in meeting here at my residence your private representative or emissary, Mr. Henry Jones Ford, Professor of Princeton University.

With Mr. Ford I discussed certain political aspects of the Philippines. He assured me that we (you and I) coincide in our thought regarding the possibility of establishing in this Archipelago a republican form of government similar to that of Switzerland under some form of guaranty or protection. I assured him that the ambition of the Filipinos to live an independent life, to have a government patterned after their own modality and uses, is universal. For this ambition the Filipinos went to war more than once, for this same ambition they are peaceful under American protection and promises.

Mr. Ford also took up the question of language and the probable status of the American officials and employees of the Philippine Government. It is my opinion that under a native government, the English language will not be stricken off the school plans nor discouraged by any means. I realize how indispensable the English language is becoming in all kinds of transactions and relations every day.

As to the status of American officials and employees I gave Mr. Ford to understand that should a radical change take place in the form of government here it would be a wise policy to let them continue in office until they resign when their positions will be gradually filled by Filipinos.

The Filipino is not prejudiced against any people or race. What Japan had done with regard to using foreigners where natives were not qualified can be repeated in the Philippines and with preference in favor of the Americans. Finally, Mr. Ford, showing great interest in the welfare of my people recommended great patience, avoiding by every means disorders and outbreaks which might entangle and make difficult the solution of the independence problem. As to this, I told Mr. Ford that no fears should be entertained. The Filipino is by nature a lover of peace, so much so that his usual peaceful mood goes sometimes beyond the prudential limit.

I state all this in writing in order to ratify and authorize with my signature all the thoughts expressed during our conference. Hoping that God will enlighten you and preserve you for the welfare of your country and my people, I remain,

                    Sincerely yours,   Emilio Aguinaldo

TLS (WP, DLC).

A Message to American Indians[1]

My Brothers: [May 24, 1913]

A hundred years ago, President Jefferson, one of the greatest of my predecessors, said to the Chiefs of the Upper Cherokees:

"My Children, I shall rejoice to see the day when the Red Men, our neighbors, become truly one people with us, enjoying all the rights and privileges we do, and living in peace and plenty as we do, without any one to make them afraid, to injure their persons, or take their property without being punished for it according to fixed laws."

This I say to you again today; but a hundred years have gone by, and we are nearer these great things then hoped for now, much nearer than we were then. Education, agriculture, the trades are the red man's road to the white man's civilization today, as they were in the day of Jefferson, and happily you have gone a long way on that road.

There are some dark pages in the history of the white man's dealings with the Indian and many parts of the record are stained with the greed and avarice of those who have thought only of their own profit, but it is also true that the purposes and motives of this great Government and of our nation as a whole toward the red man have been wise, just, and beneficent. The remarkable progress of our Indian brothers towards civilization is proof of it, and open to all to see.

During the past half century, you have seen the school house take the place of the military post on your reservations. The administration of Indian affairs has been transferred from the military to the civil arm of the Government. The education and industrial training the Government has given you has enabled thousands of Indian men and women to take their places in civilization alongside their white neighbors. Thousands are living in substantial farm houses on their own separate allotments of land. Hundreds of others have won places of prominence in the professions and some have worked their way into the halls of Congress and into places of responsibility in our State and National Governments. Thirty thousand Indian children are enrolled in Government, State and Mission schools. The great White Father now calls you his "brothers," not his "children." Because you have shown in your education and in your settled ways of life staunch, manly, worthy qualities of sound character, the nation is about to give you distinguished recognition through the erection of a monument in honor of the Indian people in the harbor of New York. The erection of that monument will usher in that day which Thomas Jefferson said he would rejoice to see, "when the Red Men become truly one people with us, enjoying all the rights and privileges we do and living in peace and plenty." I rejoice to foresee the day.

It gives me pleasure as President of the United States to send this greeting to you and to commend to you the lessons in industry, patriotism, and devotion to our common country which participation in this ceremony brings to you.

T MS (WP, DLC).
[1] The following message represents a very considerable revision by Wilson of a draft prepared about April 30, 1913, by Frederick H. Abbott, Assistant Commissioner of Indian Affairs. The draft with Wilson's changes is in the C. L. Swem Coll., NjP. Wilson dictated this message to The Phonograph on May 24.

From William Jennings Bryan

My dear Mr. President:　　　　　　Washington May 24, 1913.

I am in receipt of your letter enclosing the request of Señor Cuadra,[1] Minister of Finance of Nicaragua, who is visiting this country as Fiscal Agent, for the purpose of arranging a Nicaraguan loan with American bankers.[2] I have talked with Mr. Caudra and the retiring Minister[3]—a new Minister[4] is awaiting presentation to you—and I think it might be well for you to have a conversation with him in order that you may understand more fully the situation in Nicaragua.

I write, therefore, to ask whether it is consistent with your wishes and your engagements to fix a date for an interview with him. After you have heard from him we can discuss the subject.

I am inclined to think that the purchase of the Canal option[5] might give sufficient encouragement to the bankers to loan without the conditions which were, at their request, put into the other treaty in regard to a loan. I send you a copy of the treaty now before the Senate.[6] Senator Bacon tells me that the Democrats are nearly unanimous in opposing this treaty because they think it provides for an interference on our part in Nicaraguan affairs. They seem disinclined to endorse that principle for fear it may be regarded as a precedent.

Awaiting an expression of your wishes in the matter, and with assurances of respect, I am, my dear Mr. President,

Very sincerely yours,　W. J. Bryan

TLS (WP, DLC).
[1] Pedro Rafael Cuadra.
[2] On the diplomacy of the Taft and Wilson administrations with Nicaragua, see Link, The New Freedom, pp. 331-42, and Dana G. Munro, Intervention and Dollar Diplomacy in the Caribbean, 1900-1921 (Princeton, N. J., 1964), pp. 160-216, 388-416.
[3] Salvador Castrillo, Jr.

4 Emiliano Chamorro.
5 By the Nicaraguan-American Inter-Oceanic Canal Treaty, signed on February 8, 1913, about which see Link, p. 332, and Munro, p. 213.
6 Bryan enclosed a printed copy of the Nicaraguan-American Loan Convention of 1911. About this, see Link, p. 331, and Munro, pp. 192-94, 203.

Remarks at a Press Conference

May 26, 1913

Have we approached any nearer to recognition of Mexico in the last three or four days?

> Not so far as I can see.

Have you fully made up your mind not to recognize Mexico until the elections?

> Oh, well, I don't permit myself fast to make my mind up about the changing scene.

I know you have intimated in one of the previous talks that that was the thinking and that stood in the way—that the government was not organized or could not be organized until the elections occurred.

> Well, the government is, in a sense, organized now as a provisional government. The regular machinery of government is in large part in operation, but their plans seem to shift from time to time. That is what is puzzling me.

In your mind, is there any hazard for this country in recognizing the provisional government?

> You mean any natural hazard?

They may not come back.

> No, I suppose not.

I was thinking of the possibility of the government's being overturned—the provisional government's being overturned—in the election, and an entirely new set of men coming in, and their feeling toward this country?

> I suppose in that case the present recognition would be passing immediately.

What is the principal obstacle now, Mr. President, in recognizing Mexico?

> Well, what do you think?

Well, the economic situation, probably.

> Did you ever know a situation that had more question marks around it? Whenever I look at it, I see nothing but exclamation points. It is just a kaleidoscopic, changing scene. Nobody in the world has any certain information about the situation that I have yet found. Their information is about a month old, or it is so new it isn't verified.

If it is verified, they deliberately break it to the press.

I know only what I have seen in the dispatches. I don't know anything about it through any other channel. . . .

You can understand anything you choose in this town, if you will only keep your ears open. I should think you fellows were missing a lot of stories about the extraordinary lobbying in this town at this time.

There is a good deal written about it, Mr. President.

Somehow you haven't gotten hold of it so that the country could notice it. This town is swarming with lobbyists, so you can't throw bricks in any direction without hitting one, much inclined as you are to throw bricks. That is the most concerted and as concentrated an effort, I dare say, as has ever been made to influence governmental legislation by the pressure of private interests.

Do you refer especially to sugar?

Sugar, wool—those in particular. Those have the biggest lobbies. Of course, there are men, perfectly legitimate businessmen, who have come to town in some ways to represent their interests. I don't know that but that there is a great deal besides that going on.

I think the country knows pretty well that lobbyists are here.

I know, but you think just the usual scenery is in view.
There is a good deal more than the usual scenery in view.

They have been pressuring you, Mr. President?

No, sir, I am immune.

Can you give us some names, pictures, in connection with that, then we will start using—

Well, if I could collect this lobby around myself, I shouldn't like to be photographed with them. We can get the names out of our daily mail.

You mean, Mr. President, there is a corrupt lobby here?

I don't know that they could approach Congress in that way, but just a systematic misrepresentation of the facts and one of these organized processes by which people, just out of weakness, to please their friends, will write letters galore about things that they know nothing about. It is similar to the process of trying to get men appointed to office. I generally estimate a man in inverse proportion to the number of recommendations, because when the number passes a certain point I know there is machinery at work of the most elaborate sort, and that sort of thing is going on. But the men on the hill know that and particularly understand that. I think they do.

It would be regarded as extremely—

> It doesn't make me in the least nervous, although I would like to see these fellows made a bit ridiculous. That is what I would enjoy.

Mr. President, you said just a moment ago that you didn't think we were getting that fact out to the country. Wouldn't the most effective way to get it out be for you to authorize us to quote you on what you have just said?

> Well, I'll tell you what I'll do in a minute. I don't know what I have just said, because I am on guard in talking to you fellows this way. Before you get away from the office wire, I will try to dictate a few lines.

That will get to the country.

> All right.

JRT transcript (WC, NjP) of CLSsh (C. L. Swem Coll., NjP).

A Statement on Tariff Lobbyists

[[May 26, 1913]]

I think that the public ought to know the extraordinary exertions being made by the lobby in Washington to gain recognition for certain alterations of the tariff bill. Washington has seldom seen so numerous, so industrious, or so insidious a lobby. The newspapers are being filled with paid advertisements calculated to mislead the judgment of public men not only, but also the public opinion of the country itself. There is every evidence that money without limit is being spent to sustain this lobby, and to create an appearance of a pressure of public opinion antagonistic to some of the chief items of the tariff bill.

It is of serious interest to the country that the people at large should have no lobby and be voiceless in these matters, while great bodies of astute men seek to create an artificial opinion and to overcome the interests of the public for their private profit. It is thoroughly worth the while of the people of this country to take knowledge of this matter. Only public opinion can check and destroy it.

The Government in all its branches ought to be relieved from this intolerable burden and this constant interruption to the calm progress of debate. I know that in this I am speaking for the members of the two houses, who would rejoice as much as I would, to be released from this unbearable situation.[1]

Printed in the *New York Times*, May 27, 1913.
[1] For the impact of this statement, see Link, *The New Freedom*, pp. 187-90.

To Charles Richard Crane

My dear Friend: [The White House] May 26, 1913.

Thank you sincerely for your letter of May 23d. I congratulate you heartily on your taking over the Weekly. It is especially pleasing to me that you have secured Mr. Hapgood to take charge.

I cannot tell you how much it encourages and heartens me to have you say what you do as to the course we are taking. It is, indeed, most gratifying.

Cordially and faithfully yours,   Woodrow Wilson

TLS (Letterpress Books, WP, DLC).

To William Jennings Bryan

My dear Mr. Secretary: [The White House] May 26, 1913

Thank you for the enclosed endorsements of Dr. William H. Leavell.[1] I shall put him on the list of the men to be considered. I am, of course, at heart in sympathy with your suggestions about the various men you mention from the Southern states, but I must say there is coming to be a little point in the objection being raised that we are giving an undue proportion of offices to men south of the Mason and Dixon line. But I am going to ponder the matter very carefully, and am, as you know, at work on the list at every moment I can get.

In haste

Cordially and faithfully yours,   Woodrow Wilson

TLS (Letterpress Books, WP, DLC).
    [1] The Rev. Dr. William Hayne Leavell of Houston, Tex., former Baptist, Congregational, and Presbyterian clergyman. Appointed Minister to Guatemala, September 15, 1913.

To Frederic Yates

My dear Fred.,   The White House 26 May, 1913.

I cannot tell you what pleasure your letter[1] gave me,—gave us! The voice of a dear friend amidst the clangour of these days of rush and confusion and anxious responsibility is like sweet music and renews everything that is fresh and normal and invigorating in me. Thank you with all my heart!

Nothing has been accomplished yet,—everything is in course,— but the signs that our programme will go through are all good so far and the opinion of the country continues to back me in a most encouraging way.

We are all well, and go at our daily tasks with zest. And how often we think of you all, God bless you! The day after I am released from this great job I shall take ship for Rydal!

These are but a few, hasty lines, but they are freighted with deep affection for all three of you from all five of us.

Your sincere friend, Woodrow Wilson

ALS (F. Yates Coll., NjP).
1 Probably F. Yates to WW, April 4, 1913, ALS (WP, DLC).

From Henry Burling Thompson

Dear President Wilson: New York, N. Y. May 26, 1913.

In the old Princeton days you have invariably been patient with me in listening to advice. Considering our changed relationship, the use of the word advice now would sound almost as an impertinence. Nevertheless, I feel that a crisis has been reached on which I ought to give you my opinion.

The question of your signing or not signing the Sundry Civil Appropriation Act which contains the rider exempting labor unions and farmers' associations from the provisions of the Sherman Act has given me real anxiety.

I know that I voice the sentiments of hundreds of your friends who have as high appreciation of and admiration for you as I have, and have the welfare of your administration sincerely at heart, when I say that the approval of the bill on your part would be a source of profound sorrow to them. I am aware of the difficult situation in which you are placed, of the political exigencies and political interests, of the danger of a divided party, and all that; nevertheless, in the last analysis and stripped of all collateral issues the principle embodied in the rider is inimical to our form of government.

I have been all my life in close touch with labor and have a sincere sympathy with their ideals, and I believe in my association with them I have commanded their respect, and with this knowledge I cannot feel it is to their interest to have such exemption offered. It will result in class feeling that is injurious to both employer and employee.

I know you will appreciate that my high regard for you and my old friendship is my only warrant for intruding in such a matter. Sincerely yours, Henry B Thompson

TLS (WP, DLC).

From Edward Mandell House

On Board the Cunard R.M.S. "Mauretania."
Dear Governor: May 26 [1913].

I believe I told you that Mr. Paul Warburg had been in conference with Senator Owen and Mr. Untermeyer. I inclose you
his answer to their argument in favor of the issuance of currency by the Government.[1] His reasons seem to me to be conclusive. Why venture along uncertain paths when a well known
road can be used? For a moment before I left I thought, perhaps,
a compromise might be considered, but I doubt whether it would
be safe to conceed the least which they would be willing to accept.
The situation is a difficult one and I am sorry that I am not near
to lend what help I might.

Your very faithful,   E. M. House

ALS (WP, DLC).
   [1] This enclosure is missing.

From Louis Dembitz Brandeis

My dear Mr. President: Boston, Mass. May 26, 1913.

Replying to yours of the 22nd:

First: As to Frank P. Walsh: I met Mr. Walsh for a moment in
New York last Fall, and heard favorable reports of him and his
work from Boyd Fisher,[1] and one or two others; but I have no
information concerning him which entitles me to an opinion as
to whether or not he would be desirable for Chairman. The only
reason I have for any doubt is the fact that he lacks a national
reputation; for I found that others, of whom I have recently
inquired about him, knew as little of him as I do.

Second: As to an I.W.W. man: John Graham Brooks, Lincoln
Steffens and Walter Lippman agreed that Frank Bohn would be
the best man to represent the I.W.W. I do not personally know
Bohn, or indeed anything about him, save what I have heard from
them. I enclose a memorandum concerning him prepared by John
Graham Brooks, and in his handwriting.[2] I understand that Bohn
is from the West; that he was for some time an instructor at
Columbia; that he resigned to become an I.W.W. organizer. His
brother, William E. Bohn, was instructor at the University of
Michigan. They are both on the editorial staff of the International
Socialist Review.

My only doubt about Bohn is a technical one. I am told that
about a year ago he resigned as an active member of the I.W.W.
I presume that means that he ceased to be an organizer. He cer-

tainly appears, from his contributions to the International Socialist Review to be actively working for the cause.

Section 1 of the Industrial Relations Act speaks of "representatives of organized labor," and the question might be raised whether Bohn, under these circumstances, is a representative.

After this possible technical obstacle to selecting Bohn was brought up in conference, Steffens recommended Vincent St. John, the Secretary of the I.W.W. and the founder of the organization. Steffens says St. John is able, intelligent and representative; that he has a big reputation in labor circles, and that he is confident that St. John would contribute greatly to the work of the Commission. But Brooks says that St. John has a record of past violence, which would make his selection impossible.

I have found, in making inquiries about the various I.W.W. men, that the personal records of several of those who might naturally be selected as representative, are such as to preclude their selection.

Very cordially yours,   Louis D. Brandeis

TLS (WP, DLC).
    1 Boyd Archer Fisher, writer and social worker of New York; organizer of the Social Worker's Bureau for the Wilson and Marshall campaign of 1912; "promoter and director (without pay) of the first of New York City's 65 school social centers, in collaboration with Margaret Woodrow Wilson." Harvard College Class of 1910, *Twenty-Fifth Anniversary Report* (Cambridge, Mass., 1935), p. 251.
    2 A three-page handwritten memorandum.

From William Jennings Bryan, with Enclosures

My dear Mr. President: Washington May 26, 1913.

As I shall not be able to be present at the Cabinet meeting tomorrow, for the reason which I have given you, namely, that, not knowing that the date came on Cabinet Day, I agreed to speak at commencement exercises in New York, I enclose Memorandum made May 23 and Memorandum made today, in regard to the French loan. You will see from these that the French Ambassador last Friday disclaimed for his Government any interest in the matter and today confirms his understanding on the strength of a statement which he has received from his Government.

You will also notice that I communicated with the Chargé of the British Embassy,[1] in the absence of Ambassador Spring-Rice.

I am glad to report that Sweden today announced acceptance of the principle embodied in your peace plan, and I gave him[2] a memorandum, as I have also the French Ambassador, covering the details of the plan. Sweden makes the fifth country to accept the principle, Italy having been the first, Great Britain the second,

France the third and Brazil the fourth. I have not yet made any announcement to the public, because I am hoping for acceptance from Argentina, Peru, Norway, The Netherlands and Russia.

I am sure you are gratified, as I am, to see the acceptance of the peace plan. I am encouraged to believe that in the course of time we shall have practically all of the nations bound to us by these agreements.

The German Ambassador promised to take the matter up with his Government when he arrived there. He will be back shortly.

With assurances of respect, etc., I am,

My dear Mr. President,   Very sincerely,   W. J. Bryan

TLS (WP, DLC).
  [1] Probably Ernest Stowell Scott, First Secretary of the British Embassy.
  [2] That is, the Swedish Minister, Wilhelm August Ferdinand Ekengren.

E   N   C   L   O   S   U   R   E   I

Washington May 23, 1913.
MEMORANDUM BY THE SECRETARY.

At the suggestion of the President, I asked His Excellency, the French Ambassador, to come to the Department this (Friday) afternoon, and called his attention to the dispatch from the City of Mexico, communicating the fact that the Mexican Government was about to secure a loan from certain French banks named in the dispatch. I stated to him that the President assumed that these proposed loans were being made by the banks as private loans, made with a due understanding of the risks, and that the French Government was not at all connected with them. The Ambassador assured me that that was his understanding, although he had received no notice from his Government and relied entirely for information upon what he saw in the newspapers, but he expressed without hesitation and with emphasis his opinion that his Government had nothing to do with the loans, remarking that the banks were not the ones with which the Government was in the habit of acting. He stated, however, that he would communicate to his Government the fact that we had stated to him that we assumed that the loan was purely a private matter.

Later, on the same afternoon, I called up the British Embassy and finding His Excellency, the British Ambassador, absent on a trip to Canada, made to the Chargé, over the telephone, the same statement that I had made to the French Ambassador. The Chargé replied that they had no notice of the matter at the

Embassy aside from the newspaper notice, and that he understood that whatever loans were being made, were being made by private banks or financiers, and that the Government had no connection with them.

ENCLOSURE II

Washington

MEMORANDUM.

On this day (Monday, May 26, 1913) the French Ambassador called and said that he had communicated with his Government in regard to the Mexican loan, and had received assurance that the loan was purely a private matter in which the French Government had no interest whatever, and that the loan was made by those who were engaged in the matter at their own risk. He also suggested that, from his information, it was not entirely in the hands of citizens of France, but that some other countries were interested, the United States being named specifically.

T MSS (WP, DLC).

Julius Kruttschnitt to William Jennings Bryan

Sir: At Washington, D. C., May 26th, 1913.

Following our interview of this morning, permit me to suggest the great opportunity of the present administration to perform a great service, not only to its own citizens interested in Mexico, but to the Mexican people and the citizens of foreign nations as well, all of whom—particularly the first mentioned—are entitled to the assistance of our Government for their protection in Mexico.

The Southern Pacific Company has invested over forty millions of dollars in the construction of over 1000 miles of railway in Mexico, connecting with and designed to act as feeders to its system in the United States. It has large numbers of American citizens employed in managing and operating its Mexican lines, and these men, with their families, have for many months been exposed to violence and possible loss of life in performing duties on which their livelihood depends.

For several months, the Southern Pacific Company has been deprived of the possession of its railroad lines in Sonora and Sinaloa, which have been operated by the State Authorities with their own officers; and to prevent movement of federal troops they have destroyed large numbers of bridges and great quantities of rolling stock.

We pointed out in our conference that the present Congress, which was constitutionally elected at the time of the election of the late President Madero, has ordered an election to take place on the 26th of October, but it is very disquieting to consider the further loss of life and property that may take place in the interim, and we therefore respectfully suggest that our Government consider using its good offices to bring about an election at an early date, in other words, to attempt in this way to terminate bloodshed and the danger to American lives and property, which must otherwise continue for at least five months more.

Does it not seem, therefore, that the present administration has a great opportunity, by acting quickly, of presenting a plan to the Mexican Government urging it to call an election at an early date, instead of waiting until the 26th of October, and that such guarantee of a fair election in all of those states of which it has control, shall be given, as to command the confidence of all?

Offering our cooperation and that of our officers in any way in which it can assist, I remain,

Very respectfully yours,   J. Kruttschnitt

TLS (WP, DLC).

To Matthias Cowell Ely

My dear Mr. Ely: [The White House] May 27, 1913

Of course, I entirely agree with you about Frank Hague, but I am quite clear in my opinion that intervention on my part in respect of personal candidacies would probably do more harm than good.

I warmly appreciate your kindness in writing.

In haste

Cordially and faithfully yours,   Woodrow Wilson

TLS (Letterpress Books, WP, DLC).

To Henry Burling Thompson

My dear Friend: [The White House] May 27, 1913.

I have read with interest your letter of May 26th, and thank you for writing me. You may be sure that I shall take no action in the matter without the most serious consideration.

Cordially and sincerely yours,   Woodrow Wilson

TLS (Letterpress Books, WP, DLC).

From William Jennings Bryan

My dear Mr. President: Washington May 27, 1913.

I enclose a proposition[1] made by the gentlemen[2] whom you met yesterday in Mr. Tumulty's room. The suggestion they make is a new one, and it strikes me very favorably. I have indicated on the margin and underscored the words. Instead of asking for the recognition of Huerta, they suggest that Huerta be notified that this Government will recognize a constitutional President, if the Congress will call an election for an early date, and supervise the election so as to give a fair chance for an expression of the opinion of the people. You will notice that the gentlemen who called say:

"We would be glad to offer such aid as is within our power to effect an early election to the presidency, to the end that such a constituted President, installed and approved by the present regularly elected Congress, may receive the recognition of the United States Government."[3]

If you will make an appointment for any time tomorrow, I would like to go over the matter with you. This seems to me to offer a way out.

With assurances of my respect, I am, my dear Mr. President,
Yours sincerely,   W. J. Bryan

TLS (WP, DLC).
[1] E. Brush and S. W. Eccles to WJB, May 26, 1913, TLS (WP, DLC).
[2] Edward Brush, a vice-president of the American Smelting and Refining Co. who specialized in silver production, and Silas Wright Eccles, also a mining expert associated with the American Smelting and Refining Co.
[3] This was the portion of the letter that Bryan underscored.

From Louis Dembitz Brandeis

My dear Mr. President: Boston, Mass. May 27, 1913.

Since writing you yesterday I have another communication from Mr. Steffens in which he says that he disagrees with Mr. Brooks' judgment as to St. John,—"not his facts perhaps, but his point of view"; that "St. John is loyal and representative." Mr. St. John's address is: 164 Washington Street, Chicago.

My own opinion remains that Mr. Bohn would be much the better appointment.

If you have any doubt as to the advisability of appointing any I.W.W. man, I hope you will look at Brooks' book on "American Syndicalism."[1]   Yours cordially,   Louis D. Brandeis

TLS (WP, DLC).
[1] John Graham Brooks, *American Syndicalism: the I.W.W.* (New York, 1913).

Sir Edward Grey to Sir Cecil Arthur Spring Rice

Sir,   F. O., 27 May, 1913.

The American Ambassador came to see me to-day, and said that the President had charged him[1] with a message to say how much he desired to maintain the goodwill and cordial relations between the two countries. The Ambassador had no instructions to speak about the Panama question, but he would be ready to talk about it on some other occasion. He spoke in the very highest terms of Mr. Bryce. The Americans had ceased to regard him as an Ambassador: to them he had become *Mr. Bryce*, whose departure they felt as a personal loss to themselves.

I said that their kind feeling towards Mr. Bryce had been much appreciated here. We felt it as evidence not only of the good service that Mr. Bryce was doing for his own country, but also of their kind disposition. I cordially reciprocated the President's wishes, and said that I would do all I could to preserve the best possible relations with the United States. I should be ready to talk about the Panama Canal at any time that he desired, and also about Mr. Bryan's proposal for an international agreement that disputes should be investigated by a Commission before they were allowed to become the cause of a quarrel. I was entirely in sympathy with this idea, which had indeed been included in the General Arbitration Treaty that the Senate had not been willing to pass as it stood.   E. G.

TLI (FO 371/1859, No. 24636, PRO).
  [1] At their final meeting at the White House, on April 30, before Page sailed for Great Britain.

To William Jennings Bryan

My dear Mr. Secretary: The White House May 28, 1913

The suggestions of Mr. Edward Brush and Mr. S. W. Eccles about the Mexican matter are certainly most interesting and, I think, important. We will take them up together at an early date.
        Cordially and faithfully yours,   Woodrow Wilson

TLS (W. J. Bryan Papers, DNA).

From Matthias Cowell Ely

Dear Sir: Hoboken, N. J. May 28, 1913

I accept your views as to the inadvisability of directly and personally opposing Frank Hague, but do you not think it might be wise for you to write a letter to someone, say John J. Treacy, expressing the hope that the Progressive citizens of Jersey City, in the coming election, will vote to retain control of their own government and not to make themselves a satrapy, subject to the Essex bosses?   Yours very respectfully   Matt C Ely

TLS (WP, DLC).

Remarks at a Press Conference

May 29, 1913

Mr. President, there are reported statements that Doctor William Bayard Hale is in the City of Mexico on some mission for you, getting information or something of that sort. Could you say anything about that?

> I saw that, but, as you, I disbelieved it. It is getting to be my habit now.

You knew he was there?

> He came to see me just before Easter and told me he was going there.

Of course you will take advantage of any information?

> Oh, very greatly, yes. . . .

Mr. President, are you in sympathy with the general purpose of the Cummins resolution?[1]

> Oh, yes.

Is there any further information along that line that you could give us?

> I would tell you if there is any that I could give you fellows.

I think you probably know more about it than I do.

I mean the—the information along the line that is called for in the resolution, of course. I don't know whether you care to answer that.

> In the action of Congress as soon as—I don't know that there is. Congress can do that. Evidently they [lobbyists] don't know that there was a vote last November, so they are continuing their old practices under the impression that the Congress of the United States was built to legislate for special interests.

A bill was introduced today by Mr. Weeks of Massachusetts for registration of lobbyists, I think along the lines of the Massachusetts law.

> Yes. Well, that will do some good.

[1] Introduced by Senator Albert Cummins, Republican of Iowa. It called for the establishment of a select committee to investigate the alleged lobby and hear testimony from senators and the President. For the dénouement, see Link, *The New Freedom*, pp. 189-90.

Mr. President, are you in a position to supply the names of these lobbyists if this resolution should be passed?

 Oh, if public necessity arose, I could easily do so.

Mr. President, would you be willing to break precedent to the extent of going before that committee?

 I don't know.

Well, in another way, have you been asked to?

 No, indeed. You mean the committee to which the resolution was—

Yes, sir.

 No, I haven't.

Mr. President, you will remember congressmen the other day giving you express and cordial approval of a possible primary for the election of Presidents.

 I have always, yes sir, said that in the campaign.

Nomination?

 Yes. . . .

Mr. President, that brings up the question of the Japanese affair. Have you got any word from Japan?

 No. There hasn't been. Not a word.

Mr. President, is there anything new in a telegram to Governor Johnson in which he was asked to delay the [operation] of that bill? Reference was made to the fact that delay might offer an opportunity to remove the test of direct diplomacy. Is there any hope of doing that, despite the enactment of the bill?

 Well, I don't see that there is anything to do in that direction. The intimation there was that we needed the consultation with the Japanese government to find some way to settle it with the legislature of California with regard to what is existing now. Now, you see, there is nothing new to take up, so far as that is concerned.

I notice the Tokyo government has given out some statement that lets it be known that the California affair hadn't been adjusted to the complete satisfaction at all. . . . I thought possibly you still had some hope of reaching an agreement?

 Of course, we are always open to any suggestion that the Japanese government has to make, but it hasn't made any yet.

Would these reports there indicate a varying public opinion?

 I don't know. If we have had any, none has come to me from the State Department.

You know, it was said before that the government was rather strained. . . . Mr. President, you had, I think, some talks in the last day or two with members of Congress who were engaged in preparing currency legislation?

>Only with Mr. Glass and Senator Owen.

Now, is there a bill—could you say whether a bill is ready to be presented?

>No, there is not. I have three bills lying before me,[2] as a matter of fact, and I am generously invited to make a bill out of the three.

I thought that the professor of political economy was going to do that.

>He didn't, after all, make a draft. There were certain points I wanted his opinion on.

I have been told that the effort might be to make that a non-partisan bill, so that Republicans might support it as well as Democrats, and that the caucus might not be invoked in the House.

>Well, of course, that suggestion hadn't come to me. I hope it will be nonpartisan in this sense, that it is fair all 'round.

Is one of the bills before you Mr. Henry's bill?[3]

>No, sir, I didn't know he had one.

Well, he made a suggestion of drawing one.

>No, sir, that is not one of the three; I would be very interested to see his.

You talked with Mr. Howe[4] the other day, was that on—

>Only incidentally; we principally gossiped about affairs in Princeton.

He is a member of the American Bankers' Association?

>Yes, he is.

Have any Republican members of the House offered their assistance or cooperation in the matter of currency legislation.

>No, sir; not to me.

Mr. President, could you tell us whose bills you have before you?

>Why, I have a draft of a bill by Senator Owen, a draft by Mr. Glass, and a draft by the Secretary of the Treasury; and they are all along the same line. There is no essential divergence that I have yet discovered.

You mean that the central idea is the same, Mr. President?

>Yes, sir, in all three.

Mr. President, is there any disposition on your part to believe that

[2] The Glass bill and plans proposed by Owen and McAdoo, about which see Link, *The New Freedom*, pp. 206-10.

[3] Representative Henry had not yet introduced his bill. He introduced one on June 13 postponing action on the Federal Reserve bill and calling for a new investigation of the so-called Money Trust. See *ibid.*, 218-19.

[4] Edward Leavitt Howe, president of the Princeton Bank.

the Senate committee is sending out questions to bankers, in the apparent purpose to hear from bankers—isn't that unnecessary?

> No, sir; I think, of course, it is a perfectly natural and proper thing to do.

I think there is some feeling on the House's side—

> Of course, the gentlemen of the subcommittee of the last Committee on Banking and Currency do feel that they covered the ground pretty thoroughly in their own hearings; and they also sent out questionnaires such as the senators sent out, and got very voluminous answers, I dare say more voluminous than any prudent person would ever care to read. It greatly increases the sale of paper.

Mr. President, does one of the bills before you provide for the regulation of stock exchanges?

> No, sir.

That is to be one of the fundamentals of Mr. Henry's bill.

> Oh!

Mr. President, that reminded me of one of the other questions asked: a Republican senator said that there is a number of Republican senators who would like to vote for a sound currency bill, and they thought they would make some effort if it was possible to see the bill or know what was going into it before it has the stamp of approval of the administration, and I wondered if any advances like that have been made.

> No, sir; not yet.

I know one man, probably the same as Mr. Matthews,[5] who is, I think, a little anxious to support the bill, but he feels that before he supports the bill he thought he ought to have his opportunity to offer objections and criticisms.

> Well, he would naturally have that through the committees to which it would be referred. Of course, it ought to undergo the freest criticism after it is submitted.

Mr. President, you say you have before you the drafts of three bills with the suggestion that you make one bill out of them. Have you determined what course you are going to pursue in getting up a bill?

> No, I have not, because, frankly, I do not feel competent, myself, to draft the details of it. I will have to make up my mind which of the details are best to retain and then put it in somebody else's hand to draft it.

That would naturally be with the Secretary of the Treasury?

> Very naturally, yes, sir.

JRT transcript (WC, NjP) of CLSsh (C. L. Swem Coll., NjP), T MS (C. L. Swem Coll., NjP).
5 Unidentified.

To Louis Dembitz Brandeis

My dear Mr. Brandeis: [The White House] May 29, 1913

Thank you sincerely for your letter of May twenty-sixth. I am sorry that Mr. Walsh is not better known. I think from all that I can learn he is a man of admirable parts and quality.

My judgment is very much in suspense as to the appointment of an I.W.W. man. I shall think the matter over very deeply and carefully.

In haste, with warmest regard and appreciation.

Faithfully yours,   Woodrow Wilson

TLS (Letterpress Books, WP, DLC).

To Albert Sidney Burleson

My dear Burleson: The White House May 29, 1913

I am beginning to fear that we made a mistake about the Sacramento, California, Post Office. Fox, it seems, is acknowledged on all hands to be a lobbyist for the Southern Pacific, and the nomination has made a very bad impression out there.[1] Our best friend there, indeed one of our few friends in the editorial ranks in California, was the editor of the Sacramento Standard Union.[2]

I gather these facts from men who can not possibly have any personal interest in the matter, and deemed it my duty to call your attention to them.

Faithfully yours,   Woodrow Wilson

TLS (A. S. Burleson Papers, DLC).

[1] Wilson wrote this letter immediately after receiving a letter from Thomas J. Pence, assistant to the chairman of the Democratic National Committee, saying that Thomas Fox of Sacramento (supported by Secretary Lane) was a lobbyist for the Southern Pacific Railroad and was opposed by all California progressive Democrats and newspapers. T. J. Pence to WW, May 29, 1913, TLS (WP, DLC).

[2] L. E. Bontz, owner and manager of the *Sacramento Union*.

From Ralph Pulitzer

Dear Mr. President: New York, May 29, 1913.

I wish, with your permission, to introduce to you Mr. Alleyne Ireland,[1] who goes to Washington on my personal assignment to make a careful and accurate investigation of the nature and activities of the Lobby which I gravely fear is becoming a serious menace to the success of your tariff legislation. May I trouble you to let Mr. Ireland know whether you think it best to give

him any information which you properly can on this subject and
have him work along lines in touch with your policy in the matter, or whether you prefer to have the work done entirely independently?

I wish to take this opportunity again to thank you for your
kind letter of introduction to Colonel Goethals, which gave an
interest and instructiveness to my visit to the Canal which otherwise it could not possibly have had.

With kind regards   Faithfully yours,   Ralph Pulitzer

TLS (WP, DLC).
    [1] A member of the editorial staff of the New York *World*.

From Charles Ernest Scott

Tsingtau North China.

Honored and Revered Sir: 31 May 1913.

Your kind letter of 15 April 1913 at hand. Many thanks for
same.

Since your inauguration I have been reading with more than
usual care some of the leading vernacular Chinese papers. They
are gratified beyond measure that your administration has broken
with the "dollar diplomacy"—which policy (as we at close range
see it applied, "screwed on," out here) is disgraceful to the nations practicing it, and which the Chinese look upon as brutal
& iniquitous. Since we have pulled out of the deal America
& Americans have gone up above par with the Chinese. They feel
that Americans are their only friends. The things that we know
Russia & Russians to be practicing at Peking, & in Outer & Inner
Mongolia, & in Manchuria are beyond words. The Chinese hate
them like poison. Think of Russia & England in one fell swoop
practically taking over territory (Thibet & Mongolia) which
is larger than all the eighteen provinces combined. Their mountains are known to be stored with minerals rich beyond calcula-
tion. And Mongolia's plains, fertile & fine for grazing, can support many tens of millions of China's population overcrowded to
the South. Think of Shantung with one half the pop. of U.S.!

When merchants recently boycotted Russian banks all over
China, Russia put on the screws & forced Yuan Shi Kai to end
the boycott. Russia's indemnity for Boxer War claims are 4/10+
of all the claims allowed. . . . As the last straw that broke the
camel's back in the loan business, the Quintuple Group, under
the lead of Russia, told Yuan Shi Kai that if he did not close
with their offer of loan in May 1913, they would *all & at once*

demand their balances due on the Boxer War Indemnity! and take steps to get it or its "equivalent."

Oh, if American business men could only have come forward at that time & enabled China to defy them! There is no end of good investments for American business men to make in China, for practically everything is untouched—waiting in a crude state ready to be developed

Think of the incubus of superstition that would not allow the people to bore into their oil fields, or tap their coal deposits, or open their gold, silver, iron & copper mines lest they rouse the Old Dragon to fury! Immense quantities of pig iron are now being shipped regularly from *China to U.S.*

There is money enough among the Chinese for them to loan the Government all it needs; but the heathen heritage of centuries; the graft of which the Chinese officials are past masters; the miasmatic air of doubt, fear, suspicion, distrust—all these things & much more render the Chinese mentally powerless to function confidence! Business languishes & haltingly goes, without trust & confidence in our neighbors. Heathenism is unable to think well of others. This trusting attitude of mind is one of the many by-products of the religion of Jesus Christ. We at home don't think of this good gift of God very much; and find it hard to sense the situation here, just as we think little of the air we are breathing, or the fish of the water running through his gills. A Christian man in a heathen land has the blessings of Christianity borne in upon his soul in keen incisiveness, by contrast; and comes to realize that one of the most heinous of sins in the sons of God's favor is to depise the riches of His goodness & forbearance & long-suffering, forgetting that the GOODNESS of God should lead us to daily repentance. When it comes time for your Thanksgiving Message I wish you could help the people of our great & beloved & favored land more thoroughly to realize this truth.

I believe our people of all parties, whose opinion is worth most & whose support is most valuable—I am amazed at how even our *Massachusetts Republican* friends praise you; e. g. in Mrs Scott's home town of Holyoke, where all the many paper mills have lived & fatted off the high tariff—are *hungry* for a President to summon them to heights of *moral* endeavor; hungry to follow a President of vision, who is thoroughly religious with religion applied to life like "Father Abraham," whom the *people answered*; like your own Washington whom they followed in war & whom they trusted in counsel, because he was to be morally counted upon.

With joy we believe in you, and joy to pray for you. Mrs Scott encloses a little tribute from our *three* daughters,[1] all of whom now speak English, Chinese & German "tolerable" fairly well, without "mixin' 'em"

Sincerely Yours   Charles Ernest Scott.

ALS (WP, DLC).
    [1] It was a photograph, which Wilson acknowledged in WW to C. E. Scott, June 26, 1913, TLS (Letterpress Books, WP, DLC).

To Mary Allen Hulbert

Dearest Friend,   The White House 1 June, 1913

I have not the least idea where you are, and do not know why, in the midst of studying pardon cases and documents of every other sort, which I have a chance to examine only on Sundays, I should be stopping to write a letter which I cannot launch into space but must keep until I know your address. I suppose it is from force of habit; and that I do not know how to get comfortably through a Sunday without a chat with you. I will at least begin the little epistle, and can finish it when I learn where you are. And how devoutly I hope that that will be soon! It is uncomfortable to have lost a friend of whom I think so often, and would like to imagine as *somewhere in particular*. My thoughts are hardly interchangeable as between Trenton, New York, Nantucket, and Boston! Will you not, please, when you get, or are about to get, a definite habitat, let some dear friends of yours know as promptly as possible?

You see it's this way: We live distracting days. You are witness of that. We are at the beck and call of others (how many, many others!) and almost never have a chance to order our days as we wish to order them, or to follow our own thoughts and devices. The life we lead is one of infinite distraction, confusion,—fragmentary, broken in upon and athwart in every conceivable way; and I, for one, need fixed points upon which to base my thought at least, if I can have none on which to base my actions from hour to hour. *My friends are those fixed points.* My intercourse with them helps me restore my identity from time to time, to get the confusion out of my nervous system and feel like the real Woodrow Wilson, a fellow of fixed connections, loyal to long established, deep-rooted friendships and associations, living through his heart and his affections, his tastes and all that runs in him independent of circumstance and occupation and monetary tasks. You may judge my uneasiness, therefore, and how my daily confusions are worse confounded if my best friends are themselves eluding my imagination for days together and preventing me from following them; playing hide and seek with my mind; avioding my company! I'll have none of it, madam! Here I sit to-night feeling very much as if I were writing to an immaterial person, with no particular location in space; and you cannot imagine what an uncomfortable feeling it gives me. You have an unfair advantage, too. You know where I am not only but, if you believe what you read in the newspapers, you seem to know every movement of my busy week. Knowing me as you do, and the main things moving about me, you can easily imagine what I am thinking and what comments I am provoked to make, to those to whom I can speak without fear of being overheard or quoted, as I would speak to you; whereas I! My mind will not move *in vacuo*! I could imagine what you were doing if I could know where you are. I could even guess what you were thinking and saying. *Please* be kind and let me be at ease again in doing what I most love to do, live in thought with the friends I love, the friends who are mine whether I am in office or out, in Washington or at some unknown end of the earth. This round I live here will be all but intolerable otherwise. Where are you? What are you doing? What are you intending? Mary Hulbert in Trenton, in New York, or in Nantucket I know; but Mary Hulbert somewhere in space,—goodness knows where! how am I to know?

At last the embargo is broken (this fourth day of June in the year of our Lord nineteen hundred and thirteen) and this letter can go to Mary Hulbert of Nantucket. Your little note to Helen has come and you are once more on the map! Hurrah for that! It gives me an entirely different feeling. But this is Wednesday, the rush of the week is upon me, and I can only in desperate haste grind off this additional line or two. I am glad you are in Nantucket. I feel as if the peace of the place, and its charm, were sure to get hold of you and act on your thoughts and on your spirits; and that makes me deelpy content. I am glad that you liked the little volumes. They are bully companions. I know them of old.

We are all well, and all join in most affectionate messages.

Your devoted friend.

WWTL (WP, DLC).

To Albert Sidney Burleson

My dear Burleson: The White House June 2, 1913

Pence, who writes the enclosed letter,[1] has absolutely no interest one way or another in the matter, except for the sake of the party, and I know you will be glad to see this letter. I am afraid we have made a very serious mistake at Sacramento.[2]

In haste　　　　Faithfully yours,　Woodrow Wilson

TLS (A. S. Burleson Papers, DLC).
    [1] T. J. Pence to WW, May 29, 1913, TLS (WP, DLC).
    [2] Burleson penciled on this letter: "Stood by Fox and put him over. Sacramento went for Wilson in 1916 election and saved the state for Wilson."

From William Jennings Bryan

My dear Mr. President:　　　　　　　　Washington June 2, 1913.

We have so little time to talk over diplomatic matters, and so many things to confer about when we get together, that, with your approval, I will follow the example you have set in writing about matters between conferences.

I think it is quite important that we find a minister to China as soon as it can be conveniently done. You were making some inquiry in regard to a Professor Ross, of Wisconsin.[1] Have you found out about the matters concerning which you were uncertain? If, for any reason, you decide that he is not available, what would you think of Governor Folk for this place? The Governor is one of the first men who occured to me for this position. He has had official prominence, he has a national reputation, he is progressive and was friendly to you before the convention. He would be a valuable avdiser to the Chinese leaders in matters relating to the fundamental principles of popular government, and he is identified with the religious life of the nation, and would, I am sure, be acceptable to the missionaries. I venture to mention him for your consideration, if your mind is not already settled upon somebody.

Professor Droppers, who holds the chair of Economics at Williams College, Williamstown, Massachusetts, is, I believe, an aspirant for a diplomatic mission. New England is not very largely represented so far in the matter of appointments. Do you know Professor Droppers personally? It seems to me, from what I have heard, that he is worth considering.

Senator Hollis, of New Hampshire, has endorsed a man who impresses me very favorably, and Hollis is so staunch a supporter of progressive doctrines that you may think it best to favor him in a matter of this kind.

With assurances of great respect, I am,

My dear Mr. President,

　　　　　　　　　Very sincerely yours,　W. J. Bryan

TLS (WP, DLC).
    [1] Edward Alsworth Ross, Professor of Sociology at the University of Wisconsin.

An Aide-Mémoire from the Japanese Government[1]

[c. June 3, 1913]

The relations of geographical propinquity existing between Japan and the United States, coupled with the circumstance that both countries are steadily advancing along the same lines of peace and progress, make it entirely natural that the two peoples should come into broader and closer contact with each other, commercially, industrially and socially. Such contact may give rise to occasional worry and misunderstanding, but the relations of neighborhood are, nevertheless, inevitable and should remain unchanged. Accordingly, in the actual and unalterable situation, it is specially important that the two nations maintain between themselves genuine friendship and good accord, which will no doubt contribute to their common benefit and material well-being. That desirable end, it should be added, will be assured so long as each Power extends to the other, fair and equitable treatment in the field of legitimate activities. Whereas, if such treatment is withheld, difficulties are sure to arise, with the result that both countries will equally suffer economically and in all the various avenues of peaceful intercourse.

In these circumstances, the two neighboring countries owe it to themselves, to their traditions and aspirations, to find means by which all causes of irritation and discord shall be peacefully and permanently removed. For this purpose, it is considered essential that both peoples should meet and mingle in a spirit of mutual esteem, courtesy and toleration, and, in their various dealings with each other, should always be governed by broad rules and precepts of justice and fair play, avoiding all discriminatory treatment which may tend to hurt or wound the sense of national dignity of a self-respecting people. The Japanese people, although differing in race from the inhabitants of America and Europe, are, nevertheless, possessed of the same susceptibilities, inspired by the same aims and aspirations, and guided by the same principles, and they contemplate, with full consciousness, their high duty among the nations to contribute their best efforts in the great work of advancing the world's civilization and betterment. They welcome, with warm appreciation, the expression of high value which the United States attaches to the maintenance of the relations of good understanding between the two nations, because, in full realization of all that is meant by that expression, the Japanese Government confidently look to America—the land of noble aims and lofty ideals—for co-operation and encouragement in their endeavors in the interest of general peace and harmony.

The Japanese Government fully appreciate the action taken by the Administration in the difficult question now under discussion between the two Governments, and they earnestly hope that the President will be pleased to take the foregoing observation into favorable consideration.

T MS (WP, DLC).
[1] Handed to Wilson by Ambassador Chinda at their meeting at the White House on June 5, 1913.

To Matthias Cowell Ely

My dear Mr. Ely: [The White House] June 4, 1913

I am afraid I will seem to you very unserviceable, but really my judgment is frankly against what you advise. I see little points of irritation already which convince me that my intervention in the matter of the pending elections in Jersey City might be much more harmful than beneficial. The lines are clearly drawn and surely no voter can mistake the issue.[1]

Cordially and faithfully yours,   Woodrow Wilson

TLS (Letterpress Books, WP, DLC).
[1] In the primary election held on May 13, 1913, ten men were selected from a field of ninety-one to run for the five-man city commission. Five of the ten were Democratic adherents of Mayor H. Otto Wittpenn. Frank Hague and two of his supporters formed a second Democratic, anti-Wittpenn bloc. The two remaining candidates were former Mayor Mark Fagan, a progressive Republican, and a Republican businessman. The Hague group and the two Republicans formed a liaison of convenience. Hague cleverly portrayed himself and his allies as the progressive advocates of commission government against the "machine" of "Boss" Wittpenn. In the election on June 10, 1913, Mark Fagan had a commanding lead in votes, but Hague came in fourth, and his two Democratic cronies placed second and third, thus giving Hague control of the city commission and launching his long career as boss of Jersey City. See Richard J. Connors, *A Cycle of Power: The Career of Jersey City Mayor Frank Hague* (Metuchen, N. J., 1971), pp. 28-33.

From William Jennings Bryan

My dear Mr. President: Washington June 4, 1913.

. . . I shall leave at the White House as I go home the rejoinder which Ambassador Chinda left with me[1] this afternoon. He asks that an hour be fixed as early tomorrow as convenient when he can call in person and speak to you in regard to this rejoinder. I conclude, from what he has said, that in Japan attention has been called to the fact that he had been calling at the State Department entirely, whereas he has a right, as an Ambassador, to called upon the President directly, and I think this call is made in order to answer criticism there, or at any rate, to prevent criticism. If you will telephone me tonight, I will notify the Ambassador. . . .

I enclose also a letter to the New York bankers.[2] It was decided at the Cabinet meeting that I should prepare a letter and submit it for your approval. I have followed as nearly as I could the line you indicated. I will ask you to mail the letter so it will reach New York tomorrow morning. If you desire to make any changes, please sign my name to the amended letter and mail it. They called up by telephone today and I told them I would mail the letter tonight, indicating to them that they could quote from your statement in the Chinese Loan case in case they needed to send any dispatches before receiving the letter. . . .

We did not have time to discuss fully last night the San Domingo situation. I believe that it is important that we act immediately and that a Minister should be appointed, as well as a Receiver. The reports which we have received here point so strongly to fraud and conspiracy there that delay will be dangerous. I believe it would be well to name Mr. Vick at once as Receiver, and I would like to talk with you in regard to the man to be sent as Minister.

I am sending these things to you, so that I will not have to trespass upon your time by a call.

With assurances of my respect, etc., I am,

My dear Mr. President,

Very sincerely yours,   W. J. Bryan

TLS (WP, DLC).

[1] Japanese Ambassador to the Secretary of State, June 4, 1913, *FR 1913*, pp. 632-35.

[2] W. J. Bryan to H. B. Hollins & Co., June 4, 1913, TCL (SDR, RG 59, 893.51/1431, DNA). This letter referred the bankers to Wilson's statement on the Chinese loan (printed at March 18, 1913) and reiterated that statement's encouragement of every "legitimate" extension of trade and commerce with China, including the financing of governmental loans. However, the letter concluded, it was not the policy of the administration to single out individual firms or groups of American investors for special consideration, nor would it endorse the terms of any agreement entered upon.

Remarks at a Press Conference

June 5, 1913

Is there any intelligence with regard to the Japanese reply?

No, nothing in particular. I have just read it this morning. The Japanese Ambassador is to call on me at four o'clock and is to make his oral additions or explanations. All I can say is that the note opens a way for very interesting and further negotiations.

Does it open a way for an immediate solution, or will it take some time?

> Well, I can't judge about that. . . . How long it will take to discuss it, I can't guess.

Mr. President, then are we warranted in inferring that it does not indicate that a probable meeting or solution are inconsistent?

> Not inconsistent.

Mr. President, I hear that you are going to talk with some lawyers in New York City, also in Washington, to take it up—the question of the courts as well as the law questions. Are you asking also some lawyers who are in New York City who are up on international law who will confer with you? Of course, I don't know who they are going to be. Is that apt to be a solution, Mr. President—in the courts?

> Well of course, sooner or later, the meaning of the law would have to be determined by the courts.

I mean, will Japan take it to the courts, or we?

> Well, we wouldn't. There is no process that occurs to us now.

I thought you might instruct the Attorney General to intervene?

> No, no instructions have been given.

Mr. President, has there been a suggestion about arbitration?

> No.

Mr. President, has there been any indication on the part of Japan whether she was willing, or willing to ask on her own, that the United States should take that matter into our courts?

> No, no indication at all, sir.

Mr. President, what is the point at issue?

> Why, I thought everybody knew that.

I do not, sir.

> Why, the point at issue is the exclusion from ownership of agricultural land, at any rate in California, of those who are supposed not to be eligible to citizenship of the United States.

And what is the attitude of Japan on that subject?

> Oh, well, I can't go into the roots of that. . . .

Mr. President, yesterday there was a great slump in the stock market, and indications are that perhaps that sort of thing might continue. One of the reasons given was the reports that the administration was going to endeavor to reopen the cases against the Standard Oil and the tobacco trusts. Now it occurred to me that perhaps in view of that suspicion you would insist that Congress remain here, and then renew the currency law after the tariff bill was out of the way.

Well, I will certainly urge that, of course.
I knew you were going to urge that, but I was wondering whether
you felt quite sure you could get them to put it in effect?

> I see no reason to tell you that I can, but that is the sort of
> thing one can't be sure about because the debates are very
> long, because the questions get very repetitive. No summer
> session—

Well, I think there is plenty of time for the House to pass a currency bill before the Senate gets through with the other bill, but
it would be a question of remaining here until up to the beginning of the regular session, and I would wonder whether you
would consider that, or consult with the leaders regarding it?

> No, I haven't been up to that point. I have a very strong hope
> it won't last that long, that we will get word before—sooner
> or later.

You are going to remain here?

> Yes, sir.

Or you would until the currency bill is out of the way?

> Yes, sir. If I remain here for four years.

Does that mean, Mr. President, that you hope to get through
with the tariff bill in a comparatively short time in the Senate?

> Well, I think the situation in the Senate is entirely satis-
> factory. It is a question of how many speeches are made
> now.

Mr. President, it is suggested that you are persuaded that this
stock market flurry is caused by sinister influences and that you
are going to suggest an investigation of Wall Street methods in
that regard.

> No, sir, that is entirely without foundation. I have all my life
> been so innocent that I have never known what flurries were
> founded on. That is something too dark to the lay mind. . . .

Can you volunteer any remarks on the lobby investigation?

> No, sir. I think that speaks for itself.

Has there been any suggestion, Mr. President, that this lobby
inquiry might be made retroactive and cover the stages of the
bill in the House as well as the Senate?

> No, sir, I haven't heard any.

Mr. President, did you furnish a list of names to the committee?

> I did.

Are you willing to appear before the committee?

> They haven't asked me to, and I don't always go where I am
> not invited.

If you were requested to go, Mr. President?

> I don't know. I never cross a bridge until I get to it.

Mr. President, I wanted to inquire, sir, if you have received many letters from any Republicans in favor of just as early an enactment of the tariff law as possible, so as to put an end to the uncertainty which it creates?

Well, perhaps Tumulty could answer that question better than I can. Not very many letters of that sort have been laid before me, though some very strong letters on that legislation have been laid before me.

The *Herald* this morning had dispatches from various parts of the country, showing a very keen desire for an early enactment of the bill.

I think, of course, we can all agree that it is very desirable that it should be enacted as early as possible.

Have you any idea—

No, I haven't, but I do feel reasonably assured that the leaders of the Senate will push it as fast as they can, and I think the Finance Committee will fix the time ready to report.

That desirability seems to be very strongly in their minds.

I think it is, very.

JRT transcript (WC, NjP) of CLSsh (C. L. Swem Coll., NjP).

To Henry van Dyke

The White House June 5 1913

Would you consider favorably appointment to the Netherlands

Woodrow Wilson

T telegram (H. van Dyke Papers, NjP).

Viscount Sutemi Chinda to Baron Nobuaki Makino

2791, 2792　暗　華府発 本省着　大正2年6月6日

牧野外務大臣

珍　田　大　使

第 195 号

6月5日大統領ニ謁見貴電第 151 号覚書ヲ手交シタル上本使ハ篤ト説明ヲ加ヘ就中我ニ於テ本件ヲ重大視スル所以ニ付テハ特ニ重ヲ措キテ十分説明ヲ為シ本件ハ単リ在加州少

数日本人ノ利権問題タルニ止マラス実ニ国家ノ威厳ニ関ス
ル問題トシテ真面目ナル国論ヲ喚起セルモノナルコトヲ説
キ或ル新聞所報ノ如ク之ヲ以テ日本国ニ於ケル国内政争上
反対派ノ煽動的議論ト為スハ全然無稽ニシテ実際ハ挙国一
致深刻ナル憂慮ニ駆ラレツ、アル次第ナルコトヲ詳細縷述
シタルニ大統領ニ於テモ日本国トノ国交ハ特ニ其ノ重要視
スル所ナル旨言明セラレタル上抑モ本件ハ在加州日本人ノ
産業上優勢ナル結果トシテ加州人民自衛上已ムヲ得サルニ
出テタル次第ニシテ決シテ人種的見地ヨリ侮蔑ヲ加フル主
旨ニ非ラス即チ純然タル経済問題ニ外ナラスト雖日本国ニ
於テ本件ヲ斯ノ如ク重大視セラル、ハ全ク感情問題ニ属シ
単ニ一片ノ理論ヲ以テ之ヲ律スヘカラス従テ米国政府ニ於
テモ右ニ対シテハ尊敬ヲ以テ考量ヲ加フル所ナリト語ラレ
尚本件ヲ単ニ経済問題ナリトスル点ニ付テハ昨日国務長官
ノ所論ト略ホ同様ノ趣旨ヲ縷述セラレタルガ本使ニ於テ
我弁駁書ノ趣旨ヲ敷衍説明シタルニ対シテハ本使所論ノ理
由アルヘキハ争ハサルモ一面加州ニ於テ日本人ヲ恐怖スル
風潮ノ存在スル事実ハ枉クヘカラサル所ニシテ政事家トシ
テハ之ヲ無視スルコト能ハスト弁解セラレ尤右風潮ハ単ニ
「カリフォルニア」一州ニ限ラレ米国全体ニ非ラサルコト
ハ十分了解アリタシト云ハレタリ（続ク）

第195号ノ2

又大統領ハ我カ弁駁書ニ就テハ折角今朝来研究中ナルカ米
国政府ニ於テハ土地法ハ条約違反ノ廉ナシトノ意見ヲ有シ
居ルトコロ日本国政府ニ於テハ飽ク迄条約違反ヲ主張セラ
ルルニ付篤ト其点ヲ研究シツ、アル次第ナリ右研究ノ結果

果シテ違反ノ廉ヲ認ムルニ至ラハ米国政府ハ其責任上当然
之レカ除去ノ道ヲ講セサルヘカラス然ルニ其方法トシテハ
当国政治機関組織上之ヲ法廷ニ訴フルノ外ナキヲ以テ其際
ニハ米国政府主トナリテ訴訟ノ手段ヲ執ルヘシ尤モ米国政
府カ訴訟ノ手段ヲ執ルコトナシトスルモ相当理由アルニ於
テハ日本人ノ為メ実際ノ損害ニ対シテハ賠償ノ方法ヲ講ス
ルヲ辞セサルヘシトノ趣ヲ開陳セラレ（脱？）論トシテハ
目下ノ先決問題ハ土地法ハ果シテ条約ニ違反スルモノナリ
ヤ否ヤ研究ヲ遂クルニアリ迫テ其結果ヲ俟チ米国政府ノ執
ルヘキ手段ヲ決定スル筈ナル旨ヲ申述ヘラレタリ交談ノ要
点ハ以上ノ通ニシテ目下差迫リタル問題ハ土地法ノ条約違
反ナリヤ否ヤノ点ニアルヲ以テ我ニ於テ飽ク迄主張スル論
拠ニ関シ本使ヨリ説明ヲ試ミントセルニ対シ大統領ハ既ニ
我カ主張ハ二回ノ公文ニ依リ篤ト承知シ居ルトコロニシテ
目下専門家ヲシテ研究セシメツヽアルニ付此際特ニ本使ト
ノ間ニ法律上ノ議論ヲ交ユル要ナカルヘシトテ之ヲ避ケン
コトヲ努メラレ話題ハ主トシテ本件ヲ経済問題トナスノ点
ニ差向ケラレタルニ付本使ニ於テモ自然此点ニ重キヲ措キ
種々説明ヲ加ヘタル次第ナルカ本日大統領ノ所言ハ要スル
ニ国務長官昨日ノ談話ト大同小異ナルトコロ条約違反ノ廉
ヲ認ムルトキハ米国政府自ラ出訴スヘキ旨言明セラルタル
ハ重要ナル相違ノ点ナリ

Hw telegram (MT 3.8.2.274-2, pp. 1227-1234, JFO-Ar).

Washington, received
Confidential, No. 195.　　　　　　　　　　　　June 6, 1913

I met the President on June 5 and handed him the memorandum of your telegram No. 151, about which I gave a full
explanation. Above all I explained with great emphasis the reason why we attach so much importance to this problem. I gave
some account of the fact that the problem not only concerned
the particular interests of the few Japanese in the State of California but also concerned the dignity of our nation, and that this
had seriously aroused public opinion. Then I told him in detail
that there was no ground for such opinions, as had appeared in
the reports of a certain newspaper, which had ascribed the cause
of the development of this problem to the inflammatory arguments made by the opposition faction in Japanese internal politics, and that the fact was that a considerable anxiety has been
manifested by a consensus of our nation regarding this problem.
The President asserted that he also placed great importance upon
relations with Japan. But he added that the cause of the problem
was the industrial ascendancy of the Japanese in the State of
California against which the people of the state were obliged to
defend themselves. The Californians, he went on, never meant
to humiliate the Japanese from a racial standpoint. Then he
added that the problem was, therefore, a purely economic one,
but that because it had already changed into a matter of the
national feeling and should not be judged merely theoretically,
it should be treated with proper consideration by the United
States Government. As to the point that this problem was purely
economic, his argument was almost the same as the Secretary
of State's. In opposition to this I expatiated on the purport of
our written refutation. He agreed that my exposition was not
without ground, and he also argued that, as a political leader,
he could not afford to ignore the undeniable fact that a tendency
to fear the Japanese existed among the people of the State of
California. But he asked me to understand that this tendency
prevailed only within the State of California and not in the whole
country.

As to our written refutation, the President said that they had
been studying it with much effort since this morning. The investigation, he explained, was centered on the point whether the

escheat law was legal according to the treaty, as the United
States Government claimed, or illegal, as the Japanese government claimed. If the study resulted in the conclusion that the
law violated the treaty, he went on, the United States Government would of course assume responsibility for devising a means
of getting rid of the violation. As for the means, however, there
was nothing other than instituting a lawsuit because of the peculiar nature of the political organization of this country. In
that case, he added, the United States Government should become a plaintiff. Although it was fairly reasoned that the United
States Government might not take legal measures, it was also
remarked that the government was willing to devise some means
to compensate for the actual damages of the Japanese. He then
stated that the most urgent business was to decide whether the
escheat law violated the treaty or not, and that he would decide
what means the government should take after the conclusion of
its investigation. The meeting is summed up as above. Since the
most urgent problem was whether the escheat law violated the
treaty or not, I tried again to explain the grounds of our argument. But saying that he had known a good deal about our point
about this juridical matter, and that the experts were now studying it, the President tried to avoid a legal discussion and changed
the topic to whether this problem was an economic one or not.
Therefore I naturally also gave my attention to this issue and
added various explanations. Although the argument made by the
President today was, in sum, substantially the same as that made
by the Secretary of State yesterday, but when the United States
Government sees any possibility of a violation of the treaty, it
would itself institute legal proceedings. This was declared by
the President, and this is the important different point.

To Francis Griffith Newlands

My dear Senator: The White House June 6, 1913
     Allow me to thank you for your full letter of June fourth,[1]
explaining your position about the tariff. I sincerely hope that
before the debates are over you will find yourself convinced, as
I am entirely convinced, that the present proposals with regard
to wool and sugar are in no way in contravention either of the
action of the party in the past or of its declared purposes from
time to time in national campaigns. The opinion of the country
and of the party in favor of free wool and free sugar has steadily
and manifestly grown, until now I think it is of commanding
and determining volume. The votes of the representatives of the

party in Congress in recent years have fully prepared the country for the course now about to be pursued. It is for this reason that I have felt that in the advice I have given to those members of Congress who have consulted me in these matters I have in no way departed from the position I took before my nomination and before my election.

Cordially and sincerely yours,   Woodrow Wilson

TLS (F. G. Newlands Papers, CtY).

1 F. G. Newlands to WW, June 4, 1913, TLS (WP, DLC), arguing that it was wise national as well as party policy to reduce tariff rates gradually; that Wilson himself had taken this position during the last campaign; and that it was inequitable to put wool on the free list immediately and sugar within three years.

From Walter Hines Page

My dear Mr. President: London. June 8, 1913

Perhaps it will please you to know that the King, who gave me a prompt and cordial and rather long audience, asked in an earnest manner about your health; and, when I thanked him and gave a good report, he said that he hoped you were a robust man, seeing the heavy duties the Presidency puts on you. "The President, sir," I responded, "is of Scotch descent: does Your Majesty know of any more enduring stock?" Thus I drew a royal smile. Among other pleasant remarks that he made was that he thought it unfair to the American Ambassador that his great government did not give him a house. I told him that the personal inconvenience of the Ambassador was of less consequence than the failure properly to express, by this little omission, the high esteem in which the President and the people of the United States held his Government and the English people; and I expressed the hope that for this reason this omission might soon be made good. The King was very cordial, and since then on another occasion he has been very courteous to me.

Sir Edward Grey, the Secretary of Foreign Affairs, has been especially kind—at my formal audience with him, subsequently at a dinner to which he invited the diplomatic corps on the King's birth-day, and especially two evenings ago when he sat next me and proposed my health at the Pilgrims' dinner to me. His speech then was meant as an important utterance and it has been so received here. It may be worth your while, if I may suggest it, to have your Secretary summarize that for you. There can be no doubt of the most earnest appreciation throughout official life here of our good will.

Sir Edward is a frank and forcible man; and I now feel that

I know him well enough to talk frankly with him. He has given me a hint that he will be glad to talk about the Panama tolls matter. Having told him I have no official communication on the subject, I shall on his next regular day bring it up for informal conversation. He is greatly interested in Mr. Bryan's plan for making war harder to begin, as you will see from his speech.

My speech, in response to Sir Edward Grey's, has, I am glad to report, been cordially received by the press, as it was by the men of high station, who were kind enough to hear it.

You will pardon my troubling you with this personal note, in addition to my formal report to the Secretary of State; and I send it with the hope that you will not take the trouble to answer it.

And with the hope that you are, in fact, as well as the King and I wish you to be, I am most heartily and sincerely

Yours,   Walter H. Page

ALS (WP, DLC).

Remarks at a Press Conference

June 9, 1913

Mr. President, is the lobby investigation having the beneficial effect you expected it to have?

> That is a very interesting question. I think it is having a very beneficial effect, sir.

Would you care to say, incidentally, what the results will be?

> Oh, no. I can't predict what the results will be.

What do you think it has done so far?

> Well, I really think that these are questions which you gentlemen can answer better than I can. You see, I wouldn't have a chance to see more than a small percentage of the things that are published about that, and that is one of the ways one could tell the effects of the thing.

I thought perhaps you had noticed some effects with regard to the senators themselves, in your talks with them?

> No, sir. My hope was to relieve those who were trying to do business in Washington of a great burden. I think it is going to do that presently—in time.

Have you received any invitation yet, Mr. President, to go before the committee?

> No.

Mr. President, referring again to the currency question, have you made up your own mind, in order to be assured under the new bill, whether to use United States Treasury notes or national bank notes?

I don't know that mine is the mind to make up. That is a matter about which there has been a great deal of conference and about which there is a great deal of honest difference of opinion—as to whether the notes should be absolutely secured or not, just as you want moral character.

Have you arranged a conference with any of the members of the House Banking Committee?

Only the chairman, sir.

JRT transcript (WP, DLC) of CLSsh (C. L. Swem Coll., NjP).

To Mary Allen Hulbert

Dearest Friend,   The White House 9 June, 1913

I have still only your little line to Helen to go on, written from the Manhattan in New York and saying that you were to leave the next day for Nantucket, but that at least fixes your probable whereabouts and enables me to *imagine* what you are doing, and I shall have to be content with that until I am vouchsafed something better. It is, perhaps, a wholesome lesson for the President of the United States, lest he should begin to fancy his power very great indeed, to find that he fails of jurisdiction over his nearest friends and cannot get from them even by begging what others are urging him to accept: their confidence and their constant counsel by letter! I write in all humility, therefore, to hope that you are well and that you occasionally think kindly of your friends at Washington. Poor creatures, madam, but your own to command! It is not as cool and refreshing down here as it is at Nantucket. We have no sight of the sea from our windows. There is no fine curve of a free shore line to make us conscious of the edges of the world and of a hot continent standing away from us at far arm's length. The people about us are not naive rustic neighbours whose characters and conduct remind us of the great body of Americans whose affections and opinions make up the life of a great nation, but a sophisticated miscellany of officials and of men and women who know what they want to get from the government and from the society about it and spend night and day in search of it. We need the tonic that blows about you every hour. Our ears wait from morning till night for the voices that remind us of friends who have nothing to seek, whose affections sustain us, whose thought does not a little to guide us, that keeps us fresh with the touch of the outside world. There is no process of law by which we can obtain what we wish. There is no use trying to make use of any part of the government to get it. We must wait until some consciousness of our need comes to you and you are moved to come to our assistance with what we cannot get anywhere else. I have very often expounded this need and hunger to you; but probably you have not credited it. You have thought that what I said was just a generous way of expressing our affection and our desire to be in touch with you, while all the time I was speaking with mere literal truth. So I appeal to your generosity. Make believe that you believe me. Try the experiment of giving us what we so constantly clamour for. Play the game and judge by the consequences. Our friends are of more value to us now than they ever were before in all our lives. You have seen with what distraction our days are spent. Imagine what it would mean to you, in the midst of some such day, to be handed a letter, a long, chatty letter, full of free and intimate talk, from some one who could touch your mind with a familiar and subtle knowledge of all its tastes and ways of thinking, and to drop down in a corner by yourself and devour it. What a rest and relief it would be! How it would swing your mind back into old, delightful channels! You would turn back to your occupations with a sense of having been cheered and made normal again, and with a warm glow at your heart which nobody had known how to impart to it the day through, because everybody about you was caught in the same swirl. This is my plea. I continue to shoot these bolts of mine into the blue. I should like to know where they lodge!

We are all well. The dear folks about me will, I hope, for my sake and in response to my earnest pleading, start for New Hampshire before the end of the month. I shall, in all likelihood, not get away, except for a day or two at a time, before the autumn. This session of Congress may continue until October. But that is all right. I could not be happy elsewhere so long as there is great business going on here. This house is airy; I will curtail my office hours as the town clears of the general crowd and play more and more golf and such like proper and sedate games; long auto. drives will put ozone into my system; and I shall thrive on honest toil. Hot weather has no terrors for me. I shall envy you at Nantucket only because I should love to have such company as you are,—if not to yourself, to everyone else who has had a real taste of your quality. I shall get as much sunburn as you, and perhaps your letters, when you begin to write them, may bring me a sense of the sea! All join me in affectionate messages.

Your devoted friend,   Woodrow Wilson

You did not send me Allen's address again. I misplaced the card.

WWTLS (WP, DLC).

To Mark Sullivan

My dear Mr. Sullivan: [The White House] June 10, 1913

Will you not let me give myself the pleasure of expressing my deep appreciation of the "Comment on Congress" which appears every week in Collier's? I do not know of any page that gives me greater satisfaction or more encouragement to believe that the best influences in the country are at work to sustain right and honorable things in politics.

Cordially and faithfully yours,   Woodrow Wilson

TLS (Letterpress Books, WP, DLC).

To Charles Spalding Thomas

My dear Senator: The White House June 10, 1913

Every now and again something in what I read in the Press turns up to remind me of that splendid letter[1] you wrote in answer to those who were attempting to induce you and Senator Shafroth to leave the manifest path of loyalty and public duty. The letter was in itself tremendous and its effect has been that of a tonic.

Cordially and faithfully yours,   Woodrow Wilson

TLS (C. S. Thomas Papers, CoHi).
[1] The Editors have been unable to find a full text of Thomas's letter or to ascertain its date of composition. However, it was quoted at length in Mark Sullivan, "The Assault on the Senate," *Collier's*, LI (June 7, 1913), 9. As Sullivan's title suggests, the extracts from Thomas's letter stressed the efforts of lobbyists and special interest groups to secure changes in the Underwood tariff schedules and the danger that these efforts would wreck the entire bill and hence the future of the Democratic party.

To Maurice Francis Egan

[The White House] June 10, 1913

Would like to know if a transfer to the Court at Vienna would be agreeable to you.   Woodrow Wilson.

T telegram (Letterpress Books, WP, DLC).

From Joseph Kossuth Dixon[1]

Muskogee, Okla., June 10, 1913.

Your address to all the tribes of North American Indians in the United States was delivered to-day to the Cherokees one hundred years after the address of President Jefferson to this

historic tribe. The address was received with undoubted enthusiasm followed by the hoisting of the American flag to the native
song of Cherokee singers, followed again by the National air The
Star Spangled Banner, a historic and significant event because
of the relinquishment tomorrow of their capitol to the State of
Oklahoma and the cession of their last land title as a tribe[.]
Cherokee orders [leaders] pledged their loyalty to the flag and
rely with confidence upon your gracious words. A flag was left
flying under June skies and the fair winds of the west and thus
was notably inaugurated the Rodman Wannamaker expedition
of citizenship to the North American Indians.[2]

Joseph K. Dixon.

T telegram (WP, DLC).
    [1] Long-time associate of Lewis Rodman Wanamaker and leader of the
three expeditions to visit North American Indian tribes financed by Wanamaker
between 1908 and 1913.
    [2] Like its two predecessors, this expedition was partly intended to record
in photographs, moving picture film, and written records the way of life of
what both Wanamaker and Dixon considered to be a dying race. However, the
third expedition had as its main purpose the repetition before all of the
surviving Indian tribes of the United States of the elaborately symbolic and
romantic ceremony of raising an American flag and receiving the pledges of
allegiance of the Indians present, which Dixon briefly describes in the telegram
printed above. Dixon and his assistants visited 189 tribes in the course of a
journey covering over 27,000 miles and lasting from June to December 1913. At
each stop, the ceremony included the playing of the phonograph recording of
Wilson's message to American Indians, printed at May 24, 1913. See Joseph
Kossuth Dixon, *The Vanishing Race: The Last Great Indian Council. . . .*
3rd and rev. edn. (Philadelphia 1925), pp. xvii-xxxv; and Charles R. Reynolds,
Jr. (compiler), *American Indian Portraits from the Wanamaker Expedition of
1913* (Brattleboro, Vt., 1971), pp. 1-4.

To John Lind

[The White House] June 11, 1913

Am very earnestly desirous that you should represent the Government at the Court of Sweden. I should regard it as a great
public service if you would do so, and beg that you will be generous enough to indicate your willingness. This is a very deliberate and thoughtful choice on my part and I earnestly urge it
upon you.   Woodrow Wilson.

T telegram (Letterpress Books, WP, DLC); the telegram in the J. Lind Papers,
MnHi, is slightly garbled.

From James Alexander Reed

My dear Mr. President: Washington, D. C. June 11, 1913.

    I have been told that one Louis F. Post, of Chicago, Illinois,
is an applicant for a position in the Department of Labor, as

Assistant Secretary. I am also informed that this gentleman is not a Democrat, but is a single taxer.

I beg to suggest the advisabiilty of having his political record examined.

With great respect, I am,

Very respectfully,   Jas A Reed

TLS (WP, DLC).

From Henry van Dyke

Dear President Wilson,   Princeton, N. J. June 11. 1913.

In regard to your very gratifying proposition, my wife says that she would be honored and pleased if you should send us to the Hague to represent America. So if you think I can serve you there I am yours to command.

Faithfully   Henry van Dyke

ALS (WP, DLC).

Remarks at a Press Conference

June 12, 1913

Mr. President, a group of Louisiana men, on the stand before the lobby committee yesterday, testified that they had assurances that sugar would not go on the free list. They left the inference that the assurance is directly traceable to the President.

You notice they didn't say so at all.

No, but they left the inference very definitely, I thought. Does that—

I'll tell you a story. There was an old politician in New York who gave this advice to his son, and I hope you will ascribe the language to him and not to me. He said, "John, don't bother your head about liars. It will give you many ulcers. When there are many, deny anything. You make up your own mind it is so." That is just a story. There is one special application to it.

But you are not denying this inference?

I am not denying the *inference* by my failure to deny.

Mr. President, have you considered the possibility of establishing the civil government of the Panama Canal Zone before the canal is completed?

No, not for the moment, sir.

Is there anything new with reference to currency, Mr. President?

No, there isn't, not yet.

Have you discussed with the members of the committee the question of open hearings?

    No, they hadn't asked anything of me.

You have no idea, Mr. President, when your message will be ready for Congress?

    No, I haven't, simply because we are still working on the draft of the bill.

Have you any news from the Senate, Mr. President, with regard to the probability or possibility of passing a currency bill at this session through the Senate?

    No, I know only this—that a fair number of senators have volunteered the opinion, and the committee wrote to us, the general hope that it should be passed by this Senate.

But did they say—they did not say as to whether or not it was probable that it could be passed?

    No, but they didn't express any doubt on the subject.

Mr. President, the Banking and Currency Committee of the Senate yesterday—I mean, it was stated then by several senators—that a very heavy majority of that committee didn't think it wise to attempt currency legislation at this time.

    That hasn't reached me. I don't know it yet. Not because I doubt your statement. I am not officially informed.

It is not my statement, sir. It is a statement of the senators. Could you indicate what general lines this currency bill is going to take?

    It won't follow any general line. It will follow a genuine line.

Who is going to issue the money—the government?

    I have already said I didn't care to indicate it in general terms.

Is there anything on the recognition of Mexico?

    No, sir. . . .

Are you willing, Mr. President, to say anything about Mr. McReynolds' tobacco trust tax plan?[1]

    He didn't have any plan that I know of.

I have been misinformed.

    Yes, you certainly have.

Well, we understand from that that there is no such plan?

    There is none that I know anything about.

He hasn't made the suggestion that a graduated excise tax be imposed on tobacco products?

    No, that suggestion was made and discussed for about, I suppose, three minutes, but there has been no plan of any kind.

Somebody has been mighty misleading in the last two weeks.

Yes, I have noticed that, but we are not responsible for that. Mr. President, wasn't there some sort of agreement, understanding, that Mr. McReynolds should discuss this matter with Senator Simmons?

There was an understanding that he could discuss it with whom he pleased, yes, but he didn't propose it as a plan; and it was not thrown out except as a suggestion, to be discussed for anybody that was interested in it.

You are not willing to discuss it, then, as a suggestion?

No. As I say, I have devoted about three minutes to the suggestion since it was made.

Are you going to Cornish on the twenty-ninth?

It is my present hope that I may accompany my family there and come right back.

Does that include the Fourth if you want to?

I don't know. It would depend entirely.

Mr. President, is there anything you can say at this time as to the proposed negotiations with Japan?

Well, it's making progress in the only sense in which it could, that is to say, the State Department has in hand the formulations of the matter that we want to lay before the Japanese government. I don't know whether there has been any further development in the past few days. No, none at all that would create a more hopeful situation. The situation has been hopeful all along. I mean there hasn't been anything to cause anxiety about it.

Mr. President, will you say anything about that sundry civil bill in the reports that have been published?

No, sir. I haven't had anything to do with it one way or the other. I haven't even been consulted about it.

JRT transcript (WC, NjP) of CLSsh (C. L. Swem Coll., NjP).
1 About this matter, see Link, *The New Freedom*, pp. 417-18.

To Franklin Knight Lane

My dear Mr. Secretary: [The White House] June 12, 1913

Our little conversation just before we parted last night was, in effect, an answer to your note of the other day, but I want to acknowledge it in this way and to say how much I appreciated your thoughtfulness in writing it. I realize very keenly how unfortunate it is that so many circumstances should be combined to render it an anxious and ticklish business to change the tariff and also the basis of the currency, but I feel that if we allow ourselves to be forced to a modification of plan by the alarms and embarrassments of the moment, we shall never find the time more suited to what we wish to do, because whenever action is contemplated, the same obstructions will arise. A steady purpose and a just execution of it seems to me the only course open to us.

Always, with warmest regard,
                    Faithfully yours,   Woodrow Wilson

TLS (Letterpress Books, WP, DLC).

From William Jennings Bryan

My dear Mr. President: Washington June 12, 1913.

I spoke to you yesterday about an objection made to the British treaty by Senator Vardaman. I arranged for a ride with him this morning in order to get his point of view and I find, according to his statement, *that there is a very strong feeling in the Senate against the submission of the toll question to arbitration and that this is the foundation of the objection to the treaty.*[1] The argument made is that Great Britain having asked for arbitration under the provisions of the former treaty, the Senators who are opposed to arbitrate the toll question are afraid that ratification of this treaty, which is a renewal of the former one, might be construed as the endorsement of the position taken by Great Britain. I suggested to Senator Vardaman that the objection could be removed by a *resolution declaring that the ratification of the treaty should not be construed as a decision upon this point.* He seemed to think that that might be sufficient, although some of the Senators he was afraid might favor a resolution specifically declaring against Great Britain's contention. I tried to show him that it was unwise to anticipate this question or to attempt to decide it before it was brought before the Senate.

Talking with the French Ambassador this morning, I asked him what he thought of the resolution which I suggested to Senator Vardaman and he approved of it very heartily.

Such a resolution would not embarrass us at all, and it occurs to me that this may be an easy way out of the difficulty and enable us to secure prompt action on all the treaties. I am hastily submitting it for your consideration, because I told Vardaman that while it seemed to me a proper thing to do, I would not attempt to speak for you, and asked him not to say anything about it until I had time to present the matter to you.

Awaiting an expression of your views, I am, my dear Mr. President,   Very truly yours,   W. J. Bryan

P.S. Have been talking with Chamberlain & think I have made some progress.

TLS (WP, DLC).
 1 Italicization by Wilson.

From Henry Morgenthau

My dear Mr. President.   New York June 12. 1913

In compliance with your request I saw Mr Schiff[1] and explained to him what induced you to offer me the Turkish Mission and that you were not aware that our People were so strongly opposed to having any position made a distinctly Jewish one or having the impression continued that Turkey was the only country where a Jew would be received as our Countrys representative

Mr Schiff was pleased to hear your views and I found that he shared my desire that no Jew be appointed as Turkish Ambassador

He informed me that Secretary McAdoo had asked him over the telephone, last Sunday, to suggest a Jew for the N. Y. Sub-Treasurership and that he had written McAdoo that he knew of none. Senator O'Gorman asked me the same question last Friday & I declined to suggest any one

I wonder if they understand that this is diametrically opposed to your oft expressed policy of selecting men solely on their merits and not on account of their religion.

Why should the Jews be treated differently than any one else? Would prominent Methodists or Baptists be told here is a "Position" find one of your faith to fill it?

I write you frankly because I know you regret mistakes of this kind as much as any of us.

With sincere regards
                    Yours faithfully   Henry Morgenthau

ALS (WP, DLC).
 1 Jacob Henry Schiff, banker and philanthropist of New York, member of Kuhn, Loeb & Co., merchant bankers.

From John Lind

                    Minneapolis, Minn., June 12, 1913.

Profoundly grateful and appreciating to the fullest extent the honor and confidence suggested by your message, I do not see my way clear to accept. Personal and family considerations prevent. Reflecting convinces me that it would be questionable policy for one of foreign birth to accept a resident appointment to the country of his nativity. Complications might arise in which the most prudent conduct would not avoid criticism and embarrassment. Furthermore, I prefer to be at home where I may be able to contribute something toward the redemption of our state and the realization of the policies of the Administration.

John Lind.

T telegram (WP, DLC).

From Mark Sullivan

My dear Mr. President: New York June 12, 1913

It was very thoughtful and friendly of you to write. Naturally I was extremely surprised and pleased to get your letter.

I expect to spend several days next week in Washington and I am going to ask Mr. Tumulty if you will not let me come in and speak with you for a moment some day when you have a little leisure. I have refrained from calling in the thought that to save your time and vitality is probably as friendly a service as one can do for you.   Cordially yours,   Mark Sullivan

TLS (WP, DLC).

Sir Cecil Arthur Spring Rice to Sir Edward Grey

Rosslyn [Long Island], *June* 12, 1913.

ARBITRATION.

French Ambassador spoke to President[1] as to effect of rejection of the renewal of treaties even among nations not directly interested.

President replied that he shared his views; that opposition had come from a few members of the Senate; that he thought it would be overcome, and after some delay treaties would be probably ratified.

President gave French Ambassador impression that he would personally neglect nothing to secure a favourable result.

I think that we should bear in mind that in the opinion of all good judges submission of tolls will be refused, although arbitration treaty may be renewed, owing mainly to difficulties entailed by rejection of the other treaties, as well as increasing complications with Japan and Mexico.

Renewal would be therefore of slight practical importance.

Printed telegram (FO 317/1857, No. 26976, PRO).
[1] At the White House in the afternoon of June 9.

To Henry van Dyke

My dear Doctor van Dyke: [The White House] June 13, 1913

It cheered me very much to receive your letter of June eleventh. I am heartily glad to feel that all doubt is removed about your representing the Government at The Hague.

We enjoyed very much our little glimpse of you the other day.
        Cordially and faithfully yours,   Woodrow Wilson

TLS (Letterpress Books, WP, DLC).

To William Jennings Bryan

My dear Mr. Secretary: The White House June 13, 1913

Thank you for your letter of yesterday concerning the views of Senator Vardaman regarding the British treaty. I think that the resolution you suggest in connection with the ratification of the British treaty ought to meet the difficulties felt by some of the Senators. I am very glad indeed that you are taking an active part in arguing the matter with them, because I regard it as of the most vital consequence that the treaty should be confirmed.

I, myself, had talks yesterday with Senator O'Gorman and Senator Chamberlain regarding the treaties.
        Cordially and faithfully yours,   Woodrow Wilson

TLS (W. J. Bryan Papers, DNA).

To James Alexander Reed

My dear Senator: [The White House] June 13, 1913

I did look up the record of Mr. Post of Chicago before I issued his commission as Assistant Secretary in the Department of Labor, and, while it is not altogether "regular" as concerns party affiliation, Mr. Post is a man of peculiar fitness for the office to which I have appointed him. He has enthusiasm for the right things and, I think, will be of very great service to Secretary Wilson.

I am very much obliged to you for calling my attention to the case.   Sincerely yours,   Woodrow Wilson

TLS (Letterpress Books, WP, DLC).

From Lindley Miller Garrison

My dear Mr. President: Washington. June 13, 1913.

I have just had the pleasure of a long interview with Bishop Brent,[1] whom I met for the first time this afternoon. It was very gratifying to me, as a result of my talk with him, to find that the suggestion which I made to you of the character and extent of our next step in the Philippines,[2] not only met with the approval of his thoroughly informed mind, but that he had independently reached practically the same conclusion, and to some extent had expressed it to you in the interview he had with you the other day. He told me that the only practical difference between the suggestion that he had made to you, and the one which I told him I had made to you, was in two particulars.

He suggested that a veto power be lodged in some council. I pointed out to him that under existing legislation there was almost no question that such a veto power was now lodged in the Secretary of War; and he expressed himself as entirely satisfied with that. His other suggestion was that the legislative situation be altered by giving the Philippines a Senate. My proposition, as you know, was to not alter the existing government as to form, but to accomplish the same purpose by giving them a majority of the council. When I pointed out to him that his plan would require us to go to Congress, whereas my plan would not, he immediately concurred in the view that it would be very unwise to embark on legislation until legislation was necessary. No legislation being necessary in my proposal, he expressed himself as satisfied that we should work along that line.

He left me to go and have an interview with Mr. Quezon, having an appointment with him. He returned and has just left me. His talk with Mr. Quezon was confidential, and he promised not to reveal it. He felt at liberty, however, to say to me that he thought that if the plan which I had outlined to him were carried out, it would satisfy Mr. Quezon as the best thing to do at the present time, and would satisfy the Philippine people at the present time. He thought that we should get to it as soon as we could practically.

I think that it would be very useful if you and I could have a talk, uninterrupted by other engagements, and preferably in the evening when you would not be subject to other calls. I do feel that we ought to settle on our policy definitely and begin the framing of it and the putting of it into operation.

May I ask you to bear this in mind and look out for an opportunity to make such an appointment for me?

Sincerely yours,   Lindley M. Garrison

TLS (WP, DLC).
  [1] The Rt. Rev. Charles Henry Brent, Protestant Episcopal Bishop of the Philippine Islands since 1901.
  [2] In L. M. Garrison to WW, April 24, 1913.

From Maurice Francis Egan

Copenhagen, June 13, 1913.

Warmest thanks; most desirable honor; not sufficiently well off to accept.   Maurice Egan.

T telegram (W. J. Bryan Papers, DNA).

From Charles Henry Grasty

My dear Mr. President: Baltimore, Md. June 13, 1913.

At the end of a long search for a President of the John Hopkins University, the trustees are inclined to put an end to it by appointing a local man, Mr. William H. Buckler.[1] Before making a final decision they have come to The Sun office seeking our counsel and we advised that they ask you to suggest some names for their consideration. They told me that they had already appealed to you and that you had made a recommendation but that the Board had not accepted it. I then suggested that an effort be made to advise with you further.

This suggestion resulted in a postponement of action in the election of a president until July 7. At a meeting of the trustees last night a sub-committee of which Mr. B. Howell Griswold, Jr.[2] is the head was appointed and this committee will renew the search for a president.

They asked me to go with them to see you, and Mr. Tumulty gave me an appointment for 11:30 next Thursday. Dr. W. H. Welch, Mr. Griswold and myself look forward to seeing you at that time. I sincerely hope that you may be able to give us some inspiration and practical help in a matter that means so much to Baltimore and the cause of education in general.

I have the honor to remain,
                    Most sincerely yours,   Charles H Grasty

TLS (WP, DLC).
  [1] William Hepburn Buckler, gentleman of independent means, archeologist, former lawyer and diplomat, trustee of The Johns Hopkins University, 1904-1912.
  [2] Benjamin Howell Griswold, Jr., partner in the Baltimore banking firm of Alexander Brown and Sons and a trustee of the Johns Hopkins since 1911.

To Henry Lane Wilson

June 14/13

Replying to yours of June ninth.[1] This Government does not feel that the provisional government of Mexico is moving towards conditions of settled peace, authority and justice, because it is convinced that within Mexico itself there is a fundamental lack of confidence in the good faith of those in control at Mexico City and in their intention to safeguard constitutional rights and methods of action. This Government awaits satisfactory proof of their plans and purposes. If the present provisional government of Mexico will give the Government of the United States satisfactory assurances that an early election will be held, free from coercion or restraint, that Huerta will observe his original promise and not be a candidate at that election, and that an absolute amnesty will follow, the Government of the United States will be glad to exercise its good offices to secure a genuine armistice and an acquiescence of all parties in the program. It would be glad, also, to be instrumental in bringing about any sort of conference among the leaders of the several parties in Mexico that might promise peace and accommodation. The interests of the United States are vitally involved with conditions of peace, justice, and recognized authority in Mexico, and the Government of the United States can acquiesce in nothing which does not definitely promise these things. This message is confidential and is intended for your personal guidance in response to your request of the 9th. It is not intended as a message to the Mexican authorities.[2]

T telegram (EBR, White House Office Files, RG130, DNA).

[1] American Ambassador to Secretary of State, June 9, 1913, *FR 1913*, p. 807, urging recognition of the Huerta government and requesting that the President inform the Ambassador as to his views on recognition.

[2] There is a CLST copy of this telegram, with WWhw emendations, in WP, DLC.

From William Jennings Bryan

My dear Mr. President: Washington June 14, 1913.

Governor Osborn[1] is preparing for the trip to Haiti and Santo Domingo.[2] Owing to the fact that it is not easy to move from place to place down there in the West Indies, it has occurred to me that it might be worth while to have the gunboat PETREL, which is now at Galveston and which has asked the Department for permission to go to Havana in order to give the crew shore leave for a few days, take the Governor from Havana to Haiti and Santo Domingo, stopping at such points as he needs to visit.

I have been looking at the charts and find that the Mole St. Nicholas,[3] which we discussed, is a very desirable harbor. It is about a mile and a half across at the entrance and runs back probably between three and four miles. For the first half of the way it is a hundred feet deep or more, and then for have [half] the remaining distance runs from one hundred down to thirty-five. I am satisfied that it will be of great value to us and even if it were not valuable to us it is worth while to take it out of the market so that no other nation will attempt to secure a foothold there. I would suggest for your consideration the following proposition, namely:

That we shall negotiate for a strip of land twenty miles wide, measured ten miles each way from the center of the mouth of the harbor, the strip to run back to a point ten miles beyond the eastern line of the harbor. This will give us the entire harbor and in the neighborhood of ten miles of land all around it so that the harbor could not be attacked from the land. Second, All persons residing on the land at the time of the purchase to be permitted, upon their own application, to become American citizens. Third, Those living on the land purchased who do not desire to become American citizens, may retain their citizenship in Santo Domingo and the United States Government will purchase any land which they own, at its market value, the price to be submitted to arbitration if it cannot be agreed upon between the parties and the United States. Fourth, The price paid to be a subject of negotiation between this country and Haiti, Governor Osborn to find out what they desire and submit the sum for your consideration.

I merely submit the above suggestions as a basis for discussion. Will submit a copy of this proposition to the Secretary of War and the Secretary of the Navy and ask them to give you their opinion on the subject.

If you will let me know your wishes in regard to using the PETREL, we can have the necessary orders issued by the Navy Department at once.

In view of the disturbed condition in Mexico, I am wondering if it might not be advisable to have another battleship or two sent into the Gulf so that we may be prepared to bring Americans away in case of acute disturbance. We have three battleships down there now,—two at Veracruz, and one at Tampico. As they are battleships of the first class, they would be able to accommodate quite a large number of Americans in case they were needed at places or [of] refuge, but as a matter of precaution it has occurred to me that one or two more might, with advantage, be sent into the neighborhood.

With assurances of respect, etc., I am, my dear Mr. President,
Very sincerely yours,   W. J. Bryan

TLS (WP, DLC).
  [1] That is, Assistant Secretary of State John E. Osborne.
  [2] For the origins of this mission, the chief objective of which Bryan makes clear in this letter, see Challener, *Admirals, Generals, American Foreign Policy,* pp. 379-80.
  [3] A capacious harbor on the northwestern coast of Haiti.

From Louis Dembitz Brandeis

My dear Mr. President: Boston, Mass. June 14, 1913.

As requested at our conference on the 11th I am writing you the substance of the opinion expressed by me on the proposed currency legislation:

First: It is, of course, desirable to enact at an early date a currency bill, if an adequate, confidence-inspiring bill can be passed. But full and free discussion of any proposed measure is essential both to safety and to public confidence in its wisdom. Up to this time there has been little discussion of the currency question except that organized by the bankers.

Second: The power to issue currency should be vested exclusively in Government officials, even when the currency is issued against commercial paper. The American people will not be content to have the discretion necessarily involved vested in a Board composed wholly or in part of bankers; for their judgment may be biased by private interest or affiliation. The function of the bankers should be limited strictly to that of an advisory council. Merely placing in the Government the ultimate supervision and control over the currency issues would not afford the public adequate protection.

Third: It was suggested that a bill, providing for local boards of nine members, of whom six would be bankers, could be passed now, because of the public opinion which the bankers have been making within the past two years; that it would be desirable to so pass such a bill in order to prevent panic conditions, and that later, when the public should have become educated not to heed the cry against the Government entering the banking business, the law might be modified so as to transfer the power over the currency issue to Government officials. But a bill vesting the immediate currency-issuing power in the bankers is almost certain to meet with serious opposition, and there is a little probability of securing the passage of such a bill in time to prevent any early financial disturbance, or to quickly allay it.

Fourth: The effect which the enactment of an improved currency law would have in preventing or allaying financial disturbances has, I believe, been greatly exaggerated. The beneficent effect of the best conceivable currency bill will be relatively slight, unless we are able to curb the money trust, and to remove the uneasiness among business men due to its power. Nothing would go so far in establishing confidence among business men as the assurance that the Government will control the currency issues and the conviction that whatever money is available, will be available for business generally, and not be subject to the control of a favored few. Any currency bill which is enacted, should embody provisions framed so that the people may have some assurance that the change will enure to their benefit.

Fifth: It is a serious question whether, in case we should pass a currency bill satisfactory to the banking interests, and which contains no provisions limiting the power of the money trust, the probability of enacting later legislation to curb the money trusts would not be greatly lessened.

Sixth: The conflict between the policies of the Administration and the desires of the financiers and of big business, is an irreconcilable one. Concessions to the big business interests must in the end prove futile. The administration can at best have only their seeming or temporary cooperation. In essentials they must be hostile. While we must give the most careful consideration to their recommendations and avail ourselves of their expert knowledge, it is extremely dangerous to follow their advice even in a field technically their own.

Very cordially yours,   Louis D. Brandeis

TLS (WP, DLC).

To William II

The White House June 15, 1913.

In the sincere hope that a long continuance of Your Majesty's benignant and peaceful reign may bring the great German people increased blessings, I offer to Your Majesty the cordial felicitations of the Government and people of the United States on this 25th anniversary of Your Majesty's accession and my personal good wishes for Your Majesty's welfare.

Woodrow Wilson

T telegram signed with WWhw emendations (Letterpress Books, WP, DLC).

Remarks at a Press Conference

June 16, 1913

Mr. President, we ask the absorbing question of currency legislation. The particular thought that I have in mind this morning is,
can you explain to us the difference between the two lines of
procedure that seem to be indicated, or rather the two lines of
difference as to the issue, or proposed issue of the money, the
currency—the one the Treasury controls and the other that the
banks control? Now what is the difference, in general principle,
between Treasury control and bank control?

> Well, you will have to go to the experts to have that ex-
> plained. I really don't feel competent to explain it. I have
> never been a banker. I have never had large transactions at
> banks, so that the technique of it is something I would rather
> leave in other hands. That leads me to speak of the way
> in which we have tried to get at this thing. I don't want the
> impression to prevail for a moment that I have assumed to
> know enough to assume the authority of formulating a
> bill. I have been going over it to form my judgment about
> it as well as I could, from the suggestions that were sub-
> mitted to me by persons very much more competent than
> I am to determine the details. And, about the details, I have
> had very little opinion of my own. About the main lines, I
> have had a considerable opinion. I think the result will be
> proposals that are really and genuinely the result of com-
> mon counsel. No man's bill.

Mr. President, that comes back with the question . . . about the
main lines. There is a good deal of desire to know, and it may be
that you would be willing to say what those main lines were?

> The bill, I hope, will be so constructed that all will clear
> itself up. It is so much better to have it in definite language
> than in general language in which I might inadvertently mis-
> lead.

I might ask, then, this question—whether the bill, which is reported to be substantially agreed upon, follows those—I mean,
agreed upon, perhaps, not with yours—whether it follows those
main lines that you had in mind?

> I think so, so far as I am informed of it, it does.

Mr. President, can you tell us what gentlemen are in agreement
on that bill, for example, that represent your views and those of
Mr. Owen and Mr. Glass?

> Oh, Mr. Owen and Mr. Glass! Why I think I can say with

entire truth that there is no longer any essential variation of their views.

So there will be really only one bill?

That is what I understand, yes.

The *New York Times* gives something of what purports to be the substance of the bill, and the administration's program, on currency legislation.

I haven't seen it. I was told since I reached the office. I haven't read it.

Have you reason to hope for anything in the way of general assurances that there is going to be currency harmony?

Well, the currency is a matter about which you are bound to get perfectly genuine differences of opinion. If by harmony, you mean harmony of purpose, I am sure there will be harmony of purpose. Whether there will be entire agreement of opinion is another matter. There is no use mincing words. I have in mind all these reports that are flying about, of a great difference of opinion, many differences. I don't take any stock in them myself. I don't take any notice because the information that reaches me doesn't support that at all.

Do you still lack direct information, Mr. President, that there will be a very sizable opposition to this currency bill?

I have enough information. Several gentlemen have said, with perfect frankness, that they oppose it, that it would not be necessary to take the matter up this session. It is not a question of whether you are opposed to the currency law. It is merely a question of whether we can take it at this stage and whether we can stick it out.

One of the papers this morning intimates that Mr. Bryan has taken a position against the bill.

That is not true.

Is Mr. Bryan a factor in the making of the bill?

I don't know that he is. I have, of course, discussed the matter with him, but since our general discussion of it, I don't know of any part that he has played in it.

Well, if it is a fair question—I mean, it would be, to take an active interest?

I don't know that he has, so far as I know.

Has it been called to your attention that Mr. Henry is opposed to the bill?

I saw the speech, of course, that Mr. Henry made, demanding a full investigation of the Money Trust. Much of that speech could be interpreted as opposition, but I haven't heard anything further than that.

It might be, Mr. President, that Mr. Henry has not seen the bill yet.

I don't think he has.

Has your message been completed?

Yes, sir. That is to say, the first draft of it. I always have to put it in safekeeping a day or two, to see if it suits me.

When do you expect to send it before Congress?

I will await information until the committees are ready. I will read it in person.

Mr. President, I would like to try to make it a little easier to get this information on the currency business. We have booted it along to try to get some explanation of the thing, and I confess that I am utterly at sea and utterly ignorant of knowing what to say on currency. Any suggestions or lines that you can give us for public exploitation would be very welcome.

Well now, I appreciate the embarrassment, and I am afraid you feel that there has been some hide and seek.

Not at all.

There hasn't been. What I have been trying to do, gentlemen, is this. I want you to know just why I handle the thing as I have handled it. When we came to Washington for this session, the Democratic party was practically unanimous as to what should be done about the tariff, not as to details, of course, but as to its revision and its immediate revision. That was plain sailing. But the currency is a matter about which no party that I know of is of a single opinion. We had, therefore, to begin. As I think I told you gentlemen, we did begin to talk to each other very freely in all directions about the currency.

Now, of course, all sorts of opinions and variations of opinion have been playing upon this thing, and we will slowly eliminate the differences of opinion—honest differences of opinion—and get down to a single plan.

Now, that plan never has yet been so specifically formulated as to be worth the consideration of the business community, because the business community is interested very much more in exactly how you are going into this thing than in the general thing, how you are going to treat business in general than the machinery—the process for real, the essence of doing business.

That bill will probably, from my present information, that is to say, this result of the final agreements of opinions among those who have been working hardest on them, will probably be formulated within twenty-four or forty-eight hours. That is my intimation this morning, that being the process—this being the process of crystallization. The crystal is not yet formed.

That has been my embarrassment all along, because I don't know those lawyers out on the street, who won't be satisfied and won't approve of the final agreement, and all this time we have been coming together and, I believe, so far as my judgment guides me, on sound ground, except though, with several variations as to method. That is the whole thing. That is what has made it impossible to make a statement. I sincerely hope that this apparent failure will be lifted very soon.

Mr. President, do you hope and expect an identical bill will be introduced in both branches?

I shouldn't be surprised, although I can't state that with certainty.

Mr. President, that currency legislation shall be party legislation or nonpartisan legislation?

Although it hadn't been raised, of course I have been working entirely with my Democratic colleagues on the hill, but I state sincerely that we will have a very considerable amount of agreement on the other side of the aisle.

Have you determined, Mr. President, on any basic principles of that bill?

Oh, yes, we have been working on the basic principles all along.

Could you state any now?

No. Well, again, the embarrassment is that it should not be judged by the clothes it wears.

Let's hope it isn't hobble skirts.

No, sir, it won't be hobble skirts.

Have you had any conference with Mr. La Follette about currency?

No, I have not personally. I think Mr. Glass at noontime had a talk with him about it. That is my impression.

Mr. President, some time ago, some of the Republican senators, some on the Banking and Currency Committee, said they would welcome an opportunity to vote for some currency bill, but they would like to see it before it becomes the final administration bill. Have there been any advances of that kind made to you?

No, but I dare say that will be done.

JRT transcript (WC, NjP) of CLSsh (C. L. Swem Coll., NjP).

To Lindley Miller Garrison

My dear Mr. Secretary: [The White House] June 16, 1913

I was interested, as you were, and very greatly interested, in Bishop Brent's views. It is very valuable, indeed, to have such side lights, and such direct lights, on the situation.

Cordially yours,   Woodrow Wilson

TLS (Letterpress Books, WP, DLC).

From William Jennings Bryan, with Enclosure

My dear Mr. President: Washington June 16, 1913.

There are so many matters before this Department about which I would like to talk to you and we have so little time for discussion of these things, that I take the liberty of sending you a draft of a new treaty made by Judge Douglas[1] as attorney for Nicaragua.

He has embodied in this treaty the Platt Amendment. Extracts from the Platt Amendment are in red. The black type reproduces the Nicaraguan treaty now before the Senate except where the words in black type are underscored, these are additions.

You will notice that the $3,000,000 instead of being used as mentioned in the treaty now before the Senate is to be used as follows: $1,000,00 for the immediate needs of the Government; $2,000,000 to be used to pay the claims that may be allowed by the Joint Commission which is now sifting the claims. Some six thousand claims have been presented, of which nearly three thousand have been passed upon, with an allowance of something like $250,000. The representative insists that the allowance and payment of these claims are necessary to the maintenance of peace and order there. In the former treaty the amount was to be used for education and public works. Senator Bacon thinks that the Senate might be willing to permit the adoption of the Platt Amendment idea, but that is a personal opinion and he has not had time to make a poll of the Senate. My own preference would be to have the money used for education or permanent public works, but it may be necessary to consider the immediate needs of the Government, and as I am more interested in the securing of the option and the naval base than I am in the manner in which the money is spent, I would not regard the change as vital.

I shall be pleased to go over some of these matters with you whenever you can find leisure.

With assurances of respect, etc., I am, my dear Mr. President,
Very sincerely yours,   W. J. Bryan

TLS (WP, DLC).
¹ Charles Alexander Douglas, senior partner of the law firm of Douglas, Baker, Ruffin & Obear of Washington, which represented several Latin American governments.

E N C L O S U R E

Draft of suggested Convention between the United States and Nicaragua in substitution of the two conventions now pending before the United States Senate, one dated June 6, 1911, known as "Knox-Castrillo Convention," and the other dated February 8, 1913, commonly referred to as the "Canal Convention."¹

[The Government of the United States of America and the Government of Nicaragua, being animated by the desire to strengthen their ancient and cordial friendship by the most sincere cooperation for all purposes of mutual advantage and interest of the two nations; and the Government of Nicaragua being desirous to promote in every way economic development and prosperity under orderly and lawful government and the maintenance of its rights as secured by the Washington Conventions; and the Government of the United States being in full sympathy with these aims and desiring to lend to the Government of Nicaragua all proper assistance in these matters and also in the furtherance of its welfare and economic development; and it being the desire of both Governments to reaffirm the principle of the first paragraph of the Protocol of December 1, 1900, and to provide for the possible future construction of an interoceanic ship canal by way of the San Juan River and the Great Lake of Nicaragua or via any other route over Nicaraguan territory whenever the construction of such canal shall be deemed conducive to the interests of both countries; and the Government of Nicaragua wishing to facilitate in every way possible the successful construction, maintenance and operation of such canal and also the maintenance and operation of the Panama Canal, the two Governments have resolved to conclude a Convention to these ends, and have accordingly appointed as their plenipotentiaries, the Government of the United States, ...

¹ The text in single square brackets is from the canal convention; that in double square brackets, from the Platt Amendment; that italicized, new.

and the Government of Nicaragua, ...
who having exhibited to each other their respective full powers,
found to be in good and due form, have agreed upon and concluded the following articles:]

ARTICLE I.

[[To enable the United States to maintain the independence of
Nicaragua and to protect the people thereof, as well as for its own
defence,]] [the Government of Nicaragua grants in perpetuity
to the Government of the United States the unencumbered exclusive rights necessary and convenient to the construction,
operation and maintenance of an interoceanic canal by way of
the San Juan River and the Great Lake of Nicaragua or by way
of any other route over Nicaraguan territory, the details of the
terms upon which such canal shall be constructed, operated and
maintained to be fixed by mutual consultation between the two
Governments whenever the construction of such canal shall be
decided upon.]

ARTICLE II.

[In order to facilitate the protection of the Panama Canal and
of the canal, canal route and the rights contemplated by the
present Convention, and also to enable the United States to take
any measure or to assist the Government of Nicaragua in any
measures necessary to the ends contemplated herein, the Government of Nicaragua hereby leases for ninety-nine (99) years
to the Government of the United States the islands in the Caribbean Sea known as Great Corn and Little Corn Islands, and
covenants that, at such time and at such place on the Gulf of
Fonseca as the Government of the United States may designate,
the Government of the United States shall have the right to
establish, operate and maintain for ninety-nine (99) years a
naval base. The Government of the United States shall have the
option of renewing either or both of the above grants contained
in this article upon the expiration of the ninety-nine years afore-
said.]

ARTICLE III.

[The Government of Nicaragua hereby grants to the Government of the United States in perpetuity the right of ships of the
merchant marine of the United States to engage in coastwise
trade in Nicaragua, either by way of the aforementioned canal
or otherwise, with a right to discharge or load in part or in whole
at all Nicaraguan ports while engaged in any voyage on terms
identical with those imposed on Nicaraguan citizens or vessels.]

ARTICLE IV.

[[The Government of Nicaragua shall never enter into any treaty or other compact with any foreign power or powers which will impair or tend to impair the independence of Nicaragua, nor in any manner authorize or permit any foreign power or powers to obtain by colonization or for military or naval purposes, or otherwise, lodgment in or control over any portion of said Republic.]]

ARTICLE V.

[[The Government of Nicaragua shall not assume nor contract any public debt to pay the interest upon which, and to make reasonable sinking fund provision for the ultimate discharge of which, the ordinary revenues of the Republic of Nicaragua, after defraying the current expenses of the Government, shall be inadequate.]]

ARTICLE VI.

[[The Government of Nicaragua consents that the United States may exercise the right to intervene for the preservation of Nicaraguan independence, the maintenance of a Government adequate for the protection of life, property and individual liberty]] *and for discharging any obligations which it may assume or contract.*

ARTICLE VII.

[In consideration of the foregoing stipulations and of the purposes of this Convention, the Government of the United States shall] *upon the date of the exchange of ratifications of this Convention,* [pay] *to or* [for the benefit of the Government of Nicaragua the sum of Three Million Dollars ($3,000,000) United States gold coin of the present weight and fineness, such payment to be made] *as follows:*

One Million Dollars ($1,000,000) to the Government of Nicaragua for its immediate needs; and the remaining

Two Million Dollars ($2,000,000) [to a depositary] *or depositaries,* [an American banking corporation] *or corporations,* to be [designated] *jointly* [by the Secretary of State of the United States] *and the Minister of Finance of the Republic of Nicaragua,* [to be disbursed] *exclusively for the payment of awards and maintenance of the Nicaraguan Mixed Claims Commission,* [all such disbursements to be made by orders drawn by the Minister of Finance of Nicaragua] *upon the requisitions of the President of said Commission.*

ARTICLE VIII.

[This Convention shall be ratified by the high contracting parties according to their respective laws, and the ratifications thereof shall be exchanged at Washington, as soon as possible.]

IN FAITH WHEREOF, we, the respective plenipotentiaries, have hereunto affixed our hands and seals.

DONE IN DUPLICATE in the English and Spanish languages at   this   day of   , nineteen hundred and thirteen.

T MS (SDR, RG 59, filed with 817.812/30a, DNA).

From Elliot Hersey Goodwin[1]

Sir: Washington, D. C. June 16, 1913.

This formal request on behalf of the Chamber of Commerce of the United States of America that the Sundry Civil Bill should not receive Executive approval in its present form is based upon a referendum conducted by the Chamber among all the commercial organizations of the United States affiliated with it, which was completed on June 14. The provision of the Sundry Civil Bill which purposes to exempt labor and agricultural combinations from prosecution under the antitrust laws was the sole question submitted for consideration. In accordance with the By-laws of the Chamber, forty-five days were allowed for the vote. The result speaks clearly for itself. One hundred and sixty-nine organizations representing in their membership 106,495 firms and individuals cast 669 votes against the exemption of labor and agricultural combinations, and four organizations with a combined membership of 1,008 cast nine votes in favor of the said exemption.

Votes are apportioned according to membership. An organization with twenty-five members has one vote and an additional vote is allotted for each two hundred members in excess of twenty-five, but no organization is allowed more than ten votes.

A full analysis of the vote and a copy of the question as submitted to referendum is transmitted herewith.[2]

Very respectfully yours,
Chamber of Commerce of the United States of America.
                    Elliot H. Goodwin   General Secretary.

TLS (WP, DLC).
[1] General Secretary of the Chamber of Commerce of the United States.
[2] "Referendum No. 3," three-page T MS (WP, DLC).

To William Jennings Bryan

My dear Mr. Secretary: [The White House] June 17, 1913

I entirely approve of your suggestion about requesting the Navy Department to put the gunboat PETREL at the service of Mr. Osborn for his visit to Haiti and Santo Domingo. I take it for granted that it is within our legal power to do so without incurring unauthorized expenditures.

I am greatly interested, as you know, in Governor Osborn's visit to the island and think that he is just the right man to make it.   Cordially and faithfully yours,   Woodrow Wilson

TLS (Letterpress Books, WP, DLC).

To William Elliott Gonzales

My dear Friend: [The White House] June 17, 1913

I cannot tell you what pleasure it gave me to nominate you for the post in Cuba. I felt sure that it would be as acceptable to you as anything that I could select, and your letter confirming that impression[1] has gratified me very much indeed. May God bless you in the performance of your duties. I know that they will be performed with the highest sense of honor and responsibility.

I want you to know that Senator Tillman, of his own accord, came to me and said that he hoped that I would honor you with an appointment.
Always
     Faithfully and cordially yours,   Woodrow Wilson

TLS (Letterpress Books, WP, DLC).
[1] W. E. Gonzales to WW, June 14, 1913, TLS (WP, DLC).

To John Lind

My dear Governor Lind: The White House June 17, 1913

It was a keen disappointment to me that you did not feel at liberty to accept the appointment to Sweden. My own feeling is quite different from yours about sending as representatives to foreign countries citizens of the United States born in those countries who have won distinction here in the service of the public, but I feel that it is my duty to bow to your own conviction in that matter. It gave me great pleasure to have an opportunity to express in some way my confidence in you and my admiration for you.

    With the warmest regard and sincere regret,

        Cordially and sincerely yours,   Woodrow Wilson

TLS (J. Lind Papers, MnHi).

Jean Jules Jusserand to Stéphen Pichon

CONFIDENTIEL.

[Washington] 17 juin 1913.

Diverses communications de cette Ambassade et en particulier ma lettre du 14 et mon télégramme du 19 février dernier, ont fait savoir au Département comment ce n'était pas sans avoir couru quelque danger d'échec que notre Traité d'arbitrage, renouvelé pour 5 ans le 13 de cet mois, avait obtenu l'approbation sénatoriale.

L'événement prouve que le danger avait été plus réel qu'il ne semblait d'abord et que notre reconnaissance doit être à proportion, vis-à-vis du Sénateur Lodge qui avait bien voulu, sur ma demande, prendre l'affaire en mains et qui s'arrangea pour qu'elle fut règlée en attirant aussi peu que possible l'attention.

Le danger venait comme on sait non de mauvais sentiments à notre égard, mais du précédent ainsi créé et qui profiterait à l'Angleterre en lui facilitant assurait-on de réclamer l'arbitrage dans la question des droits de péage à Panama.

Ainsi que l'indiquait à Votre Excellence ma lettre No 341, le Traité avec ce dernier pays a été renouvelé pour 5 ans le 31 mai, et communiqué au Sénat avec ceux concernant l'Italie et l'Espagne. Nombre d'autres l'ont été depuis, celui avec la Norvège a été signé hier, et c'est parait-il le quinzième. Tous demeurent en suspens. Les ennemis de toute concession à l'Angleterre dans l'affaire des droits à Panama et en particulier des Sénateurs Chamberlain de l'Orégon et O'Gorman de New-York se sont mis en travers de la ratification et le Gouvernement du Président Wilson, si partisan de l'arbitrage et du règlement pacifique des querelles internationales, se trouve en assez fausse posture.

La situation n'est pas moins fausse pour le Gouvernement anglais dont les délégués chargés de préparer la commémoration de cent ans de paix recevaient naguère si bon accueil et faisaient de si beaux discours.[1]

Voyant que, dans cet embarras, mon collègue d'Angleterre me saurait beaucoup de gré de ce que je pourrais tenter, je me suis fait un devoir ayant occasion d'entretenir le Président, d'appeler son attention sur le très fâcheux effet que produirait dans le monde entier, l'abrogation du Traité anglo-américain, aussi anodin que le nôtre et ce n'est pas peu dire. Que penserait-on d'une nation qui prône si bruyamment l'arbitrage et qui refuse de ratifier un traité à la seule pensée qu'une question la concernant, et qui n'est du reste que d'importance secondaire, pourrait être tranchée par ce moyen? Ces remarques et d'autres venant du Représentant d'un pays ami et fort désintéressé dans l'affaire puisque son propre traité était ratifié, avaient chance de retenir l'attention. Le Président leur fit bon accueil et m'assura que rien ne serait négligé pour lui faire assurer la ratification de ce traité et de tous les autres. Je parlai de même quelques jours plus tard à M. Bryan qui me plaisanta sur ce rôle de Noé tranquille en son arche au milieu de la noyade générale; je lui expliquai qu'à l'inverse du patriarche, je souhaitais que l'arche fut ouverte à tout le monde, et refis l'exposé de mon point de vue: c'est assez pour nous que d'avoir, selon notre tradition donné l'exemple, et construit l'arche.

Sir Cecil Spring Rice m'a vivement remercié de cette marque de bon vouloir dans une circonstance où le fait que mon pays était hors de cause[2] me donnait plus de facilité qu'à lui-même peut être pour agir utilement, n'ayant pas à prendre, pour ma part, attitude de solliciteur.   [Jusserand]

CCL (N. S. États-Unis, Vol. 12, FFM-Ar).
[1] He referred to the Anglo-American commission then making plans to celebrate the centennial of the Treaty of Ghent.
[2] That is, not involved in the tolls controversy.

T R A N S L A T I O N

CONFIDENTIAL.   [Washington] June 17, 1913.

Various communications of this Embassy, and in particular my letter of the fourteenth and my telegram of February 19 last, have made known to the Department how it was not without some danger of failure that our arbitration treaty, renewed for five years the thirteenth of that month, has obtained senatorial approval.

The event proves that the danger was more real than it had seemed at first, and that our gratitude should go out to Senator Lodge, who was good enough, at my request, to take the affair in hand and who set about so that it would be settled in such a way as to attract as little attention as possible.

The danger came, as one knows, not from a lack of enthusiasm on our part, but from the precedent that would be created and from which England would assuredly profit in facilitating her claim to arbitration in the question of free Panama tolls.

Just as my letter No. 341 indicated to your excellency, the Treaty with this last named country was renewed for five years on May 31 and submitted to the Senate along with those with Italy and Spain. Many others have since been renewed—the one with Norway was signed yesterday, and it appears to be the fifteenth. We are all in suspense. The enemies of any concession to England in the Panama tolls controversy, and in particular Senators Chamberlain of Oregon and O'Gorman of New York, have set themselves to the task of thwarting ratification, and the government of President Wilson, such a strong partisan of arbitration and of the peaceful settlement of international quarrels, finds itself in an embarrassing position.

The situation is no less embarrassing for the English government whose delegates, charged with preparing the commemoration of the hundred years peace, have received not long ago so warm a welcome and engaged in such friendly discussions.

Seeing that, in this difficulty, my English colleague would be very grateful to me if I could try, and having occasion to talk to the President, I have set myself the task of drawing his attention to the very unfortunate effect which the abrogation of the Anglo-American treaty—as innocuous as ours (and that's an overstatement)—would produce on the entire world. What would one think of a nation which preaches so loudly about arbitration and which refuses to ratify a treaty at the mere thought that a question concerning it, and which on the whole is of only secondary importance, could be settled by this method?

These remarks and others coming from the representative of a friendly country and strongly disinterested in the affair, since its own treaty had been ratified, would have some chance of securing attention.

The President received these remarks warmly and assured me that nothing would be neglected on his part to assure the ratification of this treaty and of all the others.

I spoke, a few days later, on this subject to Mr. Bryan, who joked with me on this role of Noah, tranquil in his ark in the middle of the Great Flood. I explained to him that, contrary to the patriarch, I hoped that the ark would be open to everyone, and I gave an account of my point of view again: It is enough for us, according to our tradition, to have given the example and built the ark.

Sir Cecil Spring Rice has thanked me warmly for this token of good will in a circumstance in which the fact that my country was not involved made it easier for me than for him, perhaps, to act effectively, not having to take, on my part, the attitude of petitioner.   [Jusserand]

From Carter Glass

My dear Mr. President: Washington. June 18, 1913.

At the risk of being regarded pertinacious I am going to ask if you will not consider the advisability of modifying somewhat your view of bank representation on the proposed Federal Reserve Board.[1] The matter has given me much concern, and more than ever I am convinced that it will be a grave mistake to alter so radically the feature of the bill indicated. Last night when I came back to my hotel I found Mr. Bulkley[2] waiting and he sat with me until past one o'clock this morning. Knowing that he was so earnestly for a government note issue and for government control, I imagined he would be delighted with the suggested alteration. I told him of the change without first indicating my own view and much to my astonishment—and gratification—he instantly and vigorously protested, saying he had regarded the extent to which we had already put the government in control, together with the tremendous power of the Board, as the real weakness of the bill. He also said we could not escape the charge of exposing the banking business of the country to political control. As indicated to you last night, Mr. Bulkley is a strong man of the committee with whom we must reckon; hence his view of this proposed alteration fully confirms my belief that it would prove an almost irretrievable mistake to leave the banks without representation on the Central Board. You will note that the bill requires the three members selected by the banks to sever all bank connections before qualifying. Might it not be well at least to take Mr. McAdoo's suggestion and have the President select these men from a list proposed by the banks? With high esteem,
                        Sincerely yours,   Carter Glass.

TLS (WP, DLC).
    [1] Wilson had conferred with Glass, McAdoo, and Senator Owen at the White House during the evening of June 17. About this meeting, see Link, *The New Freedom*, pp. 210-12; Glass, *An Adventure in Constructive Finance*, pp. 112-13; and Willis, *The Federal Reserve System*, pp. 250-251.
    [2] Representative Robert Johns Bulkley of Ohio, a member of the subcommittee on banking and currency.

From William Gibbs McAdoo

[Washington]

Dear Mr. President,   Wednesday pm—June 18 [1913].

Mr. Glass has been here & says that it is most important that you let him know quickly when you will invite the members of the House Currency Committee, individually or collectively, to see you. He thinks you had better send the invitation to the members direct & that in view of premature publications of the plan[1] (which annoy him exceedingly) it becomes doubly important for you to act quickly, as you may be able to dissipate a good deal of discontent with the alleged secrecy about what is being done. Will you kindly advise Mr. Glass direct.

I also think it doubly important for you to see the House Committee promptly, if you have today conferred with the Senate Committee.   Hastily, Faithfully Yrs   W G McAdoo

ALS (WP, DLC).
[1] The complete text of the Federal Reserve bill as approved by Wilson, Glass, McAdoo, and Owen in a White House conference during the evening of June 18 was published in the *New York Times* and other newspapers on June 19, 1913.

A Report by William Bayard Hale[1]

Mexico City, June 18th, 1913

The administration of President Francisco Madero had undoubtedly grown unpopular by February, 1913. Mr Madero had been put into the presidency by the most fairly conducted election ever held in Mexico; though probably a bare ten per cent of the voting population had taken the trouble to go to the polls, Madero was virtually the unanimous choice of the nation.

A few months sufficed to show that the new President was unequal to the task to which he had been chosen. The ideals which he entertained in a generous heart could be applied, in a country that had all to learn of the meaning of "freedom" and "democracy," only with practical discretion; his promises of social, and particularly agrarian, reform could not be immediately realized; his most devoted supporters, once he was in power, revealed themselves in the character of self-seekers. Disillusioned, but confirmed in his belief that he had been called to a great mission, Madero adopted new methods—those, namely, of repression. He bore down on the press, proscribed his enemies, gave his generals a free hand. But he was by nature unfitted to the part of a tyrant;

[1] Hale wrote on the cover of this report: "The necessity of catching a train with this MS. renders it impossible to correct it properly. I am but a poor type-writer."

a little man, of unimpressive presence and manner, highly nervous, overwhelmed by his troubles, surrounded by incompetents, trying to be severe but yielding to his merciful instincts just when he should have been unyielding, Madero, at the end of his first year in the presidency, was in a bad way. The country was to a considerable extent unsettled; murmuring was heard from every side; the treasury was depleted, and a gang of grafters scarcely less audacious than the hated Cientificos who had wrecked Porforio Diaz's rule were in the saddle[.] In a land of settled political methods the case would have been no worse than that of a particularly incompetent Chief Executive at the end of a disastruous first year. In Mexico, it was fairly certain that, unless an early change for the better came, a popular revolution might be expected.

But the movement that broke out in the capital on the night of February 8-9 was in no sense a popular revolution. It was a conspiracy of army officers, financed by a few Spanish reactionaries, in conjunction with Cientifico exiles in Paris and Madrid.

Subscriptions towards the overthrow of Madero were passed around almost openly in the capital, with only moderate success, the principal amount used by the conspirators coming from abroad, in the shape of a draft for £12,000 payable to the Bank of London and Mexico, Vera Cruz branch; it had been intended originally for Felix Diaz's uprising of last November. Leaders in the Mexican subscription were Gen. Luis Garcia Pimentel and Inigo Noreiga. Noreiga, sometimes referred to as "the Pierpont Morgan of Mexico" had been the recipient of many grants and monopolies from the old regime; he held Porfirio Diaz's power of attorney. The active agent of the plot was Gen. Manuel Mondragon, who had accumulated much money under Diaz as a fake artillery expert. He had been entrusted with many purchases of arms; the ingenious scheme of putting his name of [on] "inventions" and collecting a royalty had been one of his methods.

Mondragon corrupted the officers (old associates of his) and persuaded the cadets of the Aspirantes military academy, at Tlalpam, a suburb of Mexico city, and they formed the nucleus of the movement.

On the night of Febroary 8, a number of cadets came into the city, on trolley cars. In the early morning they gathered before the penitentiary, where they demanded the release of Gen. Felix Diaz, in confinem[en]t awaiting trial for rebellion. After a brief parley, Diaz was released. Then they proceeded to the Santiago military prison, where they demanded and secured the release of Gen. Bernardo Reyes, a prisoner in the like case with Diaz. President Madero, against the advise of his friends, had refused to permit Reyes and Diaz to be shot as traitors when captured, according to the prevailing Mexican custom, insisting that they be properly tried.

When released, General Reyes was found dressed in the full uniform of a general in the Mexican army, assumed while waiting for the doors to open for him.

Mounting a horse, Reyes now led part of the cadets and a column of mutineering soldiers to the National Palace, in the centre of the city, arriving there a little after eight o'clock Sunday morning. Reyes had full confidence that he would be welcomed and the Palace delivered over to him, the officers in command having been bribed. He rode up as if on parade. But, in some way, the arrangement miscarried, and officers not in the plot were in charge Sunday morning. Reyes was fired on, and fell mortally wounded from his horse; the men behind him were routed, and many spectators were killed in the confused shooting that followed.

President Madero, receiving word in his palace of Chaupultepec, three miles away, about 9 o'clock mounted a horse and with a small escort rode into the city. Arriving at the end of the broad Avenida Juarez and finding the narrower streets thronged, he dismounted and went into a photographers studio opposite the unfinished National Theatre, to telephone for later news. Here he was joined by a few citizens and officers, among them Victoriano Huerta, a general in the army on leave for the treatment of his eyes. Huerta had been considered in disfavor and was known to be disappointed at not having been made Madero's minister of war, the President knowing him to be an habitual drunkard.*

Huerta now offered his services to Madero. They were promptly accepted, and Huerta was appointed commander-in-chief of the army in the city. The commission was made formal on the following day.

The President stepped out on a balcony and made a speech to the crowd, Huerta standing by his side. He then went down, remounted his horse, a splendid animal that reared and plunged in the hands of the mwn [man] who held him, commanded them to release him, and rode off, bowing to cheering crowds, alone, far ahead of his escort, to the National Palace.

General Diaz had been more successful than Reyes. Diaz's part

---

* Capt. Barr, late U.S.A., now ordinance agent of the Bethlehem Steel Company, in Mexico, tells me Madero had given him this reason for not appointing Huerta, and that he had tole Huerta, who said: "I knew that was it."

had be[e]n to take possession of the arsenal (the ciudadela) on the edge of the city. This he accomplished without opposition, and found himself in possession of a defensible fort, with the Government's reserve arms and ammunition.

That evening Madero went to Cuernavaca, capital of the neighboring state of Morelos, where the army was operating against the bands of the rebel leader Zapata, and during the night brought back a train-load of arms and ammunition and some men. By Monday morning Madero had a garrison of one thousand in the National Palace.

On Monday neither side made any important move. The President had telegraphed to Gen. Aureliano Blanquet to move with his 1200 men from Toluca, and had received word that the General was on the way.

On Tuesday, about 10 o'clock, the Government began the bombardment of the arsenal. The fire was vigorously replied to, and the city suffered severely. During the day, Government re-enforcements (but not Blanquet's men) came in, and a supply of ammunition was received from Vera Cruz. There was no movement of the mutineers from the arsenal, and no evidence of disaffection in the city at large. The American Ambassador, however, on this day told all comers at the Embassy that the Government had practically fallen and telegraphed to Washington asking for powers to force the combatants to negotiations.

On the next day, Tuesday, February 12, the mutual bombardment continued. The Ambassador took the Spanish and German ministers and, as his report to the State Department that day shows, "protested against the continuance of hostilities." "The President,["] continues Mr Wilson's report, "was visibly embarrassed and endeavored to fix the responsibility of [on] Felix Diaz."

The attitude of the American Ambassador towards President Madero had been one of undisguised contempt, from the beginning. Before the inauguration, at a dinner given Madero at the University Club in July, 1911, the Ambassador had publicly admonished the President-elect in terms of condescension that are still remembered by people of all classes in the city. Mr Wilson boasted to me that on the very day of Madero's inauguration he had reported to Washington that the end was already in sight. When Felix Diaz rose in Vera Cruz, in November, 1912, Mr Wilson, then in Kansas City, was quoted by the Associated Press as saying in an interview that Diaz was the type of man that ought to rule Mexico. Mr Wilson repudiated the interview and denied using the language. As Madero's term went on, the Ambassador became more and more outspoken in the dislike of the President, his hostility to those who, even socially, consorted with him or his family and in predictions of his early fall.

The Ambassador now took the topsy-turvy view that the President, by not surrendering instantly to the mutineers, was responsible for the bloodshed.

This view was congenial to the Spanish Minister, and to it were won the British and the German ministers. The Spanish and German ministers are not now in Mexico, but I have had the honour of meeting the British minister, and am obliged to say that I never met an individual whose character so absurdly belied his name. Mr Stronge is a silly, stuttering imbecile, the laughing-stock of the whole city, which regales itself with nothing more to its perennial delight than daily stories of Mr Stronge and the parrot by which he is constantly attended.

Mr Wilson, in response to my questions, said to me that he called into consultation, on this and subsequent occasions, only his British, Spanish and German colleagues (with once perhaps the French chargé) because they represented the largest interests here, and "the others really did not matter." At another time, Mr Wilson explained to me that it would have been difficult to reach them all, so he consulted with those representing the largest interests.

The fact is, the others were not in accord with Mr Wilson's policy. The Austrian and Japanese legations, with all the Latin-American representatives, including those of Brazil, Chile, Cuba, Guatamala and El Salvador, took the view that the constitutional government was justified in maintaining its authority, and that it was no business of foreign diplomatists to interfere against the constitutional government in a domestic conflict. Though Mr Wilson constantly endeavoree to represent his group as "the diplomatic corps," it is a fact that the numerical majority of the members of the corps acted in a contrary sense, under the Chilean and Cuban ministers.

Following the call on Madero during which Mr Wilson, Mr Stronge and Admiral von Hintze had told the President that they protested against his continuing hostilities, Mr Wilson, accompanied by Mr Stronge, went to the arsenal, called on Diaz, and, as Mr Wilson reports to Mr Knox that day, "urged that firing be confined to a particular zone."

The Ambassador had thus reached the point where he admonished the legal Government as if it were a revolt, and treated the mutineers as if they were the Government *de jure* and *de facto*.

On Wednesday and Thursday, the 13th and 14th, the battle continued; the relative positions of the combatants remained unchanged, but distressing conditions increased in parts of the city within range of the fire. The Ambassador told Mr Lascarain, Madero's prime minister and minister of foreign relations, that Madero ought to resign; as reported to Secretary Knox, Mr Wilson's language became: "Public opinion, both Mexican and foreign, holds the Federal Government responsible for these conditions."

On Thursday, the 14th (although possibly on Wednesday the 13th) the United States Consul-general in Mexico City, Mr Arnold Shanklin,* who had been driven out of the consulate by artillery fire and was now doing heroic work at the Embassy, while busy in the yard in front of the Embassy, was approached by a person of his acquaintance related to General Huerta, who asked the favor of an introduction to the Ambassador. He said:

"I have a message from the General; I believe it would be possible to have him and Diaz come to an understanding, if the Ambassador thinks that that would be a good idea. I want to see him and lay the plan before him."

The messenger went on to explain that it would not be necessary for the Ambassador to appear at all. He said that the interested parties would be satisfied if Mr Wilson were to authorize Mr. Shanklin to carry on any negotiations and otherwise repr[e]sent him. What they wanted was an understanding with the Ambassador, without involving him in any delicate responsibilities.

Mr. Shanklin replied that, so far as he was concerned, he would have no part in any such plan; however, if the messenger insisted, he would carry his request for an introduction tp [to] Mr Wilson, and the Ambassador could deal with it himself. Accordingly the Consul General went in and informed the Ambassador of the messenger's request for an introduction, explicitly stating the character of his errand, namely, that he wanted to lay before the Ambassador a plan for an understanding between the President's chief general and the rebel leader. Mr Shanklin explained that he had declined to have any part in the matter, but that he deemed it his duty to lay it before the Ambassador.

"Bring him in," said Mr Wilson. "I want to see him." Mr Shanklin brought in the messwnger, introduced him, and retired.

On Friday, the 15th, the Ambassador requested the British, Gwrman and Spanish ministers to come to the embassy. He did not invite the other members of the corps. He reports to Mr Knox:

* Mr. Shanklin is a brother of Dr. Wm. Arnold Shanklin, President of Wesleyan University.

"The opinion of my assembled colleagues was unanimous." The Spanish minister was designated to visit the National Palace and inform the President of this unanimous opinion—which was, that he should resign. Mr Madero replied tc the Spanish Minister that he did not recognize the right of diplomatists accredited to a nation to interfere in its domestic affairs; he called attention to the fact, which he feared some of the diplomatists had somehow overlooked, that he was the constitutional President of Mexico, and declared that his resignation would plunge the country into political chaos. He added that he might be killed, but he would not resign.

Later in the day, Mr Wilson went to the Palace, accompanied by the German Minister. Their object, he says, was "to confer with General Huerta." But, he goes on, "upon arrival, much to our regret, we were taken to see the President." Huerta was called in, however, and an armistice was agreed on. Returning to the embassy, the Ambassador sent the military attache to the arsenal to obtain, as he did, Diaz's consent to an armistice, over Sunday.

General Blanquet, with a regiment or two of men, arrived on Sunday, having taken a week to come forty miles, and it was soon apparent that they we[r]e not going into the fight.

Blanquet was betraying the President.

So also was the man whom the President had made his commander-in-chief,—Huerta.

Huerta had been in communication with Mr Wilson, by means of the confidential messenger, and an an [sic] understanding had been come to. During the armistice (ostensibly arranged for the bur[y]ing of dead bodies and the removal of non-combatants from the dznger zone), the details of the contemplated treachery were arranged, and before the close of the day Huerta sent word to Ambassador Wilson to that satisfactory effect. Mr Wilson's report to the State Department that night contained the eupheumistic words: "Huerta has sent me a special messenger saying that he expected to take steps tonight towards terminating the situation." (Sunday Feb 19)

The plot could not, for some reason, be carried out that night, but the messenger comes again on the morrow. This time, Mr Wilson takes Mr Knox a little more into his confidence: "Huerta has sent his messenger to say that I may expect some action which will remove Madero from power at any moment, and that plans were fully matured. * * * I asked no questions and made no comment beyond requesting that no lives be taken—except by due process of law."

That night the Ambassador told at least one newspaper man

that Madero would be arrested at noon on the morrow. Reporters were at the National Palace at the hour indicated (at least one of them with dispatches written in advance ready for swift filing), but they were disappointed. Nothing occured at the Palace at noon.

At the Gambrinus restaurant, however, that noon, the President's brother, Gustavo Madero, was arrested, after breakfasting with Huerta and other men, who, at the conclusion of the meal, seized him and held him a prisoner.

The plan of seizing the person of the President was delayed only an hour or so. At 2 o'clock, Mr Wilson had the satisfaction of telegraphing to the State Department: "My confidential messenger with Huerta has just come in," and reported Madero's arrest.

"My confidential messenger with Huerta," "the confidential messenger between Huerta and myself, a person by whom the President has requested me to reach him whenever I desire," (Wilson to Knox Feb. 28)—the anonymous figure which moves mysteriously in Wilson's reports and much more prominently in the true story of the Madero betrayal, was Enrique Zepeda, a notorious character who passes as the nephew and is the illigitimate son of Victoriano Huerta.

Enrique Zepeda is married to the step daughter of an American, Mr E. J. Pettegrew. Pettegrew says that on the Tuesday before the events now occuring, that is, on the first day of the battle, he and Zepeda arranged a meeting between Huerta and Diaz in an empty house in the city. If this is true, it would seem as if the whole bombardment were an elaborate fake, that the two generals understood each other all the time. Many other things point to this conclusion. It would then seem to be the case, if Pettegrew's story is true, that when Zepeda sought Mr Wilson's offices to bring the two generals together, it was not because his intervention was necessary, but because the conspirations wanted to let the Ambassador believe that he was "solving the situation" and to secure his promise of Washington's recognition of the government they were plotting to set up. However, as I cannot substantiate this point fully, I disregard it entirely in the further narrstive.

When Zepeda appeared at the embassy at 2 o'clock on the 18th, his hand was bleeding. He entered the basement, devoted to the offices of the secretaries and attaches, where were gathered a conxiderable number of people. Dr Ryan, a Red Cross surgeon, was present, and immediately set about dressing Zepeda's hand, Mr Shanklin holding it. Zepeda said: "I was shot helping arrest

Madero, but I didn't stop to have anything done, because I had promised the Ambassador that he should be the first man told when we had done it." At this indiscretion, the group of onlookers were hastily dispersed and the doors closed.

A few minutes later, as the Ambassador was talking with Mr E. S. A. de Lima, Manager of the Mexican Bank of Commerce (the Speyer bank) who was in the Embassy helping financially Americans in need of cash,—they were at the top of the stairs leading from the basement, a clerk came up and said "Mr Ambassador, Mr Zepeda says he must go off to carry a message to Deneral Diaz, but his hand is bleeding a good deal and it is a pity he cant remain quietly here."

"Oh, yes," said Mr Wilson, "he must not go out. Tell him he musn't stir. I will see that his message is delivered. Tell Mr Zepeda that I deeply appreciate all that he has done."

To break, here, a little away from the chronological arrangement of this story—One day, a month later, Zepeda was telling the story of the arrest. Mr C. A. Hamilton, an American mine owner of Oaxaca, broke in:

"If you people were going to do away with Madero, why in the world didn't you do it then, in the scuffle; it would have looked more natural."

"Why," replied Zepeda, "I had promised the Ambassador that we wouldn't kill him when we arrested him." This was on the evening of the 22nd of March at the house of J N Galbraith, in the hearing of MR Hamilton, Mr Galbraith, Consul General Shanklin, all of whom have (separately) repeated the remark to me, and of MR C R Hudson.

Here as well as anywhere, Zepeda's history may be traced a little further:

As his reward for his services as a go-between, Zepeda was given the post of Governor of the Federal District. (He had lately been expelled from the Mexico Country Club for immorality in the club house.) On Sunday, March 9th he gave an elaborate dinner to Mr Wilson and guests invited by the latter at the Chaupultepec Restaurant; on this occasion Mr Wilson made a speech so savage in its denunciation of the Maderos and so feank [frank] in its avowal of his part in the overthrow and his delight in it that one of the party said to me, "We looked at each other in dismay, and some of us turned pale."

On the night of March 26, this man Zepeda, after dining with "President" Huerta and drinking afterward with a party in Sylvain's Restaurant, went to the prison in which was confined Gabriel Hernandez, general in the Mexican army, ordered him dragged into the patio, shot to death and his body burned. Petroleum was poured over the body, a match was applied. Zepeda watched the corpse slowly consume, and then, with his companions, went to a house of prostitution, where he spent the rest of the night in unspeakably vile and cruel excesses such as he was already famous for.

"My confidential messenger with Huerta" is now in prison awaiting trial, but his release on the ground of insanity is expected.

On receipt of Zepeda's report, that Tuesday afternoon, Ambassador Wilson sent a message to Diaz at the arsenal, apprising him that the President had been arrested and that Heurta desired to confer with the rebel chieftain. It was agreed to hold the conference at the American Embassy. At 9 o'clock Huerta arrived at the embassy, and Mr Wilson sent Doctor Ryan and others, in an automobile flying the American flag, for Diaz, who duly returned with the party. Mr Wilson says the flag was not displayed on the return trip.

The leader of the mutiny, the traitorous commander-in-chief and the American Ambassador, with his translator, Luis d'Antin, spent the next three hours in conference in the smoking room of the embassy, framing up a plan for a new government to succeed that of the betrayed and imprisoned President. Diaz pressed his claims for the chief office, on the ground that he had fought the battle. But Huerta's claims were stronger, for, in truth, if he had not turned traitor, the revolt could not have succeeded. Three times they were on the verge of parting in anger, says the Ambassador, but his labors kept them together and finally worked out what was represented as a compromise: Huerta was to go in as Provisional President, but was to call an election and to support Diaz for the permanent presidency. A cabinet was agreed on, the Ambassador taking a leading part in this matter. He, for instance, put his veto on the naming of Vera Estañol as Minister of Foreign Relations, but consented to his going in as Minister of Education. When Zepeda was named for the governorship of the Federal District, the interpreter made a gesture of disgust, but was reproved by Mr Wilson. The Ambassador says he stipulated for the release of Madero's ministers. He made no stipulation concerning the President and Vice President.

That night, within an hour of the adjournment of the conference at the embassy, Gustavo Madero, the President's brother, was driven into an empty lot just outside the arsenal, his body riddled with bullets and thrown into a hole in the ground.

On the following day, Francisco Madero, in imprisonment and threatened with death, at the pleading of his wife and mother, and, as she said, to save their lives, not his own, signed his resignation. Vice President Pino Suarez did the same.

The arrangement was that the resignations were to be placed in the hands of the Chilean and Cuban ministers for delivery only after the two retiring officials and their families were safely out of the country. It seems however, to have been necessary for the documents to receive the authentication of the head of the cabinet, the Minister of Foreign Relations, and, while they were passing through his hands, such pressure was brought to bear upon Mr Lasdarain that he delivered the resignations directly and immediately into the hands of Madero's enemies.

Madero and Pino Suarez, however, had been promised release and safe-conduct for themselves and their families, out of the country. Mr Wilson tells me that he had been consulted by Huerta as to the best mwthod of dealing with Madero—in particular, as to whether it would be better to deport Madero, or put him into an insane asylum. "I declined to express a preference," says the Ambassador. All I said was: 'General, do what you think is best for the welfare of Mexico.'" Huerta decided, or pretended to decide, on deportation.

A train stood ready at the Mexican Railway station, to take Madero and Pino Suarez with their families down to Vera Cruz, where they were to go on board the Cuban gun-boat *Cuba* and be conveyed to a foreign shore. By nine o'clock the families, hurriedly prepared for departure, were gatherdd, waiting, on the platform. The Chilean and Cuban Ministers, who had spent the day with Madero, had announced their intention of accompanying the party down to the port, and they appeared at the station, announcing that the President and Vice President would soon follow. They did not come. About midnight the Chilean Minister left the distressed women, hurried to the Palace, and asked to see General Huerta. The General sent out word that he was very tired after a hard day's work and was resting; he would see the Minister later. Mr Riquelme waited until 2 o'clock and was still refused admittance to Huerta. He could do nothing but return to the station and advise the party to return to their homes.

In the morning it was explained that the military commandant of the port of Vera Cruz had received telegrams from Mrs Madero which had led him to reply unsatisfactorily to Huerta's instructions. The commandante is said to have replied: "By whose authority? I recognize only the authority of the constitutional President of Mexico, Francisco I Madero." It is the belief of the

Maderistas, however, that it was the decision of the Chilean and Cuban ministers to accompany the party that forbade the departure of the train, the plan having been to blow it up on the way down.

The wife and mother of Madero and relatives of Pino Suarez, relieved to learn that the men were still alive but fearing the worst, now appealed to the American Ambassador to grant the threatened men asylum in the embassy. He had opened it for a meeting-place of the plotting traitors, but he could not see his way to open it for their victims. Instead, Mr Wilson recommended that they be transferred to more comfortable quarters—from the Palace to the penitentiary. It is commonly understood that the women asked Mr Wilson to transmit in American State Department cipher a message to the President of the United States, appealing for his influence toward saving the lives of the men. Of this and another incident which nevertheless I think it well to mention, I have no proof:

It is emphatically stated to me by the leader of the Madero sympathizers in the city, Serapio Rendon, that on the 20th the American Ambassador received instructions from the State Department at Washington to inform General Huerta that improper treatment of the deposed President or Vice President would, in the opinion of the United States Government, have a most unfortunate effect, and that the Ambassador failed to communicate this message. I have no evidence that the charge is true, but Sr Rendon's averment is so positively made that the matter merits investigation.

General Huerta assumed the presidency on the 20th, carefully observing certain formalities which are held to establish the legality of his rule. The Presi[d]ent and Vice President having resigned, Madero's Minister of Foreign Relations was recognized as President for the few minutes necessary for him to appoint Victoriano Huerta Minister of Gobernation, and to resign, leaving Huerta to succeed, according to the Constitution, to the presidency.

On the 21st the American Ambassador telegraphed Secretary Knox that he would recognize the govdrnment thus set up and that he had already instructed all American consuls in the country to "urge general submission and adherence to the new government, which will be recognized by all foreign governments to-day."

The Ambassador appears to have received instructions from Mr Knox not to accord this precipitate recognition, for later in the day he telegraphs that he had had an interview with the new minister of foreign relations, Mr de la Barra, and trusts he has accomplished what the Department had in view, though he did "not resort to the refusal of full recognition."

(A reading of Mr Wilson's dispatches to the Department during the next month shows him making reports of the progress of the new government and the submission to it of all parts of the country which are so exactly opposed to the truth as to be beyond all understanding. The fact is that from the moment of Huerta's accession the country began to fall rapidly under the sway of rebellion. Today Huerta is in control of less than half the country.)

The next day was Washington's Birthday. In the morning the Ambassador and the new Minister of Foreign Relations engaged in mutual felicitations before a crowd assembled at the Washington monument; after leaving wreaths on it, a march was made to the Juarez monument, where wreaths were also left. In the late afternoon, Mr Wilson received at the embassy. The reception was attended by Huerta, Diaz, Mondragon and others of the new regime. Huerta and Wilson disappeared from the throng, and I have the authority of the Chilean Minister for the statement that Huerta and Wilson were engaged in conversation in the smoking-room, for an hour and half—during which time the Chilean Minister waited, having occasion to speak to Mr Wilson. The Ambassador omits any mention of February 22 as one of the only dates in which he reports to Mr Bryan (his long report of March 12) he had verbal or written communication with Huerta. The Chilean Minister may have been mistaken. If he be right, we have Huerta and Wilson in conference up to 7 o'clock P.M.

At 9 o'clock, the warden of the penitentiary, was visited by Col. Luis Vallestores with an order directing that the warden turn over the command of the prison to him. The retiring warden went to his home in the automobile that had brought his successor.

Very close upon the stroke of 12: that night, Francisco I. Madero and José Maria Piño Suarez were murdered. Ambassador Wilson reported to Washington the following morning that, as nearly as he could ascertain, they were killed as a result of an attempt at rescue as they were being transferred from the National Palace to the penitentiary. "I had recommended their transfer to more comfortable quarters," he explained. The story of the attempted rescue was abandoned almost as soon as it was put out. Resort to the "ley fuga," with its legend against the names of victims "killed while attempting to escape," has been a favorite method for centuries in Spanish countries, but it has neven been pretended as more than a convenient fiction.

As a matter of fact, Madero and Piño Suarez were put into two automobiles, one in each, at the Palace at 11:45, and were driven in the direction of the penitentiary, escorted by a dozen men, under the command of Major Francisco Cardenas. Cardenas, a particular comrade and henchman of Huerta, had reached the city only at 9:o'clock that night, coming from Manzanillo. The party did not go to the door of the penitentiary, but passed the street leading to it and went on to a vacant space back of the building. Here the automobile stopped. What occurred next will probably never be known exactly. According to the best evidence I have been able to gather, Piño Suarez was hauled out and shot. Then came the turn of Madero. A single bullet, in the back of the head, was his portion. The hair was singed. When the body was prepared for burial, a bruise was noticed in the forehead; it may have been the result of his fall after the fatal shot or a blow by the pistol butt before it. The murderous band, their work done, swiftly disappeared. One of the automobiles had run off, the frightened driver never stopping for a shower of bullets. Soon afterward, a peon named——, with one companion, obscure prisoners, were sent by the new warden to bring the bodies in.——took from the pockets of the dead Vice-President a number of articles, which I have handled:

A sheet of paper bearing what is apparently a cipher code; a Kansas City, Mexico and Orient Railroad pass, No. 350; a Wells-Fargo Express frank, No. 3; an occulist's and an optician's prescription, and a draft, dated Mexico City 19 February, for $2000.00 U.S. Cy., in favor of Sr. Jose Maria Piño Suarez, signed by Salvador Madero y Cia. and addressed to Sr. Ed. Maurer, 80, Maiden Lane, New York City.

In the early morning, passers-by piled stones in a little mound over the two blood-soaked spots of ground and stuck lighted candles on top.

For several days following the assasination, Huerta and his Minister of Foreign Relations talked much of investigation. No investigation has been made. No investigation is under way. Major Cardenas was put under arrest, but was soon released, and promoted Lieutenant Colonel. He is now commanding rurales in Michoacan. Only the day before this paragraph is written, he figured in the papers as having shot a prisoner in cold bold [blood].

Mr. Wilson has never made any demand for an investigation. In conversation with me, he exhibits no appreciation whatever of the nature of the deed done the night of February 22nd, after the entire group of men responsible for it had been guests at his house, no suspicion that any responsibility rested upon himself, who, in a sober view of the past, might be said to have delivered the men to death. Mr. Wilson bitterly vituperated Madero and his family, in conversation with me. He exhibits pride in the fact that he had consistently predicted Madero's fall. In reply to my question whether he thought he was in a proper diplomatic attitude in presiding at a conference of two revolting generals and in helping arrange the details of a new Presidency, when the constitutional President, to whom he was accredited, was held prisoner, the Ambassador replied that it was necessary for the good of Mexico that Madero be eliminated. To my question as to the responsibility for the death of Madero and Piño Suarez, Mr. Wilson said he took the ground that they were private citizens when they died, and that it would be an impertinence for a foreign power to demand an investigation into a purely domestic matter. He went on, with considerable violence, to say that Madero had killed hundreds illegally, and it was no concern of his how the man died. "In fact, the person really responsible for Madero's death was his wife. She was the one to blame. Madero had to be eliminated. By her telegram to Veracruz, she made it impossible to allow him to leave the Capital."

The above account of affairs in Mexico is made from the position that the movement against Madero was a conspiracy and not a popular revolution—a cuartelazo, a mili[t]ary coup, the plot of a few and not the uprising of an outraged people; & that the betrayal of the President by his generals was mercenary treachery and was not in the slightest degree a response to the sentiments of a nation, or even of the city.

I have no reason to doubt—in fact, I believe—that Ambassador Wilson was sincere in this opposite view. He undoubtedly thought that the good of the country demanded the overthrow of Madero. He had come to regard him as a Nero. Taking that view, a great deal can be said in justification of many of Mr. Wilson's acts and in extenuation of others. Taking that view, it is possible to tell the story in a very different tone, with very different accents. Indeed, there are probably omitted in this necessarily hurried story, a number of incidents that in fairness ought to be told, on any theory.

Mr. Wilson, it is fair to say, talks freely and with every appearance of candor of his part in the drama, and gives evidence in every sentence that he believes it to have been the only part humanity and patriotism (alike from the standpoint of Mexico and the United States) allowed him to play. He is evidently surprised and deeply disappointed that it is not so recognized by all. He is plainly puzzled that the country at large has repudiated the revolution, which he holds was undertaken and carried through in its behalf; deeply chagrined that it did not bring about peace.

History will probably place the responsibility for the murder of Madero elsewhere than on the shoulders of his faithful wife. Nevertheless, curious as is this illustration of the length to which an initial error can carry its victim, it is, in my judgment, absurd to picture Mr. Wilson as a malicious plotter. The worse that can truthfully be said is that, being a man of intense prejudices, he was so blinded by his hatred of Madero that he honestly mistook it for the hatred of the whole Mexican people, his own conviction for the verdict of the nation. None the less, however sincere may have been his motives, it is impossible not to conclude that Mr. Wilson's course was utterly mistaken, mischievous and tragically unhappy in its results.

It is hardly a matter of conjecture—it is a conclusion to which all facts point—that without the countenance of the American Ambassador given to Huerta's proposal to betray the President, the revolt would have failed. On Monday the 17th, the last day of the fighting, Madero was in undisputed possession of the entire city, except the arsenal and three or four houses near it still held as outposts. The mutineers had ventured on no sorties, and nothing whatever in the way of sympathy with them had appeared in any part of the city. The people had refused to rise. No sympathetic uprisings had occurred in the country. The Zapatistas, banditti long in possession of the State of Morelos and the mountains surrounding the city, had not come in, though Ambassador Wilson had daily telegraphed to Washington that they were coming. Instead, Zapata had sent word to Madero that they would suspend operations against the Federal Government until it had disposed of Felix Diaz. In brief, it was now, after a week, definitely ascertained that the Government had to do with nothing more than a single group of a few hundred men, surrounded and confined in a fort, the reduction of which was only a matter of time.

There was not a moment during the "Decena Tragica" when it would not have been possible to "end the distressing situation," "put a stop to this unnecessary bloodshed" by stern warning from the American Embassy to the traitorous army officers that the United States would countenance no methods but peaceful constitutional ones and recognize no government set up by force. President Madero was not betrayed and arrested by his officers until it had been ascertained that the American Ambassador had no objection to the performance. The plan for the immediate setting [up] of a military dictatorship would never have been formed except in the American Embassy, under the patronage of the American Ambassador, and with his promise of his Government's prompt recognition. Madero would never have been assasinated had the American Ambassador made it thoroughly understood that the plot must stop short of murder.

It cannot but be a course of grief that what is probably the most dramatic story in which an American diplomatic officer has ever been involved, should be a story of sympathy with treason, perfidy and assasination in an assault on constitutional government.

And it is particularly unfortunate that this should have taken place in a leading country of Latin America, where, if we have any moral work to do, it is to discourage violence and uphold law.

Trifling, perhaps, in the sum of miseries that have flowed from it, yet not without importance in a way, is the fact that thousands of Mexicans believe that the Ambassador acted on instructions from Washington and look upon his retention under the new American President as a mark of approval and blame the United States Government for the chaos into which the country has fallen.   Wm. Bayard Hale

T MS (SDR, RG 59, 812.00/7798 1/2, DNA).

To William Jennings Bryan

My dear Mr. Secretary: The White House June 19, 1913
    The proposed Nicaraguan treaty has my entire approval and I sincerely hope that the Senate may approve it, as well as our friends, the Nicaraguan government. I have read it very carefully.   Cordially and faithfully yours,   Woodrow Wilson

TLS (W. J. Bryan Papers, DNA).

To Francis Patrick Walsh

[The White House] June 20, 1913
    Would you be willing to serve as chairman of the Commission on Industrial Relations which I am about to appoint?
                                        Woodrow Wilson.

TLS (Letterpress Books, WP, DLC).

From Francis Patrick Walsh

Kansas City, Missouri, June 20, 1913.

With great pleasure I would be willing to serve as Chairman of the Commission of Industrial Relations. Deem it a high honor that you should think of me in this connection.

Frank P. Walsh.

T telegram (WP, DLC).

From William Jennings Bryan

My dear Mr. President: Washington June 20, 1913.

I sent you a few days ago a suggestion in regard to the purchase of the Mole St. Nicholas in Haiti. As Governor Osborn will leave Monday, I think he ought to have some general instructions as to his course of procedure.

If you will refer to my letter, you will see that it covered three points: First, the size of the concession that we should ask. I suggested a strip of land twenty miles wide, measured from the center of the mouth of the harbor, the strip to run back to a point ten miles beyond the eastern limit of the harbor so as to give us not only the harbor but enough land around it to safeguard the harbor from land attack. The second suggestion was that we assure the Haitian Government that those desiring to remain on this strip could become American citizens and that those not desiring to remain upon the strip could sell their property to this Government at its market value.

If you will give me your views upon this subject and upon any other subjects which occur to you, I should be glad to bring them to the attention of Governor Osborn so that he may be the better qualified to act when he arrives there.

I am glad that you are willing to name ex-Congressman Smith,[1] of Missouri, as minister, and I am asking whether his appointment will be acceptable so that we can make the change as soon as possible.

With assurances of respect, etc., I am, my dear Mr. President,

Very truly yours,   W. J. Bryan

TLS (WP, DLC).
[1] Madison Roswell Smith, lawyer of St. Louis; congressman, 1907-1909; Minister to Haiti, 1913-14.

Charles Henry Grasty to Joseph Patrick Tumulty

My dear Mr. Tumulty: Baltimore, Md. June 20, 1913.

We had a very satisfactory visit to the President yesterday. I was glad that we could have time enough for a discussion of the questions that were troubling us. The trustees of the University here had practically agreed on Mr. Buckler for president and I suggested that before that action was taken the President be consulted again.[1] He renewed his suggestion of Dr. Fine of Princeton upon whom the trustees had not been able to agree. In line with the President's suggestion, I am going to send Harry West to Princeton to write an article on Dr. Fine's record there.

I was deeply interested in what you told me yesterday. If we can do anything for the cause command us. I am leaving for Europe by the Imperator next Wednesday but can be reached any time as I will be in daily cable communication with The Sun office.   Sincerely yours,   Charles H Grasty

TLS (WP, DLC).
[1] William Hepburn Buckler was offered the presidency but declined it. The office remained vacant until February 1914, when it was offered to and accepted by Frank Johnson Goodnow, Eaton Professor of Administrative Law and Municipal Science at Columbia University.

To Walter Hines Page

My dear Page: The White House June 21, 1913

It was both kind and thoughtful of you to send me the little personal note you wrote on June eighth. I have read it with the greatest pleasure, not merely as a report of your happy reception in London, but also as a message from my friend who is now the Ambassador of the United States at London. I am very well, I am happy to say, pegging away at a task which would tax any man's strength, but I am cheered every day by the assistance of men like yourself.

In haste, with warmest regard,
                    Faithfully yours,   Woodrow Wilson

TLS (W. H. Page Papers, MH).

From William Jennings Bryan

My Dear Mr President   [Washington, June 21, 1913]

I enclose an interview which I prepared after talking with Mr Tumulty. Please make such corrections as you think best— striking out or adding & send to my house by messenger if you think it best to give it out tomorrow afternoon for Monday morning.[1] I have tried to make it to suit those Democrats who are friendly to me, hence the emphasis on government issues & govt control. Others will emphasis some of the other features, but as my object is to help you pass the bill I invite your frank criticism[.] With assurances etc   Yours truly   W. J. Bryan

I shall go to the House when you read the message—I have already read it with cordial approval

ALS (WP, DLC).
[1] Bryan's statement heartily endorsing the Federal Reserve bill was given to the press on June 22 and published in full, *inter alia*, in the *New York Times*, June 23, 1913.

To William Jennings Bryan

My dear Mr. Bryan,   The White House [June 21, 1913].
    It is excellent and I thank you with all my heart! I hope you will give it out for Monday.   Woodrow Wilson

ALS (W. J. Bryan Papers, DLC).

To Mary Allen Hulbert

Dearest Friend,   The White House 22 June, 1913.
    It was a great delight to hear from you, but not that you were ill and had defied the doctor, with the usual result, that you had used up your vitality utterly and could only lie like an invalid and look out of the windows to forget the house you have just set in order and catch some refreshment from the sea and the hills. I know how especially hard it must have been to go back to Nantucket this time and handle all the things that dear Mrs. Allen laid away with those tireless faithful hands of hers and her sweet zeal to save you all the trouble possible! There must have been an all but intolerable ache at your heart! I wish that at this distance there were some way to govern and divert your thoughts,—or some hypnotism we could exercise over you to make you take care of yourself and seek only the things in that lively mind of yours that relieve the strain. If some one of us could only drop you a few lines every day, be your daily companion, and *play* to you as we would wish to, perhaps we could manage you. As it is, we can hardly manage ourselves! I think that when we get through with this extraordinary experience we are going through here we will hardly know what it is to have a life and a choice of our own, seek our friends as we please, and cultivate

our own souls. It seems to grow more and more absorbing. I
seem to have less and less time that I can call, even by courtesy,
my own. Now it is the currency I have tackled. Not an hour can
I let it out of my mind. Everybody must be seen: every right
means be used to direct the thought and purpose of those who are
to deal with it and of those who, outside of Washington, are to
criticise it and form public opinion about it. It is not like the
tariff, about which opinion has been definitely forming long years
through. There are almost as many judgments as there are men.
To form a single plan and a single intention about it seems at
times a task so various and so elusive that it is hard to keep one's
heart from failing. Fortunately my heart has formed no habit
of failing. The last thing I ever think of doing is giving up. But,
among other things, this business means that I am to have no
vacation. On Friday next I shall, if I can possibly run away, accompany the family up to Cornish, staying, if Congress itself
adjourns long enough, over the fourth of July. But then I come
back for the long pull alone. I may be able to run up for a week
end at long intervals (at any rate they will seem endlessly long!),
but only if the way things are going make it wise and perfectly
safe. I could not stand the additional anxiety of seeing this heat
wilt my dear ones. I am not affected by it as Ellen is. I seem a
thorough-going Southerner. I have never tried a summer here,
of course, where summers are said to be especially fierce; but I
have tried them further South and feel sure of myself. I may get
cross (which would be a pity and a bit risky in the circumstances), but I shall not get ill. And that trip I had promised
myself to Panama now seems only too likely to fade utterly away.
My present guess is that Congress will not adjourn before the
first of October. My hope is that I can at least systematize my
pleasure as well as my business and get regular times off to play
golf or to go cruising down the river on the craft that are happily at the disposal of the President for an occasional outing.
And on Sundays I can sit down, may I not? for a chat with my
friend at Nantucket, and we may gossip about the several forms
of loneliness and the various prescriptions and forms of treatment we have heard of and tried. It will be amusing, if not helpful. And the jolly thing we have always found about one another
is, that nothing is easier than for either one of us to see, upon
the merest hint, how the other is affected by any particular
circumstance or situation, to know what will be real remedies for
real trains of thought and periods of anxiety. Think out things
for me, please madam, and I will try to do the same for you, and
we will carry on the jolliest and most profitable commerce in

notions and rallyings and suggestions that can be imagined. Neither of us can then boast to the other how lonely he (or she) is. We s[h]all simply address ourselves to the task of making it as bearable and as amusing for the other as possible. Is it a bargain?

All join me in most affectionate messages, and I am, as always and "ez a constancy"

Your devoted friend,   Woodrow Wilson

WWTLS (WP, DLC).

To Allen Schoolcraft Hulbert

My dear Allen,   The White House 22 June, 1913.

I was really distressed that I was obliged to let you get away without sitting down and having a real talk with you; and ever since you left I have had it in mind to send you the line which I am only just now able to find the time to write. You will have many opportunities in prosecuting the business you are in now to pick up the opinion of men, both those who are thoughtful and those who are not and only repeat that which they pick out from the impressions of the moment, about public affairs, about the things proposed and the things done. I wonder if you could not occasionally drop me a few lines telling me what you hear? It it [is] tremendously hard here to get the thoughts of the country as distinguished from the thoughts of Washington, and you can do me a real service if you will. I hope you will find it interesting and amusing, even, and not a burden or a bore.

I hope that you are well and that things are going well with you. I need not tell you how sincerely interested I am in everything that affects your welfare and your happiness.

With best regards,

Cordially and faithfully,   Woodrow Wilson

TLS (WC, NjP).

To William Jennings Bryan

My dear Mr. Secretary: The White House June 23, 1913

I should have covered the points about the Mole St. Nicholas more fully and explicitly than I did in my previous letter. I fully concur in the three suggestions you make: first, that the size of the concession that we should ask should be a strip of land twenty miles wide, measured from the center of the mouth of the harbor, the strip to run back to a point ten miles beyond the eastern limit of the harbor; second, that we assure the Haitian government that those desiring to remain on this strip should become American citizens and that those not desiring to remain upon the strip could sell their property to this government at its market value.

Cordially and faithfully yours,   Woodrow Wilson

TLS (W. J. Bryan Papers, DNA).

A Statement on Signing the Sundry Civil Bill

[June 23, 1913]

I have signed this bill because I can do so without in fact limiting the opportunity or the power of the Department of Justice to prosecute violations of the law, by whomsoever committed.

If I could have separated from the rest of the bill the item which authorized the expenditure by the Department of Justice of a special sum of three hundred thousand dollars for the prosecution of violations of the anti-trust law, I would have vetoed that item, because it places upon the expenditure a limitation which is in my opinion, unjustifiable in character and principle. But I could not separate it. I do not understand that the limitation was intended as either an amendment or an interpretation of the anti-trust law, but merely as an expression of the opinion of the Congress,—a very emphatic opinion, backed by an overwhelming majority of the House of Representatives and a large majority of the Senate, but not intended to touch anything but the expenditure of a single small additional fund.

I can assure the country that this item will neither limit nor in any way embarrass the actions of the Department of Justice. Other appropriations supply the Department with abundant funds to enforce the law. The law will be interpreted, in the determination of what the Department should do, by independent and I hope impartial judgments as to the true and just meaning of substantive statutes of the United States.[1]

T MS (WP, DLC).
[1] There is an undated WWsh draft; a WWT draft; and a CLST draft with WWhw emendations in WP, DLC.

Remarks at a Press Conference

June 23, 1913

Mr. President, just to start off, I wonder whether you are ready to tell us anything in answer to the criticisms of the proposal to make a purely governmental board in command of the currency situation. You don't say anything about that in your message.

No, I don't say anything about that, because I didn't want to discuss the terms of the measure. I simply wanted to urge the necessity for action by Congress. I don't want to be quoted on this, but I want to give it to you men for your own thought: There are only two choices, of course: either to give the central control to the bankers or to give it to the government. I don't see any other.

Isn't there a middle ground?

Do you mean to give it to both?

Yes, with representation of the banks.

Yes, there is, but it seems to me that is not decisive. We ought to make it a clean choice. My own feeling is that governmental control is perfectly safe. I can't imagine anybody audacious enough in a political office to play politics to that extent.

We have had some.

Yes, we have, but we have never tried them out on that line. I can only reason from comparatively small things. For example, in New Jersey the governor appoints all the judges. Now, no governor—the worst governor we have had, and we have had some pretty bad ones—has ever dared to play with the Supreme Court and the Court of Errors and Appeals. We have had a uniform quality of judges, with a very far from uniform quality of governors in New Jersey. That is because justice touches the whole community; the minute you play politics with that, the whole community knows it, and the party who dares to do it would be "chucked" and "chucked" forever—and would deserve it. I can't imagine a man even acting upon small grounds of expediency—he is a man without principle. I can't imagine anyone playing with that, because, you see, the banking system of the country will literally touch everybody.

Well, Mr. President, I was not thinking so much, and I don't think all the critics are thinking so much, of playing politics—to use that expression—with the appointments as the fact of the tremendous domination of the President at all times, through his ability to change his cabinet; and we may have a President whose views on the subject of—well, inflation, to put it roughly—were very extreme one way or the other. The fixing of a discount rate, and controlling the issue of these treasury notes, entirely apart from politics, is a mere matter of economic theory, and his power would be enormous, and there is apparently no check upon it.

You see, there is the same extreme difference among economists as to the theory of inflation. For example, there is one school of economists, and very sober, thoughtful men they are, though I utterly disagree with them, which maintains that the credit could be inflated—I mean the issue could be inflated—so long as it is no bigger than the liquid credits of the country. Of course, the fallacy there lies in what is back of the liquid credits. The minute you get beyond definite assets and bills of lading and all the other things that are extremely definite—your hopefulness of what you are going to do—then you get to not only liquid credits, but to what I should call fluid credits. The line is a line of judgment.

Mr. President, in that bill the board has the power to apportion the five hundred million dollars of the emergency currency.[1] There is nothing in that that will prevent them from giving that five hundred million to one regional bank.

I have heard that interpretation put upon it before, but I can't see it. It hasn't the power to apportion in the sense of all of it shall go here and none of it there, because the only power it has is to judge whether the credits offered are legal and sound. And any member of the regional association has the right with a certain kind of paper to call for these notes, and there must be some very special reason of unsoundness why they should not get them.

But if the full five hundred million dollars have been given to one regional bank on whatever assets are required, then there is no more of that for any other bank.

That raises the question whether five hundred millions is enough or not. That is all that it raises. And one has to admit at once that it is a perfectly arbitrary limit. It is a guess. It isn't a mere guess; it is a guess based upon the statistics. For example, in the last panic, the statistics of clearinghouse certificates—I am very poor at remembering figures, but my memory is that those certificates rose to 260 millions, but they didn't rise to anything like the level of five hundred millions. Of course, it is a debatable question as to whether that rigid limit should be set or not. I quite admit that, but, aside from the supposition that that may be all taken up in one part of the country, I don't see any danger of any power of discrimination between one section of the country and another.

Only with the fixed limit.

The fixed limit—that is a conceivable outcome.

[1] That is, new Federal Reserve currency.

Mr. President, is this intended to be a permanent law? I mean permanent in the sense of not being amended in your administration.

Oh, well, that would depend upon how it worked.

I ask you that because in the original bill, as it was drawn, there was a provision for retiring the present bond-secured currency.[2] Now that has all been stricken out.

Now, I want to explain to you gentlemen why it was stricken out; because I am giving you the benefit of all I know this morning, without desiring this to be a public discussion at all. All that the present bill provides for is additional currency. Let us leave out the gold certificates and the circulation now that isn't based upon the banks and think only of the bank issues. As I remember, there are 712 million based upon 2 per cent bonds. Now, in the case of those 2 per cent bonds of that issue, the government has no control under this bill—that is the permanent bank issue—and it remains at the same volume, no matter what the volume of business may be. The banks are making 2 per cent on the bonds, or a little less than that if they bought them at a premium, or, in addition to that, anything that they may be able to get on the currency that they lend, based upon those bonds. Now, what we are doing with this bill is to say that if the 712 millions are not enough, then additional treasury notes shall be issued upon such and such terms, to a sum not exceeding five hundred millions; but in respect of that issue the central board can determine the terms of discount and control the volume by the amount of discount, and have a general power which will enable them to see to it that these notes come in again after they have done the temporary work to which they have been assigned. In the last examination of the bill as it originally stood, we saw this: If you provide for the retirement of the 2 per cents—I mean for the refunding of the 2 per cents—and base this same kind of currency on it, you are reducing the volume of the permanent currency below the 712 millions, and, therefore, just so fast as that reduction occurs, you are making all the currency emergency currency, because you are putting it all under the control of this central board—all the rates of discount and all the general terms and arrangements made by them—unless you go to work, as the framers of this bill had not gone to work, to make another body of currency based upon the new arrangements after the 2 per cents are

2 That is, national bank notes.

gone, which would be a permanent volume and not subject
to exactly the same regulations as this emergency currency.
Do I make myself clear? In other words, we hadn't provided
the machinery by which a perfect substitution could be
made below the 712 million limit; and rather than work the
bill out with great elaboration so as to make those distinctions, we thought it best to segregate that and regard it as
a separate thing, to be treated independently.

Mr. President, when the bill creating a national bank currency
was enacted, wasn't that intended to be a sort of an emergency
currency—that is, a currency that would fluctuate in volume?

  . 	Well, I don't remember that it was. Of course, that was the
original law. It was away back just after the Civil War,
and the main object of the bill was to create a market for
the bonds of the United States.

Reading the discussions of that time, I find it was said it would
make an elastic currency, a currency that would expand or contract according to the needs of the country. But it expanded as
far as it could and stopped.

  	I can't imagine anybody saying that who knows the
processes of banking, because, you see, in order to lessen
the volume of that currency you would have to sell your
bonds or else merely arbitrarily withdraw your circulation.

Well, the argument was that a time would come when the income
from that issue would not be sufficient to warrant the bankers
to keep in it.

  	Well, that time has come now, if it ever was to come, be-
cause it couldn't very well sink below 2 per cent.

Mr. President, is this bill to be regarded as the administration bill,
or will it be subject to change—acceptable change?

  	Well, it is regarded as the administration bill in exactly the
same sense as I hope the Underwood tariff bill will be.

In general principle subject to—

  	Of course, there are details which may have to be recast. I
think the general principles are thoroughly defensible.

In the tariff bill, Mr. President, there will be certain sections of
the bill which will not be subject to compromise. Is that so with
regard to the currency bill?

  	I should think so; there are certain points built on definite
principle.

Do you regard the manner of the selection of the central board
of control as one of those principles?

  	I don't think I had better discuss that before discussion in
Congress, because I don't want to seem for a moment to shut

the doors of consideration, so far as I am concerned, on anything that is reasonable to discuss.

But it would be reasonable, would it not, Mr. President, to say that one of the principles that you feel that you would adhere to is that the government, rather than the bankers themselves, should be the dominating factor in control?

Yes, undoubtedly.

Mr. President, in that bill as originally drawn there was a provision of one-third representation of the banks on this federal board. Now the banks are compelled by this act to invest 20 per cent of their capital stock, which isn't their money but the money of their stockholders—10 paid in and a liability of 10 per cent. Now, under this bill as it was changed the banks are given no right to say what shall be done with their money that they have invested themselves, and that is the thing I think some of us were somewhat mystified about.

I don't see that, because what is done with their moneys is determined in the regional banks. The regional banks do not have to rediscount if they do not approve of the paper.

Yes, but the ultimate control is held by this Federal Reserve Board.

Yes, in a general way it is. It is regulative. It isn't a business regulation; it is a prudential regulation.

Mr. President, doesn't it say that the federal board may require these regional banks to rediscount for each other?

For each other, but not for individual banks.

But there is a varying discretion in the different regions which might make one bank very reluctant to look out for another.

That seems farfetched, because what we are trying to do is to mobilize the reserves and make all the resources of the country available, so far as possible, to every part of it. Because one of the things that we are most bent upon correcting is the present concentration of reserves and control by the discretion of a single group of bankers or by a locality of banking interests.

What makes it desirable for this central board of control to fix the discount rate? Then is the regional board itself to do that?

No, sir, the control ought to be a general control, in view of the possibility of inflation. There ought to be some authority that has a general view of what is going on in the country.

Is it safe to exercise that authority without the presence on the board of bankers?

I think it is safe, of course; that is a matter of judgment. I

don't see where we would get any better judgment from a
large number of bankers. All we need is expert advice.
I don't know anything about the question myself, but I see that
raised in the financial and commercial papers.

You see, I have this sort of feeling: A banker is in touch with
the bank of his region and has the point of view of the
banking of his region, but the minute he gets the general
—national—point of view, he really detaches himself and
ceases to be a banker.
Mr. President, the central board has no authority to fix the discount rate unless there is some emergency currency in circulation?

If none of the five hundred million is out.
Then it depends upon the general banks.

Then it depends upon the general banks of the country.
But it would ultimately fall upon the regional banks, because
they fix the rediscount rates.

Yes, so far as the paper was rediscounted, but the individual banks would have their individual issue as now up to the
bond limit and would be just as free as they are now.
Would it be correct, Mr. President, to interpret your view as
regarding this Federal Reserve Board in the same way that you
would the Interstate Commerce Commission in reference to
putting railroad men on the Interstate Commerce Commission?

Yes, I feel that there will be, when this bill is adopted, just
the same sort of change of opinion as there was about the
Interstate Commerce Commission and the public utility
boards of the states, etc. They were vigorously opposed on
very much such misgivings as are being presented just now
about this central control; with the result that at last they
were more than welcomed, because they, so to say, guaranteed the operations all along in a public way, in a way that
meant the representation of no single interest or group of
interests. I think that in the long run the bankers themselves
will be glad of this control—this direction over which they
have no control.[3]

T MS (C. L. Swem Coll., NjP).
[3] Wilson's remarks were paraphrased in a long news story in, *inter alia*, the
New York Times, June 24, 1913.

An Interview on the Banking and Currency Bill[1]

[June 23, 1913]

"I have asked congress to reform our banking and currency system at this session because of my realization of the imperative need of such action."

Woodrow Wilson, President of the United States, made this statement today to the Correspondent of the Chicago Tribune. The President received me in his office with the understanding that I was to quote him, in order that the people might obtain directly from his lips an expression of the reasons which induced him to advocate legislation now and which are responsible for his advocacy of the fundamental principles underlying the bill about to be introduced in congress.

"Our country," continued the President, "is in the dawn of a new era, an era in which an awake and intelligent people will move to realize ideals too long neglected, to perform duties too long disregarded, and to eliminate evils too long tolerated. The questions which confront us are not partisan, but national. They involve the great fundamental principles of right and justice which must be applied in every department of our national life. These principles must be established as standards of action in all our relations. Through them we will achieve that ethical development which is essential to the vitality of a free republic, create a better business system, equitable and open to the average man, under which living conditions will be made more practicable and working conditions more tolerable, and provide a fiscal system free from the greed of special privilege and private control and based upon equal and exact opportunity.

"We have taken the first step toward the realization of these principles in the tariff bill now pending in the senate. That measure strikes at the very root of special privilege not only in the adjustment of rates more in keeping with the needs of the people but in its annihilation of the system of favoritism which has benefited the rich and influential manufacturers of the country at the expense of the people. Following the enactment of that law, our business men must act to meet the changed legal conditions. Then will come expansion and new enterprise caused by the removal of the shackles which have fettered their freedom in the past."

[1] By John Callan O'Laughlin, Washington correspondent of the *Chicago Tribune*, who sent the following interview to Tumulty on June 26, 1913, for Wilson's approval. The "interview," which was not published, was actually a version of Wilson's remarks at the press conference of June 23 and Wilson's address to Congress.

The President paused and reflected for a moment. It was evident from his manner that when he said in his recent message that the proposed tariff law would emancipate business, he was not seeking for political effect but was uttering a deep conviction. It became also evident as he proceeded that he has considered profoundly the economic problems which must be solved in order to provide business with modern "tools of action," to quote the words used in his message.

"We are about to give the deathblow to the tariff monopoly," he resumed, "but we profit nothing thereby if the credit monopoly remain. It is not enough to say: 'Opportunity to engage in business is now equal,' if we do not at the same time say: 'opportunity to get credit now is equal.' There exists an alliance between the business of special privilege and credit which will enable the former to dominate in the future as in the past unless—and mark what I say—unless we free credit as we are about to free business. The dangerous centralization of control of credit places out of the reach of the many our old variety and freedom and individual energy of development. It has placed in the hands of a few men the power to direct our industrial growth, to promote enterprises in which they are interested and from which they will profit, to the exclusion of others in which they are not interested and from which they will draw no profit. That power enables them to precipitate a bankers' panic, as was the case in 1907, and to produce financial chaos through the release of the jinni in the bottle they hold. And it also effects the checking and limitation of enterprise, the numbing of individual initiative, the paralysis of thousands upon thousands of legitimate ventures the success of which would aid the prosperity of the nation through the diffusion of prosperity and the development of things the people need."

I asked the President to describe the remedy he believes will cure this evil.

"I summed up the situation in my message when I said that what business needs now and what it will continue to need will be means whereby credit, corporate and individual, and our originative brains, will be vitalized. These means I conceive to be provided by the bill formulated by the committees on banking and currency of the Senate and House. The bill is based upon solid principles of banking. It will provide an elastic currency readily responsive to sound credits, bring about the mobilization of reserves, and prevent the concentration of the money resources of the country in a few hands or for use for speculative purposes in such volume as to interfere with the needs and operations of legitimate business. It provides further for public instead of private control, thus making the banks what they should be—the servants and not the masters of business."

I suggested to the President that the proposal of Government control had aroused a great deal of opposition in banking circles.

"I am not surprised that there should be some opposition," the President replied. "Naturally certain banking interests desire to retain their grip on the finances and above all the credit of the country. But I believe the more patriotic bankers consider the matter the more convinced they will be that it is to their advantage, as it surely is to that of the people as a whole, to have the control vested in the government. We had the choice of three alternatives—to confide the central control to the government or to the bankers or to both. The last was rejected, because being a compromise it would not be satisfactory in the final analysis to the people or to the bankers. Under such a condition, the banking representatives might be expected to look after the interests of the banks irrespective of those of the people, and public suspicion might develop as to the honesty of purpose animating the board possessing the control. Moreover, this is not class legislation. It is not desirable to say that the people shall be represented and then that the bankers shall be represented, as if the latter are separate and distinct from the people. The Board should comprise men whose interests will be the people's interests, and in the latter should be included the bankers' interests.

"Eliminating the compromise arrangement, therefore, there remained the question of government or bankers' control. The inadvisability of the latter arrangement shows almost on its face. The freedom of credit for which we are striving would be dependent in case of its adoption entirely upon the will of the bankers. With government control, there is created a force which, while it will not attempt to run the business of the banks, will be clothed with some authority to prevent injustice from the banks to the general public. Under the proposed plan, recognition is given to the interests of the people, and there is established the principle of some other control of credit than arbitrary control by the banks, in exactly the same way that the interstate commerce law established the principle of control by the railroads which would enforce respect of public rights by the railroads themselves. This is a great principle. So long as it is observed, the details themselves are matters of relatively minor importance and might be subject to change either now or in the future, as the operation of the system develops new needs."

"But, Mr President," I asked, "is there not danger of politics influencing the action of the Central Board of Control?"

"It is inconceivable to me that any one in a political office would dare to play politics with a banking system which literally touches every man, woman and child in the country. A man who would act upon small grounds of expediency would be utterly without principle. I can judge in this matter only by our own experience in New Jersey. In that state, the Governor appoints all the Judges. Now no governor—and in this I include the bad as well as the good—ever has dared to play with the Supreme Court and the Court of Errors and Appeals. The result has been that we have had a uniform quality of Judges with a very far from uniform quality of Governors. That is because justice touches the whole community; the moment you play politics with it, the whole community knows it, and the Party daring to do it would be swept from and kept out of power and would deserve such a fate."

"What are the powers of the Governing Board under the bill?"

"The Governing Board has the power to regulate, but it is a prudential rather than a business regulation. It is the sole authority in the issuance of new currency, and is also empowered to fix the discount rates for the various reserve banks.

"These rates, however, apply only to discounts made by reserve banks for the other banks and not to the rates between the latter and their customers. It is to be expected that the rates fixed by the Governing Board will have an effect upon the rates charged by the banks to their customers, but it will be a moral effect only, and will not at any time approach an arbitrary interference by the Board with the business of the banks.

"The Board has supervisory authority over the reserve banks, but such authority necessarily would be exercised only with respect to the general conduct of those banks under the provision of the law itself.

"The Board could not compel a reserve bank to make discounts which for any sufficient reason it did not want to make. The management of the reserve bank would still remain the sole judge of the paper offered it for rediscount and of the amount it would be safe to accept from any single bank.

"The supervision of the reserve banks by the Governing Board should have the effect of preventing any discrimination by the reserve bank against individual banks or against any particular class of paper manifestly constituting perfectly safe security.

"I believe the effect of this supervision by the Governing Board

will be like the effect of publicity. It will restrain those in control
of the reserve banks from any inclination to use the institutions
otherwise than fairly to all concerned.

"This will be a great advance, because it will make more and
more difficult such arbitrary control of great amounts of money
by a few banks upon which other and weaker banks of necessity
have to depend for any needed accomodations. The smaller banks
will now be able to go to the reserve banks. Just as they are made
more independent, so they are made more useful to the communities they serve, and banking benefits thereby will be given
their widest distribution."

"Why was the arbitrary limit of $500,000,000 placed upon the
note issue?"

"I frankly confess we guessed at that amount, although it was
a guess based upon statistics. For example, in the last panic the
clearing house certificates issued amounted to $260,000,000,
so that the sum we fixed upon ought to be sufficient under any
and all circumstances. I quite admit it is a debatable question
as to whether a rigid limit should be set or not, and it may be
advisable not to fix any limit at all. It has been suggested that
if we have a limit of $500,000,000 the Federal Reserve Board
might turn the entire issue over to one regional bank. I do not
believe this possible. The Board has not the power to apportion
in the sense that all of the issue shall go to one district and none
to another, because the only power it has is to judge whether the
credits offered are legal and sound. Any member of the regional
association will have the right, on the offer of certain kinds of
paper, to apply for the notes and a very special reason of unsoundness would have to exist in order to justify the rejection of the
application. What we are seeking to do is to mobilize the reserves
and make all the resources of the country available so far as possible to every other part of it.

"Through the measure proposed I believe we will correct the
evil we are most bent upon correcting—that of the present concentration of reserve and control at the discretion of a single
group of bankers or by a locality of banking interests. It follows
that the control ought to be a general control in view of the possibility of inflation, an authority which knows condition[s]
throughout the country and is able to act fairly with the knowledge in mind.

"I am satisfied the bill will supply the elasticity our banking
system needs and that it will come to be viewed as a long and
necessary step in advance of existing conditions. Among other
features, it ends the deplorable condition under which the doors

of the Treasury have been wide open for the loss of gold through the exchange of this metal for legal tender paper. In the panic which began in 1893 and the bankers' panic of 1907, we witnessed the humiliating spectacle of the government being forced to appeal to the power of individuals in order to develop and carry out a plan for controlling exchanges. Under the proposed bill, the monetary resources of the country will be afforded protection in times of difficulty. The further provision for farm credits is of great importance to the farming community, as it will assure relief for borrowers in the country districts from the exorbitant rates of interest which they are compelled to pay under present conditions.

"The bill also makes for stability in banking by the requirement for frequent bank examinations and by the prohibition against speculation by national bank officers. In short, the measure is based upon standards of right and justice, and its enactment, unquestionably, will work to the advantage of all the people.

"Impressed as I am with the evils of our present banking system, and convinced that the monopoly of credits must be destroyed if the prosperous development of the nation is to be safeguarded, I consider it my duty to insist upon the passage of currency legislation during the present session. I believe the people are alive to the need. They are better informed today on the currency situation than ever before. Under such circumstances, I cannot believe any serious obstacles will be placed in the way of legislation of such vital importance, especially in view of the fact that, in conjunction with the revision of the tariff, it will be a tremendous step forward in freeing the people from the grinding slavery of monopoly."

T MS (WP, DLC).

An Address on Banking and Currency Reform to a Joint Session of Congress

[June 23, 1913]

Mr. Speaker, Mr. President, Gentlemen of the Congress:

It is under the compulsion of what seems to me a clear and imperative duty that I have a second time this session sought the privilege of addressing you in person. I know, of course, that the heated season of the year is upon us, that work in these chambers and in the committee rooms is likely to become a burden as the season lengthens, and that every consideration of personal convenience and personal comfort, perhaps, in the cases of some of us, considerations of personal health even, dictate an early conclusion of the deliberations of the session; but there are occasions of public duty when these things which touch us privately seem very small; when the work to be done is so pressing and so fraught with big consequence that we know that we are not at liberty to weigh against it any point of personal sacrifice. We are now in the presence of such an occasion. It is absolutely imperative that we should give the business men of this country a banking and currency system by means of which they can make use of the freedom of enterprise and of individual initiative which we are about to bestow upon them.

We are about to set them free; we must not leave them without the tools of action when they are free. We are about to set them free by removing the trammels of the protective tariff. Ever since the Civil War they have waited for this emancipation and for the free opportunities it will bring with it. It has been reserved for us to give it to them. Some fell in love, indeed, with the slothful security of their dependence upon the Government; some took advantage of the shelter of the nursery to set up a mimic mastery of their own within its walls. Now both the tonic and the discipline of liberty and maturity are to ensue. There will be some readjustments of purpose and point of view.[1] There will follow a period of expansion and new enterprise, freshly conceived. It is for us to determine now whether it shall be rapid and facile and of easy accomplishment. This it can not be unless the resourceful business men who are to deal with the new circumstances are to have at hand and ready for use the instrumentalities and conveniences of free enterprise which independent men need when acting on their own initiative.

It is not enough to strike the shackles from business. The duty of statesmanship is not negative merely. It is constructive also. We must show that we understand what business needs and that we know how to supply it. No man, however casual and superficial his observation of the conditions now prevailing in the country, can fail to see that one of the chief things business needs now, and will need increasingly as it gains in scope and vigor in the years immediately ahead of us, is the proper means by which readily to vitalize its credit, corporate and individual, and its originative brains. What will it profit us to be free if we

---

[1] Wilson's shorthand text at this point reads: "There will be some hardships to endure. There will follow a period of readjustment, wholesome, inevitable, but a little risky and disturbing, too, if the businessmen of the country have not had as yet prepared for their use tools, conveniences, of hardy independent enterprise which independent men need acting on their own resources."

are not to have the best and most accessible instrumentalities of commerce and enterprise? What will it profit us to be quit of one kind of monopoly if we are to remain in the grip of another and more effective kind? How are we to gain and keep the confidence of the business community unless we show that we know how both to aid and to protect it? What shall we say if we make fresh enterprise necessary and also make it very difficult by leaving all else except the tariff just as we found it? The tyrannies of business, big and little, lie within the field of credit. We know that. Shall we not act upon the knowledge? Do we not know how to act upon it? If a man can not make his assets available at pleasure, his assets of capacity and character and resource, what satisfaction is it to him to see opportunity beckoning to him on every hand, when others have the keys of credit in their pockets and treat them as all but their own private possession? It is perfectly clear that it is our duty to supply the new banking and currency system the country needs, and it will need it immediately more than it has ever needed it before.

The only question is, When shall we supply it—now, or later, after the demands shall have become reproaches that we were so dull and so slow? Shall we hasten to change the tariff laws and then be laggards about making it possible and easy for the country to take advantage of the change? There can be only one answer to that question. We must act now, at whatever sacrifice to ourselves. It is a duty which the circumstances forbid us to postpone. I should be recreant to my deepest convictions of public obligation did I not press it upon you with solemn and urgent insistence.

The principles upon which we should act are also clear. The country has sought and seen its path in this matter within the last few years—sees it more clearly now than it ever saw it before—much more clearly than when the last legislative proposals on the subject were made. We must have a currency, not rigid as now, but readily, elastically responsive to sound credit, the expanding and contracting credits of everyday transactions, the normal ebb and flow of personal and corporate dealings. Our banking laws must mobilize reserves; must not permit the concentration anywhere in a few hands of the monetary resources of the country or their use for speculative purposes in such volume as to hinder or impede or stand in the way of other more legitimate, more fruitful uses. And the control of the system of banking and of issue which our new laws are to set up must be public, not private, must be vested in the Government itself, so that the banks may be the instruments, not the masters, of business and of individual enterprise and initiative.

The committees of the Congress to which legislation of this character is referred have devoted careful and dispassionate study to the means of accomplishing these objects. They have honored me by consulting me. They are ready to suggest action. I have come to you, as the head of the Government and the responsible leader of the party in power, to urge action now, while there is time to serve the country deliberately and as we should, in a clear air of common counsel. I appeal to you with a deep conviction of duty. I believe that you share this conviction. I therefore appeal to you with confidence. I am at your service without reserve to play my part in any way you may call upon me to play it in this great enterprise of exigent reform which it will dignify and distinguish us to perform and discredit us to neglect.[2]

Printed in *Address of the President of the United States . . . June 23, 1913* (Washington, 1913).

[2] There is a WWhw and WWsh outline of this address, dated June 13, 1913, and a WWsh draft, dated "June, 1913," in the C. L. Swem Coll., NjP; a typed copy, with WWhw emendations, also in the Swem Collection; and a reading copy in WP, DLC.

ADDENDA

To Edgar Odell Lovett

My dear Lovett: Princeton, N. J. November 20th, 1908.

It gave me real pleasure to write to the Secretary of State, and he has very promptly complied with my request for a letter of introduction to the officers of our Diplomatic and Consular Service. I take pleasure in enclosing it.

It was a real pleasure to hear from you, and I particularly appreciated the thoughtful and affectionate note you sent me at the opening of the term. It touched me very much.

It is very interesting to hear of what you are doing, and I am sure that by the time this journeying is over you will feel very much settled in all your purposes. I could see in our talk at Rydal that you had already begun to see your way both negatively and affirmatively, and it will always be a real gratification to me to think that I was of some service to you in the matter.

Mrs. Wilson joins me in warmest regards to Mrs. Lovett and you, and I am, as always,

Faithfully and cordially yours,   Woodrow Wilson

TLS (E. O. Lovett Papers, TxHR).

A Tribute[1]

[c. Jan. 1, 1910]

TO THE WOMEN OF THE SOUTH

Whose purity, whose fidelity, whose courage, whose gentle genius in love and in counsel have kept the home secure, the family a school of virtue, the state a court of honour; who have made of war a season of modest heroism and of peace a time of healing; the guardians of our tranquility and of our strength.

A memory of brave men and noble women; a confidence that men are honourable and women worthy of honour, a hope that generations yet unborn will perpetuate the traditions formed in graver ages gone and loved in the days now come,—these are the foundations of a free and happy commonwealth.

WWT MS (WP, DLC).

[1] An abridged version of the following is carved on a monument to the women of the Confederacy in Rome, Ga. It was dedicated on March 9, 1910.

To Edgar Odell Lovett

My dear Lovett: Princeton, N. J. June 19th, 1909.

The enclosed letter from Benjamin Wistar Morris will explain itself. I have a very high opinion of Morris. He is a most painstaking and conscientious workman, with high ideals and a great deal of skill, and our experience with him in the building of Seventy-Nine and Patton Halls leads me to believe that he is able to calculate costs very exactly and knows what he is about on the business side.

He may lack imagination a little, but given the planning of a group of buildings and the style in which they were to be built, I should feel pretty safe in trusting him to work out something very satisfactory. The best thing about him is that he is not in the least stubborn or self-opinionated and is perfectly willing to act upon suggestions and make himself an instrument for the carrying out of the ideas of those for whom he is working. I found him most delightful in this respect, very much more so than any other architect I ever had dealings with.

It was very delightful to catch a glimpse of you here and I sincerely hope that our orbits will cross again and again, and very frequently.

Always cordially and faithfully yours,
                                    Woodrow Wilson

TLS (E. O. Lovett Papers, TxHR).

INDEX

NOTE ON THE INDEX

THE alphabetically arranged analytical table of contents at the front of the volume eliminates duplication, in both contents and index, of references to certain documents, such as letters. Letters are listed in the contents alphabetically by name, and chronologically within each name by page. The subject matter of all letters is, of course, indexed. The Editorial Notes and Wilson's writings are listed in the contents chronologically by page. In addition, the subject matter of both categories is indexed. The index covers all references to books and articles mentioned in text or notes. Footnotes are indexed. Page references to footnotes which place a comma between the page number and "n" cite both text and footnote, thus: "624,n3." On the other hand, absence of the comma indicates reference to the footnote only, thus: "55n2"—the page number denoting where the footnote appears.

We have ceased the practice of indicating first and fullest identification of persons and subjects in earlier volumes by index references accompanied by asterisks. Volume 13, the cumulative index-contents volume is already in print. Volume 26, which will cover Volumes 14-25, will appear in the near future.

The index supplies the fullest known form of names and, for the Wilson and Axson families, relationships as far down as cousins. Persons referred to by nicknames or shortened forms of names can be identified by reference to entries for these forms of the names.

All entries consisting of page numbers only and which refer to concepts, issues, and opinions (such as democracy, the tariff, the money trust, leadership, and labor problems), are references to Wilson speeches and writings. Page references that follow the symbol △ in such entries refer to the opinions and comments of others who are identified.

INDEX